Organizational Design, Development, and Behavior

Organizational Design, Development, and Behavior A Situational View

Karl O. Magnusen
Florida International University

Foreword by
Charles E. Summer
University of Washington

Scott, Foresman and Company   Glenview, Illinois
Tucker, Georgia   Oakland, New Jersey   Dallas, Texas
Palo Alto, California   Abingdon, England

To Mar and Ruth

Library of Congress Cataloging in Publication Data
Main entry under title:

Organizational design, development, and behavior

Includes bibliographies and indexes.
1. Management—Addresses, essays, lectures.
2. Organization—Addresses, essays, lectures.
I. Magnusen, Karl O., 1941–
HD31.0758   658.4'008   76-28782
ISBN O-673-15042-9

"Style or Circumstance: The Leadership Enigma," by Fred Fiedler, from *Psychology Today*, 2 (March 1969), pp. 38–43. Copyright © 1969, Ziff-Davis Publishing Company. Reprinted by permission of *Psychology Today* and Fred Fiedler.

1 2 3 4 5 6 -GBC- 80 79 78 77 76

Foreword

In this book, Karl Magnusen provides a viewpoint that fills an important gap in the textbook literature on organizational design, development, and behavior. Authors and researchers have tended to present extremely biased viewpoints on the crucial *managerial issues* or *policy issues* faced by practicing managers. They have done this because, in the formulation of experimental or theoretical insights, theorists must actually shut out the world "in buzzing confusion" to concentrate on a few limited variables, or a few limited concepts. Researchers do this by controlled observations or controlled experiments to keep out contaminating facts. Theoreticians do this by making assumptions that hold constant all the world's facts except the limited concepts in which they have a principal interest.

This bias—which results because specialists spend their lives analyzing micro "pieces" of the world—is an indispensable hallmark of good science. But it can be confusing or even dangerous for lawyers, judges, legislators, business executives, or other professionals who must make policy decisions for worldly situations. Some scholars, using the status and authority of science, imply biased solutions which will not pragmatically "work" in policy decisions. And some policy makers, unable to understand the shortcomings of underlying experimental or observational methods, begin to think they "should" follow the implied solutions suggested by social scientists. If the social scientist is a victim of what Dewey called a "trained incapacity" to see the policy problem (as contrasted with the hypothetical problem), the executive may well fall victim to following the leadership of the scientist. For, troubled by the sheer complexity of many policy situations, he or she may become dependent upon the scholar who claims to be stating "truth."

What is called for in the training of professional executives is (1) a depth of knowledge in the social sciences and (2) a healthy respect for science, *balanced by* (3) a knowledge that science can never provide final solutions to policy problems and (4) a healthy skepticism of science if used without wisdom and judgment.

Karl Magnusen helps to achieve this kind of balance in two ways. First, he has selected from the large body of literature in the behavioral sciences certain key issues of interest to the manager or policy maker: organization design; work and its discontents; job design; money motivation; leadership; group decision-making; management by objectives. Second, he has juxtaposed contrasting and sometimes contradictory viewpoints on these issues. The would-be manager is confronted with the fact that specialists on a given subject may have differing or even opposing messages about how to manage an organization.

This approach has the disadvantage of preventing closure, and of taxing the student's (and some professors') tolerance of ambiguity. It appears to be "confusing" in the structure of a course. Students may feel more comfort in a course which advocates a certain kind of job design, a certain model of leadership, or a certain "party line" on whether money is good or bad as a human motivator. It may be even more comfortable if the course reinforces this approach with "hard" research and "truth." Students may also think the professor is a more organized and knowledgeable person if the course "gives the answer" on these issues.

But far outweighing these disadvantages is the necessity for professional business school students, as opposed to students in a discipline such as psychology, to know from the beginning the real decision-making confusion faced by the manager, and to know that social science is valuable but limited in the manager's decision-making.

This book makes the tradeoff between these advantages and disadvantages. The tradeoff is made, in my opinion, to the benefit of professional business education.

Charles E. Summer

Preface

This book combines a lead essay with selected readings to examine concepts and issues in organizational design, development, and behavior. The lead essay is a critical review of different approaches to organizational analysis, including scientific management, administrative design theory, human relations, contingency theory, and organization development. Primary objectives of the essay are to emphasize the multiple entry points available for understanding organizations and to explain how comparative organizational research assists in clarifying apparently conflicting prescriptions for improved managerial and organizational effectiveness.

The essay comprises Part 1 of the book and offers a starting point for examining the situational nature of complex systems. The remaining three parts use selected readings with summary introductions to highlight and elaborate on issues brought out in the lead essay. These readings have been presented where possible in a pro-con format to emphasize opposing points of view on issues of organizational design (Part 2), organizational behavior (Part 3), and organization development (Part 4).

The book is not exhaustive in its coverage of theory, research, or practice in the areas discussed. Yet, in my judgment, the materials focus on central issues facing practitioners and researchers alike and provide a solid core of information suitable for numerous classroom applications. The book is oriented toward advanced undergraduates and beginning graduates taking courses in organizational behavior, organizational design, and organization development. Also, it should be useful as a supplement to more traditional management texts in courses where instructors want to emphasize organizational and behavioral issues. The essay has been carefully referenced to current literature, and the reading selections have been drawn from various sources, including *Academy of Management Journal, Annual Review of Psychology, Business Horizons, California Management Review, Future Shock, Harvard Business Review, Management Science, Monthly Labor Review, Organizational Dynamics,* and *Psychology Today.*

Developing this book has proved challenging, and I wish to thank a number of colleagues for their constructive remarks on the essay and other materials as the text took form, especially Steve Altman, Gary Dessler, and Enzo Valenzi (of Florida International University); and Tom Ference, Dave Lewin, John Hutchinson, Jim Kuhn, Bill Newman, Len Sayles, and Kirby Warren (of Columbia University). Other helpful critics included Orlando Behling (Ohio State University), Warren H. Schmidt (UCLA), Charles Summer

(University of Washington), and Edward T. P. Watson (Northwestern University).

I also want to thank the authors and publishers of the reading materials for permission to reprint their articles, and gratefully acknowledge the fine editorial work of Bruce Borland and Bob Johnson from Scott, Foresman. For competent manuscript typing, I am indebted to Ruth Chapman and Becky Braidman in the Division of Management at Florida International. Finally, a special note of appreciation is due Linda Rusco, whose patience, encouragement, and assistance were essential to the book's completion.

Karl O. Magnusen

Contents

1

Perspectives on Organizational Design, Development, and Behavior

INTRODUCTION

The purpose of this essay is to provide a broad overview of approaches to organizational design, development, and behavior.* The academic field dealing with this subject matter is little more than a decade old and, as Strauss has noted, remains "somewhat of an orphan," having no professional society, no leading journal, and one of the more disorganized labor markets in academia.[1] Nonetheless, the subject matter is taught in almost all major business schools and has some direct implications for aspiring managers. Goldner, for example, found that those managers who best understood organizational complexity were most successful in their careers.[2]

Unfortunately, how organizational complexity can be meaningfully analyzed has not always been made clear in the organizational literature. Theoretical development lags behind empirical research, and apparently contradictory prescriptions for managerial action abound. As examples, both task specialization and job enrichment have been found to increase productivity; both bureaucratic and nonbureaucratic structures have been found to maximize work coordination; both monetary and self-actualization needs have been found to increase motivation; and both stability and change have been found to promote organizational effectiveness.[3] Such "contradictory" prescriptions often are the result of researchers viewing organizations from different perspectives. Systems have multiple entry points for analysis, e.g., an emphasis on task, structure, people, technology, or environment, and various schools of thought have developed around these different "entry points."[4] Each school provides useful insights about organizational behavior, but sometimes overlooks the interactive nature of complex systems and the wisdom of competing viewpoints.

Except at very abstract levels of general systems theory, there is at present no unified theory of organizations.[5] Yet there is a need to understand how organizations are designed, how people react to such designs, and how managers can improve system effectiveness. Accordingly, to emphasize the importance of theoretical refinement, to systematize what is presently known, and to explain conflicting organizational prescriptions, the present essay critically examines, in chronological order of development, five major approaches to the study of organizations.

The earliest phase, *scientific management,* emphasized task variables, shop-level production activities, and assumed that human motivation occurs primarily from economic incentives. Later, *classical administrative theory,* complementary to scientific management, focused on the bureaucratic and structural aspects of organization in hopes of developing universal principles of management applicable to

*Portions of this material have appeared before in "A Comparative Analysis of Organizations" by Karl O. Magnusen. Reprinted by permission of the publisher from ORGANIZATIONAL DYNAMICS, Summer 1973. Copyright © 1973 by AMACOM, a division of American Management Associations.

all situations. Next, as a reaction to classical theory, the *human relations movement* produced numerous studies that reflected both economic and human dimensions, but provided no systematic theory of organizations.

Recently, attempts have been made to develop frameworks for the *comparative analysis of organizations*. Leading efforts here have emphasized the importance of technological or environmental variables as determinants of organizational behavior and the need to selectively apply the insights from different schools of thought. Organizations are viewed in situational or "contingency" terms and "one best way" perspectives are rejected. However, contingency thinking has not been fully explored in many applied programs aimed at organizational change. As noted in the final section of this essay, such programs seem largely dominated by an updated version of human relations called *Organization Development*. Advocates tend to promote a humanistic view of work and, for them, the model organization "is characterized by consensus, cooperative group relations, and high interaction, yet it preserves the opportunity for individual creativity because organizational members feel free to behave authentically."[6]

Progress in understanding organizations requires theoretical perspective, and the critical review of major approaches to the study of organizational systems should provoke thought and discussion while providing a focus for additional inquiry. No final solutions are offered, but an examination of the various schools should underscore the diverse entry points for organizational analysis and make clear that any one, taken alone, offers an incomplete picture of reality. By considering in broad terms the evolution of thought about organizations, the merits and problems of each perspective should become apparent. As Landsberger has noted, "Gems in isolation are worth far less than when they are strung together as a necklace. They all gain greatly by being compared and contrasted in an orderly fashion, even if we cannot yet weld them together by means of a single overarching theory."[7] It is with this awareness that the following sections have been written.[8]

SCIENTIFIC MANAGEMENT

A major stimulus to organizational research was scientific management theory. Initiated by the writings of F. W. Taylor prior to World War I, this view held that industrial unrest and waste could be eliminated and productivity increased by applying engineering methods to discover generalized technological laws from which work arrangements could be structured in one best, most efficient manner.[9] Although these methods supposedly applied to all aspects of organization, the scientific management movement remained primarily a plan for industrial shop management.

Traditionally, the maintenance of tools and the selection of work methods in industrial plants had been left to the discretion of individual workers; management simply determined the machinery to be used and the output required. According to Taylor, such an arrangement resulted in waste and low production because work methods and performance standards were left to the workers, and each would choose what was convenient instead of what was good for the firm's productivity. To eliminate these inefficiencies, Taylor suggested that management transfer control of production away from workers by standardizing machine operations and, through time and motion studies, by reducing all tasks into their simplest, unvarying components.[10] Standardization of machines and work processes would allow employees to learn their jobs more quickly, make fewer mistakes or unnecessary movements, increase their respective outputs, and make the production operation more efficient.[11]

Additional efficiencies could be obtained by selecting the right people for designated jobs, by training them in proper work methods, and by insuring their adherence to established work routines. The latter was to be accomplished through financial incentives made available from increased profits stemming from reduced waste and increased output. Incentives were linked with time and motion study results and, theoretically, stimulated employee ambition by paying workers according to their productive worth instead of the average for their class. If everyone adhered to the "objective" laws governing the work place, then the economic motives of both workers and owners could be met without argument, bargaining, or conflict.[12]

Although Taylor's view of shop management assisted in the development of industrial psychology (especially testing, selection, and training procedures), it had limitations as a means of analyzing organizational behavior. It ignored the common sense notion that the best way for one person to do a job may not be the best for another, and its narrow economic perspective on human motivation overlooked the negative psychological and group reactions of employees to task specialization and management-determined production standards. Despite Taylor's concern for the welfare of the individual, his system came under continued attack by workers (who disliked being "turned into machines") and unions (who wanted a say in the setting of standards and wage rates).[13] Finally, by focusing on technical methods of shop control, scientific management neglected the administrative component of the organization as well as problems of structure and process.

ADMINISTRATIVE DESIGN THEORY

Administrative design theory was complementary to Taylorism and shifted the concern for efficiency from the work place to the entire organization. Originating during World War I, this view grew to encompass two parallel but unrelated developments: (1) numerous managerial writings predicated on the assumption that basic similarities in organizational structure and process could be made explicit through prescriptive, universal principles of administrative action,[14] and (2) Max Weber's descriptive study of bureaucracy.[15]

Although bureaucracy technically connotes public administration, the concept exemplifies the ideal structural model used by the earlier management theorists. This structural type may be summarized as follows:[16]

1. Tasks are distributed among various members of the group as official duties, usually accompanied by the division of labor and specialization of function.
2. Offices or roles are organized into a hierarchical structure where the scope of authority of superordinates over subordinates is clearly defined.
3. A formal set of rules governing behavior is specified which ensures uniformity of organization.
4. Officials are required to assume an impersonal attitude in contacts with other officials and clients, and this produces a considerable measure of psychological distance between superiors and subordinates.
5. Employment in a bureaucracy is usually assumed to be a career for life and promotion is by merit.

Within this general framework, classical management theorists prescribed a "best way" to coordinate specialized jobs (organized by some method of departmentation—function, purpose, place, or client).[17] Unity of command, limited spans of supervision, and delegation of authority were fundamental to this coordinative process. The "one worker, one boss" principle gave the formal organizational structure a pyramidal shape and a central source from which authority flowed downward by delegation throughout the system. The principle also suggested an ideal span of supervision, usually four or six subordinates, and required that supervisors have authority equal to their positional responsibilities.[18] Managerial functions were considered to have universal characteristics in all organizations regardless of the environment or personnel involved.[19]

Despite the apparent precision of this managerial-bureaucratic approach, and its continued use, it suffers certain ambiguities when applied to real organizations. For example, the basic bureaucratic model may be interpreted differently depending upon whether the empirical or evaluative aspects of the typology are emphasized. Where the empirical aspects are used, at least three submeanings of bureaucracy can be identified: (1) an administration may be bureaucratic or not to the extent it matches Weber's ideal type, (2) an organization may be bureaucratic if some, but not necessarily all, of the Weberian characteristics are present, and (3) bureaucratic attributes may be viewed dimensionally, in which case an organization may be more bureaucratic in one dimension and less bureaucratic in another.[20] Where the evaluative aspects are used, bureaucracy may connote rationality, inefficiency, or the abuse of power.[21]

Additionally the managerial prescriptions for action often pose irreconcilable dilemmas in practice. The prescription that each employee should have only one boss, for example, provides no assistance with problems in which specialized tasks are critical to two or more departments. Similarly, the notion that authority must be equal to responsibility ignores situations involving people over whom a manager has no official control. Finally, the prescription for narrow spans of control underemphasizes the complex nature of communications in organizational systems and assumes that passing information along through hierarchical channels will be most effective.[22]

Like scientific management, administrative design theory emphasizes efficiency, an economic base to human motivation, and the need to coordinate people by detailed attention to task specialization and managerial planning. Employees are believed to prefer the security of defined job responsibilities and not to value the freedom of determining their own work assignments or approaches to problems. The theory views the organization in structured, static terms and assumes that there is "one best way" to divide up work and arrange hierarchical levels. Power-conflict relationships are ignored, the impact of the individual on the organization is overlooked, and little recognition is given to the possible consequences of bureaucracy on worker attitudes and behavior.[23]

HUMAN RELATIONS

Early Phases

The human relations view, as a multi-faceted reaction to the excessively structured classical approach, originated with a series of industrial studies directed by Elton Mayo at the Hawthorne plant of the Western Electric Company, near Chicago, between 1927 and 1932.[24] These studies initially were designed to relate productivity to such variables as illumination, fatigue, monotony, and wage incentives. After two years of confusing and inconclusive results, however, the researchers turned to a vast interviewing program to study the social and psychological factors which apparently were creating a discrepancy between how the organizational system was supposed to work (according to classical theory) and how the workers actually behaved.

The major conclusions of the Hawthorne research can be summarized as follows:[25]

1. Informal work groups have a strong influence on the organization; they establish their own production norms (either high or low) despite attempts by management to increase productivity through task specialization and economic incentives.
2. The effect of economic incentives is limited by noneconomic rewards, such as the need for individual recognition, security, and group acceptance.
3. Task specialization is inefficient when carried to an extreme.

4.   The first-line supervisor is crucial in determining work group collaboration
     for productivity; specifically, considerate and nonauthoritarian supervision
     creates high group morale which, in turn, leads to increased output.

The most notable impact of the Hawthorne studies was in the area of first-line
supervision, an emphasis reinforced by the work of Lewin and his associates on
the effectiveness of democratic leadership and group participation in decision-
making.[26] Employee-centered supervision grew in popularity as managers sought
ways to reduce industrial conflict. (Interestingly, Roethlisberger and Dickson's
report on the Hawthorne studies noted that improving face-to-face relations at
first-line levels would do little to dispel industrial conflict.)[27]

Management's concern for harmony was not entirely altruistic. The Wagner
Act of 1935 forced business to reexamine its views toward workers in light of
collective bargaining, and World War II, with its wage controls and excess profit
taxes, made good human relations attractive as a means of competing for labor
on a noninflationary basis.[28] Whatever the underlying managerial intent, the almost exclusive emphasis on supervisory training during the 1940s gave human
relations research a distinctly narrow focus.

The study of supervision merged into an analysis of industrial bureaucracy
once it was recognized that problems of supervision could arise at any level in the
hierarchy and that a foreman's leadership style depended on the kind of supervision
received from superiors. New attention was given to upper management levels and
several major studies pointed out certain dysfunctional consequences associated
with bureaucratic organizations. Merton, for example, observed that standardized
rules and procedures, designed to produce reliable employee behavior, had unintended consequences. Rules became ends in themselves and decision-making was
reduced to a routine application of procedures. Selznick showed how work specialization could cause departments to maximize their objectives at the expense of
goals crucial to the larger organization. Gouldner noted that rules defining minimum standards of behavior allowed subordinates to subvert organizational goals
of efficiency by gearing performance to the defined minimums; and, finally, Blau
showed how extreme detailing of work lowered productivity and morale.[29]

Later Phases

Results from the empirical tradition of the human relations movement cast doubt
not only on the utility of classical theory but posed challenges to its own assumptions as well. For example, research subsequent to the Hawthorne studies eventually directed attention away from the social needs of employees when it was
discovered that work groups did not influence all workers, that workers were not
always members of informal groups, and that neither employee-centered supervision nor high group morale was consistently related to productivity.[30]

During the 1950s human relations research took on a more psychological orientation. Fundamental works such as Argyris' *Personality and Organization*[31] and Maslow's *Motivation and Personality*[32] were used to demonstrate the conflict between individual and organizational goals. An emerging view of human motivation held that people seek independence, responsibility, and personal growth (higher-order needs) but that organizations stifle these tendencies through beliefs that people are basically lazy, motivated only by lower-order needs (those related to physiological and safety requirements), and responsive only to tight control by a managerial elite.

McGregor termed these different sets of assumptions about human behavior Theory X (people are lazy) and Theory Y (people are capable).[33] Theory X management allegedly creates an unhealthy situation in which employees become alienated, sullen, and unwilling to produce above minimum requirements. Sabotage of managerial control becomes a preoccupation with workers and a serious problem for organizational efficiency. By contrast, Theory Y management, which emphasizes employee participation in decision-making and personal control over work processes, supposedly improves efficiency, reduces conflict, and builds greater commitment to organizational objectives.

Theory Y perspectives gained considerable popularity during the 1960s. Particular interest was shown in the use of sensitivity training (also known as laboratory education) to examine face-to-face interactions of managers and reduce their tendencies to rely on authority relationships and bureaucratic controls. In theory, improved interpersonal competence should produce organization climates that encourage the expression of innovative or risky ideas, eliminate mistrust and negativism, and rejuvenate organizational effectiveness.[34]

In a related development, some writers have emphasized the importance of job enrichment as a way of sustaining employee expectations of personal growth and accomplishment on the job. Herzberg, for example, has argued that challenging jobs will increase both employee satisfaction and work performance.[35] His views are based on a "dual-factor" theory of motivation that considers job dissatisfaction and job satisfaction to be separate dimensions, not just polar ends of a continuum. Sources of dissatisfaction involve job *context* variables (such as company policy and administration, supervision, working conditions, interpersonal relations, and pay) while sources of satisfaction center on job *content* factors (which include opportunities for achievement, recognition, responsibility, advancement, and challenging work).

According to Herzberg, traditional management practice has tried to motivate employees by removing sources of dissatisfaction, but, while this might make work environments more tolerable, it will not result in genuine motivation—just a relative absence of job dissatisfaction. To install "internal generators" in employees, organizations must concentrate on the redesign of jobs to make them more intrinsically satisfying and meaningful.[36] Along with Argyris, Herzberg assumes that waste in human resources occurs whenever work relationships do not provide for self-actualization.

THE IDEOLOGICAL FRONT

Notice that classical and human relations theory are in many ways quite opposite, yet neither sees an insoluble dilemma between the organization's quest for rationality and the human search for happiness.[37] Classical writers tend to prescribe a *high* degree of task structure and assume that an efficient organization will be the most satisfying (because it maximizes worker pay). Humanist writers tend to prescribe a *low* degree of task structure and assume that the most satisfying organization will be the most efficient (because workers see their goals as congruent with organizational objectives).[38] However, proponents of this latter view are not agreed on actual outcomes of less programmed structures. Increases in motivation and innovation have been predicted, but so have increases in personal anxiety and struggles for power.[39]

Perhaps the most significant aspect of the entire human relations movement has been its attraction to persons with a great belief in the application of humanistic and democratic values to the workplace. Taken as universal are the personality-organization conflict, the desire for self-actualization, the importance of work, and the preferability of participatory management.[40] Yet there is evidence contrary to these articles of faith. Wool has noted that most employees are not "alienated" from their work; Fromm has long argued that most people do not seek complete freedom; Dubin has found that work is not always an important central life interest for industrial workers; and other research has shown that participatory management, successful in some instances, is undesired by certain workers, often creates conflict it is supposed to prevent, and does not inevitably lead to higher levels of work performance.[41] Further, little empirical support has been found for Maslow's need hierarchy and Herzberg's theory of motivation is clearly controversial.[42] Studies on job redesign have shown mixed results and there has been a tendency to neglect the impact of money as a motivator.[43] Finally, penetrating criticisms have been cast on the effectiveness of laboratory education (e.g., increased sensitivity reduces management decisiveness), and certain critics of the humanist approach have shown that structural (instead of attitudinal) changes can improve interpersonal relations and reduce organizational stress.[44]

The greatest weakness of the human relations approach, however, has not been its highly optimistic and normative view of human behavior. Its fundamental deficiency concerns an attempt to solve major organizational problems by drawing attention to individual and group levels of analysis while avoiding inclusive theorizing about the organization as an entity.[45] This is a continuing kind of problem—one that has been apparent in numerous writings in the organizational area.[46]

COMPARATIVE ANALYSIS OF ORGANIZATIONS: SEARCH FOR A THEORETICAL BASE

Classical and human relations writers typically have prescribed their respective views as the "best" guide for managing organizations. Objective assessments have been difficult to make, however, because neither approach has systematically examined the determinants or effectiveness of different organizational designs. Such evaluation requires comparative research, but this has been hindered for lack of any widely accepted theory of organizations.[47] General systems theory seems too abstract for purposes of comparative analysis and, although organizational typologies have been proposed by writers like Parsons, Etzioni, and Blau and Scott, these have not been productive guides either for the generation of empirical research or for practical application.[48]

Recent efforts to deal with such deficiencies have emphasized the importance of technological and environmental variables as major determinants of organizational behavior. From such work, several promising frameworks for the comparative analysis of organizations have emerged. Termed "contingency models," they offer provocative insights into the question of organizational diagnosis, have stimulated considerable interest and research, and will be discussed in the following sections on the technological and environmental "imperatives" of organizational design.

The Technological Imperative

Early in this century, F. W. Taylor related technology to productivity, yet attention was subsequently directed away from the technological aspects of work by ensuing debates over the relative importance of classical and human relations theory. However, impressive but scattered evidence throughout the 1940s and 1950s supported the importance of technology as a determinant of organizational behavior.[49]

By the early 1960s, more systematic attention was devoted to technological aspects of work, and research took a comparative approach. For example, in a study of 20 British firms, Burns and Stalker found that different rates of technical innovation were associated with different kinds of organizational structures.[50] Innovation was low in firms with "mechanistic" systems, which were characterized by distinct functional specialties, precise definitions of duties and responsibilities, and a well-defined command hierarchy. Rapid and major technical innovation, by contrast, was more evident in firms with "organic" systems, where structures were more flexible, jobs less rigorously specified, and communication resembled consultation rather than order-giving.

The most widely acknowledged research into technology was produced in the mid-1960s. While the major impetus was British in origin (this research will be discussed in the next section), receptiveness to the approach in the United States was sparked by Blauner's study of employee alienation in four industries with different technologies: printing, automobiles, textiles, and chemicals.[51] Results indicated that levels of alienation were unevenly distributed among the work forces considered, being highest in auto production and substantially lower in the other three industries. (The study provides an interesting contrast to the recent and controversial HEW study on *Work in America,* which found alienation to be more pervasive).[52]

The South Essex Studies

For purposes of comparative analysis, the most extensive and influential study to date of technology and its impact on organizational design was published in 1965 by Woodward.[53] Her research into 100 manufacturing firms in the South Essex area of England disclosed that organizational differences were not accounted for by company size, type of industry, or personality factors among executives. Further, conformity with the classical principles of organization had no relation to business success in the firms studied. Some of the most successful firms were the most conspicuous deviates.

However, when the firms were classified according to a scale of technical complexity based on nine systems of production grouped into three major categories (unit, mass, and process production—in increasing order of complexity), the data concerning organization structures fell into clear patterns. Not only were specific structures associated with each technological grouping, but within each category, companies that most nearly conformed to the median figure for each structural characteristic were most successful—success being defined in terms of profits and growth rates. High-performing firms with mass-production technologies tended to have mechanistic management systems, while high-performing firms with unit- or process-production technologies tended to have organic systems. Unit and process firms did not have identical structures, however, and neither grouping displayed the variety found among mass-production companies in the way production operations were planned and controlled.

Acknowledging that her research did not produce a general law about the relationship of technology to organizational behavior, Woodward suggested that classical management writers apparently had mass-production firms in mind when they formulated their principles of organization. She further noted that while there seems to be no "one best way" to organize manufacturing firms, there does seem to be "a particular form of organization most appropriate to each technical situation."[54]

Woodward also found that the relative importance of different functional groups and their interrelationships varied within each type of production system. Each type of technology had a "critical function", and firms above average in success not only had status systems that adequately rewarded the importance of this function, but also tended to have chief executives who had been associated with it earlier in their careers.

These "critical functions" were identified from an analysis of manufacturing cycles. In unit firms, for example, the manufacturing cycle began with marketing—finding customers by convincing them that the company could produce whatever they need. However, development—creating a custom product—was the critical activity, because demands for product quality outweighed considerations of cost or customer service. Production came last in the cycle. Interdepartmental relationships were "good" in unit firms because the manufacturing task required the close integration of functions, which, in turn, required high levels of interpersonal interaction. As Woodward noted, "In unit production, the network of relationships required to bring coordination about is also conducive to the development of satisfactory social relationships. What is best for production seems also to be best for people."[55]

In mass-production systems, the cycle started with development and long-range planning, necessitated by the considerable expenditures involved in product changes. Production was the critical function because, at least in the short run, success depended on operating efficiency, especially the reduction of unit costs. Marketing came last in the cycle, because the need for the product was known and any competitive edge was based on price and prompt deliveries. In contrast to unit firms, the functions composing the manufacturing cycle were more self-contained. Because end results did not depend on the formation of close operational relationships between development, production, and marketing, management did not have a homogeneous view of the company—instead there were sectional interests, exaggerated departmental loyalties, and mutual suspicion. Technical and social ends apparently conflict in mass-production firms, yet the conflict seemed to contribute to results. A degree of unhappiness and mutual animosity among the staff appeared necessary for commercial success.

In process production, development also was the first phase in the manufacturing cycle, because basic research was needed to expose potential new markets. Unlike either unit or mass-production firms, however, the critical function was marketing. Markets had to be assured, not only because of heavy capital expenditures for plant construction, but also because efficient operations depended on the continuous demand for products. As in unit production, production was the final phase of the cycle; but, unlike unit production, process operations—once established—were expected to run for years in a highly controlled, predictable manner.

Although the tasks of process production were more independent of each other than in either of the other production categories, the result was not a fragmented, competing structure but a two-dimensional structure with considerable intergroup harmony. The process plant may be viewed as forming an inner ring, with the research laboratories and marketing departments forming an outer ring.

Minimum coordination is required between departments or "rings," and within the plant itself, controls are built into the technological system. Consequently, Woodward observed, "As far as commercial success is concerned, the form of organization is comparatively unimportant. There is therefore no reason why the organization planner should not concentrate on building an organizational structure which meets the needs of the people employed."[56]

To summarize, then, Woodward related technology not only to organizational structures but also to power relationships. Engineering predominated in unit firms, production in mass-production firms, and marketing in process firms. Technical and social functions of management were thoroughly meshed in unit firms, partially meshed in mass-production companies, and totally separated in continuous-process firms. Conflict levels were highest in mass-production firms and seemed related to successful operations. (This implies that traditional human relations techniques that emphasize improved communications may only antagonize legitimately conflicting groups in mass-production firms and may be unnecessary in unit or process firms where the work system itself ensures the necessary interactions.)

South Essex: Later Studies
Although Woodward found specific organizational characteristics associated with different manufacturing technologies, her research did not explain why unit and process firms, at opposite ends of the technical complexity scale, sometimes resembled each other; nor did it explain why the link between technology and structure was least predictable in the mass-production category. She speculated that either the classification of technology was inadequate to deal with technical differences between mass-production firms or some other variable was an intervening influence between technology and structure.[57]

Attempts to refine measures of operations technology, however, met with little success—a point documented by Rackham.[58] Also, other research questioned the "technology causes structure" hypothesis. For example, a study by Hickson, Pugh, and Phesey of 46 diverse organizations, including 31 manufacturing firms, concluded that technology only has an impact at lower organizational levels and that system size is a more important variable.[59] Although debate continues on this point, Webber recently noted that most research points to technology having its major impact at lower organizational levels while, at higher levels, environment and overall organizational strategy make more of a difference.[60]

Woodward, of course, had recognized earlier that the "technological imperative" might be too sweeping a generalization and set out to examine the possibility that organizational structure might be less a function of technology than of the managerial control system. Yet attempts to classify control systems proved difficult, and those that resulted did not explain why managers actually selected the controls they did.[61] Reflecting on the difficulties associated with using technology and controls to predict organizational variations, Woodward and her staff decided that the common thread underlying attempts to measure technical characteristics was the concept of "variety." (This variety might depend on the nature of the product, the nature of the market, or the nature of the manufacturing processes themselves in the various systems of production.) By 1970, Woodward was searching for a broader conceptual framework and felt that "it might be more profitable to find a way of classifying technical systems by identifying the types and degree of variety within them rather than by detailed measurement of particular technical characteristics."[62]

Toward a Broader Conceptual Framework:
The Perrow Theory

A theoretical approach envisioned by Woodward already exists in the literature. Recognizing that not all organizations have a machine-based technology, Perrow sought a more generic foundation for analyzing organizations—one that uses the concepts of variability and analyzability to predict organizational structures.[63]

But, a word of caution: Perrow terms his independent variable "technology," but it is not the same production technology referred to in the South Essex studies. Instead, he is talking about knowledge technology—the characteristics used in work processes.

In Perrow's view, the technology of an organization can be determined by examining: (1) the number of exceptional cases that the organizational system must deal with, and (2) the extent to which these exceptions are analyzable. As indicated in Figure 1, by dichotomizing and cross-classifying these two dimensions, four technology quadrants can be identified, with most organizations falling within the elliptical area.

Figure 1 TECHNOLOGY VARIABLE

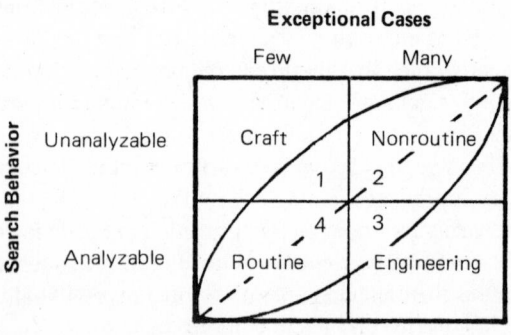

In an organization with routine operations (cell 4) few problems occur and those that do are readily analyzed. Product variety by itself may have little to do with uncertainty. For example: "Automobile firms produce an amazing variety of models and a staggering variety of parts, but these are not novel situations requiring search behavior (except in the design and engineering of model changes)."[64] By contrast, organizations with nonroutine technologies (cell 2) must deal with numerous exceptional cases that are not readily analyzed. Solutions to system crises depend on intuition, guesswork, and change. Examples of this kind of nonroutineness include aerospace firms, manufacturers of exotic metals or nuclear fuels, certain kinds of advertising agencies, and noncustodial psychiatric units.

The dotted line in Figure 1 suggests a one-dimensional scale of organizational nonroutineness; yet the Perrow framework offers two additional variants. Engineering technologies (cell 3) are similar to routinized operations in that exceptional cases can be readily understood and analyzed; but they differ in the frequency with which exceptions occur—rarely in routine firms and often in engineering firms, which must continually modify designs to meet customer needs. Craft organizations (cell 1), such as those making specialty glassware, are confronted with relatively few deviant cases requiring unique solutions but, when these exceptions occur, the intuitive search process typical of nonroutine organizations is required.

While the conceptualization given in Figure 1 may appear static, movement between cells is likely:

One may move from cell 2 to cell 1 with increasing production runs, clients served, accounts handled, research projects underway, agency programs administered and so forth, since this allows more experience to be gained and thus reduces the number of stimuli seen as exceptions. If technical knowledge increases, increasing the reliability of search procedures, one may move from cell 2 to cell 3. If both things happen—and this is the aim of most organizations—one may move from cell 2 to cell 4.[65]

To permit more routinized programs and procedures, the variability of inputs must be reduced and knowledge about them increased.

Having developed a classification system, Perrow states that certain organizational structures and goal patterns will be associated with each basic technological setting. These relationships are summarized in Figure 2. No claim is made that technology always must be an independent variable; nor is there certainty about goals being dependent variables. As Perrow notes, "occasions can be readily cited where changes in goals, for example those brought about by changes in the marketplace or the personalities of top executives, have brought about changes in the technology utilized."[66]

According to the theory, routine organizations will possess centralized, bureaucratic structures which limit the discretion and power of lower and middle management (although the latter is somewhat more powerful due to its role in developing reports for advance planning). Coordination is accomplished through

Figure 2 STRUCTURAL AND GOAL PATTERNS

	Craft Organizations				Nonroutine Organizations			
	TASK STRUCTURE							
	Discretion	Power	Coord. w/in Groups	Group Interdependence	Discretion	Power	Coord. w/in Groups	Group Interdependence
MM*	Low	Low	Planning	Low	High	High	Feedback	High
LM**	High	High	Feedback		High	High	Feedback	
	(Decentralized)				(Decentralized)			

SOCIAL STRUCTURE

Social Identity: Based on Friendship	Goal Identity: Based on a Sense of Mission

GOALS

System	Product	Derived	System	Product	Derived
Stability	Quality	Conservative	High Growth	High Quality	Liberal
Low Risk	No Innovations		High Risk	Innovative	
Moderate Profit Emphasis			Low Profit Emphasis		

TASK STRUCTURE

	Discretion	Power	Coord. w/in Groups	Group Interdependence	Discretion	Power	Coord. w/in Groups	Group Interdependence
MM**	Low	High	Planning	Low	High	High	Feedback	Low
LM**	Low	Low	Planning		Low	Low	Planning	
	(Centralized)				(Centralized)			

SOCIAL STRUCTURE

Instrumental Identity: Based on Pay, Job Security Protection from Arbitrary Authority	Task Identity: Based on Technical Satisfactions

GOALS

System	Product	Derived	System	Product	Derived
Stability	Quantity	Conservative	Moderate Growth	Quantity	Liberal
Low Risk	No Innovations		Moderate Risk	Moderate Innovations	
High Profit Emphasis			Moderate Profit Emphasis		

	Routine Organizations		Engineering Organizations

*Middle Management
**Lower Management

programmed activity and standard operating procedures that require little group interaction. Satisfaction levels of organizational members will result primarily from attention to pay, job security, and protection from arbitrary authority. System goals will include stability, high profits, and quantity output. Little risk or innovation is likely and organizational power directed toward outside social goals will be used to promote the special interests of the firm—in this case, conservative political and economic attitudes and policies.

By contrast, nonroutine organizations will have decentralized, organic structures in which both middle and lower management have high degrees of discretion and power (because problems are complex and relative expertise changes rapidly). Group interaction is considerable and coordination occurs by spontaneous feedback (mutual adjustment) instead of advance planning and use of hierarchical channels. Members will be more concerned with the organization's mission and special competencies than with pay or security, and goals emphasized will include risk and innovation over stability, growth and quality over profits, and more liberal social goals.

Craft and engineering organization have mixed characteristics. In craft firms, where few exceptional cases must be dealt with, discretion and power of lower management will be high because the supervisory area has the closest, most immediate contact with whatever unique cases develop. Coordination at these lower levels is through feedback and little interaction is required with middle management, which has more programmed and routine activities. Member satisfactions result from on-the-job friendships and knowledge of special trade skills, and goal orientations resemble those of routine organizations, except for a somewhat greater emphasis on matters of quality.

Finally, in engineering firms, where problems are analyzable but subject to many exceptions, discretion and power of lower management will be quite low. Exceptions that occur are routinely pushed up to middle management for solution and this group has considerable discretion and power in resolving problems. Coordination among middle managers is by spontaneous interaction and there is little personal contact with supervisory levels (designs are sent down and expected to be executed as given). Member satisfactions are most apt to reflect a concern for refining technical skills and abilities while goal patterns will fall into categories intermediate to those found in other technological systems.

Implications

If this reasoning is persuasive, then a number of implications follow. First, a relationship found in one organization may not be found in another unless the organizations have similar "knowledge" technologies. Second, some schools, banks, hospitals, and manufacturing firms may have more in common, because of their routine character, than nonroutine organizations in the same areas of activity. Third, organizations will try to maximize the "fit" between technology and structure in the interests of efficiency and reduced levels of unproductive conflict. Fourth, the highly structured bureaucratic form of organization (with its emphasis on rules, hierarchy, division of labor, and clear lines of authority) probably works best where the underlying technology is routine and predictable.[67]

Finally, prescriptions for certain management techniques may be more relevant in some situations than others. Consider, for example, two "steady-state" systems—one routine, the other nonroutine. The routine system, seeking greater order and control, might selectively emphasize: (1) PERT networks, (2) value analysis, (3) long-range planning, (4) system design, (5) operations research, (6) cost-effectiveness analysis, (7) decision theory, and (8) human factors engineering. By contrast, the nonroutine system, seeking flexibility and expansion of personal initiative, might selectively use: (9) business gaming, (10) sensitivity training, (11) decentralization, including profit center and unit management, (12) creativity training, (13) management grid training, (14) profit sharing, (15) motivation laboratories, and (16) job enrichment.[68] If these system states change, of course, the relative applicability of the listed techniques would also change.

A Critique of Perrow

In an exploratory study which sought empirical support for the Perrow framework, managers in 14 medium-sized manufacturing corporations in two geographical parts of the country were given questionnaires that asked about their work and organizations.[69] Of 2,841 forms distributed, 93 percent were completed and returned.

By examining managerial perceptions about the variability and analyzability of their jobs, a modal "technology" score for each organization was determined and then used to classify the respective firms into Perrow's "technology" quadrants. When this was done, however, the data showed that the companies were more homogeneous than anticipated and could be categorized only as routine or nonroutine. The craft and engineering models therefore were eliminated from further consideration. Despite this reduction in scope, results indicated that differences between the routine and nonroutine clusters of organizations were in the directions predicted for the task structure and goal sections of the theory (little support was found for social structure aspects). The magnitudes of these differences were not great, but they remained when functional groups and managerial levels of authority were held constant.

Although this study reinforces the apparent utility of the Perrow framework as a guide to organizational analysis, a number of vexing issues remain. For example, because the theory understates the importance of organizational environment, it offers few insights into the subject of change. Institutional growth and time-lags between a change in technology and subsequent change in structure are not discussed—nor is the question of whether level of technology or rate of technological change has the greater impact on organizational behavior.

The greatest challenge to the Perrow theory, however, is that it ignores the existence of multiple technologies within organizations. When a nonroutineness index was applied to functional groups within the firms discussed above, differences were found both within and between these subunits. As shown in Figure 3, production and research/development tended to be at technological extremes, with sales and finance/administration groups taking intermediate positions but tending to cluster in the routine category.

The functional subsystems also had varied task structures but, with the exception of profuction, which was highly structured, they did not follow patterns expected on the basis of technology alone. Research/development units, for example, despite their relative nonroutineness, had structural features similar to the production groups. They also were the greatest source of organizational criticism. While this criticism could result from having structures incongruent with technological requirements, more likely it resulted from the limited power of the research/development units studied. In general, sales departments were dominant, followed by production, finance/administration, and research/development. The critical point, however, is that Perrow's approach seems preoccupied with differences between organizations, to the neglect of variations within them.

Figure 3 PERCENTAGE OF FUNCTIONAL GROUPS HAVING ROUTINE AND NONROUTINE TECHNOLOGIES

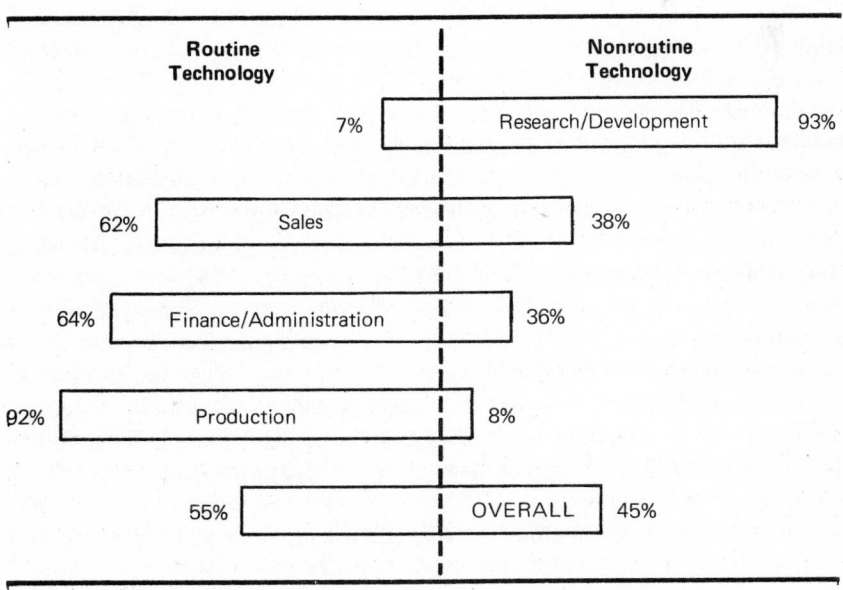

The Perrow framework, in sum, has conceptual appeal, some empirical support, and certain difficulties. It is one-sided in emphasis—as other theories have been—but this is not so much an emphasis on technology (in the sense of machine operations) as it is a focus on system uncertainty. Although Perrow makes no claim that his approach is some magical package for organizational design, he feels that his basic perspective is correct, i.e., "before an organization's problems can be solved, it is essential to determine the nature of the organization".[70]

The Environmental Imperative

The comparative frameworks of Woodward and Perrow assume that organizational structures and processes are contingent upon the demands of technology (variously defined). Another approach has been taken by Lawrence and Lorsch, who examined the relationships between organization and environment in three industrial settings chosen primarily for their different rates of technological change in both products and processes.[71] These settings or "environments" included plastics (high change), packaged foods (moderate change), and containers (low change). A total of ten organizations were studied: six plastics firms and two companies each in the other two industries. All firms used continuous-process technologies.

Observing that organizations design their subsystems to cope with different parts of the total environment, Lawrence and Lorsch first sought measures of environmental uncertainty for the marketing, production, and scientific sectors in each industry grouping. This was done by considering rates of information change, uncertainties over causal relationships, and time spans of feedback about results.

Results confirmed the researchers' expectations about the role of environment. In plastics, where pressures for innovation were greatest, the total environment was most highly diversified and uncertain. By contrast, the container environment was more predictable and stable, no doubt because innovation was less of an issue—being superseded by competitive demands for consistent, routine operations and reliable delivery services. The foods environment was intermediate in diversity.

Next, Lawrence and Lorsch measured the actual degree of differentiation among functional units as well as differences in problems of integration (coordination). Differentiation was measured along four dimensions: (1) formality of structure, e.g., formal rules and procedures vs. fewer rules and procedures; (2) time orientation, e.g., short vs. long; (3) interpersonal orientation, e.g., concern for task vs. concern for people; and (4) goal orientation, e.g., concern with market competition and customer problems vs. output, and efficiency vs. scientific advancements. Integration was examined in terms of which units needed tightest linking, the organizational level at which this linking was required, and the kinds of devices used to implement coordination.

A major finding in the study was that effective organizations (effectiveness was defined in terms of growth in profits, sales volume, and return on investment) had structures and member orientations that were congruent with ("fit") the demands of their respective environments. Thus, in plastics, and to a slightly lesser extent in foods, managers had heterogeneous outlooks. Structure was considered to be high in production, medium in sales, and low in research. Time horizons were short in production and sales but long in research. Interpersonal relations were more formal and task-oriented in production and more permissive in sales and research. Managers in container firms, however, had more homogeneous orientations and each tended to view the organization as having high structure, short time horizons, and a task emphasis in interpersonal relations.

High-performing organizations also achieved high levels of integration (defined as "the quality of the state of collaboration that exists among departments that are required to achieve unity of effort by the demands of the environment"). Although the degree (or "tightness") of integration was high in all three industries, there were differences which were accounted for by the dominant competitive issue in each environment. Where customer service was critical (containers), tightest integration was required between production and sales (to handle scheduling). Where innovation was more important (plastics and foods), interdependence had to be greatest between sales and research and between research and production (to handle new products and technological changes).

The means of accomplishing this integration varied, and a comparison of all high-performing organizations revealed both differences and similarities in effective conflict resolution procedures and practices. Differences tended to be structural in nature, while similarities related to managerial attitudes and behavior.

Successful firms in each industry, for example, used different integrating devices, with diverse environments requiring more complex mechanisms. Container firms (low differentiation) achieved integration primarily through the management hierarchy, direct managerial contacts, and paperwork systems (plans, schedules, and budgets). These methods also were used in the foods and plastics environments, but they were less important than other kinds of devices. Food organizations (moderate differentiation) relied on individual integrators, e.g., functional managers assigned to integrating roles, and on temporary cross-functional teams. Plastics firms (high differentiation), however, used formal integrating departments and permanent cross-functional teams at three levels of management.[72]

Effective companies also differed in the relative influence of various departments and the location of influence within the management hierarchy. Decision power had to be placed in units and levels where there was requisite knowledge of existing problems. Units requiring high influence were: sales in container firms (to implement customer service); sales and research in foods (to handle market and food science demands); and a separate integrating unit in plastics (to handle change). Further, in container firms, decision-making power was centralized in upper management, whereas in foods and plastics this influence was distributed more equally throughout the organization.

There were similarities among all high-performing companies as well—similarities of style in managing conflict. To begin with, managers centrally involved in achieving integration dealt with conflict by open confrontation (problem solving), instead of compromise (splitting differences), "smoothing" (trying to keep everybody happy), or "forcing" (resorting to unilateral power plays). Interestingly, Lawrence and Lorsch found that, while managers in general considered confrontation to be the most desirable mode of conflict resolution, relatively few practiced it.

Two other similarities in conflict management were important when special integrating devices were used. First, integrators felt that they were rewarded for achieving unified efforts; and second, integrators and integrating units in high-performing firms developed "balanced orientations"; i.e., they had scores on the structural, time, interpersonal, and goal dimensions that were intermediate to those of the managers and units being linked. If coordinators adopted attitudes and behavior either too similar or too dissimilar to any given department, they typically were charged with either favoritism or nonresponsiveness—the result being ineffective integration.

From this kind of comparative analysis, Lawrence and Lorsch identified several possible errors in organizational design. These included: (1) combining two different major tasks in the same unit; (2) placing similar tasks in separate units, with consequent conflict and redundancy of effort; (3) using the management hierarchy as the primary coordinating device in highly differentiated organizations; (4) using integrating devices between mildly differentiated units, which merely adds "noise" to the system; and (5) structuring and orienting an integrating unit so much like one of the sections being linked that it loses contact with the other. There are, of course, exceptions to these "errors." For example, consider the placing of similar tasks in separte units. While this may promote redundancy of effort and conflict, competition among organizational units for new innovations may be an acceptable tradeoff where high creativity or rapid development of ideas is required.

In summary, Lawrence and Lorsch found that successful organizations were able to diagnose and meet environmental requirements for differentiation and integration. These requirements were explored in several industrial settings ranging from plastics (high uncertainty) to containers (low uncertainty). Study results indicated that there is no "one best way" to organize, that organizational performance will be reduced where task structures do not "fit" environmental demands, and that certain generalizations about errors in organizational design can be made. Interestingly, the classical administrative writers used concepts similar to those emphasized by Lawrence and Lorsch but they failed to show how different systems produce different working styles.

Related Research

Attempts to systematically explain variations in organization design have been termed contingency theory. These have proved useful as partial guides for understanding the impact of technology and environment on structure, for selectively applying management techniques, and for dealing with matters of work coordination and conflict resolution. Additional research based on the Lawrence and Lorsch organization-environment model has led to other insights as well. Three such studies are illustrative and worth brief review. They concern, respectively, the question of whether to organize by product or by function; the relationship of organizational design to employee motivation; and the role of culture as an influence on organizational performance.

First, Walker and Lorsch examined the managerial dilemma of whether an organization should be structured by product or by function.[73] There are tradeoffs in each approach. While functional organization makes coordination among the various units difficult, product organization eases such problems but reduces management identification with functional goals. The basic problem here has been recognized for decades but continues to be difficult within product and market areas below the divisional level.

Based on research in two consumer foods manufacturing plants, Walker and Lorsch concluded that the functional organization leads to better results in situations where stable performance of a routine task is desired. Product organization leads to better results in situations where the task is less predictable and requires innovative problem solving. Compromises between product and functional forms might be necessary, of course, such as cross-functional teams, project management, and matrix organization (an overlay of product and functional types). But these are difficult to administer and matrix systems in particular require complex authority relationships and make heavy demands on interpersonal skills.[74]

While there is no easy solution to the product-function dilemma, an accurate assessment of the organization's basic task demands should assist greatly in making some proper choice. However, it should be noted that Walker and Lorsch have not considered the impact of information technology on organizational structures. One reason, in fact, that expanding firms turn to parallel departmentation (by product lines or geographical area) is to cope with increased difficulties of information handling. Yet if computer systems reduce information handling problems, parallel departmentation could prove undesirable, with consequent shifts back to functional organization.[75]

Second, Morse examined the relationship between organization design and individual motivation.[76] His results challenge the widespread humanist notion that formalized organizations cannot motivate people, whereas less formalized units always do. The study centered on four organizational units: two manufactured standardized containers (certain task) and two performed research and development work in communication technology (uncertain task). Each pairing belonged to the same company and included high- and low-performing units, as rated by management.

Both effective units had different structures, but in each case there was a congruence between these structures and task demands. The high-performing container section had highly structured duties, rules, procedures, and controls. By contrast, the high-performing research laboratory had a low degree of structure and more flexible control procedures. Ineffective units also had different structures, but these were inappropriate to their task demands. The low-performing container section resembled the effective research laboratory, and the low-performing laboratory resembled the successful container unit.

Most interesting, however, was the finding that managers and professionals in the two effective units had higher feelings of competence than those in the two ineffective units. According to Morse, the "fit" between task demands and organizational structures produced effective task performance and a sense of competence. Both structured and unstructured settings, then, can lead to personal motivation, a conclusion that casts further doubt on "either-or" preferences for classical or human relations theory. Morse's study emphasizes the need to consider multiple interactions among task, organization, and human variables and not to give exclusive attention to some single factor, whether it be the individual or the environment.

The third and final example of research related to the organization-environment model concerns a cross-cultural study by Reudi and Lawrence.[77] Their work compared organizational performance in German and American plastics firms. The countries selected for analysis were chosen because their plastics industries share similar market and technological characteristics.

Results indicated that the German company, a high performer by German standards, was low in performance when compared to American firms. Differentiation and integration scores were also low and the researchers felt that the cultural orientation of German managers impeded the necessary "fit" between environment and organization (i.e., high differentiation and integration scores would be anticipated for high performing plastics firms because of their dynamic environment). When compared with the American managers, the Germans were found to have stronger fears of failure, stronger desires for stable relationships and structures, and a stronger attraction to individual as against group or team activities. These characteristics apparently interfered with the creative orientations required for success in the plastics industry.

The Reudi and Lawrence study must be considered tentative (only one German firm was involved), but it does help indicate the possible impact of culture on organizational performance. Such research, along with Walker and Lorsch's study of the product-function dilemma and Morse's analysis of organizational structure and motivation, demonstrates the usefulness of the basic organization-environment model as a guide to empirical investigation and management practice. However, despite the model's important role in opening up new avenues of theory and research, it has not gone unchallenged.

Comment
Many of the challenges to Lawrence and Lorsch's work also apply to other contingency theories of organization and, for convenience, they will be discussed in that broader context. Criticism has ranged from specific methodological concern over how to measure particular variables like "environment" to more general points.[78] For example, contingency frameworks have been used primarily to describe an organization's present condition with little attention devoted to the applied process of making the organization-environment "fit" more congruent.[79] Yet, as Moberg and Koch have noted, "Just as the contingency view requires practitioners to think more like theorists, it also requires theorists to think more like practitioners."[80] If clear prescription for change based on situational demands is lacking, managers may simply use the "it depends on the situation" idea to justify current practice and avoid the systematic analysis needed to improve organizational effectiveness.[81]

Critics have also noted that while organizations must adjust their strategies, technologies, structures, and processes to changing environmental demands, a variety of organizational designs may be suitable for a particular strategy or technology, and the choice among them is an exercise in managerial judgment.[82] From this it follows that managers must resist the temptation to see a given set of situational demands producing but one acceptable solution, just as they must resist the older temptations of seeing all situations as unique (not subject to generalization) or as basically the same (and subject to universal prescription).

Finally, some writers have noted that contingency theories have dealt too exclusively with business and industrial settings despite their potential application to other kinds of systems as well, both large and small (e.g., education, health care, and governmental organizations).[83] While there has been recent progress in broadening the application of contingency theory, proponents need to recognize that the approaches offered by Woodward, Perrow, or Lawrence and Lorsch are just the beginnings of situational research and may not transfer easily to other settings. Contingency views in their present form offer special insights, with special limitations, and will not produce indisputable analyses about the "imperatives" of organizational design. The danger exists that situational models will be pressed ahead too quickly, with overstated points of convergence and understated problems of application.[84] But, given a recalcitrant gap between theory and practice, perhaps such risks are worth taking.

ORGANIZATION DEVELOPMENT

Implicit in the foregoing discussion of comparative organization theory and research is the notion that managers who understand and use contingency theory are likely to improve their abilities to diagnose organizational problems and take suitable corrective action. Most contingency theories, however, emphasize description of the organization and neglect the change processes that might lead to organizational improvement. This is not to say that change processes have been ignored; to the contrary, an entire applied field called Organization Development (OD) has emerged to deal with such matters.

The subject matter of OD is planned organizational change and, in contrast to organizational theorists, OD practitioners have shown no hesitancy about prescribing ways to make systems more effective. Sometimes neglecting careful diagnosis or comparative organizational research, they typically have promoted the idea that organizations are best improved by changing managerial attitudes, values, and organization climates in the direction of more openness, collaboration, and participation.[85] This "Theory Y" approach to management practice stems from OD's historical roots in the human relations movement and from a widespread belief among OD specialists that organizational environments are becoming increasingly complex and turbulent.[86] Toffler has popularized this latter belief in his book *Future Shock* (1970). Along with many OD writers, he argues that traditional bureaucratic structures are becoming obsolete, that more adaptive organizational systems are required, and that new levels of interpersonal skill must be developed to cope with conditions of rapid change, stress, and social upheaval.[87]

As will be seen, however, questions have been raised about the effectiveness of OD.[88] In addition, whether the environment is actually as turbulent as OD practitioners imply has been subject to debate. Perrow, for one, has suggested that the environment really has been carefully stabilized by business and government.[89] As evidence he points to administered pricing, government subsidies, planned obsolescence, and industry monopoly. In his view, the trend is not toward open, flexible, participative organizations—these are the exceptions rather than the rule.

Although the emphasis on participation and turbulent environments seems to bind the OD area together (as does agreement that OD somehow involves planning activities and extends beyond traditional management development, i.e., academic coursework taken outside the company), there is no lack of internal controversy. Practitioners have not agreed upon a definition of the field and debate continues whether OD should assist organizations in adapting to present circumstances or some future state. Further, disagreements have occurred over what represents a legitimate approach to OD, and techniques have proliferated into a confusing array of change strategies. According to Huse, OD methods have variously emphasized intrapersonal analysis (e.g., career planning and sensitivity training), personal work style (e.g., team building and intergroup development), means to link individual and organizational objectives (e.g., job redesign and management by objectives), and system-wide interventions (e.g., data surveys and Grid OD).[90]

As an example of this conflict over techniques, consider the matter of job enrichment. Many OD consultants advocate this method as a means to improve both productivity and employee involvement in work.[91] Others, however, feel that job enrichment is not a proper OD strategy, especially if it is imposed on people instead of being jointly decided upon by employees and their supervisors.[92] Such debates, unfortunately, often lose sight of the selective benefits that each technique may offer in particular situations.

As Miles recently observed, OD "has applied far more energy to the development of techniques than to the structuring of descriptive theory and research."[93] Perhaps for this very reason, OD has grown rapidly into big business. Numerous companies have OD programs of one kind or another, including General Electric, General Motors, Union Carbide, Exxon, Corning Glass, Texas Instruments, American Airlines, Hotel Corporation of America, John Hancock Insurance, IBM, Polaroid, General Foods, Armour and Company, TRW Systems, and Bank of America.[94] But, while millions of dollars have been spent on a multiplicity of programs, there is little substantive data regarding their effectiveness, even though each OD technique has shown some results in some situations.[95]

To illustrate one popular and widespread approach to organization development, the following section will critically examine Grid OD in some detail. The method is worth considering for several reasons. First, thousands of firms have adopted Grid OD in whole or in part.[96] Second, it is the most systematic and thorough OD program—one that ideally involves an entire organization at all levels of management through six phases of activity. Third, the Grid's "one best way to manage" philosophy is in direct conflict with emerging contingency approaches to organizational behavior. Finally, it has been subject to modifications aimed at making it less "ideological" and more responsive to situational theories of organization. The ensuing discussion, then, describes Grid OD, considers its effectiveness, and examines a modified Grid program. A final section reviews selected issues confronting OD as an applied profession.

Grid OD

This approach to improving organizational performance was developed and copyrighted by Blake and Mouton.[97] Based on numerous organizational studies, two key barriers to corporate excellence were found: communications and planning. According to Blake and Mouton, however, such factors are only symptomatic of deeper problems, namely, supervisors who do not understand human motivation and corporate strategy that is largely absent or poorly defined.

To counteract these barriers to performance, a six-phase program called Grid OD was developed. The first three phases work on the communication-supervision issue while the latter three emphasize the planning-strategy problem. The stages of Grid OD can be summarized briefly as follows:

Phase 1:   The Managerial Grid. Identifies each manager's style and compares it with an "ideal" or preferred style.

Phase 2:   Teamwork Development. Focuses on means for getting work teams to function better.

Phase 3:   Intergroup Development. Reduces unnecessary conflict among groups to prevent suboptimization of organizational goals.

Phase 4:   Developing the Ideal Strategic Planning Model. Attempts to design a corporate blueprint for a truly outstanding organization.

Phase 5:   Implementing the Ideal Strategic Model. Puts theory into practice by reorganizing to meet the demands of the new strategic model.

Phase 6:   Critique. Evaluates previous phases to chart progress, deficiencies, and future opportunities for achieving excellence.

Typically, top management is exposed to Phase 1 with successive exposure to lower levels of management. That is, as top management moves into Phase 2, the next lower level of management begins Phase 1.

In Blake and Mouton's view, the Managerial Grid in Phase 1 is fundamental to the success of their program because it develops an "ideal" managerial style that must be cultivated if managers are to become effective supervisors in the planning and implementation of organizational goals. They contend that every manager has a distinct style of managing which reflects varying degrees of concern for production and concern for people. These "concerns" are measured respectively along 9-point horizontal and 9-point vertical axes to produce numerous style combinations.

Basically, the Grid emphasizes five styles, with the ideal being 9-9 management (which maximizes both the concern for production and the concern for people). Various names and descriptions have been attributed to these styles, but the following are illustrative:[98]

Executive: The 9-9 manager who possesses the ideal style, i.e., who problem solves, brings conflict into the open, and uses subordinate capabilities to build organizational commitment and high performance.

Taskmaster: The 9-1 manager who emphasizes production and getting the job done, expects subordinates to know their place, and worries less about morale than whether everyone is busy and alert to performance demands.

Friend: The 1-9 manager who carefully avoids getting subordinates upset, attempts to understand employees, and does not press hard on task accomplishment.

Fencesitter: The 5-5 "middle of the road" manager in the center of the Grid who sees the conflict between production and people requirements but splits differences and compromises to avoid conflict, even though the best solutions and highest degree of commitment are not obtained.

Ostrich: The 1-1 manager who has retired on the job, performs none of the basic functions of management, and prefers to avoid problems altogether.

Blake and Mouton use a standard questionnaire to help managers identify their basic (and backup) styles. Such analysis is held to increase self-awareness, provide a common language for talking about managerial behavior, and ready people for change in the direction of genuine teamwork and joint objective setting. While Grid OD begins with a focus on individual styles, its remaining phases emphasize ever-widening degrees of system involvement. The program moves from the individual managers, to work groups, to intergroup development, to total organizational involvement. In Theory, then, Grid OD identifies a preferred management style and poses a detailed program for converting "the great majority of managers who do not currently practice the desired 9-9 mode of operation."[99] Complete implementation of Blake and Mouton's approach may take anywhere from three to five years.

Comment

Unfortunately, an accurate assessment of this program has yet to be done. There is a great deal of testimonial evidence citing Grid benefits, but very few areas of the Grid progam have been carefully studied. Many applications never get beyond Phase 1, making generalizations about the total package difficult. Further, some of the testimonial evidence is contradictory. Huse, for example, cites cases where one executive stated that his firm received 90 percent of the program's value in Phase 1, whereas another manager (from another application) asserted that the payoff was five times as great from Phase 2.[100]

Even those studies which have tried to deal systematically with complete Grid programs have not really pinpointed their effectiveness. For example, a 1964 report on Grid OD in the Sigma refinery (actually the Baytown refinery of Humble Oil) found significant changes in the direction of 9-9 management at the same time that profits rose by 160 percent. However, no control groups were used in this study to see if factors other than Grid OD were responsible for the results. The refinery was undergoing mass layoffs and new equipment changes at the time, to which management attributed about two-thirds of the results. By deduction, the remaining third of improved performance was assigned to the Grid— hardly a conclusive figure.[101]

Consider also a recent report on Grid OD as implemented at the Union Mutual Life Insurance Company of Portland, Maine. The year top management began its involvement (1972), company performance was outstanding, as it was the following year when upper management deepened its involvement in the Grid.

Again, however, cause and effect relations between Grid OD and performance were not made clear. Although the company president gave considerable credit to the Grid program, even his favorable review is difficult to assess because Union Mutual Life did not follow the six phase sequence outlined by Blake and Mouton. Managers were exposed to Phases 1 and 2 (style and teamwork seminars) as prescribed, but Phase 3 (intergroup development) was eliminated and Phases 4 through 6 were compressed. Further, the entire top management finished the entire revised program before any lower levels of management were exposed. This was an important departure from Blake and Mouton's basic approach, but top management felt strongly that it must set overall company goals before other levels of management attempted doing the same for themselves.[102]

On balance, what can be concluded about Grid OD? It is popular, usually not used as a complete package, and difficult to evaluate. Evidence does not support the contention that 9-9 management is always best and some data suggests that managers trained to be 9-1 (task) oriented move ahead faster in their careers.[103] Although the Grid is still alleged to be one of the most effective strategies for changing organizations, it has undergone modifications in practice (as in the Union Mutual case) and there are signs of interest about how Grid programs might be made responsive to the situational analysis advocated by less well-known contingency theorists. One such attempt, developed by W. J. Reddin, is particularly novel and worth special attention.

A Variant of Grid OD: The Reddin Program

Reddin views his modified Grid approach as providing a diagnostic framework for examining managerial styles along with a systematic method for planning and implementing organizational change.[104] This, of course, sounds identical to Blake and Mouton's approach. In contrast to Grid OD, however, Reddin's analysis of managerial style takes a variety of situational determinants into account and his program phases are more flexible in application. Further, Reddin emphasizes that diagnosis of organizational problems should determine the change techniques employed (unlike many OD specialists who prefer to sell prepackaged solutions).

To understand Reddin's modifications of the Grid, consider first his framework for analyzing managerial styles. Using slightly different terminology than Blake and Mouton, his Grid is built around four basic styles formed from a similar two-dimensional schematic that reflects a manager's task-orientation (TO) and relationships-orientation (RO). These basic styles are labeled Separated (low TO; low RO), Related (low TO; high RO), Dedicated (high TO; low RO), and Integrated (high TO; high RO). They correspond, respectively, to Blake and Mouton's 1-1, 1-9, 9-1, and 9-9 styles.

Unlike Grid OD, however, Reddin does not consider any single style "best" because each may be used effectively or ineffectively depending on situational elements affecting the manager. These elements include, in relative order of importance, demands made by a manager's superior, the technology employed, the organizational climate (underlying values of the system), co-workers, and sub-ordinates. All five elements are unlikely to make demands in all situations.

By analyzing his or her own operating styles and the style demands made by situational elements, a manager can produce what Reddin terms a situational flex map (see Figure 4). For a given set of circumstances, the most effective style is indicated where the dominant situational elements intersect. (The degree of variability found in each element is represented by the size of its shape compared to the total area of the map.) Thus, in Figure 4, a Related style is required for both managers. Only Manager A, however, has the current potential to use the proper style for the demands indicated. Manager B is using an inappropriate style either because of unawareness or an inability to be any more flexible than indicated.

Figure 4 SITUATIONAL FLEX MAP

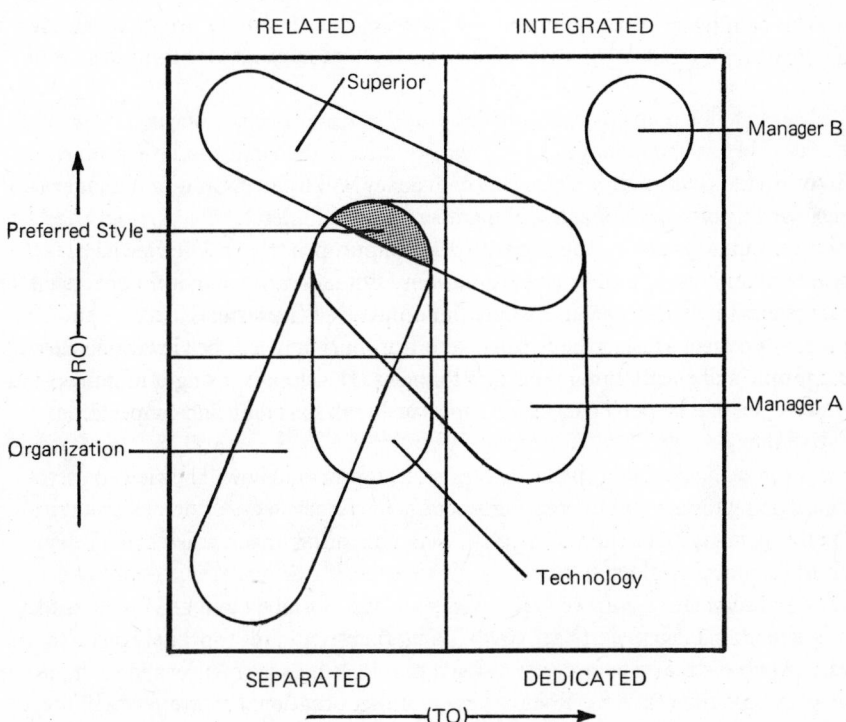

The procedure for developing flex maps is quite detailed.[105] In general, to analyze a situation and work out flex maps, managers are given two sets of twenty-item descriptors. One set applies to technology demands and the other to the four human and organizational components plus the diagnosis of managerial operating styles. Within each set, five descriptors apply to each basic style. To assess a situation, the manager involved must ask three types of questions: (1) "Which indicators describe the current technology being used?"; (2) "Which indicators describe how I should act on each of the situational components so that my effectiveness will be increased?"; and (3) "To best describe my own operating style, for which of the applicable indicators can I say, 'I do this easily and well'?"

In reviewing the style indicators for any given element, the manager checks off each item that applies. This produces a number from 0 to 5 for each of the four basic styles. If 4 or 5 descriptors apply, a "strong" rating is indicated; if 2 or 3 descriptors apply, the rating is "moderate"; and if 0 to 1 descriptors apply, the rating is "weak." In translating these to a flex map, strong ratings are indicated by a circle in the outer corner of the appropriate style area, moderate ratings are represented by a circle in the areas surrounding the origin, and weak ratings are omitted. If components of more than one basic style exist, the relevant circles are joined to form a new shape, as in Manager A's style in Figure 4. Despite this apparent complexity, it is important to recognize that flex maps are merely approximations of situational demands and are best viewed as guides for thinking about specific cases.

Once a flex map has been worked out, the degree of congruency (or incongruency) between a manager's style and situational demands can be examined. According to Reddin, this degree of congruency will influence how a manager is perceived by other organizational members. As examples:

—A manager using the *Separated* style appropriately will be viewed as properly emphasizing rules and regulations (Bureaucrat); using it inappropriately he or she will be perceived as distant and uninvolved (Deserter).

—A manager using the *Related* style appropriately will be viewed as trusting people and encouraging their development (Developer); using it inappropriately he or she will be perceived as too concerned with harmony and cooperation (Missionary).

—A manager using the *Dedicated* style appropriately will be viewed as accomplishing tasks without creating resentment (Benevolent Autocrat); using it inappropriately he or she will be perceived as creating unnecessary task pressure, hostility, and resentment (Autocrat).

—A manager using the *Integrated* style appropriately will be viewed as fostering team management (Executive); using this style inappropriately he or she will be perceived as a poor decision-maker and perhaps overconcerned with participation (Compromiser). Reddin feels that this situational awareness will not only assist individual managers in understanding how others view them but also will identify possibilities for improving the "fit" of situational components.

Situational sensitivity alone, however, is of little value. Eventually this awareness must be translated into an action program to improve managerial and organizational effectiveness. Here Reddin recommends coupling his flex map system with a management by objectives (MBO) program. (MBO programs vary in form but generally involve planned goal setting, subordinate participation in decision-making, and results-oriented appraisals.)[106] He assumes that directions for organizational change—interpersonal or structural—will emerge quite naturally as managers gain new perspectives from an analysis of situational issues affecting performance.

To implement his effectiveness program, Reddin suggests a four-phase procedure:

Phase 1:   Corporate Strategy Conference. Examines organizational goals and consolidates top executive support.
Phase 2:   Managerial Effectiveness Seminar. Instructs managers in situational analysis, examines individual styles and objectives, and assesses possible targets for change.
Phase 3:   Team or Departmental Development. Uses flex maps to consider how administrative, behavioral, or technical changes might improve the way members work together.
Phase 4:   Superior-Subordinate Workshop. Emphasizes joint objective setting, resolves misunderstandings or disagreements about ends sought, and plans for future review of performance results.

In contrast to Grid OD (and like the Union Mutual approach), Reddin's program has fewer phases and emphasizes corporate goal setting as a necessary prior step to objective setting by lower levels of management. No rigid approach is taken to implementation. Phases 1 and 4 might be reversed, for example, or other stages added (including interdepartmental sessions, meetings that focus on the interaction among successive vertical levels of management, and various kinds of periodic review conferences). How the program is handled will depend on what particular organizational goals are sought.

In summary, Reddin emphasizes the importance of diagnosis in selecting strategies for change and the essential complementarity of management and organization development. He assumes that there is no "ideal" managerial style, that multiple options exist for improving effectiveness, and that managers of a given firm know more about its problems and opportunities than external consultants who may be less problem-directed than technique-bound. Like Morse, he views motivation not as something a manager does to someone, but "as arising from a matching of all the demands of a situation."[107] Whether coupled with an MBO program or not, Reddin's basic method provides a unique way to instruct managers in situational sensitivity, style flexibility, and situational management.

Comment

Reddin has tried to bridge the gap between organization theory and practice and his rejection of a single "best" managerial style is consistent with available research, most notably that of Fiedler.[108] Yet there are some Grid-related difficulties in Reddin's approach. Little empirical evidence exists to demonstrate the effectiveness of the program and it is not entirely clear whether the TO/RO dimensions are attitudinal or behavioral in nature. Marked discrepancies may exist between a manager's view of what "style" is best and how that manager actually behaves.[109]

Further, there is some ambiguity about how the concept of participation fits into the Grid framework. Participation seems to go beyond the limited idea of interpersonal consideration implied in the RO dimension, and empirical literature has treated it separately from the TO dimension.[110] In general, studies indicate that participative leadership is preferable when decisions are not routine, when information required for decision-making cannot be standardized or centralized, when decisions need not be made rapidly, and when subordinates feel a distinct need for independence, regard their participation as legitimate, consider themselves able to contribute to the decision process, and can work without the reassurance of close supervision.[111]

Also, the MBO emphasis in Grid programs assumes positive outcomes. Proponents of MBO feel that it directs work activities toward organizational goals, provides clear standards for control, improves managerial motivation, makes better use of human resources, and provides more objective appraisal criteria. Critics of MBO, however, point to inadequate top management commitment, excessive time expenditures in goal setting activities, use of the technique as a "club" to press unrealistic goals, general paperwork problems, and managerial dislike of performance reviews.[112] Additionally, some research has shown how Grid OD and MBO may directly conflict. For example, in a study by Nord and Durand of a routine manufacturing firm, one respondent stated that "The Grid suggested that you work as a team. In MBO you just thought about yourself. MBO seemed to undermine the Grid."[113] (Contingency theorists, of course, might question the appropriateness of Grid OD and MBO in a routine manufacturing company—unless that company is evolving into a more nonroutine kind of organization.)

Despite Reddin's enthusiastic endorsement, MBO is no panacea. Implementation requires a collaborative style of management.[114] Considerable evidence, however, suggests that most efforts at MBO are autocratic, overemphasize getting subordinates to respond to management's goals, and pay little attention to each individual's personal objectives.[115] As might be expected, when MBO does not provide a genuine linkage of individual and organizational goals, resistance to change will limit the effectiveness of its application.[116]

Finally, while Reddin rejects the "one best way" philosophy of Grid OD, he apparently expects managers to become situationally aware without developing a composite view of the larger organization. No recognition is given to the broader contingency frameworks of Perrow (even though Perrow's technology cells seem remarkably congruent with Reddin's style cells) or Lawrence and Lorsch (even though their approach is useful in examining the impact of environment on structural design and patterns of coordination). In the absence of some broader view, managers may prematurely fix on Grid-like programs as the best way to consider organizational issues and consequently neglect the multiple options that exist for analyzing such problems.

Issues in Organization Development

Having reviewed the Grid programs, it seems useful to summarize several concerns about OD as an emerging applied profession. Foremost in this regard is the limited theoretical base from which OD practitioners work. Too often, organizational change is sought by focusing on individual managers and their styles of behavior. The assumption is made that if large numbers of managers change their interpersonal styles and become more participative and capable in dealing with others, then the entire organization will become more effective. Behavioral processes are emphasized while changes in structure, technology, work-flows, budgets, information systems, and external environments are overlooked—even though they may have a distinct impact on organizational behavior.[117]

Fortunately, in addition to Reddin's approach, there are signs that OD is extending its conceptual base. Huse, for example, has termed contingency theory an "exciting new development in OD," one that cuts through the "jungle of controversy" between traditionalists trying to preserve bureaucracy and OD practitioners stressing humanism and democracy in the work place.[118] Similarly, Friedlander and Brown have proposed an OD framework that simultaneously deals with technostructural and human-process aspects of organization and rejects OD efforts designed to change only the people, only the structure, or only the technology.[119]

Even if conceptual convergence occurs and OD takes more of a systems approach to organizations, there are other problems to be confronted. For example, OD's preoccupation with prepackaged solutions has hindered genuine field research, a fact amply suggested by the few long term projects done to evaluate the development of organizations over time. Granted, there have been exceptions. Marrow, et al., studied a company over several years to examine the durability of participative management,[120] and the University of Michigan's Institute for Social Research has implemented an Inter-Company Longitudinal Study.[121] But, for the most part, the OD area requires more research to identify its impact on organizations—a point underscored by Kahn's 1973 finding that only 25 percent of the OD literature contained original quantitative data.[122]

Finally, along with concerns about theoretical integration and the expansion of research, OD faces the issue of developing new power-conflict models of behavior. The area has tended to rely on "truth-love" approaches to change that emphasize personal sensitivity, openness, trust, concern, and harmony. Questions of power, vested interests, empire-building, career competition, and political advantage have been largely ignored. While this may be an adequate response in relatively closed, centralized organizations where there is basic agreement about goals (e.g., wealthy corporations), it has less application in pluralistic settings with diffuse power structures (e.g., local governments, hospitals, universities, and urban ghettoes).[123] These latter systems require insights into bargaining and negotiation processes, determinants of power, and conflict management techniques.

OD need not neglect power-conflict issues, of course, and practitioners might consider tapping the industrial relations literature which has a long tradition of dealing with strikes, grievances, mediation, arbitration, and collective bargaining. Or, closer attention might be given to business school programs that teach Machiavellian tactics to students. Such programs emphasize how power is given only grudgingly in organizations, that people seek control over others often by calculating, exploitive, secretive methods, and that individuals should consider acting dispassionately in their own self-interests.[124] This notion may seem extreme, of course, but OD has been too limited in its view of the world and needs to become more "sensitive" to other change strategies that do not fit its predominant value system of "authentic" behavior.[125] As Bennis has observed, unless power-conflict models of change are developed to complement those based on truth-love assumptions, OD "will find fewer and narrower institutional avenues open to its influence and in so doing, it will slowly and successfully decay."[126]

Elden, et al., have also emphasized the need for OD practitioners to become more conscious of competing value systems found among different organizational constituencies.[127] Such constituencies variously may seek institutional stability, greater access to and service from existing channels of wealth, power, and influence, or even fundamental social change. As these diverse expectations and demands impact on organizations, simultaneous pressures are exerted on management to improve old delivery systems for new constituencies (e.g., minorities) and provide new services for old constituencies (e.g., middle classes). This means that organizations must become better bureaucracies while parts of them are evolving nonbureaucratic forms.[128]

Further, such processes will intensify as organizations confront new post-industrial challenges regarding energy, transportation, urban development, health care, communications, and environmental protection.[129] Adaptive responses to these problem areas will require new organizational linkages that blur public-private sector interests, transcend national boundaries, and emphasize the need for managers who are "power-oriented, network-conscious, crisis-capable, value-aware, and socially pluralistic."[130] There will also be a need to communicate across social and cultural barriers—no easy task given the possibilities for misunderstanding, polarization, and violence.[131]

Whether OD will be responsive to criticism about its neglect of theory, research, and power-conflict issues remains to be seen. At stake is the distinction between "refined" professional status and "just another" passing management fad. Although critics have questioned OD's viability as a change strategy, Miles has noted that "OD may not be the answer to improving organizational and societal change processes, but it is perhaps the best arena for learning and experimentation presently available."[132] Other proponents also seem optimistic even while acknowledging that the long-run success of OD will depend on its integration with other programs aimed at organizational improvement, the degree to which additional conceptual models are developed, and "the quality and extent of research on the effectiveness of various intervention strategies."[133] As Strauss has noted, however, "Insight is much easier to obtain than implementation."[134]

SUMMARY AND CONCLUSIONS

This essay has critically examined several major approaches to organizational design, development, and behavior. Multiple entry points to the study of organizations were acknowledged, especially those of task, structure, people, technology, and environment. These basic components of organization interact but, historically, various schools of thought have developed around each. The earliest phase, scientific management, focused on task specialization and assumed human behavior to be motivated primarily by economic considerations. Administrative design theory, complementary to scientific management, stressed the bureaucratic aspects of organization and the importance of formal planning and control procedures. The human relations movement, as a response to classical management, produced a welter of findings that led to numerous people-oriented fads, including democratic supervision and sensitivity training, but provided no systematic theory of organizations as organizations.

Recently, comparative studies of organizations have resulted in several macro-level contingency frameworks for analyzing the impact of technology and environment on organizational structures, patterns of integration, conflict management, motivation, leadership styles, and system effectiveness. These approaches offer promise in assisting managers to diagnose relevant task demands, assess the extent to which subsystems must be linked, and selectively apply management or behavioral concepts and techniques. They also should help managers rethink conventional wisdom and traditional prescriptions, especially in new federalized public-private sector complexes where planning and control techniques face more iterative settings, where multiple dependency relationships require executives to become project-monitors and decision-influencers instead of order-givers and decision-makers, and where effective linkages must be developed across diverse sets of professionals and political interest groups.[135]

Although the contingency theories of organization are useful, they hardly represent final solutions. Each has distinct limitations. Woodward's research is based on production systems, yet not all firms have machine-based production units. Perrow's work seeks a more generic definition of technology, yet does not deal adequately with the question of multiple technologies within the same system. Lawrence and Lorsch emphasize organizational environments instead of technology, yet the concept of environment is handled only in very general terms. Further, none of the theories reviewed is well-linked with the others and most of the relevant research has been accomplished in industrial firms—suggesting the need for more extensive empirical ventures into other organizational sectors.

At applied levels, organization development programs, deeply rooted in the human relations movement, have only recently been influenced by emerging situational perspectives (e.g., Reddin's modification of Blake and Mouton's Grid). The major thrust of OD remains normative, with practitioners seeking to change people's values in the direction of self-worth and democratic participation. If OD is to acquire a genuine systems orientation, however, greater recognition must be given to the multiple options for initiating organizational change and improvement.

On balance, there appears to be no lack of challenge in the organizational area. Yet substantial recent progress has been made, especially in the use of situational analysis to consider organizational problems. Provocative frameworks for comparing organizations have emerged, as have novel applied techniques for dealing with organizational development. Despite a residue of old issues and the generation of many new ones, a spirit of cautious optimism about continued progress in this "orphan among fields" seems warranted. As some authors have observed, "We feel we are as confused as ever. But we think we are confused on a higher level and about more important things."[136]

NOTES

1. George Strauss, "Organizational Behavior and Personnel Relations," in W. Ginsburg, E. Livernash, H. Parnes, and G. Strauss, *A Review of Industrial Relations Research,* Vol. 1 (Madison, Wisconsin: Industrial Relations Research Association, 1970), p. 146.
2. Fred Goldner, "Success vs. Failure—Prior Managerial Perspectives," *Industrial Relations,* 9 (October, 1970), pp. 453-74.
3. Karl Magnusen, "Perspectives on Organizational Design and Development," Research Paper 21 (Revised; New York: Columbia University, Graduate School of Business, 1974), p. 1.
4. H. J. Leavitt, *Managerial Psychology* (Chicago: University of Chicago Press, 1958).
5. F. E. Kast and J. E. Rosenzweig, "General Systems Theory," *Academy of Manage-*

ment Journal, 15 (December, 1972), pp. 447-65. [See Reading 1.]

6. George Strauss, "Human Relations—1968 Style," *Industrial Relations,* 7 (October, 1967), p. 275.

7. Henry Landsberger, "The Behavioral Sciences in Industry," *Industrial Relations,* 7 (October, 1967), p. 1.

8. Other authors may prefer a different format or emphasis. As examples, see J. G. Miller, "Living Systems: The Organization," *Behavioral Science,* 17 (January, 1972), pp. 1-82, and D. S. Pugh, "Modern Organization Theory: A Psychological and Sociological Study," *Psychological Bulletin,* 66 (October, 1966), pp. 235-51.

9. F. W. Taylor, *Principles of Scientific Management* (New York: Harper, 1911). For the historical background to Taylorism, see H. Aitken, *Taylorism, at Watertown Arsenal* (Cambridge: Harvard University, 1960).

10. For one of the first statements on time and motion study, see F. B. Gilbreth, *Primer of Scientific Management* (New York: Harper, 1912).

11. The emphasis on the efficiency criterion during the period of Taylorism can be seen in H. Emerson, *Twelve Principles of Efficiency* (New York: Engineering Magazine Co., 1911).

12. F. W. Taylor, *A Piece Rate System* (London: Routledge, 1919). Also see H. L. Gantt, *Work, Wages and Profits* (New York: Engineering Magazine Co., 1919).

13. M. Nadworthy, *Scientific Management and the Unions: 1900-1932* (Cambridge: Harvard University, 1955).

14. Examples of these managerial writings include: Henri Fayol, *Industrial and General Administration,* translated by J. A. Coubrough (Geneva: International Management Association, 1930); Oliver Sheldon, *The Philosophy of Management* (London: Pitman, 1923); Luthur Gulick and L. Urwick, *Papers on the Science of Administration* (New York: Columbia University, 1937); and James D. Mooney and Alan C. Reiley, *Onward Industry* (New York: Harper, 1931).

15. Max Weber, *The Theory of Social and Economic Organization,* translated by A. M. Henderson and T. Parsons (Glencoe, Illinois: Free Press, 1947).

16. Joe Kelly, *Organizational Behavior* (Homewood, Illinois: Richard D. Irwin, 1969), pp. 267-68.

17. For the most exhaustive synthesis of this managerial-bureaucratic approach, see R. C. Davis, *The Fundamentals of Top Management* (New York: Harper, 1951).

18. A detailed analysis of these concepts may be found in Rocco Carzo, Jr., and John Yanouzas, *Formal Organizations: A Systems Approach* (Homewood, Illinois: Dorsey, 1967), pp. 43-70.

19. H. Koontz and C. O'Donnell, *Principles of Management* (4th ed.; New York: McGraw-Hill, 1968).

20. Richard H. Hall, "The Concept of Bureaucracy: An Empirical Assessment," *American Journal of Sociology,* 69 (July, 1963), pp. 32-40.

21. Nicos P. Mouzelis, *Organization and Bureaucracy* (Chicago: Aldine, 1968), pp. 51-53.

22. Two classical writers who emphasized the much neglected problem of communication were Chester Barnard, *The Functions of the Executive* (Cambridge: Harvard University, 1947), and Mary Parker Follett, *Dynamic Administration,* edited by H. C. Metcalf and L. Urwick (New York: Harper and Row, 1940).

23. For a comprehensive review and critique of administrative design theory, see J. L. Massie, "Management Theory," in J. G. March (ed.), *Handbook of Organizations* (Chicago: Rand McNally, 1965), pp. 387-422.

24. Elton Mayo, *The Human Problems of an Industrial Civilization* (New York: Macmillan, 1933); *The Social Problems of an Industrial Civilization* (Boston: Harvard

University, 1946); and *The Political Problems of an Industrial Civilization* (Boston: Harvard University, 1947).

25. The most comprehensive account of the Hawthorne studies appeared seven years after their conclusion. In this regard, see F. J. Roethlisberger and W. J. Dickson, *Management and the Worker* (Cambridge: Harvard University, 1939). For the pioneering effort on worker restriction of output, however, see S. B. Mathewson, *Restriction of Output Among Unorganized Workers* (New York: Viking, 1931). The best summary, critique, and defense of the Hawthorne investigations can be found in Henry Landsberger, *Hawthorne Revisited* (Ithaca, New York: Cornell University, 1958).

26. K. Lewin, "Group Decision and Social Change," and R. Lippitt and R. White, "An Experimental Study of Leadership and Group Life," in E. E. Maccoby, T. E. Newcomb, and E. L. Hartley (eds.), *Readings in Social Psychology* (New York: Holt, 1958), pp. 197-212 and 496-511.

27. F. J. Roethlisberger and W. J. Dickson, *Management and the Worker*, pp. 536-37.

28. George Strother, "Problems in the Development of a Social Science of Organization," in H. J. Leavitt (ed.), *The Social Science of Organizations* (Englewood Cliffs, New Jersey: Prentice-Hall, 1963) pp. 13-14.

29. See, respectively, D. C. Pelz, "Leadership Within a Hierarchical Organization," *Journal of Social Issues,* 7 (1951), pp. 49-55; Daniel Katz, Nathan Maccoby, and Nancy Morse, *Productivity, Supervision, and Morale in an Office Situation* (Ann Arbor: University of Michigan, 1951); Chris Argyris, *Executive Leadership* (New York: Harper, 1950); Robert Merton, "Bureaucratic Structure and Personality," *Social Forces,* 18 (1940), pp. 560-68; Peter Selznick, *TVA and the Grass Roots* (Berkeley: University of California, 1949); Alvin Gouldner, *Patterns of Industrial Bureaucracy* (Glencoe, Illinois: Free Press, 1954); and Peter M. Blau, *The Dynamics of Bureaucracy* (Chicago: University of Chicago, 1955).

30. See, respectively, Melville Dalton, "The Industrial 'Rate Buster': A Characterization," *Applied Anthropology,* 7 (Winter, 1948), pp. 5-18; Robert Dubin, "Industrial Workers' Worlds: A Study of the 'Central Life Interests' of Industrial Workers," *Social Problems,* 3 (January, 1956), pp. 131-42; Robert Dubin, *Leadership and Productivity* (San Francisco: Chandler, 1965), pp. 1-50; and Charles Greene, "The Satisfaction-Performance Controversy," *Business Horizons,* 15 (October, 1972), pp. 31-41 [see Reading 9].

31. Chris Argyris, *Personality and Organization* (New York: Harper, 1957).

32. A. H. Maslow, *Motivation and Personality* (New York: Harper and Row, 1954).

33. Douglas McGregor, *The Human Side of Enterprise* (New York: McGraw-Hill, 1960).

34. L. P. Bradford, J. R. Gibb, and K. D. Benne, *T-Group Therapy and Laboratory Method* (New York: John Wiley, 1964).

35. Frederick Herzberg, Bernard Mauser, and Barbara Snyderman, *The Motivation to Work* (New York: John Wiley, 1959); also, Frederick Herzberg, *Work and the Nature of Man* (Cleveland: World, 1966).

36. For applications based on Herzberg's approach, see M. Scott Myers, "Who Are Your Motivated Workers?" *Harvard Business Review,* 42 (January-February, 1964), pp. 73-88; also, W. P. Paul, Jr., K. B. Robertson, and F. Herzberg, "Job Enrichment Pays Off," *Harvard Business Review,* 47 (March-April, 1969), pp. 61-78.

37. Amitai Etzioni, *Modern Organization* (Englewood Cliffs, New Jersey: Prentice-Hall, 1964), p. 39.

38. See, for example, Rensis Likert, *The Human Organization* (New York: McGraw-Hill, 1967), and Douglas McGregor, *The Professional Manager* (New York: McGraw-Hill, 1967).

39. D. J. Hickson, "A Convergence in Organization Theory," *Administrative Science Quarterly*, 11 (September, 1966), pp. 224-37.

40. George Strauss, "Some Notes on Power-Equalization," in H. J. Leavitt (ed.), *The Social Science of Organization*, pp. 39-84.

41. See, respectively, Harold Wool, "What's Wrong with Work in America?—A Review Essay," *Monthly Labor Review*, 96 (March, 1973), pp. 38-44 [see Reading 7]; Eric Fromm, *Escape From Freedom* (New York: Farrar and Rinehart, 1941); Robert Dubin, "Industrial Workers' Worlds: A Study of the 'Central Life Interests' of Industrial Workers," p. 131; Alfred Marrow, David Bowers, and Stanley Seashore, *Management by Participation* (New York: Harper, 1967); V. Vroom, "Some Personality Determinants of the Effects of Participation," *The Journal of Abnormal and Social Psychology*, 59 (November, 1959), pp. 322-27; Nancy Morse and Everett Reimer, "Experimental Change of a Major Organizational Variable," *Journal of Abnormal and Social Psychology*, 52 (January, 1956), pp. 120-29; and R. M. Powell and J. L. Schlacter, "Participative Management: A Panacea?" *Academy of Management Journal*, 14 (June, 1971), pp. 165-73.

42. See, respectively, D. T. Hall and D. E. Nougaim, "An Examination of Maslow's Need Hierarchy in an Organizational Setting," *Organizational Behavior and Human Performance*, 3 (February, 1968), pp. 12-35; and J. G. Hunt and J. W. Hill, "The New Look in Motivation Theory for Organizational Research," *Human Organization*, 28 (Summer, 1969), pp. 100-109 [see Reading 8].

43. See, respectively, William Reif and Fred Luthans, "Does Job Enrichment Really Pay Off?" *California Management Review*, 15 (Fall, 1972), pp. 30-37, and Dale McConkey, "The 'Jackass Effect' in Management Compensation," *Business Horizons*, 17 (June, 1974), pp. 81-91. [See Readings 11 and 15.]

44. See, respectively, George Strauss, "Organizational Behavior and Personnel Relations," pp. 168-69, and E. C. Chapple and L. R. Sayles, *The Measure of Management* (New York: Macmillan, 1961).

45. For an exception in this regard, see W. Lloyd Warner and J. O. Low, *The Social System of the Modern Factory* (New Haven: Yale University, 1941).

46. As examples, see G. C. Homans, *The Human Group* (New York: Harcourt, Brace and World, 1950); Rensis Likert, *New Patterns of Management* (New York: McGraw-Hill, 1961); and R. L. Kahn, D. M. Wolfe, R. P. Quinn, J. D. Snoek, and R. A. Rosenthal, *Organizational Stress* (New York: John Wiley, 1964). These works on organization involve, respectively, an interaction model, an overlapping groups model, and an overlapping role-set model.

47. W. Richard Scott, "Theory of Organizations," in Robert Faris (ed.), *Handbook of Modern Sociology* (Chicago: Rand McNally, 1964).

48. See, respectively, T. Parsons, *Structure and Process in Modern Society* (Glencoe, Illinois: Free Press, 1960); Amitai Etzioni, *A Comparative Analysis of Complex Organizations* (New York: Free Press, 1961); and Peter Blau and William Scott, *Formal Organizations* (San Francisco: Chandler, 1962).

49. Karl Magnusen, "Perspectives on Organizational Design and Development," pp. 23-25.

50. Tom Burns and G. M. Stalker, *The Management of Innovation* (London: Tavistock, 1960).

51. Robert Blauner, *Alienation and Freedom* (Chicago: University of Chicago, 1964).

52. W. E. Upjohn Institute for Employment Research, *Work in America*, Report to the Secretary of Health, Education, and Welfare (Cambridge: M.I.T. Press, 1973).

53. Joan Woodward, *Industrial Organization: Theory and Practice* (London: Oxford

University, 1965).

54. *Ibid.*, p. 72.

55. *Ibid.*, p. 135.

56. *Ibid.*, p. 153.

57. Joan Woodward (ed.), *Industrial Organization: Behavior and Control* (London: Oxford University, 1970).

58. Jeffrey Rackham, "Technology, Control, and Organization," in Denis Pym (ed.), *Industrial Society* (London: Penguin, 1968), pp. 348-49.

59. D. Hickson, D. Pugh, and D. Pheysey, "Operations Technology and Organization Structure: An Empirical Reappraisal," *Administrative Science Quarterly,* 14 (September, 1969), pp. 378-97.

60. Ross Webber, *Management* (Homewood, Illinois: Richard D. Irwin, 1975), p. 442.

61. Joan Woodward (ed.), *Industrial Organization: Behavior and Control,* pp. 37-56.

62. *Ibid.*, p. 35.

63. Charles Perrow, "A Framework for the Comparative Analysis of Organizations," *American Sociological Review,* 32 (April, 1967), pp. 194-208.

64. _____, *Organizational Analysis* (Belmont, California: Wadsworth, 1970), p. 77.

65. _____, "A Framework for the Comparative Analysis of Organizations," p. 197.

66. *Ibid.*, p. 203.

67. *Ibid.*, p. 203.

68. The methods listed stem from a discussion in Paul Lawrence and Jay Lorsch, *Organization and Environment* (Boston: Harvard University, 1967), p. 160.

69. Karl Magnusen, "Technology and Organizational Differentiation: A Field Study of Manufacturing Corporations" (unpublished doctoral dissertation: University of Wisconsin—Madison, 1970).

70. Charles Perrow, *Organizational Analysis,* p. 85.

71. Paul Lawrence and Jay Lorsch, *Organization and Environment,* Ch. 2-6.

72. For a discussion of horizontal or lateral relationships in organizations, see L. R. Sayles, *Managerial Behavior* (New York: McGraw-Hill, 1964).

73. A. Walker and J. Lorsch, "Organizational Choice: Product versus Function," in Jay Lorsch and Paul Lawrence, *Studies in Organization Design* (Homewood, Illinois: Richard D. Irwin, 1970), pp. 36-53.

74. J. R. Galbraith (ed.), *Matrix Organizations* (Cambridge: M.I.T. Press, 1971).

75. Thomas Whisler, *Information Technology and Organizational Change* (Belmont, California: Wadsworth, 1970), pp. 37-52.

76. John Morse, "Organizational Characteristics and Individual Motivation," in Jay Lorsch and Paul Lawrence, *Studies in Organization Design,* pp. 84-100.

77. Andre Ruedi and Paul Lawrence, "Organizations in Two Cultures," in Jay Lorsch and Paul Lawrence, *Studies in Organization Design,* pp. 54-83.

78. On this methodological issue, see H. Tosi, R. Aldag, and R. Storey, "On the Measurement of the Environment," *Administrative Science Quarterly,* 18 (March, 1973), pp. 27-36; also, in the same volume, see P. Lawrence and J. Lorsch, "A Reply to Tosi, Aldag, and Storey," pp. 397-98.

79. On whether to change the organization or its environment, see J. R. Galbraith, "Organization Design: An Information Processing View," *Interfaces,* 4 (May, 1974), pp. 28-36; and W. E. Newman, "Shaping the Master Strategy of Your Firm," *California Management Review,* 9 (Spring, 1967), pp. 77-88. [See Readings 3 and 4.]

80. Dennis Moberg and James Koch, "A Critical Appraisal of Integrated Treatments of Contingency Findings," *Academy of Management Journal,* 18 (March, 1975), p. 122.

81. Raymond Miles, *Theories of Management* (New York: McGraw-Hill, 1975), p. 237.

82. R. E. Miles, C. C. Snow, and J. Pfeffer, "Organization-Environment: Concepts and Issues," *Industrial Relations,* 13 (October, 1974), p. 264.

83. Edgar Huse, *Organization Development and Change* (New York: West Publishing, 1975), p. 136.

84. Dennis Moberg and James Koch, "A Critical Appraisal of Integrated Treatments of Contingency Findings," p. 122.

85. Wendell French and Cecil Bell, Jr., *Organization Development* (Englewood Cliffs, New Jersey: Prentice-Hall, 1973).

86. Raymond Miles, "Organization Development," in G. Strauss, R. Miles, C. Snow, and A. Tannenbaum (eds.), *Organizational Behavior: Research and Issues* (Madison, Wisconsin: Industrial Relations Research Association, 1974), p. 170.

87. Alvin Toffler, *Future Shock* (New York: Random House, 1970). [See Reading 5.]

88. George Strauss, "Organizational Development: Credits and Debits," *Organizational Dynamics,* 1 (Winter, 1973), pp. 2-19.

89. Charles Perrow, "Is Business Really Changing?" *Organizational Dynamics,* 3 (Summer, 1974), pp. 31-44. [See Reading 6.]

90. Edgar Huse, *Organization Development and Change,* p. 175.

91. R. M. Ford, "Job Enrichment Lessons from AT&T," *Harvard Business Review,* 51 (January-February, 1973), pp. 96-106. [See Reading 10.]

92. Wendell French and Cecil Bell, Jr., *Organization Development,* p. 164.

93. Raymond Miles, "Organization Development," p. 169.

94. Edgar Huse, *Organization Development and Change,* p. 12.

95. *Ibid.,* p. 331.

96. William Dowling, "Using the Managerial Grid to Ensure MBO," *Organizational Dynamics,* 4 (Summer, 1974), p. 55.

97. Robert Blake and Jane Mouton, *The Managerial Grid* (Houston, Texas: Gulf Publishing, 1964). Also see their more recent book by the same publisher, *Corporate Excellence Through Grid Organization Development* (1968).

98. For example, see Larry Boulden, "Test Yourself—Do You Have What It Takes to Manage People?" *Automation,* 22 (June, 1975), pp. 50-56.

99. William Dowling, "Using the Managerial Grid to Ensure MBO," p. 56.

100. Edgar Huse, *Organization Development and Change,* p. 163.

101. R. Blake, J. Mouton, L. Barnes, and L. Greiner, "Breakthrough in Organization Development," *Harvard Business Review,* 42 (November-December, 1964), pp. 113-55.

102. William Dowling, "Using the Managerial Grid to Ensure MBO," p. 61.

103. George Strauss, "Organizational Development: Credits and Debits," p. 14.

104. W. J. Reddin, *Managerial Effectiveness* (New York: McGraw-Hill, 1970).

105. For a complete description, see W. J. Reddin and R. Stuart-Kotze, *Effective Situational Diagnosis* (4th ed.; Fredericton, Canada: Managerial Effectiveness Ltd., 1973).

106. Anthony Raia, *Managing by Objectives* (Glenview, Illinois: Scott, Foresman, 1974).

107. W. J. Reddin, *Managerial Effectiveness,* p. 160.

108. Fred Fiedler and Martin Chemers, *Leadership and Effective Management* (Glenview, Illinois: Scott, Foresman, 1974).

109. W. A. Hill, "Leadership Style: Rigid or Flexible?" *Organizational Behavior and Human Performance,* 9 (February, 1973), pp. 35-47. [See Reading 19.]

110. J. Campbell, M. Dunnette, E. Lawler, III, and K. Weick, Jr., *Managerial Behavior, Performance, and Effectiveness* (New York: McGraw-Hill, 1970), p. 416.

111. A. C. Filley and R. J. House, *Managerial Process and Organizational Behavior* (Glenview, Illinois: Scott, Foresman, 1969), pp. 404-405.

112. For a discussion of MBO advantages and disadvantages, see S. J. Carroll, Jr., and H. L. Tosi, Jr., *Management by Objectives* (New York: Macmillan, 1973).

113. Walter Nord and Douglas Durand, "Beyond Resistance to Change: Behavioral Science on the Firing Line," *Organizational Dynamics,* 4 (Autumn, 1975), p. 13.

114. Dale McConkey, "MBO—Twenty Years Later, Where do we Stand?" *Business Horizons,* 16 (August, 1973), pp. 25-36. [See Reading 24.]

115. Wendell French and Robert Hollmann, "Management by Objectives: The Team Approach," *California Management Review,* 17 (Spring, 1975), pp. 13-22 [see Reading 25]. Also see H. Levinson, "Management by Whose Objectives?" *Harvard Business Review,* 48 (July-August, 1970), pp. 125-234.

116. William Werther, Jr., and Heinz Weihrich, "Refining MBO Through Negotiations," *MSU Business Topics,* 23 (Summer, 1975), pp. 53-59.

117. Larry Greiner, "Red Flags in Organization Development," *Business Horizons,* 4 (June, 1972), pp. 17-24.

118. Edgar Huse, *Organization Development and Change,* p. 119.

119. Frank Friedlander and L. Dave Brown, "Organization Development," *Annual Review of Psychology,* 25 (1974), pp. 313-41. [See Reading 20.]

120. A. Marrow, D. Bowers, and S. Seashore, *Management by Participation.*

121. D. Bowers, "OD Techniques and Their Results in 23 Organizations," *Journal of Applied Behavioral Science,* 9 (January-February, 1973), pp. 21-43.

122. Cited in Raymond Miles, "Organization Development," p. 182.

123. Warren Bennis, *Organization Development* (Reading, Massachusetts: Addison-Wesley, 1969), p. 80.

124. "Machiavellian Tactics for B-School Students," *Business Week* (October 13, 1975), p. 86.

125. See, for example, H. Hornstein, B. Bunker, W. Burke, M. Gindes, and R. Lewicki, *Social Intervention* (New York: Free Press, 1971).

126. Warren Bennis, *Organization Development,* p. 78.

127. J. Elden, R. Goldstone, and M. Brown, "The University as an Organizational Frontier," in W. H. Schmidt, *Organizational Frontiers and Human Values* (Belmont, California: Wadsworth, 1970), pp. 87-101.

128. *Ibid.,* pp. 100-101.

129. Eric Trist, "Urban North America: The Challenge of the Next Thirty Years," in W. H. Schmidt, *Organizational Frontiers and Human Values,* pp. 77-85.

130. J. Elden, *et al.,* "The University as an Organizational Frontier," p. 101. Examples of these interorganizational forms include the NASA space complex, the Manhattan Project, and the TVA. See respectively: L. R. Sayles and M. K. Chandler, *Managing Large Systems* (New York: Harper and Row, 1971); Stephane Groueff, *Manhattan Project* (Boston: Little, Brown and Co., 1967); and Peter Selznick, *TVA and the Grass Roots.*

131. As examples, see "Poor vs. Rich: A New Global Conflict," *Time* (December 22, 1975), pp. 34-42, and Charles Perrow, *The Radical Attack on Business* (New York: Harcourt Brace Jovanovich, 1972).

132. Raymond Miles, "Organization Development," p. 191.

133. Wendell French and Cecil Bell, Jr., *Organization Development,* pp. 199-200.

134. George Strauss, "Organizational Development: Credits and Debits," p. 17.

135. L. R. Sayles and M. K. Chandler, *Managing Large Systems,* especially pp. 24 and 204.

136. F. E. Kast and J. E. Rosenzweig, *Organization and Management* (New York: McGraw-Hill, 1970), p. 613.

2

Organizational Design
Issues and Readings

Organizational design refers to the process of structuring work relationships within organizations. The process lacks architectural precision, however, because organizations are more dynamic than static. The reading materials in Part 2 have been included to further emphasize this dynamic aspect. Section A examines general systems theory and its relationship to managerial work. Section B explores strategies for organizational change, with particular attention paid to the question of whether the organization or its environment should be modified in response to increased task uncertainty. Finally, Section C reviews the debate over the actual impact of technological and environmental change on organizations and business.

Section A

Systems: First Thoughts

The term "systems" is popular with managers and researchers alike even though organizations are frequently dealt with in subsystem terms. More seems known about the components of systems than how they fit together into an integrated whole. Nonetheless, as suggested in the two articles comprising this section, system concepts provide a broad conceptual base for understanding organizations and the work that managers do in them.

The first selection, by Kast and Rosenzweig, identifies key concepts in general systems theory (GST), points out several dilemmas in applying GST to organizations, and discusses how systems theory might be made less abstract and more useful in practice. The authors view the growing emphasis on midrange contingency theories of organization as a sign of progress. However, they do not view system concepts or contingency models as a panacea for resolving organizational problems. Instead, they feel that such basic ideas will assist the understanding of complex situations and increase the likelihood of appropriate action being taken. Although many managers intuitively use systems concepts to acquire a "sense of the situation," Kast and Rosenzweig feel that if such approaches can be made more explicit, the payoff will come in better management and more effective organizations.

In the second article, Mintzberg analyzes "Managerial Work." He rejects as inadequate the traditional notion that managers "plan, organize, coordinate, and control," because such words merely describe the broad objectives of managerial work and have little meaning in the context of real systems. Accordingly, Mintzberg set out to examine what managers do by studying the chief executives of five organizations, including a consulting firm, a school system, a technology firm, a consumer goods manufacturer, and a hospital. Using a structured observation technique, he was able to identify six characteristics of managerial work and ten work roles used by chief executives to deal with job demands.

Mintzberg discusses his findings by subdividing the ten work roles into three managerial activity groupings: interpersonal contact (covering the figurehead, liaison, and leader roles), information processing (covering the nerve center, disseminator, and spokesman roles), and decision-making (covering the entrepreneur, disturbance handler, resource allocator, and negotiator roles). He feels that these ten work roles in the three behavioral groupings comprise a general specification of managerial work at all organizational levels, not just top levels.

As with general systems theory, however, Mintzberg's approach may be too broad. For example, it stops short of discussing work role variations experienced by managers in the five organizations actually studied. Despite this possible shortcoming, the article focuses needed attention on the subject of managerial work and concludes that lack of understanding in this area has been a major obstacle in the progress of management science.

General SystemsTheory: Applications for Organization and Management
Fremont E. Kast and James E. Rosenzweig

Biological and social scientists generally have embraced systems concepts. Many organization and management theorists seem anxious to identify with this movement and to contribute to the development of an approach which purports to offer the ultimate—the unification of all science into one grand conceptual model. Who possibly could resist? General systems theory seems to provide a relief from the limitations of more mechanistic approaches and a rationale for rejecting "principles" based on relatively "closed-system" thinking. This theory provides the paradigm for organization and management theorists to "crank into their systems model" all of the diverse knowledge from relevant underlying disciplines. It has become almost mandatory to have the word "system" in the title of recent articles and books (many of us have compromised and placed it only in the subtitle).*

"General Systems Theory: Applications for Organization and Management" by Fremont Kast and James Rosenzweig from ACADEMY OF MANAGEMENT JOURNAL, 15 (December 1972), 447-465. Reprinted by permission of the Academy of Management Journal and Fremont Kast.
*An entire article could be devoted to a discussion of ingenious ways in which the term "systems approach" has been used in the literature pertinent to organization theory and management practice.

But where did it all start? This question takes us back into history and brings to mind the long-standing philosophical arguments between mechanistic and organismic models of the 19th and early 20th centuries. As Deutsch says:

Both mechanistic and organismic models were based substantially on experiences and operations known before 1850. Since then, the experience of almost a century of scientific and technological progress has so far not been utilized for any significant new model for the study of organization and in particular of human thought [12, p. 389].

General systems theory even revives the specter of the "vitalists" and their views on "life force" and most certainly brings forth renewed questions of teleological or purposeful behavior of both living and nonliving systems. Phillips and others have suggested that the philosophical roots of general systems theory go back even further, at least to the German philosopher Hegel (1770–1831) [29, p. 56]. Thus, we should recognize that in the adoption of the systems approach for the study of organizations we are not dealing with newly discovered ideas—they have a rich genealogy.

Even in the field of organization and management theory, systems views are not new. Chester Barnard used a basic systems framework.

A cooperative system is a complex of physical, biological, personal, and social components which are in a specific systematic relationship by reason of the cooperation of two or more persons for at least one definite end. Such a system is evidently a subordinate unit of larger systems from one point of view; and itself embraces subsidiary systems—physical, biological, etc.—from another point of view. One of the systems comprised within a cooperative system, the one which is implicit in the phrase "cooperation of two or more persons," is called an "organization" [3, p. 65].

And Barnard was influenced by the "systems views" of Vilfredo Pareto and Talcott Parsons. Certainly this quote (dressed up a bit to give the term "system" more emphasis) could be the introduction to a 1972 book on organizations.

Miller points out that Alexander Bogdanov, the Russian philosopher, developed a theory of tektology or universal organization science in 1912 which foreshadowed general systems theory and used many of the same concepts as modern systems theorists [26, pp. 249–250].

However, in spite of a long history of organismic and holistic thinking, the utilization of the systems approach did not become the accepted model for organization and management writers until relatively recently. It is difficult to specify the turning point exactly. The momentum of systems thinking was identified by Scott in 1961 when he described the relationship between general systems theory and organization theory.

The distinctive qualities of modern organization theory are its conceptual-analytical base, its reliance on empirical research data, and above all, its integrating nature. These qualities are framed in a philosophy which accepts the premise that the only meaningful way to study organization is to study it as a system . . . Modern organization theory and general system theory are similar in that they look at organization as an integrated whole [33, pp. 15–21].

Scott said explicitly what many in our field had been thinking and/or implying—he helped us put into perspective the important writings of Herbert Simon, James March, Talcott Parsons, George Homans, E. Wight Bakke, Kenneth Boulding, and many others.

But how far have we really advanced over the past decade in applying general systems theory to organizations and their management? Is it still a "skeleton," or have we been able to "put some meat on the bones"? The systems approach has been touted because of its potential usefulness in understanding the complexities of "live" organizations. Has this approach really helped us in this endeavor or has it compounded confusion with chaos? Herbert Simon describes the challenge for the systems approach:

In both science and engineering, the study of "systems" is an increasingly popular activity. Its popularity is more a response to a pressing need for synthesizing and analyzing complexity than it is to any large development of a body of knowledge and technique for dealing with complexity. If this popularity is to be more than a fad, necessity will have to mother invention and provide substance to go with the name [35, p. 114].

In this article we will explore the issue of whether we are providing substance for the term *systems approach* as it relates to the study of organizations and their management. There are many interesting historical and philosophical questions concerning the relationship between the mechanistic and organistic approaches and their applicability to the various fields of science, as well as other interesting digressions into the evolution of systems approaches. However, we will resist those temptations and plunge directly into a discussion of the key concepts of general systems theory, the way in which these ideas have been used by organization theorists, the limitations in their application, and some suggestions for the future.

KEY CONCEPTS OF GENERAL SYSTEMS THEORY

The key concepts of general systems theory have been set forth by many writers [6, 7, 13, 71, 25, 28, 39] and have been used by many organization and management theorists [10, 14, 18, 19, 22, 23, 24, 32]. It is not our purpose here to elaborate on them in great detail because we anticipate that most readers will have been

Figure 1   KEY CONCEPTS OF GENERAL SYSTEMS THEORY

Subsystems or Components. A system by definition is composed of interrelated parts or elements. This is true for all systems — mechanical, biological, and social. Every system has at least two elements, and these elements are interconnected.

Holism, Synergism, Organicism, and Gestalt. The whole is not just the sum of the parts; the system itself can be explained only as a totality. Holism is the opposite of elementarism, which views the total as the sum of its individual parts.

Open Systems View. Systems can be considered in two ways: (1) closed or (2) open. Open systems exchange information, energy, or material with their environments. Biological and social systems are inherently open systems; mechanical systems may be open or closed. The concepts of open and closed systems are difficult to defend in the absolute. We prefer to think of open-closed as a dimension; that is, systems are relatively open or relatively closed.

Input-Transformation-Output Model. The open system can be viewed as a transformation model. In a dynamic relationship with its environment, it receives various inputs, transforms these inputs in some way, and exports outputs.

System Boundaries. It follows that systems have boundaries which separate them from their environments. The concept of boundaries helps us understand the distinction between open and closed systems. The relatively closed system has rigid, impenetrable boundaries; whereas the open system has permeable boundaries between itself and a broader suprasystem. Boundaries are relatively easily defined in physical and biological systems, but are very difficult to delineate in social systems, such as organizations.

Negative Entropy. Closed, physical systems are subject to the force of entropy which increases until eventually the entire system fails. The tendency toward maximum entropy is a movement to disorder, complete lack of resource transformation, and death. In a closed system, the change in entropy must always be positive; however, in open biological or social systems, entropy can be arrested and

---

exposed to them in some depth. Figure 1 provides a very brief review of those characteristics of systems which seem to have wide acceptance. The review is far from complete. It is difficult to identify a "complete" list of characteristics derived from general systems theory; moreover, it is merely a first-order classification. There are many derived second- and third-order characteristics which could be considered. For example, James G. Miller sets forth *165* hypotheses, stemming from open systems theory, which might be applicable to two or more levels of systems [25]. He suggests that they are *general* systems theoretical hypotheses and qualifies them by suggesting that they are propositions applicable to general systems *behavior* theory and would thus exclude nonliving systems. He does not limit these propositions to individual organisms, but considers them appropriate

may even be transformed into negative entropy—a process of more complete organization and ability to transform resources—because the system imports resources from its environment.

Steady State, Dynamic Equilibrium, and Homeostasis. The concept of steady state is closely related to that of negative entropy. A closed system eventually must attain an equilibrium state with maximum entropy—death or disorganization. However, an open system may attain a state where the system remains in dynamic equilibrium through the continuous inflow of materials, energy, and information.

Feedback. The concept of feedback is important in understanding how a system maintains a steady state. Information concerning the outputs or the process of the system is fed back as an input into the system, perhaps leading to changes in the transformation process and/or future outputs. Feedback can be both positive and negative, although the field of cybernetics is based on negative feedback. Negative feedback is informational input which indicates that the system is deviating from a prescribed course and should readjust to a new steady state.

Hierarchy. A basic concept in systems thinking is that of hierarchical relationships between systems. A system is composed of subsystems of a lower order and is also part of a suprasystem. Thus, there is a hierarchy of the components of the system.

Internal Elaboration. Closed systems move toward entropy and disorganization. In contrast, open systems appear to move in the direction of greater differentiation, elaboration, and a higher level of organization.

Multiple Goal-Seeking. Biological and social systems appear to have multiple goals or purposes. Social organizations seek multiple goals, if for no other reason than that they are composed of individuals and subunits with different values and objectives.

Equifinality of Open Systems. In mechanistic systems there is a direct cause and effect relationship between the initial conditions and the final state. Biological and social systems operate differently. Equifinality suggests that certain results may be achieved with different initial conditions and in different ways. This view suggests that social organizations can accomplish their objectives with diverse inputs and with varying internal activities (conversion processes).

---

for social systems as well. His hypotheses are related to such issues as structure, process, subsystems, information, growth, and integration. It is obviously impossible to discuss all of these hypotheses; we want only to indicate the extent to which many interesting propositions are being posed which might have relevance to many different types of systems. It will be a very long time (if ever) before most of these hypotheses are validated; however, we are surprised at how many of them can be agreed with intuitively, and we can see their possible verification in studies of social organizations.

We turn now to a closer look at how successful or unsuccessful we have been in utilizing these concepts in the development of "modern organization theory."

A BEGINNING:
ENTHUSIASTIC BUT INCOMPLETE

We have embraced general systems theory but, really, how completely? We could review a vast literature in modern organization theory which has explicitly or implicitly adopted systems theory as a frame of reference, and we have investigated in detail a few representative examples of the literature in assessing the "state of the art" [18, 19, 22, 23, 31, 38]. It was found that most of these books professed to utilize general systems theory. Indeed, in the first few chapters, many of them did an excellent job of presenting basic systems concepts and showing their relationship to organizations; however, when they moved further into the discussion of more specific subject matter, they departed substantially from systems theory. The studies appear to use a "partial systems approach" and leave for the reader the problem of integrating the various ideas into a systemic whole. It also appears that many of the authors are unable, because of limitations of knowledge about subsystem relationships, to carry out the task of using general systems theory as a conceptual basis for organization theory.

Furthermore, it is evident that each author had many "good ideas" stemming from the existing body of knowledge or current research on organizations which did not fit neatly into a "systems model." For example, they might discuss leadership from a relatively closed-system point of view and not consider it in relation to organizational technology, structure, or other variables. Our review of the literature suggests that much remains to be done in applying general systems theory to organization theory and management practice.

Some Dilemmas in Applying GST to Organizations

Why have writers embracing general systems theory as a basis for studying organizations had so much difficulty in following through? Part of this difficulty may stem from the newness of the paradigm and our inability to operationalize "all we think we know" about this approach. Or it may be because we know too little about the systems under investigation. Both of these possibilities will be covered later, but first we need to look at some of the more specific conceptual problems.

Organizations as Organisms

One of the basic contributions of general systems theory was the rejection of the traditional closed-system or mechanistic view of social organizations. But, did general systems theory free us from this constraint only to impose another, less obvious one? General systems theory grew out of the organismic views of von Bertalanffy and other biologists; thus, many of the characteristics are relevant to the living organism. It is conceptually easy to draw the analogy between living organisms and social organizations. "There is, after all, an intuitive similarity between the organization of the human body and the kinds of organizations men create. And so, undaunted by the failures of the human-social analogy through time, new theorists try afresh in each epoch" [2, p. 660]. General systems theory would have us accept this analogy between organism and social organization. Yet we have a hard time swallowing it whole. Katz and Kahn warn us of the danger:

There has been no more pervasive, persistent, and futile fallacy handicapping the social sciences than the use of the physical model for the understanding of social structures. The biological metaphor, with its crude comparisons of the physical parts of the body to the parts of the social system, has been replaced by more subtle but equally misleading analogies between biological and social functioning. This figurative type of thinking ignores the essential difference between the socially contrivd nature of social systems and the physical structure of the machine or the human organism. So long as writers are committed to a theoretical framework based upon the physical model, they will miss the essential social-psychological facts of the highly variable, loosely articulated character of social systems [19, p. 31].

In spite of this warning, Katz and Kahn do embrace much of the general systems theory concepts which are based on the biological metaphor. We must be very cautious about trying to make this analogy too literal. We agree with Silverman who says, "It may, therefore, be necessary to drop the analogy between an organization and an organism: organizations may be systems but not necessarily *natural* systems" [34, p. 31].

Distinction Between Organization and an Organization

General systems theory emphasizes that systems are organized—they are composed of interdependent components in some relationship. The social organization would then follow logically as just another system. But, we are perhaps being caught in circular thinking. It is true that all systems (physical, biological, and social) are by definition organized, but are all systems organizations? Rapoport and Horvath distinguish "organization theory" and "the theory of organizations" as follows:

We see organization theory as dealing with general and abstract organizational principles; it applies to any system exhibiting organized complexity. As such, organization theory is seen as an extension of mathematical physics or, even more generally, of mathematics designed to deal with organized systems. The theory of organizations, on the other hand, purports to be a social science. It puts real human organizations at the center of interest. It may study the social structure of organizations and so can be viewed as a branch of sociology; it can study the behavior of individuals or groups as members of organizations and can be viewed as a part of social psychology; it can study power relations and principles of control in organizations and so fits into political science [30, pp. 74–75].

Why make an issue of this distinction? It seems to us that there is a vital matter involved. All systems may be considered to be organized, and more advanced systems may display differentiation in the activities of component parts—such as the specialization of human organs. However, all systems *do not* have purposeful entities. Can the heart or lungs be considered as purposeful entities in themselves or are they only components of the larger purposeful system, the human body? By contrast, the social organization is composed of two or more purposeful elements. "An organization consists of elements that have and can exercise their own wills" [1, p. 669]. Organisms, the foundation stone of general systems theory, do not contain purposeful elements which exercise their own will. This distinction between the organism and the social organization is of importance. In much of general systems theory, the concern is primarily with the way in which the *organism* responds to environmentally generated inputs. Feedback concepts and the maintenance of a steady state are based on internal adaptations to environmental forces. (This is particularly true of cybernetic models.) But, what about those changes and adaptations which occur from *within* social organizations? Purposeful elements within the social organization may initiate activities and adaptations which are difficult to subsume under feedback and steady state concepts.

Opened and Closed Systems

Another dilemma stemming from general systems theory is the tendency to dichotomize all systems as opened or closed. We have been led to think of physical systems as closed, subject to the laws of entropy, and to think of biological systems as open to their environment and, possibly, becoming negentropic. But applying this strict polarization to social organizations creates many difficulties. In fact, most social organizations and their subsystems are "partially open" and "partially closed." Open and closed are a matter of degree. Unfortunately, there seems to be a widely held view (often more implicit than explicit) that *open-system thinking is good and closed-system thinking is bad.* We have not become sufficiently sophisticated to recognize that both are appropriate under certain conditions. For example, one of the most useful conceptualizations set forth by Thompson is that the social organization *must seek* to use closed-system concepts (particularly at the technical core) to reduce uncertainty and to create more effective performance at this level.

Still Subsystems Thinking

Even though we preach a general systems approach, we often practice subsystems thinking. Each of the academic disciplines and each of us personally have limited perspective of the system we are studying. While proclaiming a broad systems viewpoint, we often dismiss variables outside our interest or competence as being irrelevant, and we only open our system to those inputs which we can handle with our disciplinary bag of tools. We are hampered because each of the academic disciplines has taken a narrow "partial systems view" and find comfort in the relative certainty which this creates. Of course, this is not a problem unique to modern organization theory. Under the more traditional process approach to the study of management, we were able to do an admirable job of delineating and discussing planning, organizing, and controlling as separate activities. We were much less successful in discussing them as integrated and interrelated activities.

How Does Our Knowledge Fit?

One of the major problems in utilizing general systems theory is that we know (or think we know) more about certain relationships than we can fit into a general systems model. For example, we are beginning to understand the two-variable relationship between technology and structure. But, when we introduce another variable, say psychosocial relationships, our models become too complex. Consequently, in order to discuss all the things we know about organizations, we depart from a systems approach. Perhaps it is because we know a great deal more about the elements or subsystems of an organization than we do about the interrelationships and interactions between these subsystems. And, general systems theory forces us to consider those relationships about which we know the least—a true dilemma. So we continue to elaborate on those aspects of the organization which we know best—a partial systems view.

Failure to Delineate a Specific System

When the social sciences embraced general systems theory, the total system became the focus of attention and terminology tended toward vagueness. In the utilization of systems theory, we should be more precise in delineating the specific system under consideration. Failure to do this leads to much confusion. As Murray suggests:

I am wary of the word "system" because social scientists use it very frequently without specifying which of several possible different denotations they have in mind; but more particularly because, today, "system" is a highly cathected term, loaded with prestige; hence, we are all strongly tempted to employ it even when we have nothing definite in mind and its only service is to indicate that we subscribe to the general premise respecting the interdependence of things—basic to organismic theory, holism, field theory, interactionism, transactionism, etc . . . . When definition of the units of a system are lacking, the term stands for no more than an article of faith, and is misleading to boot, insofar as it suggests a condition of affairs that may not actually exist [27, pp. 50-51].

We need to be much more precise in delineating both the boundaries of the system under consideration and the level of our analysis. There is a tendency for current writers in organization theory to accept general systems theory and then to move indiscriminately across systems boundaries and between levels of systems without being very precise (and letting their readers in on what is occurring). James Miller suggests the need for clear delineation of levels in applying systems theory, "It is important to follow one procedural rule in systems theory in order to avoid confusion. Every discussion should begin with an identification of the level of reference, and the discourse should not change to another level without a specific statement that this is occurring" [25, p. 216]. Our field is replete with these confusions about systems levels. For example, when we use the term "organizational behavior" are we talking about the way the organization behaves as a system or are we talking about the behavior of the individual participants? By goals, do we mean the goals of the organization or the goals of the individuals within the organization? In using systems theory we must become more precise in our delineation of systems boundaries and systems levels if we are to prevent confusing conceptual ambiguity.

Recognition That Organizations Are "Contrived Systems"

We have a vague uneasiness that general systems theory truly does not recognize the "contrived" nature of social organizations. With its predominate emphasis on natural organisms, it may understate some characteristics which are vital for the social organization. Social organizations do not occur naturally in nature; they are contrived by man. They have structure; but it is the structure of events rather than of physical components, and it cannot be separated from the processes of the system. The fact that social organizations are contrived by human beings suggests that they can be established for an infinite variety of purposes and do not follow the same life-cycle patterns of birth, growth, maturity, and death as biological systems. As Katz and Kahn say:

Social structures are essentially contrived systems. They are made of men and are imperfect systems. They can come apart at the seams overnight, but they can also outlast by centuries the biological organisms which originally created them. The cement which holds them together is essentially psychological rather than biological. Social systems are anchored in the attitudes, perceptions, beliefs, motivations, habits, and expectations of human beings [19, p. 33].

Recognizing that the social organization is contrived again cautions us against making an exact analogy between it and physical or biological systems.

Questions of Systems Effectiveness

General systems theory with its biological orientation would appear to have an evolutionary view of system effectiveness. That living system which best adapts to its environment prospers and survives. The primary measure of effectiveness is perpetuation of the organism's species. Teleological behavior is therefore directed toward survival. But, is survival the only criterion of effectiveness of the social system? It is probably an essential but not all-inclusive measure of effectiveness.

General systems theory emphasizes the organism's survival goal and does not fully relate to the question of the effectiveness of the system in its suprasystem— the environment. Parsonian functional-structural views provide a contrast. "The *raison d'etre* of complex organizations, according to this analysis, is mainly to benefit the society in which they belong, and that society is, therefore, the appropriate frame of reference for the evaluation of organizational effectiveness" [41, p. 896].

But, this view seems to go to the opposite extreme from the survival view of general systems theory—the organization exists to serve the society. It seems to us that the truth lies somewhere between these two viewpoints. And it is likely that a systems viewpoint (modified from the species survival view of general systems theory) will be most appropriate. Yuchtman and Seashore suggest:

The organization's success over a period of time in this competition for resources—i.e., its bargaining position in a given environment—is regarded as an expression of its overall effectiveness. Since the resources are of various kinds, and the competitive relationships are multiple, and since there is interchangeability among classes of resources, the assessment of organizational effectiveness must be in terms not of any single criterion but of an open-ended multidimensional set of criteria [41, p. 891].

This viewpoint suggests that questions of organizational effectiveness must be concerned with at least three levels of analysis. The level of the environment, the level of the social organization as a system, and the level of the subsystems (human participants) within the organization. Perhaps much of our confusion and ambiguity concerning organizational effectiveness stems from our failure to clearly delineate the level of our analysis and, even more important, our failure really to understand the relationships among these levels.

Our discussion of some of the problems associated with the application of general systems theory to the study of social organizations might suggest that we completely reject the appropriateness of this model. On the contrary, we see the systems approach as the new paradigm for the study of organizations; but, like all new concepts in the sciences, one which has to be applied, modified, and elaborated to make it as useful as possible.

SYSTEMS THEORY PROVIDES THE NEW PARADIGM

We hope the discussion of GST and organizations provides a realistic appraisal. We do not want to promote the value of the systems approach as a matter of faith;

however, we do see systems theory as vital to the study of social organizations and as providing the major new paradigm for our field of study.

Thomas Kuhn provides an interesting interpretation of the nature of scientific revolution [20]. He suggests that major changes in all fields of science occur with the development of new conceptual schemes or "paradigms." These new paradigms do not just represent a step-by-step advancement in "normal" science (the science generally accepted and practiced) but, rather, a revolutionary change in the way the scientific field is perceived by the practitioners. Kuhn says:

The historian of science may be tempted to exclaim that when paradigms change, the world itself changes with them. Led by a new paradigm, scientists adopt new instruments and look in new places. Even more important, during revolutions scientists see new and different things when looking with familiar instruments in places they have looked before. It is rather as if the professional community has been suddenly transported to another planet where familiar objects are seen in a different light and are joined by unfamiliar ones as well. . . . Paradigm changes do cause scientists to see the world of their research-engagement differently. Insofar as their only recourse to that world is through what they see and do, we may want to say that after a revolution scientists are responding to a different world [20, p. 110].

New paradigms frequently are rejected by the scientific community. (At first they may seem crude and limited—offering very little more than older paradigms.) They frequently lack the apparent sophistication of the older paradigms which they ultimately replace. They do not display the clarity and certainty of older paradigms which have been refined through years of research and writing. But, a new paradigm does provide for a "new start" and opens up new directions which were not possible under the old. "We must recognize how very limited in both scope and precision a paradigm can be at the time of its first appearance. Paradigms gain their status because they are more successful than their competitors in solving a few problems that the group of practitioners has come to recognize as acute. To be more successful is not, however, to be either completely successful with a single problem or notably successful with any large number" [20, p. 23].

Systems theory does provide a new paradigm for the study of social organizations and their management. At this stage it is obviously crude and lacking in precision. In some ways it may not be much better than older paradigms which have been accepted and used for a long time (such as the management process approach). As in other fields of scientific endeavor, the new paradigm must be applied, clarified, elaborated, and made more precise. But, it does provide a fundamentally different view of the reality of social organizations and can serve as the basis for major advancements in our field.

We see many exciting examples of the utilization of the new systems paradigm in the field of organization and management. Several of these have been referred to earlier [7, 13, 19, 22, 23, 24, 31, 38], and there have been many others. Burns and Stalker made substantial use of systems views in setting forth their concepts of mechanistic and organic managerial systems [8]. Their studies of the characteristics of these two organization types lack precise definition of the variables and relationships, but their colleagues have used the systems approach to look at the relationship of organizations to their environment and also among the technical, structural, and behavioral characteristics within the organization [24]. Chamberlain used a system view in studying enterprises and their environment, which is substantially different from traditional microeconomics [9]. The emerging field of "environmental sciences" and "environmental administration" has found the systems paradigm vital.

Thus, the systems theory paradigm is being used extensively in the investigating of relationships between subsystems within organizations and in studying the environmental interfaces. But, it still has not advanced sufficiently to meet the needs. One of the major problems is that the practical need to deal with comprehensive systems of relationships is overrunning our ability to fully understand and predict these relationships. *We vitally need the systems paradigm but we are not sufficiently sophisticated to use it appropriately.* This is the dilemma. Do our current failures to fully utilize the systems paradigm suggest that we reject it and return to the older, more traditional, and time-tested paradigms? Or do we work with systems theory to make it more precise, to understand the relationships among subsystems, and to gather the informational inputs which are necessary to make the systems approach really work? We think the latter course offers the best opportunity.

Thus, we prefer to accept current limitations of systems theory, while working to reduce them and to develop more complete and sophisticated approaches for its application. We agree with Rapoport, who says:

The system approach to the study of man can be appreciated as an effort to restore meaning (in terms of intuitively grasped understanding of wholes) while adhering to the principles of *disciplined* generalizations and rigorous deduction. It is, in short, an attempt to make the study of man both scientific and meaningful [7, p. xxii].

We are sympathetic with the second part of Rapoport's comment, the need to apply the systems approach but to make disciplined generalizations and rigorous deductions. This is a vital necessity and yet a major current limitation. We do have some indication that progress (although very slow) is being made.

WHAT DO WE NEED NOW?

Everything is related to everything else—but how? General systems theory provides us with the macro paradigm for the study of social organizations. As Scott and others have pointed out, most sciences go through a macro-micro-macro cycle or sequence of emphasis [33]. Traditional bureaucratic theory provided the first major macro view of organizations. Administrative management theorists concentrated on the development of macro "principles of management" which were applicable to all organizations. When these macro views seemed incomplete (unable to explain important phenomena), attention turned to the micro level—more detailed analysis of components or parts of the organization, thus the interest in human relations, technology, or structural dimensions.

The systems approach returns us to the macro level with a new paradigm. General systems theory emphasizes a very high level of abstraction. Phillips classifies it as a third-order study [29] that attempts to develop macro concepts appropriate for all types of biological, physical, and social systems.

In our view, we are now ready to move down a level of abstraction to consider second-order systems studies or midrange concepts. These will be based on general systems theory but will be more concrete and will emphasize more specific characteristics and relationships in social organizations. They will operate within the broad paradigm of systems theory but at a less abstract level.

What should we call this new midrange level of analysis? Various authors have referred to it as a "contingency view," a study of "patterns of relationships," or a search for "configurations among subsystems." Lorsch and Lawrence reflect this view:

During the past few years there has been evident a new trend in the study of organizational phenomena. Underlying this new approach is the idea that the internal functioning of organizations must be consistent with the demands of the organization task, technology, or external environment, and the needs of its members if the organization is to be effective. Rather than searching for the panacea of the one best way to organize under all conditions investigators have more and more tended to examine the functioning of organizations in relation to the needs of their particular members and the external pressures facing them. Basically, this approach seems to be leading to the development of a "contingency" theory of organization with the appropriate internal states and processes of the organization contingent upon external requirements and member needs [21, p. 1].

Numerous others have stressed a similar viewpoint. Thompson suggests that the essence of administration lies in understanding basic configurations which exist between the various subsystems and with the environment. "The basic function of administration appears to be co-alignment, not merely of people (in coalitions) but of institutionalized action—of technology and task environment into a viable domain, and of organizational design and structure appropriate to it" [38, p. 157].

Bringing these ideas together we can provide a more precise definition of the contingency view:

The contingency view of organizations and their management suggests that an organization is a system composed of subsystems and delineated by identifiable boundaries from its environmental suprasystem. The contingency view seeks to understand the interrelationships within and among subsystems as well as between the organization and its environment and to define patterns of relationships or configurations of variables. It emphasizes the multivariate nature of organizations and attempts to understand how organizations operate under varying conditions and in specific circumstances. Contingency views are ultimately directed toward suggesting organizational designs and managerial systems most appropriate for specific situations.

But, it is not enough to suggest that a "contingency view" based on systems concepts of organizations and their management is more appropriate than the simplistic "principles approach." If organization theory is to advance and make contributions to managerial practice, it must define more explicitly certain patterns of relationships between organizational variables. This is the major challenge facing our field.

Just how do we go about using systems theory to develop these midrange or contingency views. We see no alternative but to engage in intensive comparative investigation of many organizations following the advice of Blau:

A theory of organization, whatever its specific nature, and regardless of how subtle the organizational processes it takes into account, has as its central aim to establish the constellation of characteristics that develop in organizations of various kinds. Comparative studies of many organizations are necessary, not alone to test the hypotheses implied by such a theory, but also to provide a basis for initial exploration and refinement of the theory by indicating the conditions on which relationships, originally assumed to hold universally are contingent. . . . Systematic research on many organizations that provides the data needed to determine the interrelationships between several organizational features is, however, extremely rare [5, p. 332].

Various conceptual designs for the comparative study of organizations and their subsystems are emerging to help in the development of a contingency view. We do not want to impose our model as to what should be considered in looking for these patterns of relationships. However, the tentative matrix shown in Figure 2 suggests this approach. We have used as a starting point the two polar organization types which have been emphasized in the literature—closed/stable/mechanistic and open/adaptive/organic.

We will consider the environmental suprasystem and organizational subsystems (goals and values, technical, structural, psychosocial, and managerial) plus various dimensions or characteristics of each of these systems. By way of illustration we have indicated several specific subcategories under the Environmental Suprasystem as well as the Goals and Values subsystem. This process would have to be completed and extended to all of the subsystems. The next step would be the development of appropriate descriptive language (based on research and conceptualization) for each relevant characteristic across the continuum of organization types. For example, on the "stability" dimensions for Goals and Values we would have High, Medium, and Low at appropriate places on the continuum. If the entire matrix were filled in, it is likely that we would begin to see discernible patterns of relationships among subsystems.

Figure 2   MATRIX OF PATTERNS OF RELATIONSHIPS BETWEEN ORGANIZATION TYPES AND SYSTEMS VARIABLES.

Organizational Supra- and Subsystems	Continuum of Organization Types	
	Closed/Stable/Mechanistic	Open/Adaptive/Organic
Environmental relationships		
General nature	Placid	Turbulent
Predictability	Certain, determinate	Uncertain, indeterminate
Boundary relationships	Relatively closed; limited to few participants (sales, purchasing, etc.); fixed and well-defined	Relatively open; many participants have external relationships; varied and not clearly defined
Goals and values		
Organizational goals in general	Efficient performance, stability, maintenance	Effective problem-solving, innovation, growth
Goal set	Single, clear-cut	Multiple, determined by necessity to satisfy a set of constraints
Stability	Stable	Unstable
Technical		
Structural		
Psychosocial		
Managerial		

We do not expect this matrix to provide *the* midrange model for everyone. It is highly doubtful that we will be able to follow through with the field work investigations necessary to fill in all the squares. Nevertheless, it does illustrate a possible approach for the translation of more abstract general systems theory and management practice. Frankly, we see this as a major long-term effort on the part of many researchers, investigating a wide variety of organizations. In spite of the difficulties involved in such research, the endeavor has practical significance. Sophistication in the study of organizations will come when we have a more complete understanding of organizations as total systems (configurations of subsystems) so that we can prescribe more appropriate organizational designs and managerial systems. Ultimately, organization theory should serve as the foundation for more effective management practice.

APPLICATION OF SYSTEMS CONCEPTS
TO MANAGEMENT PRACTICE

The study of organizations is an applied science because the resulting knowledge is relevant to problem-solving in on-going institutions. Contributions to organization theory come from many sources. Deductive and inductive research in a variety of disciplines provide a theoretical base of propositions which are useful for understanding organizations and for managing them. Experience gained in management practice is also an important input to organization theory. In short, management is based on the body of knowledge generated by practical experience *and* eclectic scientific research concerning organizations. The body of knowledge developed through theory and research should be translatable into more effective organizational design and managerial practices.

Do systems concepts and contingency views provide a panacea for solving problems in organizations? The answer is an emphatic *no;* this approach does not provide "ten easy steps" to success in management. Such cookbook approaches, while seemingly applicable and easy to grasp, are usually shortsighted, narrow in perspective, and superficial—in short, unrealistic. Fundamental ideas, such as systems concepts and contingency views, are more difficult to comprehend. However, they facilitate more thorough understanding of complex situations and increase the likelihood of appropriate action.

It is important to recognize that many managers have used and will continue to use a systems approach and contingency views intuitively and implicitly. Without much knowledge of the underlying body of organization theory, they have an intuitive "sense of the situation," are flexible diagnosticians, and adjust their actions and decisions accordingly. Thus, systems concepts and contingency views are not new. However, if this approach to organization theory and management practice can be made more explicit, we can facilitate better management and more effective organizations.

Practicing managers in business firms, hospitals, and government agencies continue to function on a day-to-day basis. Therefore, they must use whatever is available, they cannot wait for the *ultimate* body of knowledge (there is none!). Practitioners should be included in the search for new knowledge because they control access to an essential ingredient—organizational data—and they are the ones who ultimately put the theory to the test. Mutual understanding among managers, teachers, and researchers will facilitate the development of a relevant body of knowledge.

Simultaneously with the refinement of the body of knowledge, a concerted effort should be directed toward applying what we do know. We need ways of making systems and contingency views more usable. Without oversimplification, we need some relevant guidelines for practicing managers.

The general tenor of the contingency view is somewhere between simplistic, specific principles and complex, vague notions. It is a midrange concept which recognizes the complexity involved in managing modern organizations but uses patterns of relationships and/or configurations of subsystems in order to facilitate improved practice. The art of management depends on a reasonable success rate for actions in a probabilistic environment. Our hope is that systems concepts and contingency views, while continually being refined by scientists/researchers/ theorists, will also be made more applicable.

REFERENCES

1. Ackoff, Russell L., "Towards a System of Systems Concepts," *Management Science* (July 1971).
2. Back, Kurt W., "Biological Models of Social Change," *American Sociological Review* (August 1971).
3. Barnard, Chester I., *The Functions of the Executive* (Cambridge, Mass.: Harvard University Press, 1938).
4. Berrien, F. Kenneth, *General and Social Systems* (New Brunswick, N.J.: Rutgers University Press, 1968).
5. Blau, Peter M., "The Comparative Study of Organizations," *Industrial and Labor Relations Review* (April 1965).
6. Boulding, Kenneth E., "General Systems Theory: The Skeleton of Science," *Management Science* (April 1956).
7. Buckley, Walter, ed., *Modern Systems Research for the Behavioral Scientist* (Chicago: Aldine Publishing Company, 1968).
8. Burns, Tom and G. M. Stalker, *The Management of Innovation* (London: Tavistock Publications, 1961).
9. Chamberlain, Neil W., *Enterprise and Environment: The Firm in Time and Place* (New York: McGraw-Hill Book Company, 1968).
10. Churchman, C. West, *The Systems Approach* (New York: Dell Publishing Company, Inc., 1968).
11. DeGreene, Kenyon, ed., *Systems Psychology* (New York: McGraw-Hill Book Company, 1970).
12. Deutsch, Karl W., "Toward a Cybernetic Model of Man and Society," in Walter Buckley, ed., *Modern Systems Research for the Behavioral Scientist* (Chicago: Aldine Publishing Company, 1968).
13. Easton, David, *A Systems Analysis of Political Life* (New York: John Wiley & Sons, Inc., 1965).
14. Emery, F. E. and E. L. Trist, "Sociotechnical Systems," in C. West Churchman and Michele Verhulst, eds., *Management Sciences: Models and Techniques* (New York: Pergamon Press, 1960).
15. Emshoff, James R., *Analysis of Behavioral Systems* (New York: Macmillan Publishing Co., Inc., 1971).
16. Gross, Bertram M., "The Coming General Systems Models of Social Systems," *Human Relations* (November 1967).

17. Hall, A. D. and R. E. Eagen, "Definition of System," *General Systems, Yearbook for the Society for the Advancement of General Systems Theory,* Vol. 1 (1956).
18. Kast, Fremont E. and James E. Rosenzweig, *Organization and Management Theory: A Systems Approach* (New York: McGraw-Hill Book Company, 1970).
19. Katz, Daniel and Robert L. Kahn, *The Social Psychology of Organizations* (New York: John Wiley & Sons, Inc., 1966).
20. Kuhn, Thomas S., *The Structure of Scientific Revolutions* (Chicago: University of Chicago Press, 1962).
21. Lorsch, Jay W. and Paul R. Lawrence, *Studies in Organizational Design* (Homewood, Illinois: Irwin-Dorsey, 1970).
22. Litterer, Joseph A., *Organizations: Structure and Behavior,* Vol. 1 (New York: John Wiley & Sons, Inc., 1969).
23. ____. *Organizations: Systems, Control and Adaptation,* Vol. 2 (New York: John Wiley & Sons, Inc., 1969).
24. Miller, E. J. and A. K. Rice, *Systems of Organizations* (London: Tavistock Publications, 1967).
25. Miller, James G., "Living Systems: Basic Concepts," *Behavioral Science* (July 1965).
26. Miller, Robert F., "The New Science of Administration in the USSR," *Administrative Science Quarterly* (September 1971).
27. Murray, Henry A., "Preparation for the Scaffold of a Comprehensive System," in Sigmund Koch, ed., *Psychology: A Study of a Science,* Vol. 3 (New York: McGraw-Hill Book Company, 1959).
28. Parsons, Talcott, *The Social System* (New York: The Free Press of Glencoe, 1951).
29. Phillips, D. C., "Systems Theory—A Discredited Philosophy," in Peter P. Schoderbek, *Management Systems* (New York: John Wiley & Sons, Inc., 1971).
30. Rapoport, Anatol and William J. Horvath, "Thoughts on Organization Theory," in Walter Buckley, ed., *Modern Systems Research for the Behavioral Scientist* (Chicago: Aldine Publishing Company, 1968).
31. Rice, A. K., *The Modern University* (London: Tavistock Publications, 1970).
32. Schein, Edgar, *Organizational Psychology,* rev. ed. (Englewood Cliffs, New Jersey: Prentice-Hall, Inc., 1970).
33. Scott, William G., "Organization Theory: An Overview and an Appraisal," *Academy of Management Journal* (April 1961).
34. Silverman, David, *The Theory of Organizations* (New York: Basic Books, Inc., 1971).
35. Simon, Herbert A., "The Architecture of Complexity," in Joseph A. Litterer, *Organizations: Systems, Control and Adaptation,* Vol. 2 (New York: John Wiley & Sons, Inc., 1969).
36. Springer, Michael, "Social Indicators, Reports, and Accounts: Toward the Management of Society," *The Annals of the American Academy of Political and Social Science* (March 1970).
37. Terreberry, Shirley, "The Evolution of Organizational Environments," *Administrative Science Quarterly* (March 1968).
38. Thompson, James D., *Organizations in Action* (New York: McGraw-Hill Book Company, 1967).
39. Von Bertalanffy, Ludwig, *General System Theory* (New York: George Braziller, 1968).
40. ____, "The Theory of Open Systems in Physics and Biology," *Science* (January 13, 1950).
41. Yuchtman, Ephraim and Stanley E. Seashore, "A System Resource Approach to Organizational Effectiveness," *American Sociological Review* (December 1967).

2   Managerial Work: Analysis from Observation

Henry Mintzberg

What do managers do? Ask this question and you will likely be told that managers plan, organize, coordinate, and control. Since Henri Fayol [9]* first proposed these words in 1916, they have dominated the vocabulary of management. (See, for example, [8], [12], [17].) How valuable are they in describing managerial work? Consider one morning's work of the president of a large organization:

As he enters his office at 8:23, the manager's secretary motions for him to pick up the telephone. "Jerry, there was a bad fire in the plant last night, about $30,000 damage. We should be back in operation by Wednesday. Thought you should know."

At 8:45, a Mr. Jamison is ushered into the manager's office. They discuss Mr. Jamison's retirement plans and his cottage in New Hampshire. Then the manager presents a plaque to him commemorating his thirty-two years with the organization.

Mail processing follows: An innocent-looking letter, signed by a Detroit lawyer, reads: "A group of us in Detroit has decided not to buy any of your products because you used that anti-flag, anti-American pinko, Bill Lindell, upon your Thursday night TV show." The manager dictates a restrained reply.

The 10:00 meeting is scheduled by a professional staffer. He claims that his superior, a high-ranking vice-president of the organization, mistreats his staff, and that if the man is not fired, they will all walk out. As soon as the meeting ends, the manager rearranges his schedule to investigate the claim and to react to this crisis.

Which of these activities may be called planning, and which may be called organizing, coordinating, and controlling? Indeed, what do words such as "coordinating" and "planning" mean in the context of real activity? In fact, these four words do not describe the actual work of managers at all; they describe certain vague objectives of managerial work. ". . . they are just ways of indicating what we need to explain." [1, p. 537]

Other approaches to the study of managerial work have developed, one dealing with managerial-decision-making and policy-making processes, another with the manager's interpersonal activities. (See, for example, [2] and [10].) And some empirical researchers, using the "diary" method, have studied, what might be called, managerial "media"—by what means, with whom, how long, and where

"Managerial Work: Analysis from Observation" by Henry Mintzberg from MANAGEMENT SCIENCE, Volume 18, No. 2, October 1971, pp. B97-110. Reprinted by permission of The Institute of Management Sciences and the author.
*Numbers refer to References at the end of the article.

managers spend their time.[1] But in no part of this literature is the actual content of managerial work systematically and meaningfully described.[2] Thus, the question posed at the start—what do managers do?—remains essentially unanswered in the literature of management.

This is indeed an odd situation. We claim to teach management in schools of both business and public administration; we undertake major research programs in management; we find a growing segment of the management science community concerned with the problems of senior management. Most of these people—the planners, information and control theorists, systems analysts, etc.—are attempting to analyze and change working habits that they themselves do not understand. Thus, at a conference called at M.I.T. to assess the impact of the computer on the manager, and attended by a number of America's foremost management scientists, a participant found it necessary to comment after lengthy discussion [20, p. 198]:

I'd like to return to an earlier point. It seems to me that until we get into the question of what the top manager does or what the functions are that define the top management job, we're not going to get out of the kind of difficulty that keeps cropping up. What I'm really doing is leading up to my earlier question which no one really answered. And that is: Is it possible to arrive at a specification of what constitutes the job of a top manager?

His question was not answered.

RESEARCH STUDY ON MANAGERIAL WORK

In late 1966, I began research on this question, seeking to replace Fayol's words by a set that would more accurately describe what managers do. In essence, I sought to develop by the process of induction a statement of managerial work that would have empirical validity. Using a method called "structured observation," I observed for one-week periods the chief executives of five medium to large organizations (a consulting firm, a school system, a technology firm, a consumer goods manufacturer, and a hospital).

Structured as well as unstructured (i.e., anecdotal) data were collected in three "records." In the *chronology record*, activity patterns throughout the working day were recorded. In the *mail record*, for each of 890 pieces of mail processed

---

[1] Carlson [6] carried out the classic study just after World War II. He asked nine Swedish managing directors to record on diary pads details of each activity in which they engaged. His method was used by a group of other researchers, many of them working in the U.K. (See [4], [5], [15], [25].)

[2] One major project, involving numerous publications, took place at Ohio State University and spanned three decades. Some of the vocabulary used followed Fayol. The results have generated little interest in this area. (See, for example, [13].)

during the five weeks, were recorded its purpose, format and sender, the attention it received and the action it elicited. And, recorded in the *contact record*, for each of 368 verbal interactions, were the purpose, the medium (telephone call, scheduled or unscheduled meeting, tour), the participants, the form of initiation, and the location. It should be noted that all categorizing was done during and after observation so as to ensure that the categories reflected only the work under observation. [19] contains a fuller description of this methodology and a tabulation of the results of the study.

Two sets of conclusions are presented below. The first deals with certain characteristics of managerial work, as they appeared from analysis of the numerical data (e.g., How much time is spent with peers? What is the average duration of meetings? What proportion of contacts are initiated by the manager himself?). The second describes the basic content of managerial work in terms of ten roles. This description derives from an analysis of the data on the recorded *purpose* of each contact and piece of mail.

The liberty is taken of referring to these findings as descriptive of managerial, as opposed to chief executive, work. This is done because many of the findings are supported by studies of other types of managers. Specifically, most of the conclusions on work characteristics are to be found in the combined results of a group of studies of foremen [11], [16], middle managers [4], [5], [15], [25], and chief executives [6]. And although there is little useful material on managerial roles, three studies do provide some evidence of the applicability of the role set. Most important, Sayles' empirical study of production managers [24] suggests that at least five of the ten roles are performed at the lower end of the managerial hierarchy. And some further evidence is provided by comments in Whyte's study of leadership in a street gang [26] and Neustadt's study of three U.S. presidents [21]. (Reference is made to these findings where appropriate.) Thus, although most of the illustrations are drawn from my study of chief executives, there is some justification in asking the reader to consider when he sees the terms "manager" and his "organization" not only "presidents" and their "companies," but also "foremen" and their "shops," "directors" and their "branches," "vice-presidents" and their "divisions." The term *manager* shall be used with reference to all those people in charge of formal organizations or their subunits.

SOME CHARACTERISTICS OF MANAGERIAL WORK

Six sets of characteristics of managerial work derive from analysis of the data of this study. Each has a significant bearing on the manager's ability to administer a complex organization.

Characteristic 1. The Manager Performs a Great Quantity of Work at an Unrelenting Pace

Despite a semblance of normal working hours, in truth managerial work appears to be very taxing. The five men in this study processed an average of thirty-six pieces of mail each day, participated in eight meetings (half of which were scheduled), engaged in five telephone calls, and took one tour. In his study of foremen, Guest [11] found that the number of activities per day averaged 583, with no real break in the pace.

Free time appears to be very rare. If by chance a manager has caught up with the mail, satisfied the callers, dealt with all the disturbances, and avoided scheduled meetings, a subordinate will likely show up to usurp the available time. It seems that the manager cannot expect to have much time for leisurely reflection during office hours. During "off" hours, our chief executives spent much time on work-related reading. High-level managers appear to be able to escape neither from an environment which recognizes the power and status of their positions nor from their own minds which have been trained to search continually for new information.

Characteristic 2. Managerial Activity is Characterized by Variety, Fragmentation, and Brevity

There seems to be no pattern to managerial activity. Rather, variety and fragmentation appear to be characteristic, as successive activities deal with issues that differ greatly both in type and in content. In effect the manager must be prepared to shift moods quickly and frequently.

A typical chief executive day may begin with a telephone call from a director who asks a favor (a "status request"); then a subordinate calls to tell of a strike at one of the facilities (fast movement of information, termed "instant communication"); this is followed by a relaxed scheduled event at which the manager speaks to a group of visiting dignitaries (ceremony); the manager returns to find a message from a major customer who is demanding the renegotiation of a contract (pressure); and so on. Throughout the day, the managers of our study encountered this great variety of activity. Most surprisingly, the significant activities were interspersed with the trivial in no particular pattern.

Furthermore, these managerial activities were characterized by their brevity. Half of all the activities studied lasted less than nine minutes and only ten percent exceeded one hour's duration. Guest's foremen averaged 48 seconds per activity, and Carlson [6] stressed that his chief executives were unable to work without frequent interruption.

In my own study of chief executives, I felt that the managers demonstrated a preference for tasks of short duration and encouraged interruption. Perhaps the manager becomes accustomed to variety, or perhaps the flow of "instant communication" cannot be delayed. A more plausible explanation might be that the manager becomes conditioned by his workload. He develops a sensitive appreciation for the opportunity cost of his own time. Also, he is aware of the ever present assortment of obligations associated with his job—accumulations of mail that cannot be delayed, the callers that must be attended to, the meetings that require his participation. In other words, no matter what he is doing, the manager is plagued by what he must do and what he might do. Thus, the manager is forced to treat issues in an abrupt and superficial way.

Characteristic 3. Managers Prefer Issues That Are Current, Specific, and Ad Hoc

Ad hoc operating reports received more attention than did routine ones; current, uncertain information—gossip, speculation, hearsay—which flows quickly was preferred to historical, certain information; "instant communication" received first consideration; few contacts were held on a routine or "clocked" basis; almost all contacts concerned well-defined issues. The managerial environment is clearly one of stimulus-response. It breeds, not reflective planners, but adaptable information manipulators who prefer the live, concrete situation, men who demonstrate a marked action-orientation.

Characteristic 4. The Manager Sits Between His Organization and a Network of Contacts

In virtually every empirical study of managerial time allocation, it was reported that managers spent a surprisingly large amount of time in horizontal or lateral (nonline) communication. It is clear from this study and from that of Sayles [24] that the manager is surrounded by a diverse and complex web of contacts which serves as his self-designed external information system. Included in this web can be clients, associates and suppliers, outside staff experts, peers (managers of related or similar organizations), trade organizations, government officials, independents (those with no relevant organizational affiliation), and directors or superiors. (Among these, directors in this study and superiors in other studies did *not* stand out as particularly active individuals.)

The managers in this study received far more information than they emitted, much of it coming from contacts, and more from subordinates who acted as filters. Figuratively, the manager appears as the neck of an hourglass, sifting information into his own organization from its environment.

Characteristic 5. The Manager Demonstrates a Strong Preference for the Verbal Media

The manager has five media at his command—mail (documented), telephone (purely verbal), unscheduled meeting (informal face-to-face), scheduled meeting (formal face-to-face), and tour (observational). Along with all the other empirical studies of work characteristics, I found a strong predominance of verbal forms of communication.

Mail.
By all indications, managers dislike the documented form of communication. In this study, they gave cursory attention to such items as operating reports and periodicals. It was estimated that only thirteen percent of the input mail was of specific and immediate use to the managers. Much of the rest dealt with formalities and provided general reference data. The managers studied initiated very little mail, only twenty-five pieces in the five weeks. The rest of the outgoing mail was sent in reaction to mail received—a reply to a request, an acknowledgment, some information forwarded to a part of the organization. The managers appeared to dislike this form of communication, perhaps because the mail is a relatively slow and tedious medium to use.

Telephone and Unscheduled Meetings.
The less formal means of verbal communication—the telephone, a purely verbal form, and the unscheduled meeting, a face-to-face form—were used frequently (two-thirds of the contacts in the study) but for brief encounters (average duration of six and twelve minutes respectively). They were used primarily to deliver re-quests and to transmit pressing information to those outsiders and subordinates who had informal relationships with the manager.

Scheduled Meetings.
These tended to be of long duration, averaging sixty-eight minutes in this study, and absorbing over half the managers' time. Such meetings provided the managers with their main opportunities to interact with large groups and to leave the confines of their own offices. Scheduled meetings were used when the participants were un-familiar to the manager (e.g., students who request that he speak at a university), when a large quantity of information had to be transmitted (e.g., presentation of a report), when ceremony had to take place, and when complex strategy-making or negotiation had to be undertaken. An important feature of the scheduled meet-ing was the incidental, but by no means irrelevant, information that flowed at the start and end of such meetings.

Tours.

Although the walking tour would appear to be a powerful tool for gaining information in an informal way, in this study tours accounted for only three percent of the managers' time.

In general, it can be concluded that the manager uses each medium for particular purposes. Nevertheless, where possible, he appears to gravitate to verbal media since these provide greater flexibility, require less effort, and bring faster response. It should be noted here that the manager does not leave the telephone or the meeting to get back to work. Rather, communication is his work, and these media are his tools. The operating work of the organization—producing a product, doing research, purchasing a part—appears to be undertaken infrequently by the senior manager. The manager's productive output must be measured in terms of information, a great part of which is transmitted verbally.

Characteristic 6. Despite the Preponderance of Obligations, the Manager Appears to Be Able to Control His Own Affairs

Carlson suggested in his study of Swedish chief executives that these men were puppets, with little control over their own affairs. A cursory examination of our data indicates that this is true. Our managers were responsible for the initiation of only thirty-two percent of their verbal contacts and a smaller proportion of their mail. Activities were also classified as to the nature of the managers' participation, and the active ones were outnumbered by the passive ones (e.g., making requests vs. receiving requests). On the surface, the manager is indeed a puppet, answering requests in the mail, returning telephone calls, attending meetings initiated by others, yielding to subordinates' requests for time, reacting to crises.

However, such a view is misleading. There is evidence that the senior manager can exert control over his own affairs in two significant ways: (1) It is he who defines many of his own long-term commitments, by developing appropriate information channels which later feed him information, by initiating projects which later demand his time, by joining committees or outside boards which provide contacts in return for his services, and so on. (2) The manager can exploit situations that appear as obligations. He can lobby at ceremonial speeches; he can impose his values on his organization when his authorization is requested; he can motivate his subordinates whenever he interacts with them; he can use the crisis situation as an opportunity to innovate.

Perhaps these are two points that help distinguish successful and unsuccessful managers. All managers appear to be puppets. Some decide who will pull the strings and how, and they then take advantage of each move that they are forced to make. Others, unable to exploit this high-tension environment, are swallowed up by this most demanding of jobs.

THE MANAGER'S WORK ROLES

In describing the essential content of managerial work, one should aim to model managerial activity, that is, to describe it as a set of programs. But an undertaking as complex as this must be preceded by the development of a useful typological description of managerial work. In other words, we must first understand the distinct components of managerial work. At the present time we do not.

In this study, 890 pieces of mail and 368 verbal contacts were categorized as to purpose. The incoming mail was found to carry acknowledgements, requests and solicitations of various kinds, reference data, news, analytical reports, reports on events and on operations, advice on various situations, and statements of problems, pressures, and ideas. In reacting to mail, the managers acknowledged some, replied to the requests (e.g., by sending information), and forwarded much to subordinates (usually for their information). Verbal contacts involved a variety of purposes. In 15% of them activities were scheduled, in 6% ceremonial events took place, and a few involved external board work. About 34% involved requests of various kinds, some insignificant, some for information, some for authorization of proposed actions. Another 36% essentially involved the flow of information to and from the manager, while the remainder dealt specifically with issues of strategy and with negotiations. (For details, see [19].)

In this study, each piece of mail and verbal contact categorized in this way was subjected to one question: Why did the manager do this? The answers were collected and grouped and regrouped in various ways (over the course of three years) until a typology emerged that was felt to be satisfactory. While an example, presented below, will partially explain this process to the reader, it must be remembered that (in the words of Bronowski [3, p. 62]): "Every induction is a speculation and it guesses at a unity which the facts present but do not strictly imply."

Consider the following sequence of two episodes: A chief executive attends a meeting of an external board on which he sits. Upon his return to his organization, he immediately goes to the office of a subordinate, tells of a conversation he had with a fellow board member, and concludes with the statement: "It looks like we shall get the contract."

The purposes of these two contacts are clear—to attend an external board meeting, and to give current information (instant communication) to a subordinate. But why did the manager attend the meeting? Indeed, why does he belong to the board? And why did he give this particular information to his subordinate?

Basing analysis on this incident, one can argue as follows: The manager belongs to the board in part so that he can be exposed to special information which is of use to his organization. The subordinate needs the information but has not the status which would give him access to it. The chief executive does. Board memberships bring chief executives in contact with one another for the purpose of trading information.

Two aspects of managerial work emerge from this brief analysis. The manager serves in a "liaison" capacity because of the status of his office, and what he learns here enables him to act as "disseminator" of information into his organization. We refer to these as *roles*—organized sets of behaviors belonging to identifiable offices or positions [23]. Ten roles were chosen to capture all the activities observed during this study.

All activities were found to involve one or more of three basic behaviors—interpersonal contact, the processing of information, and the making of decisions. As a result, our ten roles are divided into three corresponding groups. Three roles —labelled *figurehead, liaison,* and *leader*—deal with behavior that is essentially interpersonal in nature. Three others—*nerve center, disseminator,* and *spokesman* —deal with information-processing activities performed by the manager. And the remaining four—*entrepreneur, disturbance handler, resource allocator,* and *negotiator*—cover the decision-making activities of the manager. We describe each of these roles in turn, asking the reader to note that they form a *gestalt,* a unified whole whose parts cannot be considered in isolation.

The Interpersonal Roles

Three roles relate to the manager's behavior that focuses on interpersonal contact. These roles derive directly from the authority and status associated with holding managerial office.

Figurehead.
As legal authority in his organization, the manager is a symbol, obliged to perform a number of duties. He must preside at ceremonial events, sign legal documents, receive visitors, make himself available to many of those who feel, in the words of one of the men studied, "that the only way to get something done is to get to the top." There is evidence that this role applies at other levels as well. Davis [7, pp. 43–44] cites the case of the field sales manager who must deal with those customers who believe that their accounts deserve his attention.

Leader.
Leadership is the most widely recognized of managerial roles. It describes the manager's relationship with his subordinates—his attempts to motivate them and his development of the milieu in which they work. Leadership actions pervade all

activity—in contrast to most roles, it is possible to designate only a few activities as dealing exclusively with leadership (these mostly related to staffing duties). Each time a manager encourages a subordinate, or meddles in his affairs, or replies to one of his requests, he is playing the *leader* role. Subordinates seek out and react to these leadership clues, and, as a result, they impart significant power to the manager.

Liaison.
As noted earlier, the empirical studies have emphasized the importance of lateral or horizontal communication in the work of managers at all levels. It is clear from our study that this is explained largely in terms of the *liaison* role. The manager establishes his network of contacts essentially to bring information and favors to his organization. As Sayles notes in his study of production supervisors [24, p. 258], "The one enduring objective [of the manager] is the effort to build and maintain a predictable, reciprocating system of relationships. . . ."

   Making use of his status, the manager interacts with a variety of peers and other people outside his organization. He provides time, information, and favors in return for the same from others. Foremen deal with staff groups and other foremen; chief executives join boards of directors, and maintain extensive networks of individual relationships. Neustadt notes this behavior in analyzing the work of President Roosevelt [21, p. 150]:

His personal sources were the product of a sociability and curiosity that reached back to the other Roosevelt's time. He had an enormous acquaintance in various phases of national life and at various levels of government; he also had his wife and her variety of contacts. He extended his acquaintanceships abroad; in the war years Winston Churchill, among others, became a "personal source." Roosevelt quite deliberately exploited these relationships and mixed them up to widen his own range of information. He changed his sources as his interests changed, but no one who had ever interested him was quite forgotten or immune to sudden use.

The Informational Roles

A second set of managerial activities relates primarily to the processing of information. Together they suggest three significant managerial roles, one describing the manager as a focal point for a certain kind of organizational information, the other two describing relatively simple transmission of this information.

Nerve Center.
There is indication, both from this study and from those by Neustadt and Whyte, that the manager serves as the focal point in his organization for the movement of nonroutine information. Homans, who analyzed Whyte's study, draws the following conclusions [26, p. 187]:

Since interaction flowed toward [the leaders], they were better informed about the problems and desires of group members than were any of the followers and therefore better able to decide on an appropriate course of action. Since they were in close touch with other gang leaders, they were also better informed than their followers about conditions in Cornerville at large. Moreover, in their positions at the focus of the chains of interaction, they were better able than any follower to pass on to the group decisions that had been reached.

The term *nerve center* is chosen to encompass those many activities in which the manager receives information.

Within his own organization, the manager has legal authority that formally connects him—and only him—to *every* member. Hence, the manager emerges as *nerve center* of internal information. He may not know as much about any one function as the subordinate who specializes in it, but he comes to know more about his total organization than any other member. He is the information generalist. Furthermore, because of the manager's status and its manifestation in the *liaison* role, the manager gains unique access to a variety of knowledgeable outsiders including peers who are themselves *nerve centers* of their own organizations. Hence, the manager emerges as his organization's *nerve center* of external information as well.

As noted earlier, the manager's nerve center information is of a special kind. He appears to find it most important to get his information quickly and informally. As a result, he will not hesitate to bypass formal information channels to get it, and he is prepared to deal with a large amount of gossip, hearsay, and opinion which has not yet become substantiated fact.

Disseminator.

Much of the manager's information must be transmitted to subordinates. Some of this is of a *factual* nature, received from outside the organization or from other subordinates. And some is of a *value* nature. Here, the manager acts as the mechanism by which organizational influencers (owners, governments, employee groups, the general public, etc., or simply the "boss") make their preferences known to the organization. It is the manager's duty to integrate these value positions, and to express general organizational preferences as a guide to decisions made by subordinates. One of the men studied commented: "One of the principal functions of this position is to integrate the hospital interests with the public interests." Papandreou describes his duty in a paper published in 1952, referring to management as the "peak coordinator" [22].

Spokesman.

In his *spokesman* role, the manager is obliged to transmit his information to outsiders. He informs influencers and other interested parties about his organization's performance, its policies, and its plans. Furthermore, he is expected to serve outside his organization as an expert in its industry. Hospital administrators are expected to spend some time serving outside as public experts on health, and corporation presidents, perhaps as chamber of commerce executives.

The Decisional Roles

The manager's legal authority requires that he assume responsibility for all of his organization's important actions. The *nerve center* role suggests that only he can fully understand complex decisions, particularly those involving difficult value tradeoffs. As a result, the manager emerges as the key figure in the making and interrelating of all significant decisions in his organization, a process that can be referred to as *strategy-making*. Four roles describe the manager's control over the strategy-making system in his organization.

Entrepreneur.

The *entrepreneur* role describes the manager as initiator and designer of much of the controlled change in his organization. The manager looks for opportunities and potential problems which may cause him to initiate action. Action takes the form of *improvement projects*—the marketing of a new product, the strengthening of a weak department, the purchasing of new equipment, the reorganization of formal structure, and so on.

The manager can involve himself in each improvement project in one of three ways: (1) He may *delegate* all responsibility for its design and approval, implicitly retaining the right to replace that subordinate who takes charge of it. (2) He may delegate the design work to a subordinate, but retain the right to *approve* it before implementation. (3) He may actively *supervise* the design work himself.

Improvement projects exhibit a number of interesting characteristics. They appear to involve a number of subdecisions, consciously sequenced over long periods of time and separated by delays of various kinds. Furthermore, the manager appears to supervise a great many of these at any one time—perhaps fifty to one hundred in the case of chief executives. In fact, in his handling of improvement projects, the manager may be likened to a juggler. At any one point, he maintains a number of balls in the air. Periodically, one comes down, receives a short burst of energy, and goes up again. Meanwhile, an inventory of new balls waits on the sidelines and, at random intervals, old balls are discarded and new ones added. Both Lindblom [2] and Marples [18] touch on these aspects of strategy-making, the former stressing the disjointed and incremental nature of the decisions, and the latter depicting the sequential episodes in terms of a stranded rope made up of fibres of different lengths each of which surfaces periodically.

Disturbance Handler.

While the *entrepreneur* role focuses on voluntary change, the *disturbance handler* role deals with corrections which the manager is forced to make. We may describe this role as follows: The organization consists basically of specialist operating programs. From time to time, it experiences a stimulus that cannot be handled routinely, either because an operating program has broken down or because the stimulus is new and it is not clear which operating program should handle it. These situations constitute disturbances. As generalist, the manager is obliged to assume responsibility for dealing with the stimulus. Thus, the handling of disturbances is an essential duty of the manager.

There is clear evidence for this role both in our study of chief executives and in Sayles' study of production supervisors [24, p. 162]:

The achievement of this stability, which is the manager's objective, is a never-to-be-attained ideal. He is like a symphony orchestra conductor, endeavoring to maintain a melodious performance in which contributions of various instruments are coordinated and sequenced, patterned and paced, while the orchestra members are having various personal difficulties, stage hands are moving music stands, alternating excessive heat and cold are creating audience and instrument problems, and the sponsor of the concert is insisting on irrational changes in the program.

Sayles goes further to point out the very important balance that the manager must maintain between change and stability. To Sayles, the manager seeks "a dynamic type of stability" (p. 162). Most disturbances elicit short-term adjustments which bring back equilibrium; persistent ones require the introduction of long-term structural change.

Resource Allocator.

The manager maintains ultimate authority over his organization's strategy-making system by controlling the allocation of its resources. By deciding who will get what (and who will do what), the manager directs the course of his organization. He does this in three ways:

(1) *In scheduling his own time,* the manager allocates his most precious resource and thereby determines organizational priorities. Issues that receive low priority do not reach the *nerve center* of the organization and are blocked for want of resources.

(2) In designing the organizational structure and in carrying out many improvement projects, the manager *programs the work of his subordinates.* In other words, he allocates their time by deciding what will be done and who will do it.

(3) Most significantly, the manager maintains control over resource allocation by the requirement that he *authorize all significant decisions* before they are implemented. By retaining this power, the manager ensures that different decisions are interrelated—that conflicts are avoided, that resource constraints are respected, and that decisions complement one another.

Decisions appear to be authorized in one of two ways. Where the costs and benefits of a proposal can be quantified, where it is competing for specified resources with other known proposals, and where it can wait for a certain time of year, approval for a proposal is sought in the context of a formal *budgeting* procedure. But these conditions are most often not met—timing may be crucial, nonmonetary costs may predominate, and so on. In these cases, approval is sought in terms of an *ad hoc request for authorization*. Subordinate and manager meet (perhaps informally) to discuss one proposal alone.

Authorization choices are enormously complex ones for the manager. A myriad of factors must be considered (resource constraints, influencer preferences, consistency with other decisions, feasibility, payoff, timing, subordinate feelings, etc.). But the fact that the manager is authorizing the decision rather than supervising its design suggests that he has little time to give to it. To alleviate this difficulty, it appears that managers use special kinds of *models* and *plans* in their decision-making. These exist only in their minds and are loose, but they serve to guide behavior. Models may answer questions such as, "Does this proposal make sense in terms of the trends that I see in tariff legislation?" or "Will the EDP department be able to get along with marketing on this?" Plans exist in the sense that, on questioning, managers reveal images (in terms of proposed improvement projects) of where they would like their organizations to go: "Well, once I get these foreign operations fully developed, I would like to begin to look into a reorganization," said one subject of this study.

Negotiator.
The final role describes the manager as participant in negotiation activity. To some students of the management process [8, p. 343], this is not truly part of the job of managing. But such distinctions are arbitrary. Negotiation is an integral part of managerial work, as this study notes for chief executives and as that of Sayles made very clear for production supervisors [24, p. 131]: "Sophisticated managers place great stress on negotiations as a way of life. They negotiate with groups who are setting standards for their work, who are performing support actively for them, and to whom they wish to 'sell' their services."

The manager must participate in important negotiation sessions because he is his organization's legal authority, its *spokesman* and its *resource allocator.* Negotiation is resource trading in real time. If the resource commitments are to be large, the legal authority must be present.

These ten roles suggest that the manager of an organization bears a great burden of responsibility. He must oversee his organization's status system; he must serve as a crucial informational link between it and its environment; he must interpret and reflect its basic values; he must maintain the stability of its operations; and he must adapt it in a controlled and balanced way to a changing environment.

MANAGEMENT AS A PROFESSION AND AS A SCIENCE

Is management a profession? To the extent that different managers perform one set of basic roles, management satisfies one criterion for becoming a profession. But a profession must require, in the words of the *Random House Dictionary,* "knowledge of some department of learning or science." Which of the ten roles now requires specialized learning? Indeed, what school of business or public administration teaches its students how to disseminate information, allocate resources, perform as figurehead, make contacts, or handle disturbances? We simply know very little about teaching these things. The reason is that we have never tried to document and describe in a meaningful way the procedures (or programs) that managers use.

The evidence of this research suggests that there is as yet no science in managerial work—that managers do not work according to procedures that have been prescribed by scientific analysis. Indeed, except for his use of the telephone, the airplane, and the dictating machine, it would appear that the manager of today is indistinguishable from his predecessors. He may seek different information, but he gets much of it in the same way—from word-of-mouth. He may make decisions dealing with modern technology but he uses the same intuitive (that is, nonexplicit) procedures in making them. Even the computer, which has had such a great impact on other kinds of organizational work, has apparently done little to alter the working methods of the general manager.

How do we develop a scientific base to understand the work of the manager? The description of roles is a first and necessary step. But tighter forms of research are necessary. Specifically, we must attempt to model managerial work—to describe it as a system of programs. First, it will be necessary to decide what programs managers actually use. Among a great number of programs in the manager's repertoire, we might expect to find a time-scheduling program, an information-disseminating program, and a disturbance-handling program. Then, researchers will have to devote a considerable amount of effort to studying and accurately describing the content of each of these programs—the information and heuristics used. Finally, it will be necessary to describe the interrelationships among all of these programs so that they may be combined into an integrated descriptive model of managerial work.

When the management scientist begins to understand the programs that managers use, he can begin to design meaningful systems and provide help for the manager. He may ask: Which managerial activities can be fully reprogrammed (i.e., automated)? Which cannot be reprogrammed because they require human responses? Which can be partially reprogrammed to operate in a man-machine system? Perhaps scheduling, information collecting, and resource-allocating activities lead themselves to varying degrees of reprogramming. Management will emerge as a science to the extent that such efforts are successful.

IMPROVING THE MANAGER'S EFFECTIVENESS

Fayol's fifty-year-old description of managerial work is no longer of use to us.
And we shall not disentangle the complexity of managerial work if we insist on
viewing the manager simply as a decision-maker or simply as a motivator of subordinates. In fact, we are unlikely to overestimate the complexity of the manager's work, and we shall make little headway if we take overly simple or narrow
points of view in our research.

A major problem faces today's manager. Despite the growing size of modern
organizations and the growing complexity of their problems (particularly those in
the public sector), the manager can expect little help. He must design his own
information system, and he must take full charge of his organization's strategy-
making system. Furthermore, the manager faces what might be called the *dilemma
of delegation*. He has unique access to much important information but he lacks a
formal means of disseminating it. As much of it is verbal, he cannot spread it
around in an efficient manner. How can he delegate a task with confidence when he
has neither the time nor the means to send the necessary information along with it?

Thus, the manager is usually forced to carry a great burden of responsibility
in his organization. As organizations become increasingly large and complex,
this burden increases. Unfortunately, the man cannot significantly increase his
available time or significantly improve his abilities to manage. Hence, in the large,
complex bureaucracy, the top manager's time assumes an enormous opportunity
cost and he faces the real danger of becoming a major obstruction in the flow
of decisions and information.

Because of this, as we have seen, managerial work assumes a number of
distinctive characteristics. The quantity of work is great; the pace is unrelenting;
there is great variety, fragmentation, and brevity in the work activities; the manager must concentrate on issues that are current, specific, and ad hoc, and to
do so, he finds that he must rely on verbal forms of communications. Yet it is on
this man that the burden lies for designing and operating strategy-making and
information-processing systems that are to solve his organization's (and society's) problems.

The manager can do something to alleviate these problems. He can learn
more about his own roles in his organization, and he can use this information to
schedule his time in a more efficient manner. He can recognize that only he has
much of the information needed by his organization. Then, he can seek to find
better means of disseminating it into the organization. Finally, he can turn to the
skills of his management scientists to help reduce his workload and to improve
his ability to make decisions.

The management scientist can learn to help the manager to the extent he
can develop an understanding of the manager's work and the manager's infor-

mation. To date, strategic planners, operations researchers, and information system designers have provided little help for the senior manager. They simply have had no framework available by which to understand the work of the men who employed them, and they have had poor access to the information which has never been documented. It is folly to believe that a man with poor access to the organization's true *nerve center* can design a formal management information system. Similarly, how can the long-range planner, a man usually uninformed about many of the *current* events that take place in and around his organization, design meaningful strategic plans? For good reason, the literature documents many manager complaints of naïve planning and many planner complaints of disinterested managers. In my view, our lack of understanding of managerial work has been the greatest block to the progress of management science.

The ultimate solution to the problem—to the overburdened manager seeking meaningful help—must derive from research. We must observe, describe, and understand the real work of managing; then and only then shall we significantly improve it.

REFERENCES

1. Braybrooke, David. "The Mystery of Executive Success Re-examined," *Administrative Science Quarterly,* Vol. 8 (1964), pp. 533-60.
2. _____ and Lindblom, Charles E. *A Strategy of Decision,* Free Press, New York, 1963.
3. Bronowski, J. "The Creative Process," *Scientific American,* Vol. 199 (September 1958), pp. 59-65.
4. Burns, Tom. "The Directions of Activity and Communications in a Departmental Executive Group," *Human Relations,* Vol. 7 (1954), pp. 73-97.
5. _____ "Management in Action," *Operational Research Quarterly,* Vol. 8 (1957), pp. 45-60.
6. Carlson, Sune. *Executive Behavior,* Strömbergs, Stockholm, 1951.
7. Davis, Robert T. *Performance and Development of Field Sales Managers,* Division of Research, Graduate School of Business Administration, Harvard University, Boston, 1957.
8. Drucker, Peter F. *The Practice of Management,* Harper and Row, New York, 1954.
9. Fayol, Henri. *Administration industrielle et générale,* Dunods, Paris, 1950 (first published 1916).
10. Gibb, Cecil A. "Leadership," Chapter 31 in Gardner Lindzey and Elliot A. Aronson (editors), *The Handbook of Social Psychology,* Vol. 4, Second edition, Addison-Wesley, Reading, Mass., 1969.
11. Guest, Robert H. "Of Time and the Foreman," *Personnel,* Vol. 32 (1955-56), pp. 478-86.
12. Gulick, Luther H. "Notes on the Theory of Organization," in Luther Gulick and Lyndall Urwick (editors), *Papers on the Science of Administration,* Columbia University Press, New York, 1937.

13. Hemphill, John K. *Dimensions of Executive Positions,* Bureau of Business Research Monograph Number 98, The Ohio State University, Columbus, 1960.
14. Homans, George C. *The Human Group,* Harcourt, Brace, New York, 1950.
15. Horne, J. H. and Lupton, Tom. "The Work Activities of Middle Managers—An Exploratory Study," *The Journal of Management Studies,* Vol. 2 (February 1965), pp. 14-33.
16. Kelly, Joe. "The Study of Executive Behavior by Activity Sampling," *Human Relations,* Vol. 17 (August 1964), pp. 277-87.
17. Mackenzie, R. Alex. "The Management Process in 3D," *Harvard Business Review* (November-December 1969), pp. 80-87.
18. Marples, D. L. "Studies of Managers—A Fresh Start?," *The Journal of Management Studies,* Vol. 4 (October 1967), pp. 282-99.
19. Mintzberg, Henry. "Structured Observation as a Method to Study Managerial Work," *The Journal of Management Studies,* Vol. 7 (February 1970), pp. 87-104.
20. Myers, Charles A. (ed.). *The Impact of Computers on Management,* The M.I.T. Press, Cambridge, Mass., 1967.
21. Neustadt, Richard E. *Presidential Power: The Politics of Leadership,* The New American Library, New York, 1964.
22. Papandreou, Andreas G. "Some Basic Problems in the Theory of the Firm," in Bernard F. Haley (ed.), *A Survey of Contemporary Economics,* Vol. II, Irwin, Homewood, Illinois, 1952, pp. 183-219.
23. Sarbin, T. R. and Allen, V. L. "Role Theory," in Gardner Lindzey and Elliot A. Aronson (eds.), *The Handbook of Social Psychology,* Vol. I, Second edition, Addison-Wesley, Reading, Mass., 1968, pp. 488-567.
24. Sayles, Leonard R. *Managerial Behavior: Administration in Complex Enterprises,* McGraw-Hill, New York, 1964.
25. Stewart, Rosemary. *Managers and Their Jobs,* Macmillan, London, 1967.
26. Whyte, William F. *Street Corner Society,* second edition, University of Chicago Press, Chicago, 1955.

Section B

Strategies for Organizational Design: Change the Organization or Change the Environment?

There is a growing emphasis on contingency theory in the organizational literature, yet much of this work is descriptive and does not attempt to design or change organizations to improve their "fit" with external environments. Unfortunately, improving this "fit" is an ongoing management process, one that raises the question of whether actions taken should focus on the organization or its environment. The two articles in this section examine this matter of strategy and offer selective advice.

The first article, by Galbraith, looks at "Organization Design" from an information processing view. The argument is made that when task uncertainty increases, organizations must either reduce the amount of information to be processed or increase their capacity to handle that information. Galbraith identifies two methods each for reducing information needs and for increasing processing capacity. In his view, these four strategies form an exhaustive set of organizational design alternatives. Management must adopt at least one of the four strategies when faced with increased task uncertainty or expect reduced performance.

There is a fifth strategy which Galbraith notes but does not discuss. Instead of changing the organization in response to uncertainty, management can operate on the environment. This option is examined in the second article—Newman's

"Shaping the Master Strategy of Your Firm." According to Newman, changing the organization may do little to improve performance if the key problem is finding new products or more responsive markets to insure organizational survival or effective growth and expansion. He feels that managers must look beyond short-run internal reorganizations and develop a master plan for relating company effort to projected future environments.

While most managers recognize the importance of having a master strategy, they are less certain how to develop one. Newman's article offers specific guidelines in this regard and complements Galbraith's work on organizational strategies for change. His examples are drawn from the business sector, but the basic analysis should prove applicable to nonprofit organizations as well.

Organization Design: An Information Processing View

Jay R. Galbraith

The Information Processing Model

A basic proposition is that the greater the uncertainty of the task, the greater the amount of information that has to be processed between decision makers during the execution of the task. If the task is well understood prior to performing it, much of the activity can be preplanned. If it is not understood, then during the actual task execution more knowledge is acquired which leads to changes in resource allocations, schedules, and priorities. All these changes require information processing *during* task performance. Therefore *the greater the task uncertainty, the greater the amount of information that must be processed among decision makers during task execution in order to achieve a given level of performance.* The basic effect of uncertainty is to limit the ability of the organization to preplan or

"Organization Design: An Information Processing View" by Jay Galbraith from INTERFACES, 4 (May 1974), pp. 28-36. Reprinted by permission of The Institute of Management Sciences and the author.

to make decisions about activities in advance of their execution. Therefore it is hypothesized that the observed variations in organizational forms are variations in the strategies of organizations to 1) increase their ability to preplan, 2) increase their flexibility to adapt to their inability to preplan, or, 3) to decrease the level of performance required for continued viability. Which strategy is chosen depends on the relative costs of the strategies. The function of the framework is to identify these strategies and their costs.

The Mechanistic Model

This framework is best developed by keeping in mind a hypothetical organization. Assume it is large and employs a number of specialist groups and resources in providing the output. After the task has been divided into specialists subtasks, the problem is to integrate the subtasks around the completion of the global task. This is the problem of organization design. The behaviors that occur in one sub-task cannot be judged as good or bad *per se*. The behaviors are more effective or ineffective depending upon the behaviors of the other subtask performers. There is a design problem because the executors of the behaviors cannot communicate with all the roles with whom they are interdependent. Therefore the design problem is to create mechanisms that permit coordinated action across large numbers of interdependent roles. Each of these mechanisms, however, has a limited range over which it is effective at handling the information requirements necessary to coordinate the interdependent roles. As the amount of uncertainty increases, and therefore information processing increases, the organization must adopt integrating mechanisms which increase its information processing capabilities.

1. Coordination by Rules or Programs

For routine predictable tasks March and Simon have identified the use of rules or programs to coordinate behavior between interdependent subtasks [March and Simon, 1958, Chap. 6]. To the extent that job related situations can be predicted in advance, and behaviors specified for these situations, programs allow an interdependent set of activities to be performed without the need for inter-unit communication. Each role occupant simply executes the behavior which is appropriate for the task related situation with which he is faced.

2. Hierarchy

As the organization faces greater uncertainty its participants face situations for which they have no rules. At this point the hierarchy is employed on an exception basis. The recurring job situations are programmed with rules while infrequent situations are referred to that level in the hierarchy where a global perspective exists for all affected subunits. However, the hierarchy also has a limited range. As uncertainty increases the number of exceptions increases until the hierarchy becomes overloaded.

3. Coordination by Targets or Goals

As the uncertainty of the organization's task increases, coordination increasingly takes place by specifying outputs, goals or targets [March and Simon, 1958, p. 145]. Instead of specifying specific behaviors to be enacted, the organization undertakes processes to set goals to be achieved and the employees select the behaviors which lead to goal accomplishment. Planning reduces the amount of information processing in the hierarchy by increasing the amount of discretion exercised at lower levels. Like the use of rules, planning achieves integrated action and also eliminates the need for continuous communication among interdependent subunits as long as task performance stays within the planned task specifications, budget limits and within targeted completion dates. If it does not, the hierarchy is again employed on an exception basis.

The ability of an organization to coordinate interdependent tasks depends on its ability to compute meaningful subgoals to guide subunit action. When uncertainty increases because of introducing new products, entering new markets, or employing new technologies these subgoals are incorrect. The result is more exceptions, more information processing, and an overloaded hierarchy.

Design Strategies

The ability of an organization to successfully utilize coordination by goal setting, hierarchy, and rules depends on the combination of the frequency of exceptions and the capacity of the hierarchy to handle them. As the task uncertainty increases the organization must again take organization design action. It can proceed in either of two general ways. First, it can act in two ways to reduce the amount of information that is processed. And second, the organization can act in two ways to increase its capacity to handle more information. The two methods for reducing the need for information and the two methods for increasing processing capacity are shown schematically in Figure 1. The effect of all these actions is to reduce the number of exceptional cases referred upward into the organization through hierarchical channels. The assumption is that the critical limiting factor of an organizational form is its ability to handle the non-routine, consequential events that cannot be anticipated and planned for in advance. The non-programmed events place the greatest communication load on the organization.

1. Creation of Slack Resources

As the number of exceptions begin to overload the hierarchy, one response is to increase the planning targets so that fewer exceptions occur. For example, completion dates can be extended until the number of exceptions that occur are within the existing information processing capacity of the organization. This has been the practice in solving job shop scheduling problems [Pounds, 1963]. Job shops quote delivery times that are long enough to keep the scheduling problem within

Figure 1   ORGANIZATION DESIGN STRATEGIES

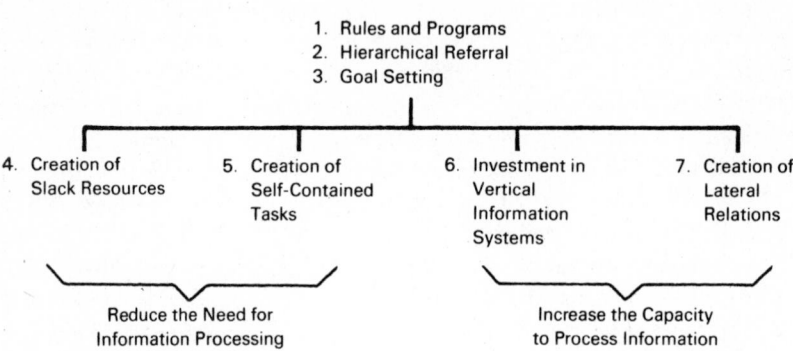

the computational and information processing limits of the organization. Since every job shop has the same problem standard lead times evolve in the industry. Similarly budget targets could be raised, buffer inventories employed, etc. The greater the uncertainty, the greater the magnitude of the inventory, lead time or budget needed to reduce an overload.

All of these examples have a similar effect. They represent the use of slack resources to reduce the amount of interdependence between subunits [March and Simon, 1958, Cyert and March, 1963]. This keeps the required amount of information within the capacity of the organization to process it. Information processing is reduced because an exception is less likely to occur and reduced interdependence means that fewer factors need to be considered simultaneously when an exception does occur.

The strategy of using slack resources has its costs. Relaxing budget targets has the obvious cost of requiring more budget. Increasing the time to completion date has the effect of delaying the customer. Inventories require the investment of capital funds which could be used elsewhere. Reduction of design optimization reduces the performance of the article being designed. Whether slack resources are used to reduce information or not depends on the relative cost of the other alternatives.

The design choices are: 1) among which factors to change (lead time, overtime, machine utilization, etc.) to create the slack, and 2) by what amount should the factor be changed. Many operations research models that are useful in choosing factors and amounts. The time-cost trade off problem in project networks is a good example.

2. Creation of Self-Contained Tasks

The second method of reducing the amount of information processed is to change the subtask groupings from resource (input) based to output based categories and give each group the resources it needs to supply the output. For example, the functional organization could be changed to product groups. Each group would have its own product engineers, process engineers, fabricating and assembly operations, and marketing activities. In other situations, groups can be created around product lines, geographical areas, projects, client groups, markets, etc., each of which would contain the input resources necessary for creation of the output.

The strategy of self-containment shifts the basis of the authority structure from one based on input, resource, skill, or occupational categories to one based on output or geographical categories. The shift reduces the amount of information processing through several mechanisms. First, it reduces the amount of output diversity faced by a single collection of resources. For example, a professional organization with multiple skill specialties providing service to three different client groups must schedule the use of these specialties across three demands for their services and determine priorities when conflicts occur. But, if the organization changed to three groups, one for each client category, each with its own full complement of specialties, the schedule conflicts across client groups disappear and there is no need to process information to determine priorities.

The second source of information reduction occurs through a reduced division of labor. The functional or resource specialized structure pools the demand for skills across all output categories. In the example above each client generates approximately one-third of the demand for each skill. Since the division of labor is limited by the extent of the market, the division of labor must decrease as the demand decreases. In the professional organization, each client group may have generated a need for one-third of a computer programmer. The functional organization would have hired one programmer and shared him across the groups. In the self-contained structure there is insufficient demand in each group for a programmer so the professionals must do their own programming. Specialization is reduced but there is no problem of scheduling the programmer's time across the three possible uses for it.

The cost of the self-containment strategy is the loss of resource specialization. In the example, the organization foregoes the benefit of a specialist in computer programming. If there is physical equipment, there is a loss of economies of scale. The professional organization would require three machines in the self-contained form but only a large time-shared machine in the functional form. But those resources which have large economies of scale or for which specialization is necessary may remain centralized. Thus, it is the degree of self-containment that is the variable. The greater the degree of uncertainty, other things equal, the greater the degree of self-containment.

The design choices are the basis for the self-contained structure and the number of resources to be contained in the groups. No groups are completely self-contained or they would not be part of the same organization. But one product divisionalized firm may have eight of fifteen functions in the divisions while another may have twelve of fifteen in the divisions. Usually accounting, finance, and legal services are centralized and shared. Those functions which have economies of scale, require specialization or are necessary for control remain centralized and not part of the self-contained group.

The first two strategies reduced the amount of information by lower performance standards and creating small autonomous groups to provide the output. Information is reduced because an exception is less likely to occur and fewer factors need to be considered when an exception does occur. The next two strategies accept the performance standards and division of labor as given and adapt the organization so as to process the new information which is created during task performance.

3. Investment in Vertical Information Systems

The organization can invest in mechanisms which allow it to process information acquired during task performance without overloading the hierarchical communication channels. The investment occurs according to the following logic. After the organization has created its plan or set of targets for inventories, labor utilization, budgets, and schedules, unanticipated events occur which generate exceptions requiring adjustments to the original plan. At some point when the number of exceptions becomes substantial, it is preferable to generate a new plan rather than make incremental changes with each exception. The issue is then how frequently should plans be revised—yearly, quarterly, or monthly? The greater the frequency of replanning the greater the resources, such as clerks, computer time, input-output devices, etc., required to process information about relevant factors.

The cost of information processing resources can be minimized if the language is formalized. Formalization of a decision-making language simply means that more information is transmitted with the same number of symbols. It is assumed that information processing resources are consumed in proportion to the number of symbols transmitted. The accounting system is an example of a formalized language.

Providing more information, more often, may simply overload the decision maker. Investment may be required to increase the capacity of the decision maker by employing computers, various man-machine combinations, assistants-to, etc. The cost of this strategy is the cost of the information processing resources consumed in transmitting and processing the data.

The design variables of this strategy are the decision frequency, the degree of formalization of language, and the type of decision mechanism which will make the choice. This strategy is usually operationalized by creating redundant information channels which transmit data from the point of origination upward in the hierarchy where the point of decision rests. If data is formalized and quantifiable, this strategy is effective. If the relevant data are qualitative and ambiguous, then it may prove easier to bring the decisions down to where the information exists.

4. Creation of Lateral Relationships

The last strategy is to employ selectively joint decision processes which cut across lines of authority. This strategy moves the level of decision making down in the organization to where the information exists but does so without reorganizing around self-contained groups. There are several types of lateral decision processes. Some processes are usually referred to as the informal organization. However, these informal processes do not always arise spontaneously out of the needs of the task. This is particularly true in multi-national organizations in which participants are separated by physical barriers, language differences, and cultural differences. Under these circumstances lateral processes need to be designed. The lateral processes evolve as follows with increases in uncertainty.

4.1. *Direct Contact* between managers who share a problem. If a problem arises on the shop floor, the foreman can simply call the design engineer, and they can jointly agree upon a solution. From an information processing view, the joint decision prevents an upward referral and unloads the hierarchy.

4.2. *Liaison Roles*—when the volume of contacts between any two departments grows, it becomes economical to set up a specialized role to handle this communication. Liaison men are typical examples of specialized roles designed to facilitate communication between two interdependent departments and to bypass the long lines of communication involved in upward referral. Liaison roles arise at lower and middle levels of management.

4.3. *Task Forces.* Direct contact and liaison roles, like the integration mechanisms before them, have a limited range of usefulness. They work when two managers or functions are involved. When problems arise involving seven or eight departments, the decision making capacity of direct contacts is exceeded. Then these problems must be referred upward. For uncertain, interdependent tasks such situations arise frequently. Task forces are a form of horizontal contact which is designed for problems of multiple departments.

The task force is made up of representatives from each of the affected departments. Some are full-time members, others may be part-time. The task force is a temporary group. It exists only as long as the problem remains. When a solution is reached, each participant returns to his normal tasks.

To the extent that they are successful, task forces remove problems from higher levels of the hierarchy. The decisions are made at lower levels in the organization. In order to guarantee integration, a group problem solving approach is taken. Each affected subunit contributes a member and therefore provides the information necessary to judge the impact on all units.

4.4. *Teams.* The next extension is to incorporate the group decision process into the permanent decision processes. That is, as certain decisions consistently arise, the task forces become permanent. These groups are labeled teams. There are many design issues concerned in team decision making such as at what level do they operate, who participates, etc. [Galbraith, 1973, Chapters 6 and 7]. One design decision is particularly critical. This is the choice of leadership. Sometimes a problem exists largely in one department so that the department manager is the leader. Sometimes the leadership passes from one manager to another. As a new product moves to the market place, the leader of the new product team is first the technical manager followed by the production and then the marketing manager. The result is that if the team cannot reach a consensus decision and the leader decides, the goals of the leader are consistent with the goals of the organization for the decision in question. But quite often obvious leaders cannot be found. Another mechanism must be introduced.

4.5. *Integrating Roles.* The leadership issue is solved by creating a new role— an integrating role [Lawrence and Lorsch, 1967, Chapter 3]. These roles carry the labels of product managers, program managers, project managers, unit managers (hospitals), materials managers, etc. After the role is created, the design problem is to create enough power in the role to influence the decision process. These roles have power even when no one reports directly to them. They have some power because they report to the general manager. But if they are selected so as to be unbiased with respect to the groups they integrate and to have technical competence, they have expert power. They collect information and equalize power differences due to preferential access to knowledge and information. The power equalization increases trust and the quality of the joint decision process. But power equalization occurs only if the integrating role is staffed with someone who can exercise expert power in the form of persuasion and informal influences rather than exert the power of rank or authority.

4.6. *Managerial Linking Roles.* As tasks become more uncertain, it is more difficult to exercise expert power. The role must get more power of the formal authority type in order to be effective at coordinating the joint decisions which occur at lower levels of the organization. This position power changes the nature of the role which for lack of a better name is labeled a managerial linking role. It is not like the integrating role because it possesses formal position power but is different from line managerial roles in that participants do not report to the linking manager. The power is added by the following successive changes:

a) The integrator receives approval power of budgets formulated in the departments to be integrated.
b) The planning and budgeting process starts with the integrator making his initiation in budgeting legitimate.
c) Linking manager receives the budget for the area of responsibility and buys resources from the specialist groups.

These mechanisms permit the manager to exercise influence even though no one works directly for him. The role is concerned with integration but exercises power through the formal power of the position. If this power is insufficient to integrate the subtasks and creation of self-contained groups is not feasible, there is one last step.

4.7. *Matrix Organization.* The last step is to create the dual authority relationship and the matrix organization [Galbraith, 1971]. At some point in the organization some roles have two superiors. The design issue is to select the locus of these roles. The result is a balance of power between the managerial linking roles and the normal line organization roles. Figure 2 depicts the pure matrix design.

Figure 2 A PURE MATRIX ORGANIZATION

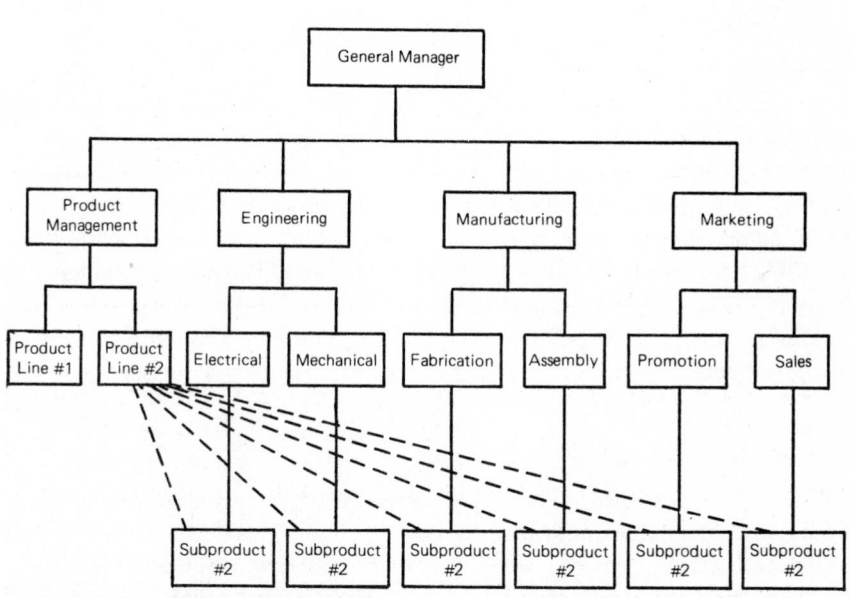

- – – = Technical authority over the product
——— = Formal authority over the product (in product organization, these relationships may be reversed)

The work of Lawrence and Lorsch is highly consistent with the assertions concerning lateral relations [Lawrence and Lorsch, 1967, Lorsch and Lawrence, 1968]. They compared the types of lateral relations undertaken by the most successful firm in three different industries. Their data are summarized in Table 1.

Table 1

	Plastics	*Food*	*Container*
% new products in last ten years	35%	20%	0%
Integrating Devices	Rules	Rules	Rules
	Hierarchy	Hierarchy	Hierarchy
	Planning	Planning	Planning
	Direct	Direct	Direct
	Contact	Contact	Contact
	Teams at 3 levels	Task forces	
	Integrating Dept.	Integrators	
% Integrators/Managers	22%	17%	0%

[Adapted from Lawrence and Lorsch, 1967, pp. 86—138 and Lorsch and Lawrence, 1968].

The plastics firm has the greatest rate of new product introduction (uncertainty) and the greatest utilization of lateral processes. The container firm was also very successful but utilized only standard practices because its information processing task is much less formidable. Thus, the greater the uncertainty the lower the level of decision making and the integration is maintained by lateral relations.

Table 1 points out the cost of using lateral relations. The plastics firm has 22% of its managers in integration roles. Thus, the greater the use of lateral relations the greater the managerial intensity. This cost must be balanced against the cost of slack resources, self-contained groups and information systems.

Choice of Strategy

Each of the four strategies has been briefly presented. The organization can follow one or some combination of several if it chooses. It will choose that strategy which has the least cost in its environmental context. [For an example, see Galbraith, 1970.] However, what may be lost in all of the explanations is that the four strategies are hypothesized to be an exhaustive set of alternatives. That is, if the organization is faced with greater uncertainty due to technological change, higher performance standards due to increased competition, or diversifies its product line to reduce dependence, the amount of information processing is increased. *The organization must adopt at least one of the four strategies when faced with greater uncertainty.* If it does not consciously choose one of the four, then the first, reduced performance standards, will happen automatically. The task information requirements and the capacity of the organization to process information are always matched. If the organization does not consciously match them, reduced performance through budget overruns, schedule overruns will occur in order to bring about equality. Thus the organization should be planned and designed simultaneously with the planning of the strategy and resource allocations. But if the strategy involves introducing new products, entering new markets, etc., then some provision for increased information must be made. Not to decide is to decide, and it is to decide upon slack resources as the strategy to remove hierarchical overload.

There is probably a fifth strategy which is not articulated here. Instead of changing the organization in response to task uncertainty, the organization can operate on its environment to reduce uncertainty. The organization through strategic decisions, long term contracts, coalitions, etc., can control its environment. But these maneuvers have costs also. They should be compared with costs of the four design strategies presented above.

Summary

The purpose of this paper has been to explain why task uncertainty is related to organizational form. In so doing the cognitive limits theory of Herbert Simon was the guiding influence. As the consequences of cognitive limits were traced through the framework various organization design strategies were articulated. The framework provides a basis for integrating organizational interventions, such as information systems and group problem solving, which have been treated separately before.

Bibliography

Cyert, Richard, and March, James, *The Behavioral Theory of the Firm,* Prentice-Hall, Englewood Cliffs, N.J., 1963.

Galbraith, Jay, "Environmental and Technological Determinants of Organization Design: A Case Study" in Lawrence and Lorsch (eds.) *Studies in Organization Design,* Richard D. Irwin Inc., Homewood, Ill., 1970.

Galbraith, Jay, "Designing Matrix Organizations," *Business Horizons,* (Feb. 1971), pp. 29-40.

Galbraith, Jay, *Organization Design,* Addison-Wesley Pub. Co., Reading, Mass., 1973.

Lawrence, Paul, and Lorsch, Jay, *Organization and Environment,* Division of Research, Harvard Business School, Boston, Mass., 1967.

Lorsch, Jay, and Lawrence, Paul, "Environmental Factors and Organization Integration," Paper read at the Annual Meeting of the American Sociological Association, August 27, 1968, Boston, Mass.

March, James, and Simon, Herbert, *Organizations,* John Wiley & Sons, New York, N.Y., 1958.

Pounds, William, "The Scheduling Environment" in Muth and Thompson (eds.) *Industrial Scheduling,* Prentice-Hall Inc., Englewood Cliffs, N.J., 1963.

Simon, Herbert, *Models of Man,* John Wiley & Sons, New York, N.Y., 1957.

4   Shaping the Master Strategy of Your Firm

William H. Newman

Every enterprise needs a central purpose expressed in terms of the services it will render to society. And it needs a basic concept of how it will create these services. Since it will be competing with other enterprises for resources, it must have some distinctive advantages—in its services or in its methods of creating them. Moreover, since it will inevitably cooperate with other firms, it must have the means for maintaining viable coalitions with them. In addition, there are the elements of change, growth, and adaptation. Master strategy is a company's basic plan for dealing with these factors.

One familiar way of delving into company strategy is to ask, "What business are we in or do we want to be in? Why should society tolerate our existence?" Answers are often difficult. A company producing only grass seed had very modest growth until it shifted its focus to "lawn care" and provided the suburban homeowner with a full line of fertilizers, pesticides, and related products. Less fortunate was a cooperage firm that defined its business in terms of wooden boxes and barrels and went bankrupt when paperboard containers took over the field.

Product line is only part of the picture, however. An ability to supply services economically is also crucial. For example, most local bakeries have shut down, not for lack of demand for bread, but because they became technologically inefficient. Many a paper mill has exhausted its sources of pulpwood. The independent motel operator is having difficulty meeting competition from franchised chains. Yet in all these industries some firms have prospered—the ones that have had the foresight and adaptability (and probably some luck, too) to take advantage of their changing environment. These firms pursued a master strategy which enabled them to increase the services rendered and attract greater resources.

Most central managers recognize that master strategy is of cardinal importance. But they are less certain about how to formulate a strategy for their particular firm. This article seeks to help in the shaping of master strategies. It outlines key elements and an approach to defining these. Most of our illustrations will be business enterprises; nevertheless, the central concept is just as crucial for hospitals, universities, and other nonprofit ventures.

A practical way to develop a master strategy is to:

Pick particular roles or niches that are appropriate in view of competition and the company's resources.

Combine various facets of the company's efforts to obtain synergistic effects.

Set up sequences and timing of changes that reflect company capabilities and external conditions.

Provide for frequent reappraisal and adaptation to evolving opportunities.

New Markets or Services

Picking Propitious Niches. Most companies fill more than one niche. Often they sell several lines of products; even when a single line is produced an enterprise may sell it to several distinct types of customers. Especially as a firm grows, it seeks expansion by tapping new markets or selling different services to its existing customers. In designing a company strategy we can avoid pitfalls by first examining each of these markets separately.

Basically, we are searching for customer needs—preferably growing ones—where adroit use of our unique resources will make our services distinctive and in that sense give us a competitive advantage. In these particular spots, we hope to give the customer an irresistible value and to do so at relatively low expense. A bank, for example, may devise a way of financing the purchase of an automobile that is particularly well-suited to farmers; it must then consider whether it is in a good position to serve such a market.

Identifying such propitious niches is not easy. Here is one approach that works well in various situations: Focus first on the industry—growth prospects, competition, key factors required for success—then on the strengths and weaknesses of the specific company as matched against these key success factors. As we describe this approach more fully, keep in mind that we are interested in segments of markets as well as entire markets.

The sales volume and profits of an industry or one of its segments depend on the demand for its services, the supply of these services, and the competitive conditions. (We use "service" here to include both physical products and intangible values provided by an enterprise.) Predicting future demand, supply, and competition is an exciting endeavor. In the following paragraphs, we suggest a few of the important considerations that may vitally affect the strategy of a company.

Elements of Demand

Demand for Industry Services. The strength of the *desire* for a service affects its demand. For instance, we keenly want a small amount of salt, but care little for additional quantities. Our desire for more and better automobiles does not have this same sort of cut-off level, and our desires for pay-television (no commercials, select programs) or supersonic air travel are highly uncertain, falling in quite a different category from that of salt.

Possible *substitutes* to satisfy a given desire must be weighed—beef for lamb, motorboats for baseball, gas for coal, aureomycin for sulfa, weldments for castings, and so forth. The frequency of such substitution is affected, of course, by the relative prices.

Desire has to be backed up by *ability to pay,* and here business cycles enter in. Also, in some industries large amounts of capital are necessarily tied up in equipment. The relative efficiency, quality of work, and nature of machinery already in place influence the money that will be available for new equipment. Another consideration: If we hope to sell in foreign markets, foreign-exchange issues arise.

The *structure of markets* also requires analysis. Where, on what terms, and in response to what appeals do people buy jet planes, sulphuric acid, or dental floss? Does a manufacturer deal directly with consumers or are intermediaries such as retailers or brokers a more effective means of distribution?

Although an entire industry is often affected by such factors—desire, substitutes, ability to pay, structure of markets—a local variation in demand sometimes provides a unique opportunity for a particular firm. Thus, most drugstores carry cosmetics, candy, and a wide variety of items besides drugs, but a store located in a medical center might develop a highly profitable business by dealing exclusively with prescriptions and other medical supplies.

All these elements of demand are subject to change—some quite rapidly. Since the kind of strategic plans we are considering here usually extends over several years, we need both an identification of the key factors that will affect industry demand and an estimate of how they will change over a span of time.

Supply Situation

Supply Related to Demand. The attractiveness of any industry depends on more than potential growth arising from strong demand. In designing a company strategy we also must consider the probable supply of services and the conditions under which they will be offered.

The *capacity* of an industry to fill demand for its services clearly affects profit margins. The importance of over- or undercapacity, however, depends on the ease of entry and withdrawal from the industry. When capital costs are high, as in the hotel or cement business, adjustments to demand tend to lag. Thus, overcapacity may depress profits for a long period; even bankruptcies do not remove the capacity if plants are bought up—at bargain prices—and operated by new owners. On the other hand, low capital requirements—as in electronic assembly work—permit new firms to enter quickly, and shortages of supply tend to be short-lived. Of course, more than the physical plant is involved; an effective organization of competent people is also necessary. Here again, the case of expansion or contraction should be appraised.

Costs also need to be predicted—labor costs, material costs, and for some industries, transportation costs or excise taxes. If increases in operating costs affect all members of an industry alike and can be passed on to the consumer in the form of higher prices, this factor becomes less significant in company strategy. However, rarely do both conditions prevail. Sharp rises in labor costs in Hawaii, for example, place its sugar industry at a disadvantage on the world market.

A highly dynamic aspect of supply is *technology*. New methods for producing established products—for example, basic oxygen conversion of steel displacing open-hearth furnaces and mechanical cotton pickers displacing century-old hand-picking techniques—are part of the picture. Technology may change the availability and price of raw materials; witness the growth of synthetic rubber and industrial diamonds. Similarly, air cargo planes and other new forms of transportation are expanding the sources of supply that may serve a given market.

For an individual producer, anticipating these shifts in the industry supply situation may be a matter of prosperity or death.

Climate of Industry

Competitive Conditions in the Industry. The way the interplay between demand and supply works out depends partly on the nature of competition in the industry. *Size, strength, and attitude of companies* in one industry—the dress industry where entrance is easy and style is critical—may lead to very sharp competition. On the other hand, oligopolistic competition among the giants of the aluminum industry produces a more stable situation, at least in the short run. The resources and managerial talent needed to enter one industry differ greatly from what it takes to get ahead in the other.

A strong *trade association* often helps to create a favorable climate in its industry. The Independent Oil Producers' Association, to cite one case, has been unusually effective in restricting imports of crude oil into the United States. Other associations compile valuable industry statistics, help reduce unnecessary variations in size of products, run training conferences, hold trade shows, and aid members in a variety of other ways.

Government regulation also modifies competition. A few industries like banking and insurance are supervised by national or state bodies that place limits on prices, sales promotion, and the variety of services rendered. Airlines are both regulated as a utility and subsidized as an infant industry. Farm subsidies affect large segments of agriculture, and tariffs have long protected selected manufacturers. Our patent laws also bear directly on the nature of competition, as is evident in the heated discussion of how pharmaceutical patents may be used. Clearly, future government action is a significant factor in the outlook of many industries.

Crucial Factors

Key Factors for Success in the Industry. This brief review suggests the dynamic nature of business and uncertainties in the outlook for virtually all industries. A crucial task of every top management is to assess the forces at play in its industry and to identify those factors that will be crucial for future success. These we call "key success factors." Leadership in research and development may be very important in one industry, low costs in another, and adaptability to local need in a third; large financial resources may be a *sine qua non* for mining whereas creative imagination is the touchstone in advertising.

We stressed earlier the desirability of making such analyses for narrow segments as well as broad industry categories. The success factors for each segment are likely to differ in at least one or two respects from those for other segments. For example, General Foods Corporation discovered to its sorrow that the key success factors in gourmet foods differ significantly from those for coffee and Jello.

Moreover, the analysis of industry outlook should provide a forecast of the *growth potentials* and the profit prospects for the various industry segments. These conclusions, along with key success factors, are vital guideposts in setting up a company's master strategy.

The range of opportunities for distinctive service is wide. Naturally, in picking its particular niche out of this array a company favors those opportunities which will utilize its strength and bypass its limitations. This calls for a candid appraisal of the company itself.

Position in Market

Market Strengths of Company. A direct measure of *market position* is the percentage that company sales are of industry sales and of major competitors' sales. Such figures quickly indicate whether our company is so big that its activities are likely to bring prompt responses from other leading companies. Or our company may be small enough to enjoy independent maneuverability. Of course, to be most meaningful, these percentages should be computed separately for geographical areas, product lines, and types of customer—if suitable industry data are available.

More intangible but no less significant are the relative standing of *company products* and their *reputation* in major markets. Kodak products, for instance, are widely and favorably known; they enjoy a reputation for both high quality and dependability. Clearly, this reputation will be a factor in Eastman Kodak Company strategy. And any new, unknown firm must overcome this prestige if it seeks even a small share in one segment of the film market. Market reputation is tenacious. Especially when we try to "trade up," our previous low quality, service, and sharp dealing will be an obstacle. Any strategy we adopt must have enough persistence and consistency so that our firm is assigned a "role" in the minds of the customers we wish to reach.

The relationship between a company and the *distribution system* is another vital aspect of market position. The big United States automobile companies, for example, are strong partly because each has a set of dealers throughout the country. In contrast, foreign car manufacturers have difficulty selling here until they can arrange with dealers to provide dependable service. A similar problem confronted Whirlpool Corporation when it wanted to sell its trademarked appliances publicly. (For years its only customer had been Sears, Roebuck and Company.) Whirlpool made an unusual arrangement with Radio Corporation of America which led to the establishment of RCA-Whirlpool distributors and dealers. Considering the strong competition, Whirlpool could not have entered this new market without using marketing channels such as RCA's.

All these aspects of market position—a relative share of the market, comparative quality of product, reputation with consumers, and ties with a distributive system—help define the strengths and limitations of a company.

Service Abilities

Supply Strengths of a Company. To pick propitious niches we also should appraise our company's relative strength in creating goods and services. Such ability to supply services fitted to consumer needs will be built largely on the firm's resources of labor and material, effective productive facilities, and perhaps pioneering research and development.

Labor in the United States is fairly mobile. Men tend to gravitate to good jobs. But the process takes time—a southern shoe plant needed ten years to build up an adequate number of skilled workers—and it may be expensive. Consequently, immediate availability of competent men at normal industry wages is a source of strength. In addition, the relationships between the company and its work force are important. All too often both custom and formal agreements freeze inefficient practices. The classic example is New England textiles; here, union-supported work habits give even mills high labor costs. Only recently have a few companies been able to match their more flourishing competitors in the South.

Access to *low-cost materials* is often a significant factor in a company's supply position. The development of the southern paper industry, for example, is keyed to the use of fast-growing forests which can be cut on a rotational basis to provide a continuing supply of pulpwood. Of course, if raw materials can be easily transported, such as iron ore and crude oil by enormous ships, plants need not be located at the original source.

Availability of materials involves more than physical handling. Ownership, or long-term contracts with those who do own, may assure a continuing source at low cost. Much of the strategy of companies producing basic metals—iron, copper, aluminum, or nickel—includes huge investments in ore properties. But all sorts of companies are concerned with the availability of materials. So whenever supplies are scarce a potential opportunity exists. Even in retailing, Sears, Roebuck and Company discovered in its Latin American expansion that a continuing flow of merchandise of standard quality was difficult to assure, but once established, such sources became a great advantage.

Physical facilities—office buildings, plants, mines—often tie up a large portion of a company's assets. In the short run, at least, these facilities may be an advantage or a disadvantage. The character of many colleges, for instance, has been shaped by their location, whether in a plush suburb or in a degenerating urban area, and the cost of moving facilities is so great that adaptation to the existing neighborhood becomes necessary. A steel company, to cite another case, delayed modernizing its plant so long that it had to abandon its share of the basic steel market and seek volume in specialty products.

Established organizations of highly talented people to perform particular tasks also give a company a distinctive capability. Thus, a good research and development department may enable a company to expand in pharmaceuticals, whereas a processing firm without such a technical staff is barred from this profitable field.

Perhaps the company we are analyzing will enjoy other distinctive abilities to produce services. Our central concern at this point is to identify strengths and see how these compare with strengths of other firms.

Finances and Management

Other Company Resources. The propitious niche for a company also depends on its financial strength and the character of its management.

Some strategies will require large quantities of capital. Any oil company that seeks foreign sources of crude oil, for instance, must be prepared to invest millions of dollars. Five firms maintain cash reserves of this size, so *financial capacity* to enter this kind of business depends on: an ability to attract new capital—through borrowing or sale of stock—or a flow of profits (and depreciation allowances) from existing operations that can be allocated to the new venture. On the other hand, perhaps a strategy can be devised that calls for relatively small cash advances, and in these fields a company that has low financial strength will still be able to compete with the affluent firms.

A more subtle factor in company capacity is its *management*. The age and vitality of key executives, their willingness to risk profit and capital, their urge to gain personal prestige through company growth, their desire to insure stable employment for present workers—all affect the suitability of any proposed strategy. For example, the expansion of Hilton Hotels Corporation into a worldwide chain certainly reflects the personality of Conrad Hilton; with a different management at the helm, a modification in strategy is most appropriate because Conrad Hilton's successors do not have his particular set of drives and values.

Related to the capabilities of key executives is the organization structure of the company. A decentralized structure, for instance, facilitates movement into new fields of business, whereas a functional structure with fine specialization is better suited to expansion in closely related lines.

Picking a Niche

Matching Company Strengths with Key Success Factors. Armed with a careful analysis of the strengths and limitations of our company, we are prepared to pick desirable niches for company concentration. Naturally, we will look for fields where company strengths correspond with the key factors for success that have been developed in our industry analyses described in the preceding section. And in the process we will set aside possibilities in which company limitations create serious handicaps.

Potential growth and profits in each niche must, of course, be added to the synthesis. Clearly, a low potential will make a niche unattractive even though the company strengths and success factors fit neatly. And we may become keenly interested in a niche where the fit is only fair if the potential is great.

Typically, several intriguing possibilities emerge. These are all the niches— in terms of market lines, market segments, or combinations of production functions —that the company might pursue. Also typically, a series of positive actions is necessary in order for the company to move into each area. So we need to list not only each niche and its potential, but the limitations that will have to be overcome and other steps necessary for the company to succeed in each area. These are our propitious niches—nestled in anticipated business conditions and tailored to the strengths and limitations of our particular company.

An enterprise always pursues a variety of efforts to serve even a single niche, and, typically, it tries to fill several related niches. Considerable choice is possible, at least in the degree to which these many efforts are pushed. In other words, management decides how many markets to cover, to what degree to automate production, what stress to place on consumer engineering, and a host of other actions. One vital aspect of master strategy is fitting these numerous efforts together. In fact, our choice of niches will depend, in part, on how well we can combine the total effort they require.

Synergy is a powerful ally for this purpose. Basically, synergy means that the combined effect of two or more cooperative acts is greater than the sum which would result if the actions were taken independently. A simple example in marketing is that widespread dealer stocks *combined with* advertising will produce much greater sales volume than widespread dealer stocks in, say, Virginia and advertising in Minnesota. Often the possibility of obtaining synergistic effects will shape the master strategy of the company—as the following examples will suggest.

Combination of Services

Total Service to Customer. A customer rarely buys merely a physical product. Other attributes of the transaction often include delivery, credit terms, return privileges, repair service, operating instructions, conspicuous consumption, psychological experience of purchasing, and the like. Many services involve no physical product at all. The crucial question is what combination of attributes will have high synergistic value for the customers we serve.

International Business Machines, for instance, has found a winning combination. Its products are well designed and of high quality. But so are the products of several of its competitors. In addition, IBM provides salesmen who understand the customer's problems and how IBM equipment can help solve them, and fast, dependable repair service. The synergistic effect of these three services is of high value to many customers.

Each niche calls for its own combination of services. For example, Chock Full o' Nuts expanded its restaurant chain on the basis of three attributes: good quality food, cleanliness, and fast service. This combination appealed to a particular group of customers. A very limited selection, crowded space, and lack of frills did not matter. However, if any one of the three characteristics slips at an outlet, the synergistic effect is lost.

Adding to Capabilities

Fuller Use of Existing Resources. Synergistic effects are possible in any phase of company operations. One possibility is that present activities include a "capability" that can be applied to additional uses. Thus, American watch companies have undertaken the manufacture of tiny gyroscopes and electronic components for spacecraft because they already possessed technical skill in the production of miniature precision products. They adopted this strategy on the premise that they could make both watches and components for spacecraft with less effort than could separate firms devoted to only one line of products.

The original concept of General Foods Corporation sought a similar synergistic effect in marketing. Here, the basic capability was marketing prepared foods. By having the same sales organization handle several product lines, a larger and more effective sales effort could be provided and/or the selling cost per product line could be reduced. Clearly, the combined sales activity was more powerful than separate sales efforts for each product line would have been.

Vertical Integration

Expansion to Obtain a Resource. Vertical integration may have synergistic effects. This occurred when the Apollo Printing Machine Company bought a foundry. Apollo was unsatisfied with the quality and tardy delivery of its castings and was looking for a new supplier. In its search, it learned that a nearby foundry could be purchased. The foundry was just breaking even, primarily because the volume of its work fluctuated widely. Following the purchase, Apollo gave the foundry a more steady backlog of work, and through close technical cooperation the quality of castings received by them was improved. The consolidated set-up was better for both enterprises than the previous independent operations.

The results of vertical integration are not always so good, however; problems of balance, flexibility, and managerial capacity must be carefully weighed. Nevertheless, control of a critical resource is often a significant part of company strategy.

Unique Services

Expansion to Enhance Market Position. Efforts to improve market position provide many examples of "the whole being better than the sum of its parts." The leading can companies, for example, moved from exclusive concentration on metal containers into glass, plastic, and paper containers. They expected their new divisions to be profitable by themselves, but an additional reason for the expansion lay in anticipated synergistic effects of being able to supply a customer's total container requirements. With the entire packaging field changing so rapidly, a company that can quickly shift from one type of container to another offers a distinctive service to its customers.

International Harvester, to cite another case, added a very large tractor to its line a few years ago. The prospects for profit on this line alone were far from certain. However, the new tractor was important to give dealers "a full line"; its availability removed the temptation for dealers to carry some products of competing manufacturers. So, when viewed in combination with other International Harvester products, the new tractor looked much more significant than it did as an isolated project.

Negative Synergy

Compatibility of Efforts. In considering additional niches for a company, we may be confronted with negative synergy—that is, the combined effort is worse than the sum of independent efforts. This occurred when a producer of high quality television and hi-fi sets introduced a small color television receiver. When first offered, the small unit was as good as most competing sets and probably had an attractive potential market. However, it was definitely inferior in performance to other products of the company and, consequently, undermined public confidence in the quality of the entire line. Moreover, customers had high expectations for the small set because of the general reputation of the company, and they became very critical when the new product did not live up to their expectations. Both the former products and the new product suffered.

Compatibility of operations within the company should also be considered. A large department store, for instance, ran into serious trouble when it tried to add a high-quality dress shop to its mass merchandising activities. The ordering and physical handling of merchandise, the approach to sales promotion, the sales compensation plan, and many other procedures which worked well for the established type of business were unsuited to the new shop. And friction arose each time the shop received special treatment. Clearly, the new shop created an excessive number of problems because it was incompatible with existing customs and attitudes.

Broad Company Goals

Summarizing briefly: We have seen that some combinations of efforts are strongly reinforcing. The combination accelerates the total effect or reduces the cost for the same effect or solidifies our supply or market position. On the other hand, we must watch for incompatible efforts which may have a disruptive effect in the same cumulative manner. So, when we select niches—as a part of our master strategy—one vital aspect is the possibility of such synergistic effects.

Master strategy sets broad company goals. One firm may decide to seek preeminence in a narrow specialty while another undertakes to be a leader in several niches or perhaps in all phases of its industry. We have recommended that this definition of "scope" be clear in terms of:

Services offered to customers.

Operations performed by the company.

Relationships with suppliers of necessary resources.

The desirability of defining this mission so as to obtain synergistic effects.

But master strategy involves more than defining our desired role in society. Many activities will be necessary to achieve this desired spot, and senior executives must decide what to do first, how many activities can be done concurrently, how fast to move, what risks to run, and what to postpone. These questions of sequence and timing must be resolved to make the strategy operational.

Strategy of Sequence

Choice of Sequence. Especially in technical areas, sequence of actions may be dictated by technology. Thus, process research must precede equipment designs, product specifications must precede cost estimation, and so forth. Other actions, such as the steps necessary to form a new corporation, likewise give management little choice in sequence. When this occurs, normal programming or possibly PERT analysis may be employed. Little room—or need—exists for strategy.

Preordained sequences, however, are exceptional in the master strategy area. A perennial issue when entering a new niche, for instance, is whether to develop markets before working on production economies, or vice versa. The production executives will probably say, "Let's be sure we can produce the product at a low cost before committing ourselves to customers," whereas the typical marketing man will advise, "Better be sure it will sell before tooling up for a big output."

A striking example of strategy involving sequence confronted the Boeing company when it first conceived of a large four-engine jet plane suitable for handling cargo or large passenger loads. Hindsight makes the issue appear simple, but at the time, Air Force officers saw little need for such a plane. The belief was that propeller-driven planes provided the most desirable means for carrying cargo. In other words, the company got no support for its prediction of future market requirements. Most companies would have stopped at this point. However, Boeing executives decided to invest several million dollars to develop the new plane. A significant portion of the company's liquid assets went into the project. Over two years later, Boeing was able to present evidence that caused the Air Force officials to change their minds—and the KC 135 was born. Only Boeing was prepared to produce the new type of craft which proved to be both faster and more economical than propeller-driven planes. Moreoever, the company was able to convert the design into the Boeing 707 passenger plane which, within a few years, dominated the airline passenger business. Competing firms were left far behind, and Convair almost went bankrupt in its attempt to catch up. In this instance, a decision to let engineering and production run far ahead of marketing paid off handsomely.

No simple guide exists for selecting a strategic sequence. Nevertheless, the following comments do sharpen the issue:

Resist the temptation to do first what is easiest simply because it requires the least initiative. Each of us typically has a bias for what he does well. A good sequence of activities, however, is more likely to emerge from an objective analysis.

If a head start is especially valuable on one front, start early there. Sometimes, being the first in the market is particularly desirable (there may be room for only one company). In other cases, the strategic place to begin is the acquiring of key resources; at a later date limited raw materials may already be bought up or the best sites occupied by competitors. The importance of a head start is usually hard to estimate, but probably more money is lost in trying to be first than in catching up with someone else.

Move into uncertain areas promptly, preferably before making any major commitments. For instance, companies have been so entranced with a desired expansion that they committed substantial funds to new plants before uncertainties regarding the production processes were removed.

If a particular uncertainty can be investigated quickly and inexpensively, get it out of the way promptly.

Start early with processes involving long lead-times. For example, if a new synthetic food product must have government approval, the tedious process of testing and reviewing evidence may take a year or two longer than preparation for manufacturing and marketing.

Delay revealing plans publicly if other companies can easily copy a novel idea. If substantial social readjustment is necessary, however, an early public announcement is often helpful.

In a particular case, these guides may actually conflict with each other; or other considerations may be dominant. And, as the Boeing 707 example suggests, the possible gains may be large enough to justify following a very risky sequence. Probably the greatest value of the above list is to stimulate careful thought about the sequence that is incorporated into a company's master strategy.

Resource Limitations

Straining Scarce Resources. A hard-driving executive does not like to admit that an objective cannot be achieved. He prefers to believe, "Where there's a will there's a way." Yet, an essential aspect of master strategy is deciding what can be done and how fast.

Every enterprise has limits—perhaps severe limits—on its resources. The amount of capital, the number and quality of key personnel, the physical production capacity, or the adaptability of its social structure—none of these is boundless. The tricky issue is how to use these limited resources to the best advantage. We must devise a strategy which is feasible within the inherent restraints.

A household-appliance manufacturer went bankrupt because he failed to adapt his rate of growth to his financial resources. This man had a first-rate product and a wise plan for moving with an "economy model" into an expanding market (following rural electrification). But, to achieve low production costs, he built an oversized plant and launched sales efforts in ten states. His contention was that the kind of company he conceived could not start out on a small scale. Possibly all of these judgments were correct, but they resulted in cash requirements that drained all of his resources before any momentum was achieved. Cost of the partially used plant and of widely scattered sales efforts was so high that no one was willing to bail out the financially strapped venture. His master strategy simply did not fit his resources.

The scarce resource affecting master strategy may be managerial personnel. A management consulting firm, for instance, reluctantly postponed entry into the international arena because only two of its partners had the combination of interest, capacity, and vitality to spend a large amount of time abroad, and these men were also needed to assure continuity of the United States practice. The firm felt that a later start would be better than weak action immediately—even though this probably meant the loss of several desirable clients.

The weight we should attach to scarce resources in the timing of master strategy often requires delicate judgment. Some strain may be endured. But, how much, how long? For example, in its switch from purchased to company-produced tires, a European rubber company fell behind on deliveries for six months, but, through heroic efforts and pleading with customers, the company weathered the squeeze. Now, company executives believe the time was wise! If the delay had lasted a full year—and this was a real possibility—the consequence would have approached a catastrophe.

Forming Coalitions. A cooperative agreement with firms in related fields occasionally provides a way to overcome scarce resources. We have already referred to the RCA-Whirlpool arrangement for distributing Whirlpool products. Clearly, in this instance, the timing of Whirlpool's entrance into the market with its own brand depended on forming a coalition with RCA.

Examples of Coalitions

The early development of frozen foods provides us with two other examples of fruitful coalitions. A key element in Birdseye master strategy was to obtain the help of cold-storage warehouses; grocery wholesalers were not equipped to handle frozen foods, and before the demand was clearly established they were slow to move into the new activity. And the Birdseye division of General Foods lacked both managerial and financial resources to venture into national wholesaling.

Similarly, Birdseye had to get freezer cabinets into retail stores, but it lacked the capability to produce them. So, it entered into a coalition with a refrigerator manufacturer to make and sell (or lease) the cabinets to retail stores. This mutual agreement enabled Birdseye to move ahead with its marketing program much faster. With the tremendous growth of frozen foods, neither the cold storage warehouse nor the cabinet manufacturer continued to be necessary, but without them in the early days widespread use of frozen foods would have been delayed three to five years.

Coalitions may be formed for reasons other than "buying time." Nevertheless, when we are trying to round out a workable master strategy, coalitions—or even mergers—may provide the quickest way to overcome a serious deficiency in vital resources.

The Right Time to Act

Receptive Environment. Conditions in a firm's environment affect the "right time" to make a change. Mr. Ralph Cordiner, for example, testifies that he launched his basic reorganization of General Electric Company only when he felt confident of three years of high business activity because, in his opinion, the company could not have absorbed all the internal readjustments during a period of declining volume and profits.

Judging the right time to act is difficult. Thus, one of the contributing factors to the multimillion-dollar Edsel car fiasco was poor timing. The same automobile launched a year or two earlier might have been favorably received. But buyer tastes changed between the time elaborate market research studies were made and the time when the new car finally appeared in dealer showrooms. By then, preference was swinging away from a big car that "had everything" toward compacts. This mistake in timing and associated errors in strategy cost the Ford Motor Company over a hundred million dollars.

A major move can be too early, as well as too late. We know, for instance, that a forerunner of the modern, self-service supermarket—the Piggly Wiggly— was born too soon. In its day, only a few housewives drove automobiles to shopping centers; and those that could afford cars usually shunned the do-it-yourself mode so prevalent today. In other words, the environment at that time simply was not receptive to what now performs so effectively. Other "pioneers" have also received cool receptions—prefabricated housing and local medical clinics are two.

No Simple Rules

The preceding discussions of sequence and timing provide no simple rules for these critical aspects of basic strategy. The factors we have mentioned for deciding which front(s) to push first (where is a head start valuable, early attention to major uncertainties, lead-times, significance of secrecy) and for deciding how fast to move (strain on scarce resources, possible coalition to provide resources, and receptivity of the environment) bear directly on many strategy decisions. They also highlight the fundamental nature of sequence and timing in the master strategy for a firm.

Master strategy involves deliberately relating a company's efforts to its particular future environment. We recognize, of course, that both the company's capabilities and its environment continually evolve; consequently, strategy should always be based, not on existing conditions, but on forecasts. Such forecasts, however, are never 100 per cent correct; instead, strategy often seeks to take advantage of uncertainty about future conditions.

This dynamic aspect of strategy should be underscored. The industry outlook will shift for any of numerous reasons. These forces may accelerate growth in some sectors and spell decline in others, may squeeze material supply, may make old sources obsolete, may open new possibilities and snuff out others. Meanwhile, the company itself is also changing—due to the success or failure of its own efforts and to actions of competitors and cooperating firms. And with all of these internal and external changes the combination of thrusts that will provide optimum synergistic effects undoubtedly will be altered. Timing of actions is the most volatile element of all. It should be adjusted to both the new external situation and the degrees of internal progress on various fronts.

Consequently, frequent reappraisal of master strategy is essential. We must build into the planning mechanisms sources of fresh data that will tell us how well we are doing and what new opportunities and obstacles are appearing on the horizon. The feedback features of control will provide some of these data. In addition, senior managers and others who have contact with various parts of the environment must be ever-sensitive to new developments that established screening devices might not detect.

Hopefully, such reappraisal will not call for sharp reversals in strategy. Typically, a master strategy requires several years to execute and some features may endure much longer. The kind of plan I am discussing here sets the direction for a whole host of company actions, and external reputations and relations often persist for many years. Quick reversals break momentum, require repeated relearning, and dissipate favorable cumulative effects. To be sure, occasionally a sharp break may be necessary. But, if my forecasts are reasonably sound, the adaptations to new opportunities will be more evolution than revolution. Once embarked on a course, we make our reappraisal from our new position—and this introduces an advantage in continuing in at least the same general direction. So, normally, the adaptation is more an unfolding than a completely new start.

Even though drastic modification of our master strategy may be unnecessary, frequent incremental changes will certainly be required to keep abreast of the times. Especially desirable are shifts that anticipate change before the pressures build up. And such farsighted adjustments are possible only if we periodically reappraise and adapt present strategy to new opportunities.

Master strategy is the pivotal planning instrument for large and small enterprises alike. The giant corporations provide us with examples on a grand scale, but the same kind of thinking is just as vital for small firms.

An Example

A terse sketch of the central strategy of one small firm will illustrate this point. The partners of an accounting firm in a city with a quarter-million population predicted faster growth in data processing than in their normal auditing and tax work, yet they knew that most of their clients were too small to use an electronic computer individually. So they foresaw the need for a single, cooperative computer center serving several companies. And they believed that their intimate knowledge of the procedures and the needs of several of these companies, plus the specialized ability of one partner in data processing, put them in a unique position to operate such a center. Competition was anticipated from two directions: New models of computers much smaller in size would eventually come on the market—but even if the clients could rent such equipment they would still need programmers and other specialized skills. Also, telephonic hook-ups with International Business Machines service centers appeared likely—but the accounting firm felt its local and more intimate knowledge of each company would give it an advantage over such competition. So, the cooperative computer center looked like a propitious niche.

The chief obstacle was developing a relatively stable volume of work that would carry the monthly rental on the proposed computer. A local insurance company was by far the best prospect for this purpose; it might use half the computer capacity, and then the work for other, smaller companies could be fitted into the remaining time. Consequently, the first major move was to make a deal—a coalition—with the insurance company. One partner was to devote almost his entire time working on details for such an arrangement; meanwhile, the other two partners supported him through their established accounting practice.

We see in this brief example:

The picking of a propitious niche for expansion.

The anticipated synergistic effect of combining auditing services with computing service.

The sequence and timing of efforts to overcome the major limiting factor.

The project had not advanced far enough for much reappraisal, but the fact that two partners were supporting the third provided a built-in check on the question of "how are we doing."

Reference

This article is adapted from a new chapter in *The Process of Management*, second edition, Prentice-Hall, Inc., 1967. Executives who wish to explore the meaning and method of shaping master strategies still further can consult the following materials: E. W. Reilley, "Planning the Strategy of the Business," *Advanced Management*, 20 (Dec. 1955), 8-12; T. Levitt, "Marketing Myopia," *Harvard Business Review*, 38:4 (July-August 1960), 45-66; F. F. Gilmore and R. G. Brandenburg, "Anatomy of Corporate Planning," *Harvard Business Review*, 41:6 (November-December 1962), 61-69; and W. H. Newman and T. L. Berg, "Managing External Relations," *California Management Review*, 5:3 (Spring 1963), 81-86.

Section C

Technological and Environmental Change, Tortoise or Hare?

The two articles in this section, by Toffler and Perrow, take opposite views of how technological and environmental change have affected organizations and business. Toffler's work, "Organizations: The Coming Ad-hocracy," is from his best-selling book *Future Shock* (which documents how technology and science have accelerated dramatically the rate of social, political, and economic change). According to Toffler, the pervasiveness of change in high-technology societies is leading to a breakdown of bureaucratic organizations. In their place are emerging new, flexible, temporary systems called "Ad-hocracies."

Toffler argues against the popular notion that organizations are becoming regimented super-bureaucracies. In his view, organizations are changing so rapidly that a three-month-old organization chart only reflects history. Although the new temporary organizational forms will not entirely replace traditional functional structures, they will change them beyond recognition. These "Ad-hocracies" will alter old loyalties, shake up lines of authority, increase the rate at which people must adapt to change, and require a level of creativity that rejects bureaucratic conformity.

The follow-up article, by Perrow, disputes the thesis of rapid social change and queries "Is Business Really Changing?" Acknowledging the substantial literature devoted to change, Perrow argues that "futurist" writers often highlight special cases that are atypical of conditions affecting most organizations. In his view, industry is still characterized by high-volume production with masses of clerks and technicians doing routine jobs.

According to Perrow, corporate business carefully controls its environment and resists technological changes that threaten its stability. This is accomplished through administered pricing, government subsidies, price fixing, planned obsolescence, tariffs, cartels, mergers, monopolies, advertising, and an ability to regulate the regulatory agencies. Far from being faced with rapid technological change, turbulent environments, and constant reorganization, business firms have produced a rate of change that Perrow calls "glacial."

5   Organizations: The Coming Ad-hocracy

Alvin Toffler

One of the most persistent myths about the future envisions man as a helpless cog in some vast organizational machine. In this nightmarish projection, each man is frozen into a narrow, unchanging niche in a rabbit-warren bureaucracy. The walls of this niche squeeze the individuality out of him, smash his personality, and compel him, in effect, to conform or die. Since organizations appear to be growing larger and more powerful all the time, the future, according to this view, threatens to turn us all into that most contemptible of creatures, spineless and faceless, the organization man.

It is difficult to overestimate the force with which this pessimistic prophecy grips the popular mind, especially among young people. Hammered into their heads by a stream of movies, plays and books, fed by a prestigious line of authors from Kafka and Orwell to Whyte, Marcuse and Ellul, the fear of bureaucracy permeates their thought. In the United States everyone "knows" that it is just such faceless bureaucrats who invent all-digit telephone numbers, who send out cards marked "do not fold, spindle or mutilate," who ruthlessly dehumanize students, and whom you cannot fight at City Hall. The fear of being swallowed up by this mechanized beast drives executives to orgies of self-examination and students to paroxysms of protest.

What makes the entire subject so emotional is the fact that organization is an inescapable part of all our lives. Like his links with things, places and people, man's organizational relationships are basic situational components. Just as every act in a man's life occurs in some definite geographical place, so does it also occur in an organizational place, a particular location in the invisible geography of human organization.

Thus, if the orthodox social critics are correct in predicting a regimented, super-bureaucratized future, we should already be mounting the barricades, punching random holes in our IBM cards, taking every opportunity to wreck the machinery of organization. If, however, we set our conceptual clichés aside and turn instead to the facts, we discover that bureaucracy, the very system that is supposed to crush us all under its weight, is itself groaning with change.

The kinds of organizations these critics project unthinkingly into the future are precisely those least likely to dominate tomorrow. For we are witnessing not the triumph, but the breakdown of bureaucracy. We are, in fact, witnessing the arrival of a new organizational system that will increasingly challenge, and ultimately supplant bureaucracy. This is the organization of the future. I call it "Ad-hocracy."

Man will encounter plenty of difficulty in adapting to this new style organization. But instead of being trapped in some unchanging, personality-smashing niche, man will find himself liberated, a stranger in a new free-form world of kinetic organizations. In this alien landscape, his position will be constantly changing, fluid, and varied. And his organizational ties, like his ties with things, places and people, will turn over at a frenetic and ever-accelerating rate. . . .

THE ORGANIZATIONAL UPHEAVAL

There was a time when a table of organization—sometimes familiarly known as a "T/O"—showed a neatly arrayed series of boxes, each indicating an officer and the organizational sub-units for which he was responsible. Every bureaucracy of any size, whether a corporation, a university or a government agency, had its own T/O, providing its managers with a detailed map of the organizational geography. Once drawn, such a map became a fixed part of the organization's rule book, remaining in use for years at a time. Today, organizational lines are changing so frequently that a three-month-old table is often regarded as an historic artifact, something like the Dead Sea Scrolls.

Organizations now change their internal shape with a frequency—and sometime a rashness—that makes the head swim. Titles change from week to week. Jobs are transformed. Responsibilities shift. Vast organizational structures are taken apart, bolted together again in new forms, then rearranged again. Departments and divisions spring up overnight only to vanish in another, and yet another, reorganization.

In part, this frenzied reshuffling arises from the tide of mergers and "demergers" now sweeping through industry in the United States and Western Europe. The late sixties saw a tremendous rolling wave of acquisitions, the growth of giant conglomerates and diversified corporate monsters. The seventies may witness an equally powerful wave of divestitures and, later, reacquisitions, as companies attempt to consolidate and digest their new subsidiaries, then trade off troublesome components. Between 1967 and 1969 the Questor Corporation (formerly Dunhill International, Incorporated) bought eight companies and sold off five. Scores of other corporations have similar stories to tell. According to management consultant Alan J. Zakon, "there will be a great deal more spinning off of pieces." As the consumer marketplace churns and changes, companies will be forced constantly to reposition themselves in it.

Internal reorganizations almost inevitably follow such corporate swaps, but they may arise for a variety of other reasons as well. Within a recent three-year period fully sixty-six of the 100 largest industrial companies in the United States publicly reported major organizational shake-ups. Actually, this was only the visible tip of the proverbial iceberg. Many more reorganizations occur than are ever reported. Most companies try to avoid publicity when overhauling their organization. Moreover, constant small and partial reorganizations occur at the departmental or divisional level or below, and are regarded as too small or unimportant to report.

"My own observation as a consultant," says D. R. Daniel, an official of McKinsey & Company, a large management consulting firm, "is that one major restructuring every two years is probably a conservative estimate of the current rate of organizational change among the largest industrial corporations. Our firm has conducted over 200 organization studies for domestic corporate clients in the past year, and organization problems are an even larger part of our practice outside the United States." What's more, he adds, there are no signs of a leveling off. If anything, the frequency of organizational upheavals is increasing.

These changes, moreover, are increasingly far-reaching in power and scope. Says Professor L. E. Greiner of the Harvard Graduate School of Business Administration: "Whereas only a few years ago the target of organization change was limited to a small work group or a single department . . . the focus is now converging on the organization as a whole, reaching out to include many divisions and levels at once, and even the top managers themselves." He refers to "revolutionary attempts" to transform organization "at all levels of management."

If the once-fixed table of organization won't hold still in industry, much the same is increasingly true of the great government agencies as well. There is scarcely an important department or ministry in the governments of the technological nations that has not undergone successive organizational change in recent years. In the United States during the forty-year span from 1913 to 1953, despite depression, war and other social upheavals, not a single new cabinet-level department was added to the government. Yet in 1953 Congress created the Department of Health, Education and Welfare. In 1965 it established the Department of Housing and Urban Development. In 1967 it set up the Department of Transportation (thus consolidating activities formerly carried out in thirty different agencies), and, at about the same time, the President called for a merger of the departments of Labor and Commerce.

Such changes within the structure of government are only the most conspicuous, for organizational tremors are similarly felt in all the agencies down below. Indeed, internal redesign has become a byword in Washington. In 1965 when John Gardner became Secretary of Health, Education and Welfare, a top-to-bottom reorganization shook that department. Agencies, bureaus and offices were realigned at a rate that left veteran employees in a state of mental exhaustion. (During the height of this reshuffling, one official, who happens to be a friend of mine, used to leave a note behind for her husband each morning when she left for work. The note consisted of her telephone number for *that* day. So rapid were the changes that she could not keep a telephone number long enough for it to be listed in the departmental directory.) Mr. Gardner's successors continued tinkering with organization, and by 1969, Robert Finch, after eleven months in office, was pressing for yet another major overhaul, having concluded in the meantime that the department was virtually unmanageable in the form in which he found it.

In *Self-Renewal,* an influential little book written before he entered the government, Gardner asserted that: "The farsighted administrator . . . reorganizes to break down calcified organizational lines. He shifts personnel . . . He redefines jobs to break them out of rigid categories." Elsewhere Gardner referred to the "crises of organization" in government and suggested that, in both the public and private sectors, "Most organizations have a structure that was designed to solve problems that no longer exist." The "self-renewing" organization, he defined as one that constantly changes its structure in response to changing needs.

Gardner's message amounts to a call for permanent revolution in organizational life, and more and more sophisticated managers are recognizing that in a world of accelerating change reorganization is, and must be, an on-going process, rather than a traumatic once-in-a-lifetime affair. This recognition is spreading outside the corporations and government agencies as well. Thus *The New York Times,* on the same day that it reports on proposed mergers in the plastics, plywood and paper industries, describes a major administrative upheaval at the British Broadcasting Corporation, a thorough renovation of the structure of Columbia University, and even a complete reorganization of that most conservative of institutions, the Metropolitan Museum of Art in New York. What is involved in all this activity is not a casual tendency but a historic movement. Organizational change— self-renewal, as Gardner puts it—is a necessary, an unavoidable response to the acceleration of change.

For the individual within these organizations, change creates a wholly new climate and a new set of problems. The turnover of organizational designs means that the individual's relationship to any one structure (with its implied set of obligations and rewards) is truncated, shortened in time. With each change, he must reorient himself. Today the average individual is frequently reassigned, shuffled about from one sub-structure to another. But even if he remains in the same department, he often finds that the department, itself, has been shifted on some fast-changing table of organization, so that his position in the overall maze is no longer the same.

The result is that man's organizational relationships today tend to change at a faster pace than ever before. The average relationship is less permanent, more temporary, than ever before.

THE NEW AD-HOCRACY

The high rate of turnover is most dramatically symbolized by the rapid rise of what executives call "project" or "task-force" management. Here teams are assembled to solve specific short-term problems. Then, exactly like the mobile playgrounds, they are disassembled and their human components reassigned. Sometimes these teams are thrown together to serve only for a few days. Sometimes they are intended to last a few years. But unlike the functional departments or divisions of a traditional bureaucratic organization, which are presumed to be permanent, the project or task-force team is temporary by design.

When Lockheed Aircraft Corporation won a controversial contract to build fifty-eight giant C-5A military air transports, it created a whole new 11,000-man organization specifically for that purpose. To complete the multi-billion-dollar job, Lockheed had to coordinate the work not only of its own people, but of hundreds of subcontracting firms. In all, 6000 companies are involved in producing the more than 120,000 parts needed for each of these enormous airplanes. The Lockheed project organization created for this purpose has its own management and its own complex internal structure.

The first of C-5A's rolled out of the shop exactly on schedule in March, 1969, twenty-nine months after award of the contract. The last of the fifty-eight transports was due to be delivered two years later. This meant that the entire imposing organization created for this job had a planned life span of five years. What we see here is nothing less than the creation of a disposable division—the organizational equivalent of paper dresses or throw-away tissues.

Project organization is widespread in the aerospace industries. When a leading manufacturer set out to win a certain large contract from the National Aeronautics and Space Agency, it assembled a team of approximately one hundred people borrowed from various functional divisions of the company. The project team worked for about a year and a half to gather data and analyze the job even before the government formally requested bids. When the time came to prepare a formal bid—a "proposal," as it is known in the industry—the "pre-proposal project team" was dissolved and its members sent back to their functional divisions. A new team was brought into being to write the actual proposal.

Proposal-writing teams often work together for a few weeks. Once the proposal is submitted, however, the proposal team is also disbanded. When the contract is won (if it is), new teams are successively established for development, and, ultimately, production of the goods required. Some individuals may move along with the job, joining each successive project team. Typically, however, people are brought in to work on only one or a few stages of the job.

While this form of organization is widely identified with aerospace companies, it is increasingly employed in more traditional industries as well. It is used when the task to be accomplished is non-routine, when it is, in effect, a one-time proposition.

"In just a few years," says *Business Week,* "the project manager has become commonplace." Indeed, project management has, itself, become recognized as a specialized executive art, and there is a small, but growing band of managers, both in the United States and Europe, who move from project to project, company to company, never settling down to run routine or long-term operations. Books on project and task-force management are beginning to appear. And the United States Air Force Systems Command at Dayton, Ohio, runs a school to train executives for project management.

Task forces and other *ad hoc* groups are now proliferating throughout the government and business bureaucracies, both in the United States and abroad. Transient teams, whose members come together to solve a specific problem and then separate, are particularly characteristic of science and help account for the kinetic quality of the scientific community. Its members are constantly on the move, organizationally, if not geographically.

George Kozmetsky, co-founder of Teledyne, Incorporated, and now dean of the school of business at the University of Texas, distinguishes between "routine" and "non-routine" organizations. The latter grapple most frequently with one-of-a-kind problems. He cites statistics to show that the non-routine sector, in which he brackets government and many of the advanced technology companies, is growing so fast that it will employ 65 percent of the total United States work force by the year 2001. Organizations in this sector are precisely the ones that rely most heavily on transient teams and task forces.

Clearly, there is nothing new about the idea of assembling a group to work toward the solution of a specific problem, then dismantling it when the task is completed. What is new is the frequency with which organizations must resort to such temporary arrangements. The seemingly permanent structures of many large organizations, often *because* they resist change, are now heavily infiltrated with these transient cells.

On the surface, the rise of temporary organization may seem insignificant. Yet this mode of operation plays havoc with the traditional conception of organization as consisting of more or less permanent structures. Throw-away organizations, *ad hoc* teams or committees, do not necessarily replace permanent functional structures, but they change them beyond recognition, draining them of both people and power. Today while functional divisions continue to exist, more and more project teams, task forces and similar organizational structures spring up in their midst, then disappear. And people, instead of filling fixed slots in the functional organization, move back and forth at a high rate of speed. They often retain their functional "home base" but are detached repeatedly to serve as temporary team members.

We shall shortly see that this process, repeated often enough, alters the loyalties of the people involved; shakes up lines of authority; and accelerates the rate at which individuals are forced to adapt to organizational change. For the moment, however, it is important to recognize that the rise of *ad hoc* organization is a direct effect of the speed-up of change in society as a whole.

So long as a society is relatively stable and unchanging, the problems it presents to men tend to be routine and predictable. Organizations in such an environment can be relatively permanent. But when change is accelerated, more and more novel first-time problems arise, and traditional forms of organization prove inadequate to the new conditions. They can no longer cope. As long as this is so, says Dr. Donald A. Schon, president of the Organization for Social and Technical Innovation, we need to create "self-destroying organizations . . . lots of autonomous, semiattached units which can be spun off, destroyed, sold bye-bye, when the need for them has disappeared."

Traditional functional organization structures, created to meet predictable, non-novel conditions, prove incapable of responding effectively to radical changes in the environment. Thus temporary role structures are created as the whole organization struggles to preserve itself and keep growing. The process is exactly analogous to the trend toward modularism in architecture. We earlier defined modularism as the attempt to lend greater durability to a whole structure by shortening the life span of its components. This applies to organization as well, and it helps explain the rise of short-lived or throw-away, organization components.

As acceleration continues, organizational redesign becomes a continuing function. According to management consultant Bernard Muller-Thym, the new technology, combined with advanced management techniques, creates a totally new situation. "What is now within our grasp," he says, "is a kind of productive capability that is alive with intelligence, alive with information, so that at its maximum it is completely flexible; one could completely reorganize the plant from hour to hour if one wished to do so." And what is true of the plant is increasingly true of the organization as a whole.

In short, the organizational geography of super-industrial society can be expected to become increasingly kinetic, filled with turbulence and change. The more rapidly the environment changes, the shorter the life span of organization forms. In administrative structure, just as in architectural structure, we are moving from long-enduring to temporary forms, from permanence to transience. We are moving from bureaucracy to Ad-hocracy. . . .

Is Business Really Changing?

Charles Perrow

Organizational theory has gradually developed a rather comprehensive paradigm for handling the impact of technological and environmental change upon organizations, which I have represented in Figure 1. Inventions and innovations in techniques and in goods and services have stimulated the growth of the "knowledge industry," and been stimulated by it. As a consequence, the environment of organizations has shown rapid and turbulent change and has led to new forms of competition. This, in turn, has stimulated both education and research, and resulted in still more innovations and inventions. The consequence for organizations, limited here to economic organizations, has been a change in the character of the workforce: more professionalization and higher skill levels; more rapid change in technologies and products; and more decentralization of authority, as those on the firing line have to make more decisions on their own and can do so because they possess the requisite skills. This creates greater instability in the environment, more innovations, and more growth in the knowledge industry. It is characteristic of our systems model that all the arrows are double-headed.

This model has been with us for several years now; it is celebrated in the works of almost all management theorists and popular authors, and is at least implicit in the work of most organizational theorists. Such widespread acceptance suggests there is a great deal in it, but I am no longer so sure, and what I want to do here

Figure 1   ORGANIZATIONAL THEORY PARADIGM

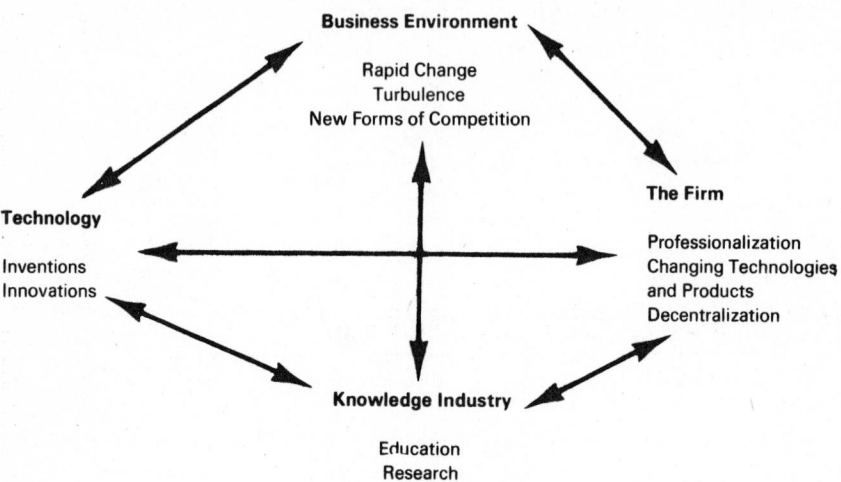

is try to convince the reader that he should not be so sure, either. I am not certain that the dominant perspective is wrong, but I think it is greatly exaggerated. It takes as given many things that should be considered quite problematical. To create the necessary skepticism about it, I shall go to the other extreme and argue against it at every point.

In contrast to this view, and frankly in a spirit of controversy, I shall emphasize the stability of the system in Figure 1 and the glacial rate of change. Let me start with the symbol of futurology that appears in the charts of Buckminster Fuller or Alvin Toffler and that pervades the writings of people like Daniel Bell and Zbigniew Brzezinski. Take the curve represented in Figure 2. Almost any behavior the futurologists are interested in can be plotted in this form. Nothing much happened for a long time, but then the increase in the behavior became exponential. The dates that one would enter at points A, B, C, et cetera would vary with the phenomenon, but the number of scientists that have been produced has increased at the rate suggested by the curve, as has the speed at which new innovations in industry can be made operational or new products marketed, the tons of metal or whatever that can be produced per hour, the velocity at which man gets about, and so on. We walked for thousands upon thousands of years on the plateau from point A to B, took horses and carriages around point B, steam engines and automobiles at C, aeroplanes and jet planes at D, and space capsules at point E, roughly 1969.

Figure 2 FUTURE SHOCK

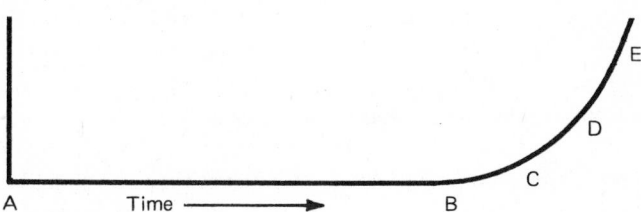

The fallacy is the evaporation of the denominator. The futurologists talk of mankind, but they ignore the world population of billions when they talk about how much faster the 10-or-so percent of Americans who use commercial flights get around today. Were they to put that small number in the numerator over the huge denominator of "mankind," the rate of change would be glacial indeed. In fact, most people in the world today don't even ride horses, let alone fly. And of course, the number who have orbited the earth is truly insignificant.

Only a tiny fraction of men are scientists. Regardless of whether this figure doubles or trebles in a few decades, the vast majority of men know nothing about what these scientists are doing, nor are their lives changed significantly by the scientists' actions, except in the case of radioactive fallout, pesticide poisonings, and so on.

The output statistics of steel for a few industrialized countries should be compared with the figures of the many nonindustrialized countries. The same is true of our organizations. When you take them all into account, rather than the few exotic ones we read about in the business journals or the exotic parts of large corporations, the overwhelming conclusion is one of stability or very slow rates of change.

PROFESSIONALIZATION

Turning now to the paradigm for organization and environment, let us start with one crucial item in Figure 1, the professionalization of the workforce, which has resulted from the knowledge explosion and education and training associated with it. It is a well-known fact that in industrialized countries the number of white-collar employees comes to exceed the number of blue-collar employees (if you count service workers as white-collar, although many are not). It happened several years ago in the United States. What is less well known is that this would not be true if females were excluded. They swell the ranks of the low-status white-collar positions and hardly are there by virtue of technological breakthroughs. In 1970, 41 percent of the females in the labor force were in clerical or sales positions. Of those classified as "professional, technical, and kindred" by the Census Bureau in 1960, 43 percent were teachers. Women are in the workforce for a shorter time than men. All this suggests that they are marginal to industry in several respects—found mostly in low-status, low-skilled, high-turnover positions.

So let's leave them out of account and look only at males. If technological change and professionalization have had a significant effect, we should expect a considerable decline in the proportion of males in the blue-collar category. Professionals, technical specialists, engineers, and the like should be manning organizations, while blue-collar workers evaporated rapidly, dried up by automation and the rapid spread of higher education.

However, over the 70-year period from 1900 to 1969, from C to E in Figure 2—a period of massive technological and organizational change—we find that the percentage of the male workforce engaged in blue-collar and service activities declined by only 13 percent. It went from 70 percent in 1900 to 57 percent in 1969, and even in the 20-year period from 1950 to 1969, the period of postwar boom and knowledge explosion, it declined by only 5 percent. Indeed, if we exclude the service workers and deal only with male manual employees, the proportion of manual workers has actually been increasing slightly in the last decade.

The proportion of professional, technical, and kindred workers, the heart of the technological revolution, is indeed up; for males, it doubled from 7 percent in 1950 to 14 percent in 1969. But 14 percent is still a small percentage of the workforce; moreover, this category appears to be heavily concentrated in two areas: aerospace and "defense" industries (for example, 19 percent of the category are engineers), and the service sector, where technological change is scarcely rampant (for example, 14 percent are teachers). To make a rough estimate, about 30 percent of this group of males are in the high-technology sector of industry, while 35 percent are in the service sector. This suggests that most of industry is not greatly affected by the doubling of the professional and technical category. Most of industry is at level C in Figure 2. To point out that TRW or a nuclear engineering firm has a large proportion of scientists or engineers is like saying the Air Force has a large proportion of people who travel at very high rates of speed. Most of industry still plods along, and plods profitably.

DECENTRALIZATION

Nevertheless, you might say there has been an obvious increase in highly trained personnel in most firms, and it should lead to more decentralization in firms. This is because the market changes are more rapid, the technology more complicated, and the skills outdated sooner, so power must be delegated to those on the firing line with the latest skills and the latest information on the environment. Furthermore, there has been a management revolution, and there are all the T-groupers, sensitivity trainers, 9,9 Grid® men, matrix managers, and the integraters. Decisions have been shoved down to lower levels. Firms are becoming more decentralized.

A rigorous definition of decentralization is impossible at present; the closer one looks, the more it looks like a meaningless term. Sometimes we seem to associate it with what some have called "organization hygiene." I suppose that most organizations today are concerned that there be less smell, safer devices, more choices as to size or color or method, less roughness, irritation, and rudeness, and less secretiveness. The social sciences have marketed a lot of products to ease human interaction and make effort more benign. I think most will agree, however, that better working conditions and more humane supervision have little to do with the decentralization of power or decision making.

The term participative management goes a bit further. It includes the hygiene sprays that are supposed to reduce alienation, but it also deals with feelings of powerlessness. The lower odors are consulted on decisions and encouraged to make their own in some areas, subject to the veto of superiors. The veto is important; it is like saying we have a democratic system of government in which people elect their leaders, but subject to the veto of the incumbent leaders. Workers and managers can have their say, make suggestions, and present arguments, and there is no doubt this is extremely desirable. It presumably results in the superior's making better decisions—but they are still his decisions.

We seem to have lost sight of something important in our packaging of pacifiers, namely, that good managements have *always* found it in their interests to utilize the skills, information, experience, and knowledge of people under them. These people know more about some things than management does, and failure to consult them not only is an affront to them, but also means that management must do much more work on its own to get the information. If it doesn't have the time or resources to do so, it makes inferior decisions. Max Weber, the much-maligned theorist of bureaucracy, was explicit about this some 60 years ago. He saw that a man has a set of skills, expertise, or experience and a sense of career with the firm. The skills, expertise, and experience can be developed, and he expects to utilize them—indeed, he wants to. It is wise, then, as we now see, to allow him the freedom to exercise these skills and to use his discretion, for that is why we employ experts and experienced people. However, he should exercise his skills in the service of organizational goals that are set for him. He is not expected, or encouraged, to inquire into the legitimacy of these goals.

Even if we move toward a more psychological model, such as the self-actualization one of Chris Argyris and others, it seems clear that self-actualization by the employee has to be on organizational terms. I don't think they would include the following as proper examples of self-actualization: organizing employees for better working conditions; exposing the cover-up of unjustified expenses in government contracts; opposing the development of chemical warfare techniques in a university research laboratory; advocating mass-transit subsidies as opposed to subsidies for highways while working for an automobile manufacturer; opposing price-fixing techniques or illegal campaign contributions at any number of large corporations; or calling for better testing of drugs and more accurate advertising in a pharmaceutical firm.

It is extremely difficult to get data demonstrating such restrictions, but one minor, though revealing, example was reported in *Look* magazine: At a stormy meeting concerning the activities of the Stanford Research Institute, a young physicist heard the president of SRI argue that no researcher was forced to undertake any project he found morally objectionable. The physicist contradicted him, saying that he had been pressured into doing chemical warfare research. The physicist was fired. As the executive vice-president of SRI put it, according to the article, "People like that have a decision to make—do they want to support the organization or not?"

Were actions such as these possible without penalty, I would agree that we would have decentralized firms. But as long as the superior can define the problem employees work on, he need not fear discussions of possible solutions. The fact that subordinates are using their expertise and skills more fully, and even with more enthusiasm, does not necessarily mean that authority or even decisions have been decentralized; it may merely mean a more effective organization (though I should add that careful critiques of research in the human relations area have as yet been unable to firmly support even that conclusion).

We hear today that large organizations have become more democratic, in that subordinates are encouraged to set their own production goals, control methods, make up their own work teams, and so on. Dog food, pacemakers, television sets, even cars are being produced by "autonomous groups." Just as no one in his right mind would instruct the maintenance staff how many sweeps of the broom were to be taken for any 6′ x 6′ area of floor, no superior should dictate how an experienced work group should go about meeting the production (and quality and scrap) standards, unless the superior really has much more expertise or experience in the matter. The good supervisor-coordinator gets the resources and monitors outputs; he doesn't give orders about task sequences if his men are competent. But the standards are still there, and nonperformance brings sanctions. And the supervisors who set the standards are still there; the men cannot vote them out of office. The ideological confusion attending the gummy word democratic is well represented by Chester Barnard, who quoted with approval an army officer in World War I who remarked that the army is the greatest of all democracies, because when the order to move forward is given, each man decides on his own whether to obey or not.

No serious organizational theorists in the United States, to my knowledge, have advocated the form of decentralization of authority that democracy seeks to provide. That is, there are no calls for workers to elect management and to have the contenders for managerial positions run on platforms such as no speed-up, better washrooms, no defense contracts, no gifts to universities, or no price fixing, let alone less pay for managers and more for workers. In Europe, especially eastern Europe, where there seems to be more progressive management in this respect, the experiment with that most anemic form of democracy, workers' councils, has had only a slight impact on organizations.

TEMPORARY ORGANIZATIONS

A more serious usage of the term decentralization occurs in connection with the appearance of temporary work groups or matrix structures, associated mostly with the name of Warren Bennis. (Dr. Bennis has lost his vision on the way to an organizational presidency, but he had many followers in this Buck Rogers school of theory who still embrace the model with which I opened this article.) Proponents of his view argue that because of rapid environmental and technological changes, those with the most relevant skills and information are in the lower reaches of the hierarchy, and they also suggest that rapid changes call for task groups that have no fixed membership. The groups form and reform, depending on the problem at hand. One is a leader at one time and a subordinate at another. The organization, then, is made up of little cells or work groups that appear and disappear according to the cycle of innovation and implementation. Upper management merely provides the resources and offers what guidance it can.

Once again, I think that the ability of top management to formulate the problem other managers are assigned so limits the range of available solutions that we find very little decentralization of authority. But even if this were not true, I think that all we have here is a slight expansion of the size of the goal-setting unit. A few elite teams are added to the goal-setting unit, while the bulk of management personnel still remains outside of it. Granted, this would constitute a form of decentralization, but I suspect that the examples given in the literature are very special and deal with very special aspects of our large firms. They will cover only a tiny minority of corporations and only a tiny minority of the employees in them. Again, I should like to refer to Figure 2; because a few men have orbited the earth, does that mean that mankind is moving any faster?

There is another important consideration. Those who argue for the reality of organic structure and its expansion write as if innovations were the only things that corporations produce. (Roy Ash some time ago took this position, pointing to pop-top disposable cans and the SST.) But after the innovations and the design, production, and marketing decisions have been made by these elite teams, an army of personnel must carry them out on a volume basis. High-volume production, with masses of workers, clerks, technicians, and personnel men doing largely routine jobs, characterizes industry, not the floating, dissolving teams of innovators and troubleshooters. To suggest otherwise is to succumb to a myth about economic organizations.

DIVISIONALIZATION

Finally, let me come to the most interesting argument of all for decentralization, found in the literature on divisionalization of large corporations. There are a number of books about divisionalization that equate it with decentralization, and some of them are very scholarly and admirable books indeed. All of them deal, at least in part, with General Motors. The first was by Peter Drucker; then came Ernest Dale; then the very influential book *Strategy and Structure,* by Alfred Du Pont Chandler, Jr., and then one by Alfred Sloan himself on his years at General Motors. The evidence given in these books supports a quite different conclusion than the one that their authors put forth (though Chandler is more circumspect about actual decentralization than the rest). The evidence strongly suggests that General Motors was quite decentralized when it was run by William C. Durant—in fact, it was the very model of a present-day conglomerate or holding company, with the main office doing little more than allocate capital among the divisions.

When Sloan came in, he radically and continuously centralized the organization. He introduced inventory-control and production-control devices and internal pricing, allotted markets to the various units, controlled capital outlays, centralized advertising and personnel, standardized parts, and routinized innovation. At every step the divisions lost autonomy. At present there is hardly an area of policy- or goal-setting that is not controlled by the very large central headquarters, and in addition, it controls an enormous number of detailed decisions, including minute aspects of styling. The functionalized exception to divisionalization at General Motors has always been the Fisher Body plant, serving all divisions. That principle is now being extended to include multidivision assembly plants, further reducing the power of the division manager.

Sloan himself takes a characteristically ambiguous position about decentralization. His book opens with praise for decentralization in General Motors; a bit later, though, he criticizes Durant, his predecessor, for allowing General Motors to be too decentralized; and still later he calls for a happy medium between centralization and decentralization. Harold Wolff, in a perceptive discussion of the General Motors structure some years ago, concluded that reading the General Motors experience as an example of decentralization was an error: "If any *one* word is needed to describe the management *structure* of General Motors as it was recast by Sloan and the brilliant group around him, then that word is not decentralization, but *centralization.*" He goes on to say that it is difficult to label the process, as distinct from the structure, but it is clear, he says, that it is not one of decentralization.

The usual way out of this labeling dilemma is to say the policy is centralized and the execution decentralized. But I contend that if policy is centralized, so is execution; the choice is execution through wasteful (and unpleasant) close supervision and direction, or execution through controlling the premises of decisions—through sharply delimiting the options available. Wolff captures it well: "The decentralized operating executives were left with smaller responsibilities than they had before. But the responsibility they did retain was total and sharply defined. They had the right to do only those things which would make the precise plans and policies of the top management work." This hardly fits the pattern of decentralized organizations that has lower-level people responding fully and freely to the turbulent environment.

There is another matter that clouds our perception of the realities of control in industry and organizations in general—the matter of scale, or volume of output, or number of things done. The head of an automotive division at General Motors is no puppet; he makes many decisions that have a great deal of impact on his division and on the corporation as a whole. But the facts that the divisions of General Motors are large and involved in very complex operations and that the division manager and his staff have a great deal to do and a great deal of responsibility do not mean that the controls exercised over them with regard to either means or ends are not great. There are simply more things to do in a large and complex organization such as a General Motors division.

The division manager is not, I understand, free to change legroom lengths, control auto frame production, formulate his own labor policies, raise capital, change the price range of his cars, engage in any significant research and development, or set up his own accounting system—let alone decide that General Motors should change its goals and policies with regard to pollution, highway sprawl, mass transit, product safety, or product warranties. Both his means and his ends are closely monitored and controlled by headquarters. There is nothing inconsistent with being both more closely controlled and having more decisions to make. As James March and Herbert Simon pointed out some time ago in their book *Organizations,* to shape the premises of decision is the key to control; it is unnecessary for members of the superior unit to make the decision themselves.

UNTANGLING THE ISSUES

I think we are only beginning to unravel some of the threads in the cloth we have woven for ourselves concerning the issues of control, delegation of authority, and decision making. I find it instructive that we can so readily assume, to use the words of Zbigniew Brzezinski, that "the increased flow of information and more efficient techniques of coordination need not necessarily prompt greater concentration of power," but can make possible a "greater devolution of authority and responsibility to the lower levels of government and society." Brzezinski's example of this summary of the model is as instructive as it is terrifying: "It is noteworthy that the U.S. Army has so developed its control systems that it is not uncommon for sergeants to call in and coordinate massive air strikes and artillery fire —a responsibility of colonels during World War II."

What Brzezinski does not note is that the ability of the U.S. Army to destroy more living things today than in World War II has increased. There are more decisions to make. The sergeant of today makes more decisions than the colonel of World War II because the lethal output of the system is so much higher. I doubt that the colonel feels robbed of authority and I doubt that he has lost any in the process. Perhaps we should begin to pull apart these two strands in our cloth—control over the premises of decision, which makes the sergeant so ready to call in massive air strikes and artillery fire, and delegation of the authority that might have given him the ability to say it is just not worth all that destruction.

The way we're conducting our research suggests, however, that we are not likely to disentangle these threads. The work of Peter Blau and his associates and of the Aston Group in England has concluded, to use Aston's terms, that the more structured the activities of an organization (that is, the greater the degree of bureaucracy), the greater the degree of decentralization of decision making or authority. But what has been measured when they speak of decentralization of authority?

I suspect that they have found that in large firms, with all their economies of scale and specialization and expert personnel, there has been an absolute increase in the output of the system. In consequence, lower managements have to make more important decisions than they do in weaker systems, but this also means that top managements have increased the importance and scope of their decisions, including those that shape the premises of lower management. It need not be a zero-sum game. Blau and Aston (and I, among many others) have not measured these kinds of decisions by top management because we are not privy to them, and, perhaps more important, not conceptually alert to them.

To say that lower management is more expert or experienced is to say that management will view the situation in the proper light and make the sensible decision in conformance with the interests of the organizational elites who control the organizations. The less the expertise, the more direct the surveillance and the more obtrusive or formal the controls; the more the expertise, the more unobtrusive the controls. The best situation of all is to hire professionals (though they do not come cheap), for someone else has socialized them and even unobtrusive controls are hardly needed. The professional, the prima donna of organizational theory, is really the ultimate eunuch, capable of doing everything well in that harem except what he should not do—and in this case that is to mess around with the goals of the organization or the assumptions that determine to what ends he will use his professional skills.

FLAWS IN THE ARGUMENT

I am quite aware that this argument has many weaknesses, and I will mention two of them. First, it is always possible to deny empirical generalizations, such as those by Blau and the Aston Group, on the grounds that the variables were not measured adequately. This is rightly called cheap criticism, but in an area as important as the centralization of authority I think it is worth raising the point quite strenuously. We should not measure decentralization by the level at which people may hire, fire, or spend a few thousand dollars without proper authorization. We must also measure the unobtrusive controls.

A more serious problem with my position is that it is difficult to know what would be a decentralized organization. Centralization seems to be inevitable, and variations in the degree are quite minor. Let me elaborate. I have argued that what we take to mean decentralization of authority generally means: (1) a larger, or more complex, or more busy organization, as there is more for people in the lower levels to do; (2) more effective bureaucratization, so that the virtues of experience, training, and expertise are more fully realized throughout the organization; (3) more effective control from the top, so that unobtrusive control has a wider scope —and this can include more effective control of the environment; and (4) better organizational hygiene, so that people are not treated so badly. This, I realize, tends to equate effective organizations with the centralization of organizations, and makes it difficult for me to be proved wrong.

This point bothers me. So let me remind you that my purpose is not to prove that the rosy new view of firms emerging from the model of our social scientists is wrong, but merely to ask for a critical pause before we continue to rush headlong into that model. My extended remarks on centralization are meant to open up the debate a bit, in the face of an ever-enlarging consensus.

I have concerned myself mainly with decentralization, but the environment and technology themselves require some brief remarks to put that part of the pattern into a critical perspective, since they are important aspects of the general consensus.

ENVIRONMENT

Is the environment really turbulent? The most important fact, but one we seem to ignore systematically, is that the environment of organizations is primarily made up of other organizations that have similar interests. The shared interests are much greater than the competitive ones. Mobil Oil and Exxon may compete furiously at the intersection of two streets in any American town, but neither of them is really threatened by this marginal competition. They work very closely together in the important matter of oil depletion allowances, our foreign policy about the Mideast, federal tax policies, the pollution issues, and private transit-versus-mass transit. In fact, they cooperate quite well with large organizations in other industries that share their interests, such as the automobile industry. And the automobile industry cooperates with, and has a stake in, the steel industry, and so on. Where, then, is the furious rate of competition? At the lower levels in the organization—the levels of the regional manager who moves prices up and down a fraction and the station manager who washes the windshields and cleans the rest rooms. Who sets the parameters of their behavior and judges them in terms of their performance? Top management. Coping with the environment, then, not only is consistent with centralized control but requires centralized control if the turbulence is going to be minor and limited to the lower echelons.

A little reflection on some obvious behavior will illustrate the stability of large firms and their ability to do three things: select the environment they wish to deal with, create new environments if necessary, and change those that threaten to produce instability. Few firms move from the top 200 in the *Fortune* listing to the next 300; few drop out of the top 500 altogether except by merger, which is, of course, a device for increasing stability and gaining control over environments. Corporations resist technological change when it suits them, and quite successfully. After inventing the transistor, AT&T declined to use it, for it would have required scrapping too much existing equipment, even though the company asked the public to put up with increasingly poor service.

The techniques for managing the environment are so well known I would hesitate to mention them, were it not for the fact that the literature on organization-environment relations and on organizational change largely ignores them. Some obvious ones are administered pricing, government subsidies, price fixing, padded cost figures, planned obsolescence, tariffs, cartels, political payoffs, special governmental aid, takeovers and mergers, and, of course, monopsony, oligopoly, monopoly, and advertising.

In the United States there is overwhelming evidence that industries are able to regulate the regulatory agencies; that the vast majority of top officials in government have come from, and will return to, private business or the law firms that service business; that despite a briefly mobilized citizenry, the heat is off the pollution area, as the main polluters control the programs and advertise their dedication—and so on and so on. There are exceptions, I readily admit—industries where the competition extends to the very top of each firm and affects large areas of policy. But, surprisingly enough, these are generally not the professionalized, technologically advanced firms, but those in the backward industries of food production, food distribution, auto parts and service, furniture, clothing, and the like. Their environments are relatively unstable because they lack size, standardization, centralized control, and mass production and mass marketing. They are 19th century industries, not 21st century industries.

TECHNOLOGICAL CHANGE

One might finally say in exasperation: "The evidence of technological change is overwhelming. Whether environments are controlled or not, surely there has been a great deal of technological change, and as a consequence, more influence on the part of technicians, engineers, scientists, and recently trained managers."

But just as the decline of the proportion of blue-collar workers in the workforce has been very slow and relatively even over the last 60 to 70 years, so has the rise in output per manhour. There have been fluctuations in this figure due to the depression of the 1930s, the war boom of the early 1940s, and more wars and recessions along the way right up to the present. Overall, though, the increase in productivity has not fluctuated greatly even from one environmental disturbance to the next. The impression is one of slow and stable change.

The reason seems to be that while most firms have routine technologies, they are only *somewhat* routine. Most are unable to automate extensively. In the large majority, new technologies have simply not created the condition for the decentralized, responsive, adaptive organization that organizational theorists seem to dream of.

I can only argue from examples here, and I shall give three of them. First, the automatic factory that was heralded as a possibility in the late 1940s and accepted as a reality by the mid-1960s is, as far as I know, still not with us. In 1965, a reporter for *Fortune,* Charles Silberman, tracked down the various references to startling examples of automation that had been served up by journalists and by social scientists. The results were very disappointing. Case after case turned out to be grossly overstated or simply not true. He could find, for example, no automated chemical complexes that had discharged their employees in droves. Most had experienced either no reduction in personnel or even some increase, and none were fully automated. After careful research, Silberman concluded that "no fully automated process exists for any major product in any industry in the U.S." Since we cannot seem to get social scientists to do this kind of work, I hope that *Fortune* magazine will send another crew out in 1975 to see if things have changed much since 1965. I don't think they will have.

The second example concerns the prima donna of technological change, computers. Again, it was *Fortune* that did the investigative work, rather than the social scientists. Tom Alexander, writing in the October 1969 issue of that magazine, concluded: "It turns out that computers have rarely reduced the cost of operations, even in routine clerical work. What they have accomplished is mainly to enable companies to speed up operations and thereby provide better service or handle larger volumes." He reported a survey by the Research Institute of America of some 2,500 companies that found that only half of those with in-house computers were certain that they were paying off—that heady enthusiasm about computers' providing total management information control systems had dissipated greatly.

Perhaps there is always waste with the adaptation of new technologies, but if so, we have been misled about its degree in this age of scientific and technological sophistication. When we look at developments like powdered metallurgy or numerically controlled machines, the story is the same. Fantastic progress is predicted but not realized, because we refuse to recognize the limits of routinization and the ability to control environments so that technological change is not required.

One last example is the Vega automobile produced by General Motors. It planned and built a completely new car and built a new plant to produce it. If automation could ever strike, it should strike here, in this key and wealthy company. (It turns out, incidentally, that the planning was completely centralized in the headquarters of General Motors and not handled by the division.) The computers in this supposedly computerized installation are limited to balancing production (though they were used in designing and making templates), and there are a few automatic welders on the production line. But as far as I can gather, there is nothing more radical in terms of technological change than this.

What allowed the company to use about 20 percent less direct labor in producing the cars was not the technology of the 1960s but that of the 1920s. First, there was the speed-up of the line, which could account for much of the labor-saving. Since it was achieved by having men work harder, we can hardly call it automation. (The line has since been slowed down as a result of high absenteeism, turnover, and wildcat strikes). Second, because there are many more interchangeable parts for all models, the number of parts was reduced and thus the complexity, allowing for longer production runs for parts. Third, the increased number of subassemblies simplified the assembly line. Fourth, there are streamlined assemblies, including the very important simplification of a one-piece roof. Finally, there is a basic model life of five years, rather than three. All of these innovations were made by the first Henry Ford, back in the 1920s. Yet the business press heralded the new plant as "the model of automation."

These examples suggest that technological change is not so widespread, continuous, and rapid as we tend to believe (as well as more wasteful of resources than we had been led to believe). I do not dispute the change that has occurred in, say, electronics, process firms, and even manufacturing, with its roller bearings and engine blocks. I am saying only that the striking examples are few, and that productivity has not taken the great leaps to be expected if these were the norm.

It is also quite possible that technological change is not impelled by market forces and scientific advancement so much as it is by government and corporate political strategy. Surely, the huge concentration of technical and scientific manpower in the defense, space, and atomic power industries is the result of political decisions. There is no free market for these products.

CONCLUSION

In conclusion, then, I have argued that there has been no rapid and drastic change in the workforce, except for the increasing employment of women in low-level, white-collar jobs in the service industry; that firms are more complex and larger, but not necessarily more decentralized, since we have been measuring only part of the control system; that the environment is not unstable and turbulent for the progressive and technologically advanced firms, but very stable, because it is controlled by the companies and managed in their common interests; and that technological change has been quite selective—far less extensive than is usually believed, resisted when it pleases firms, and well-controlled when it exists. At each point I have contradicted what I see as the dominant viewpoint on these matters in organizational theory.

Let me finally add a note to extend my contention to social and political theory. The evidence from our social and political systems also signifies overwhelming stability. The social structure of the United States has not changed much in a hundred years. There has been very little income redistribution; the class system is still quite intact; our political structures and mechanisms remain much as they were at the beginning of the century. It depends upon one's necromancy, but one interpretation of this similarity of the dominant economic, social, and political institutions is that if economic institutions do not change, we can't expect a change in the political and social ones.

SELECTED BIBLIOGRAPHY

Some of the issues raised in this paper are discussed in my recent book, *Complex Organizations: A Critical Essay* (Scott Foresman, 1972). That book deals with the concept of unobtrusive controls derived from the seminal work of James March and Herbert Simon, *Organizations* (John Wiley, 1958), the participative management school, professionalization, and the issue of environments. The statistics on the labor force are all from the usual government publications. See a more extended discussion in Richard Hamilton, *Class and Politics in the United States*

(John Wiley, 1972). The main books on General Motors are Alfred P. Sloan, *My Years with General Motors* (MacFadden-Bartell Co., 1965); Peter Drucker, *The Concept of Corporation* (Beacon Press, 1946); and Alfred Du Pont Chandler, *Strategy and Structure* (Doubleday, 1963). Harold Wolff's essay appeared in the *Harvard Business Review* (September-October 1964). The Zbigniew Brzezinski quotations come from "The American Transition," *New Republic* (September 23, 1967).

For a look at the recent literature on how bureaucracy is associated with decentralization, one has to dig into some technical, scholarly articles and books, written for academic peers rather than practitioners. The first and most accessible are Peter Blau *et al,* "The Structure of Small Bureaucracies," in the *American Sociological Review* (April 1966), and Marshall Meyer, "The Two Authority Structures of Bureaucratic Organization," in *Administrative Science Quarterly* (September 1968). See also Peter Blau, "The Hierarchy of Authority in Organization," in *American Journal of Sociology* (January 1968), and the massive tome by Blau and Richard Schoenherr, *The Structure of Organizations* (Basic Books, 1971). The English studies of the Aston Group are well summarized in John Child, "Predicting and Understanding Organization Structure," in *Administrative Science Quarterly* (June 1973).

For a debunking view of technological change that echoes my own position in part, see Victor C. Ferkiss, *Technological Man* (New American Library, 1969).

3

Organizational Behavior
Issues and Readings

Organizations are complex networks of tasks, technologies, and administrative structures linked together by individuals and groups. While Part 2 emphasized more impersonal approaches to organizational design, Part 3 focuses on selected behavioral issues. Section A examines the quality of work life in America, several basic views of employee motivation, and the relationship of job satisfaction to performance. Section B reviews the claim that job enrichment is an antidote for work apathy, and Section C draws attention to an often-neglected alternative—money as a motivator. Finally, Section D considers the situational requirements of effective leadership and the issue of whether leadership style is rigid or flexible.

Section A

Work and Its Discontents: Satisfaction and Performance

This section uses three articles to deal with the respective topics of job discontent, employee motivation, and the relationship of job satisfaction to performance. The first selection, by Wool, is a review essay which asks "What's Wrong with Work in America?" This question relates to the *Work in America* study released in 1973 by the Department of Health, Education, and Welfare (HEW). A basic and well-publicized theme in that study suggested that increasing numbers of Americans are dissatisfied with the quality of their working lives. To eliminate "blue collar blues" and "managerial discontent," the HEW report recommended "humanizing" the work place. Particular emphasis was given to job enrichment as an antidote for work apathy.

Wool, however, disputes the HEW thesis of rising job discontent. To support his case, he reassesses statistical evidence, questions the Maslow-Herzberg model of motivation which underlies the HEW prescriptions for job enrichment, and argues that American workers are more interested in spendable income than interesting, challenging work. Although Wool does not feel that all is well with the quality of work in America, he concludes that the best way to improve or eliminate undesirable jobs is through a strengthened national commitment to maximum employment policies. For him, the HEW report is a beginning on how to deal with the problems of work and not a final set of conclusions for social policy.

The second article follows up on Wool's criticism of the Maslow-Herzberg approach to motivation. In it, Hunt and Hill discuss "The New Look in Motivation Theory for Organizational Research." They analyze the Maslow-Herzberg theories, find only limited support for them, and review a more promising model of motivation proposed by Vroom. Fundamental to Vroom's approach are the concepts of "valence," "instrumentality," and "expectancy." Hunt and Hill present four empirical tests of Vroom's model, identify several questions in need of further investigation, and consider the "expectancy" model to be a major step in the direction of understanding the complexities of industrial motivation.

The final article, by Greene, takes up "The Satisfaction-Performance Controversy"—an issue that has lingered over four decades of research. Three theoretical propositions on the topic are identified. The first, and most widely believed, states that job satisfaction leads to improved work performance. The second holds that performance-related rewards cause satisfaction. Empirical evidence rejects the first proposition, however, and lends only moderate support to the second. The third, and most recent, formulation of this issue emphasizes the causal role of rewards and sees *no* inherent relationship between satisfaction and performance.

Given the inadequacies of the first two propositions, Greene focuses on the managerial implications of the "rewards" approach. He notes that while rewards cause satisfaction, only rewards based on performance cause subsequent performance. Although the key to motivation is in the linkage of rewards to performance, Greene points out that this is no easy task in practice. He discusses the reasons for this, underscores the necessity of taking individual preferences into account when setting up organizational reward systems, and concludes that the differential reward strategy has far more benefits than liabilities in resolving performance problems.

7   What's Wrong with Work in America?
–A Review Essay

Harold Wool

The rash of rank-and-file union contract rejections and wildcat strikes during the late 1960's and early 1970's, particularly the well-publicized strike by workers at the General Motors facility in Lordstown, Ohio, highlight what some are interpreting as a sort of gut revolt against work as it is organized in the American economy.

Reports of apathy, absenteeism, and even industrial sabotage among blue-collar workers, of poor morale among some white-collar workers (particularly those in repetitive dead-end jobs), of college youths' disdain of bureaucratic jobs in government or industry, and even of executives forsaking promising careers to head out to fields unknown—all these have caused some observers, notably commentators from the print and broadcast media, to question the future of work in American society. Is our commitment to the work ethic fading?

Since all of these symptoms appeared to imply some weakening of this commitment, it is not surprising that the search for a culprit has turned its spotlight on the institution of work itself—the way it is organized, its adequacy in meeting human needs, and the effects of work upon other dimensions of human welfare. A special focus of concern has been the "blue-collar worker" with the automobile assembly-line worker as the inevitable archetype. The "blue-collar blues" has become part of the media lexicon, together with knowing references to more esoteric psychological terms such as "work satisfiers and dissatisfiers," "alienation," and "anomie."

The media, moreover, have simply reflected a growing concern on the part of key officials in industry, labor, and the Government—a concern that "all is not well" among important segments of our nation's work force. An initial official effort to place these concerns in broader perspective was contained in a paper on the "Problems of the Blue-Collar Worker," prepared in early 1970 by U.S. Department of Labor staff for an ad hoc White House Task Group.[1] The paper pointed to symptoms of growing disaffection among lower-middle-income workers (those in the $5,000 – 10,000 family income range), and suggested that this was due to a

"What's Wrong with Work in America? A Review Essay" by Harold Wool from MONTHLY LABOR REVIEW, 96 (March 1973), taken from WORK IN AMERICA: REPORT OF A SPECIAL TASK FORCE TO THE SECRETARY OF HEALTH, EDUCATION, AND WELFARE, Prepared under the Auspices of the W.E. Upjohn Institute for Employment Research. Cambridge, Mass., The MIT Press, 1973.

combination of pressures: an "economic squeeze," resulting from inflationary pressures and limited advancement opportunities; a "social squeeze," reflected especially in deterioration of their communities and in racial ethnic conflicts; and a "workplace squeeze" associated with a variety of depressing working conditions, ranging from grinding monotony to unpleasant or unsafe work environments.

Further evidence that job satisfaction had become a matter of top-policy interest was provided by this reference in President Nixon's 1971 Labor Day Message: "In our quest for a better environment, we must always remember that the most important part of the quality of life is the quality of work, and the new need for job satisfaction is the key to the quality of work."

Against this backdrop, Elliot Richardson, then Secretary of Health, Education, and Welfare, approved initiation in December 1971 of a broad-gaged study of the "institution of work" and of its implications for health, education, and welfare.

The study was conducted by a 10-member Task Force, chaired by James O'Toole, a social anthropologist serving as a staff assistant in Secretary Richardson's office. Patterned after an earlier HEW study group on higher education policies, the members of the task force were apparently given full rein to develop their own thinking on the issues, independent of the usual bureaucratic constraints. The resulting report, *Work in America**, was released in December 1972, together with a cautious foreword by Secretary Richardson, which praised the report for "the breadth of its perspective and its freshness of outlook," but clearly disassociated himself and the Administration from many of its recommendations.

THE TASK FORCE VIEW

The study takes as its point of departure the premise that "work"—broadly defined as socially useful activity—is central to the lives of most adults. In addition to the obvious economic functions of work, work performs an essential psychological and social role in providing individuals with a status, a sense of identity, and an opportunity for social interaction. Referring to recent surveys as evidence, it concludes that individuals on welfare and the poor generally have the same needs and compulsions for work as do those in the economic mainstream.[2]

But, though the work ethic is still "alive" in America, the report finds that it is not "well"—and it ascribes this condition to the institution of work itself. Citing a variety of psychological studies and survey findings, the task force concludes that large numbers of American workers at all occupational levels are pervasively

---

*Work in America: Report of a Special Task Force to the Secretary of Health, Education, and Welfare, Prepared under the Auspices of the W. E. Upjohn Institute for Employment Research. Cambridge, Mass., The MIT Press, 1973. 262 pp.

dissatisfied with the quality of their working lives. Significant numbers of employed workers are locked in to "dull, repetitive seemingly meaningless tasks, offering little challenge or autonomy." And many others, including large numbers of older workers, "suffer the ultimate in job dissatisfaction" in being completely deprived of an opportunity to work at "meaningful" jobs.

The principal sources of worker discontent as seen by the authors are to be found in the confines of the individual workplace itself. The central villains of the piece are (1) the process of work breakdown and specialization associated with the pernicious influence of Frederick W. Taylor and his industrial engineer disciples, and (2) the diminished opportunities for work autonomy, resulting from the shift in locus of jobs from self-employment or small scale enterprises to large impersonal corporate and government bureaucracies. Although these trends are recognized as having been underway for many decades, what is new in the current climate, the study contends, is a revolutionary change in attitudes and values among many members of the work force—youth, minority members, and women. With higher expectations generated by increased educational achievement, these groups in particular are placing greater emphasis on the intrinsic aspects of work, its inherent challenge and interest, and less on strictly material rewards. In the case of minority workers, the study recognizes that large numbers are still concerned with the elemental needs for a job—any job—that pays a living wage, but it notes relatively high rates of discontent among black workers in many better paying jobs as well. The relegation of women to poor paying, low status jobs, and the plight of older workers, both in and out of the labor force, are also discussed.

This complex of discontents is, in turn, identified as the root cause of various ills besetting the American economy—"reduced productivity," "the doubling of man-days per year lost through strikes," and increases in absenteeism, sabotage, and turnover rates. In addition, a variety of other ills are attributed to work-related problems, including problems of physical and mental health, family instability, and drug and alcohol addiction.

Since the central diagnosis for this wide array of economic and social problems is found in the faulty organization of work, the principal remedy presented by the task force is the reorganization of work. Although "work redesign" is never explicitly defined by the authors, a number of recent experiments are cited—both here and abroad—which have had in common an extensive restructuring of jobs designed to broaden and vary the scope of workers' duties and to provide increased worker autonomy and participation in work-related decisions, often accompanied by some form of profit sharing. Collaborative efforts by labor, management and government in Norway and Sweden, resulting in a number of pilot job redesign projects, are cited as a model for emulation.[3]

Although work design is identified as the "keystone" of the report, the authors concede that this is not a sufficient solution to the problems of work—and of workers—in America. The final two chapters therefore address themselves, more generally, to a range of other work-related problems and possible solutions. Since some jobs can "never be made satisfying," an alternative approach is to facilitate movement of workers out of these jobs, through a massive midcareer retraining option or "self-renewal program" for workers.

In a concluding chapter, the report addresses itself broadly to a variety of other manpower and welfare policy issues. It endorses a "total employment" strategy, designed to produce "reasonably satisfying" jobs not only for the 5 million workers currently reported as unemployed but for an estimated 10 to 30 million additional persons who are underemployed, on welfare, or out of the labor market but who—the authors contend—would take meaningful jobs, if available. This is to be accomplished through a combination of large-scale manpower training and public employment programs and through appropriate fiscal and monetary policies. With respect to welfare reform, it is strongly critical of mandatory work provisions, as applied to welfare mothers, as reflecting a lack of appreciation of the social value of the mother's role in housekeeping and childrearing activities. The report suggests that policy emphasis be shifted to obtaining suitable employment for the fathers, while upgrading the status of housework—in part, by including housewives in the statistical count of the labor force.

EVALUATING THE REPORT

From this summary, the coolness of official response to this study will not be difficult to understand.

For somewhat different reasons, this reviewer also has mixed feelings about the value of this study as a basis for broad social policy. Its strengths—and its weaknesses—lie in its advocacy of a humanistic approach to assessment of work as a social institution. Its perspective is primarily that of the behavioral scientist, who appraises the "value" of work in terms of its total impact upon the individual—in contradistinction to the market-oriented perspective of many economists, who view work primarily as another factor contributing to the GNP and measure its "value" solely in terms of financial rewards. The task force offers insightful—if still fragmentary—documentation concerning the ways in which many jobs (both blue collar and white collar) are proving "dissatisfying" particularly to some members of the new generation. And scattered through its chapters are a number of provocative recommendations which deserve further study and followthrough. However, in its zeal to advance the cause of "humanization of work" the report suffers from overgeneralization concerning the extent and nature of work dissatisfaction and from overstatement of the potentials of work redesign as a primary solution to work-related ills.

A central theme of this study is that "a general increase in their educational and economic status has placed many American workers in a position where having an interesting job is now as important as having a job that pays well" and that the organization of work "has not changed fast enough to keep up with rapid and widescale changes in worker attitudes, aspirations and values."[4] From this premise, it is reasonable to infer that the level of worker discontent has significantly increased in recent years.

A LOOK AT AVAILABLE DATA

Yet a review of available research and statistical evidence offers very limited support for this hypothesis. For this purpose we have explored two types of data: (1) job satisfaction survey findings, and (2) those statistical indicators which have frequently been cited as manifestations of worker discontent, such as quit rates, strikes, absenteeism, and productivity.

Job satisfaction surveys.
In a recent review of the extensive literature on job satisfaction, Robert Kahn reports that some 2,000 surveys of "job satisfaction" were conducted in the United States over a period of several decades. These surveys have varied greatly in scope and design, from intensive studies of workers in a particular plant, occupation, or industry to much more general polls covering a national cross-section of the work force. In spite of these differences, Kahn—as well as earlier observers—has noted a certain consistency in the response patterns. "Few people call themselves extremely satisfied with their jobs, but still fewer report extreme dissatisfaction. The modal response is on the positive side of neutrality—'pretty satisfied.' The proportion dissatisfied ranges from 10 to 21 percent . . . Commercial polls, especially those of the Roper organization, asked direct questions about job satisfaction in hundreds of samples and seldom found the proportion of dissatisfied response exceeding 20 percent."[5] Neither Kahn nor other scholars could detect a consistent trend in job satisfaction from the available data.

Statistical indicators.
It is not unreasonable to infer, as does the task force report, that job dissatisfaction will be reflected in a variety of cost-increasing worker behaviors, such as low productivity, high voluntary turnover, high absenteeism, and increased strike activity. Research evidence based mainly on specific plant or industry studies is available to support at least some of these direct relationships, notably in the case of turnover and absenteeism. If worker discontent has been significantly increasing, some indication of this might be reflected in the overall trends of the relevant statistical indicators. Yet the evidence in this respect is inconclusive:

1. *Labor turnover.* A detailed multivariate analysis of quit rates of manufacturing workers recently completed by the Bureau of Labor Statistics indicates that year-to-year fluctu-

ations in these rates over a 20-year period are largely explained by cyclical variations in job opportunities, as measured by the rate of new hires, and that there has been *no* discernible trend in the quit rate over this period.[6]

2. *Absenteeism.* In the absence of any direct program for statistical reporting of absenteeism trends, the Bureau of Labor Statistics has analyzed data from the Current Population Survey on trends in the proportion of workers who have been absent from their jobs for all or part of a week due to illness or other personal reasons. This initial analysis does point to a small increase in worker absence rates since 1966. The average daily rate of unscheduled absences rose from 3.3 percent in 1967 to 3.6 percent in 1972, an increase of about 10 percent. The data are, however, far from conclusive, and do not provide a basis for generalization of longer-term trends or their causes.[7]

3. *Strikes.* A sharp increase in the level of strike activity was recorded in the second half of the 1960's and in the early 1970's. Man-days of idleness due to strikes rose from 0.13 percent of estimated working time in 1961—65 to 0.26 percent in 1966—71. However, the incidence of strikes normally tends to increase during inflationary periods. Strike idleness, as a percentage of working time, was actually considerably higher during the years immediately following the end of World War II (1946—50) and following the outbreak of the Korean War (1952—53) than during the more recent period of rapid price increases. Moreover, "bread and butter" issues, such as pay, benefits, job security, and union organization or security issues, have continued to account for all but a modest percentage of all strikes. In 1971, only 5.5 percent of strike idleness was attributed to plant administration or other working condition issues.[8]

4. *Productivity.* Productivity growth, as measured by output per man-hour in the private economy, which had experienced a longer-term growth trend of about 3—3½ percent a year, slackened appreciably following the mid-1960's and dropped to less than 1 percent a year in 1969 and 1970. Declines in productivity growth have occurred in the past during or immediately after periods of high economic activity. The productivity growth rate rebounded sharply, moreover, in 1971—72, thus suggesting that cyclical factors, rather than any deep-seated worker unrest, were mainly responsible for the previous decline.[9]

5. *Labor force participation.* Abstention from work or work-seeking activity is the ultimate form of rejection of work as an institution. Yet there has been no evidence of a downtrend in the overall proportion of the population, 16 years and over, reported as in the labor force. In fact, this percentage has increased over the past two decades, from 59.9 percent in 1950 to 61.3 percent in 1970.[10]

There have been some important divergent trends among different components of the working-age population. Thus, the labor force partcipation rate of men has declined from 86.8 percent in 1950 to 80.6 percent in 1970, mainly due to steady reductions in worker rates among school and college-age youth and among men 55 years and over. It is difficult, however, to interpret the decline in labor force rates for men as reflecting a rejection of work as an institution, in the face of the fact that their sisters and wives have flocked into the labor force in unprecedented numbers over this same time span, increasing their labor force participation rate from 33.9 percent in 1950 to 43.4 percent in 1970 with most of the increase occurring among married women. The desire to supplement family income was apparently a decisive factor inducing their entry into the labor force, even though these women have been disproportionately concentrated in low paying and often routine types of work.

From this necessarily brief review, it will be evident that there is little objective evidence to support an inference of a rising wave of discontent among workers, associated directly with the nature of their jobs. Fluctuations in some of the indicators, which appeared at first blush to support this hypothesis (such as labor turnover rates, strike activity and productivity growth rates) can, on closer inspection, be attributed to quite different causes, notably to the tight labor market and inflationary trends prevailing in the late 1960's and to associated labor market forces. The overall labor force participation trends—such as the sharp and sustained inflow of married women into gainful employment—simply cannot be reconciled with any hypothesis of an extensive rejection of "low quality" work. The available absenteeism data, which suggest some increase since the mid-1960's, are still too incomplete to support any broad generalizations—although they do tend to reinforce more specific reports concerning the special frustrations of the automobile industry assembly-line workers. Even the mass of survey data designed to elicit direct measures of job dissatisfaction have failed to show any consistent trend.

WHY ARE SUPPOSED TRENDS NOT VISIBLE?

If this trend has not in fact developed in visible and measurable dimensions, we may well ask "Why not?" Is it because the statistical barometers for measuring emerging social trends are too incomplete, too gross, and too insensitive for this purpose? Or is it because the theoretical constructs which lead to certain expectations as to worker behaviors and attitudes simply do not conform to reality?

Most of the available statistical indicators are clearly much too aggregative to serve as reliable indexes of worker discontent. Statistical series such as productivity and labor turnover were designed for quite different purposes. Much more disaggregation of the data, and supplementary research, is needed before we can reliably isolate the influence of specific causal factors. And we are still in the early stages of development of meaningful indexes of job satisfaction and of absenteeism. It is quite possible, therefore, that the available measures—separately and in combination—are too crude and insensitive to detect any new emerging social force.

In part, however, the explanation lies in the model of worker aspirations and behavior postulated by the social psychologists. Their point of departure is a hierarchical ordering of human needs, which, as outlined by Abraham Maslow, begins with satisfaction of basic material wants, such as food and shelter, and ascends to higher order needs, such as "self esteem" and "self actualization." An alternative formulation by Herzberg is couched in terms of "extrinsic" and "intrinsic" job factors. Extrinsic factors, such as poor pay, inadequate benefits, or poor physical working conditions may lead to job dissatisfaction, while true satisfaction depends upon the intrinsic nature of the job, its work content, and its inherent challenge and interest. But both models lead to the inference that, as the general wage level increases and physical working conditions improve, the emphasis shifts from strictly economic issues to demands for improvement in the nature of work itself.

It is difficult to challenge this scale of aspirations in the abstract. In fact, numerous surveys indicate that when workers are asked what aspects of work are most important to them, "interesting work" often heads the list, particularly among the more educated or more affluent segments of the population. Given this apparent scale of values and the rising "affluence" of American workers, why—then—have most workers not overtly attempted to change the contents of their work? For example, has the continued concentration of organized labor on "bread and butter" issues, rather than "quality of work," simply reflected a lack of sensitivity on the part of union leaders to the real needs of their members—or has it in fact reflected the priorities of their rank-and-file members?

As a broad generalization, we believe that the latter assumption corresponds much closer to reality. One fallacy in the Maslow-Herzberg model of worker aspirations, as a guide to behavior, lies in its inherently static premises. Even though individual earnings and family incomes have increased steadily over the decades, the great majority of American workers certainly do not consider themselves as "affluent," when they relate their spendable income to their spending needs, for what they now consider an acceptable standard of living. As Christopher Jencks has recently pointed out, this escalation of living standards "is not just a matter of 'rising expectations' or of people's needing to 'keep up with the Joneses' " but is due in part to the fact that with changes in our mode of life, such goods as an automobile, a telephone, or packaged foods have become an integral part of our cost of living—of participating in our social system.[11] Thus, when hard choices have to be made between a monotonous job in a regimented environment, which pays relatively well and which offers job security, and a poorer paying, less secure but more "satisfying" job, most workers—particularly those with family commitments—are still not in a position to make the trade-off in favor of meeting their "intrinsic" needs.

Moreover, most workers and most union leaders tend to be highly skeptical of the real potential of "job enrichment" as a practicable means of improving their work environment. This skepticism results from earlier experiences when worker participation, profit sharing, and similar approaches were instituted by some firms as an alternative to pay increases or as a means of staving off unionization. This point of view has recently been colorfully expressed by William W. Winpisinger, general vice-president of the International Association of Machinists:

> If you want to enrich the job, enrich the pay check. The better the wage, the greater the job satisfaction. There is no better cure for the blue-collar blues.[12]

THE QUEST FOR AUTONOMY

One of the more questionable premises made by the authors concerning the nature and sources of worker discontent is the assumption that large numbers of workers have an urge for "autonomy" at the work place and are chafing at the disciplines and controls imposed by large bureaucratic organizations—whether big business or big government. Is this in fact a major preoccupation of most workers in our society today—or is it an image created by popular emphasis on extremes: the extreme of the real frustrations of the automobile assembly-line worker, on the one hand, and of the revolt of some (probably small) fraction of upper-middle-class youth, on the other?

Certainly, one of the most "bureaucratic" organizations in modern society today is the military; no other large organization imposes equal constraints upon both the working lives and the personal lives of its labor force. Yet in 1972, while the Vietnam war was still underway, over 330,000 young men, about one-fourth of the militarily eligible manpower pool, elected to voluntarily enlist in military service. This total excludes about 85,000 additional draft-motivated enlistees, as well as many thousands of others who offered to enlist, but failed to meet physical or mental test standards. Between 1970 and 1972, voluntary (not draft-motivated) enlistments into the Army had risen by fully 80 percent, largely in response to major increases in compensation and other special inducements offered as part of the effort to move to an all-volunteer military force.[13] Numerous surveys have shown that few young men have any great illusions about the "intrinsic" aspects of most enlisted jobs: by large majorities, young high school graduates (who account for a large majority of enlistees) have recognized that civilian jobs are far preferable to military service in terms of such criteria as "freedom," "interesting work," and "highly respected job."[14] Yet, when faced with the limited range of choices open to them, large numbers of young men have been willing to accept the constraints and risks of military service in exchange for some of its visible benefits—its training and educational opportunities, its opportunity for travel and new experiences, and its material rewards.

In similar vein, prestige rankings of various civilian occupations, based on a number of surveys, have failed to reveal any consistent preference for autonomous, self-directed employment, in comparison with more regimented, but better paying and more secure occupations. Office machine operators and bookkeepers rate higher than small independent farmers in these rankings. Assembly-line workers outrank taxi drivers, in popular esteem.[15] And as we have previously noted, many millions of married women have moved from household work, which—though unpaid—has the virtue of being self-directed, into the more regimented world of gainful employment.

The foregoing comments are clearly not designed to imply that "all is well" with the quality of work in America or that, as a nation, we can afford to be complacent about some of the danger signals which have been brought to our attention. The fact that over 10 percent of employed workers express general dissatisfaction with their jobs, that many more are dissatisfied with specific aspects of their work situation, and that these proportions are much higher for youth, for women, and for minorities, is a challenge to management, unions, and the government to pursue corrective actions.

However, if our interpretation of the recent labor market behavior and attitudes of American workers is valid, it does imply a different set of criteria for measuring quality of jobs and a different set of priorities for improvement of the quality of work. Our premise is that workers have no difficulty in distinguishing between the "good" and the "bad" jobs in our economy. The least desirable jobs, typically, are inferior *both* in terms of pay and related benefits and in terms of the intrinsic nature of the work itself. Included in this category are most domestic service and hired farm labor jobs and a large proportion of the 20 million jobs occupied by workers in the private nonfarm economy which, according to a recent BLS survey, paid less than $2.50 per hour in April 1970.[16] Numerous unskilled or semiskilled jobs paying somewhat higher wages can also be included in this category because of the oppressive nature of the work and lack of advancement opportunities.

It has been possible for employers to recruit an adequate supply of workers for most of these low-level jobs because of the continued existence of a large pool of workers who have had no effective labor market choices. Included in this pool are a disproportionate number of minority members, teenaged youth, women, and recent immigrants—who share common handicaps of limited skill, limited work experience, restricted mobility, and various forms of institutionalized discrimination. These categories of workers constitute a relatively large share of the 5 million "visibly" unemployed workers and probably represent an even larger proportion of the "invisible" unemployed not included in our statistics of active job-seekers. So long as this reservoir of low-wage labor is available, employers have little incentive to increase the pay or to enhance the quality of these jobs.

The most potent strategy for improving the quality of these jobs and/or reducing their relative numbers is by reducing the size of this reserve pool of workers. It is no coincidence that the most significant progress in improving the relative status of low-wage workers in this country has been made during periods of acute wartime labor shortage, such as during World War II. It is no coincidence, either, that employer initiatives for experimentation with work redesign abroad have been most evident in countries such as Sweden and West Germany, which have managed their economies with much lower ratios of peacetime unemployment than in the United States—and have been initaited in precisely those industries, such as the automobile industry, which have most acutely felt a labor shortage situation.

The most important single set of measures which can contribute to improvements of *quality* of work in America are, thus, those designed to increase the *quantity* of work in America. This requires a much more positive national commitment to a maximum employment policy—even, if need be, at the cost of a somewhat higher level of acceptable inflation. In turn, a climate of sustained high employment can make possible more effective implementation of specific manpower and labor market policies designed to upgrade the status of workers in low level jobs and to promote equality of employment opportunity. It may, in fact, bring us closer to the era of the "post-subsistence" economy when those jobs which do not meet minimum economic *and* psychological standards will be effectively ruled out from the labor market competition.

There should be no illusion that these goals are easily attainable—either through the recommendations scattered through *Work in America* or through those proposed in the numerous other recent studies concerned with national man-power and economic policies. We can only share Secretary Richardson's expressed sentiments that this report represents "a beginning and not a conclusion."

FOOTNOTES

1. Report initially summarized in *The New York Times,* June 30, 1970, p. 1. See also Jerome M. Rosow, "The Problems of Lower-Middle-Income Workers," in Sar A. Levitan, ed., *Blue Collar Workers: A Symposium of Middle America,* (New York, McGraw-Hill, 1971), pp. 76–95.
2. For a report of one such survey, see Leonard Goodwin, "Welfare mothers and the work ethic," *Monthly Labor Review,* August 1972, pp. 35–7.
3. Some of these efforts are described by Joseph Mire in "European workers' participation in management," *Monthly Labor Review,* February 1973, pp. 9–15.
4. *Work in America,* pp. x, xi.
5. Robert L. Kahn, "The Meaning of Work: Interpretation and Proposals for Measurement," in Angus Campbell and Phillip E. Converse, *The Human Meaning of Social Change* (New York, Russell Sage Foundation, 1972), pp. 173–4.
6. Paul A. Armknecht and John L. Early, "Quits in Manufacturing: A Study of Their Causes," *Monthly Labor Review,* November 1972, pp. 31–7.
7. Based on a forthcoming BLS study on absences from work.
8. *Work Stoppages in 1971,* Summary Report, U.S. Department of Labor, June 1972, table r. 4. In 1972, strike idleness declined to 1.4 working days per thousand from 2.6 in 1971. *Work Stoppages 1972,* U.S. Department of Labor, Press Release 73–865, January 9, 1973.
9. *Economic Report of the President,* January 1973, pp. 34, 231.
10. *Manpower Report of the President, 1972,* pp. 157, 192.
11. Christopher Jencks, *Inequality: A Reassessment of the Effect of Family and Schooling in America* (New York, Basic Books, Inc., 1972), p. 5.
12. Paper presented before the annual meeting of the Industrial Relations Research Association, December 1972, at Toronto, Canada.
13. Based on unpublished data, Office of Assistant Secretary of Defense, (M&RA).
14. Harold Wool, *The Military Specialist: Skilled Manpower for the Armed Forces* (Baltimore, Md., The Johns Hopkins University Press, 1969), p. 114.
15. Paul M. Siegal, *Prestige in the American Occupational Structure,* unpublished doctoral dissertation, University of Chicago, 1971, table 5.
16. Steven Sternlieb and Alvin Bauman, "Employment characteristics of low-wage workers," *Monthly Labor Review,* July 1972, p. 11.

The New Look in Motivation Theory for Organizational Research

J.G. Hunt and J.W. Hill

During the last few years the treatment of motivation with respect to industrial and other formal organizations has more often than not been in terms of models by Maslow or Herzberg.[1] Where theories are apparently so thoroughly accepted, one naturally assumes a fairly substantial amount of data leading to empirical verification. However, as we shall show, there is relatively little empirical evidence concerning Maslow's theory; and while there are many studies bearing on Herzberg's theory, it remains controversial. After comparing these two approaches and reviewing their present status, we will describe a newer motivation theory developed by Vroom, which is similar to those developed by Atkinson *et al.* and Edwards in experimental psychology, and Peak, Rosenberg and Fishbein in social psychology.[2] It is our contention, on both theoretical and empirical grounds, that Vroom's theory, more than Maslow's or Herzberg's, is in line with the thinking of contemporary psychologists and industrial sociologists and is the best yet developed for organizational use.

THE MASLOW MODEL

Maslow's theory hypothesizes five broad classes of needs arranged in hierarchical levels of prepotency so that when one need level is satisfied, the next level is activated. The levels are: (1) physiological needs; (2) security or safety needs; (3) social, belonging, or membership needs; (4) esteem needs further subdivided into esteem of others and self-esteem including autonomy; and (5) self-actualization or self-fulfillment needs.

The original papers present very little empirical evidence in support of the theory and no research at all that tests the model in its entirety. Indeed, Maslow argues that the theory is primarily a framework for future research. He also discusses at length some of the limitations of the model and readily admits that these needs may be unconscious rather than conscious. While Maslow discusses his model and its limitations in detail, a widely publicized paper by McGregor gives the impression that the model can be accepted without question and also that it is fairly easy to apply.[3] In truth, the model is difficult to test, which is probably why there are so few empirical studies to either prove or refute the theory.

Porter provides the most empirical data concerning the model.[4] At the conscious level he measures all except the physiological needs. His samples are based only on managers, but they cover different managerial levels in a wide range of business organizations in the United States and thirteen other countries. Porter's studies have a number of interesting findings, but here we are primarily concerned with two: (1) in the United States and Britain (but not in the other twelve countries) there tends to be a hierarchical satisfaction of needs as Maslow hypothesizes; and (2) regardless of country or managerial level there is a tendency for those needs which managers feel are most important to be least satisfied.

A study by Beer of female clerks provides additional data concerning the model.[5] He examines the relationship between participative and considerate or human relations-oriented supervisory leadership styles and satisfaction of needs. He also goes one step further and argues that need satisfaction, as such, does not necessarily lead to motivation. Rather, motivation results only from need satisfaction which occurs in the process of task-oriented work. He reasons that a participative leadership style should meet this condition since it presumably allows for the satisfaction of the higher order needs (self-actualization, autonomy, and esteem). Beer found that the workers forced to arrange needs in a hierarchy (as required by his ranking method) tend to arrange them as predicted by Maslow. He also found that self-actualization, autonomy and social needs were most important, while esteem and security needs were least important, although his method (unlike Porter's) did not allow a consideration of the relationship between importance and need satisfaction. Interestingly enough, there was no significant relationship between need satisfaction and Beer's measure of motivation nor between any of the leadership style dimensions and motivation. There were, however, significant relationships between leadership style dimensions and need satisfaction. Beer concludes that the model has questionable usefulness for a theory of industrial motivation although it may provide a fairly reliable measurement of the *a priori* needs of industrial workers.

We have found only three studies that systematically consider the Maslow theory in terms of performance.[6]

The first of these, by Clark, attempts to fit a number of empirical studies conducted for different purposes into a framework which provides for progressive activation and satisfaction of needs at each of the hierarchical levels. The findings are used to make predictions concerning productivity, absenteeism, and turnover as each need level is activated and then satisfied. While the article does not explicitly test the Maslow model, it is highly suggestive in terms of hypotheses for future research that might relate the theory to work group performance.

A second study, by Lawler and Porter, correlates satisfaction of managers' needs (except physiological) with rankings of their performance by superiors and peers. All correlations are significant but low, ranging from .16 to .30. Lawler and Porter conclude that satisfaction of higher order needs is more closely related to performance than satisfaction of lower order needs. However, the differences are not very great and they are not tested for significance. For example, correlations of superior ratings for the lower order security and social needs are .21 and .23 while for the higher order esteem, autonomy, and self-actualization needs they are .24, .18, and .30. Peer correlations are similar. Thus, unlike Lawler and Porter, we conclude that in this study the correlations for lower order needs are about the same as for higher order needs.

A more recent Porter and Lawler investigation seems to provide additional support for their earlier findings by showing that higher order needs accounted for more relationships significant at the .01 level than lower order needs. However, they do not report correlations between these needs and performance and so we cannot evaluate their conclusion as we did for their earlier study.

THE HERZBERG MODEL

A second frequently mentioned motivational model is that proposed by Herzberg and his associates in 1959.[7] They used a semi-structured interview technique to get respondents to recall events experienced at work which resulted in a marked improvement or a marked reduction in their job satisfaction. Interviewees were also asked, among other things, how their feelings of satisfaction or dissatisfaction affected their work performance, personal relationships, and well-being. Content analysis of the interviews suggested that certain job characteristics led to job satisfaction, while *different* job characteristics led to job dissatisfaction. For instance, job achievement was related to satisfaction while working conditions were related to dissatisfaction. Poor conditions led to dissatisfaction, but good conditions did not necessarily lead to satisfaction. Thus, satisfaction and dissatisfaction are not simple opposites. Hence a two-factor theory of satisfaction is needed.

The job content characteristics which produced satisfaction were called "motivators" by Herzberg and his associates because they satisfied the individual's need for self-actualization at work. The job environment characteristics which led to dissatisfaction were called "hygienes" because they were work-supporting or contextual rather than task-determined and hence were analogous to the "preventative" or "environmental" factors recognized in medicine. According to this dichotomy, motivators include achievement, recognition, advancement, possibility of growth, responsibility, and work itself. Hygienes, on the other hand, include salary; interpersonal relations with superiors, subordinates, and peers; technical supervision; company policy and administration; personal life; working conditions; status; and job security.

There is considerable empirical evidence for this theory. Herzberg himself, in a summary of research through early 1966, includes ten studies of seventeen populations which used essentially the same method as his original study.[8] In addition, he reviews twenty more studies which used a variety of methodologies to test the two-factor theory. Of the studies included in his review, those using his critical incident method generally confirm the theory. Those using other methods give less clear results, which Herzberg acknowledges but attempts to dismiss for methodological reasons. At least nine other studies, most of which have appeared since Herzberg's 1966 review, raise even more doubts about the theory.[9]

While it is beyond the scope of the present article to consider these studies in detail, they raise serious questions as to whether the factors leading to satisfaction and dissatisfaction are really different from each other. A number of the studies show that certain job dimensions appear to be more important for *both* satisfaction and dissatisfaction are really different from each other. A number of the studies show that certain job dimensions appear to be more important for *both* satisfaction and dissatisfaction. Dunnette, Campbell, and Hakel, for example, conclude satisfaction *and* dissatisfaction while such dimensions as security, salary, and working conditions are less important.[10] They also raise by implication an issue concerning Herzberg's methodology which deserves further comment. That is, if data are analyzed in terms of percentage differences between groups, one result is obtained; if they are analyzed in terms of ranks within groups, another result occurs. The first type of analysis is appropriate for identifying factors which account for differences between events (as Herzberg did in his original hypothesis). The second type of analysis is appropriate if we want to know the most important factors within the event categories (which is what Herzberg claims he was doing). Analyzing the findings of Dunnette and his colleagues by the first method, we confirm Herzberg's theory; but if we rank the findings within categories, as Dunnette *et al.* also did, we find no confirmation. If we want to know whether "achievement" is important in job satisfaction we must look at its relative rank among other factors mentioned in the events leading to satisfaction, not whether it is mentioned a greater percentage of the time in satisfying events than in dissatisfying events. This distinction in analytical methods was discussed several years ago by Viteles and even earlier by Kornhauser.[11]

We conclude that any meaningful discussion of Herzberg's theory must recognize recent negative evidence even though the model seems to make a great deal of intuitive sense. Much the same can be said of Maslow's theory.

FURTHER CONSIDERATIONS IN USING THE
MASLOW AND HERZBERG THEORIES

Putting aside for the moment the empirical considerations presented by the two models, it is instructive to compare them at the conceptual level suggested in Fig.

ure 1. While the figure shows obvious similarities between the Maslow and Herzberg models, there are important differences as well. Where Maslow assumes that any need can be a motivator if it is relatively unsatisfied, Herzberg argues that only the higher order needs serve as motivators and that a worker can have unsatisfied needs in both the hygiene and motivator areas simultaneously. One might argue that the reason higher order needs are motivators is that lower order needs have essentially been satisfied. However, Herzberg presents some evidence that even in relatively low level blue-collar and service jobs, where presumably lower order needs are less well-satisfied, the higher order needs are still the only ones seen by the workers as motivators.[12]

Figure 1 MASLOW'S NEED-PRIORITY MODEL COMPARED WITH HERZBERG'S MOTIVATION-HYGIENE MODEL

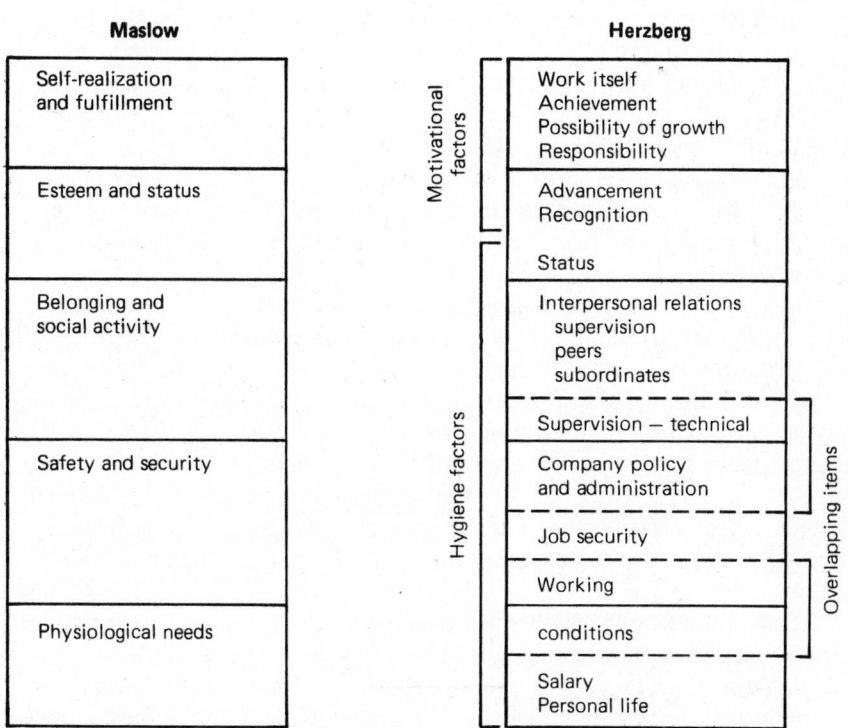

Source: Adapted from HUMAN RELATIONS AT WORK by Keith Davis. Copyright © 1967 by McGraw-Hill Book Company. Used with permission of McGraw-Hill Book Company.

Another important consideration is the relationship of these models to the accomplishment of organizational objectives. Even if there were unequivocal empirical support for the theories, there is need to translate the findings into usable incentives for promoting such objectives as superior performance, lower turnover, lower absenteeism, etc. If not, they are of little use to industrial organizations. As indicated earlier, there is relatively little evidence empirically relating Maslow's model to performance, or even to psychological well-being. Furthermore, the one Lawler and Porter study seems to show that satisfaction of higher and lower order needs are about equally related to performance, although their later investigation suggests that the former are more strongly related to performance than the latter. But we cannot tell for sure because correlations and differences between correlations are not reported.

Similarly, although Herzberg asked his respondents for effects of job events on their performance, he reports only two studies which attempt to measure performance independent of the respondent's estimate. These seem to show the performance is favorably influenced as more "motivators" are provided in the job.[13] However, insufficient data are presented to permit evaluation of the adequacy of the experimental design and performance measures. A study by Friedlander and Walton that considered employee turnover used a modification of Herzberg's technique and found that employees' reasons for staying on the job were different than their reasons for leaving.[14] The reasons for staying would be called "motivators" while those for leaving were "hygiene" factors.

We conclude that Herzberg's two-factor theory *may* be related to turnover and performance; but present studies are subject to serious criticisms. And we could find only two empirical investigations which related Maslow's model to any of these outputs.

In addition, it should be noted that neither model adequately handles the theoretical problem of some kind of linkage by which individual need satisfaction is related to the achievement of organizational objectives. Given the present formulation, it is entirely possible that there can be need satisfaction which is *not necessarily* directed toward the accomplishment of organizational goals. For example, an important organizational objective might be increased production, but workers might conceivably receive more need satisfaction from turning out a higher quality product at a sacrifice in quantity. They might also be meeting their social needs through identification with a work group with strong sanctions against "rate busting."

Finally, neither of these theories as they stand can really handle the problem of individual differences in motivation. Maslow, for example, explains that his model may not hold for persons with particular experiences. His theory is therefore nonpredictive because data that do not support it can be interpreted in terms of individual differences in previous need gratification leading to greater or lesser prepotency of a given need-category.[15] Herzberg, in similar fashion, describes seven types of people differentiated by the extent to which they are motivator or hygiene seekers, or some combination of the two, although he never relates these differences empirically to actual job performance. We turn then to a model which explicitly recognizes these issues and appears to offer great potential for understanding motivation in organizations.

THE VROOM MODEL

Brayfield and Crockett as long ago as 1955 suggested an explicit theoretical linkage between satisfaction, motivation and the organizational goal of productivity. They said:

> It makes sense to us to assume that individuals are motivated to achieve certain environmental goals and that the achievement of these goals results in satisfaction. Productivity is seldom a goal in itself but is more commonly a means to goal attainment. Therefore, . . . we might expect high satisfaction and high productivity to occur together when productivity is perceived as a path to certain important goals and when these goals are achieved.[16]

Georgopoulas, Mahoney and Jones provide some early empirical support for this notion in their test of the "path-goal hypothesis."[17] Essentially, they argue that an individual's motivation to produce at a given level depends upon his particular needs as reflected in the goals toward which he is moving *and* his perception of the relative usefulness of productivity behavior as a path to attainment of these goals. They qualify this, however, by saying that the need must be sufficiently high, no other economical paths must be available to the individual, and there must be a lack of restraining practices.

More recently, Vroom has developed a motivational model which extends the above concepts and is also related to earlier work of experimental and social psychologists.[18] He defines motivation as a "process governing choices, made by persons or lower organisms, among alternative forms of voluntary activity."[19] The concept is incorporated in Figure 2, which depicts Vroom's model graphically. Here, the individual is shown as a role occupant faced with a set of alternative "first-level outcomes." His preference choice among these first-level outcomes is determined by their expected relationship to possible "second-level outcomes."

Two concepts are introduced to explain the precise method of determining preferences for these first-level outcomes. These concepts are *valence* and *instrumentality*. Valence refers to the strength of an individual's desire for a particular outcome. Instrumentality indicates an individual's perception of the relationship between a first-level outcome and a second-level outcome or, in other words, the extent to which a first-level outcome is seen as leading to the accomplishment of a second-level outcome.

Figure 2   VROOM'S MOTIVATIONAL MODEL

Person Possessing Preference
among Various Outcomes

Goals and Associated Outcomes

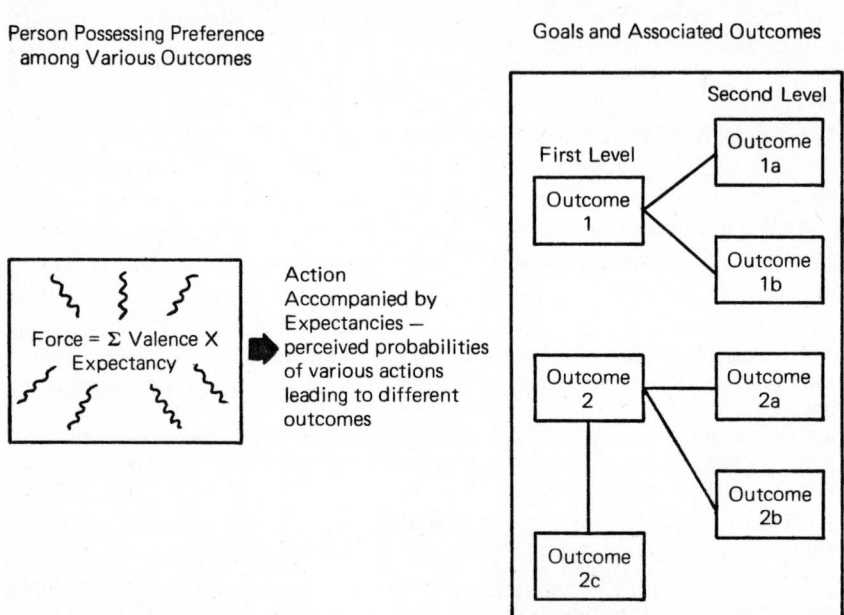

Source: Adapted from M. D. Dunnette, "The Motives of Industrial Managers," from ORGAN-
IZATIONAL BEHAVIOR AND HUMAN PERFORMANCE, Vol. 2, 1967, p. 178. (Copyright
© 1967 by Academic Press, Inc.)

Valence is measured by instructing workers to rank important individual goals in order of their desirability, or they may rate goals on Likert-type scales. Instrumentality can be measured by rating scales which involve perceived differences in the direction and strength of relationships between various first- and second-level outcomes. Important goals of industrial workers often cited in the empirical behavioral science literature are promotion, pay, pleasant working conditions and job security. The goals can be ranked by individual workers in terms of their desirability. The resulting scores are measures of valence.

In addition, each individual can be instructed to indicate on an appropriate scale the likelihood that a certain job behavior, e.g., high productivity, will lead to each of the four goals described. This score is the instrumental relationship between productivity and a specified goal. Obviously there are alternative methods of measurement available for the concepts; we will leave these for a more detailed discussion later.

Vroom expresses the valence of a first-level outcome to a person "as a monotonically increasing function of an algebraic sum of the products of the valences of all [second-level] outcomes and his conceptions of its instrumentality for the attainment of the [second-level] outcomes."[20]

For example, assume that an individual desires promotion and feels that superior performance is a very strong factor in achieving that goal. His first-level outcomes are then superior, average, or poor performance. His second-level outcome is promotion. The first-level outcome of high performance thus acquires a positive valence by virtue of its expected relationship to the preferred second-level outcome of promotion. Assuming no negative second-level outcomes associated with high performance and no other first-level outcomes that contribute to promotion, we expect motivation toward superior performance because promotion is important and superior performance is seen as instrumental in its accomplishment. Or, to put it in Vroom's terms, performance varies directly with the product of the valence of the reward (promotion) and the perceived instrumentality of performance for the attainment of the reward.

An additional concept in Vroom's theory is *expectancy*. This is a belief concerning the likelihood that a particular action or effort will be followed by a particular first-level outcome and can be expressed as a subjective probability ranging from 0 to 1. Expectancy differs from instrumentality in that it relates *efforts* to first-level outcomes where instrumentality relates first- and second-level outcomes to each other. Vroom ties this concept to his previous one by stating, "the force on a person to perform an [action] is a monotonically increasing function of the algebraic sum of the products of the valences of all [first-level] outcomes and the strength of his expectancies that the [action] will be followed by the attainment of these outcomes."[21] "Force" here is similar to our concept of motivation.

This motivational model, unlike those discussed earlier, emphasizes individual differences in motivation and makes possible the examination of very explicit relationships between motivation and the accomplishment of organizational goals, whatever these goals may be. Thus instead of assuming that satisfaction of a specific need is likely to influence organizational objectives in a certain way, we can find out how important to the employees are the various second-level outcomes (worker goals), the instrumentality of various first-level outcomes (organizational objectives) for their attainment, and the expectancies that are held with respect to the employees' ability to influence the first-level outcomes.

Empirical Tests of Vroom's Model

Vroom has already shown how his model can integrate many of the empirical findings in the literature on motivation in organizations.[22] However, because it is a relatively recent development, empirical tests of the model itself are just beginning to appear. Here we shall consider four such investigations.

In the first study, Vroom is concerned with predicting the organizational choices of graduating college students on the basis of their instrumentality-goal index scores.[23] These scores reflect the extent to which membership in an organization was perceived by the student as being related to the acquisition of desired goals. According to the theory, the chosen organization should be the one with the highest instrumentality-goal index. Ratings were used to obtain preferences for fifteen different goals and the extent to which these goals could be attained through membership in three different organizations. These two ratings were thus measures of the valences of second-level outcomes and the instrumentality of organized membership for attainment of these outcomes, respectively. The instrumentality-goal index was the correlation between these two measures. But Vroom's theory also involves consideration of expectancy, i.e., how probable is it that the student can become a member of a particular organization. The choice is not his alone but depends upon whether he is acceptable to the organization. A rough measure of expectancy in this study was whether or not the student had received an offer by the organization. If he had received an offer, expectancy would be high; if not, it would be low. The results show that, considering only organizations from which offers of employment were actually received, 76 percent of the students chose the organization with the highest instrumentality-goal index score. The evidence thus strongly supports Vroom's theory.

The next study, by Galbraith and Cummings, utilizes the model to predict the productivity of operative workers.[24] Graphic rating scales were used to measure the instrumentality of performance for five goals—money, fringe benefits, promotion, supervisor's support, and group acceptance. Similar ratings were used for measuring the desirability of each of the goals for the worker. The authors anticipated that a worker's expectation that he could produce at a high level would have a probability of one because the jobs were independent and productivity was a function of the worker's own effort independent of other human or machine pacing. Figure 3 outlines the research design.

Multiple regression analysis showed that productivity was significantly related positively to the instrumentality-goal interactions for supervisor support and money, and there was an almost significant ($p < .10$) relationship with group acceptance. The other factors did not approach significance and the authors explain this lack of significance in terms of the situational context. That is, fringe benefits were dependent not so much on productivity as on a union/management contract, and promotion was based primarily on seniority. Thus the instrumentality of productivity for the attainment of these goals was low and the model would predict no relationship.

The Galbraith and Cummings study thus supports Vroom's contention that motivation is related to productivity in those situations where the acquisition of desired goals is dependent upon the individual's production and not when desired outcomes are contingent on other factors.

Figure 3 INDIVIDUAL GOALS AND PRODUCTIVITY AS MEASURED BY VROOM'S MODEL IN ONE INDUSTRIAL PLANT

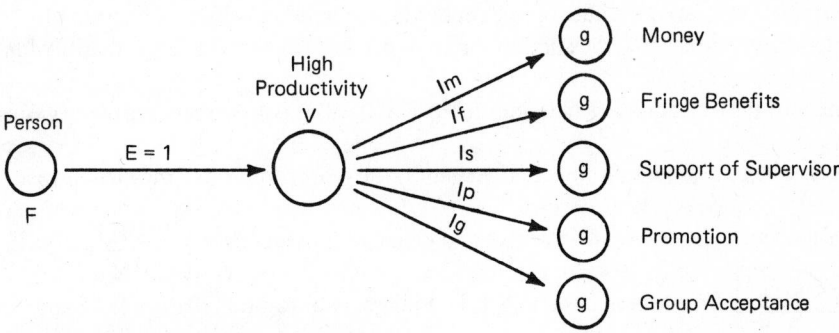

g = Desirability of a particular outcome (rating)
I = Instrumentality of production for particular outcome (rating of relationship)
E = Expectancy (= 1 here because worker sets own pace and is assumed to be capable of high productivity)
V = (Valence) the sum of the cross products of instrumentality and g
F = (Force) expectancy times the valence of productivity
Productivity = Objective measures of amount of production in relation to the production standard
Based on data from J. Galbraith and L. L. Cummings. See Reference 23.

A third study is that of Hill relating a model similar to Vroom's to behavior in a utility company.[25] Hill's model is based upon Edwards' subjective expected utility maximization theory of decision making.[26] Here one given a choice between alternatives A and/or B will select that alternative which maximizes his subjective expected utility or expected value. If the outcomes associated with action A are more desirable than those associated with B, and their probability of occurrence is greater than or equal to those associated with B, then an individual will choose behavior A over behavior B. The basic concepts are subjective expectation and subjective utility or valence. Expectation and utility are multiplicatively related and can be measured by the same techniques used to test Vroom's theory. Where a relationship is found between Subjective Expected Utility (S.E.U.) and overt behavior, it can be interpreted as support for Vroom.

The behavior considered in Hill's study is that of job bidding. This behavior is encountered in organizations that post descriptions of job openings on employee bulletin boards and encourage qualified employees to "bid" (apply) for them. Here records were kept of the number of bids made over a three-year period by groups of semi-skilled electrical repairmen matched in learning ability, seniority in grade, and age. The men were asked about the consequences of bidding and not bidding on the next higher grade job, and rated the consequence on a seven-point scale of desirability and a similar scale of probability of occurrence. Bidders were those who had bid three or more times during that time.

Fourteen different S.E.U. indices were computed from interview data to determine the relative validity of each in predicting bidding behavior. Typical of these indices were: (1) the sums of the cross products of expectation and utility for the positive consequences of bidding($\overset{+}{\Sigma}$ S.E.U.); (2) the same score for the negative consequences of bidding($\overset{-}{\Sigma}$ S.E.U.); and (3) the cross products of the *mean* expectation and utility scores for positive and negative consequences $\left[\dfrac{\overset{+}{\Sigma} \text{S.E.U.}}{N}, \dfrac{\overset{-}{\Sigma} \text{S.E.U.}}{N} \right]$. In addition to these S.E.U. indices, two traditional attitudinal and motivational measures were used. Semantic Differential scales measured each subject's respective evaluation of bidding and the next higher grade job and each subject's Need for Achievement was obtained.[27]

It was hypothesized that: (1) there would be a positive correlation between the S.E.U. indices and bidding; and (2) the S.E.U. indices would be more highly related to bidding behavior than the traditional measures.

We do not discuss relationships for all of the indices here but do consider results for one of the more comprehensive indices and those from multiple regression analysis. This index is the algebraic sum of the cross products of the positive and negative consequences of bidding minus the same score for not bidding for each individual. The correlation of this index with bidding was .26, p < .05 for a one-tailed test. The correlations between the two Semantic Differential scales and bidding were −.09 and −.25, respectively. Neither of these is significant for a one-tailed test predicting a positive correlation. The correlation between Need for Achievement and bidding was a nonsignificant .17. A multiple regression analysis determined the relative contribution of the S.E.U. indices to the prediction of bidding. A variable was selected for analysis on the basis of its relationship to the criterion and its intercorrelation with the other predictors. The multiple correlation for bidding and seven selected variables was .61, p < .05. This correlation included four S.E.U. indices, all of which had higher beta weights than the Semantic Differentials or Need for Achievement. Thus these variables accounted for more variance in the criterion than did the traditional attitudinal and motivational measures. Both hypotheses were therefore confirmed. This study adds support to the usefulness of this type of model in the study of motivation.

Finally, Lawler and Porter report a study that attempts to relate managerial attitudes to performance rankings by superiors and peers.[28] In it, 154 managers from five different organizations completed questionnaires concerning seven kinds of rewards, and their expectations that different kinds of behavior would lead to these rewards. The expectations and the ratings of the importance of instrumentality and valence, respectively, were combined multiplicatively to yield multiple correlations which were significantly related to supervisor and peer rankings of the manager's effort to perform his job well. The correlations were higher with effort to perform the job than with the rankings of job performance. Lawler and Porter predicted this result because they reasoned that job performance is influenced by variables other than motivation—e.g., by ability and role perceptions. Of course, Vroom's model is not a behavioral theory but one of motivation only. Motivation is not going to improve performance if ability is low or role perceptions are inaccurate. Vroom's model explains how goals influence effort and that is exactly the relationship found by Lawler and Porter.

CONCLUSION

Taken together, the four studies discussed in the previous section seem to show that Vroom's model holds great promise for predicting behavior in organizations. There still remain some unanswered questions. We do not know all of the goals that have positive valence in a work situation. We do not know how much of a difference in force is necessary before one kind of outcome is chosen over another. Nor do we know what combination of measures yields the best prediction in a given situation. The answers to these and other questions await further research.

One more point should perhaps be made concerning the four studies and their measurement of Vroom's concepts. While it is true that all of them used subjective measures, the model can in fact be tested with more objective devices. Instrumentality can be inferred from organization practices, expectations can be manipulated by instructions, and goals can be inferred from observed approach and avoidance behaviors. Of course, all of these techniques require assumptions concerning their relationship to the worker's subjective perceptions of the situation; but the model is certainly not bound to the methods of measurement used so far. In fact, Vroom specifies in considerable detail the different kinds of techniques that might be used to test his model.[29]

More work must be done before we can make any statements concerning the overall validity of Vroom's model. But the rigor of his formulation, the relative ease of making the concepts operational, and the model's emphasis on individual differences show considerable promise. We are also encouraged by the results of relatively sophisticated studies testing the theory. We believe it is time for those interested in organizational behavior to take a more thoroughly scientific look at this very complex subject of industrial motivation, and Vroom's model seems a big step in that direction.

NOTES

1. A. H. Maslow, *Motivation and Personality*, Harper and Row, New York; 1954; "A Theory of Human Motivation," *Psychological Review*, Vol. 50, 1943, pp. 370–396; and *Eupsychian Management*, Homewood, Illinois, Irwin-Dorsey, 1965; F. Herzberg, B. Mausner, and B. B. Snyderman, *The Motivation to Work*, Wiley, New York, 1959; and F. Herzberg, *Work and the Nature of Man*, World Publishing Co., Cleveland, Ohio, 1966, pp. 130–131. V. H. Vroom, *Work and Motivation*, Wiley, New York, 1964.

2. J. W. Atkinson, J. R. Bastian, R. W. Earl, and G. H. Litwin, "The Achievement Motive, Goal Setting, and Probability Preferences," *Journal of Abnormal and Social Psychology*, Vol. 60, 1960, pp. 27–36; W. Edwards, "Behavioral Decision Theory," *Annual Review of Psychology,* Annual Reviews Inc., Palo Alto, California, 1961, pp. 473–499; H. Peak, "Attitude and Motivation," *Nebraska Symposium on Motivation*, University of Nebraska Press, Lincoln, Nebraska, 1955, pp. 148–184; M. Rosenberg, "Cognitive Structure and Attitudinal Affect," *Journal of Abnormal and Social Psychology*, Vol. 53, 1956, pp. 367–372; M. Fishbein, "An Operational Definition of Belief and Attitude," *Human Relations*, Vol. 15, 1962, pp. 35–43.

3. D. McGregor, "Adventure in Thought and Action," *Proceedings of the Fifth Anniversary Convocation of the School of Industrial Management, Massachusetts Institute of Technology*, Massachusetts Institute of Technology, Cambridge, Massachusetts, 1957, pp. 23–30.

4. L. W. Porter, *Organizational Patterns of Managerial Job Attitudes*, American Foundation for Management Research, New York, 1964. See also M. Haire, E. Ghiselli and L. W. Porter, *Managerial Thinking: An International Study*, Wiley, New York, 1966, especially chapters 4 and 5.

5. M. Beer, *Leadership, Employee Needs, and Motivation*, Bureau of Business Research, Ohio State University, Columbus, Ohio, 1966.

6. J. V. Clark, "Motivation in Work Groups: A Tentative View," *Human Organization*, Vol. 19, 1960, pp. 199–208. E. E. Lawler and L. W. Porter, "The Effect of Performance on Job Satisfaction," *Industrial Relations*, Vol. 7, No. 1, 1967, pp. 20–28. L. W. Porter and E. E. Lawler, *Managerial Attitudes and Performance*, Irwin-Dorsey, Homewood, Illinois, 1968, pp. 148, 150.

7. Herzberg, Mausner and Synderman, *op. cit.*

8. Herzberg, *op. cit.*, chapters 7, 8. See also K. Davis, *Human Relations at Work* (Third Edition) McGraw-Hill, New York, 1967, pp. 32–36; and R. J. Burke, "Are Herzberg's Motivators and Hygienes Unidimensional?" *Journal of Applied Psychology*, Vol. 50, 1966, pp. 217–321.

9. For a review of six of these studies as well as a report on their own similar findings see M. D. Dunnette, J. P. Campbell, and M. D. Hakel, "Factors Contributing to Job Satisfaction and Job Dissatisfaction in Six Occupational Groups," *Organizational Behavior and Human Performance*, Vol. 2, 1967, pp. 143–174. See also C. L. Hulin and P. A. Smith, "An Empirical Investigation of Two Implications of the Two-Factor Theory of Job Satisfaction," *Journal of Applied Psychology*, Vol. 51, 1967, pp. 396–402; C. A. Lindsay, E. Marks, and L. Gorlow, "The Herzberg Theory: A Critique and Reformulation," *Journal of Applied Psychology*, Vol. 51, 1967, pp. 330–339. This latter study and one by J. R. Hinrichs and L. A. Mischkind, "Empirical and Theoretical Limitations of the Two-Factor Hypothesis of Job Satisfaction," *Journal of Applied Psychology*, Vol. 51, 1967, pp. 191–200, are especially useful for suggesting possible reformulations and extensions of the theory which may help overcome some of the objections voiced in the studies mentioned above.

10. Dunnette, Campbell and Hakell, *op. cit.*, pp. 169–173.
11. M. S. Viteles, *Motivation and Morale in Industry,* Norton, New York, 1953, chapter 14: A. Kornhauser, "Psychological Studies of Employee Attitudes," *Journal of Consulting Psychology,* Vol. 8, 1944, pp. 127–143.
12. Herzberg, *op. cit.,* Chapters 7–9.
13. Herzberg, *op. cit.,* Chapter 8.
14. F. Friedlander and E. Walton, "Positive and Negative Motivations Toward Work," *Administrative Science Quarterly,* Vol. 9, 1964, pp. 194–207.
15. It should be noted that the Porter and Lawler research reported above extends the Maslow model by providing an explicit linkage between need satisfaction and performance and also implicity recognizes individual motivational differences. To do these things, their research makes use of the Vroomian concepts discussed in the next section.
16. A. H. Brayfield and W. H. Crockett, "Employee Attitudes and Employee Performance," *Psychological Bulletin,* Vol. 52, 1955, p. 416.
17. B. S. Georgopoulas, G. M. Mahoney, and N. W. Jones, "A Path-Goal Approach to Productivity," *Journal of Applied Psychology,* Vol. 41, 1957, pp. 345–353.
18. This section is based especially on discussions in Vroom, *op. cit.,* Chapters 2 and 7. See also J. Galbraith and L. L. Cummings, "An Empirical Investigation of the Motivational Determinants of Task Performance: Interactive Effects between Instrumentality-Valence and Motivation-Ability," *Organizational Behavior and Human Performance,* Vol. 2, 1967, pp. 237–257.
19. Vroom, *op. cit.,* p. 6.
20. Vroom, *op. cit.,* p. 17.
21. Vroom, *op. cit.,* p. 18.
22. Vroom, *op. cit.*
23. V. H. Vroom, "Organizational Choice: A Study of Pre- and Postdecision Processes," *Organizational Behavior and Human Performance,* Vol. 1, 1966, pp. 212–225.
24. Galbraith and Cummings, *op. cit.,* pp. 237–257.
25. J. W. Hill, "An Application of Decision Theory to Complex Industrial Behavior," unpublished dissertation, Wayne State University, Detroit, Michigan, 1965.
26. Edwards, *op. cit.,* pp. 473–499.
27. For discussions of these measures see C. Osgood, G. Suci, and P. Tannenbaum, *The Measurement of Meaning,* University of Illinois Press, Urbana, Ill., 1957; A. L. Edwards, *Personal Preference Schedule Manual,* Psychological Corporation, New York, 1959.
28. E. E. Lawler and L. W. Porter, "Antecedent Attitudes of Effective Managerial Performance," *Organizational Behavior and Human Performance,* Vol. 2, 1967, pp. 122–142.
29. Vroom, *Work and Motivation, op. cit.,* Chapter 2.

9   The Satisfaction-Performance Controversy

Charles N. Greene

As Ben walked by smiling on the way to his office, Ben's boss remarked to a friend: "Ben really enjoys his job and that's why he's the best damn worker I ever had. And that's reason enough for me to keep Ben happy." The friend replied: "No, you're wrong! Ben likes his job because he does it so well. If you want to make Ben happy, you ought to do whatever you can to help him further improve his performance."

Four decades after the initial published investigation on the satisfaction-performance relationship, these two opposing views are still the subject of controversy on the part of both practitioners and researchers. Several researchers have concluded, in fact, that "there is no present technique for determining the cause-and-effect of satisfaction and performance." Current speculations, reviewed by Schwab and Cummings, however, still imply at least in theory that satisfaction and performance are causally related although, in some cases, the assumed cause has become the effect, and, in others, the relationship between these two variables is considered to be a function of a third or even additional variables.[1]

THEORY AND EVIDENCE

"Satisfaction Causes Performance"

At least three fundamental theoretical propositions underlie the research and writing in this area. The first and most pervasive stems from the human relations movement with its emphasis on the well-being of the individual at work. In the years following the investigations at Western Electric, a number of studies were conducted to identify correlates of high and low job satisfaction. The interest in satisfaction, however, came about not so much as a result of concern for the individual as concern with the presumed linkage of satisfaction with performance.

"The Satisfaction-Performance Controversy" by Charles Greene from BUSINESS HORIZONS, 15 (October 1972). Copyright® 1972 by the Foundation for the School of Business at Indiana University. Reprinted by permission.
1. Initial investigation by A. A. Kornhauser and A. W. Sharp, "Employee Attitudes: Suggestions from a Study in a factory," *Personnel Journal*, X (May, 1932), pp. 393-401.
First quotation from Robert A. Sutermeister, "Employee Performance and Employee Need Satisfaction—Which Comes First?" *California Management Review*, XIII (Summer, 1971), p. 43.
Second quotation from Donald P. Schwab and Larry L. Cummings, "Theories of Performance and Satisfaction: a Review," *Industrial Relations*, IX (October, 1970), pp. 408-30.

According to this proposition (simply stated and still frequently accepted), the degree of job satisfaction felt by an employee determines his performance, that is, satisfaction causes performance. This proposition has theoretical roots, but it also reflects the popular belief that "a happy worker is a productive worker" and the notion that "all good things go together." It is far more pleasant to increase an employee's happiness than to deal directly with his performance whenever a performance problem exists. Therefore, acceptance of the satisfaction-causes-performance proposition as a solution makes good sense, particularly for the manager because it represents the path of least resistance. Furthermore, high job satisfaction and high performance are both good, and, therefore, they ought to be related to one another.

At the theoretical level, Vroom's valence-force model is a prime example of theory-based support of the satisfaction-causes-performance case.[2] In Vroom's model, job satisfaction reflects the valence (attractiveness) of the job. It follows from his theory that the force exerted on an employee to remain on the job is an increasing function of the valence of the job. Thus, satisfaction should be negatively related to absenteeism and turnover, and, at the empirical level, it is.

Whether or not this valence also leads to higher performance, however, is open to considerable doubt. Vroom's review of twenty-three field studies, which investigated the relationship between satisfaction and performance, revealed an insignificant median static correlation of 0.14, that is, satisfaction explained less than 2 percent of the variance in performance. Thus, the insignificant results and absence of tests of the causality question fail to provide support for this proposition.

"Performance Causes Satisfaction"

More recently, a second theoretical proposition has been advanced. According to this view, best represented by the work of Porter and Lawler, satisfaction is considered not as a cause but as an effect of performance, that is, performance causes satisfaction.[3] Differential performance determines rewards which, in turn, produce variance in satisfaction. In other words, rewards constitute a necessary intervening variable and, thus, satisfaction is considered to be a function of performance-related rewards.

At the empirical level, two recent studies, each utilizing time-lag correlations, lend considerable support to elements of this proposition. Bowen and Siegel, and Greene reported finding relatively strong correlations between performance and satisfaction expressed later (the performance-causes-satisfaction condition), which

---

2. Victor H. Vroom, *Work and Motivation* (New York: John Wiley & Sons, Inc., 1964).
3. Lyman W. Porter and Edward E. Lawler, III, *Managerial Attitudes and Performance* (Homewood, Ill.: Richard D. Irwin, Inc., 1968).

were significantly higher than the low correlations between satisfaction and performance which occurred during the subsequent period (the "satisfaction-causes-performance" condition).[4]

In the Greene study, significant correlations were obtained between performance and rewards granted subsequently and between rewards and subsequent satisfaction. Thus, Porter and Lawler's predictions that differential performance determines rewards and that rewards produce variance in satisfaction were upheld.

"Rewards" as a Causal Factor

Closely related to Porter and Lawler's predictions is a still more recent theoretical position, which considers both satisfaction and performance to be functions of rewards. In this view, rewards cause satisfaction, and rewards that are based on current performance cause subsequent performance.

According to this proposition, formulated by Cherrington, Reitz, and Scott from the contributions of reinforcement theorists, there is no inherent relationship between satisfaction and performance.[5] The results of their experimental investigation strongly support their predictions. The rewarded subjects reported significantly greater satisfaction than did the unrewarded subjects. Furthermore, when rewards (monetary bonuses, in this case) were granted on the basis of performance, the subjects' performance was significantly higher than that of subjects whose rewards were unrelated to their performance. For example, they found that when a low performer was not rewarded, he expressed dissatisfaction but that his later performance improved. On the other hand, when a low performer was in fact rewarded for his low performance, he expressed high satisfaction but continued to perform at a low level.

The same pattern of findings was revealed in the case of the high performing subjects with one exception; the high performer who was not rewarded expressed dissatisfaction, as expected, and his performance on the next trial declined significantly. The correlation between satisfaction and subsequent performance, excluding the effects of rewards, was 0.00, that is, satisfaction does *not* cause improved performance.

A recent field study, which investigated the source and direction of causal influence in satisfaction-performance relationships, supports the Cherrington-

4. Donald Bowen and Jacob P. Siegel, "The Relationship Between Satisfaction and Performance: the Question of Causality," paper presented at the annual meeting of the American Psychological Association, Miami Beach, September, 1970.
Charles N. Greene, "A Causal Interpretation of Relationship Among Pay, Performance, and Satisfaction," paper presented at the annual meeting of the Midwest Psychological Association, Cleveland, Ohio, May, 1972.
5. David-J. Cherrington, H. Joseph Reitz, and William E. Scott, Jr., "Effects of Contingent and Non-contingent Reward on the Relationship Between Satisfaction and Task Performance," *Journal of Applied Psychology,* LV (December, 1971) pp. 531-36.

Reitz-Scott findings.[6] Merit pay was identified as a cause of satisfaction and, contrary to some current beliefs, was found to be a significantly more frequent source of satisfaction than dissatisfaction. The results of this study further revealed equally significant relationships between (1) merit pay and subsequent performance and (2) current performance and subsequent merit pay. Given the Cherrington-Reitz-Scott findings that rewards based on current performance cause improved subsequent performance, these results do suggest the possibility of reciprocal causation.

In other words, merit pay based on current performance probably caused variations in subsequent performance, and the company in this field study evidently was relatively successful in implementing its policy of granting salary increases to an employee on the basis of his performance (as evidenced by the significant relationship found between current performance and subsequent merit pay). The company's use of a fixed (annual) merit increase schedule probably obscured some of the stronger reinforcing effects of merit pay on performance.

Unlike the Cherrington-Reitz-Scott controlled experiment, the fixed merit increase schedule precluded (as it does in most organizations) giving an employee a monetary reward immediately after he successfully performed a major task. This constraint undoubtedly reduced the magnitude of the relationship between merit pay and subsequent performance.

IMPLICATIONS FOR MANAGEMENT

These findings have several apparent but nonetheless important implications. For the manager who desires to enhance the satisfaction of his subordinates (perhaps for the purpose of reducing turnover), the implication of the finding that "rewards cause satisfaction" is self-evident. If, on the other hand, the manager's interest in his subordinates' satisfaction arises from his desire to increase their performance, the consistent rejection of the satisfaction-causes-performance proposition has an equally clear implication: increasing subordinates' satisfaction will have no effect on their performance.

The finding that rewards based on current performance affect subsequent performance does, however, offer a strategy for increasing subordinates' performance. Unfortunately, it is not the path of least resistance for the manager. Granting differential rewards on the basis of differences in his subordinates' performance will cause his subordinates to express varying degrees of satisfaction or dissatisfaction.

---

6. Charles N. Greene, "Source and Direction of Causal Influence in Satisfaction-Performance Relationships," paper presented at the annual meetings of the Eastern Academy of Management, Boston, May, 1972. Also reported in Greene, "Causal Connections Among Managers' Merit Pay, Satisfaction, and Performance," *Journal of Applied Psychology*, 1972 (in press).

The manager, as a result, will soon find himself in the uncomfortable position of having to successfully defend his basis for evaluation or having to put up with dissatisfied subordinates until their performance improves or they leave the organization.

The benefits of this strategy, however, far outweigh its liabilities. In addition to its positive effects on performance, this strategy provides equity since the most satisfied employees are the rewarded high performers and, for the same reason, it also facilitates the organization's efforts to retain its most productive employees.

If these implications are to be considered as prescriptions for managerial behavior, one is tempted at this point to conclude that all a manager need do in order to increase his subordinates' performance is to accurately appraise their work and then reward them accordingly. However, given limited resources for rewards and knowledge of appraisal techniques, it is all too apparent that the manager's task here is not easy.

Moreover, the relationship between rewards and performance is often not as simple or direct as one would think, for at least two reasons. First, there are other causes of performance that may have a more direct bearing on a particular problem. Second is the question of the appropriateness of the reward itself, that is, what is rewarding for one person may not be for another. In short, a manager also needs to consider other potential causes of performance and a range of rewards in coping with any given performance problem.

Nonmotivational Factors

The element of performance that relates most directly to the discussion thus far is effort, that element which links rewards to performance. The employee who works hard usually does so because of the rewards or avoidance of punishment that he associates with good work. He believes that the magnitude of the reward he will receive is contingent on his performance and, further, that his performance is a function of how hard he works. Thus, effort reflects the motivational aspect of performance. There are, however, other nonmotivational considerations that can best be considered prior to examining ways by which a manager can deal with the motivational problem.

Direction

Suppose, for example, that an employee works hard at his job, yet his performance is inadequate. What can his manager do to alleviate the problem? The manager's first action should be to identify the cause. One likely possibility is what can be refered to as a "direction problem."

Several years ago, the Minnesota Vikings' defensive end, Jim Marshall, very alertly gathered up the opponent's fumble and then, with obvious effort and delight, proceeded to carry the ball some fifty yards into the wrong end zone. This is a direction problem in its purest sense. For the employee working under more usual circumstances, a direction problem generally stems from his lack of understanding of what is expected of him or what a job well done looks like. The action indicated to alleviate this problem is to clarify or define in detail for the employee the requirements of his job. The manager's own leadership style may also be a factor. In dealing with an employee with a direction problem, the manager needs to exercise closer supervision and to initiate structure or focus on the task, as opposed to emphasizing consideration or his relations with the employee.[7]

In cases where this style of behavior is repugnant or inconsistent with the manager's own leadership inclinations, an alternative approach is to engage in mutual goal setting or management-by-objectives techniques with the employee. Here, the necessary structure can be established, but at the subordinate's own initiative, thus creating a more participative atmosphere. This approach, however, is not free of potential problems. The employee is more likely to make additional undetected errors before his performance improves, and the approach is more time consuming than the more direct route.

Ability

What can the manager do if the actions he has taken to resolve the direction problem fail to result in significant improvements in performance? His subordinate still exerts a high level of effort and understands what is expected of him—yet he continues to perform poorly. At this point, the manager may begin, justifiably so, to doubt his subordinate's ability to perform the job. When this doubt does arise, there are three useful questions, suggested by Mager and Pipe, to which the manager should find answers before he treats the problem as an ability deficiency: Could the subordinate do it if he really had to? Could he do it if his life depended on it? Are his present abilities adequate for the desired performance?[8]

If the answers to the first two questions are negative, then the answer to the last question also will be negative, and the obvious conclusion is that an ability deficiency does, in fact, exist. Most managers, upon reaching this conclusion, begin to develop some type of formal training experience for the subordinate. This is unfortunate and frequently wasteful. There is probably a simpler, less expensive solution. Formal training is usually required only when the individual has never done the particular job in question or when there is no way in which the ability requirement in question can be eliminated from his job.

If the individual formerly used the skill but now uses it only rarely, systematic

7. For example, a recent study reported finding that relationships between the leader's initiating structure and both subordinate satisfaction and performance were moderated by such variables as role ambiguity, job scope, and task autonomy perceived by the subordinate. See Robert J. House, "A Path Goal Theory of Leader Effectiveness," *Administrative Science Quarterly*, XVI (September, 1971), pp. 321-39.

8. Robert F. Mager and Peter Pipe, *Analyzing Performance Problems* (Belmont, Calif.: Lear Siegler, Inc., 1970), p. 21.

practice will usually overcome the deficiency without formal training. Alternatively, the job can be changed or simplified so that the impaired ability is no longer crucial to successful performance. If, on the other hand, the individual once had the skill and still rather frequently is able to practice it, the manager should consider providing him greater feedback concerning the outcome of his efforts. The subordinate may not be aware of the deficiency and its effect on his performance, or he may no longer know how to perform the job. For example, elements of his job or the relationship between his job and other jobs may have changed, and he simply is not aware of the change.

Where formal training efforts are indicated, systematic analysis of the job is useful for identifying the specific behaviors and skills that are closely related with successful task performance and that, therefore, need to be learned. Alternatively, if the time and expense associated with job analysis are considered excessive, the critical incidents approach can be employed toward the same end.[9] Once training needs have been identified and the appropriate training technique employed, the manager can profit by asking himself one last question: "Why did the ability deficiency develop in the first place?"

Ultimately, the answer rests with the selection and placement process. Had a congruent man-job match been attained at the outset, the ability deficiency would have never presented itself as a performance problem.[10]

Performance Obstacles

When inadequate performance is not the result of a lack of effort, direction, or ability, there is still another potential cause that needs attention. There may be obstacles beyond the subordinate's control that interfere with his performance. "I can't do it" is not always an alibi; it may be a real description of the problem. Performance obstacles can take many forms to the extent that their number, independent of a given situation, is almost unlimited.

However, the manager might look initially for some of the more common potential obstacles, such as a lack of time or conflicting demands on the subordinate's time, inadequate work facilities, restrictive policies or "right ways of doing it" that inhibit performance, lack of authority, insufficient information about other activities that affect the job, and lack of cooperation from others with whom he must work.

An additional obstacle, often not apparent to the manager from his face-to-face interaction with a subordinate, is the operation of group goals and norms that

---

9. See, for example, J.D. Folley, Jr., "Determining Training Needs of Department Store Personnel," *Training Development Journal*, XXIII (January, 1969), pp. 24-27, for a discussion of how the critical incidents approach can be employed to identify job skills to be learned in a formal training situation.

10. For a useful discussion of how ability levels can be upgraded by means of training and selection procedures, the reader can refer to Larry L. Cummings and Donald P. Schwab, *Performance in Organizations: Determinants and Appraisal* (Glenview, Ill.: Scott, Foresman & Co., 1972).

run counter to organizational objectives. Where the work group adheres to norms of restricting productivity, for example, the subordinate will similarly restrict his own performance to the extent that he identifies more closely with the group than with management.

Most performance obstacles can be overcome either by removing the obstacle or by changing the subordinate's job so that the obstacle no longer impinges on his performance. When the obstacle stems from group norms, however, a very different set of actions is required. Here, the actions that should be taken are the same as those that will be considered shortly in coping with lack of effort on the part of the individual. In other words, the potential causes of the group's lack of effort are identical to those that apply to the individual.

The Motivational Problem

Thus far, performance problems have been considered in which effort was not the source of the performance discrepancy. While reward practices constitute the most frequent and direct cause of effort, there are, however, other less direct causes. Direction, ability, and performance obstacles may indirectly affect effort through their direct effects on performance. For example, an individual may perform poorly because of an ability deficiency and, as a result, exert little effort on the job. Here, the ability deficiency produced low performance, and the lack of effort on the individual's part resulted from his expectations of failure. Thus, actions taken to alleviate the ability deficiency should result in improved performance and, subsequently, in higher effort.

Effort is that element of performance which links rewards to performance. The relationship between rewards and effort is, unfortunately, not a simple one. As indicated in the figure, effort is considered not only as a function of the (1) value and (2) magnitude of reward, but also as a function of the (3) individual's perceptions of the extent to which greater effort on his part will lead to higher performance, and (4) that his high performance, in turn, will lead to rewards. Therefore, a manager who is confronted with a subordinate who exerts little effort must consider these four attributes of reward practices in addition to the more indirect, potential causes of the lack of effort. The key issues in coping with a subordinate's lack of effort—the motivation problem—or in preventing such a problem from arising involve all four of the attributes of rewards just identified.[11]

Appropriateness of the Reward
Regardless of the extent to which the individual believes that hard work determines his performance and subsequent rewards, he will obviously put forth little effort

---

11. The discussion in this section is based in part on Cummings and Schwab, *Performance in Organizations*, and Lyman W. Porter and Edward E. Lawler, III, "What Job Attitudes Tell About Motivation," *Harvard Business Review*, LXVI (January-February, 1968), pp. 118-26.

REWARDS AND EFFORT

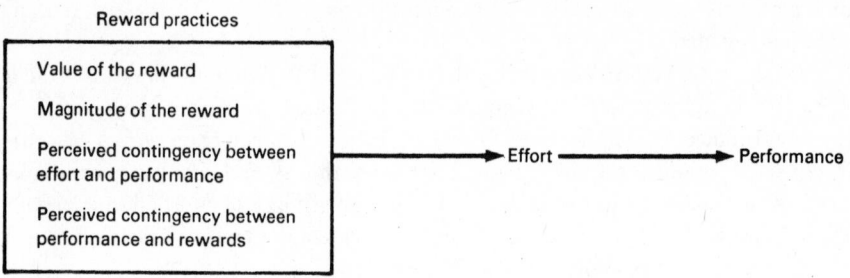

unless he *values* those rewards—that is, the rewards must have value in terms of his own need state. An accountant, for example, may value recognition from his boss, an opportunity to increase the scope of his job, or a salary increase; however, it is unlikely that he will place the same value on a ten-year supply of budget forms.

In other words, there must be consistency between the reward and what the individual needs or wants and recognition that there are often significant differences among individuals in what they consider rewarding. Similarly, individuals differ in terms of the *magnitude* of that valued reward they consider to be positively reinforcing. A 7 or 8 percent salary increase may motivate one person but have little or no positive effect on another person at the same salary level. Furthermore, a sizable reward in one situation might be considered small by the same individual in a different set of circumstances.

These individual differences, particularly those concerning what rewards are valued, raise considerable question about the adequacy of current organization reward systems, virtually none of which make any formal recognition of individual differences. Lawler, for example, has suggested that organizations could profit greatly by introducing "cafeteria-style" wage plans.[12] These plans allow an employee to select any combination of cash and fringe benefits he desires. An employee would be assigned "X" amount in compensation, which he may then divide up among a number of fringe benefits and cash. This practice would ensure that employees receive only those fringe benefits they value; from the organization's point of view, it would reduce the waste in funds allocated by the organization to fringe benefits not valued by its members. As a personal strategy, however, the manager could profit even more by extending Lawler's plan to include the entire range of nonmonetary rewards.

Rewards can be classified into two broad categories, extrinsic and intrinsic.

---

12. Edward E. Lawler, III, *Pay and Organizational Effectiveness: a Psychological View* (New York: McGraw-Hill Book Company, 1971).

Extrinsic rewards are those external to the job or in the context of the job, such as job security, improved working facilities, praise from one's boss, status symbols, and, of course, pay, including fringe benefits. Intrinsic rewards, on the other hand, are rewards that can be associated directly with the "doing of the job," such as a sense of accomplishment after successful performance, opportunities for advancement, increased responsibility, and work itself.

Thus, intrinsic rewards flow immediately and directly from the individual's performance of the job and, as such, may be considered as a form of self-reward. For example, one essentially must decide for himself whether his level of performance is worthy of a feeling of personal achievement. Extrinsic rewards, to the contrary, are administered by the organization; the organization first must identify good performance and then provide the appropriate reward.

Generally speaking, extrinsic rewards have their greatest value when the individual is most strongly motivated to satisfy what Maslow has referred to as lower level needs, basic physiological needs and needs for safety or security, and those higher level ego needs that can be linked directly to status. Pay, for example, may be valued by an individual because he believes it is a determinant of his social position within the community or because it constitutes a means for acquiring status symbols.

Intrinsic rewards are likely to be valued more by the individual after his lower level needs have been largely satisfied. In other words, there must be an adequate level of satisfaction with the extrinsic rewards before intrinsic rewards can be utilized effectively. In order to make the subordinate's job more intrinsically rewarding, the manager may want to consider several actions.

Perhaps most important, the manager needs to provide meaningful work assignments, that is, work with which the subordinate can identify and become personally involved. He should establish challenging yet attainable goals or, in some cases, it may be more advantageous for him to create conditions that greatly enhance the likelihood that his subordinate will succeed, thus increasing the potential for attaining feelings of achievement, advancement, and recognition. The manager may also consider such means as increased delegation and job enlargement for extending the scope and depth of the subordinate's job and thereby increasing the subordinate's sense of responsibility and providing greater opportunity to make the job into something more compatible with his own interests.

In short, the manager should as best he can match the rewards at his disposal, both extrinsic and intrinsic rewards, with what the subordinate indicates he needs or wants. Second, he should, by varying the magnitude and timing of the rewards granted, establish clearly in the subordinate's mind the desired effort-performance-reward contingencies.

Establishing the Contingencies

The contingency between effort and performance (that is, the extent to which the individual believes that by working harder, he will improve his performance) is largely a function of his confidence in his own abilities and his perceptions of the difficulty of the task and absence of obstacles standing in the way of successful task performance. When the effort-performance contingency is not clear for these reasons, the manager should consider several actions. He can reassign work or modify the task to be more consistent with the individual's perceptions of his own abilities; treat the problem as a "real" ability deficiency; remove the apparent performance obstacles; or simply reassure the individual.

The second contingency, the individual's belief that the rewards he receives reflect his accomplishments, is usually more difficult to establish. Here, two rather vexing predicaments are frequently encountered, both of which stem primarily from administration of extrinsic rewards. First, the instrument (usually a merit evaluation or performance appraisal device) may inaccurately measure the individual's contribution and thus his performance is rewarded in error. Reward schedules constitute the source of the second problem. Given fixed reward schedules (that is, the ubiquitous annual salary increase) adopted by the great majority of organizations, there is more frequently than not a considerable delay between task accomplishment and bestowal of the reward. As a result, the individual may not only fail to perceive the intended contingency but may incorrectly associate the reward with his behavior just prior to being rewarded. In other words, he may perceive a nonexistent contingency, and his subsequent behavior will reflect that contingency and, this time, go unrewarded.

Reward Schedules

The manner in which a given reward, or reinforcer, is scheduled is as strong a determinant of the effectiveness of that reward as is the value of the reward itself, or, for that matter, any other attribute of the reward. In organizations, the only plausible forms of reward schedules are intermittent as opposed to the continuous reward schedule in which the reward or punishment is administered after every behavioral sequence to be conditioned. In the case of the intermittent schedules, the behavior to be conditioned is reinforced only occasionally. There are four schedules of interest to the manager, each with varying effects on performance as a number of investigations in the field of experimental psychology have revealed.

1. *Fixed-interval schedule*—Rewards are bestowed after a fixed period, usually since the last reward was granted. This schedule is equivalent to the annual salary increase schedule in organizations, and its effects on performance are well-known. Typically, the individual "saves up," that is, he exerts a high level of effort just prior to the time of the reinforcement, usually his annual performance review. His performance more than likely will then taper off until the time just prior to his next annual review.
2. *Variable-interval schedule*—Rewards are administered at designated time periods, but the intervals between the periods vary. For example, a reward may be given one day after the last rewarded behavior sequence, then three days later, then one week later, and so on, but only if the behavior to be conditioned actually occurs. This schedule results in fairly consistent rates of performance over long periods of time. Praise or other forms

of social reinforcement from one's peers and superior, as an example, usually occur according to a variable-interval schedule, not by intention but simply because they are too involved with their own affairs to provide systematic reinforcement.

3. *Fixed-ratio schedule*—Reinforcement is provided after a fixed number of responses or performances by the individual. Incentive wage plans so frequently utilized in organizations constitute the prime example of this type of schedule. It is characterized by higher rates of effort than the interval schedules unless the ratio is large. When significant delays do occur between rewards, performance, much like in the fixed schedule, declines immediately after the reward is bestowed and improves again as the time for the next reward approaches.

4. *Variable-ratio schedule*—The reward is administered after a series of responses or performances, the number of which varies from the granting of one reward to the next.

   For example, an individual on a 15:1 variable-interval schedule might be reinforced after ten responses, then fifteen responses, then twenty responses, then ten responses, and so on, an average of one reinforcement for every fifteen responses. This schedule tends to result in performance that is higher than that of a comparable fixed ratio schedule, and the variation in performance both before and after the occurrence of the reward or reinforcement is considerably less.

Virtually all managers must function within the constraints imposed by a fixed-interval schedule (annual salary schedule) or fixed ratio schedule (wage incentives). However, this fact should not preclude consideration of the variable schedules, even within the framework of fixed schedules. Given their more positive effects on performance, such consideration is indeed highly desirable. It is conceivable, at least in a sales organization, for example, that monetary rewards (bonuses in this case) could be administered according to a variable-ratio schedule. From a more practical point of view, the entire range of nonmonetary rewards could be more profitably scheduled on a variable-interval basis, assuming that such scheduling was done in a systematic fashion.

CONCLUSIONS

This article has reviewed recent research concerning the relationship between satisfaction and performance and discussed the implications of the results of this research for the practicing manager. As noted at the outset, current speculation on the part of most practitioners and researchers continues to imply that satisfaction and performance are causally related, although confusion exists concerning the exact nature of the relationship. While the performance-causes-satisfaction proposition is a more recent development, the contention that satisfaction causes performance, nonetheless, remains the more widely held of the two beliefs, particularly among practitioners.

The recent research findings, however, offer only moderate support of the former view and conclusively reject the latter. Instead, the evidence provides rather strong indications that the relationship is more complex: (1) rewards constitute a more direct cause of satisfaction than does performance and (2) rewards based on current performance (and not satisfaction) cause subsequent performance.

For the manager who is concerned about the well-being of his subordinates, the implication of the finding that rewards cause satisfaction is self-evident. In order to achieve this end, the manager must provide rewards that have value or utility in terms of the subordinate's own need state and provide them in sufficient magnitude to be perceived as positively reinforcing. The manager whose goal is to increase a subordinate's performance, on the other hand, is faced with a more difficult task for two reasons. First, the relationship between rewards and performance is not a simple one. Second, there are other causes of performance—direction, the subordinate's ability, and existence of performance obstacles standing in the way of successful task performance—which the manager must also deal with.

The relationship between rewards and performance is complex because in reality there is at least one intervening variable and more than one contingency that needs to be established. An employee exerts high level effort usually because of the valued rewards he associates with high performance. Effort, the intervening variable, may be considered a function of the value and magnitude of the reward and the extent to which the individual believes that high effort on his part will lead to high performance and that his high performance, in turn, will lead to rewards.

Therefore, the manager in addition to providing appropriate rewards, must establish contingencies between effort and performance and between performance and rewards. The first contingency, the extent to which the individual believes that "how hard he works" determines his performance, is perhaps the more readily established. This contingency is a function, at least in part, of the individual's confidence in his own abilities, his perceptions of the difficulty of the task, and the presence of performance obstacles. When a problem does arise here, the manager can take those actions indicated earlier in this article to overcome an apparent ability deficiency or performance obstacle. The performance-reward contingency requires the manager, by means of accurate performance appraisals and appropriate reward practices, to clearly establish in the subordinate's mind the belief that his own performance determines the magnitude of the rewards he will receive.

The establishment of this particular contingency, unfortunately, is becoming increasingly difficult as organizations continue to rely more heavily on fixed salary schedules and nonperformance-related factors (for example, seniority) as determinants of salary progression. However, the manager can, as a supplement to organizationally determined rewards, place more emphasis on nonmonetary rewards and both the cafeteria-style reward plans and variable-interval schedules for their administration.

It is apparent that the manager whose objective is to significantly improve his subordinates' performance has assumed a difficult but by no means impossible task. The path of least resistance—that is, increasing subordinates' satisfaction—simply will not work.

However, the actions suggested concerning reward practices and, particularly, establishment of appropriate performance-reward contingencies will result in improved performance, assuming that such improvement is not restricted by ability or direction problems or by performance obstacles. The use of differential rewards may require courage on the part of the manager, but failure to use them will have far more negative consequences. A subordinate will repeat that behavior which was rewarded, regardless of whether it resulted in high or low performance. A rewarded low performer, for example, will continue to perform poorly. With knowledge of this inequity, the high performer, in turn, will eventually reduce his own level of performance or seek employment elsewhere.

Section B

Job Redesign: Antidote for Apathy?

The *Work in America* study emphasized job enrichment as a means of improving employee productivity and increasing the quality of work life. Yet the motivational assumptions underlying this prescription have not been consistently supported. So, what about the actual experience with job enrichment? Does it pay off? The materials in this section address such questions by giving an applied example of successful job enrichment and then providing three sets of criticism often neglected by proponents of job redesign.

The applied article concerns Robert Ford's discussion of "Job Enrichment Lessons from AT&T." Ford's work is among the best known in the job redesign literature and shows how work arrangements can be improved by giving employees a more meaningful slice of work. Ford examines the anatomy of a job enrichment program in detail and notes that AT&T, convinced that the program has paid off, is studying ways to go beyond the redesign of individual jobs (e.g., "job nesting" techniques). Ford lists nine lessons learned from seven years of job enrichment experience at AT&T and concludes that when the work is right, employee attitudes are right and so is performance. Unlike some job enrichment proponents, who leave the impression that employees will gladly perform more challenging work for no extra pay, Ford emphasizes that job redesign is not in lieu of cash.

The AT&T article points out the benefits of job enrichment. However, questions have been raised about the general applicability of job enrichment efforts. To illustrate, the three articles following Ford's take more critical postures. Reif and Luthans, for example, ask "Does Job Enrichment Really Pay Off?" They note that Ford's work at AT&T, despite implications to the contrary, was not completely successful even by Ford's admission. Further, according to their research, relatively few firms use job enrichment and those that do tend to concentrate on highly skilled instead of unskilled employees.

Reif and Luthans argue that not all workers want challenging jobs and further observe that some employees will resist enrichment efforts because they worry about handling the new responsibilities or losing control of work as they understand it. The authors of "Does Job Enrichment Really Pay Off?" do not intend their article to be an indictment of job redesign, only a warning that such programs are no panacea for motivational problems. In their view, job enrichment can be practiced successfully but, like all sound management programs, it must be used selectively after examining the nature of the jobs in question, the characteristics of the employees affected, and the organizational level at which the program will be implemented.

The third article, by Levitan and Johnston, continues the critical appraisal of job enrichment under the title, "Job Redesign, Reform, Enrichment—Exploring the Limitations." The authors ask: Is widespread job reform possible? Is it necessary? In developing answers, they review job enrichment studies, observe that only success stories tend to be reported, and question whether employees want more control over their work lives through participative management and humanized work. Levitan and Johnston feel that the actual possibilities for work reform are limited by economic and technological constraints and by the social demand for certain types of jobs. They do not underrate the importance of improving the quality of jobs in the labor force, but do identify broad gaps in the case for job enrichment. The need for radical work reform may not be the serious problem that some have claimed.

The final article, by Winpisinger, concerns "Job Enrichment: A Union View." As General Vice President of the International Association of Machinists and Aerospace Workers, Winpisinger notes that unionists have been skeptical of job enrichment because too often it eliminates work or seems to be a disguised attempt to get more work for less pay. (Recall that Ford's article emphasized the importance of pay but cited the reduction of the work force as a benefit of job redesign—raising the question of job enrichment for whom?) According to Winpisinger, the kind of job enrichment unions like, and have long fought for, includes better wages, shorter hours, vested pensions, and employee protection against arbitrary management authority. Coupled with the other articles in this section, the union view should help put job enrichment in perspective and temper its occasionally over-enthusiastic endorsement.

10   Job Enrichment Lessons From AT&T

Robert M. Ford

There is a mounting problem in the land, the concern of employed persons with
their work life. Blue-collar workers are increasingly expressing unhappiness over
the monotony of the production line. White-collar workers want to barter less
of their life for bread. More professional groups are unionizing to fight back at
somebody.

The annual reports of many companies frequently proclaim, "Our employees
are our most important resource." Is this a statement of conviction or is it mere
rhetoric? If it represents conviction, then I think it is only fair to conclude that
many business organizations are unwittingly squandering their resources.

The enormous economic gains that sprang from the thinking of the scientific
management school of the early 1900's—the time-and-motion study analysts, the
creators of production lines—may have ended insofar as they depend on utilizing
human beings more efficiently. Without discarding these older insights, we need
to consider more recent evidence showing that the tasks themselves can be changed
to give workers a feeling of accomplishment.

The growing pressure for a four-day workweek is not necessarily evidence
that people do not care about their work; they may be rejecting their work in the
form that confronts them. To ask employees to repeat one small task all day, at
higher and higher rates of speed, is no way to reduce the pressure for a shorter
workweek nor is it any longer a key to rising productivity in America. Work need
not be so frequently a betrayal of one's education and ability.

From 1965 to 1968 a group of researchers at AT&T conducted 19 formal
field experiments in job enrichment. The success of these studies has led to many
company projects since then. From this work and the studies of others (many of
them discussed previously in HBR), we have learned that the "lifesaving" portion
of many jobs can be expanded. Conversely, the boring and unchallenging aspects
can be reduced—not to say eliminated.

Furthermore, the "nesting" of related, already enriched jobs—a new concept
—may constitute another big step toward better utilization of "our most important resource."

First in this article I shall break down the job enrichment strategy into three
steps. Then I shall demonstrate what we at AT&T have been doing for seven years

in organizing the work beyond enrichment of individual jobs. In the course of my discussion, I shall use no illustrations that were not clearly successful from the viewpoint of both employees and the company.

While obviously the functions described in the illustrations differ superficially from those in most other companies, they are still similar enough to production and service tasks in other organizations to permit meaningful comparison. It is important to examine the nature of the work itself, rather than the external aspects of the functions.

Moreover, in considering ways to enrich jobs, I am not talking about those elements that serve only to "maintain" employees: wages, fringe benefits, clean restrooms, a pleasant atmosphere, and so on. Any organization must meet the market in these respects or its employees will go elsewhere.

No, employees are saying more than "treat me well." They are also saying "use me well." The former is the maintenance side of the coin; the latter is the work motivation side.

ANATOMY OF ENRICHMENT

In talking about job enrichment, it is necessary to go beyond such high-level concepts as "self-actualization," "need for achievement," and "psychological growth." It is necessary to specify the steps to be taken. The strategy can be broken down into these aspects—improving work through systematic changes in (a) the module of work, (b) control of the module, and (c) the feedback signaling whether something has been accomplished. I shall discuss each of these aspects in turn.

Work Module

Through changing the work modules, Indiana Bell Telephone Company scored a striking success in job enrichment within the space of two years. In Indianapolis, 33 employees, most of them at the lowest clerical wage level, compiled all telephone directories for the state. The processing from clerk to clerk was laid out in 21 steps, many of which were merely for verification. The steps included manuscript reception, manuscript verification, keypunch, keypunch verification, ad copy reception, ad copy verification, and so on—a production line as real as any in Detroit. Each book is issued yearly to the customers named in it, and the printing schedule calls for the appearance of about one different directory per week.

In 1968, the year previous to the start of our study, 28 new hires were required to keep the clerical force at the 33-employee level. Obviously, such turnover had bad consequences. From every operating angle, management was dissatisfied.

In a workshop, the supervisors concluded that the lengthy verification routine, calling for confirmation of one's work by other clerks, was not solving the basic problem, which was employee indifference toward the tasks. Traditional "solutions" were ineffective. They included retraining, supervisor complaints to the employees, and "communicating" with them on the importance to customers of error-free listing of their names and places of business in the directories. As any employee smart enough to be hired knows, an incorrect listing will remain monumentally wrong for a whole year.

The supervisors came up with many ideas for enriching the job. The first step was to identify the most competent employees, and then ask them, one by one, if they felt they could do error-free work, so that having others check the work would be pointless. Would they check their own work if no one else did it?

Yes, they said they could do error-free work. With this simple step the module dropped from 21 slices of clerical work to 14.

Next the supervisory family decided to take a really big step. In the case of the thinner books, they asked certain employees whether they would like to "own" their own books and perform all 14 remaining steps with no verification unless they themselves arranged it with other clerks—as good stenographers do when in doubt about a difficult piece of paperwork. Now the module included every step (except keytape, a minor one).

Then the supervisors turned their attention to a thick book, the Indianapolis directory, which requires many hands and heads. They simply assigned letters of the alphabet to individuals and let them complete all 14 steps for each block of letters.

In the past, new entries to all directories had moved from clerk to clerk; now all paperwork connected with an entry belonging to a clerk stayed with that clerk. For example, the clerk prepared the daily addenda and issued them to the information or directory assistance operators. The system became so efficient that most of the clerks who handled the smaller directories had charge of more than one.

Delimiting the Module.
In an interview one of the clerks said, "It's a book of my own." That is the way they felt about the books. Although not all modules are physically so distinct, the idea for a good module is usually there. Ideally, it is a slice of work that gives an employee a "thing of my own." At AT&T I have heard good modules described with pride in various ways:

- "A piece of turf" (especially a geographic responsibility).
- "My real estate" (by engineers responsible for a group of central offices).
- "Our cradle-to-grave modem line" (a vastly improved Western Electric switching-device production line).
- "Our mission impossible team" (a framemen's team, Long Lines Department).

The trouble with so much work processing is that no one is clearly responsible for a total unit that fails. In Indianapolis, by contrast, when a name in a directory is misspelled or omitted, the clerk knows where the responsibility lies.

Delimiting the module is not usually difficult when the tasks are in production, or at least physically defined. It is more difficult in service tasks, such as handling a telephone call. But modules make sense here, too, if the employee has been prepared for the work so that nobody else need be involved—in other words, when it is not necessary to say to the caller, "Let me connect you with my supervisor about that, please" or "May I give you our billing department, please?"

It is not always true that any one employee can handle a complete service. But our studies show that we consistently erred in forming the module; we tended to "underwhelm" employees. Eventually we learned that the worker can do more, especially as his or her experience builds. We do not have even one example from our business where job enrichment resulted in a *smaller* slice of work.

In defining modules that give each employee a natural area of responsibility, we try to accumulate horizontal slices of work until we have created (or recreated) one of these three entities for him or her:

1. A customer (usually someone outside the business).
2. A client (usually someone inside the business, helping the employee serve the customer).
3. A task (in the manufacturing end of the business, for example, where, ideally, individual employees produce complete items).

Any one of these three can make a meaningful slice of work. (In actuality, they are not separated; obviously, an employee can be working on a task for a *customer.*) Modules more difficult to differentiate are those in which the "wholeness" of the job is less clear—that is, control is not complete. They include cases where—

. . . the employee is merely one of many engaged in providing the ultimate service or item;

. . . the employee's customer is really the boss (or, worse yet, the boss's boss) who tells him what to do;

. . . the job is to help someone who tells the employee what is to be done.

While jobs like these are harder to enrich, it is worth trying.

Control of the Module

As an employee gains experience, the supervisor should continue to turn over responsibility until the employee is handling the work completely. The reader may infer that supervisors are treating employees unequally. But it is not so; ultimately, they may all have the complete job if they can handle it. In the directory-compilation case cited—which was a typical assembly-line procedure, although the capital investment was low—the supervisors found that they could safely permit the employee to say when sales of advertisements in the yellow pages must stop if the ads were to reach the printer on time.

Employees of South Central Bell Telephone Company, who set their own cutoff dates for the New Orleans, Monroeville, and Shreveport phone books, consistently gave themselves less time than management had previously allowed. As a result, the sale of space in the yellow pages one year continued for three additional weeks, producing more than $100,000 in extra revenue.

But that was only one element in the total module and its control. The directory clerks talked *directly* to salesmen, to the printer, to supervisors in other departments about production problems, to service representatives, and to each other as the books moved through the production stages.

There are obvious risks on the supervisors' side as they give their jobs away, piece by piece, to selected employees. We have been through it enough to advise, "Don't worry." Be assured that supervisors who try it will say, as many in the Bell System have said, "Now, at last, I feel like a manager. Before I was merely chief clerk around here."

In other studies we have made, control has been handed by the supervisor to a person when the employee is given the authority to perform such tasks as these:

- Set credit ratings for customers.
- Ask for, and determine the size of, a deposit.
- Cut off service for nonpayment.
- Make his or her own budget, subject to negotiation.
- Perform work other than that on the order sheet after negotiating it with the customer.
- Reject a run or supply of material because of poor quality.
- Make free use of small tools or supplies within a budget negotiated with the supervisor.
- Talk to anyone at any organizational level when the employee's work is concerned.
- Call directly and negotiate for outside repairmen or suppliers (within the budget) to remedy a condition handicapping the employee's performance.

Feedback

Definition of the module and control of it are futile unless the results of the employee's effort are discernible. Moreover, knowledge of the results should go directly to where it will nurture motivation—that is, to the employee. People have a great capacity for mid-flight correction when they know where they stand.

One control responsibility given to excellent employees in AT&T studies is self-monitoring; it lets them record their own "qualities and quantities." For example, one employee who had only a grade-school education was taught to keep a quality control chart in which the two identical parts of a dry-reed switch were not to vary more than .005 from an ideal dimension. She found that for some reason too many switches were failing.

She proved that the trouble occurred when one reed that was off by .005 met another reed that was off by .005. The sum, .010, was too much in the combined component and it failed. On her own initiative, she recommended and saw to it that the machine dies were changed when the reeds being stamped out started to vary by .003 from the ideal. A total variance of .006 would not be too much, she reasoned. Thus the feedback she got showed her she was doing well at her job.

This example shows all three factors at work—the module, its control, and feedback. She and two men, a die maker and a machine operator, had the complete responsibility for producing each day more than 100,000 of these tiny parts, which are not unlike two paper matches, but much smaller. How can one make a life out of this? Well, they did. The six stamping machines and expensive photometric test equipment were "theirs." A forklift truck had been dedicated to them (no waiting for someone else to bring or remove supplies). They ordered rolls of wire for stamping machines when they estimated they would need it. They would ship a roll back when they had difficulty controlling it.

Compared with workers at a plant organized along traditional lines, with batches of the reeds moving from shop to shop, these three employees were producing at a fourfold rate. Such a mini-group, where each person plays a complementary part, is radically different psychologically from the traditional group of workers, where each is doing what the others do.

(In the future, when now undreamed-of computer capacities have been reached, management must improve its techniques of feeding performance results directly to the employee responsible. And preferably it should be done *before* the boss knows about it.)

IMPROVING THE SYSTEM

When a certain job in the Bell System is being enriched, we ask the supervisory family, 'Who or what is the customer client/task in this job?" Also, "How often can the module be improved?" And then, "How often can control or feedback be improved? Can we improve all three at once?"

These are good questions to ask in general. My comments at this stage of our knowledge must be impressionistic.

The modules of most jobs can be improved, we have concluded. Responsibilities or tasks that exist elsewhere in the shop or in some other shop or department need to be combined with the job under review. This horizontal loading is necessary until the base of the job is right. However, I have not yet seen a job whose base was too broad.

At levels higher than entrance grade, and especially in management positions, many responsibilities can be moved to lower grade levels, usually to the advantage of every job involved. This vertical loading is especially important in mature organizations.

In the Indianapolis directory office, 21 piece-meal tasks were combined into a single, meaningful, natural task. There are counterparts in other industries, such as the assembly of an entire dashboard of an automobile by two workers.

We have evidence that two jobs—such as the telephone installer's job and the telephone repairman's job—often can make one excellent "combinationman's" job. But there are some jobs in which the work module is already a good one. One of these is the service representative, the highly trained clerk to whom a customer speaks when he wants to have a telephone installed, moved, or disconnected, or when he questions his telephone bill. This is sometimes a high-turnover job, and when a service representative quits because of work or task dissatisfaction, there goes $3,450 in training. In fact, much of the impetus for job enrichment came through efforts to reduce these costs.

In this instance the slice of work was well enough conceived; nevertheless, we obtained excellent results from the procedures of job enrichment. Improvements in the turnover situation were as great as 50%. Why? Because we could improve the control and feedback.

It should be recognized that moving the work module to a lower level is not the same as moving the control down. If the supervisor decides that a customer's account is too long overdue and tells the service representative what to do, then both the module and the control rest with the supervisor. When, under job enrichment procedures, the service representative makes the decision that a customer must be contacted, but checks it first with the supervisor, control remains in the supervisor's hands. Under full job enrichment, however, the service representative has control.

Exhibit I shows in schematic form the steps to be taken when improving a job. To increase control, responsibility must be obtained from higher levels; I have yet to see an instance where control is moved upward to enrich a job. It must be acknowledged, however, that not every employee is ready to handle more control. That is especially true of new employees.

Moreover, changing the control of a job is more threatening to supervisors than is changing the module. In rejecting a job enrichment proposal, one department head said to us, "When you have this thing proved 100%, let me know and we'll try it."

As far as feedback is concerned, it is usually improvable, but not until the module and control of it are in top condition. If the supervisory family cannot come up with good ways for telling the employee how he or she is doing, the problem lies almost surely in a bad module. That is, the employee's work is submerged in a total unit and he or she has no distinct customer/client/task.

When the module is right, you get feedback "for free"; it comes directly from the customer/client/task. During the learning period, however, the supervisor or teacher should provide the feedback.

When supervisors use the performance of all employees as a goad to individual employees, they thwart the internalization of motivation that job enrichment strives for. An exception is the small group of mutually supporting, complementary workers, but even in this case each individual needs knowledge of his or her own results.

Exhibit I STEPS IN IMPROVING A JOB

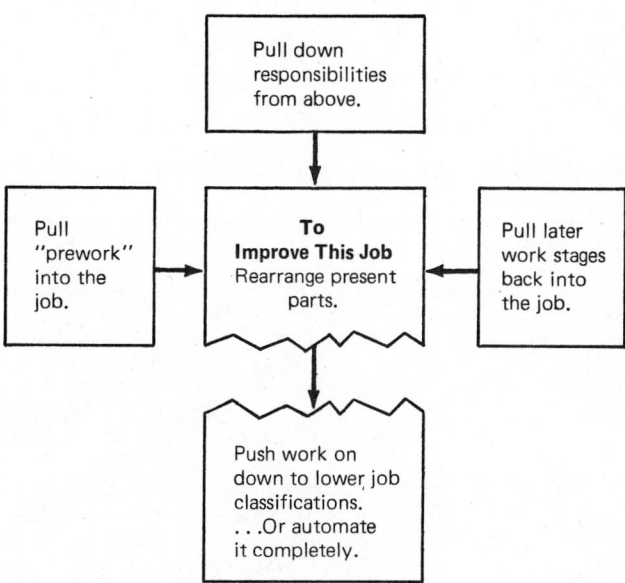

These generalizations cannot be said to be based on an unbiased sample of all jobs in all locations. Usually, the study or project locations were not in deep trouble, nor were they the best operating units. The units in deep trouble cannot stand still long enough to figure out what is wrong, and the top performers need no help. Therefore, the hard-nosed, scientifically trained manager can rightfully say that the jury is still out as to whether job enrichment can help in all work situations. But it has helped repeatedly and consistently on many jobs in the Bell System.

JOB "NESTING"

Having established to its satisfaction that job enrichment works, management at AT&T is studying ways to go beyond the enriching of individual jobs. A technique that offers great promise is that of "nesting" several jobs to improve morale and upgrade performance.

By way of illustration I shall describe how a family of supervisors of service representatives in a unit of Southwestern Bell Telephone Company improved its service indexes, productivity, collection of overdue bills, and virtually every other index of performance. In two years they moved their Ferguson District (adjacent to St. Louis) from near the bottom to near the top in results among all districts in the St. Louis area.

Before the job enrichment effort started, the service representatives' office was laid out as it appears in Exhibit II. The exhibit shows their desks in the standard, in-line arrangement fronted by the desks of their supervisors, who exercised close control of the employees.

Exhibit II   FERGUSON DISTRICT SERVICE REPRESENTATIVES' OFFICE LAYOUT BEFORE JOB ENRICHMENT

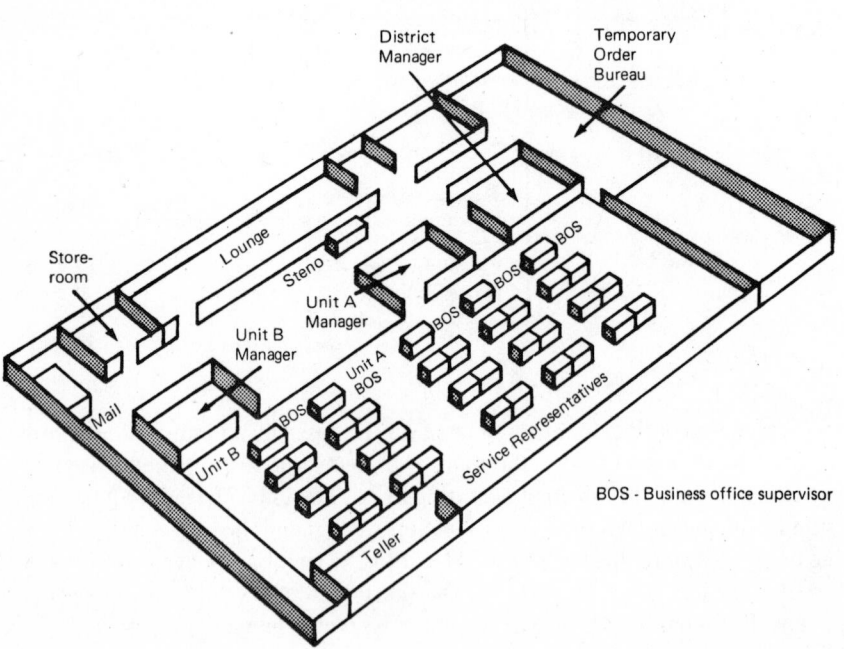

As part of the total job enrichment effort, each service rep group was given a geographical locality of its own, with a set of customers to take care of, rather than just "the next customer who calls in" from anywhere in the district. Some service reps—most of them more experienced—were detached to form a unit handling only the businesses in the district.

Then the service representatives and their business office supervisors (BOS) were moved to form a "wagon train" layout. As Exhibit III shows, they were gathered into a more-or-less circular shape and were no longer directly facing the desks of the business office supervisors and unit managers. (The office of the district manager was further removed too.)

Now all was going well with the service representatives' job, but another function in the room was in trouble. This was the entry-level job of service order typist. These typists transmit the orders to the telephone installers and the billing and other departments. They and the service order reviewers—a higher-classification job—had been located previously in a separate room that was soundproofed and air-conditioned because the TWX machines they used were noisy and hot.

Exhibit III SERVICE REPRESENTATIVES' OFFICE LAYOUT AFTER JOB ENRICH-MENT PROGRAM WAS IMPLEMENTED

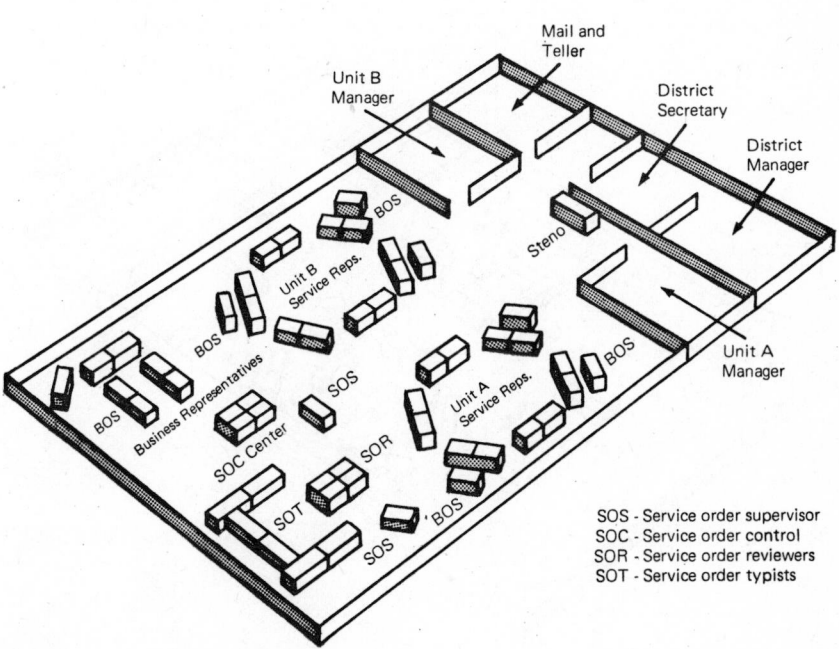

SOS - Service order supervisor
SOC - Service order control
SOR - Service order reviewers
SOT - Service order typists

When its equipment was converted to the silent, computer-operated cathode ray tubes (CRTs), the unit was moved to a corner of the service reps' room (see Exhibit III).

But six of the eight typists quit in a matter of months after the move. Meanwhile, the percentage of service orders typed "on time" fell below 50%, then below 40%.

The reasons given by the six typists who quit were varied, but all appeared to be rationalizations. The managers who looked at the situation, and at the $25,000 investment in the layout, could see that the feeling of physical isolation and the feeling of having no "thing" of their own were doubtless the real prime factors. As the arrangement existed, any service order typist could be called on to type an order for any service representative. On its face, this seems logical; but we have learned that an employee who belongs to everybody belongs to nobody.

An instantly acceptable idea was broached: assign certain typists to each service rep team serving a locality. "And while we're at it," someone said, "why not move the CRTs right into the group? Let's have a wagon train with the women

Exhibit IV   OFFICE LAYOUT AFTER SERVICE ORDER TYPISTS WERE "NESTED"

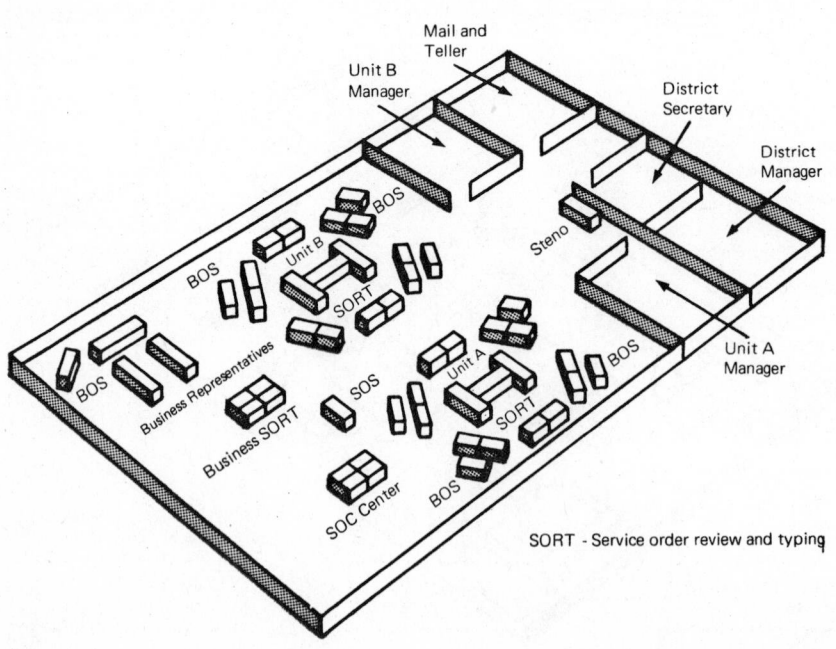

SORT - Service order review and typing

and kids in the middle." This was done (over the protest of the budget control officer, I should add).

The new layout appears in Exhibit IV. Three persons are located in the station in the middle of each unit. The distinction between service order typist and service order reviewer has been abolished, with the former upgraded to the scale of the latter. (Lack of space has precluded arranging the business customer unit in the same wagon-train fashion. But that unit's service order review and typing desks are close to the representatives' desks.)

Before the changes were started, processing a service request involved ten steps—and sometimes as many persons—not counting implementation of the order in the Plan Department. Now the procedure is thought of in terms of people, and only three touch a service order on its way through the office. (See Exhibit V.) At this writing, the Ferguson managers hope to eliminate even the service order completion clerk as a specialized position.

Has the new arrangement worked? Just before the typists moved into the wagon train, they were issuing only 27% of the orders on time. Within 30 days after the switch to assigned responsibility, 90% of the orders were going out on time. Half a year later, in one particular month, the figure even reached 100%.

These results were obtained with a 21% jump in work load—comparing a typical quarter after "nesting" with one before—being performed with a net drop

Exhibit V   OLD AND NEW PROCESSING PROCEDURES IN REQUEST-FOR-SERVICE DEPARTMENT

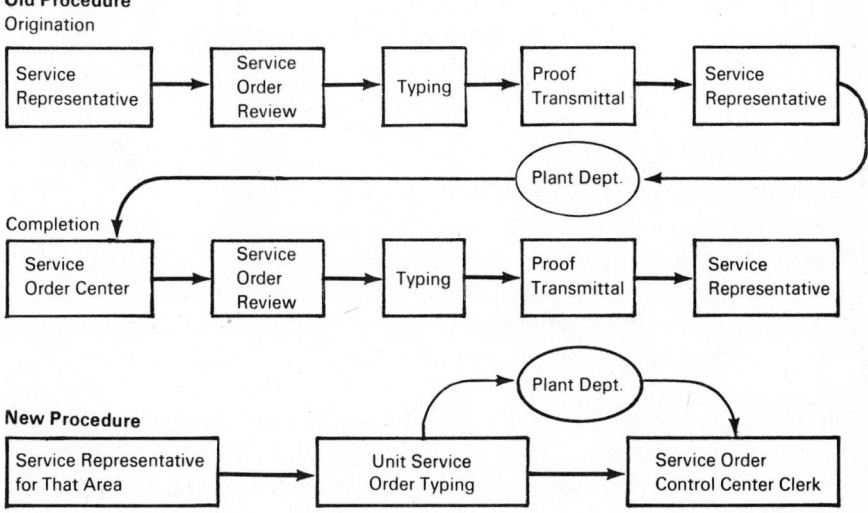

of 22 worker-weeks during the quarter. On a yearly basis it is entirely reasonable to expect the elimination of 88 weeks of unnecessary work (conservatively, 1½ full-time employees). Unneeded messenger service has been dispensed with, and one of two service order supervisor positions has been eliminated. The entire cost has been recovered already.

The service order accuracy measurement, so important in computerization, has already attained the stringent objectives set by the employees themselves, which exceeded the level supervisors would have set. Why are there fewer errors? Because now employees can lean across the area and talk to each other about a service order with a problem or handwriting that is unclear. During the course of a year this will probably eliminate the hand preparation of a thousand "query" slips, with a thousand written replies, in this one district.

And what of the human situation? When on-time order issuance was at its ebb, a supervisor suggested having a picnic for the service representatives and the typists. They did, but not a single typist showed up. Later, when the on-time order rate had climbed over 90%, I remarked, "Now's the time for another picnic." To which the supervisor replied facetiously, "Now we don't need a picnic!"

The turnover among typists for job reasons has virtually ceased. Some are asking now for the job of service representative, which is more demanding, more skilled, and better paid. Now, when the CRTs or the computer is shut down for some reason, or if the service order typist runs out of work supervisors report that typists voluntarily help the service reps with filing and other matters. They are soaking up information about the higher-rated jobs. These occurrences did not happen when the typists were 100 feet away; then they just sat doing nothing when the work flow ceased. (Because of this two-way flow of information, incidentally, training time for the job of service representative may drop as much as 50%.)

As the state general manager remarked when the results were first reported, "This is a fantastic performance. It's not enough to enrich just one job in a situation. We must learn how to put them together."

DIFFERENT CONFIGURATION

While the Ferguson District supervisory family was making a minigroup out of the service reps and their CRT typists, a strikingly different minigroup was in formation in the Northern Virginia Area of the Chesapeake and Potomac Telephone Company. There the family hit on the idea of funneling to selected order typists only those orders connected with a given central office, such as the Lewinsville frame. Soon the typists and the framemen—those who actually make the changes as a result of service orders—became acquainted. The typists even visited "their" framerooms. Now some questions could be quickly resolved that previously called for formal interdepartmental interrogations through supervisors.

At the end of the first eight months of 1972, these 9 CRT typists were producing service order pages at a rate one third higher than the 51 service order typists in the comparison group. The absence rate in the experimental unit was 0.6%, compared with 2.5% for the others, and the errors per 100 orders amounted to 2.9 as against 4.6 in the comparison group.

The flow of service orders is from (a) service rep to (b) service order typist to (c) the frameroom. The Ferguson District enjoyed success when it linked (a) and (b), while productivity for the Lewinsville frame improved when (b) and (c) were linked. Obviously, the next step is to link (a), (b), and (c). We are now selecting trial locations to test this larger nesting approach.

LESSONS LEARNED

In summary fashion, at the end of seven years of effort to improve the work itself, it is fair to say that:

1. Enriching existing jobs pays off. To give an extreme example, consider the fact that Illinois Bell Telephone Company's directory compilation effort reduced the work force from 120 persons to 74. Enriching the job started a series of moves; it was not the only ingredient, but it was the precipitating one.

2. Job enrichment requires a big change in managerial style. It calls for increasing modules, moving control downward, and dreaming up new feedback ideas. There is nothing easy about a successful job enrichment effort.

3. The nesting or configuring of related tasks—we call it "work organization"—may be the next big step forward after the enrichment of single jobs in the proper utilization of human beings.

It seems to produce a multiplier effect rather than merely a simple sum. In the Ferguson District case the job modules were not changed; the service representatives were not asked to type their own orders on the cathode ray tubes, nor were the typists asked to take over the duties of the service representatives. The results came from enriching other aspects (control and feedback) and, more important, from laying out the work area differently to facilitate interaction among responsible people.

4. While continuing job enrichment efforts, it is important not to neglect "maintenance" factors. In extending our work with job nesting, for example, we plan to experiment with "office landscaping," so called. The furniture, dividers, planters, and acoustical treatment, all must add to the feeling of work dedication. By this I mean we will dedicate site, equipment, and jobs to the employees, with the expectation that they will find it easier to dedicate themselves to customer/client/task. Especially in new installations, this total work environmental approach seems a good idea for experimentation. We will not be doing it merely to offset pain or boredom in work. The aim is to facilitate work.

5. A "pool" of employees with one job (typing pool, reproduction pool, calculating pool, and so on) is at the opposite extreme from the team or "minigroup" which I have described. A minigroup is a set of mutually supporting employees, each of whom has a meaningful module or part in meeting the needs of customer/client/task. What is "meaningful" is, like a love affair, in the eye of the beholder; at this stage, we have difficulty in describing it further.

A minigroup can have several service representatives or typists; one of each is not basic to the idea. The purpose is to set up a group of employees so that a natural, mutual dependence can grow in providing a service or finishing a task. It marks the end of processing from person to person or group to group, in separate locations or departments and with many different supervisors.

The minigroup concept, however, still leaves room for specialists. In certain Scandinavian auto plants, for example, one or two specialists fabricate the entire assembly of the exhaust pollution control system or the electrical system. Eventually, a group of workers may turn out a whole engine. In the United States, Chrysler has given similar trial efforts a high priority. The idea is to fix authority at the lowest level possible.

6. Experience to date indicates that unions welcome the kind of effort described in our studies. Trouble can be expected, of course, if the economics of increases in productivity are not shared equitably. In the majority of cases, the economics can be handled even under existing contracts, since they usually permit establishment of new jobs and appropriate wage grades between dates of contract negotiation.

An employee who takes the entire responsibility for preparing a whole telephone directory, for example, ought to be paid more, although a new clerical rating must be established. Job enrichment is not in lieu of cash; good jobs and good maintenance are two sides of the same coin.

7. New technology, such as the cathode ray tube, should enable us to break free of old work arrangements. When the Ferguson District service order typists were using the TWX machines, nesting their jobs was impractical because the equipment would have driven everybody to distraction. Installation of the high-technology CRTs gave the planners the opportunity to move together those employees whose modules of work were naturally related. This opportunity was at first overlooked.

Everyone accepts the obvious notion that new technology can and must eliminate dumb-dumb jobs. However, it probably creates more, rather than fewer, fragments of work. Managers should observe the new module and the work organization of the modules. This effort calls for new knowledge and skills, such as laying out work so attractively that the average employee will stay longer and work more effectively than under the previous arrangement.

Moreover, technology tends to make human beings adjuncts of machines. As we move toward computerized production of all listings in the white pages of the phone books, for example, the risk of an employee's losing "his" or "her" own directories is very great indeed. (Two AT&T companies, South Central Bell and Pacific Northwest Bell, are at this stage, and we must be certain the planned changes do not undermine jobs.) Making sure that machines remain the adjunct of human beings is a frontier problem which few managers have yet grappled with.

8. Managers in mature organizations are likely to have difficulty convincing another department to make pilot runs of any new kind of work organization, especially one that will cause the department to lose people, budget, or size. Individual job enrichment does not often get into interdepartmental tangles, but the nesting of jobs will almost surely create problems of autonomy. This will call for real leadership.

9. When the work is right, employee attitudes are right. That is the job enrichment strategy—get the work right.

Does Job Enrichment Really Pay Off?
William E. Reif and Fred Luthans

During the last few years, behavior-oriented management scholars and practitioners have generally extolled the virtues of Frederick Herzberg's job enrichment approach to employee motivation. Much of the management literature, especially journals aimed at the practicing manager, propose that "Job Enrichment Pays Off."[1] Lately, it has become commonplace for behavioral scientists to criticize Herzberg's research methodology but then admit the overall motivational value of the technique of job enrichment.[2] Only in a few instances have scholars or, especially, practitioners, seriously questioned the motivating effect of job enrichment.

It is widely felt to be an excellent way of motivating employees in today's organizations.

In the mad dash to modernize and get away from the Theory X (Douglas McGregor) or Systems I and II (Rensis Likert) or Immaturity (Chris Argyris) or 9, 1 (Robert Blake and Jane Mouton) approaches to the management of people, both professors of management and practicing managers may be guilty of the same thing: blindly accepting and over-generalizing about the first seemingly logical, practical and viable alternative to old style management—Herzberg's job enrichment. It now seems time to take a step back, settle down, and take a hard look at the true value that job enrichment has for motivating employees. Does job enrichment really pay off or is it merely a convenient crutch used by professors and practitioners to be modern in their approach to the management of human resources? This article attempts to provide another point of view and play the devil's advocate in critically analyzing job enrichment.

ENRICHMENT OR ENLARGEMENT?

The logical starting point in the analysis would be to see how, if at all, job enrichment differs from the older job enlargement concept. Although Herzberg, M. Scott Myers, Robert Ford and others portray job enrichment as one step beyond job enlargement, the real difference may lie more in the eyes of the definer than any actual differences in practice. The distinction between the terms becomes even cloudier when concepts such as job extension and job rotation enter the discussion. The differences between these various terms can perhaps best be depicted on a continuum of variety, responsibility, and personal growth on the job. Most job enrichment advocates carefully point out that enrichment, relative to rotation, extension, and enlargement, infers that there is greater variety, more responsibility, and increased opportunity for personal growth. Yet, for practical purposes, the differences, especially between enlargement and enrichment, may be more semantic than real. Researchers who have studied job enlargement define their term almost exactly the same way that Herzberg defines job enrichment.

Job Variety, Responsibility & Growth

Low   *High*

Rotation Extension Enlargement Enrichment

CONCLUSIONS FROM RESEARCH

To develop a framework of analysis for job enrichment, conclusions from research must first be summarized. William Reif and Peter Schoderbek's 1965 study revealed that 81 percent of the firms which responded to a mailed questionnaire survey were not using job enlargement. Of the 19 percent (forty-one firms) who were using the concept, only four indicated their experience was "very successful."[3] A more recent National Industrial Conference Board study disclosed that even though 80 percent of the responding companies expressed interest in the behavioral sciences, that even though 90 percent replied that their executives read books and articles about the behavioral sciences, and that more than 75 percent sent their executives to outside courses and seminars dealing with behavioral science concepts, there were very few firms which indicated they had put such concepts into actual practice.[4] Although a number of companies stated they were engaged in some form of job design activity, the N.I.C.B. study revealed that few have made any *sustained* effort in redesigning jobs.

The two companies which are cited most often in discussions of job enrichment are Texas Instruments and American Telephone and Telegraph. The two are given as examples of the outstanding success that can be attained when applying the job enrichment concept. However, one may question what constitutes "success." For example, Mitchell Fein, a long-time industrial engineer, assessed the Texas Instrument's job enrichment program as follows:

Texas Instruments' management was probably more dedicated to job enrichment than any other company in the world. They earnestly backed their managing philosophies with millions of dollars of efforts. After 15 years of unrelenting diligence, management announced in its 1968 report to the stockholders its program for "increasing human effectiveness," with the objective: "Our goal is to have approximately 10,000 TI men and women involved in team improvement efforts by the end of 1968 or 1969." Since TI employed 60,000, the program envisioned involving only 16 percent of its work force. The total involved was actually closer to 10 percent.[5]

In another instance, Robert Ford, who has been primarily responsible for implementing job enrichment in AT&T, reports, "Of the nineteen studies, nine were rated 'outstandingly successful,' one was a complete 'flop,' and the remaining nine were 'moderately successful.'"[6] Even more noteworthy perhaps is the fact that although Ford does not hesitate to generalize from the nineteen studies, he appears at one point to question his own optimism over the applicability of and benefits derived from job enrichment. He states: "No claim is made that these 19 trials cover a representative sample of jobs and people within the Bell system. For example, there were no trials among the manufacturing or laboratory employees, nor were all operating companies involved. There are more than a thousand different jobs in the Bell system, not just the nine in these studies."[7]

In an early study (1958), James Kennedy and Harry O'Neill published findings on the effects job enlargement had had on the opinions and attitudes of workers in an automobile assembly plant. Attitude surveys were given to both assembly line workers whose jobs were highly routine, unskilled, and paced by the assembly line, and to utility men whose jobs were quite varied. The results showed no statistical difference between the two sets of scores. This finding led Kennedy and O'Neill to conclude:

> If job content is a factor in determining how favorably workers view their supervisors and their work situation, the difference in content apparently must be along more fundamental dimensions than those observed in this study.[8]

In 1968, Charles Hulin and Milton Blood conducted an in-depth study of job enlargement. They concluded that, "The case for job enlargement has been drastically overstated and overgeneralized. . . . Specifically, the argument for larger jobs as a means of motivating workers, decreasing boredom and dissatisfaction, and increasing attendance and productivity is valid only when applied to certain segments of the work force—white-collar and supervisory workers and nonalienated blue-collar workers."[9]

Unfortunately, these studies are not widely cited in the management literature. Instead, a number of widely known and quoted management oriented behavioral scientists, among them Herzberg, McGregor, Likert, Argyris, and Blake and Mouton, are most often interpreted, sometimes wrongly, to advocate the opposite.[10] The popular position is that job enrichment is a key to successful motivation and productivity and many scholars, consultants, and practitioners actively campaign for its widespread use in modern organizations. McGregor summed up the feelings of job enrichment advocates when he said, "Unless there is opportunity *at work* to satisfy these high level needs (esteem and self-actualization), people will be deprived, and their behavior will reflect this deprivation."[11] In other words, the predominant conclusion is that people have a need to find fulfillment in their work and job enrichment provides them with the opportunity.

Why the wide divergence on the conclusions about job enrichment? Why the differences of opinion not only among scholars but also among practitioners, and between scholars and practitioners, about the efficacy of job enrichment? These are questions that the article tries to answer. The approach taken is to critically analyze the three most important concepts in job enrichment: (1) worker motivation, (2) job design, and (3) resistance to change.

WORKER MOTIVATION: ONE MORE TIME

The stated purpose of early job enlargement programs was to provide job satisfaction for unskilled blue-collar and low level white-collar (clerical) workers whose jobs were highly standardized and repetitive, operated on a short time cycle, required little knowledge and skill, and utilized only a few low-order abilities. Only a cursory review of management literature reveals that the majority of job enlargement programs in existence today are concerned with enriching the jobs of highly skilled workers, technicians, professionals, supervisors and managers, not unskilled blue- and white-collar employees. For example, in the William Paul, Keith Robertson, and Frederick Herzberg article on job enrichment in British companies, *none* of the employees in the studies could be classified as blue-collar workers.[12] Fein reports, "My experience in numerous plants has been that the lower the skills level, the lower the degree to which job enlargement can be established to be meaningful to the employees and management."[13]

The Reif and Schoderbek study discovered that of the firms using job enlargement, 73 percent used it at the supervisory level, 51 percent used it to enlarge clerical jobs, and 49 percent used it in the production area. Of the firms practicing job enlargement in the plant, 35 percent replied that the employees were primarily skilled, while only 15 percent classified the employees on enlarged jobs as unskilled.[14] In follow-up interviews three major reasons clearly emerged why it was more difficult to get unskilled workers to accept job enlargement than skilled or semi-skilled workers: (1) the unskilled prefer the status quo, (2) the unskilled seem to prefer highly specialized work, and (3) the unskilled show a lack of interest in improvements in job design which require learning new skills or assuming greater responsibility. A representative comment was: "Most unskilled workers prefer the routine nature of their jobs, and it has been my experience that they are not eager to accept responsibility or learn new skills."

In a parallel manner, the most frequent response to another question, "What are the major considerations taken into account in determining the particular job(s) to be enlarged?" was "The potential skills of employees." The survey respondents noted that in their experience, the higher the skill level of employees, the greater the probability of success with the enlarged job. Another question was, "What do you consider to be the major disadvantages of job enlargement?" The second most frequent response was that some workers were just not capable of growing with the enlarged job that was designed for them. Follow-up interviews indicated that the workers referred to by the respondents were primarily unskilled and semi-skilled blue-collar workers. Of particular interest was the response from a number of company spokesmen that in their experience many workers seemed capable of growing with the job but simply were not willing to do so. This observation was confirmed in interviews with a number of workers who had declined the opportunity to work on enlarged jobs.

The above results seem to directly contradict the commonly held motivational assumptions made by well-known behavioralists. It has become widely accepted that:

1. *Man seeks and needs meaningful work.*—Many behaviorists would contend that man's psychological well-being is dependent upon his ability to find ex-

pression and challenge in his work.

2. *Motivation is a function of job satisfaction and personal freedom.*—As was noted in a comprehensive N.I.C.B. study on job design: "Satisfaction with job content and the freedom to work on a self-sufficient independent basis are viewed as the crucial variables in the motivation to work."[15]

3. *Job content is related to job satisfaction.*—This major assumption is primarily derived from Herzberg's two-factor theory of motivation which provides the foundation for job enrichment. Herzberg implies that people are capable and desirous of greater responsibility and can be positively motivated by work which provides "meaning" to them.

These motivational assumptions do not account for why some workers show little or no interest in job enlargement. Besides the overall social and cultural impact on the values toward work, there are other specific but less widely held assumptions about worker motivation. One possible alternative assumption is that some people actually prefer highly routine, repetitive jobs. Numerous studies have pointed out that repetitive work can have positively motivating characteristics for some workers.[16] For example, Maurice Kilbridge found that assembly line workers in a television factory did not necessarily regard repetitive tasks as dissatisfying or frustrating. Also, the mechanical pacing of the conveyors was not necessarily distasteful to most workers. The Reif and Schoderbek study found that some workers preferred routine tasks because there was little thinking involved, and as a result, they were free to socialize and daydream without impairment to their productivity.[17]

Do these results suggest that workers' attitudes toward work and their ideas of what constitute satisfactory working conditions have gradually conformed to the technical requirements of our modern, industrialized society? For decades scholars and practitioners have been concerned with changing the design of work in order for it to be compatible with the psychological make-up of today's workers. In the meantime, is it possible that scholars and managers alike have failed to observe adaptation of the worker to his environment or, even more important, fundamental changes in the psychological need structure of the individual? Is there any tangible evidence which would give positive support to these intriguing possibilities?

Although not widely known to students of management, there is a small but significant literature which contradicts and is in opposition to the widely held assumptions made by job enrichment advocates. The study by Hulin and Blood is a good example. After closely analyzing practically all relevant research, they conclude that the effects of job enrichment on job satisfaction and worker motivation are generally overstated and in some cases unfounded.[18] Their study raises a number of interesting questions about the popular assumptions of worker motivation and the relationship between job enrichment, job satisfaction, and motivation. They argue that many blue-collar workers are not alienated from the work environment but are alienated from the work norms and values of the middle class. The middle class norms include: (a) positive effect for occupational achievement, (b) a belief in the intrinsic value of hard work, (c) a striving for the attainment of responsible positions, and (d) a belief in the work-related aspects of the Protestant ethic. On the other hand, these blue-collar workers do follow the norms of their own subculture. The implications are that workers who are alienated from middle class values do not actively seek meaning in their work and therefore are not strongly motivated by the job enlargement concept.

Fein's study of blue-collar and white-collar worker motivation came up with essentially the same conclusion. He states:

Workers do not look upon their work as fulfilling their existence. Their reaction to their work is the opposite of what the behavioralists predict. It is only because *workers choose not to find fulfillment in their work* that they are able to function as healthy human beings. By rejecting involvement in their work which simply cannot be fulfilling, workers save their sanity.[19]

Fein goes on to say:

. . . the concepts of McGregor and Herzberg regarding workers' needs to find fulfillment through their work are sound *only for those workers who choose to find fulfillment through their work*. In my opinion, this includes about 15-20% of the blue-collar work force. These behavioralists' concepts have little meaning for the others. Contrary to their postulates, the majority of workers seek fulfillment outside their work.[20]

Whether one agrees or disagrees with the above observation, it does raise an interesting point. One could speculate that Fein's 15 to 20 percent is about the proportion of the worker population that David McClelland and David Winter would regard as high achievers.[21] Assuming this percentage were accurate, it would be vitally important to the analysis of job enrichment. It would follow that high achievers are essentially self-motivated and would not require the external stimulus of job enrichment to perform well. By the same token, the low-achievers would not respond to job enrichment because work holds too little meaning for them to be motivated by it. They find satisfaction outside the work place.

Another interesting parallel is provided by Hulin and Blood's analysis of William F. Whyte's study of rate busters.[22] They contend that Whyte's rate busters rejected the norms of their peer group and accepted the norms of management whereas the "quota restricters" retained their peer group norms. One might safely speculate that Whyte's quota restricters belong to the group known as the "alienated from the work norms of the middle class" workers or McClelland's low-achievers or Fein's 80 to 85 percent. Thus, a plausible answer to the question, "Why isn't job enrichment used more extensively on jobs of blue-collar and low-level white-collar workers?" is that a majority of these workers may not be positively motivated by an enriched job content with the accompanying motivators.

Instead, they may be willing to exchange their minimum efforts on the job so that they can live satisfactorily outside the job.

A RE-EXAMINATION OF JOB DESIGN

Louis Davis defines job design as the "specification of the contents, methods, and relationships of jobs in order to satisfy technological and organizational requirements as well as the social and personal requirements of the job holder."[23] Traditionally, the technological requirements of work were given primary consideration in designing a job. For example, Frederick W. Taylor's work improvement efforts were directed at the task. Adjustments between technology and human needs were made in terms of the individual's adjustment to the system rather than designing the system to meet human needs. Because of the recent influence of the behavioralists, more emphasis has been devoted to the human aspects of job design. Today, the commonly expressed purpose of job design is to create more meaningful and satisfying work with the assumption being that productivity can be increased not so much by improving the technology as by improving the motivational climate.

Job enrichment is very compatible with "work is a human as well as a technical process" approach to job design. The conceptual similarity between job enrichment and the human approach to job design is very evident in the two factor motivation theory of Frederick Herzberg.[24] According to Herzberg, motivation is intrinsic to the job and the true rewards (achievement, recognition, work itself, responsibility, advancement, growth) come from doing the work, from performing effectively on the job. Many other behaviorally oriented theorists are in agreement with Herzberg's emphasis on job content, notably Argyris and McGregor who both express the desire to redesign jobs so they are capable of fulfilling esteem and self-actualization needs.

If Herzberg is correct, why hasn't job enrichment been more readily implemented into modern organizations? Possibly one of the major reasons is the failure to fully understand the significance of that part of job design which is concerned with meeting the social and personal requirements of the job holder. Everyone agrees that work is a social activity and probably most would agree that the framework for social interaction is largely an outgrowth of technology, the specific task, and the authority relationships prescribed by the formal organization. As a result, the social system or informal organization is usually structured along the lines of plant layout, machine processes, job specifications, the physical proximity of workers to each other, and operating policies and procedures. Finally, most would agree that the social system is an important means of fulfilling workers' needs for companionship, affection, reputation, prestige, respect, and status; of providing for interpersonal communication; and of helping protect the integrity and self-concept of the individual. This conclusion is brought out in a classic statement by Chester Barnard:

The essential need of the individual is association, and that requires local activity or immediate interaction between individuals. Without it the man is lost. The willingness of men to endure onerous routine and dangerous tasks which they could avoid is explained by this necessity for action at all costs in order to maintain the sense of social integration, whether the latter arises from "instinct," or from social conditioning, or from physiological necessity, or all three.[25]

It is entirely possible that for many blue-collar workers, the affiliation motive is much stronger than the Herzberg "motivators" to which job enrichment is aimed. Enriched job designs that reduce the opportunities for social interaction may have a negative rather than positive impact on worker satisfaction and productivity. The Reif and Schoderbek study found a number of workers dissatisfied with the job enrichment program for this reason. A typical response was: "I don't see my old friends anymore except during coffee breaks and at lunch. On the line a bunch of us used to talk and tell jokes all the time." [26] For these workers the only satisfaction they had experienced at work was their interaction and identification with other members of their primary group. It should not be surprising that they expressed an unwillingness to give up their group membership for the promise of more meaningful work through job enrichment. To them, a newly enriched job which threatened to destroy the established social pattern was unacceptable.

RESISTANCE TO CHANGE:
THE DILEMMA OF JOB ENRICHMENT

In the Reif and Schoderbek study, the most frequent reply (almost half of firms using job enlargement) to the inquiry "What are the major problems encountered in applying job enlargement?" was "overcoming resistance to change." By far the most frequent response to another question, "What are the major problems experienced by the workers in adjusting to job enlargement?" was "adjustment to increased duties."[27] It became clear during follow-up interviews that the two answers were related. This led to a specific investigation of why workers would resist the opportunity to work on enlarged jobs. Four basic reasons emerged as to why workers resisted job enlargement:

- First, there was anxiety expressed by some workers who felt they would not be able to learn the new and modified skills required by the job enlargement design. Was this lack of confidence in one's ability to perform efficiently on the new job justified? The answer appeared to be yes. Most of the routine jobs did not require a great amount of skill and initiative. The very routine nature of a job reduced the possibility that an employee could ever develop the necessary knowledge and skills required by the enlarged or enriched job design.

- Closely related to the feeling of inadequacy was the fear of failure. Many workers spend years developing the skills which make them highly proficient at their present jobs. Why change now? Why give up a job which affords a relatively high degree of security for one which requires learning new skills, adjusting to unfamiliar methods and operating procedures, and establishing new working relationships? Furthermore, it should be recognized that over time most workers become highly competent in performing specialized, routine tasks. Despite the seemingly unchallenging nature of a job, the worker develops a sense of pride in knowing he can execute his job better than anyone else. This feeling of accomplishment, however limited it may appear to academicians and managers, may give the employee cause to decline an offer, or react negatively, to an enriched job.

- Third, employees' attitudes toward change can be influenced by their relationship with superiors. As workers become highly proficient in their jobs, they require less direct supervision and, as a result, achieve a high degree of freedom and independence. This feeling can be quite satisfying to the worker. Initially, the move to an enriched job would require closer and more frequent supervision, especially if the worker has to rely on his supervisor for the training necessary to master new and often more difficult job skills. Going from a state of independence to even a temporary state of dependence may not be welcomed by the worker.

- A fourth reason for resisting job enrichment is characteristic of any change, at work or otherwise, and is commonly known as psychological habit.

Originally Chester Barnard, and since, many others, believed that psychological habit is a major cause of resisting change. Barnard noted that "Another incentive . . . is that of customary working conditions and conformity to habitual practices and attitudes. . . . It is taken for granted that men will not or cannot do well by strange methods or under strange conditions. What is not so obvious is that men will frequently not attempt to cooperate if they recognize that such methods or conditions are to be accepted."[28] Barnard's argument seems to directly apply to the modern job enrichment technique.

CONCLUSIONS

The preceding discussion of worker motivation, job design, and resistance to change was geared toward answering the question of whether job enrichment really pays off. Obviously, there is no simple answer. On the other hand, the preceding analysis of job enrichment has raised some very significant but badly neglected points that need emphasis. These include the following:

1.   There seems to be a substantial number of workers who are not necessarily alienated from work but are alienated from the middle class values expressed by the job enrichment concept. For these workers, job content is not automatically related to job satisfaction, and motivation is not necessarily a function of job satisfaction. These alienated workers are capable of finding need satisfaction outside the work environment. If they do experience satisfaction at work, it is not strictly the result of job content or formal job design but instead is largely influenced by social interactions with other primary group members. Job enrichment may not motivate this type of worker.

2.   For some workers, improved job design by job enrichment is not seen as an even trade for the reduced opportunity for social interaction. The present job may be considered unpleasant and boring, but breaking up existing patterns or social isolation is completely unbearable.

3.   The introduction of a job enrichment program may have a negative impact on some workers and result in feelings of inadequacy, fear of failure, and a concern for dependency. For these employees, low level competency, security, and relative independence are more important than the opportunity for greater responsibility and personal growth in enriched jobs.

These three points do not negate nor are they intended to be a total indictment of the job enrichment concept. On the other hand, they are intended to emphasize that job enrichment is not a cure-all for all the human problems presently facing modern management. This word of caution seems very appropriate at the present time. Many management professors and practitioners have jumped on the job enrichment bandwagon without carefully considering the research and analysis that is reported in this article. If nothing else, both professors and practitioners should take another hard look at their position on job enrichment as a method of motivating workers.

Like all sound management programs, job enrichment must be used *selectively* and with due consideration to situational variables such as the characteristics of the job, the organizational level, and the personal characteristics of the employees. Finally, job enrichment probably works best in organizations which have a supportive climate for innovation and change and a management which is genuinely interested in achieving greater job satisfaction for *its own sake*. Under these conditions, job enrichment can be practiced successfully and can offer great potential for the future, not only in terms of enriching the work experience for countless organizational participants, but also for increased productivity and organizational goal accomplishment.

REFERENCES

1. See William J. Paul, Jr., Keith B. Robertson, and Frederick Herzberg, "Job Enrichment Pays Off," *Harvard Business Review* (March-April, 1969), pp. 61-78.
2. See Valerie M. Bockman, "The Herzberg Controversy," *Personnel Psychology* (Vol. 24, No. 2, 1971), pp. 155-189.
3. See Peter P. Schoderbek and William E. Reif, *Job Enlargement* (Ann Arbor, Michigan: Bureau of Industrial Relations, Graduate School of Business Administration, The University of Michigan, 1969).

4. Harold M. F. Rush, "Behavioral Science—Concepts and Management Application," *Studies in Personnel Policy, No. 216* (New York: National Industrial Conference Board, 1969).
5. Mitchell Fein, *Approaches to Motivation* (Hillsdale, N.J.: 1970), p. 20.
6. Robert N. Ford, *Motivation Through the Work Itself* (New York: American Management Association, Inc., 1969), p. 188.
7. *Ibid.*, p. 189.
8. James E. Kennedy and Harry E. O'Neill, "Job Content and Workers' Opinions." *Journal of Applied Psychology* (Vol. 42, No. 6, 1958), p. 375.
9. Charles L. Hulin and Milton R. Blood, "Job Enlargement, Individual Differences, and Worker Responses," *Psychological Bulletin* (Vol. 69, No. 1, 1968), p. 50.
10. See Frederick Herzberg, *Work and the Nature of Man* (Cleveland: The World Publishing Company, 1966); also, Douglas McGregor, *Leadership and Motivation* (The MIT Press, 1966); also Rensis Likert, *The Human Organization* (New York: McGraw-Hill Book Company, 1967); also Chris Argyris, *Personality and Organization* (New York: Harper & Row, Publishers, 1957); also Chris Argyris, *Integrating the Individual and the Organization* (New York: John Wiley & Sons, Inc., 1964); and Robert Blake and Jane Mouton, *Corporate Excellence Through Grid Organizational Development* (Houston: Gulf Publishing Company, 1968).
11. Douglas McGregor, *op. cit.*, p. 40.
12. Paul, Robertson, and Herzberg, *op. cit.*
13. Mitchell Fein, *op. cit.*, p 15.
14. Peter P. Schoderbek and William E. Reif, *op. cit.*, pp. 41-72
15. Harold M. F. Rush, *Job Design for Motivation, Conference Board Report, No. 515* (New York: The Conference Board, Inc., 1971), p. 10.
16. Patricia C. Smith, "The Prediction of Individual Differences in Susceptibility to Industrial Monotony," *Journal of Applied Psychology* (Vol. 39, No. 5, 1955), pp. 322-329; also Patricia C. Smith and Charles Lem, "Positive Aspects of Motivation in Repetitive Work: Effects of Lot Size Upon Spacing of Voluntary Work Stoppages," *Journal of Applied Psychology* (Vol. 39, No. 5, 1955), pp. 330-333; also Maurice D. Kilbridge, "Do Workers Prefer Larger Jobs?" *Personnel* (Sept.-Oct., 1960), pp. 45-48; also Wilhelm Baldamus, *Efficiency and Effort: An Analysis of Industrial Administration* (London: Tavistock Publications, 1967); also Victor H. Vrooms, *Some Personality Determinants of the Effects of Participation* (Englewood Cliffs: Prentice-Hall, Inc., 1960); also Arthur N. Turner and Amelia L. Miclette, "Sources of Satisfaction in Repetitive Work," *Occupational Psychology* (Vol. 36, No. 4, 1962), pp. 215-231; and Arthur W. Kornhauser, *Mental Health of the Industrial Worker: a Detroit Study* (New York: John Wiley & Sons, Inc., 1965).
17. William E. Reif and Peter P. Schoderbek, "Job Enlargement: Antidote to Apathy," *Management of Personnel Quarterly* (Spring, 1966), pp. 16-23.
18. Hulin and Blood, *op. cit.*
19. Mitchell Fein, *op. cit.*, p. 31.
20. *Ibid.*, p. 37.
21. David C. McClelland and David J. Winter, *Motivating Economic Achievement* (New York: The Free Press, 1969).
22. Hulin and Blood, *op. cit.*, p. 49.
23. Louis E. Davis, "The Design of Jobs," *Industrial Relations* (October, 1966), pp. 21-45.
24. Herzberg, *op. cit.*

25. Chester I. Barnard, *The Functions of the Executive* (Cambridge, Mass.: Harvard University Press, 1938), p. 119.
26. Reif and Schoderbek, *op. cit.*, pp. 16-23.
27. *Ibid.*, pp. 64-70
28. Chester I. Barnard, *op. cit.*, p. 77.

Job Redesign, Reform, Enrichment — Exploring the Limitations

Sar A. Levitan and William B. Johnston

American industry has long been committed to redesign of executive and professional jobs with a view to improving the quality of work. Recently this interest in the quality of managerial, professional, and high-level sales jobs has been extended to other white-collar workers. Sometimes reports on these experiments (as well as those involving blue-collar workers) imply and occasionally state that sweeping, even radical, job reform is in the offing and can be undertaken once inertia in the workplace is overcome. But is widespread job reform possible? Is it necessary? This article considers some of the limitations on job reform. But first a few examples of the type and scope of experiments in job redesign should be considered.

In 1965, American Telephone and Telegraph Co. began experimenting with new job designs for clerical workers in an attempt to cut turnover and improve productivity. Analyzing the work of the office staffs, the job designers found most departments had compartmentalized and divided the work into essentially a paper-pushing assembly line. Few workers appreciated their work or took pride in their accomplishments. The results were high rates of turnover, low productivity, and low quality output.

To improve things, the planners analyzed the task to be performed, for ex-

From *Monthly Labor Review*, 96 (July 1973). Reprinted by permission from Sar A. Levitan and William B. Johnston, WORK IS HERE TO STAY, ALAS (Salt Lake City: Olympus Publishing Company, 1973), © 1973 by Olympus Publishing Company.

ample, service order processing, telephone book assembly, or customer billing. They reevaluated the division of labor based upon ideas of the overall job to be performed. Instead of having order-form clerks, typists, and bill verifiers, they assigned entire modules of work to individuals. Telephone book assemblers were given the entire job of processing and verifying a book or sections of a book. Billing clerks were given complete responsibility for certain accounts, rather than a single operation on each account. In many cases, typists took over tasks once routinely assigned to "higher ups." Along with job enlargement, the designers initiated changes in office layout and grouping of personnel, to facilitate communication among employees with related jobs.

Almost all of these changes had positive results. In many instances productivity rose and output was more prompt and error-free. The improvement in employee morale was often spectacular. Employees seemed to take pride in their new jobs and began to learn the jobs of those around them. Absenteeism fell sharply and turnover decreased in most cases.[1]

The AT&T methods have been duplicated in a variety of companies and situations. For example, at Bankers Trust and Merrill Lynch, Pierce, Fenner, and Smith in New York, the fractionated, time-consuming tasks of processing new stock certificates were consolidated into jobs for one worker. In both cases, significant money savings were realized, in terms of increased productivity, and in freed supervisory time.[2]

A similar job enrichment program was initiated by Xerox for its technical representatives. Machine servicemen were given more authority to decide expenses, schedule work, order inventories, interview and train new personnel, and determine workloads. After an initial adjustment period, the company found that men in the enriched jobs achieved higher performance standards than managers had previously been able to command.[3]

BLUE-COLLAR EXPERIMENTS

Work restructuring also has been tried in factories. The redesigners of blue-collar work have utilized two basic approaches—"participative management" and task reassignment—along with improvements in working conditions designed to minimize differences in status. In most cases, participative management has been favored because production technology allows little leeway in the delegation of tasks. On the assumption that even a dirty, dull, or unpleasant task can be made more acceptable if the worker has the responsibility for deciding where, when, and how fast it will be done, these plans have concentrated on developing a spirit of cooperation and teamwork on the job.

One of the oldest and most widely noted attempts at improving productivity through worker participation has been carried out at the Donnelly Mirrors Corp.

of Holland, Mich. Nearly a decade ago the company, which makes auto mirrors, dramatically expanded its concepts of incentive plans and open-line communication, instituting democratic reforms which sought to humanize assemblyline production. The employees were divided into task-oriented teams who set production goals. The workers had the authority to control the pace of product assembly and the assignment of jobs along the assembly line. In addition, all employees received salaries, rather than hourly wages, and they collectively set the rates at which they would be paid. In return for this, the employees also had responsibility for implementing productivity increases to support pay raises. In essence, the production function was delegated to the men on the line.

Reported results were impressive. The quality of production jumped sharply, even though inspectors were cut two-thirds. Scrap losses dropped by 75 percent from their former level and goods returned amounted to less than a tenth of previous volume. Productivity gains have resulted in an average salary bonus of 12 percent since the changes were instituted. Wages have risen steadily while unit production costs have fallen, enabling the company to decrease prices, expand sales, and increase profits.[4]

Donnelly's history is the most successful but not the only model of delegating responsibility to workers to increase satisfaction, productivity, and company profits. At Texas Instruments, full responsibility for janitorial service was delegated to the workers involved. The men met to decide how the work would be divided, and to set up schedules and establish standards for jobs. The sense of personal involvement made possible a reduction in manpower from 120 to 71, a rise in cleanliness evaluations from 65 to 85 percent, and a remarkable alleviation of the problem of worker turnover from 100 to 10 percent quarterly.[5]

Other plans involving changes in job tasks (for example, from assembly line to benchwork production) and job rotation have been instituted at Motorola Corp. (Plantation, Fla.), Corning Glass Co. (Medford, Mass.), the Maytag Co., and by General Foods at its Gaines Pet Food Plant (Topeka, Kans.).[6] All of these experiments have had some degree of success with respect to better employee performance, morale, and productivity.

GAPS IN THE ADVOCATES' CASE

These experiments with job redesign are all "success" stories. Indeed, most of the literature on work reform is the product of advocates reporting positive results. But there are major gaps in the case for job reform. Companies which find authoritarian controls and unchanged job rewards to be as successful as ever are not included in the surveys. Companies whose enrichment and participation plans turn sour rarely trumpet the news.

The productivity gains resulting from these projects are seldom controlled against gains from alternative innovations, and have not been followed over long enough periods to be considered permanent. Some studies have reported a "Hawthorne effect" in which productivity can be improved by either autocratic or democratic changes in management style. Thus, the experimenters may have concluded, more on faith than hard facts, that democratic techniques will eventually prove superior because of the investment in "human assets."[7] But the history of varied schemes to develop workers' sense of participation and support for corporate goals makes it clear that reforms which rely on the morale or attitudes of the work force cannot be guaranteed to last.

Just as today's young union members have little appreciation for the wages and working conditions won by earlier generations, so new workers in "humanized" plants may fail to find their work upgraded or more enjoyable. Those who were present when assembly lines were changed to benchwork, or those who remember the authoritarian supervision before the introduction of participative management, may appreciate the better quality of their work. But positive reactions resulting from innovations inevitably fade as novel systems become routines. Moreover, new arrivals will be likely to see only jobs with certain tasks, wages, and bosses. This is, of course, no argument against making changes, but they should be made because of intrinsic merits and not because they will lead to everlasting rises in productivity.

Cogent reasons suggest that the possibilities for reforming work may be limited. The projections of assembly lines abolished, jobs humanized, and productivity spiralling in the industrial world of the future are highly tentative. Neither the alternative of improving the work itself through job enrichment, nor the correlative approach of molding more satisfied employees by allowing them greater control of their work lives, is certain to have sweeping results.

LIMITS OF PARTICIPATIVE MANAGEMENT

Participative decisionmaking, profit-sharing, and autonomous work arrangements all seek to unite the individual's goals and the firm's. It is easy to see, however, that the goals of any sizable corporation and those of its employees are not easily harmonized. The ideal of communal effort in which a group of individuals are united by common beliefs to achieve a common aim is foreign to large corporate enterprises. The firm is interested in profits, with most other goals being measured by how they affect this single variable. The firm's employees, especially the production workers, are concerned with improving their lives, a goal only incidentally connected with the corporation's success and in part opposed to it because there is only one corporate revenue pie to be divided. By its nature, the corporation is not primarily concerned with workers' lives. Unless corporate enterprise were to radically alter its functions to make the welfare of its employees its first reason for being, it is hypothetical to talk of "internalizing" the firm's goals.

It has been suggested that the key to participative management is profit-sharing. But profit-sharing and even outright ownership by workers, would for any large organization be hopelessly diffused and diluted. It is doubtful that the marginal increase in income generated by full distribution of profits could do much to change workers' attitudes towards their jobs, or that a few shares of stock could do much to transform employees into members of the corporate "family." Overall, the total of all corporate after-tax profits would add less than 10 percent to employee compensation.

The idea of profit-sharing based on small production units highlights the basic goal of participative management. At bottom, all such changes seek to re-partition industry into organizations of smaller size, where the individual does not get "lost." Autonomous work groups who make their own decisions and pocket their own profits would actually be tiny companies who have become sub-contractors to the larger organizations. The breaking up of the corporation into small units may indeed be desirable from the standpoint of improving the quality of work, but it runs counter to the established principles of efficient industrial organization and is not conducive to optimizing profits.

Rhetoric about a community of interest cannot obliterate elemental conflicts between employees and employers. Many workers in subservient jobs continue to accurately perceive their work as unstimulating activity in the service of others. They see themselves neither as supporters of the free enterprise system nor as contributors to their enterprise's profit. With unflinching realism, they see themselves as bolt tighteners and machine tenders, occupations which they do not find exciting or meaningful. Inevitably, they are dissatisfied with their work and seek to change or escape it. The kind of worker control or independence which could relieve this kind of alienation is not likely to be granted without an up-heaval in corporate structures. Even then it is not clear that the new order would lead to greater work satisfaction.

ENRICHING JOBS

Paralleling the challenge to traditional ideas of work organization and super-vision are challenges to accepted rules for designing jobs and dividing tasks. Theorists of work reform emphasize that work roles are not inalterably defined by the technology of production. Underlying work redesign proposals is the ar-gument that within any technological framework there are equally productive alternatives.

Recognition that technology is not an absolute determinant of jobs does not negate its decisive influence. Without question, technology, especially its hardware, is far and away the most important factor in job design. Milling machines, computers, forklifts, and arc welders determine what tasks will be performed, dwarfing in importance work arrangements or task assignments.

The capital investment required to significantly alter methods of production is awesome. If manufacturing jobs have hardened in molds cast generations ago, much of the reason lies in the physical plant and machinery accumulated over the years. Plants manufacturing durable goods average over $25,000 of fixed capital per worker. In the oil industry, this rises to over $125,000. Because product cost in capital-intensive industries is less affected by variations in employee productivity, employers may be more willing to experiment with innovations to improve working conditions because failure would entail little risk. But changes which would require replacement of expensive capital are less appealing, particularly if managers cannot be assured the changes will lead to greater profits as well as better quality work. If changes in technology and hardware to improve the quality of work are to be made, they must also promise higher profits.

Champions of job enrichment have, of course, pitched their appeals to the profit motive. They urge that eliminating high turnover rates, raising product quality, decreasing waste, tapping firsthand knowledge for design innovations, and cutting manpower requirements are productive and profitable improvements. But even when changes in techniques and processes appear financially sound, there are other limitations to their adoption. For example, changes which are feasible in the production of small items may not apply to larger products. The inescapable problem of storing and moving large components means that assembling cars or refrigerators or engines probably can be accomplished most efficiently on a moving line. The widely heralded "benchwork" assembly methods involved products with small components, fairly lengthy assembly times, and few tools.

At some point, suggestions for enlarging jobs, increasing skills, lengthening job cycles, or rotating tasks bump into the logic which dictated division of labor in the first place. Essentially, job enrichers counsel more complex jobs with longer training times. But the present system favoring simple jobs originated as part of a long trend to greater specialization, which may be psychically expensive, but is economically cheap. It is possible that in many industries jobs have become too specialized and that workers could produce more if they had more interest in their work. Specialization may go too far and become counterproductive, but it cannot be denied that division of labor, as Adam Smith argued two centuries ago, is an essential ingredient of efficient mass production. The return to craft production may be humanly desirable, but it is impractical. Every addition to jobs which requires workers to spend more time learning the job, or alternating tools, or which entails greater inventories or duplication of tools is likely to raise unit costs. The reactions of managers to suggestions which involve new production techniques or job realignments are therefore understandably cautious. Production methods have been developed not from the arbitrary decisions of engineers, or even as a result of the inevitable progression of technology, but in a rational search for efficiency. Industrial survival of the fittest has produced a species not easily changed for the better.

Can efficient mass production ever provide challenging or creative work? A surgeon doomed to perform appendectomies for his entire career would likely come to envy a butcher who at least could carve different cuts of meat. Repetition, the foundation of mass production, slays interest. Although job rotation may hold some hope for relieving monotony, it is wishful thinking to ignore the inherent limitations on job design imposed by repeated identical operations.

It is understandable, then, that many production workers and some union leaders have tended to view workplace reforms and enriched jobs with distrust. From the vantage point of the dissatisfied worker, management, as the instigator of work redesign, is suspected of perpetrating another elaborate ploy to convince the skeptical that a lousy job is after all important or challenging or likeable. Without fundamental changes in the kinds of jobs industrial workers do, can job enrichment and motivating workers with "challenging work" be more than subtle con games? In this regard, reports of increased absenteeism, turnover, sabotage, and other visible signs of discontent do not forecast the death of the work ethic, but rather logical and long-delayed reactions by workers to jobs that are not worth doing well, or perhaps worth doing at all.

The kinds of changes which could relieve these suspicions are not likely to occur as rapidly as supporters of job enrichment hope. Personnel psychologists may sweep through factories putting glass windows in the manager's office, unlocking executive toilets, taking out time clocks, and having the workers meet on company time to set their daily schedules. But when they finish, the same machines and hands will go back to cranking out coffee pots or card tables or cookie jars. As long as processes remain the same, and machines are unable to perform all the tasks of production, job improvement for manufacturing workers will be partly just a new cosmetic on the same old crone.

SOCIAL EFFICIENCY MODEL

Recognizing the costs involved in meaningful job reform, some reformers have argued that job enrichment should control the design of production processes, even if productivity is reduced. They suggest that "social efficiency" should be given priority over considerations of purely economic efficiency.[8] The argument is that unrewarding, inhuman work has high costs in terms of social alienation, poor health, violent aggression, and other social ills. Enriching the work experience, even if it were economically costly, would be socially beneficial.

Conceptually appealing though they are, these arguments are hardly practical.

Faced with a choice between satisfying its workers and maintaining its profits, a corporation could be expected to resist job humanization. Nor is there evidence of any social groundswell of sacrificial spirit, or willingness by industrial workers to lower their standards of living in order to have more satisfying jobs. Any retreat to more primitive, costly, and "human" methods of manufacturing would require governmental intervention likely to be rejected by owners and workers.

Is it not more reasonable to assume that increased specialization and large hierarchical organizations are not accidents, but logical developments in a complex society seeking to support its growing population at an ever-rising standard of living? Whatever the price that society is paying in terms of "dehumanized" jobs in monolithic, faceless organizations, it is unrealistic to hark back to a simpler world in which organizations were small and jobs were large, as though the paradise lost could be regained. Specialized roles and specialized knowledge are essential to large organizations, and large organizations appear unavoidable in an advanced society.

To some extent, hierarchies can be leveled and the roles of individuals interchanged and broadened; but the constraints on such developments cannot be overcome by planned social change or even by violent social upheaval. Improved social efficiency cannot proceed along opposite paths to industrial efficiency, but must parallel it. Without the tremendous affluence generated in large part by efficient mass production, there would be no alternative life styles or occupations for workers to envy, and no time to invest in the education which has contributed to some workers' dissatisfaction with their jobs.

Despite all this, improvements *can* be made by rotating workers among jobs, by enlarging jobs, by expanding responsibility. Generally, managements (and unions) have done too little to change working conditions which could be improved. But there can be no gainsaying that meaningful work and maximum productivity are at odds in important ways. Until the machine entirely replaces man in the performance of routine tasks, man as adjunct to machines will likely be restless.

FALLACY OF RADICAL WORK REFORM

The limitations imposed by the imperatives of efficiency suggest that job designers face stubborn obstacles to the humanist reformation of work. The evidence that productivity will necessarily increase if jobs are humanized is far from conclusive, and an argument can be made that the technology of efficient production leaves little room for extensive job reform. Neither can a "social efficiency" model be used to justify a reduction of economic efficiency in order to improve jobs. Moreover, are workers that interested in job redesign? Is the quality of worklife the main standard by which they judge the quality of their lives? It appears that for most workers the quality of work is less important than the standard of living.

In making their case, job redesigners often use examples of workers on assembly lines in steel and textile mills, oil refineries, and machine tool factories. However, occupational data indicate the collective importance of these workers is declining. Though they have serious job problems, these workers constitute a relatively small fraction of the expanding labor force. Moreover, the advance of technology allows more production with fewer men. For example, the entire oil industry requires but 200,000 production workers, and a handful of supervisors manage to run the refineries during strikes. Thus, the most important effect of technical advance is that it shifts employment away from mechanized manufacturing processes to the jobs which are difficult if not impossible to automate—services and the professions.

Moreover, in discussing workers "trapped" in routine factory jobs, some workplace analysts often seem to see reflections of themselves: the descriptions of work sound as though the factories were filled with restless inquisitive consultants chained to assembly lines. There seem to be no placid TV watchers, none who may be pleased with simple, repetitive tasks or high wages or long weekends. From such assumptions it is not difficult for these analysts to discover great reservoirs of alienation and to claim that profound changes must be made in work. A generation too late, they are suggesting dubious solutions to problems which were gradually being solved by the elimination of such work.

One view is that the jobs of the future will demand workers who can cope with rapidly evolving technology and constantly changing environments. But a glance at the seven largest expanding occupational groups—secretaries (3.8 million); retail sales clerks (3.1 million); precollege teachers (2.7 million); restaurant workers (2.5 million); drivers and deliverymen (2.4 million); bookkeepers and cashiers (2.4 million); and cleaning workers (2.2 million)—reveals that none of these jobs is undergoing rapid change. The last great technological change in the jobs of retail sales workers was the invention of the cash register in 1879. Secretarial typing tasks have not been altered basically since the introduction of the shift register almost a century ago. Despite the proliferation of educational theories, teachers still explain concepts, assign homework, and grade tests much as they did in Abraham Lincoln's day. Janitors have witnessed the sweeping change from brooms to vacuum cleaners, and waitresses now serve bottled rather than draft beer, but few would argue that these jobs have been revolutionized by technology. (This is not to say that significant organizational changes have not occurred, such as greater use of self service, assignment of administrative duties to secretaries, and greater specialization of teaching functions.)

Another school predicts crisis in the industrial workplace as workers will increasingly reject meaningless jobs. But this prophecy ignores society's method for matching workers to jobs. The economic system determines whether a job is worth doing. Industry may find that it will have to pay higher wages for some jobs, or that the most onerous jobs will price themselves out of the market. If workers make themselves unavailable for certain jobs at any reasonable wage, then it may be expected that few employers will be willing to hire them. In return for dollar rewards, workers will either accept or reject employment. In return for tasks performed, employers will either hire or fire.

While the foregoing points up some weaknesses in the arguments for job reform, the critics of current work arrangements are far from wrong in their central thrust. In general, they hold a kernel of the truth. But repeatedly in making their arguments, the trees blind them to the forest. There *is* a problem with the design of work but not a massive problem of revolutionary significance. There *are* specific solutions but no one solution of utopian finality. Like social critics in other areas, some job reformers have become oversold on the need for change and in their ability to bring it about.

The way in which work is created is often ignored in reformers' analysis. Jobs are established by aggregate demand coupled with technological possibility. Society currently supports 828,000 janitors, 430,000 gas station attendants, and 125,000 librarians. The work these people do can be eliminated either by reducing demand for it, or by building machines to perform it. A host of factors can influence the demand for certain types of work, notably government priorities, advertising, education, and income levels. But jobs are created by the willingness of some part of society to pay for the performance of them.

Moreover, once tasks are determined they cannot be changed much. Basically, janitors sweep floors, gas station attendants pump gas, and librarians keep books on shelves, no matter what surroundings or supervision they have. More than anything else, the job itself will determine how a person will react to it. Society's requirements have already preempted much of the leeway for designing jobs. Once the tasks to be performed have been determined, work designers may shuffle the tasks among people, or put white collars on them, but work can only be truly reformed by shifts in the aggregate demand for labor. All the shuffling of assignments, rotation of duties, recombination of tasks, or restructuring of organizations and supervisory methods cannot change the basic nature of the work to be performed.

As employment shifts further away from production for survival, society should be freer to determine what work will be done based upon what people want to do. Man tends to attack the unpleasant or bothersome aspects of life first; thus, the worst work will steadily be eliminated or changed. In some future, perhaps, machines will allow everyone to work at meaningful jobs. Until then, however, work will probably continue to be organized in a way that makes it simple, easily learned, and which promotes greatest efficiency and maximum production. As yet, society continues to pay for a great variety of jobs the tasks of which some people find undesirable.

The obvious limitations of job enrichment should not be taken as mandates to maintain the status quo in the workplace. Though the experimental evidence on job reform is incomplete and the problem may not be as serious as some have claimed, job reformers are addressing issues of importance. Further research may determine that the improvements are temporary and the productivity gains disappointingly small when compared with other methods of improving productivity. But the job reform results thus far indicate that substantial improvements can be made within the framework of efficient, profitable enterprises. The upgrading of work which can be realized from redesigned jobs may not promise nirvana for all workers, but it is clearly a change for the better. The various strategies for reinvolving alienated workers deserve to be tried, not because they can be expected to solve *the* problem of the workplace but because they are likely to raise in some measure the quality of work and of life. When these innovations come to represent the wishes of workers (rather than those of productivity-minded managers or well-intentioned consultants) they should be instituted. The egalitarian ideal of enjoyable work for all may be unattainable, but a just society should aspire to no less.

FOOTNOTES

1. Robert N. Ford, "Job Enrichment Lessons from AT&T," *Harvard Business Review,* January-February 1973, p. 96.
2. Roger Rickleffs, "The Quality of Work," *The Wall Street Journal,* Aug. 21, 1972, p. 1.
3. Carl D. Jacobs, "Job Enrichment at Xerox Corporation," paper presented at the International Conference on the Quality of Work Life, Sept. 24–29, 1972, Arden House, New York.
4. Judson Gooding, "It Pays to Wake Up the Blue-Collar Worker," *Fortune,* September 1970, p. 162.
5. Neil Q. Herrick, "The Other Side of the Coin," unpublished paper delivered at the Twentieth Anniversary Invitational Seminar of the Profit Sharing Research Foundation, Evanston, Ill., Nov. 17, 1971.
6. James F. Biggane and Paul A. Stewart, "Job Enlargement: A Case Study," Louis E. Davis and James C. Taylor, eds., *Design of Jobs* (Baltimore, Md., Penguin Books, Inc., 1972), pp. 264–76. Richard E. Walton, "How to Counter Alienation in the Plant," *Harvard Business Review,* November-December 1972, pp. 70–81.
7. George Strauss, "Organizational Behavior and Personnel Relations," *Review of Industrial Relations Research,* Madison, Wis., Industrial Relations Research Association, 1970, p. 159.
8. *Work in America: Report of a Special Task Force to the Secretary of Health, Education, and Welfare, Prepared under the Auspices of the W. E. Upjohn Institute for Employment Research* (Cambridge, Mass., The MIT Press, 1973), p. 19.

13   Job Enrichment: A Union View

William W. Winpisinger

The recent rash of strikes and other labor problems at the General Motors plant in Lordstown, Ohio, has been cited by some as proof that even if the nature of the assembly line hasn't changed, the work force has. As every student of industrial relations knows, the overwhelming majority of the work force at Lordstown is young. On the basis of management's unhappy experiences with these young workers, the experts have solemnly proclaimed the discovery of a new kind of work force. They inform us that here is a generation that has never known a depression and thus has no interest in security. Here is a generation that grew up in a time of crass materialism and thus rejects the work ethic. Here is a generation that has been infected by the rebellion of youth and thus has no respect for authority. I have seen one scholarly analysis, in fact, that compares the "rebellion" at Lordstown in the early 1970's with the free speech movement at Berkeley in the early 1960's. And the conclusion was drawn that the Nation's factories, like her colleges, would never be the same again.

That kind of analysis overlooks one salient fact. The young workers at Lordstown were reacting against the same kind of grievances, in the same kind of way, as did generations of workers before them. They were rebelling against an obvious speedup. They were protesting safety violations. They were reacting against working conditions that had been unilaterally imposed by a management that was determined to get tough in the name of efficiency. Anyone who thinks that wildcats or slowdowns or even sabotage started with Lordstown doesn't know very much about the history of the American labor movement.

An almost identical series of incidents took place over much the same issues at Norwood, Ohio, at almost the same time, but very few inferences were drawn about the changing nature of the work force because, in this case, it was older workers who were involved.

Many people are viewing with alarm the decline of the work ethic in the United States. On the basis of my experience, which includes many day-to-day contacts with rank-and-file members of the Machinists union, I can assure you that the work ethic is alive and well and living in a lot of good work places.

But what the aerospace workers and auto mechanics and machinists and airline mechanics and production workers *we* represent want, in the way of job sat-

---

Abstract of a paper, "Job Enrichment: Another Part of the Forest," in PROCEEDINGS OF THE 25TH ANNIVERSARY MEETING' INDUSTRIAL RELATIONS RESEARCH ASSOCIATION, ed. Gerald G. Somers (Madison: The Association, 1973).

isfaction, is a wage that is commensurate with their skills.

If you want to enrich the job, enrich the paycheck. The better the wage, the greater the job satisfaction. There is no better cure for the "blue-collar blues."

If you want to enrich the job, begin to decrease the number of hours a worker has to labor in order to earn a decent standard of living. Just as the increased productivity of mechanized assembly lines made it possible to decrease the workweek from 60 to 40 hours a couple of generations ago, the time has come to translate the increased productivity of automated processes into the kind of enrichment that comes from shorter workweeks, longer vacations, and earlier retirements.

If you want to enrich the job, do something about the nerve-shattering noise, the heat, and the fumes that are deafening, poisoning, and destroying the health of American workers. Thousands of chemicals are being used in workplaces whose effect on humans has never been tested. Companies are willing to spend millions advertising quieter refrigerators or washing machines, but are reluctant to spend one penny to provide a reasonably safe level of noise in their plants.

If you want to enrich the jobs of the men and women who manufacture the goods that are needed for the functioning of our industrialized society, the time has come to reevaluate the snobbery that makes it noble to possess a college degree and shameful to learn skills that involve a little bit of grease under the fingernails. The best way to undermine a worker's morale, and decrease his satisfaction with himself and his job, is to make him feel that society looks down on him because he wears blue coveralls instead of a white collar. I think it is ironic that, because of prevailing attitudes, many kinds of skilled craftsmen are in short supply while college graduates are tripping over one another in search of jobs.

Some of the most dissatisfied people I know are those who got a college degree and then couldn't find a position that lived up to their expectations. And that's been especially true the last few years. There are college-trained people driving cabs today who would have had a lot more job satisfaction and made a lot more money if they had apprenticed as auto mechanics.

If you want to enrich the job, give working people a greater sense of control over their working conditions. That's what they, and their unions, were seeking in the early 1960's when management was automating and retooling on a large scale. That's why we asked for advance consultation when employers intended to make major job changes. That's why we negotiated for clauses providing retraining and transfer rights and a fair share of the increased productivity that resulted from automation.

What workers resent, and what really causes alienation, are management decisions that rearrange job assignments or upset existing work schedules without reference to the rights of the work force.

If you want to enrich the job, you must realize that no matter how dull or boring or dirty it may be, an individual worker must feel that he has not reached the end of the line. If a worker is to be reasonably satisfied with the job he has today, he must have hope for something better tomorrow.

You know this is true in universities, in government, and in management. I submit that even on assembly lines there must be some chance of movement, even if it's only from a job that requires stooping down to one that involves standing erect. But here again, we are talking about a job problem for which unionism provides an answer. And the name of that answer is the negotiated seniority clause. Perhaps workers were not thinking in terms of job enrichment when they first negotiated the right to bid on better shifts, overtime, or promotions on the basis of length of service. Perhaps they were only trying to restrict management's right to allocate jobs and shifts and overtime on the basis of favoritism. But even if they weren't thinking in terms of "job enrichment," in actual practice that's what they got.

It's true that many young workers in their 20's resent the fact that—while they have to tighten the same old bolt in the same old spot a thousand times a day—the guys in their 40's are walking up and down the line with inspection sheets or running around the factory on forklifts. They may resent it *now,* but they also know that they are accumulating seniority which they can trade for a better job of their own some day.

Yes, there are many ways in which jobs can be enriched. But I don't think those I have mentioned are what management has in mind when it talks about job enrichment. On the basis of fairly extensive experience as a union representative, I find it hard to picture management enriching jobs at the expense of profits. In fact, I have a sneaking suspicion that "job enrichment" may be just another name for "time and motion" study. As Thomas Brooks said in a recent article in the AFL—CIO *Federationist,* "Substituting the sociologist's questionnaire for the stop watch is likely to be no gain for the workers. While workers have a stake in productivity, it is not always identical with that of management. Job enrichment programs have cut jobs just as effectively as automation and stop watches. And the rewards of productivity are not always equitably shared."

I also have a feeling that what some companies call job enrichment is really little more than the introduction of gimmicks, like doing away with timeclocks or developing "work teams" or designing jobs to "maximize personal involvement" —whatever that means.

I know there are those who worry about what the younger generation is coming to, and wonder whether the rebellious young workers of today will be willing to fill their father's shoes in the factory jobs of tomorrow. But, there is little doubt, and all the studies tend to prove, that worker dissatisfaction diminishes with age. And that's because older workers have accrued more of the kinds of job enrichment that unions have fought for—better wages, shorter hours, vested pensions, a right to have a say in their working conditions, the right to be promoted on the basis of seniority, and all the rest. That's the kind of job enrichment that unions believe in. And I assure you that that's the kind of job enrichment that we will continue to fight for.

Section C

Money as a Motivator: Dollars and Sense

Herzberg's dual-factor theory of motivation suggests that money is not a motivator whereas challenging work is. Shadows have been cast on the job enrichment thesis, however, and other evidence has drawn attention to the economic aspects of work. For example, although not reprinted here, an article in the *New York Times* (January 21, 1973) headlined "The Real Cause of Workers' Discontent: Maybe It's Pay Basis Instead of a Dull Job."

Questioning the *Work in America* report, the *Times* article reviewed a study of over 2500 sewing-machine operators in 17 factories from New England to the Southwest United States (70 percent of the plants were unionized). Workers were asked to respond to a variety of questions including, "If I ever left this job it would be most of all for the following things." Given thirteen choices including job enrichment, leisure time, and better working conditions, the most frequently selected items were: (1) more job security, (2) pay equal to other plants, (3) more or different fringe benefits, and (4) a four-day, forty-hour workweek. The major conclusion? Economic factors may hold more promise than often recognized for gaining worker commitment and job performance.

The *Times* article dealt with blue-collar workers, but the same question of money as a motivator clearly has application to managerial employees. Unfortunately, with several exceptions, the exploration of pay and managerial performance has been neglected in the organizational literature. To draw attention to this important subject, articles by Lawler and McConkey have been included in this section.

Lawler's selection, "The Mythology of Management Comprehension," examines common misconceptions that managers have about the meaning and administration of pay. The article is based on a study in which managers from a wide variety of organizational settings indicated their agreement or disagreement with five statements regarding the psychological meaning of money and its link to performance. Comparing the results with other relevant research, Lawler found that many assumptions about pay were invalid or only partially valid. His discussion shows how some managers view pay as satisfying only lower-order needs, ignore the hidden costs of secret pay policies, and fail to tie pay to performance.

Lawler's work sets the stage for the second article, by McConkey, which uses parables to deal with "The 'Jackass Effect' in Management Compensation." McConkey's premise is that money will motivate but not when the "jackass effect" is present in a compensation plan. This novel effect has five variations and is present whenever managers are unclear about their expected results or when pay is not related to performance. According to McConkey, all variations of this effect can be overcome by following a plan of action which establishes management accountability, sets performance measures, and rewards achievement in an equitable way. McConkey's focus is on money, but implicitly raises the issue of management by objectives, a topic considered separately later in this book.

14   The Mythology of Management Compensation
Edward E Lawler III

A host of decisions have to be made every day concerning compensation practices, decisions that are of critical importance in determining the success of any business organization. Unfortunately, relatively little is known about the psychological meaning of money and how it motivates people. Unanswered are such critical questions as:

- How often should a raise be given?
- What are the effects of secrecy about pay?
- How should benefit programs be packaged?

In the absence of systematic knowledge, executives have had to answer these kinds of questions for themselves. Many have drawn primarily from their own and others' experience in arriving at their answers. Unfortunately, common sense derived from experience can be loaded with implicit assumptions which may not be as valid as they seem. It is my purpose here to examine a number of commonly accepted assumptions about pay and to attempt to determine if they are valid.

What are the currently accepted principles and assumptions about how pay should be administered? In order to answer this question, a study was conducted among 500 managers from all levels of management and from a wide variety of organizations. The managers were asked to indicate whether they agreed or disagreed with five statements that contained assumptions about the psychological aspects of management compensation—assumptions which have important implications for the administration of pay. The following are the five assumptions and the percentage of managers agreeing with each:

- At the higher-paid levels of management, pay is not one of the two or three most important job factors (61 percent).
- Money is an ineffective motivator of outstanding job performance at the management level (55 per cent).
- Managers are likely to be dissatisfied with their pay even if they are highly paid (54 percent).
- Information about management pay rates is best kept secret (77 percent).
- Managers are not concerned with how their salary is divided between cash and fringe benefits; the important thing is the amount of salary they receive (45 percent).

As can be seen, better than 50 percent of managers participating in the study agreed with the first four assumptions and 45 percent agreed with the last assumption.

Recently, research results have begun to accumulate which suggest that some of the assumptions may be partially invalid and some completely invalid. Let us, therefore, look at each of these assumptions and examine the evidence relevant to it.

WHAT IS THE ROLE OF PAY?

The history of the study of pay shows that we have progressed from a model of man that viewed him as being primarily economically motivated to a view that stresses social needs and the need for self-actualization. Unfortunately, in trying to establish the legitimacy of social and self-actualization needs, the proponents of this view of motivation tended to overlook the importance of pay. In some cases, they failed to mention the role of pay in their systems at all, and in other cases they implied that, because workers and managers are better off financially than they used to be, pay is less important than it was previously.

Because of this failure to deal with the role of pay, many managers have come to the erroneous conclusion that the experts in "human relations" have shown that pay is a relatively unimportant incentive and, as a result, have accepted the view that pay is a relatively unimportant job factor.[1] This is illustrated in the results of my study mentioned above. When the managers were asked to indicate how they thought the typical expert in human relations would respond to the statement that for higher-paid managers pay is not one of the most important job factors, 71 percent of the managers thought that the majority of the experts would agree with it, while 61 percent said they agreed with it themselves.

Undeniably, those writers who have stressed social and self-actualization needs have performed an important service by emphasizing the significance of non-financial incentives. It is now clear that people are motivated by needs for recognition and self-actualization as well as by security and physiological needs. But does this mean that pay must be dismissed as unimportant? I do not think the evidence justifies such a conclusion.

The belief that pay becomes unimportant as an individual accumulates more money has its roots in an inadequate interpretation of Maslow's theory of a hierarchy of needs. Briefly, Maslow's theory says that the needs which individuals seek to satisfy are arranged in a hierarchy. At the bottom of the hierarchy are needs for physical comfort. These lower-order needs are followed by such higher-order needs as social needs, esteem needs, and finally, needs for autonomy and self-actualization.

According to Maslow's theory, once the lower-order needs are relatively well satisfied, they become unimportant as motivators, and an individual tries to satisfy the higher-order needs. If it is then assumed, as it is by many, that pay satisfies only lower-level needs, then it becomes obvious that once a person's physical comforts are taken care of, his pay will be unimportant to him.[2] But this view is based upon the assumption that pay satisfies primarily lower-level needs, an assumption which I question.

PAY AS RECOGNITION

I would like to emphasize the neglected viewpoint that pay is a unique incentive—unique because it is able to satisfy both the lower-order physiological and security needs and the higher-order needs, such as esteem and recognition. Recent studies show that managers frequently think of their pay as a form of recognition for a job well done and as a mark of achievement.[3] The president of a large corporation has clearly pointed out why pay has become an important mark in the progress toward achievement and recognition for managers.

Achievement in the managerial field is much less spectacular than comparable success in many of the professions . . . the scientist, for example, who wins the Nobel prize. . . . In fact, the more effective an executive, the more his own identity and personality blend into the background of his organization, and the greater is his relative anonymity outside his immediate circle.

There is, however, one form of recognition that managers do receive that is visible outside their immediate circle, and that is their pay. Pay has become an indicator of the value of a person to an organization and as such is an important form of recognition. Thus, it is not suprising to find that one newly elected company president whose "other" income from securities approximated $125,000 demanded a salary of $100,000 from his company. When asked why he did not take a $50,000 salary and defer the other half of his salary until after retirement at a sizable tax saving, he replied, "I want my salary to be six figures when it appears in the proxy statement."[4]

It is precisely because pay satisfies higher-order needs as well as lower-order needs that it may remain important to managers, regardless of the amount of compensation they receive. For example, one recent study clearly showed (Figure 1) that although pay is slightly less important to upper-level managers (president and vice-president) than it is to lower-level managers, it is still more important than security, social, and esteem needs for upper-level managers.[5] At the lower management level, pay was rated as more important than all but self-actualization needs.

We can turn to motivation theory to help explain further why pay is important to many managers. Goals that are initially desired only as a means to an end can in time become goals in themselves. Because of this process, money may cease to be only a path to the satisfaction of needs and may become a goal in itself. Thus, for many managers, money and money making have become ends that are powerful incentives. As one manager put it when asked why his salary was important to him, "It is just like bridge—it isn't any fun unless you keep score." In summary, the evidence shows that, although pay may be important to managers for different reasons as the amount of pay they receive increases, pay remains important to all levels of management.

The evidence that is usually given to support the belief that pay is ineffective as an incentive is the finding that a number of incentive plans have failed to produce expected increases in productivity. This view is expressed well by the following statement of a company president: "Wage systems are not, in themselves, an important determinant of pace of work, application to work, or output."[6] That this view is being more widely accepted by managers in industry is reflected in the decline of the use of incentive systems at the worker level. In 1935, 75 percent of a sample of companies replied that they used wage incentive programs. By 1939 the number had fallen to 52 percent and by 1958 to 27 percent. The fact that managers have tended to stop using incentive plans for their workers points up the general disillusionment with the effectiveness of pay as an incentive among managers.

Figure 1   IMPORTANCE ATTACHED TO SIX NEEDS BY MANAGERS AT
THREE LEVELS

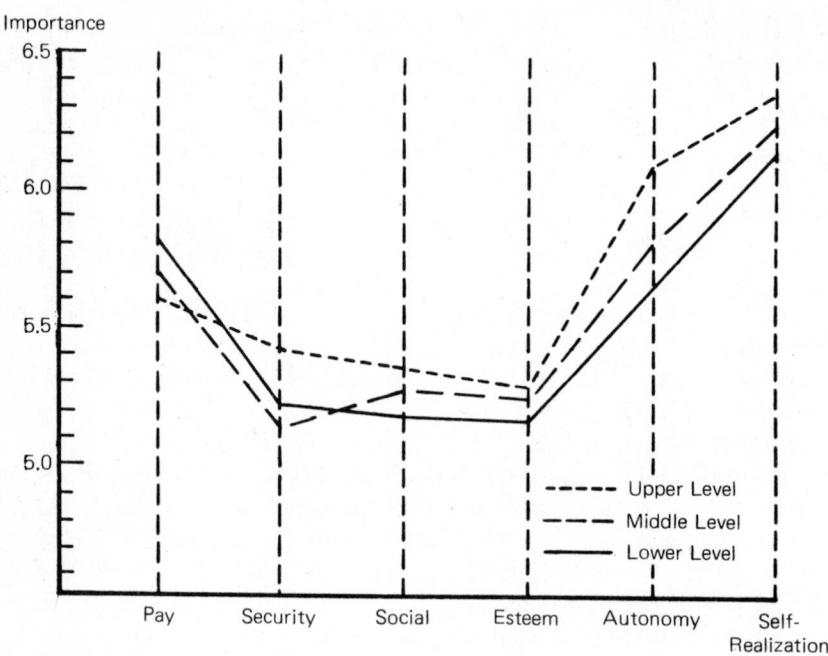

This disillusionment is also reflected in my study which showed that 55 percent of the managers sampled felt that pay is not a very effective incentive at the management level.

MANAGERS' PAY

What experiences have these managers had that might cause them to be disillusioned? I believe that one cause of the disillusionment is in the misunderstanding of how pay functions as a motivator. In current practice, the logic is that if pay is tied to productivity, then productivity should increase. This logic seems to be supported by the law of effect which states that behavior (productivity in our case) which is seen as leading to a reward (pay) will tend to be repeated.[7] However, recent research shows that one problem is that, although incentive schemes are designed to relate pay to productivity, many managers do not see them as doing this.

I have considerable evidence that many managers who work under systems which, as far as their organizations are concerned, tie productivity to pay, simply do not feel that better job performance will lead to higher pay.

I recently distributed a questionnaire to over 600 middle- and lower-level managers in a variety of organizations. These managers were asked what factors determined their pay. The consensus of these managers was that the most important factor in determining their pay was their training and experience, and not how well they performed their jobs. A look at the relationship between how well they were performing their jobs as rated by their superiors and their pay showed that they were correct. There was virtually no relationship between their pay and their rated job performance. Under these conditions, there is no reason to believe that pay will function as an incentive for higher job performance, even though these organizations claimed to have incentive pay systems.

Some other data that I collected from the same managers show one condition under which pay can be an effective incentive for high job performance. Of the managers studied, those who were most highly motivated to perform their jobs effectively were characterized by two attitudes:

- They said that their pay was important to them.
- They felt that good job performance would lead to higher pay for them.

To return to the law of effect, for these highly motivated managers, pay was a significant reward and they saw this reward as contingent upon their job performance. Thus, it would seem that one of the major limits of the effectiveness of pay as an incentive is the ability of management to design compensation programs that create the perception that pay is based upon performance.

It is not enough to have a pay plan that is called an incentive system. Not only the people who design the plan but the people who are subject to the plan must feel that it is an incentive plan. At the management level, one step in the direction of tying pay more closely to performance might be the elimination of some of the stock option and other deferred payment plans that exist now. Many of these pay plans are so designed that they destroy rather than encourage the perception that pay is based upon performance. They pay off years after the behavior that is supposed to be rewarded has taken place, and in many cases the size of the reward that is given is independent of the quality of the manager's job performance.

There are two other factors which suggest that cash payments may be particularly appropriate at this time. A recent study found that managers preferred cash payments to other forms of compensation.[8] Further, the new tax laws now make it possible to get almost as much money into the hands of the manager through salary as through stock option plans and other forms of deferred compensation.

In addition to failing to create the perception that pay is based upon performance, there are two other reasons why incentive plans may fail. Many pay plans fail to recognize the importance of other needs to individuals, and, as a result, plans are set up in such a way that earning more money must necessarily be done at the cost of satisfying other needs. This situation frequently occurs when managers are paid solely on the basis of the performance of their subordinate groups. Conflicts appear between their desire for more production in their own groups, no matter what the organizational costs, and their desire to cooperate with other managers in order to make the total organization more successful.

A second reason why incentive plans fail is that they are frequently introduced as a substitute for good leadership practices and trust between employees and the organization. As one manager so aptly put this fallacious view: "If you have poor managers you have to use wage incentives." Wage incentives must be a supplement to, and not a substitute for, good management practices.

The results of Herzberg's study of motivation have been frequently cited as evidence that pay cannot be an effective motivator of good job performance.[9] According to this view, pay operates only as a maintenance factor and, as such, has no power to motivate job performance beyond some neutral point. However, this interpretation is not in accord with the results of the study. The study, in fact, found that pay may or may not be a motivator, depending upon how it is administered. A careful reading of Herzberg shows that where pay was geared to achievement and seen as a form of recognition by the managers, it was a potent motivator of good job performance. It was only where organizations had abandoned pay as an incentive and were unsuccessful in fairly relating pay and performance that pay ceased to be a motivator and became a maintenance factor.

INCENTIVE FOR PERFORMANCE

In summary, I think the significant question about pay as an incentive is not whether it is effective or ineffective, but under what conditions is it an effective incentive. It appears that pay can be an effective incentive for good job performance under certain conditions:

When pay is seen by individuals as being tied to effective job performance in such a way that it becomes a reward or form of recognition for effective job performance.
When other needs are also satisfied by effective job performance.

The statement is frequently made that, no matter how much money an individual earns, he will want more. And indeed, as was pointed out earlier, the evidence does indicate that pay remains important, regardless of how much money an individual earns. But the assumption, accepted by 54 percent of the managers in my study, that managers are likely to be dissatisfied with their pay even if they are highly paid does not follow from this point. There is an important difference between how much pay an individual wants to earn and the amount he feels represents a fair salary for the job he is doing. Individuals evaluate their pay in terms of the balance between what they put into their jobs (effort, skill, education, etc.) and what they receive in return (money, status, etc.).[10]

Dissatisfaction with pay occurs when an individual feels that what he puts into his job exceeds what he receives in the form of pay for doing his job. Individuals evaluate the fairness of their inputs relative to their outcomes on the basis of the inputs and outcomes of other employees, usually their coworkers. Managers tend to compare their pay with that of managers who are at the same management level in their own and in other organizations. Thus, dissatisfaction with pay is likely to occur when an individual's pay is lower than the pay of someone whom he considers similar to himself in ability, job level, and job performance. But when an individual receives an amount of pay that compares favorably with the pay received by others who, he feels, have comparable inputs, he will be satisfied with his pay.

However, because an individual feels his pay is fair, it does not mean that an opportunity to make more money through a promotion or other change in inputs would be turned down, nor does it mean that more money is not desired. It simply means that at the moment the balance between inputs and outcomes is seen as equitable.

The results of a recent study of over 1,900 managers illustrates the point that managers can be, and in fact frequently are, satisfied with their pay.[11] The managers were first asked to rate on a 1 (low) to 7 (high) scale how much pay they received for their jobs. They were next asked to rate, on the same scale, how much pay should be associated with their jobs. As can be seen from Figure 2, which presents the results for the presidents who participated in the study, those executives who were paid highly, relative to other presidents, were satisfied with their pay. For this group [12] (earning $50,000 and over), there was no difference between how much pay they said they received and how much pay they thought they should receive. However, those presidents whose pay compared unfavorably with the pay of other presidents said there was a substantial difference between what their pay should be and what it was.

The same results were obtained at each level of management down to and including the foreman level. The highly paid managers at each level were quite satisfied with their pay; it was the low-paid managers at each level who were dissatisfied. In fact, highly paid foremen ($12,000 and above) were better satisfied with their pay than were company presidents who earned less than $50,000.

There is some evidence that managers can, and do, feel that they receive too much pay for their management positions. Of the 1,900 managers studied, about 5 percent reported that they received too much pay for their management positions. These managers apparently felt that their outcomes were too great in proportion to their inputs when compared with those of other managers. Although the number of managers who feel that their pay is too high is undoubtedly small, as indicated by the 5 percent figure obtained in this study, the fact that this feeling exists at all is evidence that individuals do not always feel they deserve more and more pay.

Figure 2 ATTITUDES OF CORPORATION PRESIDENTS TOWARD THEIR PAY

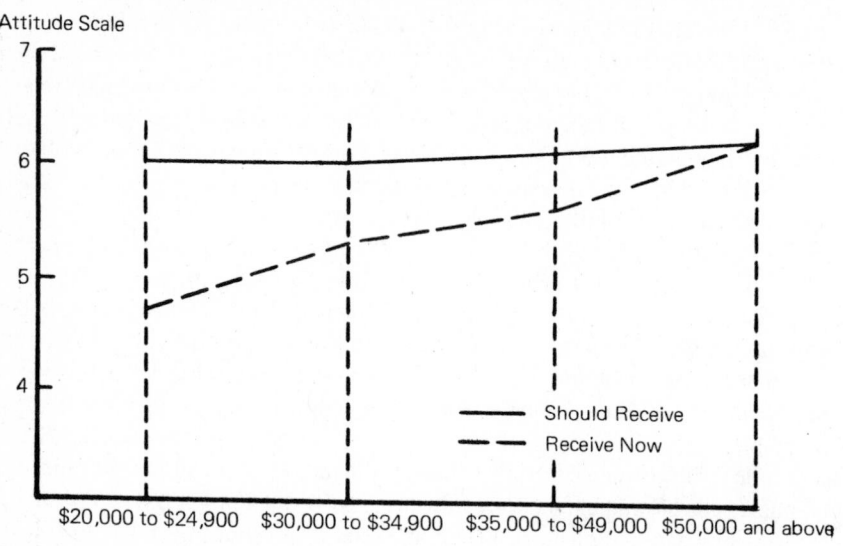

The feeling of overcompensation by some managers is also evidence that some organizations are not doing the best possible job of distributing their compensation dollars. It may be wise for organizations to give more weight to the value that subordinates and peers place on a manager's job performance when they are considering pay raises for a manager. Giving a high salary to a manager who is considered to be a poor performer by other employees can have several negative effects.

First, it can cause dissatisfaction with pay among other managers: dissatisfaction that comes about because managers who are good performers may come to see their own pay as suddenly inadequate relative to the pay of someone whom they regard as a poor performer, but who has received a raise. If such practices are followed, it is undoubtedly true that good performers will never be satisfied with their pay.

Second, and more important, giving a raise to a poor performer is a signal to other managers that pay is not necessarily based upon merit: an attitude that can destroy any motivational impetus that might be created by an otherwise well-administered compensation program. As can be seen from the results of my study of manager's assumptions about pay administration, perhaps the most commonly accepted axiom of good personnel practice is that information about management compensation rates should be kept secret. Many organizations go to great lengths to maintain this secrecy. Information about management pay rates is frequently kept locked in the company safe and the pay checks of top management receive special handling so that the size of the check is not known even by the personnel manager.

The reason typically given to defend the policy of keeping pay information secret is that secrecy helps to reduce dissatisfaction with regard to pay. According to this view, managers who do not know how much others earn are not likely to feel their pay compares unfavorably with that of other managers. Thus, personnel managers are never faced with a situation where Joe thinks he is better than Jack but knows that Jack is making more than he.

PAY RATES SECRET

However, such reasoning fallaciously assumes that secrecy policies eliminate pay comparisons. As was pointed out earlier, the evidence indicates the managers do evalute their own pay in terms of what other managers earn. What is not clear is what effect the secrecy policies have on the accuracy with which managers estimate the pay of other managers and the effects of the secrecy on how satisfying and motivating these comparisons are.

In order to gather some evidence that might serve as a basis for evaluating the effects of secrecy, I recently conducted an attitude survey. Questionnaires were completed by 563 (response rate 88.7 percent) middle and lower-level managers in seven organizations. Four of the organizations were private companies engaged in a wide variety of activities ranging from rocket manufacturing to supplying gas and electricity. The other three organizations were government agencies also engaged in a variety of activities. The four private companies all had strict secrecy policies with regard to management compensation rates, while the three government agencies did make some information public about their pay rates.

A two-part questionnaire was used. The managers were first asked to estimate the average yearly salary of managers in their organizations who were at their own level, one level above them, and one level below them. The organization provided actual average salaries in order that comparisons could be made. The managers were also asked to indicate how well satisfied they were with several aspects of their organizations' compensation systems. In addition to being asked to express their satisfaction with their own pay, they were asked to indicate whether there was too much or too little difference between their own pay and that of their superiors, and between their own pay and that of their subordinates.

The results of the study clearly showed that the managers did not have an accurate picture of what other managers in their organizations earned. Apparently, the secrecy policies were effective in keeping these managers from knowing what other managers earned. However, rather than committing random errors in estimating other managers' salaries, these managers consistently tended to overestimate and to underestimate. When the managers were asked to estimate the pay of their superiors, they consistently underestimated. When they viewed the pay of their subordinates, they consistently overestimated. One-third of the managers overestimated the pay of their subordinates by more than one thousand dollars. Similarly, they also tended to overestimate the pay of managers at their own level.

Interestingly, the managers in the government organizations were consistently more accurate in estimating the pay of other managers than were the managers in the private organizations. Because the government managers had more information about the compensation programs of their organizations, it was expected that they would be more accurate. However, this finding does serve to emphasize the point that the cause of the managers' misperceptions of other managers' pay was the secrecy policies of their organizations.

The question that now remains to be answered is what effects did these distorted pictures of what other managers earn have on the managers' job satisfaction and job performance. The effects on satisfaction with pay can be seen in the managers' answers to the three questions concerned with satisfaction with pay. They stated that there was too small a difference between their own pay and that of their superiors and also too small a difference between their own pay and that of their subordinates. These attitudes are not surprising since the managers tended to see these differences as smaller than they actually are.

EFFECTS OF SECRECY

Secrecy policies are causing some of this dissatisfaction by giving the managers inaccurate pictures of what others earn. Since managers evaluate their own pay in terms of what others earn, it is not surprising that the data show that those managers who feel their own pay is too close to that of their superiors and subordinates also feel that their own pay is too low. Undoubtedly, part of the managers' dissatisfaction with their own pay has its basis in unfavorable pay comparisons between what these managers know they make and what they think other managers make. On the basis of this evidence, it appears that one effect of secrecy policies is to increase dissatisfaction with pay.[13]

There is another way in which secrecy may contribute indirectly to both increased dissatisfaction with pay and lower motivation to perform a management job effectively. Secrecy allows a manager to avoid the responsibility of communicating to his subordinates his evaluation of their performance.

An example of what can and frequently does happen is that a manager who has to distribute raises capitalizes upon secrecy to avoid what he considers to be an unpleasant task. The manager does differentially distribute raises among his subordinates on the basis of their performance. So far, so good! However, when he explains the raises to his subordinates, if he does this at all, he tells all of them that he is satisfied with their performance. The manager may reason that he has done the right thing. "After all," he thinks, "I did reward good performance with higher pay and I didn't cause any unhappiness as I would have if I had told the poor performers how dissatisfied I was with them."

However, the differential raises have no positive effect since they do nothing to encourage the perception that pay is based upon performance. The good performer is not sure he is getting a larger raise than the poor performer, and the poor performer may feel he is being rewarded for the type of performance he has been demonstrating. Eventually, of course, the word begins to get around about how much other people got in raises (undoubtedly slightly inflated), and this information is bound to make a number of managers unhappy with their pay, as well as distrustful of their superiors.

The secrecy policies of organizations and the consequent tendency for managers to estimate incorrectly the pay of other managers may also affect the managers' motivation to perform their jobs effectively in other ways. Several studies have shown that accurate feedback about task performance is a strong stimulus to good job performance.[14] People perform better when they receive accurate information about how well they are performing relative to some meaningful standard. For managers, pay is one of the most significant and meaningful pieces of feedback information they receive. High pay is considered a sign that the manager's job performance is good. Low pay is a signal that the manager is not performing his job well and that new behavior is needed.

The results of this study indicate that, because managers have misperceptions about what other managers earn, they are unable to evaluate correctly their own pay. Because of the tendency managers have to over estimate the pay of their subordinates and peers, the majority of the managers see their pay as low and in effect are receiving negative feedback. Moreover, although this feedback suggests that they should change their job behavior, it does not tell them what type of change they should make in their behavior. In cases where managers are not doing their jobs well, this negative feedback is undoubtedly the type of information that should be communicated; in other instances, it gives a false signal to change to those managers who are performing their jobs effectively.

REDUCED MOTIVATION?

Increased pay is one of the most significant rewards that an individual receives in return for taking on the responsibilities and work associated with higher-level management jobs and, therefore, is one of the important incentives in motivating managers to work toward obtaining higher-level jobs. However, as pointed out earlier, our data indicate that managers tend to underestimate the pay of managers at higher levels. This has the effect of making the attainment of higher-level jobs less desirable because it causes managers to underestimate the rewards that are attached to the positions. Thus, the secrecy policies of organizations may be indirectly reducing the motivation of managers to gain higher-level jobs.

If, as the evidence indicates, secrecy policies have significant costs in terms of job satisfaction, motivation for effective job performance, and motivation for promotion, does it not seem logical that organizations should alter these policies? Perhaps organizations that now have secrecy policies could give out information on pay ranges and average salaries for all management levels. If they started by giving out only partial salary information, they could better prepare their employees for full disclosure, and eventually the salaries of all members of an organization should be made available to all other members of that organization. It may well be better to provide an individual with accurate information upon which to make pay comparisons than to have him make unfavorable comparisons based upon misinformation.

ROLE OF FRINGE BENEFITS

When any organization is asked to determine how much money it spends on compensation, it usually adds the money spent for salaries and fringe benefits. Similarly, an organization determines how much money an individual earns by adding his salary and the costs to them of his benefit package. Union contracts are typically spoken of as settlements involving an x cents per hour compensation package. Implicit in these measures of compensation cost is the assumption that a dollar spent on cash salary is equal to a dollar spent on life insurance or other fringe benefits. From an economic standpoint and in terms of costs to the organization, it seems reasonable that the value of a compensation package is equal to the simple sum of all its parts. It is probably the reason why 45 percent of the managers sampled endorse the view that managers are not greatly concerned with how their pay is divided among various fringe benefits.

However, I would like to suggest that dollars spent on the different parts of the compensation package may not be equal in terms of what they earn in the recipient's perception of the value of his compensation package. Several studies have shown that individuals value some compensation benefits more than others, even though the cost to the company is the same.[15] For example, one study found that employees strongly preferred receiving hospital insurance to receiving additional pension money even though the insurance and the pension plan cost the organization the same amount. In effect a dollar spent on compensation can have a different value to the recipient, depending upon the type of benefit the organization chooses to buy with it.

The studies on compensation preferences among both workers and managers show that the preferences of individuals for different benefits vary greatly, depending upon such factors as their age, sex, number of children, and marital status. For example, older workers value pension plans much more highly than do younger workers, and unmarried men value a shorter workweek more highly than do married men. These studies suggest that, at the very least, organizations may need different benefit packages in different locations, depending upon the personal characteristics of the workers in each installation.

A further step that organizations could take would be to design different packages for groups of individuals who have similar characteristics. Indeed, it may be that the optimum solution to this problem of different compensation preferences is for organizations to adopt a "cafeteria" compensation program. A "cafeteria" compensation plan would allow every employee to divide his compensation dollars among the benefits offered by his company. This would allow each employee to select the compensation options that he values most without adding to the compensation costs of the company. Previously, such a program would have been impractical because of the high costs that would be involved. However, with the advent of the computer, it is possible.

"BUFFET" BENEFITS?

"Cafeteria" wage plans would appear to have a particularly bright future among managers where union negotiations and contracts are not likely to be a hindrance. "Cafeteria" wage plans have two additional benefits that strongly argue for their use.

First, they allow employees to participate in an important decision about their jobs. Even among managers, opportunities for actual participation as contrasted with pseudo-participation are rare enough so that in every situation where participation can be legitimately and reasonably employed, it should be.

Second, "cafeteria" wage plans help to make clear to the employees just how much money is involved in their total compensation package. There are many reports of situations where employees do not even know of the fringe benefits for which their organizations are paying. With "cafeteria" wage plans, this situation would be virtually eliminated.

RESEARCH CONCLUSIONS

What are the lessons to be learned from the recent research on the psychological aspects of compensation practices? I believe that the following conclusions are warranted.

- Even at the higher paid levels of management, pay is important enough to be a significant motivator of good job performance. However, it will be a motivator only when it is seen by the managers themselves to be tied to their job performance.

* Managers can be, and in fact frequently are, satisfied with their pay when it compares favorably with the pay of other managers holding similar positions.

* Secrecy policies have significant hidden costs attached to them. The evidence indicates that secrecy may lead to lower satisfaction with pay and to a decreased motivation for promotion.

* In order to get the maximum value for money spent on compensation, organizations may have to institute "cafeteria" wage payment systems. Such a system would allow each manager to select the benefits that have the greatest value to him.

WHAT THE FUTURE HOLDS

Will organizations be willing to innovate in the area of salary administration and to implement such programs as "cafeteria" wage plans and openness about salary levels? This question can finally be answered only five or ten years from now when we will know what the wage program of the future looks like. However, there are at least two reasons for believing that organizations will be slow to consider these new programs.

First, as one critic has put it, most organizations seem intent on keeping their compensation programs up with, but never ahead of, the Joneses in a sort of "me too" behavior.[16] It is unfortunate that many organizations got so badly "burned" when they tried to install incentive wage schemes that ignored needs other than that of money. Undoubtedly, this experience has led to the current air of conservatism that exists where innovation with regard to salary administration is concerned.

Second, since none of the implications for practice that have been drawn from the results of this group of studies offers a miraculous cure for the present ills of any organizations' compensation program, slow movement may be desirable. These studies imply that there may be better ways to do things, but they also imply that there may be costs and risks involved in trying these new policies.

For example, the idea of eliminating secrecy, no matter how well handled, will probably cause problems for some employees. In particular, openness will be difficult for the relatively low-paid managers to handle. But I believe that the gains would outweigh the costs and that there would be an overall gain in motivation as a result of openness with regard to pay. I am led to this belief because, by making pay information public, pay can become an effective satisfier of such needs as esteem and recognition and thereby become optimally effective as a stimulant of effective performance. The same general point is true about "cafeteria" wage plans or tying pay more clearly to performance. There are certain costs that are associated with this type of innovative behavior, but there are also large potential gains possible where practices are successfully installed.

I have found that the top management of organizations is always questioning and testing the value of their present compensation systems, and I hope that the ideas and research results presented here will be of aid in this process of inquiry and self-correction.

NOTES

1. This is not to imply that the leading figures in the "human relations" movement do not understand the importance of pay. But, by emphasizing other rewards and by not dealing explicitly with the role of pay, they have opened the door for others to interpret their writings as implying that pay is unimportant.

2. It should be pointed out that neither Maslow nor any of the leading figures in the "human relations" movement has stated that pay satisfies only lower-order needs. Others make the interpretation that it satisfies only lower-order needs (e.g., Robert B. McKersie, "Wage Payment Methods of the Future," *British Journal of Industrial Relations*, I [March 1963]. 191-212).

3. Edward E. Lawler and Lyman W. Porter, "Perceptions Regarding Management Compensation," *Industrial Relations*, III (Oct. 1963), 41 –49; and M. Scott Myers, "Who Are Your Motivated Workers?" *Harvard Business Review*, XLII (Jan. –Feb., 1964), 72–88.

4. Arch Patton, *Men, Money, and Motivation* (New York: McGraw-Hill Book Co., Inc., 1961), p. 34.

5. Lyman W. Porter, "A Study of Perceived Need Satisfaction in Bottom and Middle Management Jobs," *Journal of Applied Psychology*, XLV (Feb. 1961), 1 –10.

6. Wilfred Brown, *Piecework Abandoned* (London: Heineman and Co. Ltd., 1962), p. 15.

7. There is evidence that the law of effect can work where a clearly perceived relationship between the behavior and the reward does not exist. However, the important point is that rewards are maximally effective when they are seen as being clearly tied to the behavior that they are intended to reward. (See, e.g., John A. McGeoch and Arthur L. Irion, *The Psychology of Human Learning* [New York: Longmans, Green and Co., 1952].)

8. Thomas A Mahoney, "Compensation Preferences of Managers," *Industrial Relations*, III (May 1964), 135 –144.

9. Frederick Herzberg, Bernard Mausner, and Barbara Bloch Snyderman, *The Motivation to Work* (New York: John Wiley and Sons, 1959).

10. J. Stacy Adams, "Wage Inequities, Productivity and Work Quality," *Industrial Relations*, III (Oct. 1963), 9 –16.

11. Edward E. Lawler and Lyman W. Porter, *op. cit.*

12. The presidents in this sample tended to come from smaller companies and, hence, the relatively low-level of their compensation.

13. Further support for this interpretation comes from the finding that there was a significant tendency for those managers who had an accurate picture of their subordinates' pay to be more satisfied with their own pay than were those managers who had an inaccurate picture of their subordinates' pay ($r = .35, p = .01$).

14. Victor H. Vroom, *Work and Motivation* (New York: John Wiley and Sons, 1964).
15. Stanley M. Nealey, "Pay and Benefit Preference," *Industrial Relations*, III (Oct. 1963), 17–28; Thomas A. Mahoney, *op. cit.;* and I. R. Andrews and Mildred M. Henry, "Management Attitudes Toward Pay," *Industrial Relations,* III (Oct. 1963), 29–39.
16. Marvin D. Dunnette and Bernard M. Bass, "Behavioral Scientists and Personnel Management," *Industrial Relations,* III (May 1963), 115–130.

15   The "Jackass Effect" in Management Compensation

Dale D. McConkey

Parable: Once upon a time there was a dumb jackass standing knee-deep in a field of carrots contentedly munching away. A wise farmer wanted the jackass to pull a loaded wagon to another field but the jackass would not walk over to the wagon. So the wise farmer stood by the wagon and held up a bunch of carrots for the dumb jackass to see. But the dumb jackass continued to contentedly munch away on his own carrots.

Moral of story: Jackasses do not work for carrots.

Underlying the approach to managerial compensation followed by many companies is the implicit assumption that well-educated managers usually can be coaxed into doing that which even the dumb jackass will not do. But the majority of managers cannot be coaxed. This observation has led to the frequently espoused premise that managers do not work for money. The premise should be expanded to provide that managers do not work for money *when the jackass effect is inherent in a compensation plan.*

The jackass effect is present in any compensation plan when the plan is not formulated and administered in a manner which preserves and furthers the only two objectives of meaningful compensation. These objectives are, first, to promote and attain equity and, second, to motivate for better performance.

Equity is attained when a manager's compensation is based on the results he has achieved and is related to a comparison of these results with the results achieved by all other managers in his organization. The motivation objective requires that the manager be convinced that extra effort and achievement on his part will result in extra compensation. He must believe his efforts will be recognized and rewarded. The manager must know this in advance of expending the efforts—not after he takes the action.

THE JACKASS EFFECT IN PRACTICE

The jackass effect commonly assumes five forms in actual practice:

Compensation is on the wrong end of the action.
The manager's accountability is so nebulous that his performance cannot be measured.
An ineffective evaluation method is used.
The compensation plan acts to level all managers into a group rather than recognize variances in individual performance.
Compensation is separated from performance.

The Wrong End

Too often compensation plans are formulated in a manner that causes a manager to take some action and, then after the action is completed, someone determines how much the manager should be paid for the action. In this approach, compensation is treated almost solely as something which follows the action. It is not unlike an owner who tells a contractor to build a house and, after the house is completed, the owner tells the builder how much he will be paid.

Compensation cannot act as a motivating force unless its future impact is well known *prior* to the action. This prior knowledge, which the manager must carry with him while he is accomplishing the action, is the key to motivating him to better performance.

An excellent example of having compensation on the wrong end of the action is provided by a large Eastern food company. It has a "discretionary bonus" plan for its managers. Practice indicates that the word "discretionary" is used advisedly. At the end of each year, the president and a few of his advisors sit down and determine which of the managers will receive a bonus and how large each payment will be. There are no established eligibility criteria to decide which managers will receive payments, and there is no formula for determining how much each of the lucky ones will receive.

Surprises abound when payments are doled out each year. Managers are surprised at their selections, and the amount each receives is a surprise. The company's plan could be aptly labeled "The Surprise Approach to Compensation." Managers cannot be motivated when they have no advance knowledge of who will receive payments or on what basis the payments are calculated.

Measurement and Measuring Tool

Only one valid basis for rewarding manager exists—the quality of their performance. The jackass effect exacts its toll when accountability is delegated in a way that performance cannot be measured and when the measuring tool (managerial appraisal or evaluation) is not geared for judging the actual results.

Measurable accountability is not established when the traditional job description is used to delegate the accountability. Traditionally, rather feeble attempts were made to assign this accountability in the form of a job description. Too often, however, these job descriptions were overly general statements of activities which the managers should pursue. No emphasis was given to the specific results the managers should achieve. Usually, the descriptions required the managers to keep busy without specifying the end results of all the effort. Thus, the managers' accomplishments could not be measured with any degree of accuracy because there was no measuring scale.

Figure 1 provides an excellent illustration of a performance evaluation form which is commonly used and which does not measure how well the accountability has been carried out. It records only the superior's perception of the degree to which the subordinate possesses the personality traits which are listed on the form. There is no correlation with the actual results achieved and thus no basis for determining what compensation the manager should receive. This approach is usually adopted as a last resort when no measurable accountability has been fixed and there is nothing tangible to measure.

The Great Leveler

Parable: Once upon a time there were six jackasses hitched to a wagon pulling a heavy load up a long steep hill. Two of the jackasses were not achievement oriented and decided to coast along and let the others do most of the pulling. Two others were relatively young and inexperienced, and had a difficult time pulling their share. One of the remaining two suffered from a slight hangover from consuming fermented barley the evening before. The sixth jackass did most of the work.

The wagon arrived at the top of the hill. The driver got down from his seat, patted each of the jackasses on the head, and gave six carrots to each. Prior to the next hill climb, the sixth jackass ran away.

Moral of the story: Never be the sixth jackass if everybody gets six carrots.

Figure 1   EXAMPLE OF TRADITIONAL PERFORMANCE EVALUATION FORM

Factor	Excellent	Above Average	Average	Below Average	Poor
Degree of cost consciousness		X			
Grasp of function	X				
Initiative		X			
Decision-making ability	X				
Application	X				
Judgment		X			
Health	X				
Appearance	X				
Loyalty	X				
Gets along with people		X			
Develops subordinates			X		
Work habits		X			
Contribution to company's progress	X				
Potential for advancement		X			
Rated by					
Reviewed by					

John Jones and Bill Smith are plant managers in the same company and each is currently earning $14,000 a year. The worth of their jobs has been evaluated by commonly accepted job evaluation techniques. The evaluations reveal that the Smith and Jones jobs are practically identical and, therefore, the following salary ranges have been established for both:

Salary Increase Schedule

Minimum	$12,000
Step 1	12,800
Step 2	13,700
Step 3	14,600
Step 4	15,600
Maximum	16,600

What happens under this plan if Jones contributes ten times as much as Smith during a particular year? What is the maximum increase in salary the outstanding producer can be granted over that of the other manager? Clearly, the maximum increase is $2,600 (the difference between their present salaries and the maximum of the range). In actual practice, it would be even less, probably $1,600 (the difference between Jones' present salary and Step 4). Thus, for making ten times the contribution of his counterpart, Jones receives only a routine merit increase. Such a small salary increase would be neither equitable to the high performance manager nor would it motivate him to continue his high performance.

Another problem resulting from utilizing only straight salaries is that every salary increase becomes a fixed cost and the manager will continue to receive it in the future regardless of the level of performance he maintains. To illustrate this point, take the above case in which the manager receives a salary increase of $1,600 for his outstanding performance. What happens next year when the manager's performance is only average? Usually, it is not advisable to reduce the salary of a manager. Thus, he will carry into future years a salary payment which he earned for his performance for only one year.

Obviously, the typical straight salary plan is not sufficiently dynamic and flexible to accommodate the differing circumstances which can and should exist in a management group. About the only way to achieve any flexibility in a straight salary plan—to recognize varying performance levels of managers—is to vary the amount and/or frequency of salary increases. Even this small amount of flexibility is not fully utilized by many organizations. As a result, it is usually advisable to add an incentive compensation plan to the salary plan. Incentive plans are discussed later in this article.

Compensation Separated From Performance

Parable: It came to pass that high unemployment among jackasses was visited upon the land, and the sixth jackass returned to climb the hill again. The hill was climbed and the driver said to the sixth jackass, "Let's sit down and discuss your performance. We'll have an appraisal interview on how well you climbed the hill."

The sixth jackass wondered where his carrots were. Noting the puzzled, eager look on the sixth jackass' face, the driver explained that the purpose of the appraisal interview was to improve hill climbing. The carrots would be discussed at some time in the future. The sixth jackass ran away again.

Moral of the story: Never be the sixth jackass when it is not certain there is food at the top of the hill.

For years, the traditionalists have advocated that superior-subordinate discussions relative to the subordinate's performance should be clearly separated from any discussion concerning how much compensation the subordinate will receive for his performance.

The premise frequently advanced in favor of making the separation is that the injection of an emotional issue like compensation into a discussion on management development would cause the less attractive subject of development to be neglected. In principle, the argument sounds plausible. However, as a practical matter, it has yet to be demonstrated that the manager is ever able to forget compensation when his performance is being discussed. On the other hand, it has been repeatedly demonstrated that, no matter what is said during the performance interview, the manager is saying to himself, "Yeah, boss, I hear you talking, but what does it mean to my paycheck?"

Thus, attempts to omit the subject of compensation often have an effect the opposite of that intended. The deliberate skirting of the subject of compensation causes it to be spotlighted in the manager's mind; frustration and a lack of trust often result.

OVERCOMING THE JACKASS EFFECT

Major policy changes and decisions are necessary in most organizations if the jackass effect is to be overcome and if equity and motivation are to be built into managerial compensation. The magnitude and impact of these changes will bear a high degree of correlation with the extent to which the organization is mismanaging its compensation program.

Equitable compensation which truly motivates better managerial performance requires an integrated "building block" approach in which each of the following components or blocks is present in the right balance:

The establishment of clear-cut accountability which can be measured
The use of a measuring system (appraisal or evaluation) which effectively determines how
   well the accountability has been carried out
The adoption of a dynamic compensation plan which recognizes wide swings in managerial
   performance
The establishment of the greatest possible direct tie between performance and rewards.

The words "integrated" and "balance" are used advisedly because compensation must be practiced as a system of interrelated parts. Too often, compensation has been looked upon in the very narrow sense as comprising only the monetary payments; the other necessary components have been omitted or slighted. Effective compensation requires a broader perspective which views compensation as illustrated in Table 1.

If one or more of these components of the integrated system fail to play their proper roles, the system is damaged—equitable motivational compensation will suffer. For example, if measurable accountability has been established (Component 1) but the evaluation or appraisal methods (Component 2) are not sufficiently reliable to measure specific achievement against the accountability, there is no basis for rewarding the manager. Similarly, it is not possible to evaluate achievement unless measurable accountability has first been established.

Table 1   COMPONENTS OF COMPENSATION

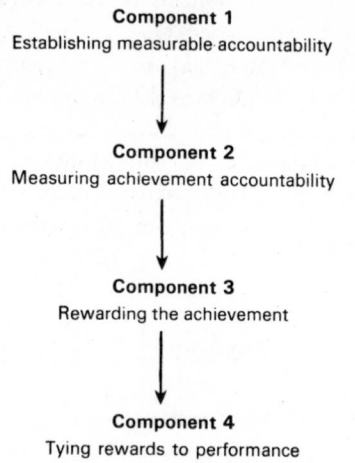

Component 1
Establishing measurable accountability

Component 2
Measuring achievement accountability

Component 3
Rewarding the achievement

Component 4
Tying rewards to performance

Clear-Cut Accountability

The only true basis for compensating a manager is to first assign him accountability for achieving specific results. His accountability must be expressed in specific terms which can be measured later to determine how much and how well he accomplished his tasks.

The more effective compensation systems require that accountability be spelled out in the form of specific, measurable objectives which the manager must achieve during a particular target period. The following are specific measurable objectives for a general manager of an operating division for a particular year:

Achieve pretax profit of $5 million
Achieve sales of $60 million
Achieve a return on investment of 12 percent
Reduce average monthly inventory by 11 percent
Complete Phase 2 of management development program.

In this example, the vague, general nature of accountability has been avoided. Instead, the division manager's accountability is now expressed in specific, clear-cut terms which can be measured and used as the basis for meaningful compensation. These objectives will be used later to illustrate how the remaining parts of the compensation system are carried out.

Measuring Performance

Once clear-cut accountability has been established, the next step is to measure the extent to which the accountability was achieved—to evaluate managerial performance. Here again, the traditionalists failed to consider the system's nature of compensation. Because the accountability was vague and general, the traditionalists did not (and could not) follow a results-oriented approach to measuring, but fell back on evaluating the manager on the basis of effort expended. The traditional approach usually took the form of the previously described evaluation procedure which emphasized "personality traits."

Obviously, it all but completely ignores examination of the critical question of what specific accountability was delegated to the manager. This approach to evaluating performance must be eliminated if effective compensation is to be achieved.

Figure 2 is a good example of a results-oriented evaluation form. It incorporates specific measurable objectives for the division manager. In this approach, the manager's performance is measured against each of the objectives for which he was accountable during the preceding year. The culmination of this matching of performance against objectives serves as the basis for determining how much compensation he should receive. This approach is consistent with one of the cardinal rules of performance evaluation—that performance appraisal must be sufficiently valid so that the results may be used for compensation purposes.

Figure 2   RESULTS-ORIENTED PERFORMANCE EVALUATION

Objectives (At beginning of year)	Results (At end of year)
Achieve pretax profit of $5 million	$ 6 million
Achieve sales of $60 million	$65 million
Achieve return on investment of 12 percent	13 percent
Reduce average monthly inventory by 11 percent	11 percent
Complete Phase 2 of management development program	Completed

Rewarding the Performance

Now that accountability has been established and performance on that accountability has been measured, the next step in the integrated system is to reward the performance in a way which promotes both equity and motivation.

While the importance of certain parts of a total compensation package such as stock options and pensions should not be minimized, they are not treated here because they are not directly related to individual performance. That is, the value of a stock option is not dependent upon individual performance but on how the investing public prices the stock, and all managers share equally in pension benefits. Two forms of compensation can and should be tied directly to individual managerial performance—salary and incentive payments.

Normally, direct compensation which is limited to salary payments is not sufficiently flexible and dynamic to recognize the wide swings or differences in performance among a group of managers. The cases of John Jones and Bill Smith, the two plant managers described earlier in this article, are vivid testimony to this premise.

Equity and motivation can best be served by utilizing both salary payments (fixed compensation) and incentive payments (variable compensation). With this approach, these direct payments can be viewed as resulting from two sources, salary payments and incentive payments.

Salary payments are rates paid for "holding down the job." The manager will always receive his salary, regardless of whether or not he receives incentive payments. The approaches and techniques for establishing salary rates are too well-known to dwell upon here. It will suffice to say that an enlightened compensation policy should provide for the payment of salaries based on the going rate for a particular managerial job based on a national average for that job. The rate should be examined at least annually to insure that it remains current.

Incentive payments are made, in addition to salary, on the basis of how well a job is accomplished. Because incentive payments are a variable form of compensation and are paid according to how well the manager performs, they provide the greatest possible opportunity to recognize any level of performance which the manager achieves (or fails to achieve). They permit compensation to be tied directly to performance on an individual basis.

If the manager's performance is below par, he receives no incentive payment—only his salary. If his performance exceeds par (his objectives), he receives above par incentive payments. For a year in which his performance was outstanding, he will receive commensurate incentive payments. All incentive payments are truly variable and based upon his varying levels of performance. An illustration of how the division general manager discussed earlier would be normally paid under an incentive plan follows.

The Weighting Problem.

The first requirement is to establish the relative weight of each of the manager's objectives *prior* to the beginning of the target year in which he is to carry out the objectives. Prior weighting of the objectives is critical; it places compensation on the beginning of the action. Only by making known the future impact of compensation prior to the action can compensation exert an influence on the action as it occurs. In the instance of the division general manager, his objectives might be weighted as shown in Table 2.

Table 2   APPLYING POINT WEIGHTS TO OBJECTIVES

Objectives	Possible Points
Achieve pretax profit of $5 million	50-100
Achieve sales of $60 million	30-80
Achieve return on investment of 12 percent	40-60
Reduce average monthly inventory by 11 percent	20-40
Complete Phase 2 of management development program	10-20

The importance of the weighting of objectives cannot be overemphasized—nor should the difficulty be minimized. It is one of the more difficult chores in formulating an incentive compensation plan and one which has caused many organizations to avoid using incentive compensation in favor of less effective but easier to develop compensation approaches. One of management's top level responsibilities is to solve problems—not walk away from them.

As an illustration, how should the manager in the simplified example in Table 2 be evaluated and rewarded if he overachieves his profit objective? Or if he overachieves both his sales and profit objectives but fails to meet his objective for return on investment (ROI)? Or if he achieves all three objectives covering sales, profit, and ROI, but is able to do so because he completely neglected his inventory reduction and management development objectives?

Obviously, the compensation policy and plan must provide for evaluating the manager on his overall performance on both quantitative factors (effectiveness— were the objectives accomplished?) and qualitative factors (efficiency—how well were the objectives accomplished?). It would be self-deflating, for example, to evaluate a manager only on effectiveness (for example, he exceeded his sales objective by 15 percent) without also looking at his efficiency (achievement of the extra 15 percent by concentrating on easy sales of fast moving products with a high cost of goods sold but with low profit margins).

The balance must be preserved by clearly indicating in advance—through the step-by-step plans or programs which should always support major objectives—how and in what proportion the objectives will be achieved. Therefore, when the target period is over and the performance is being evaluated, it is possible to determine whether the manager used good planning to achieve his objectives or whether he achieved the objective through questionable management practices.

Another policy decision is to define "minimum" performance to qualify for extra compensation. Must all objectives be achieved? If not, which objectives must be, and in what proportion? Must an increase in the sales objective be accompanied by a corresponding increase in profit and return on investment?

The Normal Award.

As each of the points shown in Table 2 is translated into incentive payment dollars (using future accomplishment as the determining basis) the manager is provided with the option of determining at what level of accomplishment he wants to work during the target period, or, expressed differently, the amount of compensation he wishes to earn. It is possible to obtain this advance knowledge about objectives (and the effects on performance which it can help bring about) by using what is commonly referred to as the "normal award" for achievement of objectives. The normal award can be defined simply as the amount of incentive compensation (commonly expressed as a percentage of base salary) which a manager can expect to receive when he fully achieves his objectives. Table 3 portrays a normal award schedule for various levels of managers.

Table 3 NORMAL AWARDS AT VARIOUS SALARY LEVELS

Salary Level	Normal Award Percentage of Base Salary
$12,000	15%
20,000	20
30,000	25
40,000	30
50,000	35
—	—
100,000	50
—	—
200,000	65

Obviously, the schedule or curve is constructed to increase the amount of the normal award at the higher levels of management. This reflects the greater potential of higher level managers to make a more substantial contribution to profits and to show greater responsibility for broader and more critical planning, decisions, and action.

Assume that the normal award for the division general manager is 35 percent of salary, and that his salary is $25,000. Two assumed levels of performance will be used to illustrate the compensation he would earn. In one case, he just achieves his objectives (par performance). In the second case, he exceeds his objectives (above par performance). The number of points he earns in both cases are shown in Table 4.

Table 4   POINTS EARNED AT VARIOUS PERFORMANCE LEVELS*

Objectives	Possible Points	Par		Above Par	
		Results	Points Earned	Results	Points Earned
$5 million profit	50-100	$5 million	50	$5 million	60
$60 million sales	30-80	$60 million	30	$60 million	33
12 percent ROI	40-60	12 percent	40	13 percent	44
Inventory reduction of 11 percent	20-40	11 percent	20	11 percent	20
Phase 2—management development program	10-20	Completed	10	Completed	10
Total			*150*		*167*

*In this example, the increased points are calculated on a one-to-one basis proportionate to the degree to which performance increased. Many companies accelerate the amount of the award at a higher rate once par performance has been achieved.

Following the "par" example used in Table 4, the division manager would receive 150 points for achieving his objectives. His normal incentive award at this point would be 35 percent of his salary, or $8,750. He would receive additional incentive compensation for the degree to which he achieves above par performance.

Once the normal award concept is adopted, the company must turn to a policy decision regarding the amount of the reward for more than 100 percent achievement of objectives. This policy should provide at least a one-for-one reward for the degree to which the objectives are exceeded. Translated into an actual example, this policy might provide payments to the manager according to Table 5.

Table 5 may be extended indefinitely; its most important feature is that for every percentage increase by which the manager exceeds his objective, his incentive payment should be increased by at least a commensurate percentage. The amounts are expressed both as a percentage of salary and in absolute dollars, since some companies relate incentive payments to the manager's salary and other companies establish absolute dollar levels which are not related to salaries. If all salaries have been established on an equitable basis, the former method is usually preferable,

Table 5 REWARDS FOR MORE THAN 100 PERCENT OBJECTIVE ACHIEVEMENT

Percent of Objective Achievement	Incentive Payment Amount	
	As Percent of Base Salary	In Absolute Dollars
100	10	x dollars
110	20	2x dollars
120	30	3x dollars
130	40	4x dollars

since it results in proportionately higher payments made to holders of higher level jobs.

Some companies limit maximum incentive payments to a certain percentage of salary. For example, the maximum payment a manager may receive is equal to 30 percent of his salary. Others use an open-ended method under which the amount of incentive payments is unlimited. The latter policy is more conducive to motivation because it emphasizes to the manager that his compensation is limited only by his accomplishments. The first policy does not provide the manager with real financial motivation to exceed his objectives by more than the point at which his compensation stops. However, for the first year or two of a new plan, to prevent incentive payments from running away while the plan and the objective-setting process are being "debugged" and refined, it may be well to establish a payment limitation. This limitation can be removed when the plan is operating effectively.

The Benefits.

The use of the weighting points and the normal award curve provide two major benefits to the manager—both of which bear heavily on equity and motivation. First, by knowing the weights prior to beginning the target year, he is able to calculate how many points he will earn at various levels of performance. For example, he knows that he will receive 30 points for achieving sales of $60 million (Table 4). If he desires to earn more points, he knows he must sell more than $60 million. He can make this decision prior to beginning his action for the target year. Second, he knows that his incentive compensation depends upon his own performance and that he has practically unlimited opportunity to earn additional compensation.

Neither time nor the purpose of this article permit the treatment here of the methods for establishing the total incentive fund for an organization as a whole or the methods for distributing portions of the total fund to various departments and divisions. It should be noted, however, that the total monies available for awarding an individual manager may be heavily influenced by the performance of the total company, his particular division or department, and, ultimately, by his own performance.

The Impact of Outside Factors

One of the more complex issues which must be considered when applying an incentive formula is how to handle the impact of outside factors over which the manager has no control. These outside factors can operate to enhance or impede his performance. For example, a few years ago a flu-like epidemic in the East caused a substantial and unanticipated demand for a leading brand of cough-drops. The sales manager for this product was able to greatly exceed his sales objective. This raised a question with respect to his incentive compensation. Should he receive additional compensation for the additional sales which did not result from his managing and planning but from factors outside of his control?

While there is not an easy or a perfect answer to this question, two general approaches are commonly followed. The first is to include a "windfall gain or loss" provision in the incentive plan. In this approach the manager's superior (and ultimately the incentive compensation committee comprised of outside directors) endeavors to isolate and evaluate the major factors which occurred and over which the manager had no control. The manager's incentive compensation may be adjusted according to this evaluation. A less desirable alternative is to consider only the results achieved without attempting to evaluate the "why." The manager's incentive sinks or swims according to the final tally.

The second approach is to evaluate the results achieved in light of the step-by-step plans developed by the manager to support his objectives. The purpose of this evaluation is to determine whether he planned (managed) his way to the results or whether he was just lucky. Evaluation of the planning process also permits an assessment of the impact of unfavorable outside events.

Regardless of which approach is used, the provisions and operations should be explained as completely as possible to all eligible managers before—not after—the target year begins.

Tying Compensation to Performance

If the equation "performance equals rewards" is to be valid, it is necessary to emphasize the interrelated nature of the two. This includes eliminating the arbitrary practice of separating performance appraisal interviews and compensation interviews. One of the traditional reasons advanced for making the separation goes to the heart of the old ineffective performance evaluation approach based on "personality traits." These were frequently used to justify just about any salary increase granted by a superior to a subordinate. For example, if a superior wanted to justify an increase for a subordinate, he would rate the subordinate as being excellent on all factors being rated. It was difficult to quarrel with the rating because it was not determined by objective results.

Thus, the traditionalists thought they could eliminate this stacking of the deck by separating the two interviews. However, any validity which this reasoning once enjoyed has now been negated by the increasing use of performance evaluation based on results. Measuring based on the specific results achieved makes it difficult to stack the deck to justify a whim or unjustified wish.

If performance is to truly equal rewards, increased emphasis should be devoted to discussing compensation as a natural and necessary part of the performance appraisal interview.

Parable: Once upon a time a farmer had six jackasses and a barn full of carrots which he kept under lock and key.

At the end of a day of wagon pulling, the farmer looked back over the day's performance of each jackass. To one of the jackasses he said, "You did an outstanding job; here are six carrots." To four of the others, he said, "Your performance was average; here are three carrots." To the remaining jackass he said, "You didn't pull your share of the load; here is one carrot."

Another day of wagon pulling dawned. The top jackass, having been properly rewarded, began the day in high spirits. The thoughts of the remaining jackasses were consumed with how they might earn more carrots through their efforts that day. The farmer had carrots available, but they had to be earned.

Moral of the story: Jackasses do work for carrots!

Section D

Leadership and Supervision: Situational Analysis

Leadership implies working with people to accomplish certain goals which may be personal or organizational in nature. By contrast, management implies a more exclusive devotion to the accomplishment of organizational objectives. Given that career success involves a blending of both personal and organizational goals, managers have shown considerable interest in the subject of leadership—as have numerous organizational researchers.

The sustained interest in leadership has produced a vast literature with an often confusing and unproductive array of results. Early studies focused on personality traits without finding any special type of individual who consistently showed signs of leadership success. Later efforts stressed the advantages of democratic supervision, but results were not consistent. Leadership seemed more researched than understood. Recently, however, progress has been made in the leadership area. Instead of emphasizing traits or participative approaches, researchers have begun to examine the conditions under which different leadership styles are most effective.

Despite such progress, the diversity of leadership research often leaves managers wondering whether their styles should be more directive or more permissive. This is especially true in day-to-day job settings where a manager may confront different work groups doing different tasks. To provide some leadership guidelines, the present section includes four articles which respectively identify different leadership patterns, discuss the impact of situational variables on style, critically review a "contingency model" of leadership, and examine the question of whether leadership style is rigid or flexible.

The first selection, by Tannenbaum and Schmidt, deals with "How to Choose a Leadership Pattern." In 1958 this article was published by the *Harvard Business Review* and, given its continued relevance, was republished in 1973 with a retrospective commentary by its authors. As will be seen in this republished version, Tannenbaum and Schmidt advocate no single best style and view managerial behavior on a continuum ranging from boss-centered to subordinate-centered leadership. For them, the successful manager is neither strong nor permissive. Instead success will depend on certain forces in the manager, subordinates, and the situation. In Tannenbaum and Schmidt's words, the successful manager is one "who maintains a high batting average in accurately assessing the forces that determine what his most appropriate behavior at any given time should be and in actually being able to behave accordingly."

Unfortunately, Tannenbaum and Schmidt do not spell out the specific circumstances under which various styles of leadership are most effective. Other investigators, however, have tried to do precisely that. The most widely known effort in this regard concerns the work of Fiedler. His article, "Style or Circumstance: The Leadership Enigma," explains an empirically based contingency model in which three situational factors (leader-member relations, tast structure, and leader position power) interact to determine whether directive or permissive leadership is most appropriate. Fiedler's research suggests that a directive approach is best when situational variables are either very favorable or very unfavorable for the leader. (By "favorable" is meant that the leader has power, a structured task, and group support). In situations of intermediate favorableness, a human-relations approach seems preferable.

Fiedler also notes that managerial styles are difficult to change. Accordingly, he recommends job engineering to make a situation more congruent with a leader's style. For example, permissive leaders facing an unfavorable situation with poor leader-member relations might seek out subordinates with backgrounds more like their own. This would make the situation more "intermediate" in favorableness and better matched to the leader's style. (Whether union contracts or company budgets would allow such personnel changes is another matter.)

Fiedler's contingency model has had a significant impact on leadership research but has not gone unchallenged. In the third article, Hunt takes up the topic of "Organizational Leadership: Some Theoretical and Empirical Considerations" and critically examines Fiedler's work. Hunt provides evidence of his own that supports the contingency model but also raises a number of questions that emerge from Fiedler's research, including the model's relevance if applied to co-acting instead of interacting groups.

The final article, by Hill, deals with the question of "Leadership Style: Rigid or Flexible?" Is it easier to change a manager's style or to reengineer the situation instead? The former view is implicit in Tannenbaum and Schmidt's work while the latter view is explicit in Fiedler's work. To examine this issue, Hill measured subordinate perceptions of their leaders' abilities to use different styles of behavior. Subjects were 124 middle- and first-level managers from accounting and research/development departments in two English companies. Results indicated that the subjects perceived their supervisors as using different styles to deal with four hypothetical (but typical) problems used in the study. Neither organizational level nor functional area affected the data, but subordinates reported that style patterns varied depending on whether interpersonal or technical problems were involved. Hill concludes that most leaders can behave flexibly enough to cope with varied situations and that "It may not be necessary either to change managers as the situation changes or to modify the situation to fit managers' styles."

How To Choose a Leadership Pattern

Robert Tannenbaum and Warren H. Schmidt

"I put most problems into my group's hands and leave it to them to carry the ball from there. I serve merely as a catalyst, mirroring back the people's thoughts and feelings so that they can better understand them. . . ."

"It's foolish to make decisions oneself on matters that affect people. I always talk things over with my subordinates, but I make it clear to them that I'm the one who has to have the final say. . . ."

"Once I have decided on a course of action, I do my best to sell my ideas to my employees. . . ."

"I'm being paid to lead. If I let a lot of other people make the decisions I should be making, then I'm not worth my salt. . . ."

"I believe in getting things done. I can't waste time calling meetings. Someone has to call the shots around here, and I think it should be me. . . ."

Each of these statements represents a point of view about "good leadership." Considerable experience, factual data, and theoretical principles could be cited to support each statement, even though they seem to be inconsistent when placed together. Such contradictions point up the dilemma in which the modern manager frequently finds himself.

NEW PROBLEM

The problem of how the modern manager can be "democratic" in his relations with subordinates and at the same time maintain the necessary authority and control in the organization for which he is responsible has come into focus increasingly in recent years.

Earlier in the century this problem was not so acutely felt. The successful executive was generally pictured as possessing intelligence, imagination, initiative, the capacity to make rapid (and generally wise) decisions, and the ability to inspire subordinates. People tended to think of the world as being divided into "leaders" and "followers."

New focus
Gradually, however, from the social sciences emerged the concept of "group dynamics" with its focus on *members* of the group rather than solely on the leader. Research efforts of social scientists underscored the importance of employee involvement and participation in decision-making. Evidence began to challenge the efficiency of highly directive leadership, and increasing attention was paid to problems of motivation and human relations.

Through training laboratories in group development that sprang up across the country, many of the newer notions of leadership began to exert an impact. These training laboratories were carefully designed to give people a first-hand experience in full participation and decision-making. The designated "leaders" deliberately attempted to reduce their own power and to make group members as responsible as possible for setting their own goals and methods within the laboratory experience.

It was perhaps inevitable that some of the people who attended the training laboratories regarded this kind of leadership as being truly "democratic" and went home with the determination to build fully participative decision-making into their own organizations. Whenever their bosses made a decision without convening a staff meeting, they tended to perceive this as authoritarian behavior. The true symbol of democratic leadership to some was the meeting—and the less directed from the top, the more democratic it was.

Some of the more enthusiastic alumni of these training laboratories began to get the habit of categorizing leader behavior as "democratic" *or* "authoritarian." The boss who made too many decisions himself was thought of as an authoritarian, and his directive behavior was often attributed solely to his personality.

New need

The net result of the research findings and of the human relations training based upon them has been to call into question the stereotype of an effective leader. Consequently, the modern manager often finds himself in an uncomfortable state of mind.

Often he is not quite sure how to behave; there are times when he is torn between exerting "strong" leadership and "permissive" leadership. Sometimes new knowledge pushes him in one direction ("I should really get the group to help make this decision"), but at the same time his experience pushes him in another direction ("I really understand the problem better than the group and therefore I should make the decision"). He is not sure when a group decision is really appropriate or when holding a staff meeting serves merely as a device for avoiding his own decision-making responsibility.

The purpose of our article is to suggest a framework which managers may find useful in grappling with this dilemma. First, we shall look at the different patterns of leadership behavior that the manager can choose from in relating himself to his subordinates. Then, we shall turn to some of the questions suggested by this range of patterns. For instance, how important is it for a manager's subordinates to know what type of leadership he is using in a situation? What factors should he consider in deciding on a leadership pattern? What difference do his long-run objectives make as compared to his immediate objectives?

Range of Behavior

Figure 1 presents the continuum or range of possible leadership behavior available to a manager. Each type of action is related to the degree of authority used by the boss and to the amount of freedom available to his subordinates in reaching decisions. The actions seen on the extreme left characterize the manager who maintains a high degree of control while those seen on the extreme right characterize the manager who releases a high degree of control. Neither extreme is absolute; authority and freedom are never without their limitations.

Now let us look more closely at each of the behavior points occurring along this continuum.

The manager makes the decision and announces it.

In this case the boss identifies a problem, considers alternative solutions, chooses one of them, and then reports this decision to his subordinates for implementation. He may or may not give consideration to what he believes his subordinates will think or feel about his decision; in any case, he provides no opportunity for them to participate directly in the decision-making process. Coercion may or may not be used or implied.

Figure 1 CONTINUUM OF LEADERSHIP BEHAVIOR

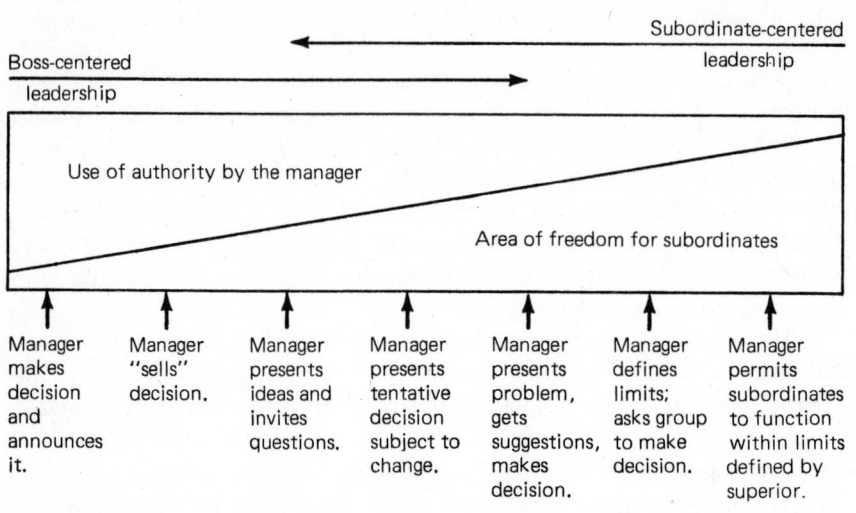

The manager "sells" his decision.

Here the manager, as before, takes responsibility for identifying the problem and arriving at a decision. However, rather than simply announcing it, he takes the additional step of persuading his subordinates to accept it. In doing so, he recognizes the possibility of some resistance among those who will be faced with the decision, and seeks to reduce this resistance by indicating, for example, what the employees have to gain from his decision.

The manager presents his ideas, invites questions.

Here the boss who has arrived at a decision and who seeks acceptance of his ideas provides an opportunity for his subordinates to get a fuller explanation of his thinking and his intentions. After presenting the ideas, he invites questions so that his associates can better understand what he is trying to accomplish. This "give and take" also enables the manager and the subordinates to explore more fully the implications of the decision.

The manager presents a tentative decision subject to change.

This kind of behavior permits the subordinates to exert some influence on the decision. The initiative for identifying and diagnosing the problem remains with the boss. Before meeting with his staff, he has thought the problem through and arrived at a decision—but only a tentative one. Before finalizing it, he presents his proposed solution for the reaction of those who will be affected by it. He says in effect, "I'd like to hear what you have to say about this plan that I have developed. I'll appreciate your frank reactions, but will reserve for myself the final decision."

The manager presents the problem, gets suggestions, and then makes his decision.

Up to this point the boss has come before the group with a solution of his own. Not so in this case. The subordinates now get the first chance to suggest solutions. The manager's initial role involves identifying the problem. He might, for example, say something of this sort: "We are faced with a number of complaints from newspapers and the general public on our service policy. What is wrong here? What ideas do you have for coming to grips with this problem?"

The function of the group becomes one of increasing the manager's repertory of possible solutions to the problem. The purpose is to capitalize on the knowledge and experience of those who are on the "firing line." From the expanded list of alternatives developed by the manager and his subordinates, the manager then selects the solution that he regards as most promising.[1]

The manager defines the limits and requests the group to make a decision.

At this point the manager passes to the group (possibly including himself as a member) the right to make decisions. Before doing so, however, he defines the problem to be solved and the boundaries within which the decision must be made.

An example might be the handling of a parking problem at a plant. The boss decides that this is something that should be worked on by the people involved, so he calls them together and points up the existence of the problem. Then he tells them:

"There is the open field just north of the main plant which has been designated for additional employee parking. We can build underground or surface multilevel facilities as long as the cost does not exceed $100,000. Within these limits we are free to work out whatever solution makes sense to us. After we decide on a specific plan, the company will spend the available money in whatever way we indicate."

The manager permits the group to make decisions within prescribed limits.

This represents an extreme degree of group freedom only occasionally encountered in formal organizations, as, for instance, in many research groups. Here the team of managers or engineers undertakes the identification and diagnosis of the problem, develops alternative procedures for solving it, and decides on one or more of these alternative solutions. The only limits directly imposed on the group by the organization are those specified by the superior of the team's boss. If the boss participates in the decision-making process, he attempts to do so with no

---

1. For a fuller explanation of this approach see Leo Moore, Too much management, too little change, *Harvard Business Review*, 41 (January-February 1956).

more authority than any other member of the group. He commits himself in advance to assist in implementing whatever decision the group makes.

KEY QUESTIONS

As the continuum in Figure 1 demonstrates, there are a number of alternative ways in which a manager can relate himself to the group or individuals he is supervising. At the extreme left of the range, the emphasis is on the manager—on what *he* is interested in, how *he* sees things, how *he* feels about them. As we move toward the subordinate-centered end of the continuum, however, the focus is increasingly on the subordinates—on what *they* are interested in, how *they* look at things, how *they* feel about them.

When business leadership is regarded in this way, a number of questions arise. Let us take four of especial importance:

Can a boss ever relinquish his responsibility by delegating it to someone else?

Our view is that the manager must expect to be held responsible by his superior for the quality of the decisions made, even though operationally these decisions may have been made on a group basis. He should, therefore, be ready to accept whatever risk is involved whenever he delegates decision-making power to his subordinates. Delegation is not a way of "passing the buck." Also, it should be emphasized that the amount of freedom the boss gives to his subordinates cannot be greater than the freedom which he himself has been given by his own superior.

Should the manager participate with his subordinates once he has delegated responsibility to them?

The manager should carefully think over this question and decide on his role prior to involving the subordinate group. He should ask if his presence will inhibit or facilitate the problem-solving process. There may be some instances when he should leave the group to let it solve the problem for itself. Typically, however, the boss has useful ideas to contribute, and should function as an additional member of the group. In the latter instance, it is important that he indicate clearly to the group that he sees himself in a *member* role rather than in an authority role.

How important is it for the group to recognize what kind of leadership behavior the boss is using?

It makes a great deal of difference. Many relationship problems between boss and subordinate occur because the boss fails to make clear how he plans to use his authority. If, for example, he actually intends to make a certain decision himself, but the subordinate group gets the impression that he has delegated this authority, considerable confusion and resentment are likely to follow. Problems may also occur when the boss uses a "democratic" facade to conceal the fact that he has already made a decision which he hopes the group will accept as its own. The attempt to "make them think it was their idea in the first place" is a risky one. We believe that it is highly important for the manager to be honest and clear in describing what authority he is keeping and what role he is asking his subordinates to assume in solving a particular problem.

Can you tell how "democratic" a manager is by the number of decisions his subordinates make?

The sheer *number* of decisions is not an accurate index of the amount of freedom that a subordinate group enjoys. More important is the *significance* of the decisions which the boss entrusts to his subordinates. Obviously a decision on how to arrange desks is of an entirely different order from a decision involving the introduction of new electronic data-processing equipment. Even though the widest possible limits are given in dealing with the first issue, the group will sense no particular degree of responsibility. For a boss to permit the group to decide equipment policy, even within rather narrow limits, would reflect a greater degree of confidence in them on his part.

DECIDING HOW TO LEAD

Now let us turn from the types of leadership which are possible in a company situation to the question of what types are *practical* and *desirable*. What factors or forces should a manager consider in deciding how to manage? Three are of particular importance:

> Forces in the manager;
> Forces in the subordinates;
> Forces in the situation.

We should like briefly to describe these elements and indicate how they might influence a manager's action in a decision-making situation.[2] The strength of each of them will, of course, vary from instance to instance, but the manager who is sensitive to them can better assess the problems which face him and determine which mode of leadership behavior is most appropriate for him.

Forces in the Manager

The manager's behavior in any given instance will be influenced greatly by the many forces operating within his own personality. He will, of course, perceive his

---

2. See also Robert Tannenbaum and Fred Massarik, Participation by subordinates in the managerial decision-making process, *Canadian Journal of Economics and Political Science,* 1950 (August), 413.

leadership problems in a unique way on the basis of his background, knowledge, and experience. Among the important internal forces affecting him will be the following:

1. *His value system.* How strongly does he feel that individuals should have a share in making the decisions which affect them? Or, how convinced is he that the official who is paid to assume responsibility should personally carry the burden of decision-making? The strength of his convictions on questions like those will tend to move the manager to one end or the other of the continuum shown in Figure 1. His behavior will also be influenced by the relative importance that he attaches to organizational efficiency, personal growth of subordinates, and company profits.[3]

2. *His confidence in his subordinates.* Managers differ greatly in the amount of trust they have in other people generally, and this carries over to the particular employees they supervise at a given time. In viewing his particular group of subordinates, the manager is likely to consider their knowledge and competence with respect to the problem. A central question he might ask himself is: "Who is best qualified to deal with this problem?" Often he may, justifiably or not, have more confidence in his own capabilities than in those of subordinates.

3. *His own leadership inclinations.* There are some managers who seem to function more comfortably and naturally as highly directive leaders. Resolving problems and issuing orders come easily to them. Other managers seem to operate more comfortably in a team role, where they are continually sharing many of their functions with their subordinates.

4. *His feelings of security in an uncertain situation.* The manager who releases control over the decision-making process thereby reduces the predictability of the outcome. Some managers have a greater need than others for predictability and stability in their environment. This "tolerance for ambiguity" is being viewed increasingly by psychologists as a key variable in a person's manner of dealing with problems.

The manager brings these and other highly personal variables to each situation he faces. If he can see them as forces which, consciously or unconsciously, influence his behavior, he can better understand what makes him prefer to act in a given way. And understanding this, he can often make himself more effective.

Forces in the Subordinate

Before deciding how to lead a certain group, the manager will also want to consider a number of forces affecting his subordinates' behavior. He will want to re-

---

3. See Chris Argyris, Top management dilemma: company needs v. individual development, *Personnel* 1955 (September), 123-24.

member that each employee, like himself, is influenced by many personality variables. In addition, each subordinate has a set of expectations about how the boss should act in relation to him (the phrase "expected behavior" is one we hear more and more often these days at discussions of leadership and teaching). The better the manager understands these factors, the more accurately he can determine what kind of behavior on his part will enable his subordinates to act most effectively.

Generally speaking, the manager can permit his subordinates greater freedom if the following essential conditions exist:

If the subordinates have relatively high needs for independence. (As we all know, people differ greatly in the amount of direction that they desire.)

If the subordinates have a readiness to assume responsibility for decision-making. (Some see additional responsibility as a tribute to their ability; others see it as "passing the buck.")

If they have a relatively high tolerance for ambiguity. (Some employees prefer to have clear-cut directives given to them; others prefer a wider area of freedom.)

If they are interested in the problem and feel that it is important.

If they understand and identify with the goals of the organization.

If they have the necessary knowledge and experience to deal with the problem.

If they have learned to expect to share in decision-making. (Persons who have come to expect strong leadership and are then suddenly confronted with the request to share more fully in decision-making are often upset by this new experience. On the other hand, persons who have enjoyed a considerable amount of freedom resent the boss who begins to make all the decisions himself.)

The manager will probably tend to make fuller use of his own authority if the above conditions do *not* exist; at times there may be no realistic alternative to running a "one-man show."

The restrictive effect of many of the forces will, of course, be greatly modified by the general feeling of confidence which subordinates have in the boss. Where they have learned to respect and trust him, he is free to vary his behavior. He will feel certain that he will not be perceived as an authoritarian boss on those occasions when he makes decisions by himself. Similarly, he will not be seen as using staff meetings to avoid his decision-making responsibility. In a climate of mutual confidence and respect, people tend to feel less threatened by deviations from normal practice, which in turn makes possible a higher degree of flexibility in the whole relationship.

Forces in the Situation

In addition to the forces which exist in the manager himself and in his subordinates, certain characteristics of the general situation will also affect the manager's behavior. Among the more critical environmental pressures that surround him are those which stem from the organization, the work group, the nature of the problem, and the pressures of time. Let us look briefly at each of these:

Type of organization

Like individuals, organizations have values and traditions which inevitably influence the behavior of the people who work in them. The manager who is a newcomer to a company quickly discovers that certain kinds of behavior are approved while others are not. He also discovers that to deviate radically from what is generally accepted is likely to create problems for him.

These values and traditions are communicated in numerous ways—through job descriptions, policy pronouncements, and public statements by top executives. Some organizations, for example, hold to the notion that the desirable executive is one who is dynamic, imaginative, decisive, and persuasive. Other organizations put more emphasis upon the importance of the executive's ability to work effectively with people—his human relations skills. The fact that his superiors have a defined concept of what the good executive should be will very likely push the manager toward one end or the other of the behavioral range.

In addition to the above, the amount of employee participation is influenced by such variables as the size of the working units, their geographical distribution, and degree of inter- and intra-organizational security required to attain company goals. For example, the wide geographical dispersion of an organization may preclude a practical system of participative decision-making, even though this would otherwise be desirable. Similarly, the size of the working units or the need for keeping plans confidential may make it necessary for the boss to exercise more control than would otherwise be the case. Factors like these may limit considerably the manager's ability to function flexibly on the continuum.

Group effectiveness

Before turning decision-making responsibility over to a subordinate group, the boss should consider how effectively its members work together as a unit.

One of the relevant factors here is the experience the group has had in working together. It can generally be expected that a group which has functioned for some time will have developed habits of cooperation and thus be able to tackle a problem more effectively than a new group. It can also be expected that a group of people with similar backgrounds and interests will work more quickly and easily than people with dissimilar backgrounds, because the communication problems are likely to be less complex.

The degree of confidence that the members have in their ability to solve problems as a group is also a key consideration. Finally, such group variables as cohesiveness, permissiveness, mutual acceptance, and commonality of purpose will exert subtle but powerful influence on the group's functioning.

The problem itself

The nature of the problem may determine what degree of authority should be delegated by the manager to his subordinates. Obviously he will ask himself whether they have the kind of knowledge which is needed. It is possible to do them a real disservice by assigning a problem that their experience does not equip them to handle.

Since the problems faced in large or growing industries increasingly require knowledge of specialists from many different fields, it might be inferred that the more complex a problem, the more anxious a manager will be to get some assistance in solving it. However, this is not always the case. There will be times when the very complexity of the problem calls for one person to work it out. For example, if the manager has most of the background and factual data relevant to a given issue, it may be easier for him to think it through himself than to take the time to fill in his staff on all the pertinent background information.

The key question to ask, of course, is: "Have I heard the ideas of everyone who has the necessary knowledge to make a significant contribution to the solution of this problem?"

The pressure of time

This is perhaps the most clearly felt pressure on the manager (in spite of the fact that it may sometimes be imagined). The more that he feels the need for an immediate decision, the more difficult it is to involve other people. In organizations which are in a constant state of "crisis" and "crash programming" one is likely to find managers personally using a high degree of authority with relatively little delegation to subordinates. When the time pressure is less intense, however, it becomes much more possible to bring subordinates in on the decision-making process.

These, then, are the principal forces that impinge on the manager in any given instance and that tend to determine his tactical behavior in relation to his subordinates. In each case his behavior ideally will be that which makes possible the most effective attainment of his immediate goal within the limits facing him.

LONG-RUN STRATEGY

As the manager works with his organization on the problems that come up day by day, his choice of a leadership pattern is usually limited. He must take account of the forces just described and, within the restrictions they impose on him, do the best that he can. But as he looks ahead months or even years, he can shift his thinking from tactics to large-scale strategy. No longer need he be fettered by all of the forces mentioned, for he can view many of them as variables over which he has some control. He can, for example, gain new insights or skills for himself, supply training for individual subordinates, and provide participative experiences for his employee group.

In trying to bring about a change in these variables, however, he is faced with a challenging question: At which point along the continuum *should* he act?

Attaining Objectives

The answer depends largely on what he wants to accomplish. Let us suppose that he is interested in the same objectives that most modern managers seek to attain when they can shift their attention from the pressure of immediate assignments:

1. To raise the level of employee motivation;
2. To increase the readiness of subordinates to accept change;
3. To improve the quality of all managerial decisions;
4. To develop teamwork and morale;
5. To further the individual development of employees.

In recent years the manager has been deluged with a flow of advice on how best to achieve these longer-run objectives. It is little wonder that he is often both bewildered and annoyed. However, there are some guidelines which he can usefully follow in making a decision.

Most research and much of the experience of recent years give a strong factual basis to the theory that a fairly high degree of subordinate-centered behavior is associated with the accomplishment of the five purposes mentioned.[4] This does not mean that a manager should always leave all decisions to his assistants. To provide the individual or the group with greater freedom than they are ready for at any given time may very well tend to generate anxieties and therefore inhibit rather than facilitate the attainment of desired objectives. But this should not keep the manager from making a continuing effort to confront his subordinates with the challenge of freedom.

CONCLUSION

In summary, there are two implications in the basic thesis that we have been developing. The first is that the successful leader is one who is keenly aware of those forces which are most relevant to his behavior at any given time. He accurately understands himself, the individuals and group he is dealing with, and the company and broader social environment in which he operates. And certainly he is able to assess the present readiness for growth of his subordinates.

But this sensitivity or understanding is not enough, which brings us to the

---

4. For example, see Warren H. Schmidt and Paul C. Buchanan, *Techniques that produce teamwork* (New London, Arthur C. Croft Publications, 1954); and Morris S. Viteles, *Motivation and morale in industry* (New York, W. W. Norton, 1953).

second implication. The successful leader is one who is able to behave appropriately in the light of these perceptions. If direction is in order, he is able to direct; if considerable participative freedom is called for, he is able to provide such freedom.

Thus, the successful manager of men can be primarily characterized neither as a strong leader nor as a permissive one. Rather, he is one who maintains a high batting average in accurately assessing the forces that determine what his most appropriate behavior at any given time should be and in actually being able to behave accordingly. Being both insightful and flexible, he is less likely to see the problems of leadership as a dilemma.

RETROSPECTIVE COMMENTARY

Since this **HBR** Classic was first published in 1958, there have been many changes in organizations and in the world that have affected leadership patterns. While the article's continued popularity attests to its essential validity, we believe it can be reconsidered and updated to reflect subsequent societal changes and new management concepts.

The reasons for the article's continued relevance can be summarized briefly:

The article contains insights and perspectives which mesh well with, and help clarify, the experiences of managers, other leaders, and students of leadership. Thus it is useful to individuals in a wide variety of organizations—industrial, governmental, educational, religious, and community.

The concept of leadership the article defines is reflected in a continuum of leadership behavior (see Figure 1 in original article). Rather than offering a choice between two styles of leadership, democratic or authoritarian, it sanctions a range of behavior.

The concept does not dictate to managers but helps them to analyze their own behavior. The continuum permits them to review their behavior within a context of other alternatives, without any style being labeled right or wrong.

(We have sometimes wondered if we have, perhaps, made it too easy for anyone to justify his or her style of leadership. It may be a small step between being nonjudgmental and giving the impression that all behavior is equally valid and useful. The latter was not our intention. Indeed, the thrust of our endorsement was for the manager who is insightful in assessing relevant forces within himself, others, and the situation, and who can be flexible in responding to these forces.)

In recognizing that our article can be updated, we are acknowledging that organizations do not exist in a vacuum but are affected by changes that occur in society. Consider, for example, the implications for organizations of these recent social developments:

The youth revolution that expresses distrust and even contempt for organizations identified with the establishment.

The civil rights movement that demands all minority groups be given a greater opportunity for participation and influence in the organizational processes.

The ecology and consumer movements that challenge the right of managers to make decisions without considering the interest of people outside the organization.

The increasing national concern with the quality of working life and its relationship to worker productivity, participation, and satisfaction.

These and other societal changes make effective leadership in this decade a more challenging task, requiring even greater sensitivity and flexibility than was needed in the 1950s. Today's manager is more likely to deal with employees who resent being treated as subordinates, who may be highly critical of any organizational system, who expect to be consulted and to exert influence, and who often stand on the edge of alienation from the institution that needs their loyalty and commitment. In addition, he is frequently confronted by a highly turbulent, unpredictable environment.

In response to these social pressures, new concepts of management have emerged in organizations. Open-system theory, with its emphasis on subsystems' interdependency *and* on the interaction of an organization with its environment, has made a powerful impact on managers' approach to problems. Organization development has emerged as a new behavioral science approach to the improvement of individual, group, organizational, and interorganizational performance. New research has added to our understanding of motivation in the work situation. More and more executives have become concerned with social responsibility and have explored the feasibility of social audits. And a growing number of organizations, in Europe and in the United States, have conducted experiments in industrial democracy.

In light of these developments, we submit the following thoughts on how we would rewrite certain points in our original article.

The article described forces in the manager, subordinates, and the situation as givens, with the leadership pattern a resultant of these forces. We would now give more attention to the *interdependency* of these forces. For example, such interdependency occurs in: (a) the interplay between the manager's confidence in his subordinates, their readiness to assume responsibility, and the level of group effectiveness; and (b) the impact of the behavior of the manager on that of his subordinates, and vice versa.

In discussing the forces in the situation, we primarily identified organizational phenomena. We would now include forces lying outside the organization, and would explore the relevant interdependencies between the organization and its environment.

In the original article we presented the size of the rectangle in Figure 1 as a given, with its boundaries already determined by external forces—in effect, a closed system. We would now recognize the possibility of the manager and/or his subordinates taking the initiative to change those boundaries through interaction with relevant external forces—both within their own organization and in the larger society.

The article portrayed the manager as the principal and almost unilateral actor. He initiated and determined group functions, assumed responsibility, and exercised control. Subordinates made inputs and assumed power only at the will of the manager. Although the manager might have taken into account forces outside himself, it was *he* who decided where to operate on the continuum—that is, whether to announce a decision instead of trying to sell his idea to his subordinates, whether to invite questions, to let subordinates decide an issue, and so on. While the manager has retained this clear prerogative in many organizations, it has been challenged in others. Even in situations where he has retained it, however, the balance in the relationship between manager and subordinates at any given time is arrived at by interaction—direct or indirect—between the two parties.

Although power and its use by the manager played a role in our article, we now realize that our concern with cooperation and collaboration, common goals, commitment, trust, and mutual caring limited our vision with respect to the realities of power. We did not attempt to deal with unions, other forms of joint worker action, or with individual workers' expressions of resistance. Today, we would recognize much more clearly the power available to *all* parties, and the factors that underlie the interrelated decisions on whether to use it.

In the original article, we used the terms "manager" and "subordinate." We are now uncomfortable with "subordinate" because of its demeaning, dependency-laden connotations and prefer "nonmanager." The titles "manager" and "nonmanager" make the terminological difference functional rather than hierarchical.

We assumed fairly traditional organizational structures in our original article. Now we would alter our formulation to reflect newer organizational modes which are slowly emerging, such as industrial democracy, intentional communities, and "phenomenarchy."[5] These new modes are based on observations such as the following:

Both manager and nonmanagers may be governing forces in their group's environment, contributing to the definition of the total area of freedom.

A group can function without a manager, with managerial functions being shared by group members.

A group, as a unit, can be delegated authority and can assume responsibility within a larger organizational context.

Our thoughts on the question of leadership have prompted us to design a new behavior continuum (see Figure 2) in which the total area of freedom shared by manager and nonmanagers is constantly redefined by interactions between them and the forces in the environment.

---

5. For a description of phenomenarchy, see Will McWhinney, Phenomenarchy: A suggestion for social redesign, *Journal of Applied Behavioral Science,* May 1973.

Figure 2 CONTINUUM OF MANAGER–NONMANAGER BEHAVIOR

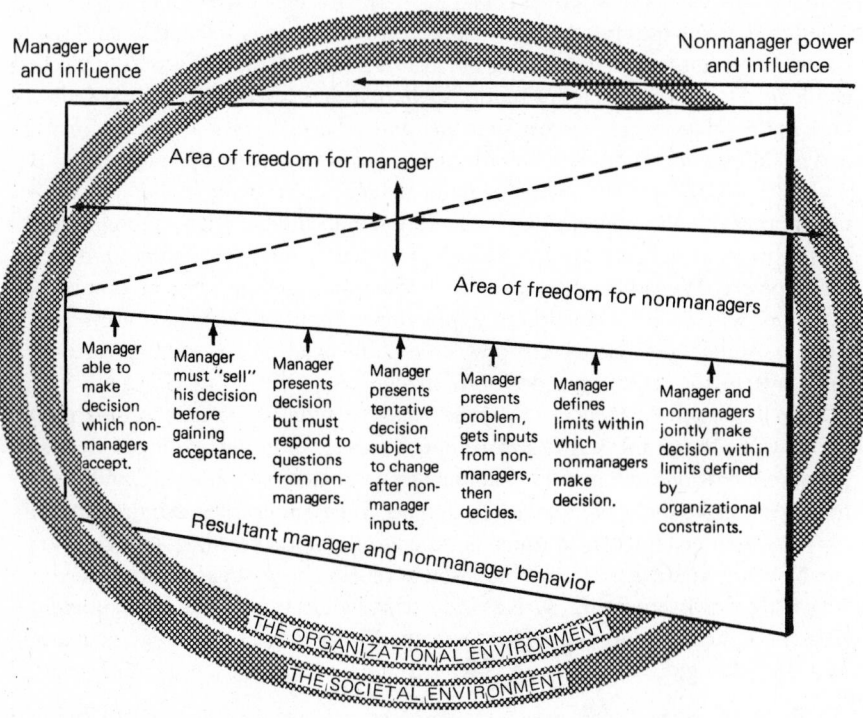

The arrows in the exhibit indicate the continual flow of interdependent influence among systems and people. The points on the continuum designate the types of manager and nonmanager behavior that become possible with any given amount of freedom available to each. The new continuum is both more complex and more dynamic than the 1958 version, reflecting the organizational and societal realities of the 1970s.

Style or Circumstance:
The Leadership Enigma

Fred E. Fiedler

What is it that makes a person an effective leader?

We take it for granted that good leadership is essential to business, to government, and to all the myriad groups and organizations that shape the way we live, work, and play.

We spend at least several billions of dollars a year on leadership development and executive recruitment in the United States. Leaders are paid 10, 20, and 30 times the salary of ordinary workers. Thousands of books and articles on leadership have been published. Yet we still know relatively little about the factors that determine a leader's success or failure.

Psychologists have been concerned with two major questions in their research on leadership: How does a man become a leader? What kind of personality traits or behavior makes a person an *effective* leader? For the past 15 years, my own work at the University of Illinois Group-Effectiveness Research Laboratory has concentrated on the latter question.

Psychologists used to think that special personality traits would distinguish leaders from followers. Several hundred research studies have been conducted to identify these special traits. But the search has been futile.

People who become leaders tend to be somewhat more intelligent, bigger, more assertive, more talkative than other members of their group. But these traits are far less important than most people think. What most frequently distinguishes the leader from his co-workers is that he knows more about the group task or that he can do it better. A bowling team is likely to choose its captain from good rather than poor bowlers, and the foreman of a machine shop is more likely to be a good machinist than a poor one.

In many organizations, one only has to live long in order to gain experience and seniority, and with these a position of leadership.

In business and industry today, the men who attain a leadership position must have the requisite education and talent. Of course, as W. Lloyd Warner and James C. Abegglen of the University of Chicago have shown, it has been most useful to come from or marry into a family that owns a large slice of the company's stock.

Becoming a leader, then, depends on personality only to a limited extent. A person can become a leader by happenstance, simply by being in the right place at the right time, or because of such various factors as age, education, experience, family background, and wealth.

Almost any person in a group may be capable of rising to a leadership position if he is rewarded for actively participating in the group discussion, as Alex Bavelas and his colleagues at Stanford University have demonstrated. They used light signals to reward low-status group members for supposedly "doing the right thing." However, unknown to the people being encouraged, the light signal was turned on and off at random. Rewarded in this unspecified, undefined manner, the low-status member came to regard himself as a leader and the rest of the group accepted him in his new position.

It is commonly observed that personality and circumstances interact to determine whether a person will become a leader. While this statement is undoubtedly true, its usefulness is rather limited unless one also can specify how a personality trait will interact with a specific situation. We are as yet unable to make such predictions.

Having become a leader, how does one get to be an effective leader? Given a dozen or more similar groups and tasks, what makes one leader succeed and another fail? The answer to this question is likely to determine the philosophy of leader-training programs and the way in which men are selected for executive positions.

There are a limited number of ways in which one person can influence others to work together toward a common goal. He can coerce them or he can coax them. He can tell people what to do and how to do it, or he can share the decision-making and concentrate on his relationship with his men rather than on the execution of the job.

Of course, these two types of leadership behavior are gross over-simplifications. Most research by psychologists on leadership has focused on two clusters of behavior and attitudes, one labeled autocratic, authoritarian, and task-oriented, and the other as democratic, equalitarian, permissive, and group-oriented.

The first type of leadership behavior, frequently advocated in conventional supervisory and military systems, has its philosophical roots in Frederick W. Taylor's *Principles of Scientific Management* and other early 20th Century industrial engineering studies. The authoritarian, task-oriented leader takes all responsibility for making decisions and directing the group members. His rationale is simple: "I do the thinking and you carry out the orders."

The second type of leadership is typical of the "New Look" method of management advocated by men like Douglas McGregor of M.I.T. and Rensis Likert of the University of Michigan. The democratic, group-oriented leader provides general rather than close supervision and his concern is the effective use of human resources through participation. In the late 1940s, a related method of leadership training was developed based on confrontation in unstructured group situations where each participant can explore his own motivations and reactions. Some excellent studies on this method, called T-group, sensitivity, or laboratory training, have been made by Chris Argyris of Yale, Warren Bennis of State University of New York at Buffalo, and Edgar Schein of M.I.T.

Experiments comparing the performance of both types of leaders have shown that each is successful in some situations and not in others. No one has been able to show that one kind of leader is always superior or more effective.

A number of researchers point out that different tasks require different kinds of leadership. But what kind of leader? To answer this question, I shall present a theory of leadership effectiveness that spells out the specific circumstances under which various leadership styles are most effective.

We must first of all distinguish between leadership style and leader behavior. Leader behavior refers to the specific acts in which a leader engages while directing or coordinating the work of his group. For example, the leader can praise or criticize, make helpful suggestions, show consideration for the welfare and feelings of members of his group.

Leadership style refers to the underlying needs of the leader that motivate his behavior. In other words, in addition to performing the task, what personal needs is the leader attempting to satisfy? We have found that a leader's actions or behavior sometimes does change as the situation or group changes, but his basic needs appear to remain constant.

To classify leadership styles, my colleagues and I have developed a simple questionnaire that asks the leader to describe the person with whom he can work least well:

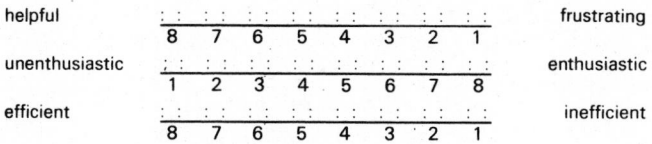

LEAST-PREFERRED CO-WORKER

Think of the person with whom you can work least well. He may be someone you work with now, or he may be someone you knew in the past. Use an X to describe this person as he appears to you.

helpful	8 7 6 5 4 3 2 1	frustrating
unenthusiastic	1 2 3 4 5 6 7 8	enthusiastic
efficient	8 7 6 5 4 3 2 1	inefficient

From the replies, a Least-Preferred-Co-Worker (LPC) score is obtained by simply summing the item scores. The LPC score does not measure perceptual accuracy, but rather reveals a person's emotional reaction to the people with whom he cannot work well.

In general, the high-scoring leader describes his least-preferred co-worker in favorable terms. The high-LPC leader tends to be "relationship-oriented." He gets his major satisfaction from establishing close personal relations with his group members. He uses the group task to gain the position of prominence he seeks.

The leader with a low score describes his least-preferred co-worker in unfavorable terms. The low-LPC leader is primarily "task-oriented." He obtains his major satisfaction by successfully completing the task, even at the risk of poor interpersonal relations with his workers.

Since a leader cannot function without a group, we must also know something about the group that the leader directs. There are many types of groups, for example, social groups which promote the enjoyment of individuals and "counteracting" groups such as labor and management at the negotiating table. But here we shall concentrate on groups that exist for the purpose of performing a task.

From our research, my associates and I have identified three major factors that can be used to classify group situations: (1) position power of the leader, (2) task structure, and (3) leader-member personal relationships. Basically, these classifications measure the kind of power and influence the group gives its leader.

We ranked group situations according to their favorableness for the leader. Favorableness here is defined as the degree to which the situation enables the leader to exert influence over the group.

Group Situation Model TASK-ORIENTED GROUPS ARE CLASSIFIED IN A THREE-DIMENSIONAL MODEL USING THE THREE MAJOR FACTORS AFFECTING GROUP PERFORMANCE

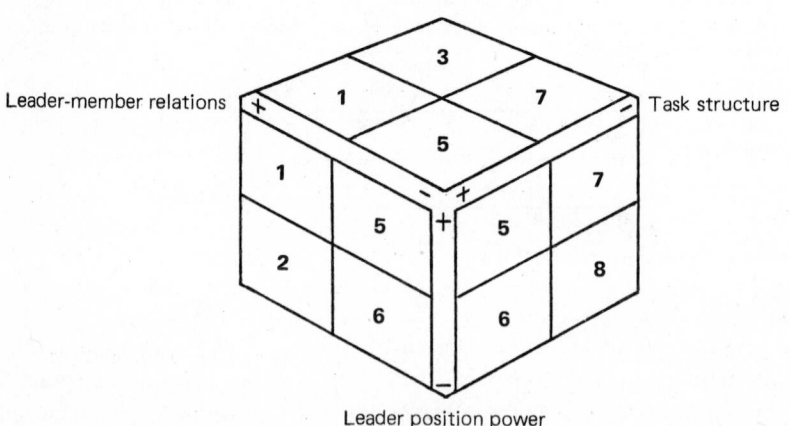

Leader-member relations

Task structure

Leader position power

Based on several studies, leader-member relations emerged as the most important factor in determining the leader's influence over the group. Task structure is rated as second in importance, and position power as third.

Under most circumstances, the leader who is liked by his group and has a clear-cut task and high position power obviously has everything in his favor. The leader who has poor relationships with his group members, an unstructured task, and weak position power likely will be unable to exert much influence over the group.

The personal relationships that the leader establishes with his group members depend at least in part upon the leader's personality. The leader who is loved, admired, and trusted can influence the group regardless of his position power. The leader who is not liked or trusted cannot influence the group except through his vested authority. It should be noted that a leader's assessment of how much he is liked often differs markedly from the group's evaluation.

Task structure refers to the degree the group's assignment can be programmed and specified in a step-by-step fashion. A highly structured task does not need a leader with much position power because the leader's role is detailed by the job specifications. With a highly structured task, the leader clearly knows what to do and how to do it, and the organization can back him up at each step. Unstructured tasks tend to have more than one correct solution that may be reached by any of a variety of methods. Since there is no step-by-step method that can be programmed in advance, the leader cannot influence the group's success by ordering them to vote "right" or be creative. Tasks of committees, creative groups, and policy-making groups are typically unstructured.

Position power is the authority vested in the leader's position. It can be readily measured in most situations. An army general obviously has more power than a lieutenant, just as a department head has more power than an office manager. But our concern here is the effect this position power has on group performance. Although one would think that a leader with great power will get better performance from his group, our studies do not bear out this assumption.

However, it must be emphasized that in some situations position power may supersede task structure (the military). Or a very highly structured task (launching a moon probe) may outweigh the effects of interpersonal relations. The organization determines both the task structure and the position power of the leader.

In our search for the most effective leadership style, we went back to the studies that we had been conducting for more than a decade. These studies investigated a wide variety of groups and leadership situations, including basketball teams, business management, military units, boards of directors, creative groups, and scientists engaged in pure research. In all of these studies, we could determine the groups that had performed their tasks successfully or unsuccessfully and then correlated the effectiveness of group performance with leadership style.

Now by plotting these correlations of leadership style against our scale of group situations, we could, for the first time, find what leadership style works best in each situation. When we connected the median points on each column, the result was a bell-shaped curve.

The results show that a task-oriented leader performs best in situations at both extremes—those in which he has a great deal of influence and power, and also in situations where he has no influence and power over the group members.

The Effective Leader DIRECTIVE LEADERS PERFORM BEST IN VERY FAVORABLE OR IN UNFAVORABLE SITUATIONS. PERMISSIVE LEADERS ARE BEST IN MIXED SITUATIONS. GRAPH IS BASED ON STUDIES OF OVER 800 GROUPS.

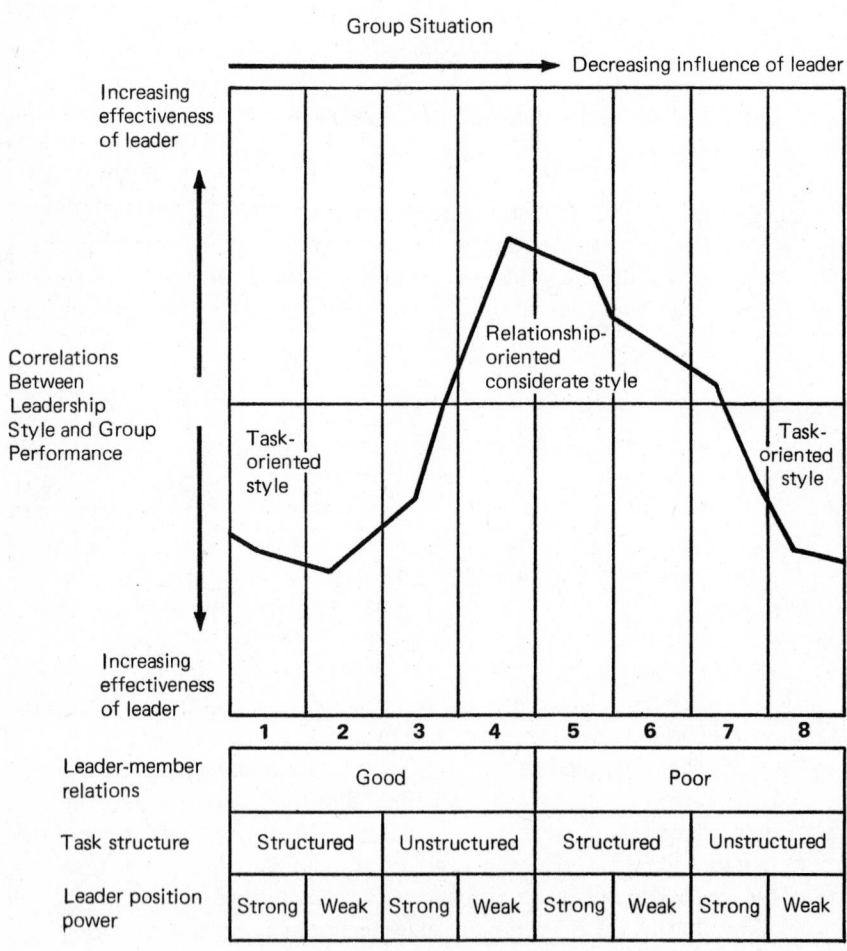

Relationship-oriented leaders tend to perform best in mixed situations where they have only moderate influence over the group. A number of subsequent studies by us and others have confirmed these findings.

The results show that we cannot talk about simply good leaders or poor leaders. A leader who is effective in one situation may or may not be effective in another. Therefore, we must specify the situations in which a leader performs well or badly.

This theory of leadership effectiveness by and large fits our everyday experience. Group situations in which the leader is liked, where he has a clearly defined task and a powerful position, may make attempts at nondirective, democratic leadership detrimental or superfluous. For example, the captain of an airliner can hardly call a committee meeting of the crew to share in the decision-making during a difficult landing approach. On the other hand, the chairman of a voluntary committee cannot ask with impunity that the group members vote or act according to his instructions.

Our studies also have shown that factors such as group-member abilities, cultural heterogeneity, and stressfulness of the task affect the degree to which the leader can influence members of the group. But the important finding and the consistent finding in these studies has been that mixed situations require relationship-oriented leadership while very favorable and very unfavorable job situations require task-oriented leaders.

Perhaps the most important implication of this theory of leadership is that the organization for which the leader works is as responsible for his success or failure as is the leader himself.

The chances are that *anyone* who wants to become a leader can become one if he carefully chooses the situations that are favorable to his leadership style.

The notion that a man is a "born" leader, capable of leading in all circumstances, appears to be nothing more than a myth. If there are leaders who excel under all conditions, I have not found them in my 18 years of research.

When we think of improving leadership performance, we tend to think first of training the leader. Personnel psychologists and managers typically view the executive's position as fixed and unchangeable and the applicant as highly plastic and trainable. A man's basic style of leadership depends upon his personality. Changing a man's leadership style means trying to change his personality. As we know from experiences in psychotherapy, it may take from one to several years to effect lasting changes in a personality structure. A leader's personality is not likely to change because of a few lectures or even a few weeks of intensive training.

It is doubtful that intensive training techniques can change an individual's style of leadership. However, training programs could be designed to provide the opportunity for a leader to learn in which situations he can perform well and in which he is likely to fail. Laboratory training also may provide the leader with some insights into his personal relationships with group members.

Our theory of leadership effectiveness predicts that a leader's performance can be improved by engineering or fitting the job to the leader. This is based, at least in part, on the belief that it is almost always easier to change a leader's work environment than to change his personality. The leader's authority, his task, and even his interpersonal relations with his group members can be altered, sometimes without making the leader aware that this has been done.

For example, we can change the leader's position power in either direction. He can be given a higher rank if this seems necessary. Or he can be given subordinates who are equal or nearly equal to him in rank. His assistants can be two or three ranks below him, or we can assign him men who are expert in their specialties. The leader can have sole authority for a job, or he may be required to consult with his group. All communications to group members may be channeled through the leader, making him the source of all the inside information, or all members of the group can be given the information directly, thus reducing the leader's influence.

The task structure also can be changed to suit the leader's style. Depending upon the group situation, we can give the leader explicit instructions or we can deliberately give him a vague and nebulous goal.

Finally, we can change the leader-member relations. In some situations it may be desirable to improve leader-member relations by making the group homogeneous in culture and language or in technical and educational background. Interdisciplinary groups are notoriously difficult to handle, and it is even more difficult to lead a group that is racially or culturally mixed. Likewise, we can affect leader-member relations by giving a leader subordinates who get along well with their supervisor or assign a leader to a group with a history of trouble or conflict.

It may seem that often we are proposing the sabotaging of the leader's influence over his group. Although common sense might make it seem that weakening the leader's influence will lower performance, in actuality our studies show that this rarely happens. The average group performance (in other words, the leader's effectiveness) correlates poorly with the degree of the leader's influence over the group.

In fact, the findings from several studies suggest that a particular leader's effectiveness may be improved even though the situation is made less favorable for him.

The leader himself can be taught to recognize the situations that best fit his style. A man who is able to avoid situations in which he is likely to fail, and seek out situations that fit his leadership style, will probably become a highly successful and effective leader. Also, if he is aware of his strengths and weaknesses, the leader can try to change his group situation to match his leadership style.

However, we must remember that good leadership performance depends as much upon the organization as it does upon the leader. This means that we must learn not only how to train men to be leaders, but how to build organizations in which specific types of leaders can perform well.

In view of the increasing scarcity of competent executives, it is to an organization's advantage to design jobs to fit leaders instead of attempting merely to fit a leader to the job.

Organizational Leadership: Some Theoretical and Empirical Considerations
J. G. Hunt

A recurring problem among managers has been that of determining the type of leader behavior or leadership style necessary to promote effective work groups. Research in this area appears to yield contradictory results. Some studies have shown that leadership styles denoting directive, authoritarian, task-oriented, or similar behavior promote effective group performance; others have shown that human relations-oriented or nondirective leader behavior gives better results. [1].

To resolve these conflicting results Fiedler has developed the "Contingency Model" theory which proposes that situations be classified in terms of their favorableness for the leader to exert influence over group members. The theory hypothesizes that a task-oriented leader will obtain better performance than a relationship-oriented leader under conditions very favorable or very unfavorable for the leader. On the other hand, the relationship-oriented leader will perform best under "moderately favorable" conditions [2].

This paper discussed the Contingency Model together with a recent empirical test in which it was validated in three business organizations. The model is then considered in terms of its theoretical implications within organizations. Finally, some new research directions are discussed.

"Organizational Leadership: Some Theoretical and Empirical Considerations" by J. G. Hunt in BUSINESS PERSPECTIVES, 4 (Summer 1968), 16-24. Reprinted by permission of the publishers.

DESCRIPTION OF THE CONTINGENCY MODEL

The measure of leadership style used by Fiedler and in the present study is what
Fiedler has termed the leader's "esteem for his least preferred coworker" (LPC).
A leader is asked to think of the one person with whom he has been able to work
the least well (his least preferred coworker) and to describe him on scales such as
the following:

> Pleasant : 8 : 7 : 6 : 5 : 4 : 3 : 2 : 1 : Unpleasant
> Friendly : 8 : 7 : 6 : 5 : 4 : 3 : 2 : 1 : Unfriendly

The least preferred coworker does not have to be someone with whom the
leader is presently working but can be someone with whom he has worked in the
past; thus he can be a past or present peer, subordinate, or superior. From 18 to
21 adjective scales have typically been included in the LPC measure. The LPC
score is the sum of the total number of one to eight point-item scores. A person who
describes his least preferred coworker relatively favorably is termed a "high LPC"
leader, while one who describes him unfavorably is called a "low LPC" leader [2].

After much research, Fiedler has interpreted the LPC score as a dynamic
trait which results in different leader behavior as the situation changes. This behavior is influenced not only by the situation but by the personal needs which the
leader seeks to satisfy. The low LPC individual gains need satisfaction from successful task performance, while the high LPC person gains satisfaction through
successful interpersonal relations. Thus, high and low LPC leaders seek to satisfy
different needs in the group situation, and their behavior varies according to the
ease with which a given situation allows them to achieve need satisfaction. Based
on the above interpretation, Fiedler has designated high LPC leaders as "relationship-oriented" and low LPC leaders as "task-oriented" [2].

The Contingency Model theory postulates that group effectiveness is contingent upon leadership style and the favorableness of the situation for the leader to
exert influence over his group members. While many dimensions might be used
to operationally define the leader's situation, Fiedler's earlier research led him to
use three: leader-member relations, task structure, and position power.

Leader-member relations have been operationally defined in terms of group
member sociometric acceptance of the leader or in terms of the leader's perception
of "group atmosphere." This latter measure asks the leader to use the same bipolar
adjective format as the LPC scale to describe his work group. According to Fiedler,
a leader who describes his group favorably feels well accepted by group members
and sees the group as low in tension [2].

Task structure refers to the extent to which task requirements are clearly
specified as in routine assembly-line work versus being ambiguous and undefined
as in creative research. Four variables developed by Shaw have been used to mea-

sure this dimension. These are (a) goal clarity—the extent to which the task's ob‑
jectives are defined; (b) goal-path multiplicity—whether there is one or more
than one way of reaching the goal; (c) decision verifiability—the degree to which
the outcome can be evaluated; and (d) solution specificity—whether there is one
or more than one possible outcome [3].

Position power denotes the power or authority delegated by the formal or‑
ganization regardless of the leader's willingness or ability to use it. A simple check
list has been used to measure it [2].

Fiedler has arranged these variables in eight different cells to form a "favor‑
ableness for the leader" continuum as in Figure 1.

Ordering of these dimensions is based on Fiedler's assumption that leader-
member relations are most important and position power is the least important.
It is assumed that favorable relations will allow a leader to do what would be dif‑
ficult for a person without favorable relations. A lack of power can be at least par‑
tially compensated for by favorable relations or task structure [2].

When the cells are arranged as above and the correlations between leader
LPC and group performance within each of them are plotted, the "performance
curve" shown in Figure 1 is obtained. This curve is based on twelve years of re‑
search and shows the within-cell median correlations of 15 different studies rep‑
resenting over 800 groups [2]. Thus each median correlation is based on a number
of separate samples each of which contains several leaders and work groups.

The curve shows that the correlation between leader LPC and group perfor‑
mance is negative in Cells I, II, III, and VIII, positive in Cells IV and V, and ap‑
proximately zero in Cell VII. Thus the low LPC, task-oriented leader tends to
obtain better group performance under very favorable *and* very unfavorable con‑
ditions while the high LPC, relationship-oriented leader does better under moder‑
ately favorable circumstances.

TESTING THE MODEL IN BUSINESS

Fiedler conducted one major validation study in cooperation with the Belgain Navy
which provided support for the major hypothesis of the model [4]. However, this
study was an experiment carried out with specially set up groups and tasks. The
present study was designed to further test the theory by attempting to validate it
in business and industrial organizations [5].

Hypotheses

The model was originally formulated in terms of "interacting groups"—those
which require higher member interdependence for task completion. It seemed im‑
portant to test whether or not it could be extended to "coacting groups"—those

Figure 1 CORRELATIONS BETWEEN LEADER LPC AND GROUP PERFORMANCE WHEN GROUP-TASK SITUATIONS ARE ORDERED IN TERMS OF "FAVORABLENESS FOR THE LEADER"

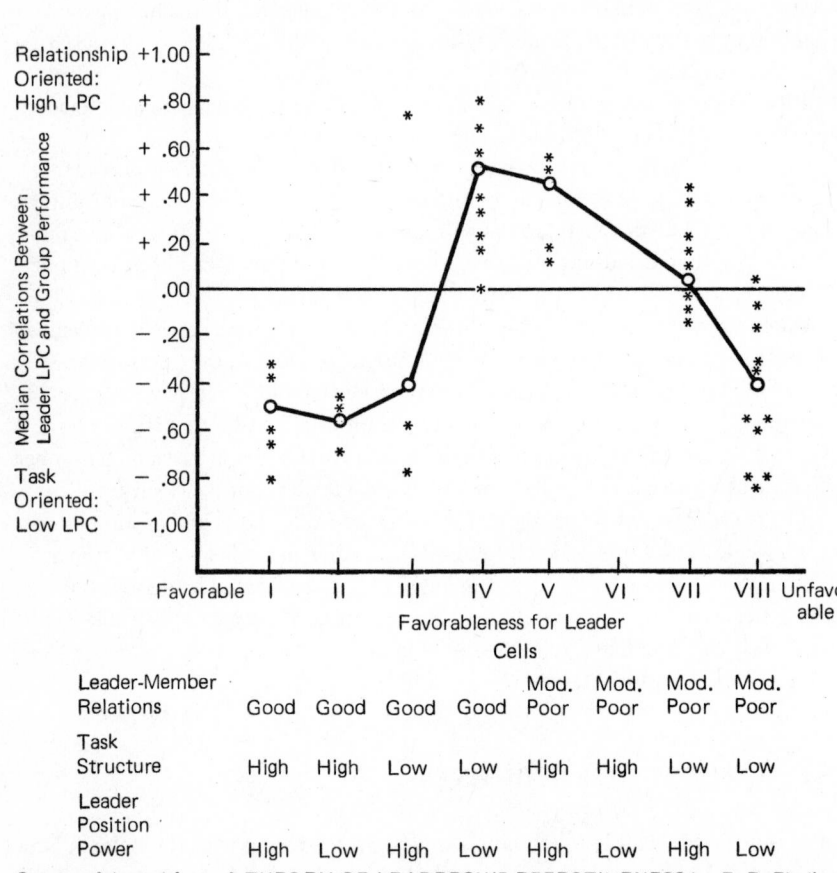

Cells	I	II	III	IV	V	VI	VII	VIII
Leader-Member Relations	Good	Good	Good	Good	Mod. Poor	Mod. Poor	Mod. Poor	Mod. Poor
Task Structure	High	High	Low	Low	High	High	Low	Low
Leader Position Power	High	Low	High	Low	High	Low	High	Low

in which members are relatively independent in task completion. Hypotheses therefore considered both kinds of groups. These hypotheses were also formulated on the assumption that position power would be high in the business organizations sampled and hence data would be available to test Cells I, III, V, and VII.

The following hypothesis was therefore tested for interacting groups:

When group-task situations are ordered along a favorableness for the leader continuum there will be a negative correlation between supervisor LPC and group performance under very favorable leader conditions, while there will be a positive correlation under a situation intermediate in favorableness.

An identical hypothesis was formulated for coacting groups but on an exploratory basis.

Method

To test the hypotheses the following steps were necessary: (*a*) obtain leadership style data in terms of LPC for work-group supervisors, (*b*) classify samples into cells considering leader-member relations, task structure, and position power, (*c*) correlate within each cell supervisor LPC and work-group performance, and (*d*) test these correlations for statistical significance as indicated below.

Samples

In selecting samples, the main considerations were to find a substantial number of groups performing the same task and to have valid and reliable performance measures. We also hoped to find groups with well-structured tasks as well as those with relatively unstructured tasks so that as many cells of the model as possible could be tested. The following five sets of groups in three organizations met these requirements:

Sample	Number of Groups
1. Company X: Research firm in atomic energy field	
a) Research chemists	18
b) Skilled craftsmen	1
2. Company Y: Grocery chain	
a) Meat departments	21
b) Grocery departments (entire store except meat departments)	24
3. Company Z: Farm and earth-moving machinery manufacturer	
Management teams of general foreman or superintendent and	
subordinate first-line production foremen	15

Measures

Instruments were similar or identical to those described previously. The LPC scale was used to measure leadership style of the work-group supervisors while the group-atmosphere scale was used to evaluate leader-member relations. The task structure and position power measures were modified to fit a business or industrial context.

Samples were classified as primarily coacting or interacting on the basis of an interview with a company official familiar with the extent to which the duties of the sampled units required within-group interdependence. Thus, the research chemists, meat departments, and production management teams were classified as interacting; the shop craftsmen and grocery departments were considered to be coacting.

Performance of research chemists and shop craftsmen was measured by using ratings of three or more officials familiar with their work. Objective productivity figures were available for the supermarket meat and grocery departments as well as the Company Z production foreman sample.

Data Analysis

Each of the hypotheses was tested as follows: (a) Spearman rank order correlations between manager LPC and work unit performance were computed for the samples within each cell; (b) for each cell the probability that a correlation of the magnitude and direction found in (a) would occur by chance was determined; and (c) each of these probabilities was combined and tested for over-all significance using a one-tailed test [6].

Results

Figure 2 superimposes the present results on Fiedler's curve of median correlations. Interacting samples are found in Cells I, III, V, and VII, and all correlations except the one for the low-task structure research chemists fall close to the curve. A combined significance test on the correlations of the seven samples in Cells I, III, and V shows them to be significant at slightly better than the .05 level. (Results in Cell VII were not included in the significance test since an essentially zero correlation was predicted. However, their average is zero which tends to support the predicted near-zero correlation even though it has not been tested statistically.) On the basis of these results the first hypothesis was therefore accepted.

Coacting samples are found in Cells I and V, and all four correlations fall close to the curve. These combined correlations are significant at better than the .01 level. This hypothesis was also accepted and it was concluded that the model

Figure 2 CORRELATIONS BETWEEN SUPERVISOR LPC AND GROUP EFFECTIVE-
NESS SUPERIMPOSED ON A CURVE OF MEDIAN CORRELATIONS IN
FIEDLER'S MODEL

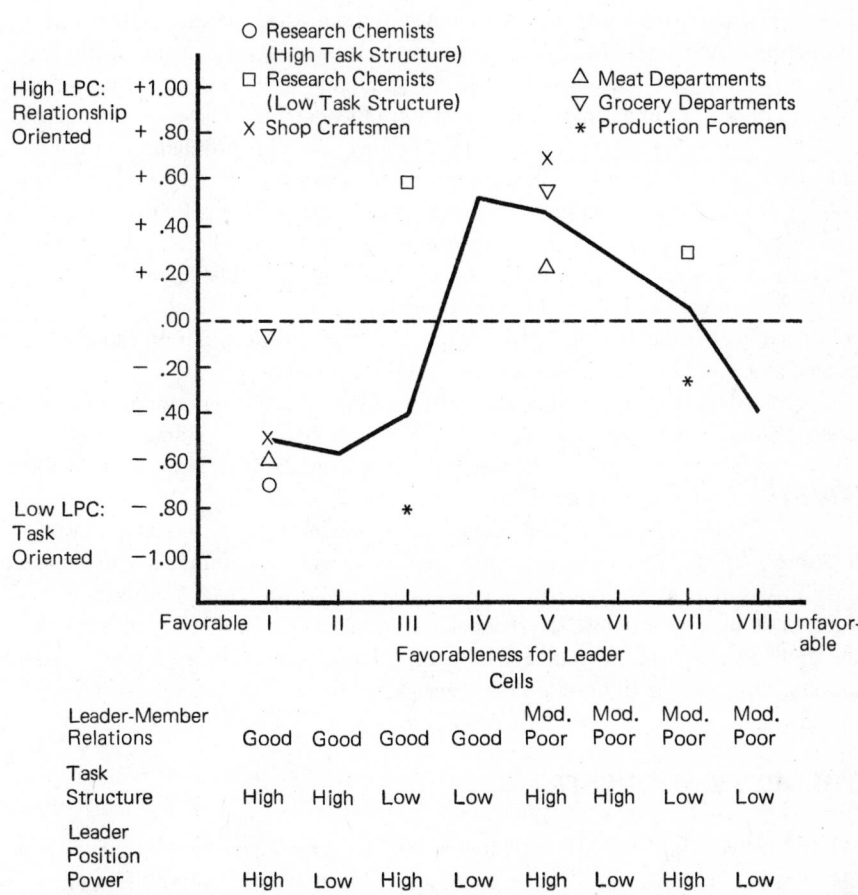

predicts performance for both interacting and coacting groups in the samples tested
here. Although only four cells were tested, if as seems reasonable, position power
is generally high in most business and industrial organizations, then these four
cells are the really relevant ones for testing the model. Hence we might argue that
these four cells constitute a comprehensive test of the Contingency Model in these
kinds of firms.

USEFULNESS OF MODEL

While the importance of a "situational" approach to leadership has been recognized for many years [7], this model is the first to provide an operational conceptual scheme for systematically classifying situational as well as other variables. Thus the model provides a badly needed beginning toward reconciling many of the conflicting results found in leadership research. It has also made a significant start toward encompassing the classes of variables that have been suggested by Sanford as being important in a comprehensive theory of leadership. These are (a) the leader and his psychological attributes, (b) the follower with his problems, attitudes, and needs, and (c) the group situation in which followers and leaders relate to one another [8]. The model presently considers leadership style which falls under the first category as does the leader's perception of group atmosphere. Task structure and position power fall under the group situation category. The favorableness for the leader concept, as discussed below, provides a framework which should allow consideration of other variables within the leader and group situation categories as well as a number of variables within the follower category.

The model is an impressive one because of the extensive amount of empirical evidence used in developing it—15 studies of over 800 groups conducted over a 12-year period. Furthermore, the previously discussed Belgian Navy study and the present study lend supporting evidence.

In addition to its theoretical importance, a model such as this has potential usefulness for manager selection and placement as well as training. It also opens up possibilities in terms of organizational design or what Fiedler [2] has termed "organization engineering." Here work unit dimensions would be modified to fit the leadership style of the manager in charge. Thus it may make new tools available for obtaining a better fit between managerial abilities and organizational requirements.

THEORETICAL QUESTIONS

While Fiedler's model as presently formulated is useful for the reasons mentioned above, it also makes a significant contribution in terms of the kinds of theoretical questions it poses. These questions point out new directions which leadership research might take. We consider three of these:

1. An examination of leadership style assuming that the remaining variables are treated as in the present model.
2. An examination of the extension or refinement of the intervening variables of leader-member relations, task structure, and position power with leadership style considered in terms of the presently used LPC.
3. An examination of intervening variables beyond those presently used, assuming LPC is used to measure leadership style.

Leadership Style

An important theoretical problem is that we know little about the behavior of high and low LPC leaders. As previously indicated, Fiedler has interpreted LPC in terms of leader need satisfaction and argues that high LPC leaders achieve need satisfaction through successful interpersonal relations, while low LPC leaders achieve satisfaction through successful task completion. Unfortunately, this interpretation tells us little about the actual behavior of the two kinds of leaders. Fiedler has devoted a great deal of research to this problem, but it is complicated because the behavior of the two kinds of leaders appears to change as the situation in which the leaders are operating makes it easy or hard for them to achieve need satisfaction. Thus, we might expect that sometimes there would be a significant correlation between LPC and measures of leadership style used by other researchers and sometimes not. And, indeed, available studies suggest that this is the case. Typical of these is a study by Meuwese and Fiedler [9] which shows a significant relationship between LPC and the Ohio State dimension of "consideration" (discussed below). An unpublished study by the author shows significant relationships for this dimension in some work-group samples but not in others.

This leader behavior is an extremely important issue because without understanding it we cannot explain why the model "works." We need to have an understanding of the manner in which specified leader behavior interacts with the intervening variables to influence group performance. One approach to this problem is to obtain behavioral data for high and low LPC leaders in each cell of the model. These data could be procured either by observation and classification into different behavior categories or by obtaining group member perceptions of a leader's behavior.

An alternative approach would be to use leadership style measures other than LPC and see the kind of performance curve generated as data are collected for each cell of the model. In other words, "To what extent does the favorableness for the leader concept predict performance when a behavioral measure of leadership style is used?"

Table 1 summarizes leadership style measures used in some of the better known previous research. This table shows that a number of these dimensions appear to be logically related. Furthermore, a study by Argyle, Gardner, and Cioffi gives empirical support to this view [10]. They considered the first five of these dimensions and found significant and fairly substantial intercorrelations between them. Thus, they concluded that "employee centered" supervisors tended to be· "democratic," to supervise in a "general way," and to be relatively "nonpunitive." It may therefore be reasonable to consider these variables as subdivisions of a more underlying variable. The "consideration" dimension used in the Ohio State studies appears to include the essence of these other dimensions as well as "human-relations competence." The "differentiation of role" and "administrative competence" dimensions appear to be related; the Ohio State "initiating structure"

Table 1   LEADERSHIP STYLE MEASURES USED IN PREVIOUS STUDIES

Study	Dimension	Definition
Michigan* Southern California	Closeness of Supervision	Degree to which supervisor checks up on his men frequently, gives detailed and frequent instructions, and in general limits their freedom to do work in their own way.
Michigan Southern California	Pressure for Production	Degree to which supervisor attempts to keep up production by putting pressure on subordinates, criticizing their efforts, urging them to speed up, and emphasizing deadlines and targets.
Michigan Southern California	Employee Orientation (Production Centered vs. Employee Centered)	Degree to which supervisor emphasizes production as opposed to keeping his employees happy.
Southern California	Democratic vs. Authoritarian	Degree to which supervisor listens to ideas, reasons with his men, explains to them as fully as possible and discusses the work and possible changes with them as opposed to a supervisor who knows his own mind, gives orders crisply, expects men to know what he wants, and relies on his superior knowledge to solve problems.
Michigan Southern California	Discipline	Degree to which supervisor takes punitive action based on the weight and authority of his position as opposed to using tact or persuasion to correct employee infractions of regulations.
Michigan	Differentiation of Role	Degree to which supervisor performs supervisory functions such as planning, coordination of activities, etc., as opposed to doing subordinate functions.

*For the specific studies conducted by the University of Michigan and the University of Southern California see Argyle, Gardner, and Cioffi, "The Measurement of Supervisory Methods," in *Human Relations*, Vol. 10 (1957), pp. 295–314.

dimension appears to tap a somewhat similar concept. "Technical competence" appears to be similar to what is termed below "task relevant ability," and hence is considered here in that context rather than as a part of leadership style [11].

The concepts implicit in the "initiating structure" and "consideration" dimensions appear to identify leader behaviors basic to almost any kind of group. Bass [12] further supports use of these dimensions by arguing that they can safely be equated to categories of leader behavior identified by Wherry, Rupe, and Roach. Thus we are interested in considering the kind of performance curve which

Study	Dimension	Definition
Mann[†]	Administrative Competence	Degree to which supervisor performs functions required to coordinate activities of one organization family with another; the ability to think and act in terms of the total system within which he operates. Includes planning, programming, and organizing work; assigning tasks, responsibility, and authority; inspecting and following up work; and coordinating efforts and activities of different organizational members and units.
Mann[†]	Human Relations Competence	Degree to which supervisor uses pertinent knowledge and methods for working with and through people.
Mann[†]	Technical Competence	Degree to which supervisor uses pertinent knowledge, methods, and equipment necessary for performance of specific tasks, and for the direction of such performance.
Ohio[‡] State	Initiating Structure	Degree to which supervisor organizes and defines the relationship between himself and subordinates, defines the role of each subordinate, and establishes well-defined patterns of organization, channels of communication, and ways of getting the job done.
Ohio State[‡]	Consideration	Degree to which supervisor exhibits behavior indicative of friendship, mutual trust and respect, and "good human relations" between himself and his subordinates.

[†] See F. Mann, "Toward an Understanding of the Leadership Role in Formal Organization," in R. Dubin, et al., *Leadership and Productivity* (San Francisco: Chandler, 1965).
[‡] See Stogdill, R., and Coons, A., *Leader Behavior: Its Description and Measurement* (Research Monograph No. 88. [Columbus: Bureau of Business Research, Ohio State University, 1957]).

might result from using "consideration" and "initiating structure" measures of leadership style. These measures would give an indication of the leader's behavior as seen by subordinates.

We are faced with an immediate problem, however. There is a question about handling these two dimensions which are often independent of each other [13]. As a starting point, research might be conducted to examine the kind of performance curve generated for each dimension separately. It might be found, for example, that one dimension generated a curvilinear relationship similar to LPC, while the other did not. Or perhaps one dimension would show a sharply changing curve from one cell to another, while the other would show a virtually flat curve. It seems likely, however, that there is an interactive effect between the two dimensions and that they should be tested simultaneously.

One way of simultaneously treating these dimensions when they are independent would be to consider them in the following four combinations: *(a)* high initiating structure—high consideration, *(b)* low initiating structure—low consideration, *(c)* high initiating structure—low consideration, and *(d)* low initiating structure—high consideration. It seems likely that the performance curves for each of these combinations would differ.

This kind of knowledge would allow the model to consider variables used by other researchers. Furthermore, since we could relate perceived leader behavior to other dimensions, we would gain a better idea about why the model shows this kind of relationships.

MODERATOR VARIABLES

As indicated above, a second research direction is to examine some questions concerned with leader-member relations, task structure, and leader position power.

Leader-Member Relations

We are concerned here with the extent to which the leader's perception of group atmosphere and subordinate acceptance of the leader can be considered as interchangeable variables in the model. From a theoretical standpoint they appear different. The former is a leader perceptual variable while the latter is a subordinate perceptual variable or a type of "situational" variable in the sense that it is external to the leader. It is possible, however, that the two kinds of dimensions might play a similar role in the model in terms of their interaction with the other variables in influencing group effectiveness. Therefore we need empirical research to test the interchangeability of these two variables and to provide a basis for further theorizing concerning their influence in the model.

Task Structure

Triandis has suggested that worker "task relevant ability," e.g., aptitude or intelligence, and task structure probably would interact with each other to influence performance [14]. Thus it appears that a different leadership style might be more appropriate where there was a match between ability and structure, for example, high structure—low ability, than where the two were mismatched. We might thus expect some difference in the relationship between different ability-structure combinations and the other intervening variables considered. It is proposed that the following four combinations be examined: *(a)* high ability—high structure, *(b)* high ability—low structure, *(c)* low ability—high structure, and *(d)* low ability—low structure. The fourth condition would presumably call for more structured behavior from the supervisor than the other conditions, which in turn would appear to differ in the amount of human relations behavior required.

Power

The present concept is concerned with the power the organization grants to a supervisory position. Yet we all know that two managers occupying the same position may have sharply different abilities to use rewards and punishment officially at their disposal. Pelz has referred to this as upward influence—a supervisor's ability to influence his boss so that the supervisor can utilize the power at his disposal. He has shown that helpful and restraining behavior on the part of supervisors has very different effects on employee satisfaction depending upon the supervisor's upward influence [15]. Patchen carries this finding further by showing that, among other things, upward influence and a supervisor's willingness to use it interact to influence employee productivity norms [16].

Hence it seems reasonable to examine this upward influence concept of power as a Contingency Model dimension. The focus shifts from power inherent in the position to power at the leader's disposal because of his upward influence. This still leaves the question of the extent to which a leader utilizes this power with respect to his employees. It may be obvious to a supervisor's subordinates that because of his upward influence he has much power at his disposal, but he may not choose to use it.

Before this question is considered it would seem wise to examine the relationship between power utilization and leadership style. It might be hypothesized that a low LPC (task-oriented) leader would tend to highly utilize his available power, while his high LPC (relationship-oriented) counterpart would not. Power utilization might also be related to other measures of leadership style. If there is not a strong relationship between power utilization and leadership style, then it would seem reasonable to extend the concept to include it. If, on the other hand, such a relationship does exist, it is suggested that the concept be extended to include upward influence only.

CONSIDERATION OF OTHER DIMENSIONS

A third research direction is to examine other dimensions which might be included in a leadership model. If we think in terms of the favorableness for the leader concept, what intervening variables might be considered?

The present model uses three classes of variables to influence the relationship between leader LPC and group performance. These are group variables—position power, task variables—task structure, and leader variables—leader member relations measured by the leader's perception of "group atmosphere." It does not specifically consider subordinate variables such as personality, attitude, or ability which, as indicated above, a comprehensive theory of leadership might contain [17]. This class of variables would include such subordinate dimensions as authoritarianism, need for independence, and task relevant ability which was discussed above in conjunction with task structure. Such variables as group cohesiveness, group member heterogeneity, and group status congruence might be considered as other possible group variables. Task variables, in addition to task structure, might include task complexity as well as technology, e.g., process technology versus small batch or job shop technology can influence the effectiveness of a given leadership style [18].

Leader variables present a problem. It may be that "group atmosphere" is a special case which is only relevant when leadership style is measured using LPC. It would seem that the leader's perception of his acceptance by group members might produce different behavior in a high LPC leader than in one low in LPC and hence influence group performance. If this were the case, it probably would not be a relevant variable when leadership style was measured in terms of behavioral dimensions such as those discussed earlier. Other possible leader dimensions such as personality variables might better be considered as being alternative ways of conceiving leadership style rather than as intervening variables. However, leader task relevant ability would probably be an exception. It does not seem to readily fit into the leadership style category; yet it seems reasonable to classify it as a special kind of moderator dimension interacting with leadership style and other intervening variables to influence group performance.

Thus the model being proposed would use task variables, group variables, subordinate personality, attitude and ability variables, and leader task relevant ability variables to operationally define the favorableness for the leader concept. Now, obviously this is a large number of classes to consider and, of course, the number of individual variables is even larger. What we can expect to find is interchangeability among many of these variables: one variable will interact with leadership style in the same way as another and thus affect group output in the same way. Consequently we might expect, for instance, that group cohesiveness and group member homogeneity might be used interchangeably. In this way it might ultimately be possible to specify a few variables which serve the same functions in the model as a large number of other variables.

COACTING VERSUS INTERACTING GROUPS

The previous discussion concerned itself with interacting (high group member interdependence) groups only. These are the kinds of groups used to formulate the

Contingency Model. However, results of the present study introduce one more theoretical issue of importance. That issue is concerned with whether the same kind of model will be useful for interacting as opposed to coacting groups. Results of this study indicate that the same kind of model is applicable to both kinds of groups discussed. However, this finding needs to be examined in future research. Fiedler conducted two studies of coacting groups before his model was developed and found the correlations between LPC and performance to be in the opposite direction from that which would be predicted by the model [2].

We might also theorize that the leader's major functions would be different in the two kinds of groups and therefore require a different leadership effectiveness model. An important leader function in interacting groups would seem to be concerned with coordination of subordinate activities, while a primary function in coacting groups might be stressing psychological support and encouragement and stressing individual motivation.

Perhaps the particular kind of coacting groups is important here. The groups in Fiedler's two studies had, respectively, tension-arousing and highly creative coacting tasks. These kinds of tasks may be so different from the production coacting tasks of this study that a different kind of leadership style is required. The coacting groups examined here do not appear to be involved with particularly anxiety-arousing or creative tasks.

The importance of this issue receives additional support from Dubin. He makes the point that an increasing proportion of jobs will be performed individually rather than in groups; hence group theories of leadership may not be appropriate [19].

REFERENCES

1. For support of the authoritarian position see, for example, C. Hawkins, "A Study of Factors Mediating a Relationship between Leader Rating Behavior and Group Productivity," unpublished doctoral dissertation, University of Minnesota, 1962; M. E. Shaw, "A Comparison of Two Types of Leadership in Various Communication Nets," *Journal of Abnormal and Social Psychology,* Vol. 50 (1955), pp. 127−34. For support of the human relations position see, for example, R. Likert, *New Patterns of Management.* New York: McGraw-Hill Book Co., 1961.
2. F. E. Fiedler. *A Theory of Leadership Effectiveness.* New York: McGraw-Hill Book Co., 1967.
3. M. E. Shaw. "Scaling Group Tasks: A Method for Dimensional Analysis." Gainesville, Florida: Department of Psychology, University of Florida, 1963.
4. F. E. Fiedler. "The Effect of Leadership and Cultural Heterogeneity on Group Performances: A Test of the Contingency Model," *Journal of Experimental Social Psychology,* Vol. 2 (1966), pp. 237−64.

5. For more details of the methodology and results of this study see J. G. Hunt, "Fiedler's Leadership Contingency Model: An Empirical Test in Three Organizations," *Organizational Behavior and Human Performance,* Vol. 2 (1967), pp. 290–308.

6. M. Gordon, E. Loveland, and E. Cureton, "An Extended Table of Chi-Square for Two Degrees of Freedom, for Use in Combining Probabilities from Independent Samples," *Psychometrika,* Vol. 17 (1952), pp. 311–15.

7. See, for example, O. Tead. *The Art of Leadership.* New York: McGraw-Hill Book Co., 1935; W. Jenkins, "A Review of Leadership Studies with Particular Reference to Military Problems," *Psychological Bulletin,* Vol. 44 (1947), pp. 54–79.

8. F. Sanford. *Authoritarianism and Leadership.* Philadelphia: Institute for Research in Human Relations, 1950.

9. W. Meuwese, and F. E. Fiedler, "Leadership and Group Creativity under Varying Degrees of Stress." Urbana, Ill.: Group Effectiveness Research Laboratory, University of Illinois, 1966.

10. M. Argyle, G. Gardner, and F. Cioffi, "The Measurement of Supervisory Methods," *Human Relations,* Vol. 10 (1957), pp. 295–314.

11. These conclusions are similar but not identical to those of D. Bowers and S. Seashore, "Predicting Organizational Effectiveness with a Four Factor Theory of Leadership," *Administrative Science Quarterly,* Vol. II (1966), pp. 238–63.

12. B. Bass. *Psychology and Organizational Behavior.* New York: Harper & Bros., 1960.

13. While often independent of each other, under some circumstances these dimensions appear to be correlated. See, for example, S. Nealey, and M. Blood, "Leadership Performance of Nursing Supervisors at Two Organizational Levels." Urbana, Ill.: Group Effectiveness Research Laboratory, University of Illinois, 1967.

14. H. Triandis. "Notes on the Design of Organizations," in J. Thompson, (Ed.), *Approaches to Organizational Design.* Pittsburgh, Pa.: University of Pittsburgh Press, 1966.

15. D. Pelz, "Influence: A Key to Effective Leadership in the First-Line Supervisor," *Personnel,* Vol. 29 (1952), pp. 3–11.

16. M. Patchen. "Supervisory Methods and Group Performance Norms," *Administrative Science Quarterly,* Vol. 7 (1962), pp. 275–93.

17. There is an exception to this statement if leader-member relations are considered in terms of subordinate acceptance of the supervisor. This would be a form of subordinate attitude.

18. Do not confuse complexity and structure. For example, a missile countdown is highly structured but also highly complex.

19. R. Dubin. "Supervision and Productivity: Empirical Findings and Theoretical Considerations," in R. Dubin, G. Homans, F. Mann, and D. Miller, *Leadership and Productivity.* San Francisco: Chandler Publishers, 1965.

Leadership Style: Rigid or Flexible?
Walter A. Hill

There is a growing acceptance of a contingency theory of leadership effectiveness in both academic and managerial circles. This approach contends that different leadership behaviors are required in different situations in order to achieve effectiveness. As Rubin and Goldman (1968, p. 153) have pointed out, "The effective manager then must be able, not only to respond differently to different individuals, but must himself be flexible enough to change with them as they and the situation change."

One of the more interesting questions posed by an acceptance of a contingency model is whether a leader can behave flexibly enough to cope with varied situations or whether it is necessary either to replace the leader as the situation changes or to modify the situation to fit the leader's capabilities. There is a disagreement over this issue. Schmidt and Tannenbaum (1958, p. 101) suggested that a leader is capable of exhibiting a wide range of behavior when they state:

The successful leader is one who is able to behave appropriately in light of these perceptions. If direction is in order, he is able to direct; if considerable participative freedom is called for, he is able to provide such freedom. Thus, the successful manager of men can be primarily characterized neither as a strong leader nor as a permissive one. Rather, he is one who maintains a high batting average in accurately assessing the forces that determine what his most appropriate behavior at any given time should be and in actually being able to behave accordingly.

Fiedler, (1965, p. 115), on the other hand, did not feel that a leader is capable of varying his behavior to a large degree. He stated:

Fitting the man to the leadership job by selection and training has not been spectacularly successful. It is surely easier to change almost anything in the job situation than a man's personality and his leadership style.

As the contingency model grows in importance, it will become necessary to discover the extent to which a leader can vary his behavior.

The major purpose of this paper is to learn if subordinates perceive that their leaders would use the same style of leadership for a variety of problems or if they perceive that their leaders would alter their style as they are confronted with different situations. The secondary aim of this paper is to discover if a tendency toward a rigid leadership style varies with either functional area or organizational level.

METHODOLOGY

The data on leadership flexibility reported in this paper was collected as part of a larger study of Decision Difficulty and Individual Effectiveness which the author conducted with managers in two English companies. Leadership flexibility was defined as subordinate managers' perceptions of the degree to which their superiors would use different leadership styles in different situations.

Since the author could not locate a sampling instrument whose validity and reliability had been established in the United Kingdom culture, he constructed his own. The instrument was presented sequentially with three different groups: 30 managers in accounting and research and development departments of an electronics components firm, 35 students in a postexperience course (these students either held or were on leave from full-time managerial or engineering jobs), and 15 managers in a small engineering-oriented firm. Each of the subjects was asked to read the questionnaire and to indicate whether or not the situations posed and the styles presented were realistic and generalizable across both functions and firms as well as understandable in the context of the overall study. Although it was not possible to attain quantitative measures of validity and reliability, personal interviews with selected subjects did not reveal any major deficiencies in the instrument.

The final form of the questionnaire described four possible leadership styles which a supervisor could employ. *Style A* was a directive, "I'll take charge and set it right" approach; one in which the manager was not too concerned with the feelings and attitudes of his subordinates because he believed that these matters were not part of his job. *Style B* also was a directive approach but the superior who employed this style realized the need to maintain good human relations although this was clearly secondary to his primary concern with getting the job done. *Style C* was a nondirective, participative approach where the supervisor's primary concern was the development and maintenance of positive feelings and attitudes among his subordinates. This manager realized, however, that he must insure that wise decisions were made and implemented by his subordinates. The last approach, *Style D,* also was nondirective and participative. The superior who used this approach placed primary emphasis on developing and maintaining positive feelings and attitudes among his subordinates with the underlying philosophy that if he could do this, the people would solve their own problems thus freeing him from insuring that adequate decisions and implementation procedures would be devised. The four styles, then, were defined to illustrate varying emphasis on task and interpersonal orientations. *Style A* has a predominant task orientation. *Style B* has a primary task and secondary interpersonal orientation. *Style C* has a primary interpersonal and secondary task orientation. *Style D* has predominant interpersonal orientation.

The questionnaire also contained four typical but hypothetical managerial problems. These situations were devised to vary along the two dimensions of complex — simple and interpersonal — technical. The first two problems were complex as there were many alternative solutions, conflicting criteria which were to be met, and no immediate way existed to prove that a decision was correct. The first problem was complex from a human relations standpoint since the decision involved an emotionally charged interpersonal problem. The second problem was complex from a technical standpoint as the problem was difficult but largely not interpersonal in nature. The last two problems were simple relative to the first two. Once again, one involved an interpersonal and the other a technical problem.

Degrees of Style Flexibility

Since there were four styles which could be used in each of the four situations, five degrees of style flexibility could be distinguished. Style rigidity (Category A) was defined to occur when a subordinate stated that his superior would use the same style, irrespective of what style, for each of the four situations. The next least flexible posture (Category B) was defined to occur when a subordinate responded that his supervisor would use one style, irrespective of what style, for three of the situations and a different style in the fourth case. A greater degree of flexibility (Category C) was defined to occur when a subject stated that his superior would use two different styles, irrespective of the styles, but each of the styles would be employed in two situations. An even more flexible stance (Category D) was defined to exist if the respondent replied that his supervisor would use three different styles where one would be used twice and the other two once. The most flexible behavior (Category E) was defined to occur if the subordinate believed that his manager would use four different styles for the four cases. Since the degree of leadership style flexibility (or rigidity) was defined according to subjects' perceptions of how their supervisors would respond to four hypothetical, but typical managerial problems, not by actual measurements of supervisory behavior, it is possible that the responses may be projective rather than descriptive.[1]

Respondents were informed that the purpose of the questionnaire was to "identify the style which your supervisor uses to solve the typical problems which

---

1. Since the four problems were typical, ones which most supervisors have to deal with, it was assumed that subordinates would indicate the style their supervisor had used when faced with each of the problems.

arise in your department." Each subject was asked to indicate which of the four styles his supervisor would use in solving each of the four problems. Respondents were specifically instructed not to indicate the style their superiors should use but the style they would use when confronted with the hypothetical problems.

Subjects

Participants were chosen from two large manufacturers of electronic components located in the Midlands, England. The first group of subjects were members of a research and development laboratory which employed approximately 750 professional and technical personnel. This laboratory, designated Company A, R & D, employed 27 middle managers and 60 first level supervisors. Questionnaires were distributed to each of the 87 managers. Usable returns were received from 18 middle managers and 34 first level managers—a response rate of 60%.

The second group of subjects were chosen from accounting and research and development managers in Company B. The accounting managers, designated Company B, Accounting, were all employed in factories where they were responsible for such functions as cost accounting, standard costing, shop control, and materials control. Nine middle managers and 33 first level managers were asked to participate in the study. Usable returns were received from eight middle managers and 30 first level supervisors—90% response.

The research and development laboratory in Company B employed approximately 170 research scientists, as well as supporting personnel. Questionnaires were distributed to 15 middle managers and 23 first level managers. Usable responses were received from 14 middle managers and 20 first level managers—a 90% response.

RESULTS

Table 1 reports subjects' perceptions concerning the leadership style their supervisors would use in dealing with four typical but hypothetical problems. The data indicate the degree of flexibility attributed to superiors by their subordinates who were classified both by functional area and organizational level. The first hypothesis tested was that all subordinates would state that their superiors would use the same style, irrespective of what style, to respond to each of the four situations. The expected chi-square distribution under this hypothesis was that all responses from each of the three groups would fall in Category A in Table 1. The data in the Category A column indicate that only eight, five, and four respondents from the three groups, respectively 17 of 124 subjects (14%), stated that their supervisors would use the same style for all four problems (no one style was predominantly reported). An overall chi-square test revealed a value of 92.39 ($df = 8$) which was significant at the .001 level thus indicating rejection of the hypothesis. Additional chi-square tests were run for middle, first level, R & D, and accounting managers with resulting chi-square values of 32.51 ($df = 8$), 60.04 ($df = 8$), 61.97 ($df = 4$), and 30.42 ($df = 4$), respectively all significant at the .001 level.

It can be concluded that the respondents in this sample did not believe that their supervisors would use the same leadership style to deal with all four problems whether their responses were considered in the aggregate or subdivided by either functional area or organizational level. Although these results cannot prove conclusively that managers use different styles when tackling different problems because such proof requires actual observation of leadership behavior, they do indicate that subordinates felt their supervisors would use different styles.

The second hypothesis tested was that there would be no difference between the proportion of middle and first level managers who reported that their superiors would use the same style, irrespective of what style, to respond to each of the four situations. Although the responses in Category A, Table 1, indicate a higher proportion of first level supervisors (15 vs 10%) stated that their superiors would use the same style in all the situations, the resulting t value of .758 ($df = 122$) indicate no differences between the responses of the two groups when they were separated by organizational level.

The third hypothesis tested was that there would be no difference between the proportion of accounting and research and development managers who reported that their superiors would use the same style, irrespective of what style, to respond to each of the four situations. Although the responses in Category A, Table 1, indicate that a higher proportion of research and development managers (15 vs 11%) reported that their superiors would use the same style in all four situations, the resulting t value of .588 ($df = 122$) indicates no differences between the two groups when they were separated by functional area.

Since subordinates did not report that their superiors would use the same style to deal with each of the four problems, it was conceivable that they did not attribute any pattern to their supervisors' responses. A fourth hypothesis tested was that subjects would report that their supervisor would use the four styles randomly to deal with the four hypothetical problems. The expected distribution under the randomness assumption was that 2, 19, 14, 56, and 9% of the responses would fall in Categories A, B, C, D, and E, respectively. Table 2 reports the observed and expected number of respondents who attributed varying degrees of style flexibility to their superiors. An overall chi-square test revealed a value of 127.67 ($df = 8$) which significant at the .001 level thus indicating that the randomness hypothesis should be rejected. Additional chi-square tests showed that the hypothesis could not be supported when the respondents were subclassified as middle managers ($\chi^2 (8) = 33.86$), first level managers ($\chi^2 (8) = 109.57$), research and development managers ($\chi^2 (4) = 100.26$) or accounting managers ($\chi^2 (4) = 23.45$).

Table 1 SUBORDINATES' PERCEPTIONS OF THEIR SUPERVISORS' LEADERSHIP STYLE FLEXIBILITY[a]

	Total number of respondents		Category A Supervisor would use same style for all situations		Category B Supervisor would use one style for three situations and another style for the fourth situation		Category C Supervisor would use one style for two situations and another different style for the other two situations		Category D Supervisor would use three styles		Category E Supervisor would use all four styles	
	N	%	N	%	N	%	N	%	N	%	N	%
Company A, R & D												
Middle managers	18	100	2	11	6	33	3	17	7	39	0	0
First-level managers	34	100	6	18	10	29	8	24	8	24	2	6
Total managers	52	100	8	15	16	31	11	21	15	29	2	2
Company B, R & D												
Middle managers	14	100	2	14	3	21	5	36	2	14	2	14
First-level managers	20	100	3	15	1	5	6	30	10	50	0	0
Total managers	34	100	5	15	4	12	11	32	12	35	2	6
Company B, accounting												
Middle managers	8	100	0	0	2	25	2	25	4	50	0	0
First-level managers	30	100	4	13	3	10	10	33	13	43	0	0
Total managers	38	100	4	11	5	13	12	32	17	45	0	0
Totals												
Middle managers	40	100	4	10	11	28	10	25	13	32	2	5
First-level managers	84	100	13	15	14	17	24	29	31	37	2	2
Total managers	124	100	17	14	25	20	34	27	44	35	4	3

[a] Percentages may not equal 100 because of rounding procedures.

Table 2 LEADERSHIP STYLE FLEXIBILITY: OBSERVED AND EXPECTED VALUES[a]

	Total re-spondents		Category A Supervisor would use same style for all situations		Category B Supervisor would use one style for three situations and another style for the fourth situation		Category C Supervisor would use one style for two situations and another different style for the other two situations		Category D Supervisor would use three styles		Category E Supervisor would use all four styles	
	N	%	Expected	Observed	Expected	Observed	Expected	Observed	Expected	Observed	Expected	Observed
Company A, R & D	52	100	1.04	8	9.88	16	7.28	11	29.12	15	4.68	2
Company B, R & D	34	100	.68	5	6.46	4	4.76	11	19.04	12	3.06	2
Company B, accounting	38	100	.76	4	7.22	5	5.32	12	21.28	17	3.42	0
Totals	124	100	2.48	17	23.56	25	17.36	34	69.44	44	11.16	4

[a]The sum of expected values may not equal the number of respondents (N) because of rounding procedures.

The data in Tables 1 and 2 show that subordinates reported they did not believe that their supervisors would either use the same style (irrespective of what style) or randomly employ styles to deal with the four typical but hypothetical problems. These attributions suggest the possibility that some other pattern of style usage may exist, at least in the minds of the subjects. For example, a manager may be perceived to deal with simple problems, irrespective of whether they are technical or interpersonal, in a directive manner and handle complex problems in a nondirective way or he may be seen as resolving technical problems, irrespective of whether they are simple or complex with Style A and dealing with interpersonal problems with Style D.

Although the questionnaire was not designed to ascertain if subordinates perceived that their superiors would vary their styles as a function of any specific problem dimension, it did contain four problems which varied on two dimensions; complex–simple and interpersonal–technical. While the author recognizes that respondents made predictions about their superiors' behavior in only four, specific problem situations and therefore any generalizations concerning the relationship of these responses to the general task dimensions of complex–simple and interpersonal–technical may be limited by specific-problem variance, a *post hoc* analysis of Category C responses was performed to determine if responses followed these dimensions more frequently than would be expected by chance. Table 3 reports the expected and observed number of subjects whose responses were divided along either the complex–simple or technical–interpersonal dimension or along neither of the two dimensions. Tests indicated a significant difference at the .001 level ($t(123) = 6.88$) between the expected and observed number of subjects who responded that their supervisors would use one style for interpersonal problems, and another different style for technical problems.

DISCUSSION

The major purpose of this paper was to determine if subordinates perceived that their superiors would use the same leadership style, irrespective of what style, for each of four typical but hypothetical problems. The results reported in Table 1 indicate that only 14% of the subjects reported that their supervisors would use the same leadership style for all four problems; 86% replied that their superiors would exhibit some degree of style flexibility across the four situations. These data suggest that the true proportion of managers who are perceived by their subordinates to rely upon only one style to handle problems which confront them should be revised from 100 to 14% with a 95% confidence that the true proportion perceived as using the same style would fall between 8 and 20%.

Table 3 CATEGORY C RESPONSES BROKEN DOWN ALONG GENERAL TASK DIMENSIONS: EXPECTED AND OBSERVED VALUES[a]

	N	Subordinates' responses divided along the technical-interpersonal dimension				Subordinates' responses divided along the complex-simple dimension				Subordinates' responses not divided along either the technical-interpersonal or the complex-simple dimensions			
		Expected		Observed		Expected		Observed		Expected		Observed	
	N	N	%	N	%	N	%	N	%	N	%	N	%
Subjects' responses	124	5.79	4.67	22	17.74	5.79	4.67	9	7.26	5.79	4.67	3	2.42

[a] The expected values for each of the three columns were derived by multiplying the probability that a response would fall in Category C strictly by chance (.14) by one third, because the response could fall into three different states in Category C.

Although behavioral flexibility is often thought to be associated with the organizational level at which a manager is located, it did not affect these results, i.e., first-level managers were no more or less likely than middle managers to report that their superiors' leadership style was rigid. Functional area did not affect the results either; i.e., accounting managers were no more or less likely than R & D managers to report that their superiors' style was rigid. These results suggest that the perceived style rigidity that was reported may have been more a function of personality variables and perceptual expectations of subordinates than of either functional area or organizational level.

Regardless of the cause of style flexibility, it seems safe to conclude that, at least from the subordinates' viewpoint, managers can exhibit some degree of style flexibility thus obviating the need to either replace the manager as the situation changes or to modify the situation to fit the leader's capabilities. One must still determine, of course, which managers are capable of what degree of style flexibility; this will not be an easy problem to solve.

The perceived ability of managers to modify their style as they are confronted with different problems was corroborated further by the data in Table 2 which indicate that subjects did not believe that their supervisors would choose their response styles randomly. It can be concluded that, if managers are not perceived either to use one style all the time or to employ styles randomly, some response pattern must exist. The data in Table 3 indicate that the type of problem confronting the manager may influence the style his subordinates perceive he would use. A significant tendency was for subordinates to report that their supervisors would use one style to handle interpersonal problems and another, different style to tackle technical problems. It would appear that further research to learn the degree to which perceived style varies with other task dimensions may prove fruitful.

Although there are several reasons why leaders might adopt a consistent response pattern toward certain types of problems and not others, a particularly appealing one is that they develop a good deal of confidence and experience little anxiety when confronted with certain types of problems while other types make them uncertain and insecure. If this is true, and conversations with managers suggests it is, a manager under favorable circumstances may be more willing and able to vary his style to meet changing situational requirements. This same leader may feel threatened by other types of problems and adopt a very rigid style to mask his uncertainty and to reduce his anxiety. Research is now underway to determine if a manager's score on the Bass Orientation Inventory can predict the flexibility of his style toward certain sets of problems. It may be that supervisors who score high on task orientation, as distinguished from interpersonal or self orientation, may feel more confident and less anxious when confronted with technical problems and will exhibit greater style flexibility when coping with these problems. These same supervisors may become quite rigid when dealing with interpersonal problems regardless of the degree of complexity involved.

One other explanation seems very feasible; i.e., managers really do not vary their styles but subordinates think they do. This may occur because some subordinates may place greater importance and interest in a specific class of problems, e.g., interpersonal ones. This emphasis may influence their expectations concerning what behavior is appropriate for their supervisor. If this does occur, the same behavioral act may be judged to possess varying degrees of flexibility by the subordinates; i.e., some may believe the act was authoritarian; others may feel it was democratic. This line of reasoning would corroborate the belief that supervisors really have only one leadership style. The author has rejected this explanation because his personal observations of and discussions with managers have led him to believe that they are capable of and do vary their leadership styles.

The fact that one manager can behave more flexibly than another does not imply that he will be more effective. It seems more reasonable to suggest that effective performance requires the implementation of styles appropriate to situational demands. The ability to employ different leadership styles is important only if the situations which confront a manager require such flexibility. There may be situations which are so stable that the adoption and consistent use of one style is most effective. Unfortunately, the design of this study did not enable the author to assess properly the situational demands placed upon the subjects and leaves him with no alternative but to make the usual plea for more research. It does seem important, however, that future studies of leadership effectiveness incorporate the technical – interpersonal dimension. Although the operational difficulties of this separation are recognized, most real life problems vary in both technical and interpersonal elements and our research efforts should recognize this.

CONCLUSION

The growing acceptance of a contingency theory of leadership effectiveness represents a significant step forward in the leadership literature. One important question raised by the acceptance of such a theory, however, is the ability of managers to employ a variety of leadership styles. The data reported in this paper suggest that managers were not perceived by their subordinates to rely solely upon one style. Although some managers were perceived to adopt a certain style for certain types of problems, a good deal of style flexibility generally was perceived by subordinates. This conclusion suggests that most leaders can behave flexibly enough to cope with varied situations. Thus, it may not be necessary either to change managers as the situation changes or to modify the situation to fit managers' styles.

Although there are still many important questions which must be answered before our knowledge concerning leadership effectiveness is adequate, some of the more pressing ones are: Can a manageable typology of situational variables be constructed? Can measures of managerial effectiveness be developed for each of these situations so that a "best" style can be determined for each typological case? Can this "best" style be made consistent with subordinates and superiors' expectations concerning the role? Can managers' preference for problem types be identified? To what extent can a manager volitionally control his behavior? What are the most effective means of teaching managers to be sensitive to situational requirements and to adapt their styles to meet these demands? When these questions are answered, we will know a great deal more about leadership effectiveness.

REFERENCES

FIEDLER, F. E. Engineering the job to fit the manager. *Harvard Business Review,* 1965, 43, 115–122.

FIEDLER, F. E. Personality, motivational systems, and behavior of high and low LPC persons. Technical Report, 70–12, Organizational Research Unit, Department of Psychology, University of Washington, September, 1970, p. 1.

RUBIN, I. M., & GOLDMAN, M. An open system model of leadership performance. *Organizational Behavior and Human Performance,* 1968, 3, 143–156.

TANNENBAUM, R., & SCHMIDT, W. H. How to choose a leadership pattern. *Harvard Business Review,* 1958, 36, 95–101.

4

Organization Development: Issues and Readings

To ensure organizational effectiveness, managers must continually realign or change existing organizational structures and processes. This is a challenging task under the best of circumstances, and the materials in Part 4 have been included to emphasize this point. Section A offers a broad "state-of-the-art" review of the organization development area and examines the durability of certain organizational improvement efforts. Section B looks at the assets and liabilities of group problem solving and discusses strategies for the management of different types of decision tasks. Section C explores the development and refinement of management by objectives and suggests a method for improving linkages between MBO and OD practitioners. Finally, Section D adds a unique perspective on performance issues by analyzing positive reinforcement techniques and the correlates of organizational effectiveness.

Section A

Planned Change and Its Durability

The OD literature has proliferated in recent years, with diverse groups of practitioners emphasizing the advantages of their respective approaches to organizational improvement. Not surprisingly, there has been a growing interest among managers in the careful examination of OD and its various techniques. While Part 1 of this book looked selectively at OD, the present section broadens coverage of the area by including a critical review of the field plus an article that considers the durability of planned organizational change.

The review article, "Organization Development," is by Friedlander and Brown. In contrast to many OD specialists, they conceptualize OD not just in human-process terms, but in techno-structural terms as well. After explaining their theoretical framework, Friedlander and Brown identify several research issues in applied behavioral science. Next, they proceed to the main body of their review which examines techno-structural methods of change (e.g., sociotechnical interventions and job redesign) and human-process techniques (e.g., survey feedback, team building, and intergroup development). Their work suggests that human-process methods have more effect on attitudes while certain techno-structural approaches have more impact on performance variables. Friedlander and Brown also discuss several comparative OD studies, point out that many OD efforts are multi-faceted (making unambiguous evaluation of results difficult), and conclude that OD needs a more general theory of planned change than currently exists.

The second article, by Seashore and Bowers, is one of the few studies that considers the "Durability of Organizational Change." Seashore and Bowers report on an OD effort begun by the Harwood Company when it bought its major competitor, the Weldon Company. Harwood had an established tradition of participative management whereas Weldon had a long tradition of centralized, authoritarian management. After the takeover, Harwood management began a program to rebuild and renew the Weldon firm along the lines of Harwood's more participative style. This program began in 1962 and lasted for two years. Results were largely positive, with improvements in profits and employee morale. Yet there was concern over the long-run impact of the development effort and, in mid-1969, part of the original research team returned to Weldon to consider the durability of earlier changes.

According to Seashore and Bowers, the follow-up analysis showed that Weldon had remained a successful, more participative organization. Although the changes at Weldon included plant modernization and improved pay, the researchers credit results to the participative climate. Given the extensiveness of the change effort, however, such attribution might be questioned. It could be argued, for example, that the major cause of success at Weldon stemmed from employee concern over possible loss of jobs under a new management—leading to adaptive behavior regardless of improved work processes, better pay, or more flexible supervisory attitudes.

Seashore and Bowers emphasize the primary importance of human-process variables in organizational change. Though subject to some debate, their work confronts directly a complicated issue—the "durability of change" over time. Relatively few studies have tackled this issue despite a clear need for longitudinal research in the OD area. Whatever the underlying cause of success at Weldon, the Seashore and Bowers article remains one of the better case illustrations of planned organizational change, surpassed only by Marrow, Bowers, and Seashore's original Harwood-Weldon study—*Management by Participation* (New York: Harper and Row, 1967).

20 Organization Development

Frank Friedlander and L. Dave Brown[1]

INTRODUCTION

Organization development (OD) has emerged both from the demands of a changing environment and from knowledge provided by the evolution of the applied behavioral sciences. . . . The framework we shall use in reviewing OD views organizations as composed of people with different sets of values, styles, and skills; technologies with different characteristics; and processes and structures which reflect different kinds of relationships between people or between people and their work (114). Processes and structures are the integrating mechanisms for (a) applying human resources to technological processes for task accomplishment, and (b) facilitating the utilization of technological processes for human fulfillment. From this perspective OD is a method for facilitating change and development in people (e.g. styles, values, skills), in technology (e.g. greater simplicity, complexity) and in organizational processes and structures (e.g. relationships, roles) (80). The objectives of OD generally can be classified as those optimizing human and social social improvement or as those optimizing task accomplishment or more likely as some (often confused) blend of the two.

Our concept of organization develpment calls for change in technology and structure (technostructural) or change in individuals and their interaction processes (human-processual), rather than efforts to change only the people, only the structure/process, or only the technology of the organization. The rationale behind this decision is twofold. First, the organizational processes and structures are the major linkage between the human and technological inputs into the organization; process and structure are thus core concepts of the organization as a system. Second, much of the literature on change indicates the relative impotence of efforts to change only technology (e.g. industrial engineering, operations research, and scientific management approaches), only people (e.g. selection methods, sensitivity groups, and most training), or only the structure (e.g. rearrangements and reorganizations based only on structural elements). For example, strong resistance or failure is often encountered in efforts to change only the organization structure (59), only the technology of the organization (163), or only the individual (46, 47, 71, 81).

[1] This review was supported in part by the National Institute of Mental Health, U.S. Public Health Service (Research Grant 5 RO1 MH 20719).

Figure 1 APPROACHES TO ORGANIZATION DEVELOPMENT

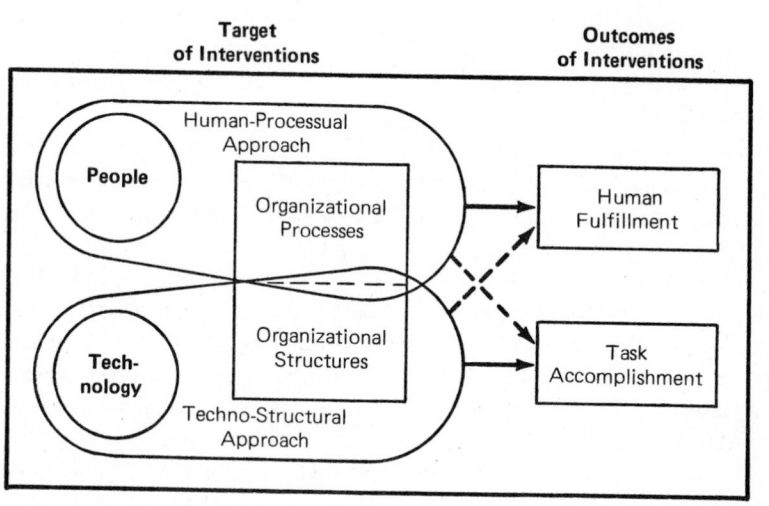

The framework for our discussion of OD is pictured in Figure 1. An organization includes people, technology, and process/structure. These components interact in the technostructural and human-processual systems on behalf of the objectives of human fulfillment and task accomplishment. Although we have not pictured it in Figure 1, the environment obviously interacts with all of these components in terms of input to and output from the organization.

As indicated in Figure 1, the human-processual and technostructural change approaches converge at the interface of the organization process and structure. Both process and structure are concerned with authority, communication, decision-making, goal-setting, and conflict resolution. But process implies the implementation of these as dynamic behavioral events and interactions, whereas structure describes these as ongoing sets of durable roles and relationships. Attitudes and behavior are clearly affected by both process (130) and structure (137). Over time, structures can be changed by processes that are inconsistent with them and processes are constrained and facilitated by organizational structures. Since process and structure are embedded in each other, it is almost impossible to create lasting change in one without modification of the other. Yet there are those who focus on changing organizational structures with no involvement in the behavioral processes in which these structures are embedded, and those who are totally concerned with changing processes, oblivious of the ongoing structures which underlie these processes.

If organizations can be viewed as composed of three components (people, technologies, and structures), so also can OD itself be understood by this model. It is at once a set of personal values, a set of change technologies, and a set of processes or structures through which the change agent relates to the organizational system. Thus OD interventions can be described in terms of the degree to which they incorporate values of humanism, democracy, economics, and science; the degree to which they utilize such technologies as team building, job design, and survey feedback; the degree to which they incorporate collaborative or unilateral relationships between change agent and organization; and the degree to which they are intended to optimize human/social benefit or productivity/performance objectives.

The values of the more humanistic and democratic approaches to OD are stated rather explicitly in the literature. Many of these stem from the Theory Y assumptions of McGregor (128). Tannenbaum & Davis (160), for example, clearly state these as values in transition in society: toward a positive and confirming view of man as a whole person, in process; toward encouraging the effective expression of feelings, authenticity, risk, confrontation, and collaboration. . . .

The objectives of OD are obviously colored by these values. They include creating an open problem-solving climate, supplementing the authority of role and status with the authority of knowledge and competence, locating decision-making and problem-solving as close to information sources as possible, building trust and collaboration, developing a reward system which recognizes the organizational mission and the growth of people, helping managers to manage according to relevant objectives rather than past practices, and increasing self-control and self-direction for people within the organization (42,155). Others see OD objectives as increased problem-solving capacity (15,155), cultural change (42), or re-education (86, 174).

The relationships of OD practitioners to organizational systems vary from facilitative-collaborative to unilateral-directive. In the latter, the change agent gathers data, analyzes it, reports his findings to senior management, and recommends changes. In the more facilitative role, the change agent helps others engage in exploration, diagnosis, and development. Phases in the facilitative-collaborative process include helping the organization identify problems, set priorities, develop data, plan action strategy, test and implement alternatives, and evaluate the change effort (20, 109, 120, 124).

The main body of this review is divided into these two sections: technostructural and human-processual change approaches. We exclude studies and conceptualizations not encompassed in one of these two approaches. We omit studies which were not concerned with change per se, or which were not field studies in organizational settings. We have also not considered some approaches because of space limitations or inclusion in previous reviews: e.g. management by objectives, pay and incentive systems, staffing systems.

RESEARCH ISSUES IN ORGANIZATION DEVELOPMENT

As in most of the applied behavioral sciences, research and theory on OD follow practice. This may reflect either the difficulties of doing research on OD or the impotence of research in creating practical theory and contributing to improved practice. The first explanation locates responsibility in organizational systems for lack of cooperation and appreciation of research; the second locates responsibility in research for lack of relevance and applicability to the organization.

Research on organizations, even stable organizations, presents a host of difficulties. Organizations are complex systems, with many relevant variables that combine in intricate interactions. The student of organizations must cope with size, complexity, and sluggish responses to events. Controlled comparisons are difficult, and the costs of developing a large sample of organizations can be astronomical. Behavioral science is just beginning to grapple with the social psychology of research, and organizational researchers must cope with issues like the attitude toward the research of the respondent's boss (2) and the obvious need by respondents to benefit from the research (78). . . .

In one sense the very dilemmas that OD research faces are its opportunities to create a new approach to knowledge-getting and knowledge-giving. It faces these dilemmas because, unlike many disciplines, it is a humanistic, change-oriented, professionally practiced field. Its current research methods are based on traditions that knowledge-getting and knowledge-giving are separate; the evaluation and validation of change lead to understanding development processes; that external rigor, control, and standardization are ideal methodological characteristics; that knowledge necessarily produces change.

Most research reported in this review, for example, has taken an evaluative stance, utilizing reliable pre- and post-measures selected and administered by the researcher to increase his knowledge of change and development in the "other" (e.g. the person, group, organization, etc). Pre-post measures provide for the practitioner and the client systems data at only two points in time, rather than a continous picture of the interactive developmental process. Continuous documentation (e.g. a detailed case study) provides data on the ongoing interactive processes which occurred, but does not provide immediate feedback to guide subsequent action steps. The issue is somewhat similar to suggesting to a person about to shave his face to look at yesterday's photographs of his preshave and postshave face instead of looking in the mirror. A moving picture would provide continuous data, but still not the immediate feedback or client control that shaving in a mirror provides. Thus for consultant and client relevance, research is most useful if it provides immediate continuous feedback of the process and progress of intervention and development. OD theory based on this kind of research would provide the greatest validity on change processes and might also provide the most relevance to practitioners. . . .

TECHNOSTRUCTURAL APPROACHES

Technostructural approaches to OD refer to theories of and interventions into the technology (e.g. task methods and processes) and the structure (e.g. the relationships, roles, arrangements) of the organization. Technostructural approaches are rooted in the fields of engineering, sociology, psychology, economics, and open systems theory. Change interventions are intended to affect the work content and method and to affect the sets of relationships among workers. Within the broad heading of technostructural development are included sociotechnical systems perspectives, job design and enlargement, and job enrichment. These methods are easier to separate in theory than in practice, but the conceptual distinction among them has implications that are important enough to warrant their preservation in this discussion.

Sociotechnical systems and job design are, in part, a reaction to and an emergence from two earlier and still current perspectives of change: (*a*) scientific management and industrial engineering which focus upon the physical environment and physiological requirements of workers; and (*b*) psychology and social psychology, which focus on the social relationships and personal needs of the workers. Proponents of sociotechnical systems and job design criticize the physical approach for treating social groups and individuals mechanistically, and criticize the psychological approach for ignoring the technology of the organization or treating it as unchangeable. Further criticism is that both approaches treat the organization as a closed system, dealing with intraorganizational issues in piecemeal fashion and ignoring the important linkages between the organization and its environment (60).

The concept of sociotechnical systems has been applied to the work initiated in England, particularly at the Tavistock Institute. Sociotechnical interventions are directed at the fit between the technological configurations and the social structure of work units. The term "job design" until recently has been applied to developments in the U.S., particularly those initiated at the University of California at Berkeley. Job design studies have sought to manipulate the configuration of technology, as in task designs and assignments making up jobs, and to explore the effects of these changes on personal, social, and organizational phenomena (60). We have grouped job design studies together with job enlargement studies since the methodologies are similar. Job design and enlargement are concerned with increasing satisfaction and performance, although there seems to be greater concern in job design to enhance performance, and greater concern in job enlargement to enhance job satisfaction. Job enrichment is derived from theories of motivation, whereas job enlargement is based on industrial engineering principles. In job enrichment, work functions from a vertical slice of the unit are brought together into a single job to increase the challenge of that job (and therefore the motivation of the jobholder); in job enlargement, work functions from horizontal slices of the work unit are consolidated to provide greater variety and a sense of the whole task.

There are also differences in scope among these three approaches. Sociotechnical systems take into account the entire system, job design focuses upon sets of inter-related functions, and job enrichment is concerned primarily with single jobs. Successful job enrichment, for example, may enrich a single job at the expense of other jobs in that unit. Sociotechnical systems, on the other hand, frequently rearrange relationships among roles or tasks or the sequence of activities.

Sociotechnical Systems

In one of the earliest studies in sociotechnical systems, Trist & Bamforth (163) found that two different social systems in British coal mining were associated with very different levels of productivity, absenteeism, and accidents. Traditional coal mining utilized small, cohesive work groups working as autonomous teams, each establishing its own system of work with each worker performing a variety of tasks. Technological advances led to a change in which work groups of about 40 men in three shifts were formed, with their activities spread over a wide area. The task requirements prohibited close interpersonal relations and group identification; workers were assigned to narrow tasks and paid on an individual rather than a team basis. The longwall method resulted in lower performance, higher absenteeism, feelings of passivity and indifference, and emotional strain. When many of the social and group relationships were reintroduced into a "composite longwall method," productivity, attendance, safety, and morale were substantially improved (70, 164).

Rice (140), another member of the Tavistock group, applied similar concepts in an Indian weaving mill. Installation of automatic looms and task specialization led to a decline in the quantity and quality of woven products. Rice introduced a number of changes: the number of job levels was reduced from nine to three, tasks were made interchangeable, and semiautonomous work groups were created and placed in charge of a set of looms. During the following 2 years, productivity rose, wasted-cloth rate declined, and morale rose dramatically. . . .

The Tavistock group is now heavily involved in experiments in "industrial democracy" being carried out at the national level in Norway. In collaboration with workers, employers, and the Norwegian government, a number of field experiments in the effects of different work philosophies and sociotechnical arrangements have been carried out. Though the results available are only preliminary, there is evidence (70a, 160a, 162a) that the changes do indeed have important effects on both productivity and alienation.

Job Design and Job Enlargement

Like the sociotechnical systems approach, job design and enlargement focus upon both the technical aspects of the job and the social structures which support it. They also attempt to increase satisfaction and performance by building in greater variety, discretion, feedback, identity, and responsibility for whole task completion.

In one of the earliest studies in job design, Marks (125), as reported in Davis & Canter (61), conducted an experiment on the shop floor to change the configuration of technology through task design and job assignments. For example, operations, inspection, and securing of materials were combined into one job and performed at individual work stations. This design resulted in improvements in output, quality, production flexibility, and job attitude. In a similar study (57) in which assembly jobs were changed over to more independent bench jobs, production time decreased and quality increased. Preference for self-pacing was found as the reason for preferring bench jobs, but social interaction and work interaction showed sharp reductions. Similar results have been found for enlargement of maintenance jobs (63). . . .

Alderfer (3) concludes in a review that job enlargement results in increased overall job satisfaction and greater meaningfulness of work. Lawler (111) reviewed ten studies and found quality improvements in all, but productivity increases in only four. Davis (60) explains such improvements as a consequence of increased number and variety of tasks, self-determination of pacing, increased responsibility for quality, increased discretion of work methods, and sense of work completion. Alderfer (3) found that enlarged jobs are judged by non-jobholder experts as requiring more technical competence and opportunity for innovation, more variety of duties, and more need to deal with people. Incumbents of enlarged jobs reported increased satisfaction with opportunities to use their skills and abilities and decreased satisfaction with their relations with superiors. Friedman (82) reports a study in which interaction and communication between foremen and workers increased, resulting in increased prestige for workers. . . .

Alderfer (3) suggests that differing results of job enlargement on interpersonal relations is contingent upon the technology. In continuous process technology, where there is a high demand for interdependency among employees, job enlargement may place greater stress on these interdependencies, resulting in lowered satisfaction.

Job Enrichment

Job enrichment is the restructuring of the content of a set of jobs or functions which are vertically related to enhance the employee's opportunity for responsibility, achievement, challenge, and growth. It generally involves collapsing various vertical functions into a single more responsible function. Proponents of job enrichment are somewhat critical of job enlargement, claiming that job enlargement condenses the boredom and monotony of several jobs into one job. Job enrichment as an organizational process evolved from the two-factor motivation theory developed by Herzberg, Mausner & Snyderman (99); the theory stresses that man's needs at work are met essentially by the nature of his work. The major motivators that can be built into work are increased achievement, recognition, responsibility, advancement, task capability, and knowledge. . . .

There are a number of reviews of job enrichment applications (10, 122, 143) and several additional accounts of application findings (129, 135). Although the number of well-designed studies is too few to make broad generalizations, there are indications that job enrichment has positive effects on satisfaction and motivation (72). There is reason to believe that the quality of production increases more than the quantity (10, 111), although this applies to applications which combine job enrichment and enlargement. In much of the literature, the concept of "motivation" is used as a convenient device to explain increased performance or satisfaction. The direct effect on motivation of job enrichment programs is unexplored.

There are a number of questions regarding the relative impact of the process through which changes are introduced and implemented and the impact of the restructured job. In some studies employees participated in decisions, while in others only supervisors influenced the restructuring. The assumption which underlies directive implementation is that task related experiences lead to changes in attitudes and needs (89, 122); changed work experience will result in attitude change, rather than vice versa. In connection with this, Hackman & Lawler (92) and Alderfer (3) suggest that experiencing higher order need satisfaction will result in the development of higher order needs.

Job enrichment and job enlargement generally ignore individual and technological differences; most proponents assume that job enrichment or enlargement are applicable and relevant regardless of the individual concerned and regardless of the technology of the organization. But Turner & Lawrence (165) found that enriched jobs resulted in greater satisfaction and less absenteeism for small-town workers but not for urban employees. Similarly, Hulin & Blood (103) and Blood & Hulin (33) found that workers who hold traditional values about work and achievement respond positively to complex jobs, but more alienated (urban, blue-collar) workers respond negatively to complex jobs. Hackman & Lawler (92) report positive correlations between job complexity (variety, autonomy, task identity, feedback) and motivation, satisfaction and performance *only* for employees with higher order need strength (e.g. for accomplishment, growth, challenge, variety, participation). Wanous (170) found that higher order need strength accounted for more of the relationships between job complexity and positive outcomes than either the blue-collar, urban distinction made by Hulin & Blood (103) or the Protestant ethic values distinction made by Blood (32). Standing (156) found that the degree of satisfaction within a single set of jobs varied as a function of the cognitive complexity of the employee. The degree of satisfaction with the work itself was in inverted U-shaped function of cognitive complexity. These studies suggest a contingency theory in which the probability of job enrichment and enlargement resulting in increased performance or satisfaction is contingent upon the needs of the employee, his cognitive complexity, and his cultural milieu.

Similarly, increases in performance and satisfaction resulting from these changes may be contingent upon the technology of the organization. Task identity, for example, may be difficult to establish in a continuous process technology, but autonomy and feedback seem easier to implement in an automated process technology than in heavy assembly work (31). Several organizations are finding job enrichment and enlargement simply impossible given their huge investments in stationary equipment. Other contingencies which the organization may face include lack of sufficient skills to take on more demanding work, short-term lowered performance which frequently accompanies organizational change, union resistance or disinterest (143).

The sociotechnical studies reviewed in this section consistently indicate increased performance and productivity—a finding that is less clear for job design/enlargement or job enrichment. The evidence on job enrichment is too sparse as yet to make unqualified claims as to its effectiveness; more research is needed. All three approaches seem to result in quality increases, lowered absenteeism, and lowered turnover. The evidence for production time decreases and cost savings is mixed for job enlargement and job enrichment. In terms of attitudinal change, job satisfaction tends to increase as a result of job enlargement and job enrichment. Job enlargement, however, tends to result in a more socially isolated role for the workers, which increases both the need and difficulty in relating to others with whom their tasks are interdependent. Sociotechnical systems avoid this issue by social restructuring of the work group, resulting in clear increases in group morale. . . .

HUMAN PROCESSUAL APPROACHES

Human process intervention focuses on the human participants and the organization processes (e.g. communication, problem-solving, decision-making) through which they accomplish their own and the organization's goals. This orientation to OD is rooted in the academic fields of psychology, social psychology, and anthropology and in the applied disciplines of group dynamics and the human relations movement. Human process-orientation change agents tend to value human fulfillment highly and to expect improved organizational performance to follow on improved human functioning and processes (152). These two don't necessarily go hand in hand, even though it may be more comfortable to assume this. . . .

Although practitioners have developed a number of alternative interventions concerned with human processes in organizations (cf. Beckhard 20, Fordyce & Weil 73, Burke & Hornstein 42, French & Bell 75), most research efforts focus on three general areas of process-oriented intervention: survey feedback, group development, and intergroup development. These three intervention strategies are founded on some common assumptions: sharing information can be valuable, particularly when it hitherto has remained unshared but has influenced organizational processes (like some covert feelings); confronting and working through differences among people who must work together can enhance collaboration; participation in decision-making can lead to increased commitment. Survey feedback involves organizational groups in discussing diagnostic data and planning action steps. Group development activities emphasize improving group abilities to accomplish their tasks. Intergroup development interventions press for improved management of the interfaces between groups. These three forms of intervention are at least potentially compatible, and often are used in sequence, beginning with survey feedback and moving to group and intergroup development activities.

Survey Feedback

Survey feedback is a process in which data is systematically collected (usually by questionnaires) from members of an organization, analyzed in summary fashion, and fed back selectively to organization members. To varying degrees, outside staff and organization members collaboratively design the questions to be asked, jointly analyze and interpret the data, and feedback in meetings to organization units from which the data was collected for purposes of diagnosis and potential change. The intervention has developed from traditional attitude surveys which were administered to employees and fed back to management; in recent years findings have been presented to employee respondents as well, partly to gain their cooperation in future studies. Such feedback has now taken on clear organizational development purposes as well (36, 130), on the assumption that discrepancies between organizational ideals and actual responses to the survey will generate motivation for change (136).

Early participation of organization members in the design and collection of data is likely to increase the relevance of the feedback (123, 130, 132). Organization members may be asked to develop questions for the survey, or they may be interviewed to determine what issues are relevant (130). Early involvement in one study increased awareness of interpersonal problems between supervisors and subordinates (7).

The part played by organizational superiors in the feedback meetings is critical. Baumgartel (17) found that perception of supervisory behavior changed as a consequence of increased information flow and problem confrontation between hierarchical levels after feedback. Chase (49) reports that the feedback process tended to equalize power even in a highly threatening environment, and Klein, Kraut & Wolfson (108) report that use of line managers rather than personnel representatives to feed back data resulted in more satisfaction and greater perceived utilization of the data. Participation of superiors in discussion of the feedback may facilitate effective use of the information. On the other hand, a resistant or antagonistic superior can undermine the process; Alderfer & Ferris (7) suggest that managers meet in peer groups to prepare for feedback of potentially threatening results before meeting with their subordinates in family groups. . . .

It seems clear that survey feedback meetings can lead to attitudinal changes by participants. Miles et al (130) report improved satisfaction with decisions even though they were not implemented); Mann (123) found improvement in attitudes toward work, supervisors, progress, and group ability to get the job done; Bowers (35) reports improvement in organizational climate, managerial task and interpersonal leadership, and satisfaction; Brown (38) found increased participant involvement in the organization. But the longer term changes in individual behavior or organizational performance appear to be contingent on more than just survey feedback. Despite highly successful meetings and increased satisfaction, Miles et al. (130) found that few action steps or structural changes emerged from the meeting and so little change occurred. Brown (38) notes that the higher involvement did not persist without follow-up, and Frohman (83) found that more change occurred with consultant follow-up than without it.

The research literature suggests that the effectiveness of survey feedback can be increased by collaborative involvement of the participants, participation of unit management, facilitation by an outside consultant, and specific decisions about follow-up and action steps. There is evidence that survey feedback can be an effective "bridge" between diagnostic activities (e.g. interviewing or questionnaire administration) and active intervention, since its primary effects seem to be on attitudes and perceptions of the situation. But there is little evidence that survey feedback alone leads to changes in individual behavior or organizational performance.

Group Development Intervention

OD practitioners have emphasized the importance of the work group rather than the individual (40, 102). Group development interventions like "team-building," according to French & Bell, are "probably the most important single group of (OD) interventions" (75, p. 112).

Descriptions of different forms of team-building technology are easily obtained (e.g. Clark 53, 54; French & Bell 75; Fordyce & Weil 73; Golembiewski 86; Burke & Hornstein 42). Beer (21) classifies the different approaches to group development according to the primary issues they treat: (a) goal-setting activities (18, 20) that establish clear goals for the team to achieve; (b) interpersonal relations development (12, 13, 152) to improve the quality of interaction among team members; (c) role analysis work (65, 95) for increased clarity about each member's role and responsibilities; and (d) "Managerial Grid" group development (26) to prepare the group for later phases in the grid OD program.

The literature contains a number of case studies of group development activities from the vantage point of the consultant (69, 110). But these case studies offer little more than the flavor of the experience.

The impact of team-building activities has been explored systematically by several investigators. Argyris (12) and Harrison (93) report interview, observation, and questionnaire data from three groups of managers, two of which experienced T-group training and a comparison group. The study was frankly exploratory and suffers from methodological problems, but the data suggested changes in values and behavior of participants occurred. In a subsequent study, Argyris (13) trained an executive group to be more "interpersonally competent"; times series analysis of tape recordings suggested that the training affected executive meeting behavior, though only anecdotal evidence for the relationship between the changed behavior and increased effectiveness was available. In a larger study, Friedlander (76) found that four trained teams reported significantly higher levels of group effectiveness, mutual influence, and personal involvement and participation than did the eight control groups. Schmuck, Runkel & Langmeyer (148) trained the faculty of a junior high school and compared the experimental faculty with the faculties of several similar schools. The experimental faculty reported more positive perceptions of the principal, the staff meetings, and the level of innovations in teaching, and they espoused more norms consistent with laboratory values than the controls; the authors also report anecdotal data about positive changes. . . .

There remains a dearth of evidence for the effects of team building external to the group developed. Harrison (93) noted that the changed interpersonal perceptions of Argyris' T-group participants did not generalize to the participants' subordinates. Bigelow (25), on the other hand, found that participation in group development activities affected teachers in the classroom, even through the group development activities were not designed to change classroom behavior. Analysis of tapes of teacher classroom behavior indicated that participants became more integrative and less dominative than controls, and that student perception of relationships with their peers improved in the classrooms with trained teachers. Fosmire, Keutzer & Diller (74) report the results of group development with the entire faculty of a new high school. Their intervention led to increased interpersonal openness and acceptance of conflict among the faculty and to increased perceptions by students of the faculty as responsive and themselves as responsible.

Though none of the research designs is flawless, there is convergent evidence that group development activities affect participant attitudes and sometimes their behavior as well. These effects may also "spill over" in some fashion to other organization members. It remains unclear, however, what mechanisms operate in successful team development activities, or what critical conditions must be satisfied for successful generalization of learnings outside the team, or what effects group development has on actual task performance.

Intergroup Relations Development

Problems at the interfaces between groups in an organization are endemic in modern organizations, and they are a matter of central concern to OD practititioners

(23, 75). Lawrence & Lorsch (113) suggest that intergroup relations problems are an inevitable correlate of the differentiation of organizational subsystems to meet and deal with environmental complexity. Important conflict has been reported between different departments in business organizations (68, 151), between headquarters and field teams (30), between field and administrative officers of the State Department (23), between a management development program and other subsystems in a bank (4), between union and management representatives (29, 30), among different occupational specialties in coal mines (164), and between potential merger partners (34).

There is no shortage of ideas for managing intergroup conflict. Some theories have been developed in social psychological research (154), others from work with organizations (141). Neilsen (133) describes seven strategies for intervening in intergroup conflict that vary in the degree to which they deal with behavior alone or with both behavior and attitudes. Walton (167) has suggested four interventions for third parties to help manage intergroup conflict: 1. reduce the potential for conflict (e.g. change structure or personnel); 2. resolve substantive issues (e.g. make the decisions); 3. help manage manifest conflict (e.g. be a referee); 4. facilitate a change in the relationships.

The first two alternatives require power over the combatants, an option that some technostrucural consultants have used to great effect. Trist et al. (164), for example, eliminated counterproductive intergroup conflict among coal miners by changing the sociotechnical system. But most human process consultants have no such power or they decline to use it. They have preferred the latter two interventions: helping manage manifest conflict and facilitating relationship changes. Walton (168) offers some provocative insights into the complexities of the third party role; his approach involves improving intergroup relations by improving relations between their representatives. A more common approach has been to foster a general "problem-solving" approach to the relations between groups. . . .

Intergroup development interventions to change relationships and manage conflict in practice are based on information sharing, confrontation of differences, and working through to new understandings. The prototype design requires groups to develop lists of their perceptions of themselves, the other group, and their views of the other group's perceptions of them, and then to use the lists as input to developing better understanding of each other and to creating future action plans. This design was developed by Blake and his colleagues (29, 30), but it has been used and recommended by many others (e.g. Beckhard 20; French & Bell 75).

There is very little systematic research on the effectiveness of such interventions in the field. Case studies abound (e.g. Black, Mouton & Sloma 29), but they leave many questions about the efficacy of the intervention unresolved. Golembiewski & Blumbert (87, 88) report attitudinal changes after a workshop that included confrontation among several groups from the same organization, but while participant attitudes changed in the ways predicted by the investigators, no data were collected on the consequences of the intervention for individual behavior or organizational performance. Further, effects of the intergroup intervention may have been confounded by a simultaneous confrontation between the participants and the consultants (who, after all, constituted an extra-organizational group that was potentially a unifying "external enemy" for all participants).

It is painfully evident that more research is needed before much can be said about the utility of the present process-oriented technology for managing intergroup relations. There is a good deal of activity going on, but relatively little in the way of unambiguous findings available. We simply do not know much about whether OD interventions lead to better management of intergroup relations or not. . . .

COMPARATIVE STUDIES OF OD INTERVENTIONS

One approach to comparison of OD interventions has been to examine successful and unsuccessful interventions reported in the literature. Greiner (91) compared 18 studies of organization change (technostructural, human-processual, multifaceted, and non-OD approaches) and found three features that distinguished successes: (a) successes consistently arose from strong internal and external pressures for change; (b) successes followed a consistent pattern from initial pressures to the gradual involvement of many levels including top management in diagnosis and change activities; and (c) successes were characterized by shared decision-making rather than unilateral or delegated decisions. . . .

But Greiner's (91) study did not evaluate alternative interventions. Bowers (35) has compared empirically the impacts over time of four interventions—interpersonal process consultation, task process consultation, laboratory training (group development), and survey feedback—and two control conditions—data handback and no treatment—on a host of attitudinal variables. Survey feedback, interpersonal process consultation, and data handback led to positive changes on a majority of the dependent measures, while task process consultation led to no change, and laboratory training and no treatment led to negative changes. Further analysis indicated that changes in perceived organizational climate (human resources primacy, communication flow, motivational climate, decision-making practices, technological readiness, and lower-level influence) influenced the impacts of the interventions; without positive climate changes no interventions had very positive effects, and with them even laboratory training helped. The only intervention that directly improved organizational climate, however, was survey feedback. . . .

MULTIFACETED ORGANIZATION
DEVELOPMENT

There are a number of reports of organization development activities with organizations as a whole. Some are anecdotal case studies (e.g. Beckhard 18; Davis 64;
Alschuler 9), and some evaluations of interventions based on attempts to collect
"harder" data, albeit with design problems (e.g. Blake et al. 28; Huse & Beer 105;
Zand, Steele & Zalkind 175). Relatively few reports, however, combine interventions into both technostructure and human processes with systematic efforts to
evaluate the interventions' effects or to account theoretically for the phenomena
observed.

Whyte & Hamilton (173) report work that predates the term "OD," but that
fits under the OD rubric. With only a hazy theory of organizational change, the
authors began an avowedly exploratory project with the "Tremont Hotel" in
1945. They observed and interviewed people in five departments and top management, and developed solutions to problems through group meetings of those involved. The organizational changes that resulted included redefined roles, improved productivity and safety records, decreased turnover, and improved interpersonal relations.

Another pioneering study was reportedly by Jaques (106), who began work
in the late 1940s with the Glacier Metal Company in England. He reports five
cases of work with company subsystems that requested the help of the research
team, whose task was: ". . . developing methods of offering technical assistance to
groups that requested the help of the team in exploring underlying and concealed
forces—whether psychological, cultural, structural, or technological—that were
impeding their progress or otherwise reducing their efficiency" (106, p. 306).
The team observed and interviewed members at work, and offered their impres-
sions and interpretations at group meetings to help clarify underlying issues. Although Jaques claims no responsibility for organizational changes, it is clear from
his descriptions that the interventions of the research team often influenced discussion and decisions taken.

Seashore & Bowers (149) studied an explicit attempt to change three of an
organization's five departments through several interventions including problem-
solving meetings, seminars, survey feedback, and personal coaching and counsel-
ing. Results supported the hypothesis that the interventions contributed to positive
change on pre-established dimensions, and that the experimental groups changed
more positively than the controls.

In a subsequent study, the same authors collaborated with Marrow to study
the changes in the Weldon Manufacturing Corporation after its acquisition by a
competitor (126). The new owners launched a change program that included tech-

nical system changes, widespread training, more careful selection, revised payment systems, and increased participation in decision-making and problem-solving at all levels. Results included positive attitude changes, increased return on capital and production efficiency, and decreased turnover and absenteeism relative both to past performance and to the company's major competitor. Follow-up research 7 years later (150) indicated that many changes were durable over that period.

Hill (100) studied a major sociotechnical change process in the Tavistock tradition of OD at Shell UK Limited. Carefully orchestrated interventions to clarify company objectives and values, share them with all levels, and then to share responsibility for increasing profitability and for meeting community needs led to positive changes in understanding, levels of individual skill, and organizational climate. Of 23 departments, 15 reported organizational or procedural changes, 10 reported job design changes, 10 reported changes in responsibility and commitment, and 5 reported improved performance. There were also changes in plant design, staff appraisal systems, manpower planning, and job enrichment programs.

Finally, Lawrence & Lorsch (112) have developed a "contingency theory" of organization that describes organizational structure and process contingent on the environmental uncertainty. They have explored the implications of contingency theory for OD and reported change efforts in a variety of organizations that seek to take into account the interfaces between individuals, groups, the organization, and its environment. Although only crude efforts at evaluation have been made, the theory is one of the most promising yet available in OD, in that it attempts to account systematically for both structural and processual variables and interventions at various levels in the organization. . . .

Of the six cases, three—Whyte & Hamilton (173), Jaques (106), and Lawrence & Lorsch (112)—emphasize exploration of the processes of organizational change, and their primary contribution is to conceptual formulations of those processes. The others—Seashore & Bowers (149), Marrow, Bowers & Seashore (126), and Hill (100)—emphasize careful evaluation of explicit interventions into organizational structures and processes on behalf of planned change. The evidence suggests that such projects can lead to changes in organizational performance as well as changes in individual attitudes and behavior.

Examination of the six reports also suggests some other observations. First, OD is not a short-term process; on the contrary, these cases took years to bear fruit. Second, it is important to have the support and active involvement of top management in the project; without that support it is difficult to gain commitment from lower levels. Third, in these projects interventions were made at several levels of the organizational hierarchy; support of top management by itself is not a sufficient condition for success. Finally, unambiguous evaluation of OD interventions is exceedingly difficult to arrange even with professional researchers involved as in these cases.

CONCLUSIONS

We have described OD as a planned change effort where the intervention is at the individual and process (human-processual) levels or the technological and structural (technostructural) levels. Excluded from our concept of OD are change efforts which deal only with individuals and do not make parallel efforts to change the structures and processes in which these individuals live and work, change efforts which focus entirely upon the technological factors and do not consider the structures and processes needed to support these changed technologies, and change efforts which impose structural reorganization without considering human or technological needs and demands. We have therefore reviewed studies of change which deal with the technostructural or human-processual aspects of the organization, and have found these to be reasonably effective beginnings for organizational change.

In general, human-processual approaches (survey feedback, group, and intergroup methods) have a number of positive effects on the attitudes of those involved. There is little evidence, however, that organizational processes actually change, or that performance or effectiveness is increased. Of the technostructural approaches, sociotechnical systems has the clearest effect on performance, while all three methods (sociotechnical, job design and enlargement, job enrichment) tend to increase satisfaction with work. These findings, however, may be colored by the fact that almost all technostructural interventions have been done with blue-collar or lower level white-collar workers, whereas most human-processual interventions were done with white-collar management groups. In blue-collar jobs, where more concrete criteria of performance are available, increased effectiveness may be easily measured. On the other hand, higher level white-collar jobs deal increasingly with abstract performance criteria that make measurement difficult. Little is reported in the literature about using human-processual approaches with blue-collar workers, or about using technostructural approaches with management level employees. This may be due to the inapplicability of different methods to different levels, or it may reflect the difficulty in measuring abstract criteria as noted above.

In one sense, sociotechnical systems, job design/enlargement, and job enrichment are theories about the appropriateness of certain social and technological structures rather than change methods. They have emerged from theories which attempt to understand and explain the current condition of personal, social, and technical systems. On the other hand, survey feedback, group, and intergroup methods have emerged from efforts to invent processes for development, influence, and movement. They may be methods for getting a change process moving, but it is never clear what their structural implications are. Increased integrations of the two approaches, we think, will increase the present capacity of OD to influence organizational effectiveness toward both human fulfillment and task accomplishment.

We believe that OD needs to explore various technologies, different sorts of change agent-client relationships, and alternative values currently emerging in our society. OD needs a framework to encompass this diversity that would encompass different values, different technologies, and different relationships contingent on different planned outcomes of intervention.

Some of the potential richness and diversity of OD are represented in its application to wider planned social change activities. Goodstein & Boyer (90) intervened on behalf of the community in a municipal agency; Walton (169) tried to develop solutions to international border questions in an intergroup workshop with country representatives; Wedge (172) describes an effort to intercede between antagonists in international conflict; Levin & Stein (115) and Duhl & Steetle (67) report interventions or attempts to intervene in community conflicts. These efforts have been marginally successful at best, and they may represent only the publishable tip of an iceberg of complete failures. OD today is a long way from being the general theory and technology of planned social system change we would like to see it become.

Why so? If we are to develop a more general theory of planned change, wh is necessary? OD has been developed within and for an extremely narrow range o. organizations: by far the most common consumer of OD to date has been business and industry. A more general theory of planned change must come to grips with a number of issues that OD at present ignores.

The future of OD rests in part on its values and the degree to which its practice, theory, and research are congruent with those values. Thus far, most OD is initiated by the organization—for the purpose of furthering such organizational goals as increased performance. We seldom question the merits of these goals as part of the OD process. Though most OD practitioners and researchers in some degree value both organizational task accomplishment *and* human fulfillment, there is an organizational press in favor of the former. OD as a field runs the risk of encouraging and implementing subtle but persuasive forms of exploitation, curtailment of freedom, control of personality, violation of dignity, intrusion of privacy—all in the name of science and of economic and technological efficiency. Within the hierarchical fabric of everyday organizational power struggles, OD researcher/consultants typically represent the control needs of management. The needs of those lower in the organization for a higher quality of life, for an expanded range of occupational and life choices may seldom be known or acted upon by the consultant. The only choice for many such employees is to remain in or leave their organization. Ross (142) points out that many value discussions in the field at the moment skate over some fundamental questions about present societal arrangements: OD may well be another organizational palliative, engaged in "making some people happier at the job of making other people richer" (142, p. 583). We need to consider in more depth what values are central to planned change and what implications those values have for client selection (or creation), permissible strategies and tactics, appropriate use of fees and other compensation. OD as a field is faced with decisions about the balance it can and will strike between changing institutions to increase human development and changing people to promote institutional development. The two goals are rarely consistent with each other.

Theoretically most of OD has adopted what Walton (166) has called the "attitude change strategy" for social change, which is based on shared information, trust among the parties, collaboration, and free choice. Less attention has been paid to the "power strategy" for social change, which is based on information management, distrust, conflict, and coercion (though many OD interventions borrow the power of the establishment to enact changes). More effective OD will require more elaboration of the theory of power from the points of view of both the powerful and the powerless (e.g. Gamson 85), and so will a broader theory of planned change.

Finally, broader applications of a theory of planned change will require expanded intervention technologies. Such technologies might include techniques for training advocates (51), tactics for organizing a power base and a client system where none existed before (8), technologies for information management and control for social ends (161), or rational strategies for the management of violence (134).

We are saying that current OD theory and practice may be a small part of a rich, broad, far-reaching, relevant field of planned change. As the wider field is legitimized and developed, and as broader technologies and theories are developed, these will feed back into and enrich the field of OD.

If the practice and theory of OD is to merge into a broader field of planned change, what role will research play in this transformation? We believe that research will either play a far more crucial role in the advancement of this field, or become an increasingly irrelevant appendage to it. Thus far it has utilized its techniques primarily for evaluation and validation, and its current techniques are well adapted to this. Thus far it has chosen to play a relatively uninvolved and distant role in the change-practice situation. Thus far it has focused on producing data for research needs rather than practice needs. As a result, we have theory from an external research perspective only. We have generally failed to produce a theory of change which emerges from the change process itself. We need a way of enriching our understanding and our action synergistically rather than at one or the other's expense—to become a science in which knowledge-getting and knowledge-giving are an integrated process, and one that is valuable to all parties involved. We believe that a theory of planned change must be a theory of practice, which emerges from practice data and is of the practice situation, not merely about it.

Literature Cited

2. Alderfer, C. P. 1968. Organizational diagnosis from initial client reactions to a researcher. *Hum. Organ.* 27:260–65
3. Alderfer, C. P. 1969. Job enlargement and the organizational context. *Personnel Psychol.* 22:418–26
4. Alderfer, C. P., 1971. Effect of individual, group and intergroup relations on attitudes toward a management development program. *J. Appl. Psychol.* 55:302–11
7. Alderfer, C. P., Ferriss, R. 1972. Understanding the impact of survey feedback. See Ref. 42, 234–43
8. Alinksy, S. D. 1972. *Rules for Radicals.* New York: Vintage
9. Alschuler, A. 1972. Toward a self-renewing school. *J. Appl. Psychol.* 8:577–600
10. Anderson, J. W. 1970. The impact of technology on job enrichment. *Personnel* 47:29–37
12. Argyris, C. 1962. *Interpersonal Competence and Organizational Effectiveness.* Homewood, Ill.: Dorsey
13. Argyris, C. 1965. *Organization and Innovation.* Homewood, Ill.: Irwin-Dorsey
15. Argyris, C. 1970. *Intervention Theory and Method.* Reading, Mass.: Addison-Wesley
17. Baumgartel, H. 1959. Using employee questionnaire results for improving organizations. *Kans. Bus. Rev.* 2–6
18. Beckhard, R. 1966. An organization improvement program in a decentralized organization. *J. Appl. Behav. Sci.* 2:3–25
20. Beckhard, R. 1969. *Strategies of Organizational Development.* Reading, Mass.: Addison-Wesley
21. Beer, M. 1974. The technology of organization development. In *Handbook of Industrial and Organizational Psychology,* ed. M. D. Dunnette. Chicago: Rand McNally
23. Bennis, W. G. 1969. *The Nature of Organization Development.* Reading, Mass.: Addison-Wesley
24. Bennis, W. G., Benne, K. D., Chin, R., Eds. 1969. *The Planning of Change.* New York: Holt, Rinehart & Winston, 2nd ed.
25. Bigelow, R. C. 1971. Changing classroom interaction through OD. See Ref. 147, 71–85
26. Blake, R. R., Mouton, J. S. 1968. *Corporate Excellence Through Grid Organizational Development.* Houston: Gulf Publ.
28. Blake, R. R., Mouton, J. S., Barnes, L. B., Greiner, L. E. 1964. Breakthrough in organizational development. *Harvard Bus. Rev.* 42:37–59
29. Blake, R. R., Mouton, J. S., Sloma, R. L. 1965. The union-management intergroup laboratory: strategy for resolving intergroup conflict. *J. Appl. Behav. Sci.* 1:25–57
30. Blake, R. R., Shepard, H. A., Mouton, J. S. 1964. *Managing intergroup Conflict in Industry.* Ann Arbor: Found. Res. Hum. Behav.
31. Blauner, R. 1964. *Alienation and Freedom.* Univ. Chicago Press
32. Blood, M. R. 1969. Work values and job satisfaction. *J. Appl. Psychol.* 53:456–59
33. Blood, M. R., Hulin, C. L. 1969. Alienation, environmental characteristics, and worker responses. *J. Appl. Psychol.* 51:284–90
34. Blumberg, A., Wiener, W. 1971. One from two: facilitating an organizational merger. *J. Appl. Behav. Sci.* 9:21–43
35. Bowers, D. G. 1973. OD techniques and their results in 23 organizations: the Michigan ICL Study. *J. Appl. Behav. Sci.* 9:21–43
36. Bowers, D. G., Franklin, J. F. 1972. Survey-guided development: using human resources measurement in organizational change. *J. Contemp. Bus.* 1:43–55

38. Brown, L. D. 1972. Research action: organizational feedback, understanding, and change. *J. Appl. Behav. Sci.* 8:697–774

40. Burke, W. W. 1971. A comparison of management development and organization development. *J. Appl. Behav. Sci.* 7:569–79

42. Burke, W. W., Hornstein, H. A., Eds. 1972. *The Social Technology of Organization Development.* Fairfax, Va.: NTL Learning Resources Corp.

46. Campbell, J. P. 1971. Personnel training and development. *Ann. Rev. Psychol.* 22:291–306

47. Campbell, J. P. Dunnette, M. D. 1968. Effectiveness of T-group experiences in managerial training and development. *Psychol. Bull.* 70:73–104

49. Chase, P. 1968. A survey feedback approach to organization development. In *Proceedings of the Executive Study Conference.* Princeton: Educ. Test. Serv.

51. Chesler, M. A., Lohman, J. E. 1971. Changing schools through student advocacy. See Ref. 147, 185–211

53. Clark, J. V. 1970. Task group therapy 1: goals and the client system. *Hum. Relat.* 23:263–77

54. Ibid. Task group therapy 2: intervention and problems of practice, 383–403

57. Conant, E. H., Kilbridge, M. D. 1965. An interdisciplinary analysis of job enlargement: technology, costs and behavioral implications. *Ind. Labor Relat. Rev.* 18:377–95

59. Dalton, M. 1965. Managing the managers. *Hum. Organ.* 14:4–10

60. Davis, L. E. 1966. The design of jobs. *Ind. Relat.* 6:21–45

61. Davis, L. E., Canter, R. R. 1956. Job design research. *J. Ind. Eng.* 7:275

63. Davis, L. E., Werling, R. 1960. Job design factors. *Occup. Psychol.* 34:109–32

64. Davis, S. A. 1967. An organic problem-solving method of organizational change. *J. Appl. Behav. Sci.* 3:3–21

65. Dayal, I., Thomas, J. M. 1968. Operations KDE: developing a new organization. *J. Appl. Behav. Sci.* 4:473–586

67. Duhl, L. J., Steetle, N. J. 1969. Newark: community or chaos, a case study of the medical school controversy. *J. Appl. Behav. Sci.* 5:537–72

68. Dutton, J. M., Walton, R. E. 1972. Interdepartmental conflict and cooperation: two contrastive studies. In *Managing Group and Intergroup Relations,* ed. J. W. Lorsch, P. R. Lawrence, 285–309. Homewood, Ill.: Irwin-Dorsey

69. Dyer, W. G., Maddocks, R. F., Moffitt, J. W., Underwood, W. J. 1970. A laboratory-consultation model for organization change. *J. Appl. Behav. Sci.* 6:211–27

70. Emery, F. E., Trist, E. L. 1960. Sociotechnical systems. In *Management Sciences: Models and Techniques,* ed. C. W. Churchman, M. Verhulst. New York: Pergamon

70a. Emery, F. E., Thorsrud, E. 1969. *Form and Content in Industrial Democracy.* London: Tavistock

71. Fleishman, E. A. 1953. Leadership climate, human relations training, and supervisory behavior. *Personnel Psychol.* 6:205–22

72. Ford, R. N. 1969 *Motivation Through Work Itself.* New York: Amenaan Manage. Assoc.

73. Fordyce, J. K., Weil, R. 1971. *Managing with People.* Reading, Mass.: Addison-Wesley

74. Fosmire, F., Keutzer, C., Diller, R. 1971. Starting up a new senior high school. See Ref. 147, 87–112

75. French, W. L., Bell, C. H. 1973. *Organization Development.* Englewood Cliffs, N.J.: Prentice-Hall

76. Friedlander, F. 1967. The impact of organizational training laboratories upon effectiveness and intervention of ongoing work groups. *Personnel Psychol.* 20:289–308

78. Friedlander, F. 1970. Emerging blackness in a white research world. *Hum. Organ.* 29: 239–50
80. Friedlander, F. 1972. Congruence in organization development. *Proc. 31st Ann. Meet. Acad. Manage. 1971,* 153–60
81. Friedlander, F., Greenberg, S. 1971. The effect of job attitudes, training and organization climate upon performance of the hard-core unemployed. *J. Appl. Psychol.* 55: 287–95
82. Friedman, G. 1961. *The Anatomy of Work.* Glencoe, Ill.: Free Press
83. Frohman, M. A. 1970. *An empirical study of a model and strategies for planned organizational change.* PhD thesis. Univ. Michigan
85. Gamson, W. 1968. *Power and Discontent.* Homewood, Ill.: Dorsey
86. Golembiewski, R. T. 1972. *Renewing Organizations.* Itasca, Ill.: Peacock Publ.
87. Golembiewski, R. T., Blumberg, A. 1967. Confrontation as a training design in complex organizations: attitudinal changes in a diversified population of managers. *J. Appl. Behav. Sci.* 3:525–47
88. Golembiewski, R. T., Blumberg, A. 1968. The laboratory approach to organization change: confrontation design. *Acad. Manage. J.* 11:199–210
89. Goodman, P., Baloff, N. 1968. Task experience and attitudes toward decision making. *Organ. Behav. Hum. Perform.* 3:202–16
90. Goodstein, L. D., Boyer, R. K. 1972. Crisis intervention in municipal agency: a conceptual case history. *J. Appl. Behav. Sci.* 8:318–40
91. Greiner, L. E. 1967. Patterns of organizational change. *Harvard Bus. Rev.* 45:119–28
92. Hackman, J. R., Lawler, E. E. 1971. Employee reactions to job characteristics. *J. Appl. Psychol.* 55:259–86
93. Harrison, R. 1962. Impact of the laboratory on perceptions of others by the experimental group. See Ref. 12, 261–71
95. Harrison, R. 1972. Role negotiation: a tough minded approach to team development. See Ref. 42, 84–96
99. Herzberg, F., Mausner, B., Snyderman, B. B. 1959. *The Motivation to Work.* New York: Wiley
100. Hill, P. 1971. *Towards a New Philosophy of Management.* New York: Barnes and Noble
102. Hornstein, H. A., Bunker, B. B., Hornstein, M. G. 1971. Some conceptual issues in individual and group oriented strategies of intervention into organizations. *J. Appl. Behav. Sci.* 7:557–67
103. Hulin, C. L., Blood, M. R. 1968. Job enlargement, individual differences, and workers' responses. *Psychol. Bull.* 69:41–45
105. Huse, E. F., Beer, M. 1971. Eclectic approach to OD. *Harvard Bus. Rev.* 49:103–12
106. Jaques, E. 1952. *The Changing Culture of a Factory.* New York: Dayden
108. Klein, S. M., Kraut, A. I., Wolfson, A. 1971. Employee reactions to attitude survey feedback: study of the impact of structure and process. *Admin. Sci. Quart.* 16:497–514
109. Kolb, D. A., Frohman, A. L. 1970. An organization development approach to consulting. *Sloan Manage. Rev.*
110. Kuriloff, A. H., Atkins, S. 1966. T-group for a work team. *J. Appl. Behav. Sci.* 2:63–93
111. Lawler, E. E. 1969. Job design and employee motivation. *Personnel Psychol.* 22: 426–35

112. Lawrence, P. R., Lorsch, J. W. 1967. *Organization and Environment*. Boston: Div. Res., Harvard Bus. Sch.
113. Lawrence, P. R., Lorsch, J. W. 1969. *Developing Organizations: Diagnosis and Action*. Reading: Addison-Wesley
114. Leavitt, H. J. 1965. Applied organizational change in industry: structural, technological, and humanistic approaches. In *Handbook of Organizations*, ed. J. G. March. Chicago: Rand McNally
115. Levin, G., Stein, D. D. 1970. System intervention in a school community conflict. *J. Appl. Behav. Sci.* 6:337 – 52
120. Lippitt, R., Watson, J., Westley, B. 1958. *The Dynamics of Planned Change*. New York: Harcourt, Brace
121. Locke, E. A. 1968. Toward a theory of task motivation and incentives. *Organ. Behav. Hum. Perform.* 3:157 – 89
122. Maher, J. R. 1971. *New Perspectives in Job Enrichment*. New York: Van Nostrand-Reinhold
123. Mann, F. C. 1961. Studying and creating change. See Ref. 24, 605 – 15. 1st ed.
124. Margulies, N., Raia, A. P. 1972. *Organization Development: Values, Process, and Technology*. New York: McGraw-Hill
125. Marks, A. R. N. 1954. *An investigation of modifications of job design in an industrial situation and their effects on some measures of economic productivity*. PhD thesis. Univ. California, Berkeley
126. Marrow, A. J., Bowers, D. G., Seashore, S. E. 1967. *Management by Participation*. New York: Harper and Row
128. McGregor, D. 1960. *The Human Side of Enterprise*. New York: McGraw-Hill
129. Meyers, S. M. 1964. Who are your motivated workers? *Harvard Bus. Rev.* 42:73 – 88
130. Miles, M. G., Hornstein, H. A., Callahan, D. M., Calder, P. H., Schiavo, R. S. 1969. The consequences of survey feedback: theory and evaluation. See Ref. 24, 456 – 68
132. Neff, F. W. 1965. Survey research: a tool for problem diagnosis and improvement in organizations. In *Applied Sociology*, ed. S. M. Miller, A. W. Gouldner. New York: Free Press
133. Neilsen, E. H. 1972. Understanding and managing intergroup conflict. See Ref. 68, 329 – 43
134. Oppenheimer, M. 1969. *The Urban Guerilla*. Chicago: Quadrangle
135. Paul, W. J., Robertson, K. B., Herzberg, F. 1969. Job enrichment pays off. *Harvard Bus. Rev.* 47:61 – 78
136. Peak, H. 1955. Attitude and motivation. In *Nebraska Symposium on Motivation*, ed. M. R. Jones. Lincoln: Univ. Nebraska
137. Porter, L. W., Lawler, E. E. 1965. Properties of organization structure in relation to job attitudes and job behavior. *Psychol. Bull.* 64:23 – 51
140. Rice, A. K. 1958. *Productivity and Social Organization: The Ahmedabad Experiment*. London: Tavistock
141. Rice, A. K. 1969. Individual, group and intergroup processes. *Hum. Relat.* 22:565 – 84
142. Ross, R. 1971. OD for whom. *J. Appl. Behav. Sci.* 7:58 – 85
143. Rush, H. M. F. 1971. *Job Design for Motivation*. New York: Conf. Board Rep. 515
147. Schmuck, R. A., Miles, M. B., Eds. 1971. *OD in Schools*. Palo Alto: National Press
148. Schmuck, R. A., Runkel, P. J., Langmeyer, D. 1969. Improving organizational problem solving in a school faculty. *J. Appl. Behav. Sci.* 5:455 – 90

149. Seashore, S. E., Bowers, D. G. 1963. *Changing the structure and functioning of an organization.* Monogr. 33, Univ. Michigan Survey Res. Center

150. Seashore, S. E., Bowers, D. G. 1970. Durability of organizational change. *Am. Psychol.* 25:227–33

151. Seller, J. A. 1963 Diagnosing interdepartmental conflict. *Harvard Bus. Rev.* 41:121–32

152. Shepard, H. A. 1965. Changing interpersonal and intergroup relations in organizations. See Ref. 114, 1115–43

154. Sherif, M., Harvey, O. J., White, B. J., Hood, W. R., Sherif, C. 1961. *Conflict and Cooperation: the Robbers' Cave Experiment.* Norman, Okla.: Univ. Book Exch.

155. Sherwood, J. J. 1971. An introduction to organization development. *Exp. Publ. Syst. APA* 11

156. Standing, T. E. 1973. Satisfaction with the work itself as a function of cognitive complexity. *Proc. 81st Ann. Conv. APA*

160. Tannenbaum, R., Davis, S. A. 1969. Values, man and organizations. *Ind. Manage. Rev.* 10:67–86

160a. Thorsrud, E. 1969. A strategy for research and social change in industry: a report on the industrial democracy project in Norway. *Soc. Sci. Inform.* 9 (5): 65–90

161. Torezyner, J. 1972. The political conflict of social change: a case study of innovation in adversity in Jerusalem. *J. Appl. Behav. Sci.* 8:287–317

162a. Trist, E. 1970. A socio-technical critique of scientific management. Presented at Edinburgh Conf. Impact Sci. Technol. Edinburgh Univ.

163. Trist, E. L., Bamforth, K. W. 1951. Some social and psychological consequences of the longwall method of coal getting. *Hum. Relat.* 4:3–38

164. Trist, E. L., Higgin, G. W., Murray, H., Pollock, A. B. 1963. *Organizational Choice.* London: Tavistock

165. Turner, A. N., Lawrence, P. R. 1968. *Industrial Jobs and the Worker.* Cambridge, Mass.: Harvard Univ. Grad. Sch. Bus. Admin.

166. Walton, R. E. 1965. Two strategies of social change and their dilemmas. *J. Appl. Behav. Sci.* 1:167–79

167. Walton, R. E. 1967. Third party role in interdepartmental conflict. *Ind. Relat.* 7:29–43

168. Walton, R. E. 1969. *Interpersonal Peacemaking: Confrontations and Third Party Consultation.* Reading, Mass.: Addison-Wesley

169. Walton, R. E. 1970. A problem-solving workshop on border conflicts in Eastern Africa. *J. Appl. Behav. Sci.* 6:453–89

170. Wanous, J. P. 1973. Individual differences and employee reactions to job characteristics. *Proc. 81st Ann. Conv. APA*

172. Wedge, B. 1971. A psychiatric model for intercession in intergroup conflict. *J. Appl. Behav. Sci.* 7:733–61

173. Whyte, W. F., Hamilton, E. L. 1964. *Action Research for Management.* Homewood, Ill.: Irwin-Dorsey

174. Winn, A. 1969. The laboratory approach to organizational development: a tentative model of planned change. *J. Manage. Stud.* 6:157

175. Zand, D. E., Steele, F. I., Zalkind, S. S. 1969. The impact of an organizational development program on perceptions of interpersonal, group, and organizational functioning. *J. Appl. Behav. Sci.* 5:393–410

21   Durability of Organizational Change

Stanley E. Seashore and David G. Bowers

The aim of this article is to add a modest footnote to the growing literature concerning planned change in the structure and function of formal organizations. The question asked is whether changes that have been planned, successfully introduced, and confirmed by measurements, over but a relatively short span of time, can survive as permanent features of the organization. Will such a changed organization become stabilized in its new state, or will it continue the direction and pace of change, or perhaps revert to its earlier state?

This report will include a brief review of an earlier effort to change an organization, a presentation of some new data about the present state of the organization, and some first speculations about the meaning of the data for the understanding of psychological and social phenomena in formal organizations.

BACKGROUND

The earlier events against which our new data are to be set are reported rather fully elsewhere (Marrow, Bowers, & Seashore, 1967). A brief review of the essential facts will set the stage.

In late 1961 the Harwood company purchased its major competitor, the Weldon company. This brought under common ownership and general management two organizations remarkably similar in certain features and remarkably different in others. Both made and marketed similar products using equipment and manufacturing processes of a like kind; were of similar size in terms of business volume and number of employees; served similar and partially overlapping markets; were family-owned and owner-managed firms; and had similar histories of growth and enjoyed high reputation in the trade.

The differences between the two organizations are of particular interest. The Harwood company had earned some prominence and respect for their efforts over many years to operate the organization as a participative system with high value given to individual and organizational development, as well as to effective perfor-

"Durability of Organizational Change" by Stanley Seashore and David Bowers from AMERICAN PSYCHOLOGIST, 25 (March 1970), pp. 227-233. Copyright © 1970 by the American Psychological Association. Reprinted by permission of the American Psychological Association and the authors.
1. The assistance of Edith Wessner is acknowledged.

mance. The Weldon company had for years been managed in a fashion that prevails in the garment industry, with a highly centralized, authoritarian philosophy and with secondary concern for individual development and organizational mainte- nance. The two organizations were, in 1962, rather extreme examples from the continuum vaguely defined by the terms *authoritarian* versus *participative*. Mea- surements in both firms in 1962 confirmed that the difference was not merely im- pressionistic, but was represented in quantitative assessments of the organizational processes for planning, coordination, communication, motivation, and work per- formance, and was represented as well in member attitudes. The two firms were also sharply contrasting in their performance in 1962, even though over a longer span of years their business accomplishments had been similar. In 1962 Weldon, in sharp contrast to Harwood, was losing money, experiencing high costs, gener- ating many errors of strategy and work performance, suffering from member dis- affection with consequent high absenteeism and high turnover. Weldon, despite its technical, fiscal, and market strengths, was near the point of disaster.

The new owners set out on a program to rebuild the Weldon enterprise ac- cording to the model of the Harwood company. The ultimate aim was to make the Weldon firm a viable and profitable economic unit within a short period of time. A rather strenuous and costly program was envisioned, including some moderniza- tion of the plant, improved layout and flow of work, improvements in records and production control methods, and product simplification, as well as changes in the human organization. The renewal program concerning the organization itself concerns us here.

The approach to organizational change can be characterized briefly in three respects: (*a*) the conception of the organizational characteristics to be sought; (*b*) the conception of processes for changing persons and organizational systems; and (*c*) the linking of the social system to the work system.

The guiding assumptions or "philosophy" on which the change program was based included elements such as the following:

1. It was assumed that employees would have to gain a realistic sense of security in their jobs and that this security would have to arise basically out of their own successful efforts to improve their organization and their performance, not out of some bargained assurances.
2. The introduction of substantial change in the work environment requires that employees have confidence in the technical competence and humane values of the managers and supervisors; this confidence can be earned only if it is recipro- cated by placing confidence in the employees.
3. In a situation of rapid change it is particularly necessary to use procedures of participation in the planning and control of the work and of the changes; such procedures are needed at all levels of the organization.
4. The rebuilding of an organization may require an input of technical resources

and capital on a substantial scale—not unlike the investments required to rework a technology or control system of a factory.

5. Management involves skills and attitudes that can be defined, taught, and learned, and these skills and attitudes need not be confined to high rank staff; each member of the organization, at least in some limited degree, must learn to help manage his own work and that of others related to him.
6. Guidelines such as these are not readily understood and accepted unless they can be linked to concrete events and to the rational requirements of the work to be done and the problems to be solved.

The conception of change processes incorporated in the rebuilding of the Weldon organization emphasized the application of multiple and compatible change forces. The physical improvements in work resources and conditions were to be accompanied by informational clarity, enhanced motivation through rewards, and ample skill training and practice. That is, change was to be introduced simultaneously at the situational, cognitive, motivational, and behavioral levels so that each would support the others.

The linking of the social organization to the work system was to be accomplished through efforts, however limited, to design work places, work flows, information flows, and the like in a manner not merely compatible with but integral with the associated social organization and organizational processes.

The program of rebuilding the organization was carried out by the local management with substantial assistance and stimulation from the new owners and from a variety of consultants, including psychologists. The general planning and guidance of the program were influenced primarily by Alfred Marrow, Board Chairman of the Harwood Corporation and Fellow of Division 14. The role of the Institute for Social Research was not that of change agent, but rather that of observing, recording, measuring, and analyzing the course of events and the change that resulted.

The change program was successful in important respects. Within two years there occurred improvements in employee satisfactions, motivations, and work performance. The organization took on characteristics of an adaptive, self-controlling, participative system. The firm as a business unit moved from a position of loss to one of profit. At the end of 1964, after two years of change effort, the factory was abandoned as a research site, the rate of input of capital and external manpower into the change program diminished substantially, and the factory and its organization were expected to settle down to something like a "normal" state.

EXPECTATIONS ABOUT CHANGE

From the start of this organizational change program there was a concern about the long-run consequences of the program, and there was uncertainty about the permanence of change. The following quotations from our earlier report illustrate the intentions, hopes, and doubts (Marrow et al., 1967):

> the whole organization, from the plant manager down to the production workers, were taken into an exercise in joint problem-solving through participative methods in groups, with a view toward making such procedures a normal part of the management system of the plant [p. 69].
>
> The refreezing of Weldon in a new and more effective state is not regarded as a permanent thing, but as another stage in the evolution and continuous adaptation of the organization. Some features of the conversion plan explicitly include the provision of built-in capacities for easier change in the future [p. 232].
>
> Will the changes at Weldon last? The only evidence we have at the present time is that the change from a predominantly "authoritative" to a dominantly "consultative" type of management organization persisted for at least two years in the view of the managers and supervisors involved. Surely there exist forces toward a reversion to the old Weldon form of organizational life; it remains an uncertainty whether they will or will not win over the new forces toward consolidation of change and further change of the intended kinds [p. 244].

In mid-1969, four and one-half years after the termination of the intensive change program, Dr. Bowers and I invited ourselves back to the Weldon plant for a follow-up measurement of the state of the organization. This remeasurement consisted of a one-day visit to the plant by a research assistant who administered questionnaires to managers, supervisors, and a sample of the employees.[1] In addition, certain information was abstracted from the firm's records, and the views of the plant manager were solicited as to changes that had taken place and possible reasons for change. We can turn directly to a few tables and figures representing the changes and the situation as of 1969.

RESULTS

First, we present some data from the production employees. Table 1 shows selected items from our questionnaire survey bearing on the issue of whether there has occurred a decline, a rise, or a stabilization of the attitudes, satisfactions, and optimism of the employees. The table shows the percentage of employees giving the two most favorable responses, of five offered, to each question. The columns represent the results in 1962 before the change program began, in 1964 at the conclusion of the formal change effort, and in 1969.

The general picture is one of the maintenance of earlier gains in the favorability of employee attitudes or the further improvement in attitudes. This observation holds for seven of the nine indicators. The remaining two deserve brief special comment.

Satisfaction with supervisors declined during the period of the active change program but has remained relatively high and constant since 1964. The initial de-

Table 1   CHANGES IN JOB ATTITUDES

Item	1962 %	1964 %	1969 %
Company better than most	22	28	36
Own work satisfying	77	84	91
Satisfied with pay system	22	27	28
Company tries to maintain earnings	26	44	41
Satisfied with supervisor	64	54	54
Like fellow employees	85	86	85
Group cohesiveness	25	23	30
Plan to stay indefinitely	72	87	66
Expect future improvement in situation	23	31	43

cline is viewed as a consequence of the substantial change in the supervisors' role during the active change program. During that period, the supervisors acquired substantially more responsibility and authority as well as some new activities and duties that are thought to have removed the supervisors from a peerlike to a superior status relationship with the operators, which they retain now. This interpretation is, of course, speculative but made before the 1969 data were in hand.

The decline in the proportion of employees planning to stay on indefinitely is rather difficult to assess. The rise between 1962 and 1964 can be attributed to the improvement in pay and working conditions in that period. The subsequent decline is to be accounted for, partly, by the fact of recent production expansion and the presence on the payroll of a relatively large number of turnover-prone short-service employees. One might also speculate that rising prosperity during the period might have increased the attractiveness of marriage, child bearing, or retirement for these female employees. In any case, the decline in the percentage committed to long job tenure appears to be at odds with the general rise in job satisfactions and in the marked rise in optimism about the future improvement in the Weldon situation. We should add that the decline in percentage committed to long tenure is confirmed by the fact of a moderate rise in actual turnover rates in recent months.

Table 2 shows a few selected items bearing on the question whether the rise in satisfactions and expectations is accompanied by some loss in productivity concern and task orientation. The data, again, are from employee questionnaire responses (except for the last line) and show changes from 1962 to 1964, and then to 1969.

Five of the indicators reflect a rise in level of task orientation and production concern since the end of the formal change program. The remaining items are not negative, but merely indeterminate. There is clearly a rise in recent years in the

Table 2 CHANGE IN TASK-ORIENTATION INDICATORS

Item	1962 %	1964 %	1969 %
Company quick to improve methods	18	24	31
Company good at planning	22	26	35
Not delayed by poor services	76	79	90
Produce what rates call for	44	67	53
Expect own productivity to improve	63	55	62
Peers approve of high producers	58	58	66
Closeness of task supervision	38	27	47
Desired closeness of supervision	57	52	64
Mean productivity (% of standard)	87	114	?

percentage of employees who say the firm is quick to improve work methods, good at planning, provides efficient services (maintenance, supplies, scheduling), who report that their peers approve of high producers, and who themselves desire frequent and ready access to supervisory help. Two sets of data require special comment.

The data on productivity, three lines in the table, should be considered as a set. The numbers show that the self-report of "Nearly always producing what the rates call for" rose substantially during the active change program, and this is confirmed by the actual productivity records of the firm as shown in the last line "Mean productivity against standard." During the same period the percentage of employees expecting a further gain in their own productivity declined, as it should have considering that more employees were approaching the firm's hoped-for level of high productivity and earnings. By 1969 there was some decline in the percentage reporting high productivity and a corresponding rise in the percentage expecting a future rise in their productivity; this pair of related changes appears to reflect the presence on the staff of an increasing number of relatively new employees not yet up to the level of skill and performance they may reasonably expect to attain. There is a crucial item of missing data in the last line of the table; for technical reasons, we have not been able to calculate the current actual productivity rate in a form that allows confident comparisons with the earlier figures. Our best estimate is that productivity has been stable with a slight decline in recent months arising from the recent introduction of additional inexperienced employees.

Attention is also suggested to the pair of lines in Table 2 concerning closeness of supervision. At all three times of measurement, these production workers desired more close supervision than they actually experienced; these employees, unlike those in some other organizations, see their supervisors to be potentially helpful in improving productivity and increasing piece-rate earnings. The decline in experienced closeness of supervision during the period 1962–64 matches other evidence to be presented later that during this period there was a substantial change in the supervisors' role that diverted the supervisors from immediate floor supervision and left a temporary partial shortage of this service to production workers. The figures show that by 1969 this supervisory deficit has been recouped and more. This sustains our general view that during the years following the Weldon change program there has been not a decline in concern for task performance among employees and in the organizational system generally but rather a further gain in task orientation.

The change in supervisory behavior mentioned earlier is shown in Figure 1. We attempted at the three points in time to measure the extent to which supervisors, in the view of employees, engaged in behaviors we categorize as "supportive," "goal emphasizing," and "work facilitating." (Two additional dimensions of leader behavior that we now use in describing organizations are not represented here because they were not yet identified in 1962; we chose to continue use of the initial measurement methods rather than to update them.)

Figure 1 CHANGE IN THREE DIMENSIONS OF SUPERVISORY LEADERSHIP BEHAVIOR

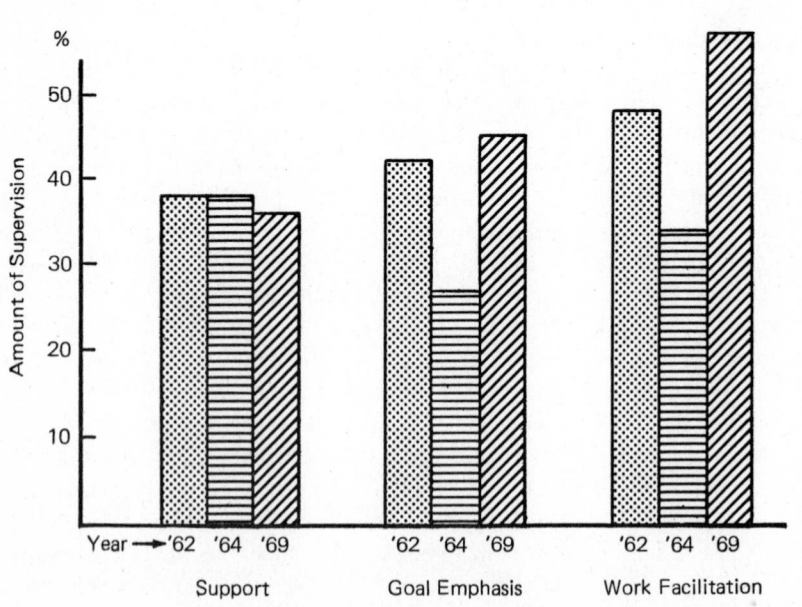

Figure 1 shows that the amount of supervisory supportiveness experienced by employees remained constant during the 1962–64 period and has risen slightly since then. Goal emphasis and work facilitation both dropped during the active change program, for reasons mentioned earlier, and have since risen above their 1962 levels. These data sustain our belief that the Weldon organization since 1964 has increased its expression of concern for production goals and its provision of conditions for effective work performance, and at no cost of declining concern for employee attitudes and satisfactions.

One more set of data from the employees is pertinent here, namely, their description of the amount and hierarchical distribution of control in the Weldon organization. One of the explicit aims of the change program was that of increasing the total amount of control and of altering the distribution of control so that lower rank people—supervisors and operators—would have some added degree of control. This was accomplished during the change program period to a very limited and nonsignificant degree. Subsequent changes have been in the direction intended and more substantial in degree. The data are shown in Figure 2. In 1969, compared with the earlier periods, there is more control being exercised in total, with a notable increment in the case of the headquarters staff, a further small decline for the local plant management, and increments for the supervisors and for the employees. There appears to have been a change of modest degree, more or less as hoped for, and there has clearly not been a reversion to the original condition of concentrated control in the hands of the plant manager.

We turn now to some indicators of the state of the Weldon organization from the views of the supervisors and managers. The data presented in Figure 3 are derived from Likert's assessment instrument "Profile of Organizational and Performance Characteristics" (Likert, 1961, 1967). Most readers will have some acquaintance with this instrument and the theory and research data that it expresses, but a brief characterization might be helpful. The instrument used is a 43-item graphic-scale rating form that allows the respondent to describe his own organization as it presently functions and as he ideally would like it to function. The items are so chosen and arranged that the respondent may report a syndrome of organizational characteristics that locates the organization on a scale ranging from "authoritative" to "participative." Likert discerns four regions of this scale, named Systems 1, 2, 3, and 4, with word labels ranging from "Authoritarian" through "Benevolent Authoritarian" and "Consultative" to "Participative." The conception is analogous to McGregor's "Theory X" and "Theory Y" scale, and also to Blake's two-dimensioned matrix. To put it somewhat disrespectfully, the bad guys are thought to have and to prefer System 1 organizations while good guys aspire to and approach the System 4 state. The results for Weldon, 1962, 1964, and 1969 are represented in Figure 3.

At the left of the field are two graph lines showing the state of the Weldon organization in 1962, first as rated by the Institute for Social Research research

Figure 2 CHANGE IN AMOUNT AND HIERARCHICAL DISTRIBUTION OF CONTROL

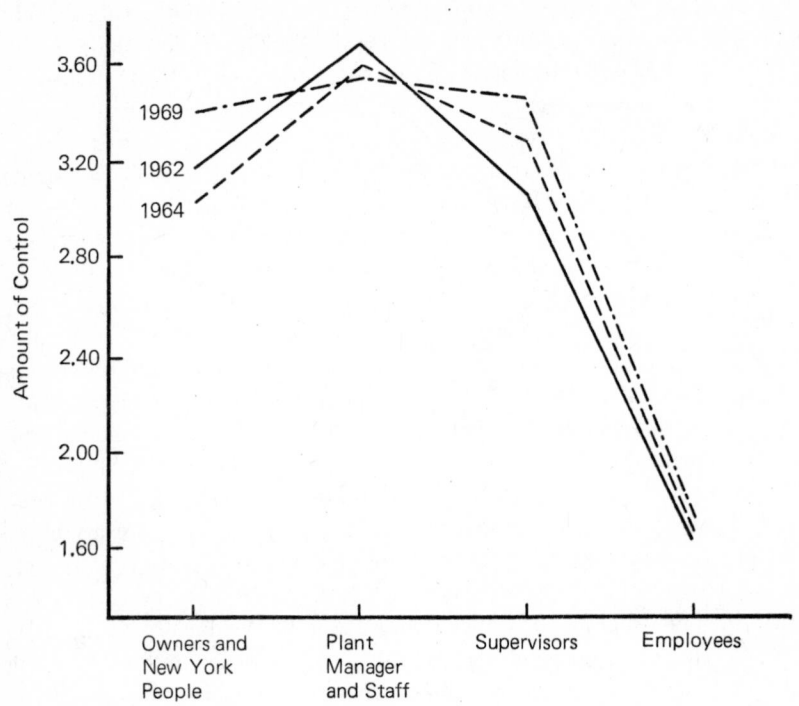

team from interview protocols and observations, and next and somewhat more favorably as rated by the supervisors and managers on the scene. Weldon at that time was described to be autocratic—in some respects rather harshly autocratic and in some respects more benevolently autocratic. The state of the organization in 1964 and in 1966 is represented in the next two lines. These data are from supervisors and managers; they indicate a pattern of change that is substantial in magnitude and wholly compatible with the intentions embodied in the Weldon change program. There was no regression toward the earlier state during the 1964–66 period. The right-hand line represents the results of our 1969 assessment; it shows that in the view of the managers and supervisors at Weldon, the organization has progressed still further toward their ideal of a participative organizational system.

A final remark should be made about measured changes in Weldon before we turn to a consideration of the meaning of these data. Some readers will be interested in business outcomes as well as in the attitudes and behavior of the members

Figure 3 CHANGE IN PROFILE OF ORGANIZATIONAL CHARACTERISTICS

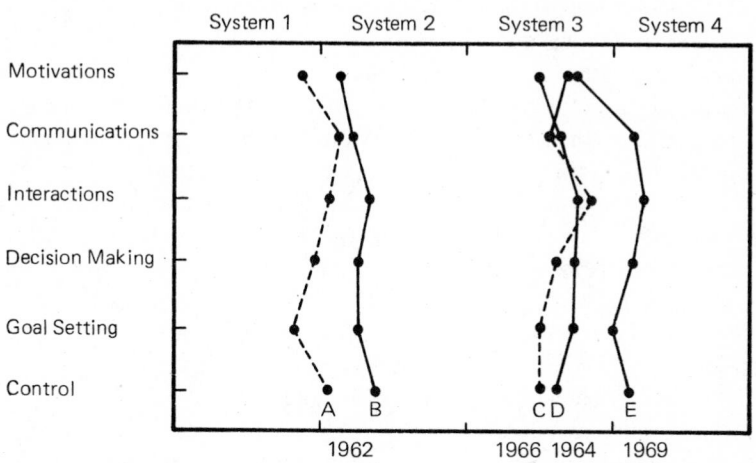

of the organization. Briefly, Weldon moved from a position of substantial capital loss in 1962 to substantial return on investment in 1964; this direction of change in profitability has continued through 1968, the last year of record. Employee earnings which rose substantially between 1962 and 1964 have been sustained at a relatively high level. During the period since 1964 there have been substantial gains in efficiency and volume for the factory as a whole. New products and work methods have been introduced. By such business indicators, Weldon is a successful organization.

DURABLE CHANGE

The evidence we must weigh, although somewhat mixed and with a few contrary elements, appears to sustain the conclusion that the Weldon organization, far from reverting to its prior condition, has during recent years made additional progress toward the organizational goals envisioned by the owners and managers in 1962, and envisioned as well by supervisors and production employees at a somewhat later time. This outcome invites speculations about the psychological and social forces that are at work.

We confess a brief regret that there was not an opposite outcome, for we are rather better equipped with ideas about organizational stability and regression than we are with ideas about organizational change and continuing development.

For example, before the data became available, we were prepared to make some remarks about the "Hawthorne effect"—about the superficiality and transient quality of organizational and behavioral changes induced under conditions of external attention and pressure; but it boggles the mind to think of a "Hawthorne effect" persisting for over eight years among people half of whom were not on the scene at the time of the original change. Similarly, we were prepared to make wise remarks about cultural forces, habits, and the natural predilection of managers for nonparticipative methods; these we thought would help explain a reversion to the prevailing conditions in organizations. We were prepared to assert that in the absence of contrary environmental forces, external influences, and purposive continuing change efforts of a vigorous kind, an organization would migrate back to some more primitive form of organizational life.

Clearly we need to appeal to other ideas than these. We are, all of us, ill prepared to do so. Two recent and fairly comprehensive reviews of organizational change strategies (Leavitt, 1965; Shepard, 1965) say nothing about the permanence or continuation of change processes except for a remark by Shepard that "change in the direction of collaboration-consensus patterns [participative patterns] . . . facilitates growth, change and adaptation to new environmental challenges and opportunities [p. 1141]."

A first explanatory idea rests on the possibility that the heavy investment of external talent, money, and effort that characterized the original change period at Weldon has been continued during the subsequent years. We are assured that this is not the case. There has indeed been some additional use of external consultants, but at a modest rate that is considered normal and permanent. There has indeed been further improvement and change in the work system and the production facilities, but at no more than a permanently sustainable rate. There has indeed been a continuation of certain organizational activities introduced as part of the original change program, but these are regarded as normal operating procedure and not as special change efforts. Economic conditions have been favorable to the firm, but they were also favorable at the distressed time preceding the change of ownership in 1962.

We believe that there are three other lines of explanation that do bear scrutiny. These thoughts about the Weldon experience are not offered with any sense of great insight or of conceptual innovation. They are offered only as suggestions for lines of inquiry and emphasis in future organizational research. The first concerns the provision of "lock-in" devices that make difficult the reversal of the original change.

It was mentioned earlier that the original change program contained some notions of seeking mutually reinforcing change actions across the psychological, organizational, and technological domains. A central idea was to make structural changes in the organization that matched the work system and that did not violate reasonable assumptions about the values and motives of individual members. For example, the revitalized piece-rate pay system was viewed to be viable only if sustained by the provision of assured services that allowed high earnings, a revision of the record and information flow system that assured instant supervisory response to low earnings, and a moderating of the prior job assignment system so that a production employee could become skilled in the work assigned. The idea of systemic consistency is surely an elementary one, no more than common sense—a habit of thought for those who have learned to view the factory as a total system in which all elements are interdependent. The interdependence of elements tends to preserve, to enhance, and to "lock in" the central characteristics of the system and thus to prevent retrogression.

A second factor in Weldon's continuation of intended change might lie in the earlier legitimation of concern about organizational processes. This is speculative, for we have no ready way to assess the extent to which there was implanted the habit of deliberate and self-conscious examination of the potential side effects of the many policy and operating decisions, usually technical or economic in origin, that arise daily. One of the fragmenting features of many organizations is the tendency to isolate problems, to treat them as if they could be optimally resolved without reference to their broader context. An organization habituated at all levels to think about, discuss openly, and to weigh properly the full range of elements in the organizational system might well have unusual capacities for self-maintenance and self-development.

A third possible explanation of the maintenance of the changes at Weldon and their further development under conditions of limited continuing external influence might lie in the inherent merit of the participative organizational model. Could it be that people who have experienced a taste of it get hooked, know what they want, and lend their effort to maintaining it? A glance at the newspaper headlines on almost any day will suggest that some of our fellow citizens do not like what they are experiencing in formal organizations and have thoughts of having something better, by force if necessary.

REFERENCES

Leavitt, H. J. Applied organizational change in industry. In J. G. March (Ed.), *Handbook of organizations*. Skokie, Ill.: Rand-McNally, 1965.

Likert, R. *New patterns of management*. New York: McGraw-Hill, 1961.

Likert, R. *The human organization*. New York: McGraw-Hill, 1967.

Marrow, A. J., Bowers, D. G., & Seashore, S. E. *Management by participation*. New York: Harper & Row, 1967.

Shepard, H. A. Changing interpersonal and intergroup relationships in organizations. In J. G. March (Ed.), *Handbook of organizations*. Skokie, Ill.: Rand-McNally, 1965.

Section B

Group Decision-Making: Pros, Cons, and Contingencies

OD practitioners often view group decision-making as fundamental to organizational improvement efforts. Yet even this standard prescription requires thoughtful analysis. Accordingly, the two articles in this section consider group problem solving and the related issue of managerial adjustment to new decision situations.

In the first selection, Maier discusses "Assets and Liabilities in Group Problem Solving." He points out that group methods are not always superior to individual efforts. Their effectiveness will depend on the nature of the problem encountered, the goal to be achieved, and the skill of the group's leader. On balance, however, Maier feels that if the liabilities inherent in groups are avoided and assets capitalized on, groups have the potential for exceeding the results of a superior individual functioning alone.

The companion article, by Delbecq, looks at "The Management of Decision-Making Within the Firm." Delbecq acknowledges the need for a situational approach to group problem solving but notes that managers are sometimes slow in adjusting group behavior when decision-making requirements change. He argues that if managers can improve their ability to classify decision tasks they will be more effective in redefining the behavior of their managerial team as it moves from one task type to another. To assist managers in this regard, Delbecq identifies three categories of decision-making (routine, creative, and negotiated) and discusses their different requirements for group structure and process. Finally, to clarify problems of implementing these different strategies, Delbecq considers their relationship to traditional organizational models.

Assets and Liabilities in Group Problem Solving

Norman R. F. Maier

A number of investigations have raised the question of whether group problem solving is superior, inferior, or equal to individual problem solving. Evidence can be cited in support of each position so that the answer to this question remains ambiguous. Rather than pursue this generalized approach to the question, it seems more fruitful to explore the forces that influence problem solving under the two conditions (see reviews by Hoffman, 1965; Kelley & Thibaut, 1954). It is hoped that a better recognition of these forces will permit clarification of the varied dimensions of the problem-solving process, especially in groups.

The forces operating in such groups include some that are assets, some that are liabilities, and some that can be either assets or liabilities, depending upon the skills of the members, especially those of the discussion leader. Let us examine these three sets of forces.

GROUP ASSETS

Greater Sum Total of Knowledge and Information

There is more information in a group than in any of its members. Thus problems that require the utilization of knowledge should give groups an advantage over individuals. Even if one member of the group (e.g., the leader) knows much more than anyone else, the limited unique knowledge of lesser-informed individuals could serve to fill in some gaps in knowledge. For example, a skilled machinist might contribute to an engineer's problem solving and an ordinary workman might supply information on how a new machine might be received by workers.

Greater Number of Approaches to a Problem

It has been shown that individuals get into ruts in their thinking (Duncker, 1945; Maier, 1930; Wertheimer, 1959). Many obstacles stand in the way of achieving a goal, and a solution must circumvent these. The individual is handicapped in that he tends to persist in his approach and thus fails to find another approach that might solve the problem in a simpler manner. Individuals in a group have the same failing, but the approaches in which they are persisting may be different. For example, one researcher may try to prevent the spread of a disease by making man immune to the germ, another by finding and destroying the carrier of the germ, and still another by altering the environment so as to kill the germ before it reaches man. There is no way of determining which approach will best achieve the desired goal, but undue persistence in any one will stifle new discoveries. Since group members do not have identical approaches, each can contribute by knocking others out of ruts in thinking.

Participation in Problem Solving Increases Acceptance

Many problems require solutions that depend upon the support of others to be effective. Insofar as group problem solving permits participation and influence, it follows that more individuals accept solutions when a group solves the problem than when one person solves it. When one individual solves a problem he still has the task of persuading others. It follows, therefore, that when groups solve such problems, a greater number of persons accept and feel responsible for making the solution work. A low-quality solution that has good acceptance can be more effective than a higher-quality solution that lacks acceptance.

Better Comprehension of the Decision

Decisions made by an individual, which are to be carried out by others, must be communicated from the decision-maker to the decision-executors. Thus individual problem solving often requires an additional stage—that of relaying the decision reached. Failures in this communication process detract from the merits of the decision and can even cause its failure or create a problem of greater magnitude than the initial problem that was solved. Many organizational problems can be traced to inadequate communication of decisions made by superiors and transmitted to subordinates, who have the task of implementing the decision.

The chances for communication failures are greatly reduced when the individuals who must work together in executing the decision have participated in making it. They not only understand the solution because they saw it develop, but they are also aware of the several other alternatives that were considered and the reasons why they were discarded. The common assumption that decisions supplied by superiors are arbitrarily reached therefore disappears. A full knowledge of goals, obstacles, alternatives, and factual information is essential to communication, and this communication is maximized when the total problem-solving process is shared.

GROUP LIABILITIES

Social pressure

Social pressure is a major force making for conformity. The desire to be a good group member and to be accepted tends to silence disagreement and favors consensus. Majority opinions tend to be accepted regardless of whether or not their objective quality is logically and scientifically sound. Problems requiring solutions based upon facts, regardless of feelings and wishes, can suffer in group problem-solving situations.

It has been shown (Maier & Solem, 1952) that minority opinions in leaderless groups have little influence on the solution reached, even when these opinions are the correct ones. Reaching agreement in a group often is confused with finding the right answer, and it is for this reason that the dimensions of a decision's acceptance and its objective quality must be distinguished (Maier, 1963).

Valence of Solutions

When leaderless groups (made up of three or four persons) engage in problem solving, they propose a variety of solutions. Each solution may receive both critical and supportive comments, as well as descriptive and explorative comments from other participants. If the number of negative and positive comments for each solution are algebraically summed, each may be given a *valence index* (Hoffman & Maier, 1964). The first solution that receives a positive valence value of 15 tends to be adopted to the satisfaction of all participants about 85 percent of the time, regardless of its quality. Higher-quality solutions introduced after the critical value for one of the solutions has been reached have little chance of achieving real consideration. Once some degree of consensus is reached, the jelling process seems to proceed rather rapidly.

The critical valence value of 15 appears not to be greatly altered by the nature of the problem or the exact size of the group. Rather, it seems to designate a turning point between the idea-getting process and the decision-making process (idea evaluation). A solution's valence index is not a measure of the number of persons supporting the solution, since a vocal minority can build up a solution's valence by actively pushing it. In this sense, valence becomes an influence in addition to social pressure in determining an outcome.

Since a solution's valence is independent of its objective quality, this group factor becomes an important liability in group problem solving, even when the value of a decision depends upon objective criteria (facts and logic). It becomes a means whereby skilled manipulators can have more influence over the group process than their proportion of membership deserves.

Individual Domination

In most leaderless groups a dominant individual emerges and captures more than his share of influence on the outcome. He can achieve this end through a greater degree of participation (valence), persuasive ability, or stubborn persistence (fatiguing the opposition). None of these factors is related to problem-solving ability, so that the best problem solver in the group may not have the influence to upgrade the quality of the group's solution (which he would have had if left to solve the problem by himself).

Hoffman and Maier (1967) found that the mere fact of appointing a leader causes this person to dominate a discussion. Thus, regardless of his problem-solving ability a leader tends to exert a major influence on the outcome of a discussion.

Conflicting Secondary Goal: Winning the Argument

When groups are confronted with a problem, the initial goal is to obtain a solution. However, the appearance of several alternatives causes individuals to have preferences and once these emerge the desire to support a position is created. Converting those with neutral viewpoints and refuting those with opposed viewpoints now enters into the problem-solving process. More and more the goal becomes that of winning the decision rather than finding the best solution. This new goal is unrelated to the quality of the problem's solution and therefore can result in lowering the quality of the decision (Hoffman & Maier, 1966).

FACTORS THAT SERVE AS ASSETS OR LIABILITIES, DEPENDING LARGELY UPON THE SKILL OF THE DISCUSSION LEADER

Disagreement

The fact that discussion may lead to disagreement can serve either to create hard feelings among members or lead to a resolution of conflict and hence to an innovative solution (Hoffman, 1961; Hoffman, Harburg, & Maier, 1962; Hoffman & Maier, 1961; Maier, 1958, 1963; Maier & Hoffman, 1965). The first of these outcomes of disagreement is a liability, especially with regard to the acceptance of solutions; while the second is an asset, particularly where innovation is desired. A leader can treat disagreement as undesirable and thereby reduce the probability of both hard feelings and innovation, or he can maximize disagreement and risk hard feelings in his attempts to achieve innovation. The skill of a leader requires his ability to create a climate for disagreement which will permit innovation without risking hard feelings. The leader's perception of disagreement is one of the critical factors in this skill area (Maier & Hoffman, 1965). Others involve permissiveness

(Maier, 1953), delaying the reaching of a solution (Maier & Hoffman, 1960b; Maier & Solem, 1962), techniques for processing information and opinions (Maier, 1963; Maier & Hoffman, 1960a; Maier & Maier, 1957), and techniques for separating idea-getting from idea-evaluation (Maier, 1960, 1963; Osborn, 1953).

Conflicting Interests versus Mutual Interests

Disagreement in discussion may take many forms. Often participants disagree with one another with regard to solutions, but when issues are explored one finds that these conflicting solutions are designed to solve different problems. Before one can rightly expect agreement on a solution, there should be agreement on the nature of the problem. Even before this, there should be agreement on the goal, as well as on the various obstacles that prevent the goal from being reached. Once distinctions are made between goals, obstacles, and solutions (which represent ways of overcoming obstacles), one finds increased opportunities for cooperative problem solving and less conflict (Hoffman & Maier, 1959; Maier, 1960, 1963; Maier & Solem, 1962; Solem, 1965).

Often there is also disagreement regarding whether the objective of a solution is to achieve quality or acceptance (Maier & Hoffman, 1964b), and frequently a stated problem reveals a complex of separate problems, each having separate solutions so that a search for a single solution is impossible (Maier, 1963). Communications often are inadequate because the discussion is not synchronized and each person is engaged in discussing a different aspect. Organizing discussion to synchronize the exploration of different aspects of the problem and to follow a systematic procedure increases solution quality (Maier & Hoffman, 1960a; Maier & Maier, 1957). The leadership function of influencing discussion procedure is quite distinct from the function of evaluating or contributing ideas (Maier, 1950, 1953).

When the discussion leader aids in the separation of the several aspects of the problem-solving process and delays the solution-mindedness of the group (Maier, 1958, 1963; Maier & Solem, 1962), both solution quality and acceptance improve; when he hinders or fails to facilitate the isolation of these varied processes, he risks a deterioration in the group process (Solem, 1965). His skill thus determines whether a discussion drifts toward conflicting interests or whether mutual interests are located. Cooperative problem solving can only occur after the mutual interests have been established and it is surprising how often they can be found when the discussion leader makes this his task (Maier, 1952, 1963; Maier & Hayes, 1962).

Risk Taking

Groups are more willing than individuals to reach decisions involving risks (Wallach & Kogan, 1965; Wallach, Kogan, & Bem, 1962). Taking risks is a factor in acceptance of change, but change may either represent a gain or a loss. The best guard against the latter outcome seems to be primarily a matter of a decision's quality. In a group situation this depends upon the leader's skill in utilizing the factors that represent group assets and avoiding those that make for liabilities.

Time Requirements

In general, more time is required for a group to reach a decision than for a single individual to reach one. Insofar as some problems require quick decisions, individual decisions are favored. In other situations acceptance and quality are requirements, but excessive time without sufficient returns also represents a loss. On the other hand, discussion can resolve conflicts, whereas reaching consensus has limited value (Wallach & Kogan, 1965). The practice of hastening a meeting can prevent full discussion, but failure to move a discussion forward can lead to boredom and fatigue-type solutions, in which members agree merely to get out of the meeting. The effective utilization of discussion time (a delicate balance between permissiveness and control on the part of the leader), therefore, is needed to make the time factor an asset rather than a liability. Unskilled leaders tend to be too concerned with reaching a solution and therefore terminate a discussion before the group potential is achieved (Maier & Hoffman, 1960b).

Who Changes

In reaching consensus or agreement, some members of a group must change. Persuasive forces do not operate in individual problem solving in the same way they operate in a group situation; hence, the changing of someone's mind is not an issue. In group situations, however, who changes can be an asset or a liability. If persons with the most constructive views are induced to change the end-product suffers; whereas if persons with the least constructive points of view change the end-product is upgraded. The leader can upgrade the quality of a decision because his position permits him to protect the person with a minority view and increase his opportunity to influence the majority position. This protection is a constructive factor because a minority viewpoint influences only when facts favor it (Maier, 1950, 1952; Maier & Solem, 1952).

 •The leader also plays a constructive role insofar as he can facilitate communications and thereby reduce misunderstandings (Maier, 1952; Solem, 1965). The leader has an adverse effect on the end-product when he suppresses minority views by holding a contrary position and when he uses his office to promote his own views (Maier & Hoffman, 1960b, 1962; Maier & Solem, 1952). In many problem-solving discussions the untrained leader plays a dominant role in influencing the outcome, and when he is more resistant to changing his views than are the other participants, the quality of the outcome tends to be lowered. This negative leader-influence was demonstrated by experiments in which untrained leaders were asked to obtain a second solution to a problem after they had obtained their first one (Maier & Hoffman, 1960a). It was found that the second solution tended to be superior to the first. Since the dominant individual had influenced the first solution, he had won his point and therefore ceased to dominate the subsequent discussion which led to the second solution. Acceptance of a solution also increases as the leader sees disagreement as idea-producing rather than as a source of difficulty or trouble (Maier & Hoffman, 1965). Leaders who see some of their participants as troublemakers obtain fewer innovative solutions and gain less acceptance of decisions made than leaders who see disagreeing members as persons with ideas.

THE LEADER'S ROLE FOR INTEGRATED GROUPS

Two Differing Types of Group Process

In observing group problem solving under various conditions it is rather easy to distinguish between cooperative problem-solving activity and persuasion or selling approaches. Problem-solving activity includes searching, trying out ideas on one another, listening to understand rather than to refute, making relatively short speeches, and reacting to differences in opinion as stimulating. The general pattern is one of rather complete participation, involvement, and interest. Persuasion activity includes the selling of opinions already formed, defending a position held, either not listening at all or listening in order to be able to refute, talking dominated by a few members, unfavorable reactions to disagreement, and a lack of involvement of some members. During problem solving the behavior observed seems to be that of members interacting as segments of a group. The interaction pattern is not between certain individual members, but with the group as a whole. Sometimes it is difficult to determine who should be credited with an idea. "It just developed," is a response often used to describe the solution reached. In contrast, discussions involving selling or persuasive behavior seem to consist of a series of interpersonal interactions with each individual retaining his identity. Such groups do not function as integrated units but as separate individuals, each with an agenda. In one situation the solution is unknown and is sought; in the other, several solutions exist and conflict occurs because commitments have been made.

The Starfish Analogy

The analysis of these two group processes suggests an analogy with the behavior of the rays of a starfish under two conditions; one with the nerve ring intact, the other with the nerve ring sectioned (Hamilton, 1922; Moore, 1924; Moore &

Doudoroff, 1939; Schneirla & Maier, 1940). In the intact condition, locomotion and righting behavior reveal that the behavior of each ray is not merely a function of local stimulation. Locomotion and righting behavior reveal a degree of coordination and interdependence that is centrally controlled. However, when the nerve ring is sectioned, the behavior of one ray still can influence others, but internal coordination is lacking. For example, if one ray is stimulated, it may step forward, thereby exerting pressure on the sides of the other four rays. In response to these external pressures (tactile stimulation), these rays show stepping responses on the stimulated side so that locomotion successfully occurs without the aid of neural coordination. Thus integrated behavior can occur on the basis of external control. If, however, stimulation is applied to opposite rays, the specimen may be "locked" for a time, and in some species the conflicting locomotions may divide the animal, thus destroying it (Crozier, 1920; Moore & Doudoroff, 1939).

Each of the rays of the starfish can show stepping responses even when sectioned and removed from the animal. Thus each may be regarded as an individual. In a starfish with a sectioned nerve ring the five rays become members of a group. They can successfully work together for locomotion purposes by being controlled by the dominant ray. Thus if uniformity of action is desired, the group of five rays can sometimes be more effective than the individual ray in moving the group toward a source of stimulation. However, if "locking" or the division of the organism occurs, the group action becomes less effective than individual action. External control, through the influence of a dominant ray, therefore can lead to adaptive behavior for the starfish as a whole, but it can also result in a conflict that destroys the organism. Something more than external influence is needed.

In the animal with an intact nerve ring, the function of the rays is coordinated by the nerve ring. With this type of internal organization the group is always superior to that of the individual actions. When the rays function as a part of an organized unit, rather than as a group that is physically together, they become a higher type of organization—a single intact organism. This is accomplished by the nerve ring, which in itself does not do the behaving. Rather, it receives and processes the data which the rays relay to it. Through this central organization, the responses of the rays become part of a larger pattern so that together they constitute a single coordinated total response rather than a group of individual responses.

The Leader as the Group's Central Nervous System

If we now examine what goes on in a discussion group we find that members can problem-solve as individuals, they can influence others by external pushes and pulls, or they can function as a group with varying degrees of unity. In order for the latter function to be maximized, however, something must be introduced to serve the function of the nerve ring. In our conceptualization of group problem solving and group decision (Maier, 1963), we see this as the function of the leader. Thus the leader does not serve as a dominant ray and produce the solution. Rather, his function is to receive information, facilitate communications between the individuals, relay messages, and integrate the incoming responses so that a single unified response occurs.

Solutions that are the product of good group discussion often come as surprises to discussion leaders. One of these is unexpected generosity. If there is a weak member, this member is given less to do, in much the same way as an organism adapts to an injured limb and alters the function of other limbs to keep locomotion on course. Experimental evidence supports the point that group decisions award special consideration to needy members of groups (Hoffman & Maier, 1959). Group decisions in industrial groups often give smaller assignments to the less gifted (Maier, 1952). A leader could not effectually impose such differential treatment on group members without being charged with discriminatory practices.

Another unique aspect of group discussion is the way fairness is resolved. In a simulated problem situation involving the problem of how to introduce a new truck into a group of drivers, the typical group solution involves a trading of trucks so that several or all members stand to profit. If the leader makes the decision the number of persons who profit is often confined to one (Maier & Hoffman, 1962; Maier & Zerfoss, 1952). In industrial practice, supervisors assign a new truck to an individual member of a crew after careful evaluation of needs. This practice results in dissatisfaction, with the charge of *unfair* being leveled at him. Despite these repeated attempts to do justice, supervisors in the telephone industry never hit upon the notion of a general reallocation of trucks, a solution that crews invariably reach when the decision is theirs to make.

In experiments involving the introduction of change, the use of group discussion tends to lead to decisions that resolve differences (Maier, 1952, 1953; Maier & Hoffman, 1961, 1964a, 1964b). Such decisions tend to be different from decisions reached by individuals because of the very fact that disagreement is common in group problem solving and rare in individual problem solving. The process of resolving difference in a constructive setting causes the exploration of additional areas and leads to solutions that are integrative rather than compromises.

Finally, group solutions tend to be tailored to fit the interests and personalities of the participants; thus group solutions to problems involving fairness, fears, face-saving, etc., tend to vary from one group to another. An outsider cannot process these variables because they are not subject to logical treatment.

If we think of the leader as serving a function in the group different from that of its membership, we might be able to create a group that can function as an intact organism. For a leader, such functions as rejecting or promoting ideas according to his personal needs are out of bounds. He must be receptive to information contributed, accept contributions without evaluating them (posting contributions on a chalk board to keep them alive), summarize information to facilitate integration, stimulate exploratory behavior, create awareness of problems of one member by others, and detect when the group is ready to resolve differences and agree to a unified solution.

Since higher organisms have more than a nerve ring and can store information, a leader might appropriately supply information, but according to our model of a leader's role, he must clearly distinguish between supplying information and promoting a solution. If his knowledge indicates the desirability of a particular solution, sharing this knowledge might lead the group to find this solution, but the solution should be the group's discovery. A leader's contributions do not receive the same treatment as those of a member of the group. Whether he likes it or not, his position is different. According to our conception of the leader's contribution to discussion, his role not only differs in influence, but gives him an entirely different function. He is to serve much as the nerve ring in the starfish and to further refine this function so as to make it a higher type of nerve ring.

This model of a leader's role in group process has served as a guide for many of our studies in group problem solving. It is not our claim that this will lead to the best possible group function under all conditions. In sharing it we hope to indicate the nature of our guidelines in exploring group leadership as a function quite different and apart from group membership. Thus the model serves as a stimulant for research problems and as a guide for our analyses of leadership skills and principles.

CONCLUSIONS

On the basis of our analysis, it follows that the comparison of the merits of group versus individual problem solving depends on the nature of the problem, the goal to be achieved (high quality solution, highly accepted solution, effective communication and understanding of the solution, innovation, a quickly reached solution, or satisfaction), and the skill of the discussion leader. If liabilities inherent in groups are avoided, assets capitalized upon, and conditions that can serve either favorable or unfavorable outcomes are effectively used, it follows that groups have a potential which in many instances can exceed that of a superior individual functioning alone, even with respect to creativity.

This goal was nicely stated by Thibaut and Kelley (1961) when they

wonder whether it may not be possible for a rather small, intimate group to establish a problem solving process that capitalizes upon the total pool of information and provides for great interstimulation of ideas without any loss of innovative creativity due to social restraints [p. 268].

In order to accomplish this high level of achievement, however, a leader is needed who plays a role quite different from that of the members. His role is analogous to that of the nerve ring in the starfish which permits the rays to execute a unified response. If the leader can contribute the integrative requirement, group problem solving may emerge as a unique type of group function. This type of approach to group processes places the leader in a particular role in which he must cease to contribute, avoid evaluation, and refrain from thinking about solutions or group *products*. Instead he must concentrate on the group *process*, listen in order to understand rather than to appraise or refute, assume responsibility for accurate communication between members, be sensitive to unexpressed feelings, protect minority points of view, keep the discussion moving, and develop skills in summarizing.

REFERENCES

Crozier, W. J. "Notes on Some Problems of Adaptation." *Biological Bulletin,* 1920, **39,** 116–129.

Duncker, K. "On Problem Solving." *Psychological Monographs,* 1945, **58** (5, Whole No. 270).

Hamilton, W. F. "Coordination in the Starfish: III. The Righting Reaction as a Phase of Locomotion (righting and locomotion)." *Journal of Comparative Psychology,* 1922, **2,** 81–94.

Hoffman, L. R. "Conditions for Creative Problem Solving." *Journal of Psychology,* 1961, **52,** 429–444.

Hoffman, L. R. "Group Problem Solving." In L. Berkowitz (Ed.), *Advances in experimental social psychology,* Vol. 2. New York: Academic Press, 1965. Pp. 99–132.

Hoffman, L. R., Harburg, E., & Maier, N. R. F. "Differences and Disagreement as Factors in Creative Group Problem Solving." *Journal of Abnormal and Social Psychology,* 1962, **64,** 206–214.

Hoffman, L. R., & Maier, N. R. F. "The Use of Group Decision to Resolve a Problem of Fairness." *Personnel Psychology,* 1959, **12,** 545–559.

Hoffman, L. R., & Maier, N. R. F. "Quality and Acceptance of Problem Solutions by Members of Homogeneous and Heterogeneous Groups." *Journal of Abnormal and Social Psychology,* 1961, **62,** 401–407.

Hoffman, L. R., & Maier, N. R. F. "Valence in the Adoption of Solutions by Problem-solving Groups: Concept, Method, and Results." *Journal of Abnormal and Social Psychology,* 1964, **69,** 264–271.

Hoffman, L. R., & Maier, N. R. F. "Valence in the Adoption of Solutions by Problem-solving Groups: II. Quality and Acceptance as Goals of Leaders and Members." Unpublished manuscript, 1967. (Mimeo)

Kelley, H. H., & Thibaut, J. W. "Experimental Studies of Group Problem Solving and

Process," In G. Lindzey (Ed.), *Handbook of social psychology*. Cambridge, Mass.: Addison-Wesley, 1954. Pp. 735 – 785.

Maier, N. R. F. "Reasoning in Humans: I. On Direction." *Journal of Comparative Psychology*, 1930, **10**, 115 – 143.

Maier, N. R. F. "The Quality of Group Decisions as Influenced by the Discussion Leader." *Human Relations*, 1950, **3**, 155 – 174.

Maier, N. R. F. *Principles of human relations*. New York: Wiley, 1952.

Maier, N. R. F. "An Experimental Test of the Effect of Training on Discussion Leadership." *Human Relations*, 1953, **6**, 161 – 173.

Maier, N. R. F. *The appraisal interview*. New York: Wiley, 1958.

Maier, N. R. F. "Screening Solutions to Upgrade Quality: A New Approach to Problem Solving Under Conditions of Uncertainty." *Journal of Psychology*, 1960, **49**, 217 – 231.

Maier, N. R. F. *Problem solving discussions and conferences: Leadership methods and skills*. New York: McGraw-Hill, 1963.

Maier, N. R. F., & Hayes, J. J. *Creative management*. New York: Wiley, 1962.

Maier, N. R. F., & Hoffman, L. R. "Using Trained 'Developmental' Discussion Leaders to Improve Further the Quality of Group Decisions." *Journal of Applied Psychology*, 1960, **44**, 247 – 251. (a)

Maier, N. R. F., & Hoffman, L. R. "Quality of First and Second Solutions in Group Problem Solving." *Journal of Applied Psychology*, 1960, **44**, 278 – 283. (b)

Maier, N. R. F., & Hoffman, L. R. "Organization and Creative Problem Solving." *Journal of Applied Psychology*, 1961, **45**, 277 – 280.

Maier, N. R. F., & Hoffman, L. R. "Group Decision in England and the United States." *Personnel Psychology*, 1962, **15**, 75 – 87.

Maier, N. R. F., & Hoffman, L. R. "Financial Incentives and Group Decision in Motivating Change." *Journal of Social Psychology*, 1964, **64**, 369 – 378. (a)

Maier, N. R. F., & Hoffman, L. R. "Types of Problems Confronting Managers." *Personnel Psychology*, 1964, **17**, 261 – 269. (b)

Maier, N. R. F., & Hoffman, L. R. "Acceptance and Quality of Solutions as Related to Leaders' Attitudes Toward Disagreement in Group Problem Solving." *Journal of Applied Behavioral Science*, 1965, **1**, 373 – 386.

Maier, N. R. F., & Maier, R. A. "An Experimental Test of the Effects of 'Developmental' vs. 'Free' Discussions on the Quality of Group Decisions." *Journal of Applied Psychology*, 1957, **41**, 320 – 323.

Maier, N. R. F., & Solem, A. R. "The Contribution of a Discussion Leader to the Quality of Group Thinking: The Effective Use of Minority Opinions." *Human Relations*, 1952, **5**, 277 – 288.

Maier, N. R. F., & Solem, A. R. "Improving Solutions by Turning Choice Situations into Problems." *Personnel Psychology*, 1962, **15**, 151 – 157.

Maier, N. R. F., & Zerfoss, L. F. "MRP: A Technique for Training Large Groups of Supervisors and Its Potential Use in Social Research." *Human Relations*, 1952, **5**, 177 – 186.

Moore, A. R. "The Nervous Mechanism of Coordination in the Crinoid *Antedon rosaceus.*" *Journal of Genetic Psychology*, 1924, **6**, 281 – 288.

Moore, A. R., & Doudoroff, M. "Injury, Recovery and Function in an Aganglionic Central Nervous System." *Journal of Comparative Psychology*, 1939, **28**, 313 – 328.

Osborn, A. F. *Applied imagination*. New York: Scribner's, 1953.

Schneirla, T. C., & Maier, N. R. F. "Concerning the Status of the Starfish." *Journal of Comparative Psychology*, 1940, **30**, 103 – 110.

Solem, A. R. "1965: Almost Anything I Can Do, We Can Do Better. " *Personnel Administration,* 1965, **28,** 6 – 16.

Thibaut, J. W., & Kelley, H. H. *The social psychology of groups.* New York: Wiley, 1961.

Wallach, M. A., & Kogan, N. "The Roles of Information, Discussion and Consensus in Group Risk Taking." *Journal of Experimental and Social Psychology,* 1965, **1,** 1 – 19.

Wallach, M. A., Kogan, N., & Bem, D. J. "Group Influence on Individual Risk Taking." *Journal of Abnormal and Social Psychology,* 1962, **65,** 75 – 86.

Wertheimer, M. *Productive thinking.* New York: Harper, 1959.

The Management of Decision-Making Within the Firm: Three Strategies for Three Types of Decision-Making

Andre L. Delbecq

Recent theory concerned with group problem-solving suggests that different types of decision making require different group structures and processes. The administrator who "manages" the decision-making process must, therefore, organize the executive team in different ways as he deals with the variety of decision-making situations within the firm.

Every practicing administrator is well aware of these qualitative differences in the problem-solving situations which he and his management team face. Further, even without conscious effort on his part, the management group will often change its pattern of communication and individual managers will adjust their roles, as the management team faces different tasks. Research evidence shows that over time, problem-solving groups tend to adjust their behavior in keeping with changes in the nature of group problem-solving.[1]

On the other hand, the process of adjustment to new decision-making situations is often slow, usually incomplete, and occasionally nonexistent. Managers develop expectations about appropriate behavior in decision-making meetings with

"The Management of Decision-Making Within the Firm: Three Strategies for Three Types of Decision-Making," Andre L. Delbecq, *Academy of Management Journal,* December 1967, Vol. 10, No. 4, pp. 329 – 339. Reprinted by permission of the Academy and the author.

their superiors, so that their behavior falls into a pattern with limited variability which may be appropriate for some types of decision making, but highly inappropriate for other decision-making situations.[2] However, if the manager is highly sensitive to differences in the decision-making tasks faced by the management team, and can verbally redefine both his own and his subordinates' roles in a fashion congruent with the new decision-making situation, research indicates that the management group can much more readily change its behavior as the result of such role redefinition in order to adjust to a new decision-making situation.[3]

The purpose of this article is to set forth three decision-making strategies, each of which is tailored to a different type of problem-solving situation encountered within the firm. Further, each strategy will be examined to determine the degree to which it differs from the logic of classical organization models. It is hoped that this examination of the three different strategies will fulfill the following purposes:

1. The administrator will become more sensitive to the kind of group structure and process which each of the three problem-solving tasks demands,
2. The problems of implementing the strategies within a traditional formal organization culture will be clearer, and
3. The implications for the redesign of traditional formal organization models to facilitate greater flexibility for problem-solving can be suggested.

THE RELEVANCE OF "TASK" FOR GROUP STRUCTURE

Since the body of this article proposes that managers should reorganize group structure and process as they face different types of decision tasks, a word about the relevance of task as a variable around which to construct "organization" is appropriate. It is axiomatic to say that individual behavior is goal directed,[4] and that group behavior is purposeful or goal directed as well.[5] The task of a group is normally thought of, however, only in terms of the stated goal of the group's activity. Thus, there are familiar typologies of groups based on stated goals. For example, Wolman classifies groups as being Instrumental Groups (which individuals join for the satisfaction of "to take" needs, e.g., business associations), Mutual Acceptance Groups (in which "give" and "take" motives are important, e.g., friendship relations), and Vectorial Groups (which people join for the purpose of serving a lofty goal).[6]

Another typology dealing with organizations as macro-groups is that of Scott and Blau who speak of Mutual Benefit Associations (where the prime beneficiary is the membership), Business Concerns (where the owner is the prime beneficiary), Service Organizations (where the client group is the prime beneficiary), and Commonweal Organizations (where the prime beneficiary is the public at large).[7]

What is not immediately apparent in each of these descriptive typologies is that task, as a variable, affects several dimensions of the system (regardless of whether one is referring to a small group or a large organization) including:

1. *Group Structure:* In terms of the relationship between the individual members,
2. *Group Roles:* In terms of the behavior required of individual group members which are necessary to facilitate task accomplishment,
3. *Group Process:* In terms of the manner of proceeding toward goal accomplishment,
4. *Group Style:* In terms of the social-emotional tone of interpersonal relationships (e.g., the amount of stress on individual members, the congeniality of interpersonal relations, the perceived consequences of individual and group success or failure),
5. *Group Norms:* Relative to each of the preceding four dimensions.

Thus, in treating task as merely the end goal, many of the theoretical as well as the practical implications of the group's or organization's tasks are not made explicit. For example, when mutual benefit organizations are compared with business concerns, one would expect the former to be characterized by greater dispersion of power (structure), broader membership participation in goal setting (roles and process), greater emotional support of individual members (style), and stronger egalitarianism (norms).

In a similar fashion, the problem-solving "task" faced by a particular managerial team, within a particular organization, at a particular point of time, likewise must affect the structure, roles, process, style, and norms of the management team if the group is to optimally organize itself to deal with its task.[8]

STRATEGIES FOR GROUP PROBLEM SOLVING

Against this background, we can now proceed directly to classify decision situations as found in groups and organizations and to specify group strategies implied in behaviorally oriented group and organization studies appropriate for dealing with each of the situations.[9]

Strategy One: Routine Decision Making

The first decision situation with which we will deal is the routine decision-making situation. In Simon's terminology, this is the "programmed" decision-situation; in Thompson's terminology, the "computational" decision.[10] Here, the organization or group agrees upon the desired goal, and technologies exist to achieve the goal. In such a situation, the following strategy can be specified as consistent with behavioral models:

1. *Group Structure:* The group is composed of specialists, with a coordinator (leader).
2. *Group Roles:* Behavior is characterized by independent effort, with each specialist contributing expertise relative to his own specialty, including the coordinator (leader) who specializes in coordination across task phases.
3. *Group Process:* At the beginning of the planning period, specialists, with the coordinator, specify the productivity objectives. Subsequently, excepting occasional joint meetings to review progress, coordination of specialist endeavors is generally obtained by means of dyadic (two-person) communication between specialists.
4. *Group Style:* Relatively high stress is characteristic. Stress is achieved through quality and quantity commitments and time constraints, agreed upon in joint consultation at the beginning of the planning period. Responsibility is decentralized within areas of specialization, but coordination is centralized in the coordinator.
5. *Group Norms:* Norms are characterized by professionalism (high sense of individual responsibility and craftsmanship); commitment to shared team objectives relative to quantity and quality of output; economy and efficiency.

The above strategy evidences both similarity and dissimilarity when compared with classical organizational models. It is similar in that there is a clear division of labor, functional and structural specialization (specialization in work, and between work and coordination), and centralized coordination.

On the other hand, this "optimal" model is dissimilar in several significant ways. To begin with, responsibility is obtained primarily through team commitments to group objectives, dealing with both the quantity and quality of the output. This commitment, elicited through joint discussion between the specialists and the coordinator at the beginning of the planning period, places responsibility on both the team members and the coordinator, rather than locating responsibility solely in the coordinator.

Control is obtained in two ways. First, the coordinator provides the feedback mechanism for the team by monitoring the progress of individual specialists to assure conformity to shared productivity and time objectives. Situations where actual performance deviated from prior commitments are brought to the shared attention of the team, which institutes appropriate correction measures. Thus, discipline rests upon joint commitments rather than upon superordinate sanctions.[11] Second, because motivation is task-intrinsic, specialists are "normatively" expected to be "self-controlled" through professional, reference-group standards. Authority is likewise decentralized based upon specialist expertise and shared norms.

Since responsibility, authority, and discipline are shared within the management team, there is less status disparity between the coordinator and the specialist than is the case between supervisor and subordinates in traditional organization models. Indeed, coordination is seen as a type of specialization, rather than as a function of superior personal attributes, or positional status. As a consequence, there is a propensity for fluid changes in group personnel; different task experts bring to bear their differentiated competences at different points of time as the group encounters various phases of decision making in the completion of a project. Further, the role of the coordinator may shift between the specialists on occasions, as the coordination requirements demand different admixtures of skills at various phases of project management.

Admittedly, the strategy assumes high quality personnel in terms of both task skills and interpersonal skills. Further, it requires a degree of autonomy for both individual specialists and each specialist team, an autonomy which must be predicated on personal and organizational maturity. It also assumes that the objectives of the organization and each group can be integrated into a meaningful, internally consistent ends-means chain, where, at each level and between each area, objectives can be translated in terms of appropriate technologies.

Nonetheless, although a "pure" strategy (best approximated in project management, matrix management, or task-force groups), movement towards such a model for structuring groups dealing with "routine" tasks appears capable of avoiding many of the dysfunctions of classical organizational models, while captivating the advantages of division of labor, specialization, centralized coordination, and task-intrinsic motivation.

Strategy Two: Creative Decision Making

The second decision situation with which we will deal is the creative decision-making situation. Here we are talking about decision making which in Simon's terminology is "heuristic" and in Thompson's terminology is "judgmental."[12] The central element in the decision making is the lack of an agreed-upon method of dealing with the problem; this lack of certitude may relate to incomplete knowledge of causation, or lack of an appropriate solution strategy. In such a situation, the following strategy can be specified as consistent with behavioral models:[13]

1. *Group Structure:* The group is composed of heterogeneous, generally competent personnel, who bring to bear on the problem diverse frames of reference, representing channels to each relevant body of knowledge (including contact with outside resource personnel who offer expertise not encompassed by the organization), with a leader who facilitates creative (heuristic) processes.
2. *Group Roles:* Behavior is characterized by each individual, exploring with the entire group all ideas (no matter how intuitively and roughly formed) which bear on the problem.

3. *Group processes:* The problem-solving process is characterized by:
    (a) spontaneous communication between members (not focused in the leader)
    (b) full participation from each member
    (c) separation of idea generation from idea evaluation
    (d) separation of problem definition from generation of solution strategies
    (e) shifting of roles, so that interaction which mediates problem solving (particularly search activities and clarification by means of constant questioning directed both to individual members and the whole group) is not the sole responsibility of the leader
    (f) suspension of judgment and avoidance of early concerns with solutions, so that emphasis is on analysis and exploration rather than on early solution commitment.
4. *Group Style:* The social-emotional tone of the group is characterized by:
    (a) a relaxed, nonstressful environment
    (b) ego-supportive interaction, where open give-and-take between members is at the same time courteous
    (c) behavior which is motivated by interest in the problem, rather than concern with short-run payoff
    (d) absence of penalties attached to any espoused idea or position.
5. *Group Norms:*
    (a) are supportive of originality, and unusual ideas, and allow for eccentricity
    (b) seek behavior which separates source from content in evaluating information and ideas
    (c) stress a nonauthoritarian view, with a relativistic view of life and independence of judgment
    (d) support humor and undisciplined exploration of viewpoints
    (e) seek openness in communication, where mature, self-confident individuals offer "crude" ideas to the group for mutual exploration without threat to the individual for "exposing" himself
    (f) deliberately avoid credence to short-run results, or short-run decisiveness
    (g) seek consensus, but accept majority rule when consensus is unobtainable. [14]

Obviously, the above prescription for a strategy to deal with creativity does not easily complement classical organization theory. Structural differentiation and status inequality (other than achieved status within the group) are deemphasized. The decisive, energetic, action-oriented executive is a normative misfit. Decisions evolve quite outside the expected frame of reference of the "pure" task specialist. Communication is dispersed, rather than focused in a superior or even a coordinator. Motivation is totally task-intrinsic, the pleasure being much more in the exploration than in an immediately useful outcome. Indeed, the very personnel who thrive by excellent application and execution of complex technologies in the first strategy, find the optimal decision rules for the second strategy unnatural, unrealistic, idealistic, and slow.

Nonetheless, although all members of any organization will not find both of the strategies equally comfortable, it can be expected that most organizational members can approximate the strategy given appropriate role definitions. The point, here, is that the group structure and process which is called for to facilitate creativity is intrinsically different from our first strategy. While the first strategy called for an internally consistent team of complementary specialists who are "action" oriented, the second strategy calls for a heterogeneous collection of generalists (or at least generically wise specialists not restricted to the boundaries of their own specialized frame of reference, and even, not necessarily of the immediate group or organization) who are deliberately and diagnostically patient in remaining problem-centered. The membership, roles, processes, style, and norms of strategy two are more natural to the scientific community (or a small subset thereof) than to the practicing executive. The general implications, however, must await the exposition of the third strategy.

Strategy Three: Negotiated Decision Making

The third decision situation with which we will deal is the negotiated decision-making strategy. In this instance, we are concerned with a strategy for dealing with opposing factions which, because of differences in norms, values or vested interests, stand in opposition to each other, concerning either ends or means, or both.[15] Organization theory has never given much attention to groups in conflict, since several elements of classical models precluded such open conflict. One element was, of course, the existence of monocratic authority. At some level in the hierarchical system, authority to "decide" was to be found. Parties representing various opinions might be given a hearing, but ultimately Manager X was to make the decision. Another element in classical thought which precluded open conflict was the conviction, however utopian, that conflict was merely symptomatic of inadequate analysis. Adequate problem-solving would surely show that the conflict was artificial and that an integrative decision could be reached. Thus, the study of mechanisms for negotiation between groups in conflict was left to the student of political science and social conflict and was excluded from organizational models.

Nonetheless, the realities of conflict have been ubiquitous. Present models encourage the sublimation of conflict, veiling it in portended rationality. As one wag expressed the matter, "If people don't agree with me, it isn't that I am wrong, or that they are right, but merely that I haven't been clear." In spite of Trojan efforts at "clear communication," the elimination of all conflict through analysis is, indeed, a utopian desire. There have been, and will be, instances where the organization finds itself encompassing two "camps," each supported by acceptable values and logic, and each committed to a different course of action, relative to either means, ends, or both. The question remains, then, as to what would be an appropriate strategy in those cases where "analysis" cannot provide an acceptable solution to both parties since the disparate opinion or positions are based on assumptions and premises not subject to total decision integration.

The following strategy can be specified:

1. *Group Structure:* The group is composed of proportional representation of each faction (but with the minority never represented by less than two persons), with an impartial formal chairman.[16]

2. *Group Roles:* Each individual sees himself as a representative of his faction, seeking to articulate and protect dominant concerns of the group he represents, while at the same time negotiating for an acceptable compromise solution.

3. *Group Processes:* The problem-solving process is characterized by:
    (a)   orderly communication mediated by the chairman, providing opportunity for each faction to speak, but avoidance of factional domination
    (b)   formalized procedures providing for an orderly handling of disputation
    (c)   formalized voting procedure
    (d)   possession of veto power by each faction
    (e)   analytical approaches to seeking compromise, rather than mere reliance on power attempts.

4. *Group Style:* Group style is characterized by:
    (a)   frankness and candor in presenting opposing viewpoints
    (b)   acceptance of due process in seeking resolution to conflicts
    (c)   openness to rethinking, and to mediation attempts
    (d)   avoidance of emotional hostility and aggression.

5. *Group Norms:* Group norms are characterized by:
    (a)   desire on the part of all factions to reach agreement
    (b)   the perception of conflict and disagreement as healthy and natural, rather than pathological
    (c)   acceptance of individual freedom and group freedom to disagree
    (d)   openness to new analytical approaches in seeking acceptable compromise
    (e)   acceptance of the necessity of partial agreement as an acceptable, legitimate, and realistic basis for decision making.

There is, obviously, no parallel in either structure or norms to the above strategy in classical organizational models. The acceptance of open conflict; provision for due process between conflicting groups; openness to compromise; evolution of policy and objectives through negotiation; and "representative groups" while found in the "underworld" in most organizations, are outside the general organizational model. Indeed, managers involved in "negotiations," either in the personnel (labor relations) or marketing (customer relations) areas, find it difficult to articulate the legitimacy of many of their decisions except through rationalizations.

CONCLUSIONS AND IMPLICATIONS

Both the propensities for groups to change the nature of their interaction as they change task, and/or task phases, and the prescriptions for group strategies dealing with differentiated decision situations as set forth above, indicate that the structure and processes of groups must be related to changes in the characteristics of the decision-making tasks. Whether one agrees with each proposition in each of the decision strategy models set forth in this article or not, the fact that each of the decision-making situations is endemically different is difficult to refute.

On the other hand, formal organizations as conceived in present organizational models are presumably structured in terms of the predominant type of task encountered by the system. (Thus, the "bureaucratic" model is based on facilitating "routine" decision making; the labor union council is structured to deal with negotiated decision making; etc.) Since task is, in the most pertinent sense, what members of the organization subjectively define it to be as they respond to the situation in which they find themselves, the internal features of a decision group within the organization will generally be conditioned by the predominant structured roles created to deal with the "typical" decisions encountered in day-to-day organizational tasks. As a result, role expectations and behaviors conditioned in the central organizational system (the formal organization) may inhibit the decision task performance in the subsystem (the decision-making committee, conference, or task force).

Since there are several types of decisions to be made within complex organizations, with each general type calling for a different group structure and process, a major role of the manager in such a system is the evoking of appropriate changes in behaviors on the part of the managerial team as it moves across task types by means of role redefinition. This assumes that the manager can classify decision tasks according to the models presented here, or some other conceptual scheme, and that the managerial team can respond with congruent role flexibility. Earlier pilot research by the author indicates that such flexibility seems to be within the capacities of a large portion of the population given appropriate role redefinition by the superior.[17]

In the real sense, then, management of the decision-making process is management of the structure and functioning of decision groups, so that these decision-making processes become congruent with changes in the nature of the decision-making task being undertaken at a particular point of time within the organization.

Finally, we spent considerable time delineating the "task-force," "systems management" or "matrix organizational" approach (strategy one)[18] as the appropriate strategy for routine decision making purposefully, since it seems to provide a mechanism for integrating various types of decision making at various phases of project management within a flexible structure. It is felt that strategy one avoids the structural rigidity of formal organization models such as "bureaucracy." There is no reason, for instance, why "creative" or "negotiated" strategies cannot be incorporated into the objectives and standards-setting decision sessions at the beginning of the planning period. Further, there is no reason why personnel other than the "task specialists" cannot mediate the decision making by participation in these early decision phases. Thus, by dropping the assumption of "agreed-upon technologies" and "agreed-upon objectives," and incorporating strategies two and three into these early planning sessions, or intermittently juxtaposing these strategies with strategy one, the possibility for incorporating decision-making flexibility into the "project management" context of strategy one seems not only feasible, but a desirable movement in the direction of fluid group structures and processes. Such movement toward organizational fluidness is more congruent with the need for role flexibility as the management team moves across decision strategies at various phases of project planning and implementation.

REFERENCES AND NOTES

1. Harold Guetzkow and Herbert A. Simon, "The Impact of Certain Communication Nets upon Organization and Performance in Task Oriented Groups," *Management Science,* 1 (1955), 233–250; Rocco Carzo, Jr., "Organization Structure and Group Effectiveness," *Administrative Science Quarterly* (March, 1963), pp. 393–425.
2. Leonard Berkowitz, "Sharing Leadership in Small, Decision-Making Groups," *Journal of Abnormal and Social Psychology* (1953), pp. 231–238; Andre L. Delbecq, "Managerial Leadership Styles in Problem-Solving Conferences," *Academy of Management Journal,* VII, No. 4 (Dec., 1964), 255–268.
3. Andre L. Delbecq, "Managerial Leadership Styles in Problem-Solving Conferences: Research Findings on Role Flexibility," *Academy of Management Journal,* VIII, No. 1 (March, 1965), 32–43.
4. Harold J. Leavitt and Ronald A. H. Mueller, *Managerial Psychology* (Chicago: University of Chicago Press, 1964), pp. 8–9.
5. Robert T. Golembiewski, *The Small Group* (Chicago: University of Chicago Press, 1962), p. 181.
6. Benjamin Wolman, "Instrumental, Mutual Acceptance and Vectorial Groups," Paper read at the Annual Meeting of the American Sociological Association, August, 1953
7. Peter M. Blau and W. Richard Scott, *Organizations, A Comparative Approach* (San Francisco: Chandler Publishing Company, 1962).

8. W. C. Schutz, "Some Theoretical Considerations for Group Behavior," *Symposium on Techniques for the Measurement of Group Performance* (Washington, D.C.: U.S. Government Research and Development Board, 1952), pp. 27–36.

9. The reader should be clearly forewarned that each of the strategies is the author's own conceptualization. While an extensive review of the literature, both theoretical and empirical, underlies each strategy, it is not meant to be implied that the strategy represents a model about which scholars universally agree. Rather, the strategies represent the theoretical position of the author which is consistent with much of the literature, but is admittedly open to question and refinement.

10. J. Thompson and Arthur Tuden, "Strategies, Structures and Processes of Organizational Decision," *Comparative Studies in Administration,* ed. Thompson et al. (Pittsburgh,Pa.: University of Pittsburgh Press, 1959), pp. 198–199; H. Simon, *The New Science of Management Decisions* (New York: Harper Brothers, 1960), Chapters 2, 3.

11. For a treatment of the manner in which group norms control individual behavior, see Andre T. Delbecq and Fremont A. Shull, "Norms, A Feature of Symbolic Culture: A Major Linkage Between the Individual, the Small Group and Administrative Organization," *The Making of Decisions,* ed. W. J. Gore and J. W. Dyson (N.Y.: The Free Press of Glencoe, 1964), pp. 213–242.

12. Herbert A. Simon and Allen Newell, "Heuristic Problem Solving: The Next Advance in Operations Research," *Operations Research Journal* (Jan.–Feb., 1958); Thompson and Tuden, *op. cit.*

13. Particularly useful models dealing with individual and group creativity can be found in William E. Scott, "The Creative Individual," *Journal of Management* (Sept., 1965); Larry Cummings, "Organizational Climates for Creativity," *Journal of the Academy of Management* (Sept., 1965); Victor A. Thompson, "Bureaucracy and Innovation," *Administrative Science Quarterly* (June, 1965); Gary Steiner, *The Creative Organization* (Chicago: University of Chicago Press, 1965); and Norman R. F. Maier, *Problem-Solving Discussions and Conferences* (New York: McGraw-Hill, 1963).

14. In development of the above model, we have consciously avoided the issue of "nominal" groups (where members work without verbal interaction in generating solution strategies) vs. "interacting" groups. While preliminary evidence favors "nominal" groups in generating ideas, the question as to the appropriateness of the nominal group strategy for the total decision process (i.e., evaluation as well as idea generation) remains in question.

Further, the experimental tasks used in the studies may be different in kind from organizational decision making. In any event, the above model seems quite adaptable to separation into nominal and interacting processes at various phases, using modifications which do not vitiate the general tenor of the model. For a discussion of nominal vs. interacting groups, see Alan H. Leader, "Creativity in Management," Paper read at the Midwest Division of the Academy of Management, April 8, 1967; P. W. Taylor, P. C. Berry, and C. H. Block, "Does Group Participation When Using Brainstorming Facilitate or Inhibit Creative Thinking?" *Administrative Science Quarterly,* III (1958), 23–47.

15. In this respect, we assume a position different from that of Thompson and Tuden in their earlier model who posit that "compromise" decision making is predicated on disagreement about ends. Thompson and Tuden, *op. cit.*

16. The justification for the minority never being represented by less than two persons is that it is difficult for one person to represent his group across the boundary and that a minority of one is easy prey for a majority coalition of two members, let alone more than two.

17. Andre L. Delbecq (March, 1965). We agree that some individuals will find it impossible to assume flexible roles due to their particular developmental history which results in a fixated behavior pattern. We also agree that some roles will be more natural than others for individuals due to their developmental history. We disagree, however, with the notion that the normal population cannot assume at least functionally relevant roles in accordance with the various strategies, a point which appears to be the position of some theorists. A more conservative viewpoint than ours is assumed by Abraham Zaleznic in *Human Dilemmas of Leadership* (New York: Harper & Row, 1965).

18. For an elaborated treatment of "Matrix Organization" see Fremont A. Shull, *Matrix Structure and Project Authority for Optimizing Organizational Capacity* (Monograph, Business Research Bureau, Southern Illinois University, Carbondale, Illinois, 1965); Warren Bennis, "Beyond Bureaucracy," *Transactions* (Summer, 1965); John F. Mee, "Ideational Items: Matrix Organization," *Business Horizons* (Summer, 1964), pp. 70–72; and Carl R. Praktish, "Evolution of Project Management," Paper read at Midwest Academy of Management, April, 1967.

Section C

Management by Objectives: Development and Refinement

Management by objectives has existed for over two decades, yet there is considerable uncertainty about what MBO involves. This uncertainty reflects the diversity of MBO applications throughout business, industry, and government. To assist an understanding of MBO, the two articles in this section review its development and suggest a preferred method of implementation.

The first selection, by McConkey, is titled "MBO—Twenty Years Later, Where Do We Stand?" It traces the evolution of MBO, examines the extent of adoption, discusses MBO's impact on managing, and points out a number of pitfalls to which the system can succumb. McConkey notes that while MBO has not been a 100 percent success, its overall effect has been dramatic even though there still exists the need to refine parts of the system, especially in the areas of management appraisal and compensation. He concludes that the key word in management by objectives is "management" and that users who adopt MBO without careful attention to its participative philosophy will do so on a "planned failure basis."

Interestingly, although successful implementation of MBO requires a collaborative style of management, many OD practitioners do not recognize MBO as a "legitimate" OD technique. (Even Friedlander and Brown's broad-ranging review of the OD area neglected MBO applications). The reason for this becomes apparent in the second article—French and Hollmann's "Management by Objectives: The Team Approach."

According to French and Hollmann, most MBO variations reinforce an autocratic style of management and thus have certain deficiencies. For example, autocratic MBO neglects the interdependent nature of most jobs, does not integrate the objectives of all managers in a unit, and hampers the supervisor-subordinate relationship. The authors recommend strengthening MBO by linking it more closely with OD's emphasis on teamwork.

Group approaches to MBO are not new, but most do not offer guidelines for implementation. French and Hollmann's work is unique in this regard because it proposes a nine-point strategy for building group problem solving into the MBO process. The result is "collaborative" management by objectives (CMBO). French and Hollmann recognize that CMBO will not be accomplished easily in most organizations and that its initial success will depend on top management support. Nonetheless, they assert that CMBO has merit in practice and "can help people, teams, and units become more goal-directed without undermining efforts to maintain or create a participative, responsive team climate in the organization."

24   MBO–Twenty Years Later, Where Do We Stand?

Dale D. McConkey

Management by objectives—or any management approach which has existed for a number of years and has received widespread acclaim—should be subject to review and evaluation. The review should address itself to providing answers to the following major questions:

What have been the most significant milestones in the development and application of the approach?
To what extent has MBO been adopted?
What has been its major impact on the management process and the manager's job?
Is it a viable approach for continuing development and application?

MILESTONES IN MBO

Although it is difficult to apply the description "milestone" to only some elements in a series of events, certain events can be singled out as the most significant in the evolution of MBO. The *first* concerns the translation of the MBO concept into reality. "Objectives" of one variety or another have been known and used by managers since Biblical times. It remained for Peter Drucker, writing in 1954, to utilize them as the basis for a management system.[1] Drucker, always the able catalyst to management thinking, set the stage by proposing that objectives would serve as the vehicle for administering and directing a systems approach to managing an organization. Others would develop the system and render it operative. Approximately fifteen years after Drucker's lucid pronouncement, MBO has become a practical reality embodied, successfully and unsuccessfully, in thousands of various and diverse organizations throughout the world. Concept has been translated into practice.

The *second* milestone concerns the three-stage evolution of MBO from its fledgling stage to the present. Initially, almost complete emphasis was devoted to improving the performance of the individual manager—by providing him with goals toward which to strive and by according him recognition for his achievements.

Next, emphasis switched to the organization as a total entity, and the goal was overall organizational effectiveness on a short-range basis. Finally, the long-run future of the organization was emphasized by balancing and directing the results of individual managers to achieve organizational priorities.[2]

The *third* milestone was realized when MBO advanced from a special-purpose management tool or technique into a full-fledged management system.

The early efforts of the pioneers in MBO arose primarily from a complete disenchantment with the techniques then popular for evaluating or appraising managerial performance. The evaluation techniques of the late 1950s measured the degree to which managers were thought to possess, or to fail to possess, highly subjective traits or factors. Factors commonly evaluated were cost awareness, grasp of function, initiative, innovation, punctuality, loyalty, cooperation, potential for advancement, and other qualities. The traits were not keyed to actual results achieved, and two evaluations of the same manager could differ by 180 degrees because of the orientation and prejudices of the examiners.

Gradually, measurable objectives and results replaced evaluations of traits. This required the development of effective objectives for managers and here we see the beginnings of the new system. The development of objectives appropriate for

1. Peter F. Drucker, *The Practice of Management* (New York: Harper & Row, 1954).
2. See Robert A. Howell, "Managing by Objectives—A Three-Stage System," *Business Horizons*, Vol. XIII (February 1970), pp. 41–5.

use in evaluating performance paved the way for allowing objectives to serve as the focal point for all other major parts of the management process.

EXTENT OF ADOPTION

The precise extent to which MBO has been adopted is impossible to gauge. To date there are no valid findings or data on the number of organizations which have adopted MBO. Any attempt to arrive at the number is complicated by the need for a definition of the degree of MBO which an organization must practice to be included in the data. Moreover, the collection of data would be further confused because of the uncertainty concerning what MBO is.

Some managers classify themselves as MBO practitioners simply because they operate with budgets. Others do so because they work with general goals and objectives, and others because they believe they are following a few MBO principles—as they understand them. And still others profess to be full-fledged MBO managers because they give their subordinates some voice in decision making.

The above variations notwithstanding, there is no question that MBO has been adopted extensively. Applications are found in abundance in large and small companies and in all areas of the business sector—in both capital goods and consumer goods companies and in companies with product lines as divergent as turbines and facial tissues and with goals as different as producing a product and providing a service.

The nonprofit sector, having witnessed the attention devoted to MBO in the private sector, has begun to adopt MBO at a rather startling pace. This trend is discernible among government units, in hospitals and the health-care field, among religious organizations, and in educational systems.

Service organizations—whose growth is outpacing manufacturing entities—constitute another vital area of growth. Many insurance companies, banks, and retail establishments are presently exploring and adopting the MBO system.

A pattern of adoption within geographical locations is also evident. From the United States, MBO has spread to England, Europe, Japan, Canada, and other parts of the globe.

Thus, MBO has been widely adopted and is being extensively practiced. This adoption is not based upon its proven value, but upon its logical appeal. To date, there has been no validation through a representative sample of the degree to which MBO increases organizational or managerial effectiveness. . . . No correlation has been established between MBO and the specific profitability levels of a company or between MBO and the definite levels of effectiveness of managers. To ask whether such correlations can ever be established—in light of the numerous known variables—is to pose an extremely difficult question.

However, it can be demonstrated, without attempting to quantify the results, that practicing MBO in depth does result in improved communication, coordination, control, and motivation of managers. These desirable ends are considered the minimum an organization should expect from its MBO efforts, and there is little, if any, disagreement that these benefits do accrue when MBO is employed for at least two to three years.

Before proceeding to a discussion of the specific changes which MBO has helped bring about, the absence of "pure" MBO systems must be indicated. If pure MBO is defined as a system in which all of the commonly accepted principles of MBO are practiced in A to Z fashion, few, if any, organizations actually practice MBO.

Major differences exist in the applications of MBO, in the procedures for accomplishing the applications, and in the degree of conviction with which MBO is pursued. For example, some organizations embrace the method primarily as a means of evaluating their managers, while others use it primarily for planning. Still others employ MBO as the overall management system. Even within different divisions of the same company, there are considerable differences in the approach and applications. For example, in one multibillion dollar, multidivision company, some divisions are practicing MBO as a way of life while other divisions have barely heard of it.

IMPACT ON MANAGING

The impact of MBO on the management process and on the manager has been profound and dramatic. Nowhere is this impact more demonstrable than in the change in the very definition of "management."

Formerly, if a person were asked to define management, he might reply, "It's getting things done through people." If pressed to amplify his definition, he might add "by planning, organizing, directing, and controlling." This rather common and traditional definition of management was rendered obsolete by a recent study completed by a committee of the Association of Consulting Management Engineers and reported by the Business Management Council.[3] This study concluded that management is comprised of three steps: establishing objectives, directing the attainment of objectives, and measuring results.

The accompanying figure portrays the "management wheel" which resulted from the study. The three major steps in managing are divided into their eleven elements. Thus, in lieu of defining management by general terms or by citing a list of functions which the manager carrys out, management now is defined as comprising three major steps—all highly oriented toward objectives. Now the former

---

3. *BMC Report Number 1* (New York: Business Management Council, 1968).

Elements of Managing

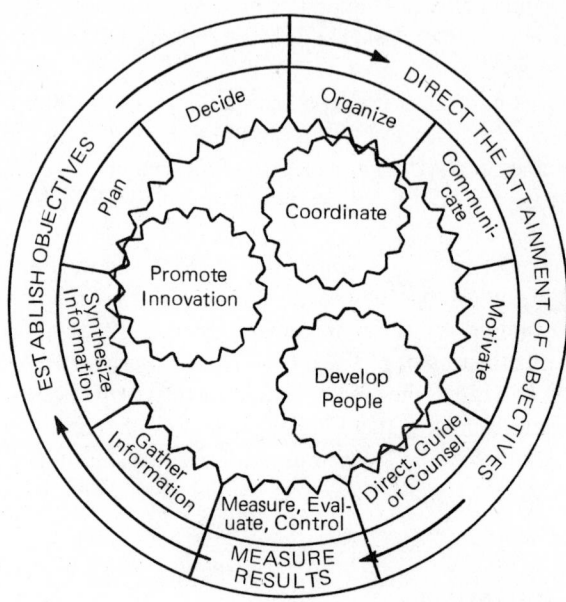

main functions are subfunctions of the three larger steps. This change in emphasis and the rationale leading to the change have brought about far-reaching changes in many of the traditional approaches to the manager's job. Several of these key changes are described in subsequent sections of this article.

Not the least of these changes has been the major distinction established between "running" a business and "managing" a business. Those who run a business are usually frantically busy doing many different things—often working excessively long hours—and hoping that something will happen. Those who manage a business make things happen by deciding what they should be doing and then lining up all of their resources and actions to make it happen. The latter are usually in control of their operations while the former frequently have operations which are out of control.

Management Styles

Twenty years of MBO experience have demonstrated that MBO enjoys a better chance for success if its practitioners follow a particular management style. The more successful companies have been those whose management can be characterized by a balanced, participative style, one which encourages maximum participation while discouraging permissiveness. For obvious reasons, MBO will be least successful with an autocratic management. While MBO can achieve some measure of success in a bureaucratic atmosphere, its effectiveness will be greatly decreased by the excess of red tape, controls, and procedures.

The balanced, participative style is usually defined as one in which the maximum number of the following attributes is actually practiced in a maximum degree:

In-depth delegation
Maximum participation in the objective setting and planning processes
Managers permitted to make some mistakes
Change encouraged and planned for
Policies and procedures minimal and subject to change when necessary
Controls tight but only the minimum imposed to keep the unit in control
A meaningful reward system
A high degree of self-management, self-discipline, and self-control on the part of managers.

Experience has proven that MBO cannot be successfully foisted on the wrong management style. The entire management style and approach must be supportive of MBO or it will not reach its success potential.

Increased Use of Behavioral Sciences

More and more, MBO is raising the status of behavioral scientists from mere voices crying in the wilderness to valuable and recognized members of the management process. According to the author's concept, management thinking passed through three stages of development on its way to the fourth stage, the MBO system.

Stage 1—Stage 1 was exemplified by the birth and adoption of the so-called "scientific management" approach. This stage relied heavily on a more impersonal approach to managing people, and was characterized by emphasis on standards, work measurement, and methods improvements. Its leading advocates were Taylor and the Gilbreths.

Stage 2—This stage, a swing to paying more attention to the human or personal factor in managing people, was a natural outgrowth of the emphasis on the impersonal approach of Stage 1. Much of the thinking of Stage 2 can be attributed to Elton Mayo and those who follow his work.

Stage 3—Stage 3 can be described as an era of discontinuity—an era in which a sizable chasm developed between the purists, who advocated the scientific management approach (frequently the hard-nosed production managers who looked

down their noses at behavioral scientists whom they frequently regarded as social-
ist theorizers), and the behavioral scientists, who often regarded scientific managers as hard-nosed profit-seekers with inadequate regard for the human factor
and with little appreciation of the how and why of motivating people.

Stage 4—The end of Stage 3 came in the late 1950s. The move to participative
management within the MBO system started a narrowing of the gap between
impersonal and personal management approaches. MBO, while continuing to emphasize the importance of achieving the necessary objectives of the organization,
also placed a premium on marshalling and directing all of the human assets toward those objectives. Applications of the behavioral sciences were evident. This
trend continues to grow as MBO serves increasingly as a marrying agent.

Increasing Use of Staff Managers

Prior to MBO, the staff manager was frequently regarded as a necessary evil, as
one who dealt with intangibles which could not be measured. Often he received
neither the opportunity to make a profit-oriented contribution nor acceptance and
recognition for his accomplishments when they were achieved.

The advanced applications of MBO now permit staff managers to write
measurable objectives, to measure rather finitely their contributions against their
objectives, to receive deserved recognition in the process, and to take their proper
place as members of the profit-making team. With staff managers currently averaging 20 to 40 percent of an organization's total manpower budget, their increased utilization must be credited as being one of MBO's greater contributions.
While some organizations have been slow to bring staff managers into the MBO
system, the number which now consider staff managers as an integral part of
MBO is steadily increasing.[4]

Appraising Managers

One of the most dramatic changes brought about by MBO has been its impact on
measuring managerial performance. MBO has been instrumental in a three-stage
progression concerning managerial appraisals.

Stage 1 (pre-MBO) was a period in which the emphasis was on measuring
performance by rating traits; Stage 2 switched the emphasis to measurement
based primarily on achievement of preset objectives; and Stage 3 concentrates on
measures designed to evaluate managers both on the degree to which objectives
were achieved and on how efficiently the objectives were achieved. Table 1 highlights the major characteristics of each of these stages.[5]

---

4. See Dale D. McConkey, *Management by Objectives for Staff Managers* (New York: Vantage Press, 1972).
5. For an in-depth discussion of the third stage, see Harold Koontz, *Appraising Managers as Managers* (New York:
American Management Association, 1972).

Table 1   HISTORY OF APPROACHES TO MANAGERIAL APPRAISAL

STAGE 1 Measuring by Traits Pre-MBO	STAGE 2 Measuring by Objectives 1955-72	STAGE 3 Measuring by Objectives and Efficiency 1972-
Emphasis was on measuring managers based on trait factors, such as health, initiative, loyalty, punctuality, and grasp of function.	Emphasis was on measuring managers based on degree to which they achieved, or failed to achieve, their objectives.	Emphasis was on objectives and how efficiently managers achieved their objectives.
This was an extremely weak approach because it was not related to results which the manager achieved.	This was a much better approach as it was results-oriented. However, it emphasized effectiveness: were the objectives achieved or not? It failed to consider efficiency: was the achievement based on good management practices?	This has the added advantage of coupling effectiveness (were the objectives achieved?) with efficiency: did the manager accomplish the results by luck or by sound management?

Job Description

MBO has all but eliminated the traditional job description which catalogued what the company required of the job—not of the manager in the job. The emphasis in MBO descriptions is on the manager because the system recognizes that it is the man who makes the job in the managerial ranks (see Table 2 for a comparison of the differences between the traditional and the MBO job description and Table 3 for an illustration of what an MBO job description should be).

It is not possible to overemphasize the importance of the document which describes the manager's accountability. This document serves as the basis for evaluating the manager's performance, for rewarding him, and for gauging the countless other actions relating to individual performance. The total of all these activities determines the future of the total entity.

Compensation Practices

MBO has had a pronounced impact on compensation practices, both in the basis on which payments are made and in the form the payments take.

Basis for Compensating—Prior to the widespread adoption of MBO, it was quite common for compensation to be based on so-called "merit" principles.

Table 2   COMPARISON OF TRADITIONAL AND MBO JOB DESCRIPTIONS

	Traditional	MBO
Major thrust	Heavily oriented to long statements of activities	Oriented to objectives
Change factor	Seldom changes unless major function is added or subtracted from the job	Objectives portion changes at least once each year
Priorities	Lack of change precludes recognizing changing priorities	Changing priorities are recognized through changing objectives
Improvement	Lack of recognition of change precludes inclusion of improvement as a factor	Continual improvement can be programmed into the changing objectives
Orientation	Heavily job-tailored; frequently ignores the man and differences in men	Man-tailored; individual strengths can be capitalized on

Table 3   EXAMPLE OF MBO JOB DESCRIPTION

JOB TITLE: Vice-President and General Manager, Operating Division B

PURPOSE
Management of Division B to achieve growth and profits according to approved plans

RESPONSIBILITIES (relatively stable from year to year)
1. Planning to achieve long- and short-term objectives
2. Monitoring the efficient execution of approved plans
3. Development and administration of division policy and procedures and of standards of performance; implementation of corporate policies and procedures
4. Marketing for Division B services
5. Operations —Maintenance
         —Job quality
         —Safety
         —Efficiency
         —Equipment design and construction supervision
6. Personnel and financial services not provided by corporate office

ACCOUNTABILITY
1. Achieve pretax return of 11 percent on capital employed
2. Achieve minimum sales of $27 million
3. Achieve pretax profit of $3 million
4. Increase profit contribution at division level by 4 percent over 1972
5. Develop at least one new product with potential sales volume of $100,000 annually

However, merit was a highly elusive term, and few organizations succeeded in realizing it in actual practice. Too often, for example, merit became synonymous with longevity. Invariably, there was a tenuous connection between a manager's compensation and the results he achieved or the contribution he made.

As often as not, compensation plans did everything possible to destroy the prime objectives of compensation: promoting equity and motivation. Rewards which were not tied to specific results—and were not given to the manager in proportion to the results he achieved—could hardly be considered equitable or a motivating force to encourage better performance. MBO has precipitated fundamental changes by insisting that compensation be tied closely to achievement of objectives and paid in proportion to the degree to which the objectives are achieved or exceeded.

Form of Payments—Incentive compensation, in one form or another, has been around for many years, but it remained for MBO to give real meaning and purpose to its use. Formerly, incentive payments were often limited to a small percentage of an organization's top managers and were usually handed out on a profit-sharing basis in which payments were related more to total organizational performance than to the individual performance of the manager. This too has changed. The percentage of managers covered by incentive plans is on the increase.

Incentive payments are viewed more and more from the standpoint of the contribution of the individual manager. Even though the company as a whole may have enjoyed record profits, there is no guarantee that the individual manager will share in the bonanza. Emphasis is placed on his individual record (results).

Recognizing the limitations imposed by salary payments (fixed vs. variable compensation costs, inability to recognize wide swings in individual performance, and the failure of salaries to emphasize a direct tie-in with profitability), many companies are stressing variable incentive payments over straight salaries. The group of managers whose total compensation contains a significant amount of incentive compensation is definitely enlarging. Arch Patton, a leading researcher on executive compensation, has stated that a successful MBO system in the United States seems to require an incentive plan for sound ongoing administration.[6]

Thus, MBO has reoriented the basis of compensation from nebulous merit to results, changed the emphasis of payments from salary to incentives, and increased the number of managers participating in incentive plans. Of at least equal importance in the rewards process, MBO has provided the possibility for recognizing contributions when promotion time arrives.

Planning

Probably no other aspect of the management process has received such a substantial jolt from MBO as planning has. Formerly, planning was "an exercise in

---

6. Arch Patton, "Does Performance Appraisal Work," *Business Horizons*, Vol. XVI (February 1973), p. 89.

writing" tolerated to satisfy the company's requirements; now, its value and help to the individual manager is increasingly appreciated. More important, the manager recognizes the real need for planning. He can appreciate why it is necessary.

Edward Green, one of the authorities in the area of corporate planning, has compared what he terms the traditional approach to planning with the more modern approach, which is markedly oriented toward MBO. Table 4 outlines Green's comparision.

Delegation

MBO has at last brought real meaning to the definition of delegation. Formerly, delegation was defined as "getting things done through other people." This wholly inadequate definition failed to recognize that "things" can be good, bad, or indifferent. Unfortunately, the much-touted delegation was approached in the same inadequate fashion.

Now delegation is approached in a manner which is conducive to more positive results. Under MBO, a subordinate is not told to go out and do something or to get things done. Instead, he is delegated specific objectives or end results for which he is accountable. Both he and his boss know the specific end results which he must achieve.

One of the cardinal mandates of MBO is that the manager must have sufficient authority to accomplish his objectives. For the first time, in many instances, managers are receiving clear definitions of the authority they may exercise. Statements such as "he shall enjoy authority commensurate to carry out his job" are rapidly giving way to rather finite statements of authority.

The impact of MBO on the overall management process and especially its effect on delegation have provided a viable foundation for practicing participative management. Delegating by specific objectives permits a manager to determine much of his own destiny—to help set his objectives, to do much of his own planning to achieve the objectives, to operate with the authority he knows he has, and to take the initiative when corrective action is required. The emphasis on delegating end results permits participation and helps considerably in preventing permissive management.

In an era in which one of the popular buzz-words of the day is "job enrichment"—with attention so far directed almost exclusively to the employee instead of the manager—MBO has made considerable strides in enriching the manager's job. The practice of MBO in depth culminates in each manager becoming "president" of his own little "company" within the total organization. When this end is reached, the manager experiences substantial job enrichment because his destiny depends largely upon his own efforts.

Table 4   COMPARISON OF OLD AND NEW PLANNING APPROACHES

	Static Planning (Old Way)	vs.	Dynamic Planning (New Approach)
Purpose	Get a "plan"		Achieve optimum results
Basic premise	Forecasts are accurate		Future is unpredictable
Technique	Static, periodic		Dynamic, continuous
Process	Rigid, formal, prescribed		Flexible, selective adaptation
Management style	Traditional, authoritative		Decentralized, participative
Responsibility	Top management VP, planning Centralized planning staff		Every manager Director, planning services Decentralized planning coordinators

Types of planning
  Strategic
  Operational
  Logistic
	Separate plans		Integrated planning

Functional planning
  Marketing
  Financial
  Personnel, and so on
	Separate plans		Integrated planning

Time spans
  Short
  Medium
  Long-range
	Separate plans		Integrated planning

Support	Resistance and resentment		Enthusiastic participation
Durability	Tapers off to discouragement		Growing value and enthusiasm
Cost/benefits	Too much time-effort-paper Higher cost Limited benefits		Better decisions and programs Less time and effort Better results

SOURCE: Edward J. Green, "The Communication Crisis," Marshall Allan Robinson lecture, University of Pittsburgh, 1972.

Decision Making

The decision-making process also has come in for its share of change as a result of MBO. Two aspects of MBO have been causative forces in this change. The first is the feedback and data, tailored and directed to the individual manager, and the second is the structuring of strict accountability for each manager.

Feedback—Advocates of decentralization have long advocated that decisions should be made at the lowest possible level of management at which all information necessary to the decision comes together. However, the principle has been honored more in the breach than in practice.

Some of the reasons why the principle was not widely practiced concern the characteristics of the data many managers receive: an overabundance of raw data but little of the selected intelligence required for decision making; data prepared for the needs of the manager's superior instead of for the manager; and data collected for costing and revenue purposes rather than for use by the manager.

MBO places a premium on data prepared under the best principles of enlightened responsibility accounting—the right data, at the right time, at the right place, for the right manager. Now, with in-depth delegation and the proper data, decisions can be made at the lowest possible level, nearest the point of action, and at the time the action is taking place.

Accountability—Prior to MBO's requirement for strict accountability by individuals, decisions often were delayed because of what one writer has referred to as decision drift, that is, the tendency to avoid decision making when it is not clear who should make the decision. Often, the timid manager will purposely delay or ignore making a decision unless he is forced to make it. The undesirable expedient of decision making by committee often results.

MBO, by clearly defining who is accountable for what, pinpoints the manager who should make a particular decision. This has definitely lessened procrastination and avoidance of decision making.

A VIABLE APPROACH

Some Pitfalls

As noted elsewhere in this article, MBO has not been a 100 percent success. Many systems have been failures—absolute failures. Others, while not failing completely, have failed to deliver the benefits of which they are capable—failures by degree. Both types of failures have resulted from succumbing to the numerous pitfalls which can develop in the system.

The experience of various and diverse organizations over roughly twenty years has singled out a number of reasons for the failure of some organizations to make their mark with MBO.[7] The pitfalls include:

Considering MBO a panacea
Lacking participation by subordinates in setting objectives
Leaving out staff managers
Delegating executive direction of the program
Creating a "paper mill" with forms and procedures
Failing to provide feedback to the individual manager
Emphasizing techniques over the system
Implementing too quickly
Failing to reward performance
Having objectives which are not supported by adequate plans
Failing to revise the system based on experience
Being impatient for results
Endeavoring to overquantify objectives
Stressing objectives instead of the system
Dramatizing short-term objectives
Omitting periodic reviews of performance
Omitting refresher training with respect to refinements and managers new to the system
Failing to blend individual objectives into the whole
Managing without the necessary "guts"
Lacking ability or willingness to delegate.

Many of these pitfalls occur from poor initial implementation of the MBO system within the organization. Many of the outstanding MBO failures can be traced to this critical implementation stage—generally in the decision to adopt MBO in the first instance or in the manner in which the system was installed.[8]

MBO Time Shock

The progressive use of MBO within an organization has an attendant time shock to managers. F. D. Barrett, president of Management Concepts, Ltd., describes this shock feature as threefold, coming about when the manager realizes that:

Writing meaningful objectives requires several days, not just a few hours
The time required to realize the full impact of MBO is not a matter of months but a few years
A pronounced change takes place in the amount of time the manager spends actually "managing" rather than "doing." Increasingly, doing gives way to managing.[9]

7. Adapted from Dale D. McConkey, "20 Ways to Kill MBO," *The Management Review* (October 1972), pp. 4–13.
8. For an in-depth treatment of implementation, see Dale D. McConkey, "Implementation—The Guts of MBO," *Advanced Management* (July 1972), pp. 13–18.
9. F. D. Barrett, "The MBO Time Trip," *The Business Quarterly* (Autumn 1972), pp. 44–47.

Unfortunately, the impact of this time shock has been too little appreciated by some organizations, and the effectiveness of their MBO approaches has suffered. The impact of this shock—actually it is a necessary period of transition—can neither be ignored nor brought to a forced conclusion. It is as necessary and natural as the progression of a child from adolescence to adulthood. Any attempt to move too rapidly or to fail to gain from the experience arising from the requisite steps will result in an inferior development process.

FUTURE OF MBO

Since the application and impact of MBO are yet unfolding any evaluation must be a dynamic one. However, evidence to date indicates that the effect of MBO has been most dramatic—both on the overall approach to managing and on the many parts of the management process.

Probably its signal benefit has been its insistence on improving organizational effectiveness through improving the effectiveness of the individual manager. This transition has been well summarized by Barrett in his comparison between "Model A" management, pre-MBO, and "Model B" management, after MBO (see Table 5). The average organization—the author dislikes the term but is hard pressed to come up with a better description—should expect that this transition will start to take place three to five years after beginning its MBO system.

Table 5   TRANSITION IN MANAGEMENT STYLES UNDER MBO

Pre-MBO	Post-MBO
Day-to-day managing	Future-focused
Amateur, seat-of-pants	Full-fledged professional
Inward-looking	Outward-looking
Product-oriented	People-oriented
Organization-oriented	Consumer-oriented
Activities-oriented	Results-oriented
Administration of routine	Creation of innovations
Emphasis on "how to"	Emphasis on "what to"
Emphasis on money, machines, materials	Emphasis on people, minds, time
Centralized, technocratic, functional control	Decentralized initiative from subordinates
Authoritarian style	Participative style
Directives and supervision	Delegation and reporting
Individualism	Teamwork

SOURCE: Reprinted by permission of the author, F. D. Barrett, "The MBO Time Trip." *The Business Quarterly* (Autumn 1972), pp. 44-45.

MBO and its benefits are too well established, having survived the test of about twenty years of practice, to be considered a passing fancy or a fad. The system has earned its place as part of the permanent management scene. The future will bring the continued use and increased applications of MBO. Real progress remains to be made in several major areas. Managers must become more adept at setting top priorities. As all of an organization's efforts are geared through MBO to meeting top priorities, management's efforts must be directed to insuring that the most desirable priorities are selected. Otherwise, MBO causes an organization to become increasingly efficient at something it should not be doing in the first place.

Having set the optimum priorities, management must increase its competence in planning to achieve the priority objectives. Failure to develop better planning expertise will render it impossible to exploit the full potential of priority objectives.

Other areas of the MBO system necessitate continual refinement. For example, even though much excellent work has been done in relating managerial appraisal to actual contribution, more work remains to be done on this subject. Similarly, additional progress must be made to establish a more direct correlation between a manager's contributions and his rewards. The tie-in presently is not direct enough.

Lastly, the effectiveness of MBO in general will continue to suffer unless an organization's management recognizes that the key word in Management by Objectives is "Management" and not "Objectives." MBO is a whole new way of life for many organizations. It is a way of managing. Those organizations which embrace the system without recognizing this and without first examining their management philosophy and practice will continue to adopt MBO on a "planned failure" basis. Even worse, they will become easy prey for the increasing number of MBO advocates with a solution who are running around looking for a problem.

The utilization of the remarkable and continuing growth in numbers of workers in the "knowledge industry" represents another area of high potential payback from MBO. The system has much to commend it for application to these workers. The failure to align their efforts to priorities and full utilization of their talents will constitute a costly oversight for their organizations.

Experience has proven that MBO, by itself, will accomplish nothing but chaos. In the hands of a capable management which is ready for it and knows how to use it, it has much to offer. For the right management, it holds promise of a bright future.

25   Management by Objectives: The Team Approach

Wendell L. French and Robert W. Hollmann

Study of the many books, articles, case studies, speeches, and discussions about management by objectives (MBO) indicates that most forms of this approach tend to reinforce a one-to-one leadership style. It is also apparent that MBO efforts vary from being highly autocratic to highly participative among organizations and even within some organizations. In this article we present a case and strategy for *collaborative* management by objectives (CMBO), a participative, team-centered approach. This approach has a number of unique features that will minimize some of the deficiencies in more traditional versions, but as we shall see, the skills involved and the organizational climate required for its optimal effectiveness may not come easily.

ONE-TO-ONE MBO

Let us first compare the autocratic and participative characteristics of one-to-one versions of MBO. Examples 1a through 1d in Table 1 illustrate how this form can differ along the autocratic-participative continuum. In one contemporary version of MBO, the superior prepares a list of objectives and simply passes them down to the subordinate. In a second version, the superior prepares the subordinate's list of objectives and allows him or her ample opportunity for questions and clarification. In a third version, the subordinate prepares his own list of objectives and submits this list to his superior for discussion and subsequent editing and modification by the superior. And in a fourth version, the superior and subordinate independently prepare lists of the subordinate's objectives and then meet to agree upon the final list. Similar degrees of subordinate participation also can occur at other steps in the MBO process (in determination of objective measures of performance and in the end-of-the-period evaluation, for example). Obviously many variations are possible, but the point is that the different versions of one-to-one MBO can fall anywhere along the traditional autocratic-participative continuum.

Table 1 OBJECTIVE SETTING IN DIFFERENT VERSIONS OF MBO

Degree of Subordinate Influence on Objectives	Very Little	Some	Moderate	Considerable
	1a	**1b**	**1c**	**1d**
Individual Orientation	Superior prepares list of sub-ordinate's objectives and gives it to subordinate.	Superior prepares list of sub-ordinate's objectives; allows opportunity for clarification and suggestions.	Subordinate prepares list of his objectives; superior-subordi-nate discussion of tentative list is followed by editing, modi-fication, and finalization by superior.	Superior and subordinate inde-pendently prepare list of sub-ordinate's objectives; mutual agreement reached after ex-tensive dialogue.
	2a	**2b**	**2c**	**2d**
Team Orientation	Superior prepares individual lists of various subordinates' objectives; hands out lists in group meeting and explains objectives.	Superior prepares unit and indivi-dual objectives; allows oppor-tunity for questions and sugges-tions in group meeting.	Superior prepares list of unit ob-jectives which are discussed in group meeting; superior de-cides. Subordinates then pre-pare lists of their objectives, discuss with superior; indivi-duals' objectives discussed in team meeting with modifica-tions made by superior after extensive dialogue.	Unit objectives, including team effectiveness goals, are devel-oped among superior, subordi-nates, and peers in a group meeting, usually by consensus; superior and subordinates later independently prepare lists of subordinates' objectives, reach temporary agreement; subordi-nates' objectives finalized after extensive discussion in team meeting.

DEFICIENCIES IN ONE-TO-ONE MBO

Disregarding the likely long-range inadequacies of any autocratic form of MBO, we believe that the one-to-one mode has a number of critical deficiencies. First, one-to-one MBO does not adequately account for the interdependent nature of most jobs, particularly at the managerial and supervisory levels. Second, it does not assure optimal coordination of objectives. And third, it does not always improve superior-subordinate relationships, as is widely claimed by MBO proponents (we do not know whether a team approach always will improve relations either, but we are much more optimistic about the latter). These deficiencies pertain to all versions of one-to-one MBO, regardless of how autocratic or participative, although we believe that the deficiencies would be more salient under autocratic supervisory behavior. Let us examine these limitations more closely.

Managerial interdependence

A number of writers have pointed out that one-to-one, superior-subordinate MBO does not recognize the interdependent or complementary nature of managerial jobs.[1] We concur with this criticism and believe that effective implementation of MBO requires a "systems view" of the organization. Each manager functions in a complex network of vertical, horizontal, and diagonal relationships, and his success in achieving his objectives is often (if not always) dependent upon the communication, cooperation, and support of other managers in this network.

The relevance of managerial interdependence is particularly evident when MBO is used with staff managers. A number of authors have described the difficulties in applying MBO to staff positions.[2] We need not reiterate their ideas here, except to stress the point that the advisory and supportive nature of staff work dictates that a staff manager's objectives be highly interrelated with the activities and objectives of other managers, both line and staff. Furthermore, staff objectives are often more qualitative than quantitative, and therefore more difficult to set and measure. Asking the staff manager to set either qualitative or quantitative objectives in isolation from those upon whom his attainment of these objectives is largely dependent does not make good sense.

An indication of the lack of attention to the interdependent nature of managerial jobs can be found in two recent works, one including descriptions of MBO programs in four British firms,[3] the other including five American companies.[4] Eight of the nine companies require that forms be filled out in the MBO programs, but in only one company's form is there any space for the manager to specify the extent to which his objectives require involvement of other managers.

Coordination of objectives

Another deficiency is associated with this interdependency. One of the highly touted advantages of MBO is that it results in effective coordination of objectives;

that is, there is better integration (including minimization of gaps and duplication) of the objectives of all managers in the work unit. While this is certainly a desirable benefit, it must be recognized that one-to-one MBO places the responsibility for such coordination entirely upon the superior, since he is the only person in the MBO process to have formal contact with all subordinate managers. In effect, the superior is required to function as a "central processing center of objectives."

We believe that one-to-one MBO simply does not provide the opportunity for maximum coordination of objectives. The superior may be able to marginally, or even adequately, coordinate the objectives of his immediate subordinates on a one-to-one basis, but this procedure does not really do justice to the subtleties of interdependent relationships. Under such circumstances, except for information transmitted informally and sporadically between peers in on-the-job interaction, subordinate managers have little knowledge or understanding of each other's objectives. On the other hand, if these subordinates were provided with the opportunity for dynamic interactive processes in which their objectives are systematically communicated and adjusted, final objectives probably would be more effectively coordinated.

The deficiency in the coordination of objectives is magnified in cases of managers performing highly interrelated tasks but working in different departments. For example, a sales manager in a marketing division organized along product lines needs to coordinate his objectives with those of the appropriate production manager responsible for manufacturing the product. The sales manager may meet his objective of a 5-percent increase in the sales of product X, but the organization is likely to suffer a loss of future sales and customers if the manufacturing output of product X, which is based upon the production manager's objectives, is inadequate to meet these sales commitments. One-to-one MBO between the sales and production managers and their respective superiors provides no systematic method for integrating their objectives, and accordingly, these two managers must rely entirely upon their own initiative for the development of integrative mechanisms. Quite frankly, we doubt that this haphazard approach results in optimal coordination.

Improved superior-subordinate relationships

The participative, or mutual involvement, form of one-to-one MBO is extolled largely for the improvement in superior-subordinate relationships it is expected to bring about. Not all research supports this claim, however. For example, Tosi and Carroll found that even after an intensive and carefully planned MBO program that stressed subordinate participation, subordinate managers did not feel that the superior-subordinate relationship had improved significantly in terms of helpfulness on the part of the superior.[5] While the researchers offered no specific empirical reasons for this finding, other authors have suggested factors that might provide some explanation.

Kerr believes that the typical organization hierarchy creates a superior-subordinate status differential that acts as a deterrent to the expected improvement in relationships.[6] For instance, when MBO is conducted in a somewhat autocratic manner the status differential inhibits the subordinate from challenging the decisions of his boss or the objectives he has established. Even in cases of greater subordinate involvement, status differences may hinder attainment of the desired ideal mutuality in the MBO process. A similar note is struck by Levinson, who believes that rivalry between a boss and his subordinate can easily impede the creation or maintenance of a positive relationship.[7] It is important to point out that Tosi and Carroll also found that the same MBO program stressing increased subordinate participation resulted in no significant increase in subordinates' perceived influence in the goal-setting process.[8] Perhaps superior-subordinate status differentials or rivalry were operating in this organization.

Incompatibility between the superior's role as a coach and his role as a judge may also hamper the superior-subordinate relationship. Researchers at The General Electric Company concluded that the two primary purposes of performance appraisal (performance improvement and salary adjustment) are in conflict.[9] They suggested that these two purposes could be better accomplished in two separate interviews—a proposal with which we agree. Yet even in this approach, it is easy to see the difficult position in which the superior is placed: prior to and during one interview he is expected to *constructively* evaluate the subordinate's performance and help him formulate plans for improvement, while in the second interview he is expected to *judiciously* evaluate the subordinate's performance in order to make crucial salary recommendations and to inform the subordinate of his decision. Only an exceptionally talented person could shift adroitly between these two roles (especially with the same subordinate), and it is our opinion that most managers have great difficulty doing so. Thus, an MBO program that requires the superior to have complete responsibility in performing these incompatible roles, even in separate interviews, could easily strain rather than improve superior-subordinate relationships.

TEAM COLLABORATION IN MBO

We believe that MBO could be strengthened considerably by increasing the opportunities for systematic collaboration among managers. Furthermore, MBO programs based on cooperative teamwork and group problem solving would represent a positive step toward rectifying some of the deficiencies found in one-to-one MBO. Ironically, in his original description of MBO, Drucker said, "Right from the start . . . emphasis should be on team-work and team results,"[10] but it doesn't look to us as if the MBO movement has gone this way. A number of other authors have called for group or peer goal setting and evaluation in MBO,[11] but with few exceptions,[12] suggestions for a group approach to MBO generally have not been augmented with systematic guidelines or frameworks for implementation.

MBO programs described in the literature and in operation that *do* acknowledge the collaborative dimension can be classified in three categories. First, there are programs that superficially refer to the need for some sort of collaborative effort during the MBO process. For example, the MBO instruction manual may include a statement such as: "Each manager should exert maximum effort to ensure that his objectives are effectively coordinated with those of other managers in his work group." Under this unsystematic approach, then, collaboration is left entirely to each manager's own initiative.

Second, there are programs that provide some formal means for collaboration (see examples 2b and 2c in Table 1). For instance, Wikstrom describes one company program that includes "cross-checking meetings" in which managers present their tentative goals, check the impact of these goals on one another, and make adjustments before finalizing the goals.[13] In a similar vein, Raia suggests team reviews between the superior and his subordinates.[14] Based upon a joint problem-solving approach, these regular review sessions are intended to measure the team's progress toward its goals and to improve team relationships. Raia also encourages the use of a "responsibility matrix" to identify the degree to which various other management positions are related to the major activities a manager performs to accomplish his specific objectives.[15] In essence, then, programs in this second category include collaboration as a tangential aspect of an essentially one-to-one approach.

Third, there are MBO programs that include systematic collaboration as an integral part of the entire process (see example 2d in Table 1). The three-day team objectives meeting described by Reddin illustrates this approach.[16] In this program each team (superior and his immediate subordinates) concentrates on such matters as team-effectiveness areas, team-improvement objectives, team decision making, optimal team organization, team meeting improvements, team-effectiveness evaluation, and team-member effectiveness. Such collaborative approaches appear to have many features congruent with contemporary organization development (OD) and are qualitatively quite different from one-to-one approaches.

MBO AND OD CONTRASTED

One way to describe how CMBO differs qualitatively from a one-to-one approach is to contrast the one-to-one version with the emerging field of OD, which has a strong emphasis on team collaboration. Organization development, in the behavioral-science meaning of the term,[17] is a broader strategy for organizational improvement than is MBO, but it can include the collaborative version as we shall describe it. For instance, Blake and Mouton's six-phase grid OD program in-

Table 2 TRADITIONAL MBO COMPARED WITH OD

What Traditional (One-to-One) MBO Seems to Do	What OD Seems to Do
1. Assumes there is a need for more goal emphasis and/or control.	1. Assumes there may be a variety of problems; a need for more goal emphasis and/or control may or may not be a central problem.
2. Has no broad diagnostic strategy.	2. Uses an "action-research" model in which system diagnosis and rediagnosis are major features.
3. Central target of change is the individual.	3. Central target of change is team functioning.
4. Asks organization members to develop objectives for key aspects of their jobs in terms of quantitative and qualitative statements that can be measured.	4. Asks organization members to provide data regarding their perceptions of functional/dysfunctional aspects of their units and/or the total organization.
5. Emphasizes avoidance of overlap and incongruity of goals. Assumes things will be better if people understand who has what territory.	5. Emphasizes mutual support and help. Assumes that some problems can stem from confusion about who has what responsibilities, but also looks at opportunities for mutual help in the many interdependent components across jobs.
6. Focuses on the "formal" aspects of the organization (goals, planning, control, appraisal).	6. Initially taps into "informal" aspects of the organization (attitudes, feelings, perceptions about both the formal and informal aspects—the total climate of the unit or organization).
7. Focuses on individual performance and emphasizes individual accountability.	7. Focuses on system dynamics that are facilitating or handicapping individual, team, and organizational performance; emphasizes joint accountability.
8. Stresses rationality ("logical" problem solving, man's economic motives).	8. Legitimizes for discussion nonrational aspects (feelings, attitudes, group phenomena) of organization life as well as rationality; frequently legitimizes open exploration of career and life goals.
9. Focuses on organizational end results of the human-social system (particularly as measured by "hard data") such as sales figures, maintenance costs, and so forth.	9. Focuses on both ends and means of the human-social system (leadership style, peer relationships, and decision processes, as well as goals and "hard data").
10. Has little interpersonal-relations "technology" to assist superior and subordinate in the goal-setting and review processes.	10. Has extensive interpersonal relations, group dynamics, and intergroup "technology" for decision making, communications, and group task and maintenance processes.

cludes teamwork development (phase 2) and intergroup development (phase 3), both of which include collaborative goal setting.[18] In fact, they suggest that MBO can be "introduced as the culminating action of Teamwork Development."[19]

Some of the differences, as we see them, between the traditional one-to-one MBO and OD are shown in Table 2. Traditional MBO concentrates on the individual, on goal setting for the individual, on rationality, and on end results. In contrast, OD focuses on how individuals see the functioning of their teams and the organization, on nonrationality, as well as rationality, and on means as well as ends. In addition, OD has a recurring component of system diagnosis that seems to be minimal or absent from the traditional forms of MBO. Further, OD efforts usually move toward legitimizing open discussion of individual career and life goals, which most MBO programs largely ignore.

A STRATEGY FOR COLLABORATIVE MBO

Contemporary organization-development efforts can provide insights and some of the technology for more widespread emergence of collaborative forms of MBO. We would like to propose a nine-phase strategy for Collaborative MBO. Basically, the essential process is one of overlapping work units interacting with "higher" and "lower" units on overall organizational goals and objectives, unit goals and objectives, and individuals interacting with peers and superiors on role definition and individual goals and objectives.

Phase I: Diagnosis of Organizational Problems
A collaborative organizational diagnosis, by discussions or questionnaires involving a cross-section of organization members, suggests the usefulness of a CMBO effort in solving *identified problems*. It appears to us that MBO, as frequently practiced, is a solution in search of a problem. For a variety of reasons, including the existence of a strong goal emphasis under some other name, overwork of many key people in the organization, or problems requiring other solutions, MBO may not be timely or appropriate.

Phase II: Information and Dialogue
Workshops on the basic purposes and techniques of CMBO are held with top management personnel, followed by workshops at the middle- and lower-management levels. These workshops can be conducted by qualified members of the personnel or training departments, by line managers trained in the approach, or if the organization prefers, by a qualified consultant. Having top-level managers conduct the workshops with middle and lower managers may speed up the process of shifting toward the more supportive climate necessary for CMBO.

Phase III: Diagnosis of Organizational Readiness

This diagnosis, based upon interviews and group meetings, must indicate an interest in and a willingness to use the process on the part of several organizational units, especially those at the top of the organization. Ideally, a number of over-lapping units should express a desire to implement CMBO; for example, in addition to the president of a manufacturing firm and his immediate subordinates expressing interest, the manufacturing director and his immediate subordinates may want to be involved, and two of these subordinate managers may wish to start the process with their subordinate teams, and so forth. Favorable interest in CMBO from a few units randomly scattered throughout the organization would probably be inadequate to create enough interaction and momentum to give the approach a fair try. A good deal of diagnosis of organizational readiness will have already occurred in the information-and-dialogue phase. Similarly, diagnosis of organizational readiness may reveal the need for supplemental CMBO work-shops for some units or for suspending the CMBO effort.

Phase IV: Goal Setting—Overall Organization Level

Overall organization goals and specific objectives to be achieved within a given time period are defined in team meetings among top executives, largely on the basis of consensus. It is important that this phase be an interactive process with middle and lower levels of the organization; inputs about organization goals and objectives from subordinate managerial and supervisory levels must be obtained during (or before) this phase.

Phase V: Goal Setting—Unit Level

Unit goals and objectives essential to achieving overall organization goals and objectives are defined in team situations, largely by consensus. Again, this is an interactive process between higher units and their respective subordinate units.

Phase VI: Goal Setting—Individual Level

This phase begins with individual managers developing their specific objectives in terms of results to be achieved and appropriate time periods. Personal career and development goals are part of this "package." If desired, the manager's superior may simultaneously develop a list of objectives for the subordinate. The superior and subordinate discuss, modify, and tentatively agree on the subordi-nate's objectives. These discussions are followed by group meetings in which team members discuss each other's objectives, make suggestions for modification, and agree upon each manager's final list of objectives.

Phase VI assumes that there is agreement on the major responsibilities and parameters of the team members' roles. If major responsibilities need to be re-viewed or redefined, the following sequence is used as the preliminary stage of phase VI: (1) individual team members list their major responsibilities; (2) individual team members meet with their superior to discuss, modify, and tentatively agree upon their major responsibilities; and (3) team members discuss and work toward consensus on their major responsibilities in group meetings.

Phase VII: Performance Review

On a continuing basis, either the subordinate or the superior initiates discussion whenever progress toward objectives should be reviewed; matters of team concern are discussed in regularly scheduled team meetings. Particularly relevant at this stage are occasions when internal or external factors suggest the need for revision in the original set of goals and objectives; if appropriate, these revisions should be made in collaborative team meetings.

At the end of the agreed-upon time period, each manager prepares a report on the extent to which his objectives have been achieved and discusses this report in a preliminary meeting with his superior. These reports then are presented by each individual in a group meeting, with the discussion including an analysis of the forces helping and hindering attainment of objectives. This review process occurs at all levels (organization, unit, and individual) and ordinarily would start at the lower levels as a convenient way to collate information.

Phase VIII: Rediagnosis

Diagnosis needs to reoccur, but at this phase it is the CMBO process itself that needs examining, as well as the readiness of additional units to use CMBO. Is the CMBO process helping? hindering? in what way? What is the process doing to the relationships between superiors and subordinates and within teams? Something has gone awry if goal setting and performance review are perfunctory or avoided, if the process seems unattached to the basic processes of getting the work of the organization done, or if relationships are becoming strained. On the other hand, if superiors and subordinates and teams find that the process is challenging and stretches and develops their capabilities, and if they feel good about it, the CMBO process is probably on the right track toward increased organizational effectiveness. Ideally such diagnosis should be ongoing as the CMBO process evolves.

Phase IX: Recycle

Assuming that rediagnosis has resulted in the decision to continue the CMBO effort, the cycle of phases IV through VIII is repeated, probably once a year at the overall organization level. Ongoing individual and team progress reviews may result in modification of unit- or individual-level goals more often than once a year. Through periodic problem sensing and rediagnosis, the details of the process will undoubtedly be modified to more adequately meet the needs of teams and individuals. The nine-phase strategy for implementing CMBO is presented in Figure 1.

Figure 1   A STRATEGY FOR IMPLEMENTING COLLABORATIVE MANAGEMENT BY OBJECTIVES

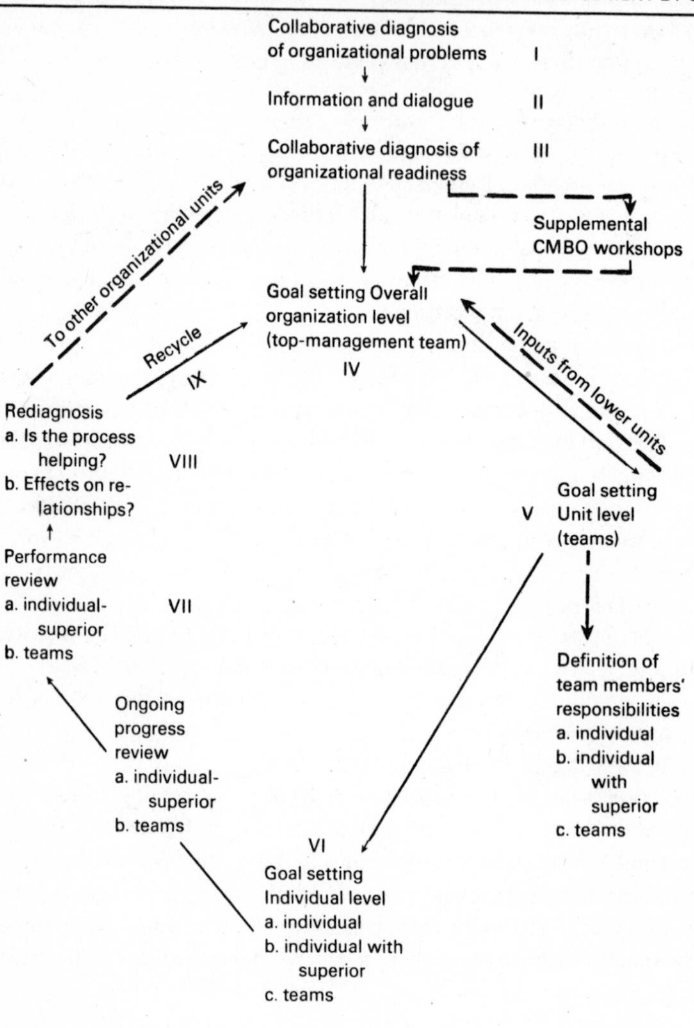

Collaborative diagnosis
of organizational problems   I
↓
Information and dialogue   II
↓
Collaborative diagnosis of   III
organizational readiness

Supplemental
CMBO workshops

To other organizational units

Recycle
IX

Goal setting Overall
organization level
(top-management team)
IV

Inputs from lower units

Rediagnosis
a. Is the process
   helping?   VIII
b. Effects on re-
   lationships?
↑
Performance
review
a. individual-   VII
   superior
b. teams

Goal setting
V   Unit level
     (teams)

Ongoing
progress
review
a. individual-
   superior
b. teams

Definition of
team members'
responsibilities
a. individual
b. individual
   with
   superior
c. teams

VI
Goal setting
Individual level
a. individual
b. individual with
   superior
c. teams

SOME CONTINGENCIES

CMBO is not likely to be an easy process for many organizations. Initial successes depend upon a strong desire on the part of the top-management team to cooperate with and help each other. In addition, the process requires some modicum of skill in interpersonal relations and group dynamics. Training in these skills can accompany the CMBO effort, or if an OD effort is under way, such skills will be emerging as part of this broader process.

Proper timing in the introduction of CMBO is also very important. CMBO is by no means a managerial panacea; it should be introduced only when diagnosis suggests its applicability and usefulness as well as organizational readiness. A CMBO effort can be time-consuming, and strong resistance can occur if the process is thoughtlessly superimposed at the wrong time—for example, during a period when people are preoccupied and harried with the annual budgeting process or faced with a major external threat to the organization. It is equally important to recognize that the utility of diagnosing organizational readiness is contingent upon the adequacy of information presented to managers in the CMBO work-shops (phase II).

Successful expansion of the process to lower levels of the organization requires commitment to and skills in participative management, as well as a willingness and ability to diagnose the impact of the goal-setting and review processes on or-ganization members and organizational functioning. Such a diagnosis of how things are going might result, for instance, in temporarily postponing phase VI. Successful completion of phases I through V and the appropriate team aspects of phases VII through IX might in itself be a major achievement and a move forward in organizational effectiveness. Developing effective group dynamics takes time and an organization should proceed with caution in this area. A major shift to a col-laborative mode cannot be made overnight.

THE MERITS OF CMBO:
RESEARCH AND PRACTICE CLUES

There are a number of clues to the merits of a Collaborative MBO approach (that is, the kind that has a team emphasis, is truly collaborative, and exists in a climate of mutual support and help) in research reports and in practice. Likert cites a study of a sales organization in which salesmen held group meetings at regular intervals to set goals, discuss procedures, and identify results to be achieved before the next group meeting.[20] During these meetings the superior acted as a chair-man; he stressed a constructive, problem-solving approach, encouraged high performance, and provided technical advice when necessary. The results of the study showed that salesmen using group meetings had more positive attitudes toward their jobs and sold more on the average than salesmen not using group meetings. According to Likert:

Appreciably poorer results are achieved whenever the manager, himself, analyzes each man's performance and results and sets goals for him. Such man-to-man interactions in the meetings, dominated by the manager, do not create group loyalty and have far less favorable impact upon the salesmen's motivation than do group interaction and decision meetings. Moreover, in the man-to-man interaction little use is made of the sales knowledge and skills of the group.[21]

Another recent study found that managers' perceptions of the supportiveness of the organizational climate and their attitudes toward MBO were significantly related.[22] A supportive climate was viewed in terms of such features as high levels of trust and confidence between superiors and subordinates, multidirectional communication aimed at achieving objectives, cooperative teamwork, subordinate participation in decision making and goal setting, and control conducted close to the point of performance (self-control). Essentially, this climate was seen as comparable to Likert's Participative Group (System 4) management system.[23] The results of the study showed significant ($p < 0.01$) positive correlations between the supportiveness of the climate and how effective managers believed the MBO process to be. Managers' evaluations of MBO effectiveness were assessed in six areas: (1) planning and organizing work, (2) objective evaluation of performance, (3) motivation of the best job performance, (4) coordination of individual and work-group objectives, (5) superior-subordinate communication, and (6) superior-subordinate cooperation. Even more important was the significant ($p < 0.01$) positive correlation between supportiveness of the climate and managers' overall satisfaction with MBO as it related to their jobs.[24]

Holder describes how consensus decision making has been used at Yellow Freight System, Inc. since the early 1950s.[25] Work groups in the firm are organized according to the "linking-pin concept"[26] and decisions, including those dealing with managers' objectives, are made on a consensus basis within each work group. The writer's account is unclear as to whether consensus MBO operates throughout the management hierarchy; however, his description indicates that it extends to at least the regional-manager level. Although Holder provides no objective measure of effectiveness, he suggests that the length of time for which the program has been used attests to its success.

Finally, in explaining a job-enrichment program in a European chemical company, Myers reports: "In 1970, more than 40,000 additional employees conferred in work teams and functional groups to define criteria against which their performance could be measured and to set tangible goals."[27] According to Myers, the program has (a) moved decision making down to the levels where the work is performed, (b) resulted in better integration of individual and organizational goals, (c) required managers to rely upon interpersonal competence rather than official authority to get results, and (d) reduced the traditional barrier between management and nonmanagement. We think this experience is particularly significant; if operative work groups can effectively set objectives in a collaborative environment, it seems reasonable to expect that managers would also be able to do so.

CONCLUSIONS

The findings of these studies and organizational programs help confirm our belief that Collaborative Management by Objectives can work. We feel that CMBO, as we have described it, is congruent with a participative, team-leadership style and can avoid many of the dysfunctional spinoffs of the prevailing one-to-one versions of MBO. We do not wish to imply, however, that CMBO will work in all organizations and under any circumstances. Care must be taken to ensure that appropriate conditions are present before and that necessary skills emerge during the implementation of CMBO.

Successful application of CMBO requires that managers be motivated to shift the climate of the organization, or at least the climate of those units using CMBO, in the direction of more teamwork, more cooperation, more joint problem solving, and more support. While a team approach per se would tend to diminish the dysfunctional consequences of status differentials and could shift the locus of commitments among people away from the one-to-one arena toward the lateral or interdependent team arena, a team approach void of mutual support and group skills could create more problems than it would solve. Training of work teams in skills of communication, group processes, and joint problem solving is vital to this shift toward a more supportive climate.

Equally vital to the success of CMBO are skills in diagnosis—both the original diagnosis that identifies the need and readiness for CMBO and the subsequent diagnoses that tune into managers' perceptions of the functional and dysfunctional aspects of the CMBO process and their assessment of the emerging climate. Such continuous "tracking" will be hard work, but the resulting opportunities for modification and other corrective action should make the CMBO process that much more relevant to the needs of the organization and its members.

The nine-phase strategy we have proposed is one way of introducing more systematic collaboration into the MBO process. While it will undoubtedly take considerable effort and attention to make the CMBO strategy work well, this approach can help people, teams, and units become more goal-directed without undermining efforts to maintain or create a participative, responsive team climate in the organization.

REFERENCES

1. See, for example, Gerard F. Carvalho, "Installing Management by Objectives: A New Perspective on Organization Change," *Human Resource Management* (Spring 1972), pp. 23–30; Robert A. Howell, "A Fresh Look at Management by Objectives," *Business Horizons* (Fall 1967), pp. 51–58; Charles L. Hughes, "Assessing the Perfor-

mance of Key Managers," *Personnel* (January-February 1968), pp. 38–43; Bruce D. Jamieson, "Behavioral Problems with Management by Objectives," *Academy of Management Journal* (September 1973), pp. 496–505; Harold Koontz, "Making Managerial Appraisal Effective," *California Management Review* (Winter 1972), pp. 46–55; and Harry Levinson, "Management by Whose Objectives?" *Harvard Business Review* (July-August 1970), pp. 125–134.

2. See, for example, Thomas P. Kleber, "The Six Hardest Areas to Manage by Objectives," *Personnel Journal* (August 1972), pp. 571–575; Dale D. McConkey, "Staff Objectives Are Different," *Personnel Journal* (July 1972), p. 477 ff;   and Burt K. Scanlan, "Quantifying the Qualifiable, or Can Results Management Be Applied to the Staff Man's Job?" *Personnel Journal* (March 1968), p. 162 ff.

3. John W. Humble, ed., *Management by Objectives in Action* (New York: McGraw-Hill, 1970).

4. Walter S. Wikstrom, *Managing by- and with-Objectives* (New York: National Industrial Conference Board, 1968).

5. Henry Tosi and Stephen J. Carroll, Jr., "Improving Management by Objectives: A Diagnostic Change Program," *California Management Review* (Fall 1973), pp. 57–66.

6. Steven Kerr, "Some Modifications in MBO as an OD Strategy," *Proceedings, 1972 Annual Meeting,* Academy of Management, 1973, pp. 39–42.

7. Harry Levinson, "Management by Objectives: A Critique," *Training and Development Journal* (April 1972), pp. 3–8; see also Levinson, op. cit.

8. Tosi and Carroll, op. cit.

9. Herbert H. Meyer, Emanual Kay, and John R. P. French, Jr., "Split Roles in Performance Appraisal," *Harvard Business Review* (January-February 1965), pp. 123–129.

10. Peter F. Drucker, *The Practice of Management* (New York: Harper & Bros., 1954), p. 126.

11. See, for example, Carvalho, op. cit.; Wendell French, *The Personnel Management Process: Human Resources Administration,* 3d ed. (Boston: Houghton Mifflin, 1974); Howell, op. cit.; Charles L. Hughes, *Goal Setting* (New York: American Management Association, 1965), p. 123; Jamieson, op. cit.; Kerr, op. cit.; and Levinson, "Management by Whose Objectives?" op. cit.

12. A notable exception is W. J. Reddin, *Effective Management by Objectives: The 3-D Method of MBO* (New York: McGraw-Hill, 1971), chapter 14. Also see Wendell French and Cecil H. Bell, Jr., *Organization Development: Behavioral Science Interventions for Organization Improvement* (Englewood Cliffs, N.J.: Prentice-Hall, 1973), pp. 167–168; and Anthony P. Raia, *Managing by Objectives* (Glenview, Ill.: Scott, Foresman, 1974).

13. Wikstrom, op. cit., pp. 22–23.

14. Raia, op. cit., p. 110.

15. Ibid., pp. 75–78.

16. Reddin, op. cit.

17. French and Bell, op. cit., p. 15.

18. Robert R. Blake and Jane S. Mouton, *Corporate Excellence Through Grid Organization Development* (Houston: Gulf Publishing, 1968); and Robert R. Blake and Jane S. Mouton, *Building a Dynamic Corporation Through Grid Organization Development* (Reading, Mass.: Addison-Wesley, 1969).

19. Blake and Mouton, *Corporate Excellence,* p. 110.

20. Rensis Likert, *The Human Organization* (New York: McGraw-Hill, 1967), pp. 55 – 59.
21. Ibid., p. 57.
22. Robert W. Hollmann, "A Study of the Relationships Between Organizational Climate and Managerial Assessment of Management by Objectives," unpublished Ph.D. dissertation, University of Washington, 1973.
23. Likert, op. cit.; and Rensis Likert, *New Patterns of Management* (New York: McGraw-Hill, 1961).
24. Hollmann, op. cit.
25. Jack J. Holder, Jr., "Decision Making by Consensus," *Business Horizons* (April 1972), pp. 47 – 54.
26. Likert, *New Patterns of Management* and *The Human Organization*.
27. M. Scott Myers, "Overcoming Union Opposition to Job Enrichment," *Harvard Business Review* (May-June, 1971), pp. 37 – 49.

Section D

Systems and Second Thoughts

The reading units in this book began with a section on "Systems: First Thoughts," which discussed general systems theory and managerial work. This final section also deals with managers and systems, but from a slightly different perspective. The two articles included here focus on performance issues. One proposes a unique method for improving employee performance; the other reviews a debate over whether universalistic or contingency approaches to management offer the best guides for determining organizational effectiveness.

The first article, by Beatty and Schneier, takes up motivation theory once again and offers "A Case for Positive Reinforcement." The authors argue that job enrichment (JE) and MBO, well-known and popular remedies for ineffective job performance, have certain weaknesses that positive reinforcement (PR) can offset. In their view, PR is relatively easy to use, emphasizes rewards over punishment, and can be used in all job settings because it deals with job behavior instead of job content (as in JE) or job objectives (as in MBO).

Beatty and Schneier see PR programs as compatible with other remedies for poor performance but feel that PR's emphasis on behavioral feedback offers a more immediate way to reward desired outcomes. They do not see PR as a motivational panacea, however, and recognize certain practical difficulties with the method. For example, PR advocates must face the problem of specifying desirable types of managerial behavior. Additionally, they must deal with situations in which behavior rewarded by management is punished by other work groups. Despite such complications, PR has had some organizational successes, most notably at Emery Air Freight. According to Beatty and Schneier, use of positive reinforcement should help managers diagnose the effectiveness of organizational reward systems and, in broader terms, encourage research into the various components of managerial work.

The final article, by Child, asks "What Determines Organization Performance?" This issue is particularly slippery and has led to considerable debate among businessmen and researchers alike. One contending group believes that specific factors universally determine organizational performance. By contrast, another group rejects the universalist position and promotes a contingency view, one that links performance to the interaction of situational variables.

In an attempt to resolve this debate, Child studied 82 British companies in six industries and developed ten propositions regarding the managerial correlates of organizational effectiveness. Half support the universal approach and half support the contingency view. Child spells out the practical implications of his findings, identifies points of compatibility, and specifically rejects doctrinaire thoughts on what causes performance. He concludes that systems effectiveness "is not the prey of random and uncontrollable forces." Rather, "there are usually several ways of securing an effective match between a company's internal organization and the contingencies it faces."

A Case for Positive Reinforcement

Richard W. Beatty and Craig Eric Schneier

Many managers can easily differentiate between their good and poor employees and appreciate the consequences of poor performance in terms of an organization's profit, productivity, and competitive advantage. The causes of poor performance have been examined frequently, and solutions have been offered in the form of improved techniques for selecting better employees, training programs to teach needed skills, and motivational schemes designed to increase the quantity and quality of performance on the job.

Managers, however, are involved only indirectly with selection and training problems; these matters are usually the primary responsibility of psychologists, personnel technicians, and other experts. Essentially, selection is a problem of picking the person to fit the job. Such a person possesses the knowledge, skills, and abilities needed to perform well, or can be trained if required. Industrial psychology and personnel administration have made some important advances in the areas of selection and training to aid managers. But the manager is usually left with ineffective employees, often described as having motivation problems, after the "experts" have departed. The major assumption underlying this type of performance problem is that the employee has the abilities and skills to perform well, but lacks the willingness to do so.

In attempting to solve motivation problems, two well-publicized performance improvement remedies have been proposed, each with a large and zealous following. These two approaches are job enrichment (JE) and management by objectives (MBO). Both have strengths and weaknesses, and each is applicable to different aspects of the motivation problem. However, these remedies are not the only ones available. The explicit systematic use of positive reinforcement (PR) is another approach, one with great potential for improving performance at work.

The major assumptions, advantages, and disadvantages of each of these three methods will be discussed and a case made for the use of PR as an alternative method for resolving motivation problems. PR can be used compatibly with JE and MBO.

JOB ENRICHMENT

JE is a motivational technique, familiar to most managers, which emphasizes the need for challenging and interesting work. It suggests that jobs be redesigned so that intrinsic satisfaction is derived from doing the job. In its best applications, JE leads to a "vertically" enhanced job by adding functions from other organizational levels, making the job contain more variety and challenge, and offer autonomy and pride to the employee. The essence of JE is thus to change the content of jobs and make the work more challenging and meaningful.

JE makes several assumptions about people which are frequently accepted as universal truths and which need to be made more explicit. First, JE assumes that when intrinsic satisfaction is offered, extrinsic rewards (those from outside the immediate job) become secondary in importance. Second, JE assumes that extrinsic rewards (for example, pay and working conditions), if effective at all, are only effective as motivators in the short run. Third, JE assumes that people require self-actualization on the job and look to jobs rather than off-the-job activities as their primary sources of satisfaction and self-actualization.

If we accept these assumptions concerning the reasons for the lack of motivation which leads to good performance, JE would seem to be an appropriate remedy for monotonous, routine jobs; for jobs with large accident, turnover, and absenteeism rates; or for organizations in which employees feel alienated or powerless.

There are problems, however. JE cannot be successfully applied to all jobs. For example, many management jobs have been enriched with autonomy and responsibility, yet performance is lacking. There are also obvious problems in the implementation of JE; employees may want more and more say in policy formation, causing management to feel threatened with loss of power and control. Finally, for employees who want off-the-job satisfaction or are primarily concerned with work as a means to an end (for example, a bigger bag of groceries, a mortgage payment, or a new car), JE may simply not be appropriate.

In short, JE operates on the major premise that satisfaction, gained through self-actualization and challenge on the job, leads to high performance. But the existence of a direct causal sequence from satisfaction to performance has been doubted for some time. C. N. Greene, among others, has suggested that a reverse relationship (performance →satisfaction) may be more accurate.[1] That is, performance may be the cause—not the result—of satisfaction at work. The situations for which JR is applicable, its assumptions about motivation, and its motivational consequences are summarized in the accompanying table.

MANAGEMENT BY OBJECTIVES

The second remedy often proposed for motivation problems, MBO, is concerned with job performance, not job satisfaction. In MBO, employees help determine performance goals and are evaluated on the degree to which they attain these goals. Employees are made aware of what is expected of them and judged according to the "results." They are left free, within limits, to choose their own means of attaining their objectives. MBO usually proceeds through the following phases: goal setting, action planning, implementation, and review and evaluation. Many variants of the process are currently in vogue, however.

MBO, like JE, is founded on a set of implicit motivational assumptions. The MBO approach assumes that high performance can be achieved when employees know the specified goals, participate in the goal-setting process, and know the results. All of these are assumed to lead to increased employee motivation. With MBO, the cause of poor performance rests with ill-defined goals of the job, rather than job content, as in JE.

MBO would thus be appropriate where job results are not well understood and performance standards are ambiguous; where criteria for appraisal are inadequate or covertly subjective; where control problems are significant; where role conflict and/or role ambiguity exists; and where communication between superior and subordinates is poor. In such situations, MBO, because it develops explicit goals for which individuals and organizations are held accountable, could improve performance.

---

1. Charles N. Greene, "The Satisfaction-Performance Controversy," *Business Horizons* (October 1972), pp. 31–41.

JOB ENRICHMENT, MANAGEMENT BY OBJECTIVES, AND POSITIVE REINFORCEMENT: COMPATIBLE SOLUTIONS TO THE MOTIVATION PROBLEM

Problem Diagnosis	Motivational Assumptions	Job-Type Applicability	Time Frame for Distribution of Rewards	Motivational Consequences/Implications	
				Positive	Negative
		JOB ENRICHMENT			
Jobs are extremely monotonous, segmented and routine. Apathy, absenteeism, and turnover are excessive.	JE assumes that intrinsic rewards from job content (for example, challenge and autonomy) are the keys to long-run motivation because people want to satisfy higher level needs on the job.	JE is best for lower level jobs because these are typically routine and repetitive.	JE assumes that workers receive intrinsic satisfaction upon completion of a challenging job.	Jobs are more interesting and challenging; thus people are motivated to improve quality and to lower absenteeism and turnover.	Employees may feel that they have more to say about their jobs than they really do or than management intended. Some employees may not want challenging jobs, but simply a chance to earn money in order to satisfy their needs off the job.
		MANAGEMENT BY OBJECTIVES			
Jobs are ill-defined, and performance criteria are ambiguous and subjective. Employees feel they do not know where they stand and what is required of them.	MBO assumes that people will work to attain objectives to which they are committed. This commitment is attained by allowing employees to participate in goal setting.	MBO is difficult to apply to higher level jobs because these often have the most ambiguous objectives or standards.	MBO formally dispenses feedback in the appraisal interview. Informally, feedback can be dispensed by supervisors at any time.	MBO can reduce ambiguity related to one's job, promote communication between superiors and subordinates, and allow effort to be directed to organizational goals.	By emphasizing results rather than behavior, MBO can ignore such factors as discretion and judgment and can overquantify job objectives. Employees may feel that their participation in goal setting is not authentic. They may be defensive and anxious about their evaluations and try to cover up their mistakes to make their performance look good.
		POSITIVE REINFORCEMENT			
Behavioral objectives are not specified or are ambiguous. There is heavy reliance on punishment and threat, and little provision for rewarding employees.	PR assumes that desired behavior must be positively reinforced in order to sustain it, that variable schedules of reinforcement are powerful for controlling behavior, and that punishment has some negative side.	PR can be applied to all jobs because it does not involve job content. Instead, it involves the relationship between job behavior and its consequences.	PR allows dispensed reinforcement to be of any one of several schedules (for example, continuous, fixed, or variable).	Performance can be improved if desired behavior is specified and linked to valued consequences. The use of punishment at work often leads to escape and avoidance behaviors rather than to an increase in desired behavior.	The same behavior can receive both positive and negative reactions from different groups, thus putting employees in a conflict situation. Identifying desired behavior is time consuming and costly; it requires detailed observation by supervisors, who are often already overburdened.

However, as in the case of JE, the assumptions on which MBO are based may not be universally applicable. Even if objectives are clearly identified and communicated, effective performance may not result. Employees may feel that the objectives are those of management and are determined irrespective of their needs. Further, there may be instances when the results have been produced by circumstances beyond the employee's control (for example, budget cuts and market deficiencies), despite considerable effort and desired job behavior. Thus, the relationship between job behavior and job performance may not be so direct as is often assumed in MBO. When employees see that behavior does not lead to desired results, perhaps because of factors beyond their control, they may quit trying.

The goal-setting process in MBO may also lead to an overemphasis on quantifiable results at the expense of collaboration and teamwork. MBO can cause suboptimization when one division or department attempts to maximize its objectives at the expense of other divisions' goals, and can cause minimally acceptable results to become organizational norms by the establishment of minimum outputs. Furthermore, organizations can be overburdened with the paperwork often required by MBO systems.

Finally, although good MBO programs stress continual feedback, perhaps the greatest deficiency in the implementation of MBO is failure to provide immediate feedback from management to employees. Often feedback comes only at prescribed intervals, such as the six- and twelve-month formal performance review sessions, and thus is often not received by employees immediately after performing a job. This is in direct contrast with what we know about the timing of effective feedback.

The improbability of universal application of MBO is due both to its primary focus on job results, while often ignoring job behavior, such as effort, and the practical problems often associated with its implementation. MBO is thus not a complete remedy to the problem of poor performance, although there are situations in which it is certainly applicable (see table).

An analysis of the motivational assumptions of JE and MBO shows that each may be effective in some instances, but neither is a panacea. Both approaches see the root of the problem as being in the nature of jobs—job content in the case of JE and job objectives in the case of MBO. Although JE and MBO can be effective remedies to performance problems, they are often seen as the only remedies, and thus they may be overused and applied indiscriminately, irrespective of the cause of poor performance. Another solution, Positive Reinforcement (PR) can offset the major weaknesses of both JE and MBO.

POSITIVE REINFORCEMENT

The emphasis in a PR program is placed on the desired job behavior that leads to job outcomes or results, rather than results alone; on providing direct links between job behavior and rewards; and on the use of positive reinforcement, rather than punishment or the threat of punishment.

At the base of the PR approach is the relationship between behavior and its consequences. Consequences can be viewed as outcomes in an individual's environ-ment related to the demonstration of certain behaviors which may be thought of as positive and desirable (for example, praise from a supervisor) or negative and undesirable (for example, a disciplinary lecture). In both cases, the frequency of behavior may be increased as the result of these consequences. If the consequence does, in fact, increase the occurrence of the behavior it is called a reinforcer. For example, praise—a positive reinforcer—when dispensed after the employee arrives at work on time may increase the occurrence of punctuality. A negative reinforcer —a disciplinary lecture—dispensed after tardy arrival may also increase the occurrence of punctuality. However, increases in the occurrences of desired be-havior through the use of an aversive stimulus are effective only if the person sub-stitutes the desired behavior for the undesired behavior in order to avoid the aversive stimulus. (This may not necessarily be the case, as will be discussed later.)

Therefore, reinforcers (positive and negative) can be effective in controlling desired job behavior if they are closely linked to the performance they are meant to control. When reinforcement does not immediately follow the desired behavior, it loses much of its effectiveness because an employee fails to associate the con-tingent relationship between the cause (for example, desired job behavior) and the effect (for example, reward).

If we can specify behavior in the work setting that leads to effective perfor-mance, identify reinforcers that control behavior, and dispense positive reinforce-ment upon evidence of the desired behavior, we can improve performance.

Obviously, this procedure is already practiced; organizations do offer posi-tive reinforcement for desired performance. However, the process is usually done poorly and unsystematically, with lengthy time lags and indirect ambiguous re-lationships between behavior and consequences. Further, negative reinforcement and punishment, rather than positive reinforcement, may be relied upon too heavily. These practices violate the major concepts of the PR model. Before ex-panding this point, a few more concepts of the PR model need to be introduced.

Schedules of Reinforcement

The idea of schedules or frequency of reinforcement is also critical to the PR ap-proach. Reinforcement can be dispensed on a "continuous" schedule, in which every appropriate behavior is reinforced, as in piece rate and commission pay plans, or on a "variable" schedule, in which only a proportion or ratio of desired behaviors is reinforced. Reinforcement can also be dispensed at fixed intervals of time, as when employees receive a weekly or biweekly salary, or where wages are computed on the basis of an interval of time (for example, hourly).

In fact, few work settings use variable or intermittent schedules in which they vary the scheduling of positive reinforcement for effective performance. For example, it is possible to reward an employee after five successful demonstrations of a specific job behavior, then after ten demonstrations, and so on. The number of behaviors required for reinforcement under this schedule may vary from one to ten, but will average around five per reward.

An example of the power of this variable ratio schedule is the slot machine. Reinforcement in the form of winning is not dispensed each time nor on a regular basis, but on a random or intermittent basis. Therefore, the player is highly motivated to continue playing; the next play may be a winner.

Continuous and variable schedules may differ in their effect upon desired behavior. When a reinforcer is withdrawn from a person accustomed to a continuous schedule, the person soon stops demonstrating the desired behavior, but if the reinforcer is removed from a person accustomed to a variable schedule he may continue to demonstrate desired behavior over a long period of time. Thus, the variable schedule is a more efficient and powerful tool in that fewer reinforcers tend to prolong the demonstration of desired behaviors.

Punishment

Unlike reinforcement, punishment influences behavior by presenting a negative stimulus or withdrawing a positive stimulus in order to reduce the frequency of undesirable behavior. The relationship between punishment and negative reinforcement is often confused; they differ in that punishment is designed to remove behavior from a repertoire while negative reinforcement generates behavior.

The punctuality example may help show how these two ideas are related. As stated earlier, negative reinforcement increases the frequency of an alternative behavior as a person seeks to avoid an aversive stimulus. But punishment decreases the frequency of behavior. In negative reinforcement, an aversive stimulus (a disciplinary lecture) that follows a behavior (arriving late to work) may increase the frequency of a desired behavior (punctuality) as this behavior removes the aversive stimulus. This occurs if punctuality is the next response in the employee's behavior repertoire when certain behavior is removed.

However, increased absenteeism may be the behavior strengthened by the negative reinforcement of tardiness. For example, if a person finds himself arising late in the morning and unable to get to work on time, he may decide to take the whole day off to avoid the disciplinary lecture. But the disciplinary lecture, when known to follow late arrival for work, is punitive if it decreases the frequency of future tardiness.

Decreasing the frequency of an undesirable behavior may not lead to the increase of a desired behavior or strengthen any specific alternative behavior. For example, to avoid the punishment associated with tardiness, an employee may resort to a series of undesired behaviors, such as increased absenteeism, lying about illness, or having other employees clock him in. These behaviors avoid punishment, but are damaging to the organization. They are, however, readily observed in organizations relying too heavily on punishment.

Because punishment often suppresses undesired behavior and does not necessarily replace undesirable behaviors with desirable ones, desirable behaviors must simultaneously be positively reinforced; otherwise, proper responses may not be learned. For example, a child brings home an unsatisfactory report card and the parent commands the child, "Never bring home a report card like that again!" To escape punishment, the child may learn not to bring the report card home or to duplicate the parent's signature on the card. What the child has not learned is how to improve his or her grades through hard work, because such behavior has not been rewarded by the parent. In addition, the child may also learn to dislike the parent, because the parent is a punishing agent, just as an employee may learn to dislike a punishing supervisor, and resort to absenteeism, turnover, or cover-up of mistakes to escape punishment.

The PR Model in Organizations

Perhaps the best-known example of the PR model is Emery Air Freight's experience under the direction of Edward Feeney, in which feedback is given to employees to show how actual performance differs from the employee's own perceptions and from company standards. This feedback is very important; it requires employees to change their behavior in the desired direction to receive positive reinforcement (often in the form of praise) and recognize when they are surpassing previous performance levels.

Emery's annual savings from the use of PR in one program alone (the use of containers for shipments) has been reported to be $650,000.[2] This system does not attempt to make jobs intrinsically rewarding (as JE does) or rely on mutual goal setting to help further structure job goals (as MBO does). Instead, the system concentrates upon immediate feedback on actual job behavior and uses positive reinforcement in the form of praise.

Lesser known examples of the success of the PR model include training programs where positive reinforcement is used systematically to hasten learning; an organization which gives cash bonuses for perfect attendance; a hardware store which uses a lottery to reward those with exemplary attendance records; and a manufacturing organization in which attendance is significantly improved by the use of variable schedules to dispense rewards. In another example, Michigan

---

2. For reports of Feeney's efforts, see "At Emery Air Freight: Positive Reinforcement Boosts Performance," *Organizational Dynamics* (Winter 1973), pp. 41–50, and "Performance Audit, Feedback, and Positive Reinforcement," *Training and Development Journal* (November 1972), pp. 8–13.

Bell Telephone experimented with PR and reported that the absenteeism of 1,000 operators was cut almost in half when schedules were changed to permit immediate reinforcement.

CRITICISMS OF JE AND MBO

The PR approach is also critical of traditional methods of rewarding performance in organizations. Ambiguous relationships too often exist between performance and rewards because they fail to specify the behavior necessary in order to receive rewards. In fact, in many job situations rewards are offered not for performing well or even adequately, but for not performing poorly, with no provisions for rewarding excellent performance.

Further, we are guilty of neglecting what we know about the importance of immediate feedback. Techniques like MBO can help identify excellent performance, but the evaluation process in MBO is typically held some time after performance; therefore, the effect of the reward given for that performance is considerably lessened. For example, in a recent discussion of the use of money to motivate managers, Sidney R. Wilson noted an inconsistency: "Rarely is there an identifiable relationship between changes in compensation (salary, bonus, or stock) and personal performance. Even if there were, the reward comes so long after the performance that it could not possibly have any incentive value."[3]

Further, because rewards are often not contingent upon desired behaviors, employees do not know precisely why they received a reward. Perhaps more important, they do not know specifically what must be done in order to receive awards. Thus, we often not only fail to build a direct relationship between desired behavior and reward and fail to reward immediately after the observation of desired behavior, but also we may be actually reinforcing poor performance. This is because many rewards appear to be available to employees regardless of performance level. If we pay an employee every week and offer little or no reinforcement during that period, we are actually reinforcing both desired and undesired behaviors.

Management by Exception or Punishment?

In addition to the ineffective use of rewards through systems such as MBO, the technique known as management by exception can be seen as a means of negative reinforcement or as punishment. If management by exception is used, employees know that only when something goes wrong will they be contacted by a super-

---

3. Sidney R. Wilson, "Motivating Managers With Money," *Business Horizons* (April 1972), pp. 15–24.

visor. They may be docked in pay or called into the supervisor's office or somehow be confronted. Therefore, they may not be working for rewards, but may be merely trying to avoid punishment.

This approach may be satisfactory in accomplishing desired behavior if the desired behavior is the next in the person's response hierarchy. If not, as previously noted, desired behavior may not be forthcoming and unfortunate side-effects such as avoidance and dislike of the punishing manager may occur.

Motivational Assumptions of PR

Like other remedies for improving performance, PR is based on certain assumptions about motivation. PR assumes that at least some people derive job satisfaction through extrinsic rewards rather than through the work itself. Such persons may find intrinsic satisfaction in off-the-job activities which are permitted by jobs which provide extrinsic, tangible rewards such as money.

Further, the assumption made in JE that employees' higher level needs can be properly diagnosed by managers so that they can then design jobs to fulfill these needs is not necessary in the PR system; it relies on general extrinsic reinforcers such as pay, which can subsequently be exchanged by employees to meet their needs as they perceive them. The implications of PR's motivational assumptions are noted in the figure.

The Carrot and the Stick

Many charge that PR is a manipulative scheme—a device to control employee behavior via the carrot and stick (reward-punishment) philosophy of management. There are several responses to this criticism. One is that organizations presently attempt to control behavior by offering rewards and punishment for performance, but are doing an ineffective job. This is due to the lack of systematic planning and, as shown, to over-emphasis of the use of the stick. PR can alleviate the harmful effects of punishment by concentrating on positive reinforcement.

PR also specifies an individual's job objectives in behavioral terms so that employees know precisely what is expected of them. This approach is more in the interest of employees than seducing them with human relations training or with shallow attempts to permit participation in either the design of jobs or performance evaluations, while actually requiring unwavering conformity to management standards and goals.

Problems and PR

There are practical problems with PR, which must be resolved through careful planning and experimentation, as well as philosophical issues which can evoke controversy and emotion from participants. One practical issue is the specification of desired behavior. Identification of behavioral objectives is often easy for many routine and/or entry-level jobs; however, managerial jobs may be unprogrammed and entail many different responsibilities. A behavioral analysis of managerial positions is a difficult yet necessary prerequisite to the implementation of PR.

Even if we specifically identify desired behaviors, these behaviors may simultaneously be rewarded by management and punished by work groups or families. For example, high output may attract praise from supervisors and scorn from coworkers, who see it as leading to higher output quotas. Hard work and long hours may be positively reinforced by the organization but resented by one's family. Further, a PR program may require that a supervisor observe subordinate behavior more frequently in order to dispense PR. Such additional demands may be resented.

Philosophical issues can also hinder the effectiveness of a PR program. As was noted, many believe that PR is tantamount to the manipulation and control of people by reward and punishment, and images of white rats in Skinner's experiments come to mind. As Walter Nord has stated, this view is in direct contradiction to the image many people would prefer to have of themselves: "Modern Americans, especially of the managerial class, prefer to think of themselves and others as being self-actualizing creatures operating at the top of Maslow's need hierarchy, rather than as animals being controlled and even manipulated by their environment."[4]

Of course, these charges have been addressed by proponents of PR. Practical problems can be alleviated as we study jobs, especially managerial jobs, in behavioral terms. This necessitates, of course, detailed observation, identification, and analysis of what people do at work, which should produce categorizations of work activities and their frequencies. Proponents of PR would also argue that we are controlling work behavior now, but that by relying so heavily on punishment and negative reinforcement, we are not doing it effectively. PR may not lead to the resentment and emotional stress which often accompanies punishment.

Of course, the practical problems, as well as the reservations many have about the implications of PR, can be overcome principally by experimenting in actual organizational settings and by citing the persuasive evidence of successful implementations which continue to appear in the literature.

THE COMPATIBILITY OF PR

A most advantageous aspect of the PR system is its compatibility with the other remedies for performance problems, JE and MBO, as well as with present person-

---

4. Walter Nord, "Beyond the Teaching Machine: The Neglected Area of Operant Conditioning in the Theory and Practice of Management," *Organizational Behavior and Human Performance* (November 1969), pp. 375–401.

nel practices. PR offers organizations a way to more objectively and immediately reward performance at all levels and in all jobs, to facilitate specification of desired performance levels, and to deemphasize punishment and its harmful effects.

Intrinsic motivation (for example, JE) is not universally applicable, nor is it sufficient to sustain performance. External rewards still control performance to a large extent. Structuring jobs, providing feedback, and allowing for participation in goal setting are likewise not sufficient as they are not applicable to all employees and jobs. Therefore, it is suggested that all three possible solutions to performance problems be explored. Obviously, in many cases more than one solution may be necessary.

Further, a diagnosis of the task, the people, and the structure of organizations should precede attempts to apply a technique to motivational problems, whether it be JE, MBO, or PR. The interdependency of these variables is vital because they can form a situation which can limit the applicability of any one technology to improve performance. In his discussion of JE, John Morse supports this point: "Job enrichment is a design mechanism that either fits or does not fit the task and technology to which it is being applied. It is also a design mechanism and technique that either fits or does not fit the personality of the individuals whose jobs are being enriched."[5]

This statement is equally applicable to MBO and PR. It suggests that the effective application of a specific technique to alleviate the motivation problem hinges upon the congruence of existing variables in the organization with the assumptions that a particular technique makes about the problem. As can be seen from the table, each of the three techniques results from somewhat different diagnoses of the motivation problem. Each has a certain range of job-type applicability, time frame, and positive and negative consequences for the organization and its employees. There are at least three ways to deal with motivation problems; all three should be considered and perhaps used in combination.

Poor employee performance is perhaps the most pervasive problem in organizations today. We have attributed poor performance to two general causes. The first, which can be called the deficiency problem, occurs when employees do not possess the necessary abilities, skills, or attributes. This problem can be alleviated by selection strategies and training programs.

There may still exist a problem of poor performance, however, even when the employees possess the proper abilities, skills, and attributes. We have termed this a motivational problem, the second cause of poor performance. We have argued that it is perhaps the more serious problem in organizations. Two well-publicized remedies have been offered—JE and MBO—but these, and their many variants, have been effective only to a limited degree.

---

5. John Morse, "A Contingency Look at Job Design," *California Management Review* (Fall 1973), pp. 67–75.

A third solution to the problem of improving job performance through a motivation technique is available. This solution is PR, which focuses on actual behavior rather than on measures of effectiveness by emphasizing positive rewards rather than punishment and by systematically recognizing the power of immediate feedback and different reinforcement schedules. An analysis of PR often reveals the current ineffective and illogical use of rewards presently offered in organizations.

We have offered a contingency approach to the motivation problem. The contingency concept implies that there is only one best way to solve organization problems, but that there may be several equally effective programs. The contingency or situational approach necessitates a thorough diagnosis of the organization's setting in order to identify the problems that exist and to identify techniques which are effective for these specific problems.

When a manager diagnoses poor performance as a motivation problem rather than a deficiency problem, the following steps should be taken:

The manager should assess the job for its ability to offer challenging work to employees. If more intrinsic motivation is thought to be necessary, he can look into JE as a partial solution.

The manager should assess the objectives of the job to determine whether or not they have been communicated to the worker, have been defined specifically, and whether the worker has received feedback about his results relative to these goals. If there are deficiencies here, MBO may be investigated as a partial solution.

The manager should assess the extrinsic rewards offered to the worker in a job. Are they of sufficient quantity and types to improve performance? Are they offered soon after proper performance? Are they contingent upon evidence of performance? Are rewards substituted with threat of punishment or punishment to control behavior? To the extent that these questions are unsatisfactorily answered, PR as a partial solution to the motivation problem needs to be investigated.

It is time that managers recognize the power of rewards and punishment for controlling work behavior and performance in organizations. They should systematically and explicitly examine the unintended consequences of their inadequate use of contingencies of reinforcement, their overemphasis on threat and punishment, and their ineffective use of rewards and schedules of reinforcement in the work setting.

27 What Determines Organization Performance? The Universals vs. the It-All-Depends

John Child

Background: This article is largely based on a research program involving 82 British companies selected among six industries to provide contrasting environments. Two of the industries were in the service sector: advertising and insurance (predominantly ordinary life insurance). Four were manufacturing, with two of these being science based—electronics (predominantly instruments and components) and pharmaceuticals. The other two manufacturing industries were chocolates-and-sweets and family newspapers. The companies chosen provided a clustering within each industry around six different size levels, of 150, 300, 500, 1,000, 2,500, and 6,000 employees.

Information on the organization, technology, location, scale, ownership, policy, and background of each company was obtained chiefly through interviews with its senior managers and specialists. In 78 of the companies, the researchers followed up this investigation within one to two weeks with a questionnaire to senior and departmental managers asking them about the nature of their jobs, their personal attitudes toward matters such as change and innovation, and how they would characterize typical behaviors at their level in the company. Completed replies returned by 787 of the 888 managers contacted were the source of data on managerial characteristics. Statistics on the profit and growth performance of the companies were collected from their internal records and accounts.

One school of management thought maintains that, irrespective of the circumstances, certain factors, attributes—call them what you will—universally determine the performance of any organization. The opposing school (newer, and perhaps for that reason just as doctrinaire) argues that universals are not reflections of reality, that the effect of any factor on organizational performance varies with the objectives, size, markets, and other characteristics of the particular organization. This is the contingency school.

Which school is correct? Research, including our own investigations, discourages dogmatism, permits tentative generalizations, and indicates strongly the need for further research. Based on the research to date, however, ten propositions are advanced here about the factors that determine organizational performance; half of these propositions refer to universal attributes, while the other half lend themselves to a contingency approach to organizational performance.

But first, a few caveats that qualify what follows.

The question of what determines the levels of performance achieved by organizations still defies a sure answer. The problem is extremely complex because, as Jonathan Boswell said in his *The Rise and Fall of Small Firms*, "A vast number of influences on performance are at work. Some of these are quantifiable, others aren't; some are external to the firm, others are internal and managerial, and of the latter many are subtly interwoven."

Both universalistic and contingency perspectives assume that it is possible to identify factors that will to some degree determine levels of performance. A major difficulty, however, lies in the fact that performance is not simply a dependent variable. The performance levels achieved by an organization constitute a vital input of information to its managers that is likely to stimulate them to make adjustments in policies and modes of operation. These adjustments may be an attempt to correct a poor level of performance or to accommodate the consequences of good performance, such as a growth in scale, and so to sustain the favorable trend. In other words, it is unrealistic to regard performance *only* as a variable dependent on other factors.

This conclusion has important implications for the interpretation of the kind of data it has been practicable to obtain in most research studies. These data are cross-sectional in nature, deriving from measurements taken in a single time period, rather than from a close examination of how performance and other variables change in association with one another over time. Within certain limits, such studies can provide useful clues as to what factors are associated with different levels of performance, but they cannot address the question of how performance acts as part of a continuing cycle of organizational change. This means that they cannot demonstrate what causes good or bad performance. Problems of interpretation will therefore arise.

For instance, in my own research into 82 British companies, I found that less profitable and slower-growing firms used manpower budgets and other cost controls more than did high performers. The implications of this correlation are ambiguous. To what extent do manpower budgets contribute to lower performance because of their intrinsic inflexibility and because they focus managers' attention on departmental considerations, rather than on broader needs? On the other hand, to what extent is manpower budgeting instituted or intensified as a response to poor performance, in an attempt to keep manpower costs to a minimum and to control a staffing situation that may be getting out of hand? My impression is that in practice a period of poor performance often stimulated an intensification of financial controls.

These introductory remarks contain the elements of a simple framework that will be used to bring together the more salient research findings on the performance of organizations. This framework is sketched out in Figure 1 in terminology that applies particularly to business organizations. Briefly, the strategy and plans that are formulated are regarded as major determinants of an organization's

Figure 1 PERFORMANCE IN THE CONTEXT OF ORGANIZATIONAL BEHAVIOR

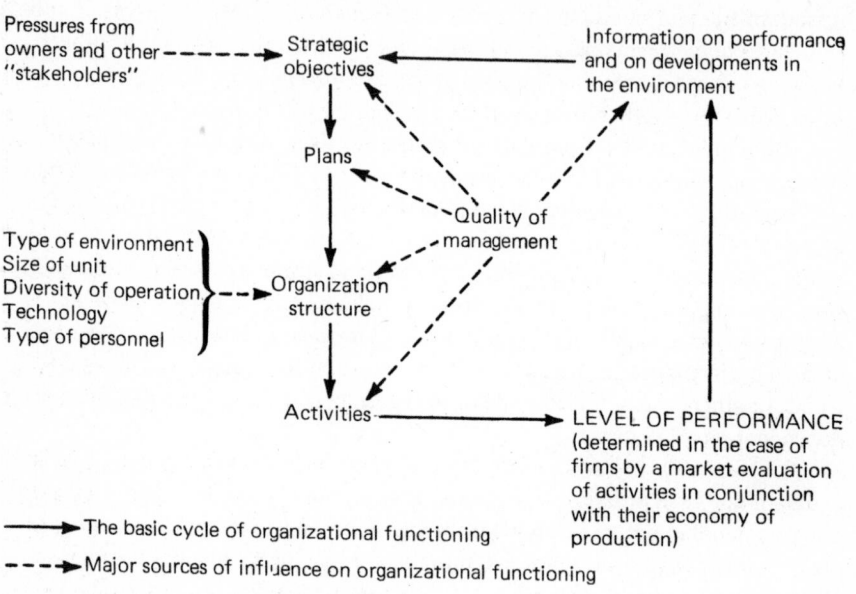

Pressures from owners and other "stakeholders" - - - - → Strategic objectives ← Information on performance and on developments in the environment

Plans

Quality of management

Type of environment, Size of unit, Diversity of operation, Technology, Type of personnel } - - - → Organization structure

Activities ——————→ LEVEL OF PERFORMANCE (determined in the case of firms by a market evaluation of activities in conjunction with their economy of production)

——————→ The basic cycle of organizational functioning

- - - -→ Major sources of influence on organizational functioning

activities, and hence a critical influence on its eventual performance. Strategic decisions are responses to pressures imposed on managers by the various participants within the organization and its environment, with managers' own stakes in ownership being a strongly influencing factor. The design of organization structure in the light of situational contingencies is included as a potential determinant of how effectively the tasks of the organization are carried out. The quality of management is regarded as a pervasive element that can affect all aspects of organizational behavior.

The managerial, strategic, and organizational factors that have emerged as correlates of performance will now be discussed separately, with research findings organized around the ten major propositions mentioned earlier.

MANAGERIAL CORRELATES OF PERFORMANCE

"The good manager" is the keynote of one of the most popular universalistic theories about performance. This theory holds that the successful leadership of any organization will depend on the presence of certain qualities of character, drive, competence, and dedication among its managers. Thus, a British survey carried out in the early 1960s concluded that "thrusting" managerial attitudes "are considerably more likely to lead to high and profitable growth than are the sleepy attitudes and practices with which they are contrasted."

Youth, technical qualification, and a stake in the ownership of the organiza-tion are among the factors often thought of as promoting more effective management. For example, in recruiting, the relative merits of youth, with its supposed adaptability and energy, as against the experience of more mature applicants, have often occasioned debate. What are the facts?

Proposition 1: Organizations run by younger teams of top managers will tend to achieve higher levels of performance.

The journal *Management Today* found in its 1973 survey of the boards of the 200 largest British companies that those having the oldest boards showed lower profitability and growth than companies with the youngest directors. As the journal put it, there was no refutation here of "the common-sense view that companies dominated by conservatively reared older men are less likely to produce dynamic performance."

Our research at the Aston Management Centre did not find that the age of senior managers correlated systematically with company profits, but it did relate to growth in sales, income, and assets measured over a five-year period. In each one of six industries sampled, younger managements typically achieved higher rates of company growth. At their best, the "young Turks" achieved quite outstanding growth performances. Although there was a lot of variation in the levels attained, the least successful young teams did no worse than the least successful older managements. Two economists, Peter Hart and John Mellors, have also independently looked at the age of company chairmen and the growth of net assets in four British industries and reached the same conclusion: The growth of companies controlled by older men tends to be slower, although less volatile.

So a fairly general link seems to exist between youthful management and more rapid growth. But how should we interpret this observation? After all, it may signify little more than that faster-growing companies recruit and promote younger people more rapidly into senior vacancies. Is youth among managers just a consequence of growth already achieved?

Favoring this argument is the fact that managers in faster-growing companies tended to have had shorter periods of service with the company and to have reached their present posts via fewer intermediate positions. On the other hand, they had not on the whole been in their present jobs for any less time than had managers in slow-growing companies.

The personal qualities that we found to characterize younger managers support the view that age is, indeed, an operative influence. Younger managers were more likely to press actively for change and innovation within their companies. They questioned prevailing systems of formal rules and authority more keenly. They also had greater confidence in their own abilities to succeed in the high positions they held than did older managers. The confident attitudes and behavior found among younger managers are just the kind likely to promote a striving for innovation and rapid growth.

Comparisons of individual companies illustrate these general findings. An example is the best and the worst performers among the 15 insurance companies in the Aston study. Let us call them Company A and Company B. These two organizations had such distinctive climates that they were immediately apparent to the visitor. In Company A, the high performer, there was an atmosphere of busyness, yet the staff appeared relaxed, friendly, and well turned out. Despite the hustle and bustle, appointments were always kept punctually and staff members seemed to know of and take an interest in each other's movements. The initial appearance of Company B to the visitor was in marked contrast. Staff members were casual to the point of indifference; there was little animation in their behavior; the whereabouts of senior managers were often unknown (particularly around the middle of the day); and appointments were not kept on several occasions.

Company A's senior management team had an average age of 34 years, compared with 50 years in Company B. When we applied statistical measurements of attitudes and behavior, the managers in the two companies contrasted sharply. In Company A, formal rules and routines were adhered to with less than half the degree of rigidity found in Company B. Some 50 percent more pressure for change and innovation was reported among managers in Company A. The young management team in that company expressed itself as being almost twice as ready to take risks when necessary, and also preferred to have more variety and challenge in its work. It is worth noting that a study by Victor Vroom and Bernd Pahl of 1,500 managers from 200 U.S. companies found a consistent and significant relationship between younger age and a greater willingness to take risks.

I have devoted some space to the question of youthful management because it may be an influence on performance that applies in most types of organization and upon which managers can act. Research findings to date point to the need for career systems that allow young people of proven ability and appropriate experience to advance rapidly to senior positions. The other side of this coin is the justification of the practice found in some American corporations where, after the age of 50 or so, senior executives may be transferred into less demanding positions.

In British industry, the rapid promotion of able men and women who are still in their prime is slowly becoming more usual, but a planned transfer of older people to less responsible positions, as opposed to more brutal methods like dismissal or compulsory early retirement, is not. This always tends to be resisted by the older executives who hold power in company managements, and it is important for transfers of this kind not to entail a loss of remuneration and privilege. The question remains, nevertheless, whether holding down top management positions is to be primarily a reward of age and long service or a recognition of who is best able to meet the requirements of the job—quite possibly a relatively young man.

Proposition 2: Organizations run by formally better-qualified teams of top managers will tend to achieve higher levels of performance.

The reasoning behind this proposition is the straightforward notion that the possession of formal qualifications is likely to indicate that managers have a certain level of attested expertise and ability. This potential influence on levels of performance cannot, of course, be entirely separated from the age factor, since younger managers tend more often to possess these formal qualifications than do older managers.

Some evidence emerges from British studies that the financial success of companies is generally greater when a relatively high proportion of their directors have formal professional qualifications. D. P. Barritt found this to be the case after studying the profits of larger British companies in the 1950s. More recently, in the mid-1960s, a study by Roger Betts of 23 companies, chiefly in construction and plastics, found that those achieving a higher rate of growth in profits had a greater average number of formal qualifications held per director. In both industries, the successful companies had a significantly higher proportion of directors concerned with research and development and (it appeared) possessing scientific qualifications.

There is some support, then, for the proposition that formally qualified management teams will achieve superior performance. And the balance within top executive or directorial teams of types of qualifications may also relate to success. For example, in the study of Betts just cited, there was evidence that poor-performing companies had a heavy weighting of men with production and engineering backgrounds. Another study of 93 major British companies achieving the highest and lowest rates of return on capital during the period 1966−72 found that the high performers had more directors with accounting qualifications, while the low performers had more directors with engineering qualifications. This proportionate relationship of directors' qualifications appeared to be more closely associated with organizational performance than the total number of qualifications within the board.

Proposition 3: Organizations run by managers with a substantial personal stake in their ownership will tend to achieve higher levels of performance.

A major theme in writings on the "managerial revolution" is that managers who do not have a significant personal stake in the ownership of corporations will devote more attention to objectives other than the maximization of profit. One such objective is growth, which many commentators have concluded will furnish considerable advantages to managers in terms of higher remuneration, prestige, sense of achievement, and so on.

A number of studies have been made in the United States and Britain of the relation between the control of companies and their levels of performance. Overall, the results suggest that companies with a concentration of ownership control (rather than dispersed ownership) tend to have higher rates of profit *and* higher rates of growth, but differences in levels of performance have often not been significant, and the measures of ownership influence have been formalistic and indirect.

In our studies, we have found that where there was a greater concentration of ownership control, chief executives attached particularly great importance to maximizing profits and growth: There were, however, no significant links between the ownership control factor and rates of profit actually achieved, and the only significant link with growth was found in the tendency for owner-controlled companies to have a more rapid growth in net assets over a five-year period.

Rather fewer studies have looked at managers' stockholdings in relation to company performance, but the results that emerge are more clear-cut, indicating that when managers have greater personal stake in ownership, the performance of companies tends to be superior. For example, a study by Steve Nyman of the 100 largest British commercial and industrial companies found that higher levels of stockholding by directors were significantly associated with higher rates of growth. A larger stake in ownership was also associated with the achievement of higher rates of profit, although this result was only just statistically significant. Given higher growth and higher profitability, it is not surprising that a greater stake in ownership was also associated with a higher stock market rating and a higher price-earnings ratio.

In short, there is a clear tendency for the company in which control is linked with a stake in ownership to be a superior performer. The motivational implications of this relationship for all types of organizations are significant, since they suggest that whenever managers have a direct personal stake in the success of an undertaking, its performance will be enhanced. There is also a suggestion here that the objectives held by managers may influence the performance of their organizations, which leads us to a consideration of strategic factors.

Proposition 4: The performance standards set by an organization's management will be influenced by the norms of performance among other organizations of a similar type.

Strategy deals with the objectives established for an organization and the effort to attain them. For example, if we establish the objective of sustaining a given annual rate of growth, this may mean diversification into a faster-growing industry in order to achieve the objective. There is ample evidence that normal rates of profit and growth vary among industries and that these variations can have an important influence on the performance of firms, especially smaller ones whose activities are usually confined to a single industry. In addition to reflecting certain shared economic circumstances having to do with size of markets, growth of overall demand, structure of the industry, and so forth, the differentiation of company performance levels by industry also reflects the presence of shared standards by which many firms are content to judge themselves. This phenomenon—of managements' assessing performance against localized, rather than general, standards—is likely to be even more widespread outside the business sphere, where mechanisms to enforce universal economic standards such as stock market ratings are absent. It is this consideration that underlies the proposition made above.

We also expect that the mix of objectives held by an organization's senior managers will have an impact on its performance. The exact formulation of objectives may well result from an appraisal of what can realistically be attained in the light of the organization's previous performance. The type of objectives held by top management is, nevertheless, likely to be an active influence upon performance because of the ways in which objectives shape plans and activities. Moreover, the singlemindedness of managements is important, first because effort may be dissipated in trying to achieve too many different aims at once, and second, because the more conflict among senior managers over objectives, the less integrated will be their efforts toward reaching a common goal. Hence, we arrive at the fifth proposition.

Proposition 5: The less dispersed top-management objectives are and the more agreement there is among senior managers as to which objectives have priority, the more successful the organization will be in attaining them.

Chief executives in our study of British firms were asked to rate the importance to their companies of ten possible objectives, scoring each of them separately along five-point scales. Nearly all of the respondents gave very high priority to maximizing net profit over the long term (five years) and to achieving a high rate of growth. Because of this strong measure of agreement, the rating of these objectives did not discriminate between successful companies and others.

The evaluation of certain other objectives did differentiate. In the more profitable companies, with above-average rates of return for their industries on sales and on net assets, chief executives attached lower importance to a high level of distributed dividends, but greater importance to a high level of rewards and benefits for employees. In more profitable firms they also showed less concern for the company's prestige. In the faster-growing companies, chief executives attached low importance to maximizing short-term profits over a 12-month period, to paying out a high level of dividends, and to "service to the wider community."

A comparison of three sugar confectionary companies with contrasting performance profiles illustrates these points in greater detail. Company X was a poor performer by any criterion. Company Y had an outstanding growth record and had maintained an average level of profitability. Company Z was highly profitable and had achieved an average level of growth. As Figure 2 shows, the chief executive of all three companies attached considerable importance to major objectives such as maximizing long-term profitability, growth, and market share. In Company X, however, the chief executive hardly discriminated in his assessment among these objectives and others in the list we gave him. In the two better-performing companies, less importance was attached to objectives like prestige, a high dividend payout, and service to the community. In growth-Company Y, innovation was given a high rating. In Company Z, which was securing high margins on high-quality traditional lines, less emphasis was given to growth and market share than in Company Y, and somewhat more stress was placed on maximizing profits in the short term.

Findings like these, even though they concern chief executives' views alone, suggest that the mix of strategic objectives selected for a business may influence its performance. In the sample as a whole, the companies achieving greater commercial success were those whose top managements were more singleminded in pursuing longer-term profit and growth objectives. Chief executives in these companies also paid considerable attention to the building up of internal strengths, such as providing favorable conditions for employees and retaining surpluses within the business to finance further profitable expansion.

In companies where chief executives attach more importance to external points of reference, such as prestige, serving the community, and paying higher dividends, financial performance tends to be poorer. Whether this association between a lower concern for external interests and superior performance can continue through the 1970s, with the present growing insistence on company social responsibility, remains to be seen. On the whole, though, the message of these findings seems clear: If you want to manage a successful business, concentrate on a few key

Figure 2   RATING OF OBJECTIVES IN THREE CONFECTIONERY COMPANIES*

Objective	Ratings of importance**		
To maximize:	Company X	Company Y	Company Z
1. Net profit over five years	5	5	5
2. Rate of growth	5	5	4
3. Market share	4	5	4
4. Employee rewards	4	5	5
5. Net profit over one year	5	3	4
6. Prestige	5	3	2
7. Innovation	4	5	2
8. Assets and reserves	4	2	1
9. Dividends distributed	4	2	1
10. Service to the wider community	4	1	1

* Company X was a small, family firm with low profitability and low growth, old product and old technology. Company Y was an American-owned firm of small to medium size, with average profitability and rapid growth, some new products and advanced technology. Company Z was a medium-size subsidiary, with high profitability and average growth, and traditional high-quality products, enjoying high margins on low-cost technology.

** 5—extremely important
4—very important
3—moderately important
2—not very important
1—not at all important

objectives and avoid distractions. This also implies, of course, that careful thought should be given to the selection of key objectives in the first place.

Further support for Proposition 5 comes from a study by David Norburn, who compared 21 British companies with varying levels of financial performance. He found that the more successful companies were characterized by a greater degree of consensus among top executives about who was responsible for setting long-term objectives and about the priority of objectives their organizations should follow. In poor-performing organizations he found both more disagreement and a wider spread of objectives. Norburn also found that successful company managements possessed better information on their environments. It is likely that superior, well-integrated information will assist managers to agree on which objectives deserve priority.

There are more strategic factors associated with performance than can be considered here, but there is enough evidence to indicate that as a general rule, attention to the formulation of strategy will have beneficial effects on performance. For instance, the systematic planning of expansion policies among American firms is related to superior economic performance. A comparative study of acquisition behavior among American companies carried out by Igor Ansoff and his colleagues lends further support to Proposition 5, because the firms more successful in terms of profit and growth were found to have restricted their attention to a more limited range of possible acquisitions and to have evaluated these more thoroughly.

ORGANIZATION STRUCTURE AND PERFORMANCE

Managerial attributes and the quality of strategy appear to have some relation to levels of performance in most organizations, even though the organizations differ in their environment, diversity, size, technology, and personnel. When we turn to a third possible influence on performance, the design of organization structure, we find most authorities taking the view that the type of situation is vital. This is the contingency approach mentioned earlier, which states that the design of organization most appropriate for high performance can be formulated only with contingent circumstances in mind. According to this theory, there are no general principles of organization.

The argument goes as follows: Contingent factors such as the type of environment or the size of the organization have some direct influence on levels of success. There may, for example, be economies of scale open to the larger organization. Certain environments, such as particular industries, may be more beneficent and provide greater opportunity. Second, it is assumed that a set of structured administrative arrangements consciously adapted to the tasks that are to be done, to the expectations and needs of people performing the tasks, to the scale of the total operation, to its overall complexity, and to the pressures of change being encountered will themselves act to promote a higher level of effectiveness than will a structure ill-suited to these contingencies. Organization structure is seen in this way to modify the effects of contingencies upon performance. Last, the all-pervasive quality of management affects both strategic decisions as to the type of conditions under which the organization will seek to operate and the design of its internal structure.

Environment

According to contingency theory, different approaches to organizational design are conducive to high performance, depending on whether or not the environment in which the organization is operating is variable and complex in nature, or stable and simple. Variability in the environment refers to the presence of changes that are relatively difficult to predict, involve important departures from previous conditions, and are likely, therefore, to generate considerable uncertainty.

Complexity of the environment is said to be greater the more extensive and diversified the range of an organization's activities, which correspondingly take it into more diverse sectors of the environment. These diverse sectors are all relevant areas of external information that it should monitor. There is evidence that the degree of environmental variability is a more important contributor to uncertainty among managerial decision makers than is complexity. I shall discuss variability now and return to complexity in a later section on diversity of operations.

Proposition 6: In conditions of environmental variability, successful organizations will tend to have structures with the following characteristics: (1) arrangements to reduce and to structure uncertainty; (2) a relatively high level of internal differentiation; and (3) a relatively high level of integration achieved through flexible, rather than formalized, processes.

This mouthful of a proposition attempts to distill the essence of what we know so far about a highly complex issue. Among possible arrangements to reduce and structure the uncertainty generated by a changing environment are a closer liaison with the separate independent organizations upon which one's own organization is highly dependent as supplier or customer (even to the extent of vertical or horizontal integration), and attempts to secure a better quality of intelligence from outside the organization.

The critical nature of a variable environment and the need for liaison with outside organizations and for a significant intelligence activity all mean that an organization is under pressure to employ specialist staff in boundary or interface roles—that is, in positions where they form a link with the outside world, scooping in and evaluating relevant information. This may well take the form of setting up more specialist departments and thereby increasing the internal differentiation of the organization.

If there are many new significant external changes to which an organization has to adapt, and if it has become fairly differentiated to cope with these, then there will be all the more need to achieve a degree of integration among its personnel that not only offsets their specializations from one another but, over and above this, permits them to react swiftly to new developments in a coordinated manner. Flexible, rather than highly formalized, methods of coordination and information-sharing will be required. This generally means a greater amount of face-to-face participation in discussions and decision making, with an emphasis on close lateral relations among members of different departments instead of formal links up and down hierarchies or via periodic formal meetings. This mode of working also implies a higher degree of delegation, particularly when it comes to operational decisions.

Various studies that have examined organizational performance in relation to structure and variable environments have produced sufficiently consistent findings to support the conclusions we have just made. Each study, of course, examines the structural elements I have mentioned in more detail. In the United States there is the well-known work of Paul Lawrence and Jay Lorsch, as well as studies by Robert Duncan, Pradip Khandwalla, Anant Negandhi, and Bernard Reiman, among others. Of British studies, Tom Burns' and G. M. Stalker's is the best known.

Our own research at Aston indicated that companies in the variable science-based environment characterizing electronics and pharmaceuticals that were achieving above-average levels of growth tended to rely less on formal procedures and documentation than did slow-growing companies. Among firms in more stable environments, high-growth companies relied more (but only marginally so) on formalized methods of integration than did less successful firms.

These organizational differences between high- and low-growth companies located in contrasting environments were most marked in certain areas of management. Within the stable sector, faster-growing companies had significantly more formalization in the production area, especially in matters like defining operator tasks, training operators, and recording their performance. The faster-growing companies in variable environments particularly made little use of formal training procedures, standardized routine personnel practices, and formal hierarchical channels for communication or seeking and conveying decisions.

Size of Unit

Here the major proposition is this:

Proposition 7: Organizations that increase their degree of formalization to parallel their growth in size will tend to achieve higher levels of performance.

Critics contend that the problem of the large organization is the dead weight of bureaucratic administration that it takes on. In an attempt to hold together its many divisions and departments, the large organization emphasizes conformity to the rules, a trait that has prompted the observation that "a new idea has never come out of a large corporation." Many studies of organization have confirmed that large scale does indeed breed bureaucracy in the form of highly compartmentalized jobs and areas of work, elaborate procedural and paperwork systems, long hierarchies, and delegation of routine decisions to lower-level managers within precise discretionary limits.

Much as critics may decry bureaucracy, we found that in each industry the more profitable and faster-growing companies were those that had developed this type of organization in fuller measure with their growth in size above the 2,000-or-so employee mark. At the other end of the scale, among small firms of about 100 employees, the better performers generally managed with very little formal organization. The larger the company, the higher the correlation between more bureaucracy and superior performance.

Poorly performing large companies tend to specialize their staff less, to have less developed systems and procedures, and to delegate decision making less extensively. It is also worth noting that among the poorly performing companies the strength of the relation between changes in size and changes in structure is noticeably reduced, compared with that among high performers.

Comparisons of larger companies within the same industry clearly illustrate this trend. For example, we studied three of the largest national daily newspaper groups. One was the superior performer by a substantial margin, in terms of growth, return on net assets, and return on combined circulation plus advertising sales. Although this particular group was the smallest of the three big companies in numbers employed, it operated a highly formalized type of organization—it had developed a more elaborate set of procedures and systems covering a wider range of activities than had the other two companies, and it relied heavily on written communication and records. Indeed, its most distinguishing feature lay in this heavier use of documentation, especially job descriptions, manuals, work records, and the like.

The newspaper industry represents a relatively stable environment. When the nature of each organization's environment is taken into account, as well as its size, the association between organization and performance becomes more complicated. The need for companies operating in a more variable environment to keep a check on the formality in their organization, especially its routine-enforcing elements, probably explains why it is the successful companies in a more stable environment that most rapidly take on a formal bureaucratic type of structure as they grow larger. The rate at which companies tend to develop bureaucratic structures as their size increases varies according to the environment and performance in the following sequence from low to high: below-average performers in stable environments; below-average performers in variable environments; above-average performers in variable environments; above-average performers in stable environments.

Managers, it appears from our research, have to take note of multiple contingencies, such as environment plus size, when planning the design of their organization. When there is not much variability in the environment, the need to develop organization to suit size becomes relatively more dominant. In this environment, the better-performing companies tend to develop formalized structures at a faster rate as they grow than do poor performers. When the environment is a variable one, however, these differences in structural development are reduced, because the contingency of coping with uncertainty tends to offset the contingency of coping with large scale. We found that in a variable environment, the rate of increase in formalization accompanying growth in scale is higher for good performers, but the absolute level of their formalization only reaches that of poor-performing companies at a size approaching 10,000 employees. The picture is complex indeed, as most practical managers are well aware!

Diversity of Operations

Now comes the eighth proposition:

Proposition 8: Organizations that group their basic activities into divisions once these activities become diversified will tend to achieve higher levels of performance.

This proposition expresses the fundamental argument for the divisionalized organizational structure that has become the dominant form among large business firms today and that can also be seen in some large public undertakings. Organizations having a spread of different products or services, and having outlets in a number of regions, operate in a complex total environment. Such organizations are also likely to be large. Because of both their size and their diversity, they will almost certainly experience communications difficulties.

To overcome these problems, it is logical to create decentralized, semiautonomous operating units or divisions, for these can group formal relationships in a way that reflects the necessities of exchanging information and coordination around common problems. These commonalities may center around product groups, favoring a product division type of organization, or they may center on geographical regions, favoring an area division structure. If both product and regional coordination are equally vital, then a mixed, or "grid," structure may be logical.

The detailed research of John Stopford and Louis Wells supports the argument that these divisionalized arrangements work. American multinational corporations that have divisionalized their structures in response to a diversity of activities tend to be superior performers. The more successful firms have in most cases adopted the kind of divisionalization—international divisions, global area divisions, global product divisions, mixed or grid structures—that considerations such as product diversity and level of involvement in foreign business would logically dictate.

Technology

This brings us to the ninth proposition:

Proposition 9: Organizations that design their work flow control and support structures to suit their technologies will tend to achieve higher levels of performance.

The term technology is employed in almost as many different senses as there are writers on the subject. The analyses offered by Charles Perrow and Joan Woodward are the best known and best developed. Perrow's definition of technology in terms of variability of inputs and availability of known techniques to handle these comes close to what most have in mind when they speak of variability in the environment and its generation of uncertainty. To this extent, Perrow's recommendations for structural design tend to be borne out by the findings of studies on organizational performance under different environmental conditions.

Woodward's view of technology is based on the physical organization of work flows. Does the organization have heavy plant and a rigid sequence of production, as in car assembly? Or does it have fairly light plant and flexible production, as in the manufacture of some electronic instruments and in service industries? Woodward's pioneering studies suggested that when organizations design structural attributes to fit their technologies, they secure a superior level of performance. Unfortunately, neither Woodward nor subsequent investigators adopting her approach have employed precise measures of performance.

The research we conducted indicated that the pattern of specialization in production and ancillary areas such as production control and maintenance was predictable in terms of the technology employed. In addition, the proportion of total employment allocated to some of the ancillary functions varied along with differences in technology. For example, more rigid technologies, such as those of a process type, tend to have relatively few production control specialists and internally specialized production control departments. Most control is actually built into the technology itself.

These associations between technology and the structure of employment lead one to ask whether, along with environment, size, and diversity, there is some logic of adjustment to contingencies here. If there is, does the extent to which organizations adapt to the logic predict differences in their performance?

The closeness of fit between technology and the pattern in which roles were specialized did not vary significantly between good- and poor-performing companies. What did distinguish the more successful firms was that they tended to vary their investment in manpower devoted to production support activities according to differences in their technology. For instance, among companies using heavy plant and more rigid production systems, the more profitable and faster-growing ones had significantly larger percentages of their total employment given over to maintenance activities. In other words, allocation of manpower in relation to technological requirements appears to improve performance.

Type of Personnel

Now let's consider the last proposition:

Proposition 10: Organizations that adopt forms of administrative structure consistent with the expectations and perceived needs of their personnel will tend to achieve higher levels of performance.

This proposition is a cornerstone of the behavioral study of organizations. Readers of *Organizational Dynamics* will already be familiar with the work of Chris Argyris, Frederick Herzberg, Rensis Likert, Douglas McGregor, and others who have argued for structures and styles of management that secure a higher degree of commitment to the organization from employees by more adequately meeting their expectations and their needs as mature adults. In a broader context, moves to enrich jobs and the developments in industrial codetermination now under way in Europe also reflect an implicit faith in Proposition 10, since they start from the premise that employees' expectations and perceived needs are not being fulfilled adequately by existing organization forms.

The results of many research studies indicate that the proposition is valid. Indeed, some would call it a truism. While it is unnecessary to review familiar ground, some qualifications are in order. The proposition refers to the expectations and perceived needs of personnel. This reference to the perceptual level is important, for whatever the order of man's universal psychological needs, it is clear that different types of people do not have the same requirements of their work at the conscious perceptual level. One has only to compare the professional employee with the manual worker to realize that sociocultural factors are crucial in shaping different expectations as to what constitute legitimate conditions of work. Similarly, research of a cross-cultural nature has indicated that different supervisory styles are effective with employees located in different cultural milieux where different attitudes toward work and authority are evident. In short, Proposition 10 indicates the managements need to spend time ascertaining the expectations of different groups among their employees if they want to have a reliable idea of which arrangements will secure the willing commitment of those employees.

CONCLUSION

I have discussed ten propositions, of which half support the universalistic argument on organizational performance and half support the contingency argument. These two arguments have sometimes been regarded as completely opposed, but the findings of research indicate several ways in which they are compatible.

In essence, the contingency approach stresses that managers should secure and evaluate information on their operating situation and that they should adapt the design of their organizational structure when necessary. It will quite possibly prove to be a general rule that managerial qualities such as the personal flexibility and drive associated with youth or the thrust for performance spurred on by a personal stake in stock appreciation enhance a company's ability to adjust to new contingencies. This is a universalistic type of statement, which includes two of the propositions I have advanced; it is nevertheless quite compatible with a contingency view of organizational design.

A further example of compatibility between the two arguments can be provided. The priority top managements give to different objectives is probably a factor that always influences the performance profiles that they attain. At the same time, the performance of any two companies having identical sets of objectives is unlikely to be the same, because this will also be determined by how they decide to adjust to prevailing contingencies.

The practical implications of the first five universalistic propositions have already been discussed. The first two draw attention to the desirability of selecting and developing managers who possess a combination of relative youth and relevant qualifications. Proposition 3 supports the general thrust of research on motivation and reward by indicating that the performance of organizations is enhanced when they grant their managers a sizable personal stake in their development. The fourth and fifth propositions indicate how the objectives management selects can shape performance, and how a greater degree of boardroom consensus over objectives will increase the chances of achieving good performance. These last two propositions speak for the practical importance of good communication, information sharing, and other hallmarks of effective integration among top executives.

The thrust of the last five propositions, and supporting research, is that the design of organization is likely to influence a company's performance. The problem has to be worked out in the context of each company's own circumstances. Several evaluations have to be made before deciding on the form of organization that is most appropriate. First, we must assess the nature of present and future contingencies. In other words, just what kind of institution are we, and what do we want to be in terms of markets, size, type of production, and so on? Second, what are the organizational requirements imposed by relevant contingencies? For example, a large unit will have particular problems of coordination and communication. What alternative organizational designs might satisfy these requirements?

Third, if different contingencies pose the dilemma of conflicting requirements, what policies could we formulate to modify the contingencies themselves? Some companies, for example, that seek to enter a faster-growing but more variable market or that seek to combine successful new product development with economies of large-scale, standardized "bread and butter" operations are finding that they can circumvent the size contingency by setting up small, internally flexible, venture-management units or similar companies-within-companies.

The important point is that there are usually several ways of securing an effective match between a company's internal organization and the contingencies it faces. This fact tends to be overlooked by those who share the present-day public concern about large bureaucratic firms and other institutions. A bureaucracy can be operated in different ways, and not necessarily with the proverbial "dead hand." And even if large scale brings too much bureaucracy to permit desirable levels of participation and sensitivity to change, there are in most areas of activity various possibilities for devolving units into smaller ones without incurring any loss in their efficiency.

In conclusion, it is already possible to identify certain managerial and organizational factors that are related to company performance, but in the future it will be necessary to go further and initiate experiments and changes in these variables that, it is hoped, will demonstrate how far they actively determine performance. It is, however, abundantly clear that company performance is not the prey of random and uncontrollable forces.

SELECTED BIBLIOGRAPHY

Most writings on the performance of organizations have been by economists, who have only infrequently examined managerial or organizational factors. Robin Morris and Adrian Wood, in editing *The Corporate Economy* (Macmillan, 1971) have, however, drawn together recent theoretical and empirical studies that take such factors into account. Jonathan Boswell's *The Rise and Decline of Small Firms* (Allen and Unwin, 1973) examines the performance of small firms in Britain, giving particular attention to problems of management succession. *Attitudes in British Management* (Penguin, 1966) contrasts "thrusting" and "sleeping" managerial attitudes, which it claims are associated with marked differences in company performance. Paul R. Lawrence and Jay W. Lorsch, in *Organization and Environment* (Harvard Business School, 1967), provides a classic statement of the contingency approach. Within the contingency school, Tom Burns and G. M. Stalker, in *The Management of Innovation* (Tavistock, 1961), consider the implications of environmental differences. John M. Stopford and Louis T. Wells, in *Managing the Multinational Enterprise* (Basic Books, 1972), concentrate on diversity of operations, while Joan Woodward's *Industrial Organization: Theory and Practice* (Oxford University Press, 1965) reports studies on technology, organization, and performance. More detailed accounts of the author's own research into performance will appear in the *Journal of Management Studies* in October 1974 and February 1975.

Author Index

Subject Index